T&T CLARK COMPANION
TO HENRI DE LUBAC

Forthcoming titles in this series include:

T&T Clark Companion to Prayer,
edited by Ashley Cocksworth & John C. McDowell

Titles already published include:

T&T Clark Companion to the Atonement,
edited by Adam J. Johnson
T&T Clark Companion to the Doctrine of Sin,
edited by Keith L. Johnson and David Lauber
T&T Clark Companion to Methodism,
edited by Charles Yrigoyen Jr
T&T Clark Companion to Reformation Theology,
edited by David M. Whitford
T&T Clark Companion to Augustine and Modern Theology,
edited by C. C. Pecknold and Tarno Toom
T&T Clark Companion to Liturgy,
edited by Alcuin Reid

T&T CLARK COMPANION TO HENRI DE LUBAC

Edited by Jordan Hillebert

LONDON • NEW YORK • OXFORD • NEW DELHI • SYDNEY

T&T CLARK
Bloomsbury Publishing Plc
50 Bedford Square, London, WC1B 3DP, UK
1385 Broadway, New York, NY 10018, USA
29 Earlsfort Terrace, Dublin 2, Ireland

BLOOMSBURY, T&T CLARK and the T&T Clark logo
are trademarks of Bloomsbury Publishing Plc

First published in Great Britain 2017
Paperback edition first published 2021

Copyright © Jordan Hillebert, 2017

Jordan Hillebert has asserted his right under the Copyright,
Designs and Patents Act, 1988, to be identified as Author of this work.

For legal purposes the Acknowledgements on p. xiii constitute
an extension of this copyright page.

Cover image © Shutterstock

All rights reserved. No part of this publication may be reproduced or
transmitted in any form or by any means, electronic or mechanical,
including photocopying, recording, or any information storage or retrieval
system, without prior permission in writing from the publishers.

Bloomsbury Publishing Plc does not have any control over, or responsibility for,
any third-party websites referred to or in this book. All internet addresses given
in this book were correct at the time of going to press. The author and publisher
regret any inconvenience caused if addresses have changed or sites have
ceased to exist, but can accept no responsibility for any such changes.

A catalogue record for this book is available from the British Library.

A catalog record for this book is available from the Library of Congress.

ISBN: HB: 978-0-5676-5722-0
PB: 978-0-5677-0113-8
ePDF: 978-0-5676-5721-3
eBook: 978-0-5676-5723-7

Typeset by Integra Software Services Pvt. Ltd.

To find out more about our authors and books visit
www.bloomsbury.com and sign up for our newsletters.

For Fr Isaac Poobalan and Fr Ian Michael

CONTENTS

Contributors — x
Acknowledgements — xiii
Foreword: A Paradoxical Humanism
    Rowan Williams — xiv
Abbreviations of Frequently Cited
Works by Henri de Lubac — xx

Part 1
HENRI DE LUBAC IN CONTEXT

Chapter 1
INTRODUCING HENRI DE LUBAC
    Jordan Hillebert — 3

Chapter 2
NEO-SCHOLASTICISM OF THE STRICT OBSERVANCE
    Tracey Rowland — 29

Chapter 3
THE INFLUENCE OF MAURICE BLONDEL
    Francesca Aran Murphy — 57

Chapter 4
RESSOURCEMENT
    Jacob W. Wood — 93

Chapter 5
HENRI DE LUBAC AND THE SECOND VATICAN COUNCIL
    Aaron Riches — 121

Part 2
KEY THEMES IN THE THEOLOGY OF HENRI DE LUBAC

Chapter 6
THE MYSTICAL BODY: ECCLESIOLOGY AND SACRAMENTAL THEOLOGY
    Gemma Simmonds, CJ — 159

Chapter 7
THE CHRISTIAN MYSTERY OF NATURE AND GRACE
  Nicholas J. Healy Jr.   181

Chapter 8
THE SPIRITUAL INTERPRETATION OF SCRIPTURE
  Kevin L. Hughes   205

Chapter 9
AN INHUMAN HUMANISM
  Patrick X. Gardner   225

Chapter 10
ON RELIGION
  David Grumett   247

Chapter 11
KNOWING GOD
  D. Stephen Long   269

Chapter 12
A THEOLOGY OF HISTORY
  Cyril O'Regan   289

Chapter 13
MYSTICISM AND MYSTICAL THEOLOGY
  Bryan C. Hollon   307

Chapter 14
AN EMERGING CHRISTOLOGY
  Noel O'Sullivan   327

Part 3
A THEOLOGICAL LEGACY

Chapter 15
HENRI DE LUBAC AND A DESIRE BEYOND CLAIM
  Jean-Yves Lacoste (Translation by Oliver O'Donovan)   351

Chapter 16
HENRI DE LUBAC AND PROTESTANTISM
  Kenneth Oakes   373

Chapter 17
HENRI DE LUBAC AND RADICAL ORTHODOXY
   Simon Oliver   393

Chapter 18
HENRI DE LUBAC AND POLITICAL THEOLOGY
   Joseph S. Flipper   419

Chapter 19
HENRI DE LUBAC AND THE CHRISTIAN LIFE
   Nicholas M. Healy   445

Bibliography   466
Index   488

CONTRIBUTORS

Joseph S. Flipper (PhD, Marquette University) is Assistant Professor of Theology and Assistant Director of the Ethics and Social Justice Center at Bellarmine University, Louisville, Kentucky. He is author of *Between Apocalypse and Eschaton: History and Eternity in Henri de Lubac* (Fortress Press, 2015).

Patrick X. Gardner (PhD, University of Notre Dame) is currently a Lilly Postdoctoral Fellow in Humanities at Valparaiso University.

David Grumett (PhD, University of Cambridge) is Lecturer in Christian Ethics and Practical Theology at the University of Edinburgh. He is author of *De Lubac: A Guide for the Perplexed* (T&T Clark, 2007) and of articles and chapters on several aspects of de Lubac's theology, including in the *International Journal of Systematic Theology*, *The Journal of Religion*, and *Modern Theology*.

Nicholas J. Healy, Jr. (DPhil, Oxford University) is Associate Professor of Philosophy at the John Paul II Institute for Studies on Marriage and Family. He is an editor of the North American edition of *Communio: International Catholic Review*. He is the author of *The Eschatology of Hans Urs von Balthasar: Being as Communion* (Oxford University Press, 2005) and, together with David L. Schindler, *Freedom, Truth, and Human Dignity: The Declaration on Religious Freedom* (Eerdmans, 2015).

Nicholas M. Healy (PhD, Yale University) is Professor of Theology and Religious Studies at St John's University, New York. His recent publications include *Hauerwas: A (Very) Critical Introduction* (Eerdmans, 2014) and *Thomas Aquinas: Theologian of the Christian Life* (Ashgate, 2003).

Jordan Hillebert (PhD, University of St Andrews) is Tutor in Theology at St Padarn's Institute and Honorary Lecturer at Cardiff University. His recent publications include 'The Death of God and the Dissolution of Humanity' (*New Blackfriars* 95: 1060).

Bryan C. Hollon (PhD, Baylor University) is Professor of Theology at Malone University. He is author of *Everything Is Sacred: Spiritual Exegesis in the Political Theology of Henri de Lubac* (Cascade, 2008).

Kevin L. Hughes (PhD, University of Chicago) is Associate Professor of Theology and Religious Studies at Villanova University. His publications include *Constructing Antichrist: Paul, Biblical Exegesis, and the Development of Doctrine in the Early*

Middle Ages (CUA Press, 2005) and 'The "Fourfold Sense": De Lubac, Blondel, and Contemporary Theology' (*The Heythrop Journal* 42, 4).

Jean-Yves Lacoste (PhD, Paris; STD, Toulouse) is Honorary Professor at the Australian Catholic University. His recent publications include *From Theology to Theological Thinking* (UVA Press, 2013), *L'intuition sacramentelle, et autres essais* (Paris, 2014), and *Recherches sur la parole* (Louvain-la-Neuve, 2014).

D. Stephen Long (PhD, Duke University) is Cary M. Maguire University Professor of Ethics at Southern Methodist University. He recently published *The Perfectly Simple Triune God: Aquinas and His Legacy* (Fortress Press, 2016) and *Saving Karl Barth: Hans Urs von Balthasar's Preoccupation* (Fortress Press, 2014).

Francesca Aran Murphy (PhD, University of London) is Professor of Systematic Theology at the University of Notre Dame. She is editor of the Illuminating Modernity series with Bloomsbury Press. Her most recent book is *Illuminating Faith* (Bloomsbury, 2014).

Kenneth Oakes (PhD, University of Aberdeen) is Assistant Professor of Systematic Theology at the University of Notre Dame. He is author of *Karl Barth on Theology and Philosophy* (OUP, 2012) and *Reading Karl Barth: A Companion to Karl Barth's Epistle to the Romans* (Wipf & Stock, 2011), editor of *Christian Wisdom Meets Modernity*, and co-author of *Illuminating Faith: An Invitation to Theology*. His articles, reviews, and translations have appeared in *Modern Theology*, *The Thomist*, *Pro Ecclesia*, and the *International Journal of Systematic Theology*.

Oliver O'Donovan FBA, FRSE (DPhil, Oxford University) is Honorary Professor of Divinity at the University of St Andrews. He is author of *Self, World and Time* and *Finding & Seeking* (Eerdmans, 2013–2014) and translator of *Persons: The Difference between 'Someone' and 'Something'*, by Robert Spaemann (Oxford, 2006).

Simon Oliver (PhD, University of Cambridge) is the Van Mildert Professor of Divinity at Durham University, UK. He is author of *Philosophy, God and Motion* (Routledge, 2005) and *Creation: A Guide for the Perplexed* (Bloomsbury, 2017), and editor, with John Milbank, of *The Radical Orthodoxy Reader* (Routledge, 2009).

Cyril O'Regan (PhD, Yale University) is Huisking Professor of Theology at the University of Notre Dame. His recent publications include *Anatomy of Misremembering (1): Balthasar's Response to Philosophical Modernity. Vol. 1: Hegel* (Crossroad, 2014) and *Theology and the Spaces of Apocalyptic* (Marquette University Press, 2009).

Noel O'Sullivan (PhD, Institut Catholique de Paris) lectures in systematic theology at the Pontifical University of Maynooth, Ireland. His first published work is *Christ* *and Creation* (Oxford: Peter Lang, 2009). He is currently preparing a book on the priesthood. A Canon of the Cathedral Chapter of his diocese, he is Dean of Cork.

Aaron Riches (PhD, University of Nottingham) teaches theology at the Seminario Mayor San Cecilio, in the archdiocese of Granada, Spain, and is a joint faculty member of the Instituto de Teología 'Lumen Gentium' and the Instituto de Filosofía 'Edith Stein'. He is author of *Ecce Homo: On the Divine Unity of Christ* (Eerdmans, 2016).

Tracey Rowland (PhD, Cambridge University; STD, Pontifical Lateran University) is Professor of Theology at the John Paul II Institute (Melbourne) and the University of Notre Dame (Australia). She is a member of the International Theological Commission and on the editorial board of *Communio: International Catholic Review*, which was founded by Henri de Lubac, among others. Her most recent book is *Catholic Theology* (Bloomsbury, 2017).

Gemma Simmonds, CJ (PhD, University of Cambridge) is a sister of the Congregation of Jesus and a Senior Lecturer in Pastoral and Social Studies and Theology at Heythrop College, University of London. She is Director of the Religious Life Institute and a former President of the Catholic Theological Association of Great Britain. Her translation work includes Henri de Lubac's *Corpus Mysticum* (SCM Press, 2006). Her publications include 'Kenotic Authority in the Church', in A. Carroll et al. eds, *Towards a Kenotic Vision of Authority in the Catholic Church* (Council for Research in Values & Philosophy, 2015); and 'Jansenism and Ressourcement', in Gabriel Flynn and Paul Murray, eds, *Ressourcement: A Movement for Renewal in Twentieth-Century Catholic Theology* (OUP, 2012).

Rowan Williams (DPhil, Oxford University) was the 104th Archbishop of Canterbury (2002–2012). He is presently Master of Magdalene College, Cambridge. His recent publications include *On Augustine* (Bloomsbury, 2016) and *The Edge of Words: God and the Habits of Language* (Bloomsbury, 2014).

Jacob W. Wood (PhD, The Catholic University of America) is an Assistant Professor of Theology at Franciscan University of Steubenville. His publications include 'Henri de Lubac, Humani Generis, and the Natural Desire for a Supernatural End' in *Nova et Vetera* (English Edition) (forthcoming); 'Augustine and Henri de Lubac' (with C. C. Pecknold) in *The T&T Clark Companion to Augustine and Modern Theology* (T&T Clark, 2013); and *Speaking the Love of God: An Introduction to the Sacraments* (Emmaus Road, 2016).

ACKNOWLEDGEMENTS

The initial conversations leading to the publication of this volume occurred nearly three years ago, while I was completing a doctoral thesis on the theology of Henri de Lubac at the University of St Andrews. It was under the advice and warm encouragement of my doctoral supervisor, Professor John Webster, that I was put in contact with Anna Turton and the wonderful team at T&T Clark. I am certain that without John's prompting and constant support, this project never would have seen the light of day. Like so many, I mourn deeply the loss of such a tremendous teacher, theologian, and friend. I hope that this volume serves in some small way as a testament to his influence and generosity of spirit.

Special thanks belong to the contributors to this volume – for their dedication, their insights, and their shared enthusiasm for introducing readers to the 'primeval forest' (in the words of Hans Urs von Balthasar) of de Lubac's writings and ideas. As well as Anna Turton, Miriam Cantwell of T&T Clark assisted greatly (and patiently!) in bringing this project to completion. The greatest debt of gratitude belongs, as ever, to my wife, Krisi. The final year of a PhD and the first year of teaching are busy enough without the editorial responsibilities of a project such as this one. I am immensely grateful for her patience, love, and support throughout.

Finally, this volume is dedicated to Fr Isaac Poobalan and Fr Ian Michael for their pastoral care and spiritual direction during the writing and editing of this volume.

Jordan Hillebert
Cardiff
Feast of St Francis, 2016

FOREWORD: A PARADOXICAL HUMANISM

Rowan Williams

Henri de Lubac's writing might be taken as a touchstone for defining and identifying a particular style of Christian humanism – or more specifically Catholic humanism. Echoing Maritain, he was an advocate for an 'integral' humanism; and for once, the word 'humanism' does indeed have some resonances of its Renaissance usage. Like those who claimed the title in the fifteenth and sixteenth centuries, de Lubac is a writer who takes care of the business of writing. Just as earlier humanists turned their backs, stylistically as well as intellectually, on a rather sclerotic scholasticism, so de Lubac both turns away from what one of our authors nicely calls 'Strict Observance' neo-Thomism and also seeks fresh idioms and registers for theological reflection. This makes it difficult at times to pin down his views on specific doctrinal questions with quite the exactitude his critics – and sometimes his friends – would have wished: several of these essays note that he is not particularly interested in pronouncing on contested sub-themes in dogmatics (look, for example, at the study in these pages of his Christology). His style lends itself more to a brilliantly varied *evocation* of the world of reference within which dogma functions. 'Dogma', he writes in *Paradoxes of Faith*,[1] 'is a vast domain which theology will never wholly exploit' (p. 228). At the same time, he is careful to insist that this must not be understood as an apologia for impressionistic and edifying flannel. The true theologian must emerge 'beyond' the realm of tough specialist work, not avoid it by remaining 'beneath' it; and it is a betrayal 'to cite the needs of souls, or the necessity of a current language and the superiority of concrete and living words over abstractions and technicalities' as an excuse for abandoning the intellectual labour which is what the church needs from its divines (p. 37).

Paradoxes of Faith is one of the best introductions to de Lubac because it is so full of such pointed remarks to the would-be Christian intellectual – to himself, of course, in wry recognition of certain temptations he would have identified. As we are reminded several times in this collection, de Lubac saw human being itself as a paradox, so it is natural that he should reflect theologically in the mode of deliberately paradoxical, sometimes gnomic, aphorism. It is a good introduction because it shows de Lubac at work in the crucible of language; he is consciously shaping maxims for theological practice and intellectual practice more generally that will carry the tension of his basic theological vision without letting it fall apart; he is crafting a language appropriate for its subject matter. These tightly condensed

---

1. San Francisco: Ignatius Press, 1987; all page references in the text are to this edition.

paragraphs are meditations on how to think – how to think about the faith, but also about how to think faithfully, in the widest possible sense. Intellectual maturity or intellectual excellence is not about the search for intellectually impressive and complex structures, nor is it to do with a quest for total self-transparency or immediacy, thought grasping the naked substance of self. 'Intelligence does not naturally look for what is "intelligent": it looks for what is true. The man who turns his intelligence away from its end by seeking intelligent things is really no longer intelligent' (pp. 103–104). And again, 'It is not sincerity, it is Truth which frees us ... To seek sincerity above all things is perhaps, at bottom, not to want to be transformed' (p. 127).

'Not to want to be transformed'; that is a startlingly vivid definition of the ultimate sin of the intellect in de Lubac's eyes, and it helps to explain why he is so insistent, in these meditations, on the necessary incompleteness of the intellect's work, even in theology. The intellect is oriented towards truth, but that truth is ultimately identical with love (cf. p. 114); so the intellect's perfection is unimaginable without some notion of perfection in 'ontological' truthfulness, alignment with a reality that is self-giving and transfigures through its gift. 'The possession of the true can be perfect only in the possession of being' (p. 116). This is where the apparently technical debates about 'natural' and 'supernatural' intentionalities and completions have their real ground; and de Lubac is clear that what we need to say about the inherent orientation of the created self/soul/mind towards God is rooted in what we believe about *God* before any consideration of what we believe about humanity. Truth is loving, so ultimately truth is inseparable from gift; God can give no other gift than God, and so God lovingly transforms wherever truth is properly sought and found. And if we turn this in a slightly different direction, we should have to conclude that 'When we are right without praying, without loving, our "right" bears but the fruits of death' (p. 167). It is this stress on the austerity of truth, the demand of truthfulness as the demand that reality itself makes upon our minds, that makes de Lubac the very opposite of a relativist. 'Orthodoxy: the most necessary and the least adequate thing in the world' (p. 223); we must speak properly of God and we must know with the most sharply refined clarity that our most 'proper' speech is never free from ambiguity. Yet 'there is a hidden complicity in us' that allows even this ambiguity to be effective (p. 197). However incomplete our words, there is something that is still truly and rightly said if we are open to the inseparable act of infinite being, love and truth, because of what we are in the order of creation, because our thinking itself is possible only through the gift of that infinite act.

'We would rather not be some one ourselves than meet that Some One' (p. 214). De Lubac's frame of reference is not humanistic in any bland sense that simply expects the best of humanity, and *Paradoxes of Faith* can be read as a series of meditations on the habits of untruthfulness as well as a celebration of the human. Faced with a truth that is transformingly active, we are afraid, and do what we can to replace such a truth with a manageable fiction. Ironically – and this has even more resonance for the twenty-first century than for de Lubac's contemporaries – the safest such fictions, those of a mechanistic and impersonal universe, require us to abandon any notion of personal dignity or liberty; and we willingly accept such Faustian bargains in order not to fall into the hands of love. This is why the liberation of intellect and the renewal of the life of the spirit are so closely intertwined. We must battle against the 'domestication' of the spirit (p. 213), restoring to it its proper location in an 'uncertain and threatened life' (p. 115), just as we respect the labour of intellect, for (de Lubac quotes St Thomas), 'Those who obtain something without trouble, keep it without love' (p. 188). Even an intellectual rebellion against God may do more for faith than an intellectual confidence about God, since what matters is the awareness of 'confrontation' with a truth that is as much foreign to us as the love and longing for it is native to us (p. 216). 'We can accept night. We cannot fail to struggle with contradiction' (p. 176). The avoiding of suffering is not an option in the life of the spirit or the mind ('In the order of the spirit, a method of painless birth will never be found', p. 186); we do not cultivate it, but accept the weight of frustration and work to remove the simply contradictory – to arrive, we might say, at the basic and unavoidable contradiction between the impulse to make our suffering a self-serving drama and the recognition that we must learn to inhabit with grace the place where we actually are. We 'poison' our suffering 'by living [our] memories in resentment and [our] anticipations in fear and anxiety' (p. 179).

Beatitude, the bliss we are made for, is something different from happiness (p. 201), the contentment we demand in the terms we can manage. De Lubac is consistently clear that what is offered in revelation and grace is not domesticable, not predictable or calculable in terms of what we think we need to complete us. The paradox at the centre of his thinking – and at the centre of the theology he re-presents out of the tradition – is that we are indeed 'naturally' oriented towards relation with the infinite God, but that the realization of this relation radically alters what we conceive as natural. In a bold step, de Lubac contrasts Christianity with 'religion' in general: religion (including, says de Lubac, modern substitutes, cultural or ideological, for older systems) gives us back what we want, restoring a time 'before our history', a mother's breast; Christianity offers an encounter with the Father in the Garden, restoring not our indeterminate infancy but our hopeful youth (p. 216). There is a palpable sideways reference here to the world of post-Freudian, even Lacanian, thought, though it is not clear how much de Lubac would want to be pressed on the maternal/paternal contrast in those more technical terms. The image is one designed to clarify the ways in which Christian faith builds upon and transfigures the desire we begin from rather than promising a fulfilment we can imagine in advance. Just as 'the craftsman respects the resistance of matter' (p. 148), the worker in the field of the spirit accepts the resistance of what is encountered, because it is this which will eventually allow what is new to appear, not a plain repetition of the familiar and consoling. It is worth noting that de Lubac makes this point specifically in the context of labouring for Christian unity, to warn against seeking to achieve it 'too cheaply': what the 'craftsman' works on is the densely compacted reality of diverse Christian lives responding to what they perceive as truth. Unity in such terms is of course elusive, to say the least; yet 'each step towards it nevertheless constitutes an absolute gain... because it increases charity' (p. 155). And such charity is intrinsically connected to the conviction that what we seek is not full mutual transparency but the love that enable us to live with a difference always diminishing but never annihilated (p. 158, on how mutual transparency can be a form of the mere unity of 'the herd').

There is therefore another paradox: to speak in these ways about the transformation of our engagement with truth, in mind and heart, is to commend a kind of maximalism; yet if that maximalism produces only a bellicose perfectionism, we have failed to see the point. 'The greatest corruption', says de Lubac, is misconceiving the good as the useful, and so missing the truly radical ('to make us fall short of the Gospel every day through the desire of making it fully effective some day', p. 193). That is to say, our worst temptation will be to see our Christian identity in terms of cumulative movement towards some kind of universal utilitarian good. But this obscures for us the fact that the good is demanded of us wholly in every moment through (and only through) our surrender to the loving truth that is God. That surrender is always imperfect, but what is surrendered *to* is always already complete in its self-gift. So the knife-edge we have to walk is between different kinds of infidelity: we can be unfaithful to the wholeness of the gift and become trapped in our own striving for a perfect future; we can be unfaithful to the demand of surrender and become trapped in an idle and uncommitted dependence on what is now an abstract hope in God's providential action. What has to be recognized is that the gospel announcement of how God acts is necessary for the life and well-being of the world. It is not *our achievement as Christians* that is necessary (p. 59). Yet if that announcement is to be authentic and credible, it must be made out of surrender.

'"How can I present Christ?" – As you love him' (p. 215). If our doctrines feel remote to us or stale or implausible, we have to ask what has become of our own inner kindling by the truth that has laid hold of us. The failing of 'modernism', says de Lubac, is that the revisionist looks at faith as it is in himself or herself: it *looks* like a rigid and atrophied thing, so it must be rejected. But what is necessary is in fact a conversion into the life of the continuing tradition, an acceptance of the teaching at a new level of prayerful seriousness (p. 217). Once again, surrender is what is demanded. But it is not a surrender to some external command, some 'human system' (p. 223), which will always be 'sterilizing'; surrender to the living truth is always fertile. And one of the implications of surrender is that we shall be seeking truth rather than sincerity ('We are only sincere when we are not thinking about it', p. 114). Here as elsewhere, de Lubac is quietly but consistently responding to an existentialist stress on 'authenticity' in faith or act – the quest for the action that is inalienably, uniquely, even arbitrarily, mine and no one else's; this quest is seductively close to the quest for a truth that is apprehended with genuine personal intensity and clarity, but it is tragically and catastrophically vitiated by its constant turning towards itself, towards its own interiority, in the doomed search for transparency.

As all these quotations make plain, de Lubac's 'humanism' is very far from being an uncritical affirmation of natural human goodness, even of natural orientation towards God in some senses of that language. We are indeed so constituted that we cannot be ourselves without Christian revelation; the catch is that we are so deeply at odds with ourselves as not to be able to grasp this. We are oriented, in other words, towards *revelation*, to an irruption of God's truth that simultaneously fulfils and judges our natural life and desire; we are not so made that we smoothly advance towards the knowledge of God without the specific historical gift that is Christ ('Christianity is not one of the great things of history: it is history which is one of the great things of Christianity', p. 145). So it makes no sense to argue that we must 'Humanize before Christianizing' (p. 69): 'If the enterprise succeeds, Christianity will come too late: its place will be taken. And who thinks that Christianity has no humanizing value?' We cannot imagine that it is possible to construct a complete human identity which can (only?) *then* be confronted with the truth of the gospel; our incomplete humanity is repeatedly engaged from beyond with the reality that makes it alive in this engagement. There is no static and un-relational human completeness; and the relation that above all completes is relation with the grace of God in Christ. Otherwise we shall have a world of 'dead souls' (p. 86).

Much more could be quoted from *Paradoxes of Faith*; but the themes identified here may help the reader to see a little of how de Lubac's thought inhabits the tension between affirmation of the human aptitude for receiving what God has to give and denial that this can ever mean a conditioning of what theology says by the apparent needs of the world as it has constructed itself. 'Nothing excellent can come from one who aims first at a public' (p. 34); and if we want to talk, as so often we do, about the importance of 'prophetic' witness, we had better remember that prophecy is almost by definition what is not heard and received by its immediate context (pp. 199–200). De Lubac's humanism is indeed a paradoxical position, but an intensely theological one, for which both history and metaphysics matter. And this balance of concerns means that he is able to be equally robust about the folly of perfectionism (and so of naive reformism) and the danger of softening the austerity of the gospel's demand for conversion. As various essays in this collection will set out in more detail, his significance in laying the foundations for Vatican II's more generous approach to non-Christian religion is tightly balanced with his impatience at the ecclesial utopianism which came in the wake of the Council, the assumption that the renewal of the Catholic Church could be conceived as a matter of 'modernising' or otherwise adjusting to changing cultural norms. His distance from any variety of progressivism in the post-conciliar era was more than an ageing man's disillusion; as this rapid survey of his aphorisms suggests, it was grounded in a remarkably integrated metaphysical and indeed cultural sensibility, acutely aware of the likelihood of fashionable self-deception. But it should also indicate how little he was a conservative as such: he insists unsparingly on the risks of conformism, of orthodoxy without substance and without love or humility. A sympathetic reader of Newman, he knows as clearly as does the English Cardinal that doctrinal definition is a sort of stopgap for our ignorance rather than a claim to comprehend, and that inhabiting tradition is a far more rich and engaged matter than repeating correct formulations. 'A man's faith can go down to zero without even being shaken by doubt' (p. 21); so we need to understand where doubt and frustration, intellectual and spiritual must be faced and acknowledged in the labour of theology – conscious also of the crucial self-examination that may tell us that our problem lies with our own unwillingness to be transfigured.

The church 'disappoints and irritates us' (p. 235); we shall never arrive at a situation where the institution simply corresponds to itself – or to our utopian plans for it. What matters is that it 'at the same time pursues its irreplaceable mission among us, which does not cease for a single day to give us Jesus Christ' (p. 235). This mixture of realism about human failure and realism about divine faithfulness is what makes de Lubac so abidingly positive and demanding a theologian: a humanist, but (paradoxically?) a rare diagnostician of human untruthfulness in the face of an eternal truth eternally engaged in love.

ABBREVIATIONS OF FREQUENTLY CITED WORKS BY HENRI DE LUBAC

AMT	*Augustinianism and Modern Theology*
ASC	*At the Service of the Church*
BC	*A Brief Catechesis on Nature and Grace*
C	*Catholicism: Christ and the Common Destiny of Man*
CF	*The Christian Faith*
CM	*Corpus Mysticum: The Eucharist and the Church in the Middle Ages*
CPM	*The Church: Paradox and Mystery*
CR	*Christian Resistance to Anti-Semitism*
DAH	*The Drama of Atheist Humanism*
DG	*The Discovery of God*
HS	*History and Spirit: The Understanding of Scripture According to Origen*
MC	*The Motherhood of the Church*
ME	*Medieval Exegesis*
MP	*More Paradoxes*
MS	*The Mystery of the Supernatural*
PF	*Paradoxes of Faith*
S	*Surnaturel*
SC	*The Splendor of the Church*
TF	*Theological Fragments*
TH	*Theology in History*

See Bibliography for complete bibliographic information.

Part I

HENRI DE LUBAC IN CONTEXT

Chapter 1

INTRODUCING HENRI DE LUBAC

Jordan Hillebert

In February 1976, on the occasion of his eightieth birthday, Henri de Lubac received a letter from Pope Paul VI, writing 'to express our fatherly joy, to display the high opinion we have of you, and to thank you as you well deserve, in our name and that of the Church'. Among the 'impressive gifts' bestowed upon de Lubac by God – Paul VI mentions de Lubac's ministry as a priest in the Society of Jesus, his contribution as *peritus* (theological expert) during the Second Vatican Council (1962–1965) and his years as a professor at the Catholic Institute of Lyons – the pope extols de Lubac for his prodigious literary output:

> These cost you hard work, pain, and some hardships. In them your holy and awesome task was ever to seek the truth with utmost care, to follow the venerable footsteps of the Fathers, and to embrace the established traditions of our forebears... The gifts you brought to your writing and the principles you followed are the sources of their enduring freshness.[1]

The pope's words attest not only the erudition and vitality of de Lubac's writings but also the remarkable change of fortune in de Lubac's academic and ecclesial career. Less than thirty years earlier, de Lubac was believed by many to have been implicated in Pope Pius XII's encyclical concerning 'some false opinions threatening to undermine the foundations of Catholic doctrine'.[2] In 1950, de Lubac was removed from his teaching responsibilities in Lyons on account of 'pernicious errors on essential points of dogma',[3] and for more than a decade thereafter he remained a largely marginalized figure. De Lubac's writings assuredly cost him 'some hardships' – hardships shared by a number of other prominent Jesuit and Dominican theologians throughout the 1940s and 1950s

---

1. Henri de Lubac includes this letter in the Appendices to ASC, pp. 379–82.
2. Pius XII, *Humani Generis*: Encyclical Letter Concerning Some False Opinions Threatening to Undermine the Foundations of Catholic Doctrine (12 August 1950), *Acta Sanctae Sedis* 42 (1950): pp. 561–78.
3. ASC, p. 68.

and indicative of the tumultuous landscape of mid-century Roman Catholic theology.

It is difficult to overstate the significance of de Lubac's contribution to this controversial and immensely fecund era in Roman Catholic thought. Along with such thinkers as Marie-Dominique Chenu (1895–1990), Yves Congar (1904–1995), Henri Bouillard (1908–1981), and his one-time pupils Jean Daniélou (1905–1974) and Hans Urs von Balthasar (1905–1988), de Lubac was one of the leading exponents of what would come to be referred to as *ressourcement* – a mode of theologizing at variance with the then-regnant forms of neo-scholastic theology which would come to play a decisive role in the theological developments of the Second Vatican Council (1962–1995). These *ressourcement* theologians sought to revitalize the discipline of theology from the often-arid and overly rationalist (syllogistic) theology ensconced in the seminary textbooks of the first half of the twentieth century by means of a return to earlier theological voices. In so doing, they likewise sought to facilitate the Church's engagement with contemporary thought and culture.

Without denying the historical and theological significance of this collective venture or de Lubac's own commitment to the task of *ressourcement*, one must be careful not to allow this impressive chorus to drown out de Lubac's own momentous contribution to modern Christian thought. De Lubac's works – demonstrating mastery over a staggering array of figures, epochs, and intellectual disciplines – have left an indelible mark in the areas of historical, philosophical, and dogmatic theology. His achievement as a Roman Catholic theologian has been likened to that of his Protestant contemporary Karl Barth (1886–1968). Indeed, in recent years, one of de Lubac's most influential interpreters has argued that de Lubac was 'a greater theological revolutionary' than his Swiss counterpart.[4] The publication of de Lubac's epochal *Surnaturel* (1946) has been deemed by disciples and critics alike as 'the most influential event in Catholic theology of the twentieth century',[5] 'almost as important an event of cultural revision as *Being and Time* or the *Philosophical Investigations*'.[6] Few modern theologians have done as much to set the contemporary theological agenda as Henri de Lubac.

And yet, for all this, there remains a surprising dearth of scholarly engagement with de Lubac's writings in the English-speaking world.[7] While few today would

---

4. John Milbank, 'The Programme of Radical Orthodoxy', in Laurence Paul Hemming, ed., *Radical Orthodoxy? – A Catholic Enquiry* (Aldershot: Ashgate, 2000), p. 35.

5. Guy Mansini, 'The Abiding Theological Significance of Henri de Lubac's *Surnaturel*', *The Thomist* 73 (2009): p. 593.

6. Milbank, *The Suspended Middle: Henri de Lubac and the Renewed Split in Modern Catholic Thought*, 2nd ed. (Grand Rapids, MI: William B. Erdmans Publishing Company, 2014), 70.

7. Some notable exceptions are Paul McPartlan, *The Eucharist Makes the Church* (Edinburgh: T&T Clark, 1993); Susan K. Wood, *Spiritual Exegesis and the Church in the Theology of Henri de Lubac* (Grand Rapids, MI: William B. Eerdmans, 1998); Milbank,

deny his importance, de Lubac has received considerably less attention than such contemporaries as Karl Rahner or Hans Urs von Balthasar. Expositions of de Lubac's thought are often relegated to larger treatments of the *nouvelle théologie* (an originally pejorative title given to those mid-century exponents of *ressourcement*).[8] There are some indications that things are beginning to change. The employment (though often somewhat eccentric) of de Lubac's *Surnaturel* thesis by exponents of 'Radical Orthodoxy' and the return to prominence of neo-scholastic readings of Thomas Aquinas have done much in recent years to garner attention to de Lubac's work. However, it remains to be seen whether either will serve as a catalyst for the kind of careful and sustained attention that de Lubac's theology requires and deserves. The former runs the risk of instrumentalizing de Lubac's project for other theological agendas – effectively marshalling de Lubac as a proponent of Radical Orthodoxy *avant la lettre*[9] – while the latter tends to restrict attention to debates surrounding the proper interpretation of the Common Doctor. In both cases, de Lubac's rich vision of the Christian faith and the larger concerns animating his theological project remain conspicuously in the background.

It is to this lacuna that the present volume is addressed. The chapters that follow seek not only to introduce readers to the prolific contribution of Henri de Lubac but also to shed new light on this important and complex figure by considering his immediate context (Part I), the principal themes canvassed in his writings (Part II), and his continuing theological legacy (Part III). The current chapter offers something of an introduction to this volume by way of locating de Lubac's work within the narrative of a unitary life and project. Like every writer, de Lubac was in important respects a product of his circumstances. 'Descartes's wet-nurse is more responsible than he himself believed for all that he drew from his *cogito*', de Lubac once remarked.[10] So it is with de Lubac – his ideas did not emerge and develop in a vacuum, but were continually derived from and formulated in response to the experiences of a twentieth-century, French, Jesuit priest and professor. There are other good reasons for situating de Lubac's ideas within the contours of his biography. De Lubac is one of those rare theologians whose life is every bit as interesting and instructive as his writings. Seriously wounded during the First World War, hunted by the Gestapo for his 'spiritual resistance' to

---

The Suspended Middle; David Grumett, *De Lubac: A Guide for the Perplexed* (London: T&T Clark, 2007); Bryan C. Hollon, *Everything Is Sacred: Spiritual Exegesis in the Political Theology of Henri de Lubac* (Oregon: Cascade Books, 2009); Noel O'Sullivan, *Christ and Creation: Christology as the Key to Interpreting the Theology of Creation in the Works of Henri de Lubac* (Oxford: Peter Lang, 2009); Joseph S. Flipper, *Between Apocalypse and Eschaton: History and Eternity in Henri de Lubac* (Minnesota, MN: Fortress Press, 2015).

8. Cf. Hans Boersma, *Nouvelle Théologie and Sacramental Ontology: A Return to Mystery* (Oxford: Oxford University Press, 2009); Jürgen Mettepenningen, *Nouvelle Théologie – New Theology: Inheritor of Modernism, Precursor of Vatican II* (London: T&T Clark, 2010).

9. This is the argument advanced by Edward T. Oakes, 'The Paradox of Nature and Grace: On John Milbank's *The Suspended Middle*', *Nova et Vetera* 4:3 (2006): p. 682.

10. 'On Christian Philosophy', *Communio* 19 (Fall, 1992): p. 485.

Nazism and the Vichy regime during the Second, and subject to a wholly different form of warfare within the Society of Jesus throughout the 1940s and 1950s, de Lubac was anything but an ivory tower academic. Finally, writing at the age of seventy-nine, de Lubac himself notes, 'nearly everything I have written has been as a result of circumstances that were often unforeseen, in scattered order and without technical preparation'.[11] De Lubac's frank, if characteristically modest, confession reveals the necessity of attending to the circumstances that occasioned his writings. However, one must not presume that the 'occasional' nature of de Lubac's work precludes a significant unity. As we intend to demonstrate in this chapter, nearly all of de Lubac's writings are animated by a twofold concern. That is, de Lubac is continuously occupied with demonstrating both the unity of the Church's polyphonic tradition and the ability of that tradition to 'make sense' of the enigma of human existence and the history within which each individual life finds its meaning. For de Lubac, the task of *ressourcement* is closely allied to the Church's contemporary mission as a 'witness and agent of fundamental meaning'.[12] The mystery to which the Church throughout history bears witness and apart from which the Church 'has no existence, value or efficacy',[13] is the only means whereby the 'problem' of human being attains its resolution. 'In revealing to us the God who is the end of man, Jesus Christ, the Man-God, reveals us to ourselves.' This is the animating principle behind nearly all of de Lubac's writings, not least his work on the supernatural. The dynamism of human existence is teleologically ordered to the supernatural gift of Godself – that gift revealed as it is realized in the person and works of Jesus Christ, without whom 'the ultimate foundation of our being would remain an enigma to us'.[14]

Early Life and Education

Henri Marie-Joseph Sonier de Lubac was born in Cambrai, in the north of France, on 20 February 1896. The third of six children, de Lubac was raised in the faith and practices of a devout Catholic family. 'I have immense gratitude for my parents. They always gave us the example of duty, constancy, self-sacrifice, and piety.'[15] The circumstances surrounding de Lubac's birth provide a valuable glimpse, not only of the extent of his parents' religious commitment, but also of the mounting tension between the Catholic Church in France and the laicist policies of the Third Republic at the turn of the century. On 29 March 1880, Minister of Education (and future prime minister) Jules Ferry instigated a series

---

11. ASC, p. 143.
12. De Lubac, 'The Total Meaning of Man and the World', *Communio* 35 (Winter, 2008): p. 628; citing Paul Ricoeur, 'Sciences humaines et conditionnements de la foi', *Recherches et Débats* 14 (1965): p. 140.
13. CPM, p. 15.
14. De Lubac, 'The Total Meaning of Man and the World', pp. 626–27.
15. De Lubac, *Mémoire sur l'occasion de mes écrits* (Paris: Cerf, 2006), pp. 11–12.

of decrees dissolving a number of 'unauthorized' religious congregations in France. At the time, a large portion of the nation's children were educated in Church schools by members of religious orders, and the decrees of March 29 were part of a larger attempt to protect French youth from the illiberal and ultimately anti-republican influence of the Roman Catholic Church. Among the protestors of these decrees was a nineteen-year-old Maurice Sonier de Lubac (1860–1936) who, while escorting a group of Capuchin fathers from Lyons, became involved in a brawl and injured a counter-protester by striking him in the face with the hilt of his sword. De Lubac was fined for carrying an unauthorized weapon and encouraged by his employer, the Bank of France, to take up his post somewhere outside Lyons. De Lubac was sent first to Lille, then to Verdun, and finally to Cambrai where, in 1896, his wife Gabrielle (née Baurepaire; 1867–1963) gave birth to their son, Henri.[16]

Despite the decrees of 1880 and the so-called *lois d'exception* of 1901 and 1904 (which resulted in the expulsion of some twenty thousand religious schools and the closure of ten thousand congregation schools in France), de Lubac received the entirety of his primary education in religious schools, first in Bourg-en-Bresse (1898–1902) and then in and around Lyons (1902–1911). While a student at the Jesuit college of Notre Dame de Mongré (1909–1911), and under the spiritual direction of Fr Eugène Hains, SJ, de Lubac began to discern a vocation to the religious life. In 1913, a year after his eldest sister, Louise, joined the Carmelite Order, de Lubac entered the novitiate of the Society of Jesus. It would be another seven years, however, before de Lubac began his formal training. In 1914, de Lubac was drafted into military service, and from 1915 to 1918, he served as an infantry soldier during the First World War. On All Saints Day, 1917, de Lubac sustained a shrapnel wound to the head, from which he suffered for years of earaches and continuous bouts of dizziness. As one of his students later recounts, 'The schoolmaster was a suffering man who brought back home from the First World War a serious head injury that impeded his work for days and weeks on end. Quite often we found him in an easy chair or stretched out on his bed, scarcely able to speak.'[17] It was not until an operation in 1954 that de Lubac finally recovered from the injuries sustained during the war.

It was during the war years that de Lubac also dates his first serious theological reflections. While stationed in Eparges, de Lubac gained the friendship of an unbelieving primary-school teacher. The two spoke frequently and debated on matters pertaining to philosophy and religion. According to de Lubac, these conversations were the initial inspiration for his book *The Discovery of God*.[18]

---

16. For a more detailed account of 'L'affaire de Lubac', cf. Georges Chantraine, *Henri de Lubac, t. I: De la naissance à la démobilisation (1896–1919)* (Paris: Cerf, 2007), pp. 57–58.

17. Xavier Tilliette, 'Henri de Lubac achtzigjährig', *Internationale Katholische Zeitschrift Communion* 5 (1976): p. 187, n. 12; cited in Rudolf Voderholzer, *Meet Henri de Lubac: His Life and Work* (San Francisco: Ignatius Press, 2008), p. 49.

18. ASC, p. 42.

This work, in many respects the most speculative and idiosyncratic of all de Lubac's writings, was intended 'to lend a helping hand to a few people in their search for God'.[19] In it, de Lubac argues for a pre-conceptual apprehension of God as the necessary condition for all finite acts of knowing and willing. This 'transcendental affirmation of God' sets in motion reason's quest to arrive at an explicit knowledge of the Absolute. This dynamism, in turn, finds its place of repose only in the supernatural revelation of Godself and the assimilating work of the Holy Spirit. Though more overtly 'apologetic' than de Lubac's other works, *The Discovery of God* attests de Lubac's lifelong occupation with modern unbelief. This occupation – which de Lubac often describes as a *confrontation*[20] – informs not only his engagement with such thinkers as Feuerbach, Comte, and Nietzsche, but also his many writings on the supernatural. For according to de Lubac, certain theological convictions inherited from late scholasticism concerning the relative autonomy of 'pure nature' left the Church ill-protected against (if not complicit in) the rise of atheistic humanism in the nineteenth and twentieth centuries.

De Lubac began his theological training in earnest in 1920, receiving much of his education in England on account of the strictures placed upon the religious orders in France. After a semester studying humanities at St Mary's College, Canterbury (1920), de Lubac completed his philosophical training in Jersey, England (1920–1923), before studying theology, first at the Jesuit theologate at Ore Place, Hastings (1924–1926), and finally at Fourvière, Lyons (1926–1928). As a student, de Lubac immersed himself in the writings of Irenaeus, Augustine, and especially Aquinas, as well as such contemporaries as Pierre Rousselot (1878–1915), the transcendental Thomist Joseph Maréchal (1878–1944), and the lay Catholic philosopher Maurice Blondel (1861–1949). The latter played a particularly crucial role in de Lubac's intellectual development.[21] De Lubac first discovered the writings of Blondel during his years of philosophy at Jersey – at which time he found himself perpetually at odds with the rigid neo-scholasticism of his instructors. What de Lubac discovered in Blondel was a philosophically rigorous defence of the intrinsic relation between human nature and the supernatural – between reason and revelation, philosophy and theology. According to Blondel, the problem of human destiny cannot be avoided. Human beings act, whether consciously or unconsciously, under the impulse of a particular finality. And yet, as Blondel seeks to demonstrate in an exacting (and often exhausting!) phenomenology of human action, human beings are incapable of attaining the end they necessarily seek. Philosophy thus arrives at

---

19. DG, p. 206; English translation of *Sur les chemins de Dieu* (Paris: Aubier, 1956), an expanded and revised edition of *De la connaissance de Dieu* (Paris: Editions du Témoignage Chrétien, 1945).

20. Cf. Henri de Lubac, 'Nature and Grace', in T. Patrick Burke, ed., *The Word in History* (New York: Sheed and Ward, 1966), p. 27.

21. Cf. Maurice Blondel, *Action (1893): Essay on a Critique of Life and a Science of Practice* (Indiana: University of Notre Dame Press, 2007); *The Letter on Apologetics and History and Dogma* (Michigan: William B. Eerdmans Publishing, 1964).

the postulate of the 'supernatural' as that which is both absolutely *necessary* for human beings and ultimately *inaccessible*. The dynamism of thought and action betray the 'supernatural insufficiency' of human nature.[22] According to de Lubac, it was Blondel who 'launched the decisive attack on the dualist theory which was destroying Christian thought', and it was largely due to his influence that 'we have consciously ceased to conceive of the natural and the supernatural orders as though they were two superposed storeys without any inner connections'.[23] Writing to Blondel in 1932, de Lubac states his own ambition to defend 'on the level of the most positive theology' the relation between nature and the supernatural suggested in Blondel's philosophy.[24] That is, whereas Blondel sought to demonstrate the supernatural insufficiency of human nature 'from below', de Lubac hoped to provide a theological interpretation of the dynamism of human existence 'from above' – on the basis of humanity's revealed destination to the graced enjoyment of God.

Two Programmatic Works

De Lubac was ordained priest in 1927 and completed his theological studies the following year. Due to the early retirement of Fr Albert Valensin, de Lubac was hurriedly appointed to the chair of fundamental theology at the Theology Faculty of Lyons in September 1929 – a post for which, having never obtained a doctorate, de Lubac felt greatly underprepared. Though lecturing 'downhill' at the Université Catholique, de Lubac resided primarily at the Jesuit scholasticate overlooking Lyons at Fourvière.[25] It was here that de Lubac served in an unofficial capacity as theological mentor to a number of prominent Jesuit students, including Jean Daniélou, Hans Urs von Balthasar, and the philosopher Xavier Tilliete (b. 1921). According to Balthasar, de Lubac referred his students 'beyond scholasticism to the Church fathers, generously making his notes and excerpts available to us'. As Tillliette recounts: 'he conducted a sort of clandestine teaching ministry; professors and students both visited his room regularly. He himself was never concerned about having "disciples" – "One is your Master" – but rather about inspiring them to be diligent theologians. Their studies were supposed to give form to their existence and train them to be witnesses to Christ'.[26] It was from

22. Blondel, *Letter on Apologetics*, p. 141.
23. BC, pp. 37–38.
24. De Lubac includes this exchange with Blondel in ASC, pp. 183–88.
25. De Lubac initially spent five years at the Jesuit residence on rue d'Auvergne (an old shack that was demolished shortly afterward) before transferring to Fourvière. Cf. ASC, p. 16.
26. Hans Urs von Balthasar, *Test Everything: Hold Fast to What Is Good* (San Francisco: Ignatius Press, 1989), p. 11; Tilliette, 'Henri de Lubac achtzigjährig': p. 187, n. 12; both citations included in Voderholzer, *Meet Henri de Lubac*, pp. 48–49.

this 'clandestine teaching ministry', along with that of de Lubac's confrère Henri Bouillard, that the so-called School of Fourvière took shape in the 1930s and 1940s, before coming under censure by the Father General of the Society in the early 1950s (of which more shall be said shortly).[27]

De Lubac's opening lecture at the Université Catholique de Lyons is in many respects programmatic for the approach to theology undertaken in his subsequent works.[28] In it, de Lubac mounts a provocative challenge to both the 'immanentism' of secular modernity (the theoretical refusal of all appeals to transcendence) and what he describes as the 'extrinsicism' of modern Roman Catholic theology (theological appeals to an order of nature in abstraction from humanity's supernatural finality). De Lubac begins his lecture with a critical assessment of contemporary forms of apologetics – apologetics forged largely in reaction to the rationalism of the Enlightenment project and the fideism and/or traditionalism to which many in the Church (particularly in France) sought refuge. According to this school of thought, the task of apologetics is concerned primarily with establishing the *fact* of revelation 'scientifically' on the basis of such 'external evidences' as the miracles and fulfilled prophecies recorded in scripture. The supernatural *content* of revelation is thus relegated to the domain of theology, while the task of apologetics is restricted to the rational demonstration of the credibility of the Christian religion. According to de Lubac, the error in this approach to apologetics consists in:

> ...conceiving of dogma as a kind of 'thing in itself', as a block of revealed truth with no relationship whatsoever to natural man...According to these theologians, when the apologist wishes to pass from reason to faith, he has only to establish a completely extrinsic connection between the two...He has only to observe, with the support of certain signs, that 'God has spoken' in history. And, just as it has never been his business to ask what man might be expecting, he is not to concern himself with what God has said.[29]

In place of such extrinsic accounts of the relationship between theology and apologetics, de Lubac's lecture gestures in the direction of an alternative construal of these two disciplines based upon a more 'traditional' (and Blondelian) account of the relation between nature and the supernatural. Rather than considering apologetics and theology in abstraction from one another – as two largely autonomous enterprises corresponding to the heteronomous realms of nature and the supernatural – de Lubac insists upon their compenetration. For according to

---

27. De Lubac always maintained that the 'Fourvière School' was a myth, concocted by theological opponents (notably Fr Reginald Garrigou-Lagrange of the Angelicum in Rome) in an attempt to associate and thereby condemn an assortment of otherwise independent thinkers and ideas. Cf. Henri de Lubac, *A Theologian Speaks* (Los Angeles, CA: Twin Circles Publishing Company, 1985), pp. 33–35.

28. Later published as 'Apologetics and Theology', in TH, pp. 91–104.

29. Ibid., p. 93.

de Lubac, 'there is no better way... for *giving an explanation* of our Faith... than to work with all our strength for its *understanding*. We must, by the *fides quaerens fidem* [faith seeking understanding], step forward to meet the *intellectus quaerens fidem* [understanding seeking faith]'.[30] Nature is teleologically ordered to the supernatural. Reason finds its place of fulfilment only in the revelation of God. As such, the credibility of the Christian faith resides, not primarily in external proofs, but rather in the intelligibility of faith itself and in the understanding of all things (including the dynamism of reason) in the light of this truth. According to de Lubac, it is therefore doctrine that 'attracts and conquers intelligence'.[31] De Lubac concludes his inaugural lecture by insisting that this conquering of the intelligence by doctrine, this compenetration of theology and apologetics, is the proper task of fundamental theology. It is the task, in other words, to which de Lubac understood himself to have been appointed as the chair of fundamental theology at the Université Catholique de Lyons.

If it is to de Lubac's inaugural lecture that we look for the principle motivating his approach to theology – the apologetic urgency of the Church's own reflection upon the revealed content of Christian belief – it is in his first book that we discover the main themes investigated in subsequent writings. Originally published in 1938, *Catholicisme* remains one of the most accessible and comprehensive introductions to de Lubac's entire oeuvre. This patchwork of lectures and previously published articles is not, as some of its earliest readers and reviewers supposed, a work on the *Catholica* per se – it is not a treatise on the Catholic Church. It is not exclusively, or even primarily, a work of ecclesiology. *Catholicism* is an exploration of the irreducibly social and historical dimensions of the Christian faith. It advances a theology of history along the axis of the restoration of humanity's abrogated unity – 'the recovery of supernatural unity of man with God, but equally of the unity of men amongst themselves'.[32] As de Lubac argues in *Catholicism*, this work of supernatural reunion is accomplished in Jesus Christ, extended historically through the sacrament of Christ's restorative presence, the Church, and consummated at the eschaton 'in the unity of the Body of Christ now fully perfected'.[33]

As Balthasar notes in his introduction to de Lubac's theology, the major works that followed *Catholicism* 'grew from its individual chapters like branches from a tree'.[34] The ecclesiology set forth in ch. 2, for instance, is developed at greater length in such works as *The Splendor of the Church*, *The Church: Paradox and Mystery*, and *The Motherhood of the Church*. Underlying each of these works is the conviction famously set forth in *Catholicism*: 'If Christ is the sacrament

---

30. Ibid., p. 98.
31. Ibid., p. 97.
32. C, p. 35.
33. Ibid., p. 120.
34. Hans Urs von Balthasar, *The Theology of Henri de Lubac* (San Francisco: Ignatius Press, 1991), p. 35.

of God, the Church is for us the sacrament of Christ; she represents him, in the full and ancient meaning of the term; she really makes him present.'[35] The Church is both a creature and an instrument of Christ's restorative benefits – the community of those reconciled to God in Christ and the continuation of Christ's reconciling work. In its insistence upon the sacraments as 'instruments of unity' (ch. 3), *Catholicism* anticipates the theological upshot of the historical investigations undertaken in *Corpus Mysticum*: the definitive fruit (*res tantum*) of the sacraments (and the Eucharist in particular) is the unity of the Church. Thus, while it is true that the Church 'produces' the Eucharist through the ministry of her ordained priesthood, it is equally the case that the Eucharist 'produces' the Church. By the Spirit of Christ, the Church *becomes* the body of which it partakes in the Eucharist. 'Thus everything points to a study of the relation between the Church and the Eucharist, which we may describe as standing as cause to each other. Each has been entrusted to the other, so to speak, by Christ.'[36] The chapter of *Catholicism* devoted to the interpretation of scripture (ch. 6) paves the way for de Lubac's voluminous contribution to the history of 'spiritual exegesis'.[37] This foray into the intricacies of Christian allegorical interpretation is scarcely an aside in *Catholicism*. Rather, what de Lubac discovers in patristic and medieval readings of scripture is a common grammar for 'making sense' of the contingencies of history more generally. For according to de Lubac, in learning to read the entirety of scripture (and hence the historical events to which scripture bears authoritative witness) in the light of the revelation of God and the reconciliation of humanity in Jesus Christ, one learns to read history qua history Christologically. Thus, as de Lubac insists in the 'Preface' to the first volume of his *Medieval Exegesis*, spiritual exegesis contains 'a whole theology of history... It organizes all of revelation around a concrete center, which is fixed in time and space by the Cross of Jesus Christ'.[38] In the historically circumscribed life and ministry of Jesus Christ, the purpose of history itself is rendered intelligible to those belonging in history to Christ's mystical body.

Finally, *Catholicism* contains one of de Lubac's earliest engagements with the phenomenon of atheist humanism. As de Lubac indicates in the book's 'Introduction', *Catholicism* was written with an eye to secular critiques of Christianity for being exclusively preoccupied with matters pertaining to individual salvation. Thus, whereas Marxist teleology culminates in the 'free development of each' as the condition for the 'free development of all', Christian soteriology (so the argument runs) restricts its hope to the soul's anagogical escape from the vicissitudes of history in the lone vision of God. In an important sense, the entirety of *Catholicism* is a rejoinder to this caricature of the Christian

---

35. C, p. 76.
36. SC, p. 133.
37. Cf. *History and Spirit: The Understanding of Scripture according to Origen*; *Medieval Exegesis*, 3 vols. The fourth volume of *Exégèse médiévale* has not yet been translated into English.
38. ME, v. I, p. xix.

gospel. 'We are accused of being individualists even in spite of ourselves, by the logic of our faith, whereas in reality Catholicism is essentially social.'[39] However, de Lubac goes further than simply debunking individualist construals of Christianity. In the final chapter of *Catholicism*, de Lubac turns the tables on Christianity's detractors, arguing that *only* Christian appeals to transcendence secure the accomplishment of a truly collective destiny for humanity. For if nothing transcends the dialectic of immanently historical processes – if humanity is simply the totality of beings relegated to particular moments in time – then it is not *humanity* that attains some final liberation, but only a conglomerate of future individuals. It is therefore necessary 'that humanity should have a meeting place in which, in every generation, it can be gathered together, a center to which it can converge, an Eternal to make it complete, an Absolute which, in the strongest and most real sense of the word, will make it *exist*'.[40] Immanence is guaranteed by transcendence. The end (*telos*) of history is eschatology. What we discover in the concluding chapter of *Catholicism* is therefore a rehearsal of the main thesis set forth in *The Drama of Atheist Humanism* (1944): 'Exclusive [atheistic] humanism is inhuman humanism.'[41] It is also the conviction permeating de Lubac's many writings on nature and the supernatural: the perfection of human society, like the perfection of every individual, entails 'the irruption of a wholly different principle'.[42] Nature attains its completion only through the supernatural.

In responding to 'communitarian' critiques of Christianity, and in compensating for the overly juridical approach to ecclesiology in a great deal of contemporary Roman Catholic literature,[43] *Catholicism* is very much a work of its time. Even so, it remains one of the key texts of twentieth-century Catholic theology. *Catholicism* is a towering work of doctrinal synthesis – at once constructive and deeply conversant with earlier theological voices. As Joseph Ratzinger (now Pope Emeritus Benedict XVI) remarks in his Foreword to the 1988 English edition, 'It fascinated theologians in the fifties everywhere and his [de Lubac's] insights quickly became the common patrimony of theological reflection.'[44] Balthasar, who did much to secure the work's international readership by translating it into German, describes *Catholicism* as 'the first authentic breakthrough into a more liberated view of the Church'. He recalls with some embarrassment a birthday celebration in honour of Yves Congar at which the master of ceremonies declared to Fr Congar, 'no matter how important your work may be, that of de Lubac, not yours, has achieved the decisive breakthrough'.[45] By the end of the 1940s, the success of *Catholicism* helped to secure de Lubac's place as one of the leading Catholic intellectuals in France.

39. C, p. 15.
40. Ibid., p. 354.
41. DAH, p. 14.
42. Ibid., p. 466.
43. Cf. C, p. 314.
44. Ibid., p. 12.
45. Balthasar, *Test Everything*, p. 14.

The War Years

De Lubac's second major work was *Corpus Mysticum* – a historical and theological investigation of the semantic drift of the words 'corpus mysticum' (mystical body) from signifying originally the eucharistic mystery to eventually designating the corporate body of the Church. In *Corpus Mysticum*, de Lubac attempts to showcase the extent to which debates in the eleventh and twelfth centuries (anticipating later debates at the time of the Reformation) concerning the 'real presence' of Christ in the Eucharist led to the unfortunate neglect of the sacrament's role in the formation of the ecclesial body. While the completion of *Corpus Mysticum* came immediately on the heels of *Catholicism*, setting the pace for the staggering succession of works that would span the next fifty years, the outbreak of war in 1939 prevented it from emerging from the printers until 1944. In the meantime, beginning especially with the German invasion and the occupation of northern France in 1940, de Lubac's intellectual energies were devoted largely to confronting the 'neopaganism' of Nazism and the attendant nationalism and anti-Semitism now vying for the soul of France. As de Lubac laments in a letter to his Jesuit superiors on 25 April 1941, not even the Church was immune from the 'Hitlerian virus' sweeping the country.[46] Following the Fall of Paris and the armistice of Compiègne in 1940, which officially placed the north and west of France under German control, Maréchal Pétain (1856–1951) was elected prime minister of France, governing the country's 'free zone' from Vichy in collaboration with Hitler's Reich. Still smarting from the laicist policies of the Third Republic and the Church's cultural marginalization throughout much of the early twentieth century, a growing number of French Catholics (clergy included) were tempted to see the hand of divine governance at work in the sudden rise of the Vichy regime, which championed the traditional values of 'Work, Family and Country' and instituted a number of policies favourable to the Church in France.[47] As de Lubac writes to his superiors:

> It seems that we have become, in large measure, dupes of the necessity in which we find ourselves of participating in the official lie... We hear some of [our Christian leaders] publicly express satisfaction with the present situation from the religious point of view; hyperboles abound on their lips and in their writings; they speak freely of 'providential defeat', of 'miracles', and so forth.[48]

From Lyons, the 'capital of the Resistance', de Lubac played a leading role in the Church's 'spiritual resistance' to Nazism. In June 1941, two weeks after the order was given in the *Journal officiel* for a census to be taken of all Jews in France,

---

46. Later published as 'Letter to My Superiors', TH, pp. 428–39.
47. Cf. Joseph Komonchak, 'Theology and Culture at Mid-Century: The Example of Henri de Lubac', *Theological Studies* 51 (1990): p. 597; Julian Jackson, *France: The Dark Years, 1940–1944* (Oxford: Oxford University Press, 2001), pp. 268–71.
48. TH, p. 434.

de Lubac co-authored a widely circulated declaration condemning Vichy's anti-Semitic policies and propaganda.[49] On 10 August 1942, following the great roundup of Jews in Paris and similar operations in the south, de Lubac was sent by the Archbishop of Lyons (Cardinal Gerlier) to consult with the Archbishop of Toulouse (Cardinal Saliège) for the purpose of preparing a joint intervention. From this meeting arose a pastoral letter which was secretly distributed to the priests of both dioceses and simultaneously read in pulpits throughout the unoccupied zone. During the war years, de Lubac wrote and lectured often on the dangers of Nazi ideology. Along with such figures as Pierre Chaillet, Gaston Fessard, Jean Daniélou, and Yves de Montcheuil, de Lubac contributed regularly to the production and distribution of the *Cahiers du Témoignage chrétien* – a clandestine series of pamphlets intended to encourage Christians to organize resistance to Nazism on theological grounds. Of the contributors to the *Cahiers*, Fr Chaillet narrowly escaped being arrested by swallowing incriminating papers moments before his interrogation by the Gestapo, and Fr de Montcheuil was tragically executed in 1944. De Lubac himself was hunted by the Gestapo and forced to flee Lyons in 1943. He remained hidden away in Vals until the departure of the German army in 1944.

As well as confronting head-on the anti-Christian commitments funding Nazism, de Lubac devoted a number of lectures and essays throughout the war years to demonstrating the extent to which the present crisis owes its genesis to a confluence of ideologies emerging a century earlier. These writings were eventually compiled and included in de Lubac's massively influential *The Drama of Atheist Humanism* – a work that emerged before the liberation of Paris and which went through four editions by 1950.[50] In *The Drama of Atheist Humanism*, de Lubac argues that the dissolution of humanity is the inevitable consequence of the 'death of God' as heralded by such prophets of atheist humanism as Ludwig Feuerbach, Auguste Comte, and (most persuasively) Friedrich Nietzsche. Each of these thinkers in his own way rebelled against the tyranny of transcendence, seeking to liberate human beings from God in order to secure humanity's own immanent dignity. According to the advocates of atheist humanism, humanity must reclaim the 'divine' attributes mistakenly attributed to God. God must die that man might truly live. On the contrary, de Lubac insists: 'If man takes himself as god, he can, for a time, cherish the illusion that he has raised and freed himself. But it is a

---

49. The 'Chaine Declaration' was written by Abbé Joseph Chaine (professor of Old Testament at the Catholic Institute of Lyons), de Lubac, Louis Richard (professor of dogma), and Fr Joseph Bonsirven (a priest in residence at the Fourvière scholasticate). It was distributed anonymously beginning 17 June 1941. De Lubac includes the full text in CR, pp. 66–68.

50. As de Lubac acknowledges in the preface to later editions, Vichy censures during the Occupation prevented him from making explicit the relation between the ideologies canvassed in *The Drama of Atheist Humanism* and Nazi Neopaganism. 'This explains, on the one hand, some of the emphases and, on the other hand and in particular, some of the omissions, some of the silences' (DAH, p. 15).

fleeting exaltation! In reality, he has merely abased God, and it is not long before he finds that in doing so he has abased himself.'[51] In abolishing transcendence, humanity unmoors itself from the source of its own true dignity and vocation. Immanence thus collapses under the weight of a falsely attributed Absolute. The death of God eventually gives way to the death of humanity. This, de Lubac suggests, is the ideological backdrop to the horrors of the present era. It is also, we might add, the rationale for the emergence of what Emmanuel Levinas refers to as 'an atheism that *is not* humanist' in the years immediately following the Second World War.[52] As Jean-Paul Sartre declares in his widely celebrated (and even more widely contested) post-war manifesto, *L'existentialisme est un humanisme*, 'there is no human nature, because there is no God to have a conception of it'.[53]

De Lubac's criticisms of the conditions leading to the rise and success of Nazism were hardly restricted to the advocates of atheist humanism. According to de Lubac, the Church likewise bears significant responsibility for the present crisis. Indeed, as de Lubac declares in a 1941 lecture, 'At the root of everything, it must be said, there is a failure among Christians.'[54] On the one hand, de Lubac insists, the faith has become a means to civic order in accord with Napoleon's purely utilitarian maxim: 'A religion is necessary for the people.' De Lubac obviously has in mind a number of Pétain's Catholic supporters for whom religion served a primarily conservative social agenda. On the other hand, for many a sincere believer, faith has become a strictly private affair. This privatization of the Christian faith effectively evacuates public discourse of any theological account of the common good. The project of cultural construction is thus relegated to largely atheological – or explicitly *anti*-Christian – influences. In a lecture delivered the following year, de Lubac aims his critiques more directly at the teaching office of the Church, addressing the culpability of priests and theologians for the 'disappearance of the sense of the sacred' in modern France.[55] More specifically, de Lubac targets the methodological and theological commitments enshrined in the seminary manuals of the day. At the level of method, such theology all too often proceeds in the manner of an esoteric science, similar to other sciences with the sole exception that theology's first principles are derived from revelation rather than from reason or experience. According to de Lubac, theology is thereby abstracted from the contingencies and concerns of history, mystery is conflated with the mere boundaries of deductive reasoning, and the self-revelation of God is reduced to a static depository of timeless propositions.

---

51. Ibid., pp. 67–68.
52. Levinas, 'On Maurice Blanchot', in *Proper Names* (London: Athlone Press, 1996), pp. 127–28. See Jordan Hillebert, 'The Death of God and the Dissolution of Humanity', *New Blackfriars* 95:1060 (November 2014): pp. 674–88.
53. Sartre, *Existentialism and Humanism* (London: Methuen & Co, 1968), p. 28.
54. 'Christian Explanation of Our Time', TH, p. 441.
55. 'Internal Causes of the Weakening and Disappearance of the Sense of the Sacred', TH, pp. 223–40.

It is little wonder that such modes of theologizing fail to find a contemporary audience. More importantly, at the level of doctrine, the neo-scholastic manuals posit a strictly extrinsic relation between nature and the supernatural. In an effort to protect the gratuity of the supernatural, nature was granted a level of autonomy heretofore unrealized in the history of Christian thought, while the supernatural was relegated to 'some distant corner' where, according to de Lubac, 'it could only remain sterile'. There was therefore 'an unconscious conspiracy' between secularism and a certain theology. The latter concerned itself strictly with the supernatural truths of revelation. Secularism meanwhile took root and developed within an order wholly sufficient unto itself in isolation from the claims of the supernatural. The lines of demarcation were thus drawn and agreed upon by both parties, theology supplying the metaphysical warrant for its own marginalization. As de Lubac elsewhere insists, a confrontation with atheistic immanentism thus entails a return to a more traditional rendering of the relation between nature and the supernatural, one that takes seriously humanity's ontological ordination to the supernatural. It was this particular theological vision that de Lubac sought to rehabilitate in his *Surnaturel*, that epochal text that was completed during the Occupation and that would introduce de Lubac to a wholly different form of 'warfare' throughout the late 1940s and 1950s.

Surnaturel

De Lubac's writings on the supernatural span six decades, comprising four monographs and numerous articles.[56] The subject had occupied de Lubac since his days as a student. At St Mary's College in Canterbury, de Lubac encountered Pierre Rousselot's thesis on the *Intellectualisme de saint Thomas* which, according to de Lubac, first awakened him to metaphysical problems.[57] In Rousselot's work, de Lubac discovered an alternative to neo-scholastic readings of the Angelic Doctor, one that prioritized the intellect's need and *innate desire* for 'that supernatural complement that takes place in the Beatific Vision'.[58] This rendering of the dynamism of human reason was soon reinforced by de Lubac's reading of Blondel on Jersey. Finally, while a student of theology at Ore Place, de Lubac was encouraged by then-Professor of Scripture Joseph Huby to verify whether the teaching of Aquinas on the subject of the supernatural 'was indeed what was claimed by the Thomist school around the sixteenth century, codified in

---

56. Cf. *Surnaturel*; 'Duplex Hominis Beatitudo', *Communio* 25 (Winter 2008): pp. 599–612; 'The Mystery of the Supernatural', TH, pp. 281–316; *Augustinianism and Modern Theology*; *The Mystery of the Supernatural*; and *A Brief Catechesis on Nature and Grace*.

57. ASC, p. 65. Rousselot was killed in the spring of 1915 at the Battle of Les Eparges, a year before de Lubac himself was stationed at Eparges.

58. Rousselot, *The Intellectualism of Saint Thomas* (New York: Sheed and Ward, 1935), pp. 178–79.

the seventeenth and asserted with greater emphasis than ever in the twentieth'.[59] Huby's invitation set de Lubac to work over the next four years until teaching responsibilities forced him to abandon the project for nearly a decade.[60] It wasn't until June of 1940, while evading the German army in La Louvesc, that de Lubac returned to his notes on the supernatural:

> I spent several days up there putting a little order into it. Soon there was the return from our exodus... and I gave no more thought to it. But when, in 1943, being hunted by the Gestapo, I had to flee once more, I carried along my notebook. Hidden away in Vals, which I could not leave and where I could not engage in any correspondence, I thus had something to occupy my retreat... When I came back to Lyons soon after the departure of the German army, it was ready to be delivered to the printer.[61]

What emerged from the printers in 1946 was scarcely what one might expect from such a contentious publication. As the French historian Étienne Fouilloux remarks, the appearance of *Surnaturel* was 'quite the opposite of a media campaign for an anticipated bestseller'.[62] The sheer size of the tome (roughly 500 pages of densely argued prose), the modest number of copies (700 in its first run), and a litany of untranslated Latin citations would have seemed to destine *Surnaturel* to a rather limited and specialist audience. Few could have anticipated that this largely esoteric collection of historical studies would be the catalyst for one of the most significant theological controversies of the twentieth century.

What de Lubac advances in *Surnaturel* and subsequent writings on the topic is both a refutation of the neo-scholastic theory of 'pure nature' and a positive construal of humanity's innate ordination to the beatific vision. The system of pure nature to which de Lubac devotes his polemic is less an isolated doctrine than a series of interrelated principles and theological convictions intended to safeguard the gratuity of the supernatural without compromising the integrity of created nature. This system posits a twofold finality for human beings – a purely natural beatitude corresponding to the natural desire of human beings and their connatural end and a supernatural beatitude surpassing the capacities of human nature and the limitations of natural desire. According to the advocates of pure nature, both ends reside strictly in the contemplation of God. However, whereas one's natural beatitude consists in the contemplation of God *according to his or her natural powers* (the knowledge of God sought after by the philosophers), supernatural

---

59. ASC, p. 35.

60. In the meantime, de Lubac published portions of his research in 'Deux augustiniens fourvoyés', *Recherches de science religieuse* 21 (1931), pp. 422–43, 513–40; 'Remarques sur l'histoire du mot "surnaturel"', *Nouvelle revue théologique* 61 (1934): pp. 225–49, 350–70.

61. ASC, p. 35.

62. Fouilloux, 'Henri de Lubac at the Moment of the Publication of *Surnaturel*', in Serge-Thomas Bonino, ed., *Surnaturel: A Controversy at the Heart of Twentieth-Century Thomistic Thought* (Florida: Sapientia Press, 2009), p. 4.

beatitude is possible *only by the light of glory* in the beatific vision (the knowledge of God enjoyed by the saints). Thus, while the former is to a certain extent 'owed' to human beings as a matter of right, insofar as it lies within the powers of human nature to attain, the latter is strictly gratuitous, exceeding the proportionality of created nature and only ever received in the form of a divine gift.

De Lubac's misgivings with the theory of pure nature converge upon three main lines of criticism. In the first place, as we noted above, de Lubac was convinced that the theory left the Church ill-equipped in confronting the immanentism of secular modernity. 'The unbeliever found it easy to withdraw into his indifference in the very name of what theology was telling him: if my very nature as a man truly has its end in itself, what should oblige or even arouse me to scrutinize history in the quest for some other vocation perhaps to be found there?'[63] According to this schema, de Lubac insists, the supernatural is at best an unnecessary 'superstructure' and at worst an intrusion upon humanity's immanently sufficient order of existence. Second, de Lubac was unimpressed by the theory's historical pedigree. That is to say, de Lubac's response to the line of inquiry suggested by Fr Huby was decidedly negative – the theory of pure nature proffered by Thomists in the sixteenth century has little to do with the doctrine of St Thomas. The Common Doctor, in company with Augustine, Bonaventure, Duns Scotus, and the entirety of eastern theology, never envisaged for human beings 'an end at once transcendent and natural, consisting in a knowledge of God other than the beatific vision.'[64] According to de Lubac, the theory of pure nature was developed initially by Denys the Carthusian (1402–1471) *in opposition to* the writings of St Thomas and only later introduced into the Thomist commentarial tradition by the Dominican Cardinal Cajetan (1469–1534).[65] Finally, and most importantly, de Lubac argues that the theory of pure nature subsumes human beings within a univocal account of created nature, thereby betraying the unique ontological status of human persons. According to the advocates of pure nature, 'all being must have its connatural end, proportioned to its nature and of the same order as it.'[66] This unassailable principle, however faithful to the cosmology of Aristotle, does little justice to the history of Christian reflection on the dignity of humanity's creation in the divine image. As St Thomas neatly summarizes this anthropological consensus, 'The rational creature in this surpasses all creation, because he has the capacity for the highest good through divine vision and enjoyment, *although for this he needs the divine help of grace*.'[67] To be human is therefore to be uniquely and fittingly ordered to the reception of God's self-bestowal in grace.

In contradistinction to the theory of pure nature, de Lubac thus insists upon what he refers to as a more 'paradoxical' construal of the drama of human

---

63. De Lubac, 'Nature and Grace', in T. Patrick Burke, ed., *The Word in History* (New York: Sheed & Ward, 1966), p. 32.
64. S, p. 109.
65. Cf. S, p. 105; AMT, p. 113; MS, pp. 144–45.
66. 'The Mystery of the Supernatural', TH, p. 104; see also S, p. 114.
67. Thomas Aquinas, *De malo*, q.1, c.5; cited in AMT, p. 171; emphasis added.

existence. First, de Lubac maintains that *human beings are ordered to a single finality*. Humanity's ultimate end is supernatural, granted by the light of glory in the beatific vision of God. 'Natural' beatitude – the felicitous condition of humanity's relation to any number of proximate goods – participates proleptically in this perfect happiness *without* constituting in itself a transcendent end. Second, de Lubac insists upon *an intrinsic relation between being and finality*. According to de Lubac, the advocates of pure nature err in considering finality, not as 'a destiny inscribed in the very structure of the being and which, ontologically, he cannot avoid', but rather as 'a destination received more or less from outside and after the fact'.[68] For de Lubac, finality is something ontological, something intrinsic to the creature that cannot be altered without altering in turn the very nature of that being itself. To insist therefore that human beings alone (at least among corporeal beings) are ordered to a supernatural end is to insist likewise on a radical disproportionality between human beings and other 'beings of nature'. Finally, according to de Lubac, the principal expression of this disproportionality and the basic ontological implication of humanity's supernatural finality is the dynamism of the 'unquiet heart' – humanity's *natural desire for the supernatural*. As de Lubac famously declares in the concluding chapter of Surnaturel, '*L'esprit est donc désir de Dieu*'.[69] The human spirit just is the desire for God. This desire is not, as some of de Lubac's later interpreters would insist, an inchoate participation in the grace that fulfils human nature.[70] Rather, the longing for God is 'a longing "born of a lack," and not arising from "the beginnings of possession"'.[71] According to de Lubac, this desire is at once absolute, unconditioned, and inefficacious. That is to say, the desire for God imposes itself necessarily upon our nature (we cannot not desire it); is antecedent to all finite acts of knowing and willing (it is not elicited by some prior object of knowledge); and places no obligation upon God to fulfil it.

Lightning Strikes Fourvière

At the time of *Surnaturel*'s publication, de Lubac was already an object of some suspicion among a number of influential Thomists. His involvement as co-editor of *Sources chrétiennes* (a translation series of patristic works into contemporary French) and his contribution to the Fourvière series *Théologie* (which aimed 'to go to the sources of Christian doctrine, to find in it [*sic*] the truth of our life'[72]) elicited charges of historical relativism and antipathy to the 'scientific consensus' of scholastic theology.[73] De Lubac and a number of his Fourvière colleagues were

---

68. 'The Mystery of the Supernatural', TH, p. 296.
69. S, p. 483.
70. Cf. Milbank, *The Suspended Middle*, 43–44.
71. MS, p. 84.
72. ASC, p. 31; quoting Henri Bouillard.
73. Cf. Marie-Michel Labourdette, 'La théologie et ses sources', *Revue thomiste* 46 (1946): pp. 353–71.

accused of championing a 'new theology' (*nouvelle théologie*), which could only lead to 'scepticism, fantasy, and heresy'.[74] With the publication of *Surnaturel*, the line of attack was extended from matters of methodology to the realm of positive doctrine. According to his critics, in insisting, 'there can only be for man one end: the supernatural end, which the Gospel proposes and theology defines as the "beatific vision"',[75] de Lubac was guilty either of subsuming the gratuity of the supernatural to the gratuity of creation or worse, positing an exigency in human nature for the supernatural. This suspicion of exigency was only exacerbated by de Lubac's construal of the *desiderium naturae*. For how could God possibly be free to grant or withhold a finality inscribed in the very depths of human being? (On the contrary, de Lubac always maintained that exigency runs in the exact opposite direction: 'if there is in our nature a desire to see God, this can only be because God wills for us this supernatural end which consists in seeing him. It is because, willing it and never ceasing to will it, he places and never ceases to place this desire in our nature').[76]

In September of 1946, at the outbreak of controversy, the newly elected Superior General of the Society of Jesus, Fr Janssens, assured de Lubac that neither he nor the pope held him in any suspicion. Janssens provided further proof of his confidence when, in January of the following year, he confided to de Lubac the direction of the Jesuit periodical *Recherches de science religieuse*. Within a few months, however, the mounting criticisms of de Lubac's work led Fr Janssens to reassess the situation. Desperate to avoid magisterial involvement, Janssens subjected *Surnaturel* to the scrutiny of four anonymous censors. By March 1948, de Lubac was instructed to submit all of his writings to both Provincial and Roman censors, and in February 1950, de Lubac was instructed to resign as editor of *Recherches* and cease all teaching by the summer. Shortly thereafter, 'lightning struck Fourvière'.[77]

In June of 1950, the order was given to remove de Lubac and four of his confreres from their religious duties in Lyons. According to Janssens, such extreme measures were provoked by 'pernicious errors on essential points of dogma'.[78] De Lubac was swiftly sent off to rue de Sèvres in Paris, at which time (on the very day of his arrival), Pope Pius XII's encyclical *Humani generis* appeared in the French Roman Catholic newspaper *La Croix*. Of particular relevance to the fate of de Lubac was a line in the encyclical warning of certain theologians who 'destroy the gratuity of the supernatural order, since God, they say, cannot create intellectual beings without ordering and calling them to the beatific vision'.[79] The Pope's words were immediately taken as an incrimination of de Lubac's work on the supernatural,

---

74. Réginald Garrigou-Lagrange, 'La nouvelle théologie. où va-t-elle?', *Angelicum* 23 (1946): pp. 126–45.
75. S, p. 493.
76. Ibid., pp. 486–87.
77. ASC, p. 67.
78. Ibid., p. 68.
79. Pius XII, *Humani generis*, p. 25.

thus lending papal credence to the charges brought against him by his neo-scholastic opponents.[80] In the weeks following the publication of the encyclical, the order was given to withdraw from Jesuit libraries three of de Lubac's books (*Surnaturel, Corpus Mysticum,* and *Connaissance de Dieu*) as well as a volume of *Recherches* containing one of de Lubac's essays on the supernatural. For the next decade, de Lubac remained a largely marginalized figure. Numerous ministries were refused him, and for most of the 1950s he was prevented from teaching and publishing in the field of theology.

Rehabilitation and the Threat of Intrinsicism

Even 'in exile', de Lubac's writing continued at a feverish pace. Since theology was initially closed to him, de Lubac took the opportunity to publish three works on Buddhism[81] – a subject that had interested de Lubac for more than two decades during which he had lectured regularly on the history of religions at the Université Catholique. De Lubac had long been struck by the originality and multiformity of Buddhism, as well as by its spiritual depths. This foray into world religions nevertheless confirmed his conviction of 'the extraordinary unicity of the Christian Event', what he referred to often as *la Nouveauté chrétienne* (the Christian Newness).[82] In 1956, de Lubac set to work on what would eventuate as four volumes on the history of medieval exegesis. However historical the line of inquiry taken in *Medieval Exegesis*, the inspiration for these four volumes was, like all of de Lubac's works, chiefly theological. As we noted above, what de Lubac discovered amidst the diverse schema advanced by patristic and medieval exegetes with respect to the 'multiple senses' of scripture was a shared theological conviction concerning the historical primacy of Christ. Rather than evacuating history of its own proper density and meaning in favour of some 'timeless truth' (the modus operandi of Hellensitic philosophic allegory), Christian spiritual/allegorical interpretation sought to explicate the events and telos of history in the light of the singular history of Jesus of Nazareth.

As early as 1956, there were some signs (however faint) that the air of suspicion surrounding de Lubac was beginning to settle. De Lubac returned to

---

80. De Lubac always denied being incriminated in *Humani generis*. Indeed, he notes that the relevant sentence in the encyclical actually reproduces his own writing on the subject from two years earlier (ASC, p. 71; referring to 'The Mystery of the Supernatural', TH, p. 118). However, without denying that God *could* have created intellectual beings without ordering them to the supernatural, de Lubac is nevertheless adamant that in the present order of human existence, human beings are teleologically ordered to the beatific vision.

81. *Aspects du Bouddhisme* (Paris: Editions du Seuil, 1951) [trans. *Aspects of Buddhism* (London: Sheed & Ward, 1953)]; *La recontré du Buddhisme et de l'Occident* (Paris: Aubier, 1952); *Amida* (Paris: Editions du Seuil, 1955).

82. ASC, p. 32.

Lyons (though not to Fourvière), where he was permitted to give instruction at the Catholic Faculties on the subjects of Hinduism and Buddhism. De Lubac was also permitted to publish *Sur le chemins de Dieu*, an enlarged edition of the heretofore-censured *Connaissance de Deiu*, including a postscript responding to his critics. In 1958, de Lubac received letters from both Pope Pius XII and Fr Janssens indicating (in the former) a renewed confidence in de Lubac's work and (in the latter) the acknowledgement of a certain complicity in the 'misunderstandings' surrounding de Lubac's misfortunes throughout the 1950s.[83] With the accession of Pope John XXIII later that year, de Lubac's rehabilitation took an enormous leap forward. The new Pope made known his displeasure with the events surrounding *Humani generis* and, as a sign of goodwill, had a large donation made to *Sources chrétiennes*. In August of 1960, Pope John XXIII openly confirmed his confidence in de Lubac by selecting him as a consulter to the Preparatory Theological Commission for the Second Vatican Council. From there, de Lubac went on to serve in an official capacity as *peritus* to the Council. He was involved in revising the famous Schema 13, which served as the foundation for the Pastoral Constitution on the Church in the Modern World (*Gaudiem et spes*), and the influence of his theology is clearly evident in the dogmatic constitutions on revelation (*Dei verbum*) and the Church (*Lumen gentium*). While de Lubac's theology continued to face some concerted opposition throughout the 1960s (as indeed it does till to this day), by the close of the final session of the Vatican Council, de Lubac was once more in good standing with the magisterium and his Jesuit superiors. De Lubac continued to publish well into his eighties, penning among other works two 'commentaries' on the Vatican II documents,[84] three more books on the subject of the supernatural,[85] a monograph on the Renaissance philosopher Pico della Mirandola,[86] and two volumes on the apocalyptic legacy of Joachim of Fiore.[87]

While de Lubac's pre-conciliar writings regularly attracted the ire of 'conservatives' (both political and theological) within the Church, de Lubac now found himself increasingly at odds with certain 'progressive' trends in post-conciliar theology. In particular, de Lubac laments the 'gnostic elitism' and critical disposition adopted by a number of contemporary theologians in relation to both the conciliar documents and the magisterium. Indeed, these thinkers, rarely named by de Lubac (with a couple notable exceptions[88]), receive his fiercest polemic to date. Responding to Pope John XXIII's clarion call for *aggiornamento* (bringing up to date) at the outset of the Council, these theologians sought rupture

---

83. Ibid., pp. 89–91.

84. *La Révélation divine* (Lyon: Ed. La Bonté, 1966); and *Athéisme et sens de l'homme: une double requite de Gaudium et Spes* (Paris: Cerf, 1968).

85. *Augustinianism and Modern Theology*; *The Mystery of the Supernatural*; and *A Brief Catechesis on Nature and Grace*.

86. *Pic de La Mirandole: Études et discussions* (Paris: Aubier-Montaigne, 1974).

87. *La Postérité spirituelle de Joachim de Flore*, 2 vols (Paris: Lethielleux, 1978), p. 81.

88. Cf. de Lubac's accusation of Hans Küng's 'theological charlatanism' (MP, p. 72)!

with the Church's living tradition rather than renewal from within.[89] The 'openness to the world' advocated and evinced in *Gaudium et spes* was likewise pressed into the service of an ecclesial and theological conformism to the ideologies of secular modernity.[90] Claiming for itself the title of true heir to the 'spirit of Vatican II', this 'para-Council', 'which often deserved the name anti-Council',[91] proffers a 'radical "transformation", which is to say, the secularization of the Church, which is to say, by its true name, apostasy. It is apostasy that is covered up by the successive tinsel of the "spirit of the Council", "secularization", "pluralism", and so on'.[92]

It is unfair simply to attribute such remarks to an aged conservatism or de Lubac's blind allegiance to Pope Paul VI (both charges levelled against de Lubac by his contemporaries).[93] Rather, de Lubac's opposition to post-conciliar 'progressivism' was every bit as indebted to a particular construal of the supernatural as his opposition to neo-scholastic integrism throughout the 1940s and 1950s. That is to say, de Lubac was convinced that both neo-scholasticism and certain trends in post-conciliar theology mitigate the necessity of the supernatural. The former, in its avowal of a purely natural teleology, relegated the supernatural to an arbitrary 'superstructure'. The latter had a tendency to naturalize the supernatural, eliding the necessary distinction between nature and the economy of grace. This line of criticism is evident throughout a number of de Lubac's later writings. For instance, while generally sympathetic to the theology of Karl Rahner (1904–1984), de Lubac took issue with his famous construal of 'anonymous Christianity'. According to de Lubac, Rahner's thesis underplays the transfigurative novelty of the supernatural. For, 'In Jesus, there has appeared to us not only someone who reveals to man what man already was but also … someone who, revealing the depths of God, changes man radically'.[94] More to the point: an 'implicit Christianity' does little justice to the necessity of *metanoia* as the antecedent condition for humanity's supernatural enjoyment of God. Similarly, without denying the urgency of the Church's commitment to the betterment of human society, de Lubac warns against a false equivalence between social liberation and the supernatural in-breaking of God's kingdom. 'We must, then, take care not to confuse the "progress of this world" … with the "new creation". We must avoid slipping from the conversion of heart … to the unfolding of history (dialectic or not) that bears "as in its womb" the societies of the future.'[95] Finally, and most forcefully, de Lubac challenges Schillebeeckx's portrayal of the Church as the 'sacrament of the world' – the visible manifestation of what grace is always already accomplishing in 'human-

---

89. Cf. BC, p. 236.
90. Cf. ASC, p. 150.
91. BC, p. 238.
92. MP, p. 45.
93. Cf. ASC, p. 148.
94. CPM, p. 90.
95. BC, p. 101.

existence-in-the-world'.⁹⁶ To the contrary, as we have seen, for de Lubac the Church is the 'sacrament of *Christ*', the continuation of Christ's reconciling work and the harbinger of humanity's eschatological unity.

Whereas *Surnaturel* was the primary vehicle for de Lubac's assault upon extrinsicism, his magisterial two-volume *La Postérité spirituelle de Joachim de Flore* takes up his later occupation with theological *intrinsicism* (the immanentizing of the supernatural within human nature and/or history). According to the twelfth-century abbot and apocalypticist Joachim of Fiore (1135–1202), history unfolds along three stages in the progressive actualization of human freedom. The final stage, what Joachim terms the 'age of the Spirit', will occur within history (prior to the Final Judgment) and will consist of the perfection of divine knowledge and human fellowship. At this stage, the institutional Church and its sacramental cultus will give way to an unmediated fellowship between the 'spiritual men' (*viri spirituales*) of history's final epoch. Just as de Lubac noted a certain complicity between the neo-scholastic theory of pure nature and the anthropology of secular humanism, so in *La Postérité spirituelle* de Lubac traces the evolution of Joachimite apocalypticism into secular narrations of history. That is, according to de Lubac, Joachimite appeals to a future 'age of the Spirit' *within history* led ultimately to the immanentizing of eschatology in secular philosophies of history and the eclipse of Christology and ecclesiology in a great deal of modern theology. Thus, according de Lubac, the champions of the 'Spirit of Vatican II' are actually the spiritual heirs of Joachim of Fiore. Post-conciliar appeals to an immantentist/revolutionary eschatology and the necessity of the Church's radical transfiguration betray the spectre of the Calabrian abbot.

It is a testament to de Lubac's independence as a thinker with respect to intellectual fads – an independence inspired by his dependence upon the sources of the Church's living tradition – that he should spend so much of his career ecclesiastically marginalized only to be dismissed by many in his later years as a 'court theologian'. Increasingly *passé* from the vantage of a certain post-conciliar orthodoxy, the latter decades of de Lubac's life nevertheless brought with them a number of just recognitions of his accomplishments both as an academic and as a servant of the Church. Already in 1959 (prior to his full ecclesial rehabilitation), de Lubac was elected as a member of the *Académie des sciences morales et politiques*, one of the five branches of the prestigious Institute of France. In 1969, alongside such theologians as Karl Rahner, Hans Urs von Balthasar, and Joseph Ratzinger, de Lubac was selected as a member of the International Theological Commission, a newly commissioned advisory panel to Pope Paul VI. Finally, on 2 February 1983, just before his eighty-seventh birthday, de Lubac was made cardinal by Pope John Paul II.

On 4 September 1991, following a stroke that deprived him of his ability to speak, Cardinal de Lubac died under the care of the Little Sisters of the Poor in Paris.

---

96. Cf. de Lubac, 'The "Sacrament of the World"?', BC, pp. 191–234.

The Unity of a Theological Project

Writing in 1975 with respect to the scope of his own work, de Lubac remarks, 'It would be fruitless to seek in such a diverse collection of writings the elements of any truly personal philosophical or theological – or, as some have said, "gnoseological" – synthesis, whether to criticize or adopt it.'[97] De Lubac made no attempt to offer a systematic presentation of his thought in the manner of, for instance, Rahner's *Foundations of Christian Faith*. There is no single key for unlocking the Lubacian corpus. Faced with the sheer breadth of de Lubac's writings, one never quite shakes the feeling expressed by Balthasar that one is 'at the entrance to a primeval forest. The themes could hardly be more diverse, and the gaze of the researcher glides seemingly without effort over the whole history of theology – and of thought itself'.[98] Nevertheless, as de Lubac acknowledges, it is possible to discern in his work a certain unity of intent. 'Without claiming to open up new avenues to thought, I have sought rather, without any antiquarianism, to make known some of the great common areas of Catholic tradition. I wanted to make it loved, to show its ever-present fruitfulness.'[99] It was this lifelong occupation with 'the great common areas of Catholic tradition' that led to de Lubac's involvement in *Sources chrétiennes* as well as to such overtly historical works as *Corpus Mysticum* and *Medieval Exegesis*. However, it can be said that de Lubac's entire oeuvre belies the modern bifurcation of 'historical' and 'dogmatic' theology. His more constructive ventures in Christian dogmatics (works like *Catholicism* and *The Splendor of the Church*) are always a 'thinking with' and a 'speaking after' the tradition's diverse and collective witness to the 'deep and permanent unity of the faith'.[100] Conversely, his more historical investigations always presuppose a shared encounter with the object of Christian faith – the mystery of Jesus Christ to which the scriptures and tradition bear witness. For de Lubac, it is this shared belonging to the mystery of God in Christ that secures both the unity and the diversity of the Church's theological tradition. For the mystery always and inevitably exceeds – and indeed *disrupts* – the concepts and the logic by which it is rendered intelligible. The history of theology is not, therefore, the accumulation of propositions according to which the mystery becomes less and less 'mysterious' (more and more subject to rational control). It is rather the history of the Church's ongoing attempt to bear faithful and intelligent witness to the gift of God's self-revelation.[101] This witness will employ a variety of concepts. It will critically appropriate all sorts of culturally conditioned idioms and habits of thought. It will become 'all things to all people' so that it might 'by any means save some'. But the mystery to which the Church bears witness is unchanging. And it is the unity of this mystery, discerned by the Spirit of Christ within the Church, that gives to the tradition its permanent unity.

---

97. ASC, p. 143.
98. Von Balthasar, *The Theology of Henri de Lubac*, p. 23.
99. ASC, p. 143.
100. Ibid., p. 144.
101. Cf. de Lubac, 'The Problem of the Development of Dogma', TH, pp. 248–80.

Finally, as we indicated at the outset of this chapter, de Lubac's theology is perpetually animated by the conviction that this mystery to which the Church attests is the only means whereby the dynamism of human existence and the drama of history more generally find their meaning. It is something of a refrain throughout de Lubac's writings: 'At the same time that the God-man Jesus Christ reveals God to us, He reveals us to ourselves. Without God the ultimate recesses of our being remain an enigma to us.'[102] As de Lubac insists already in his opening lecture at the Université Catholique, the Church's apologetic task is first and foremost the exposition of the Church's doctrine. The Church recalls to human beings the sublimity of their vocation and the calamity of their present condition by testifying resolutely to the supernatural object of its hope. The Church likewise anticipates, however imperfectly, the supernatural reunion to which history itself is teleologically ordered as both the recipient and the instrument of Christ's reconciling work.

---

102. De Lubac, 'Nature and Grace', pp. 34–35.

Chapter 2

NEO-SCHOLASTICISM OF THE STRICT OBSERVANCE

Tracey Rowland

The most prominent schools of twentieth-century and contemporary Catholic theology can usually be traced back to one of two orientations – an orientation which is focused on eighteenth-century issues about rationality and universal human nature or an orientation which is focused on nineteenth-century issues about history, tradition, and human particularity. Broadly it may be argued that the pre-conciliar theological establishment, especially as it was represented in the Roman academies, was focused on responding to the intellectual criticisms of Catholicism which arose in the eighteenth century, while the Vatican II generation, influenced by existentialism in philosophy and the salvation history debates in Protestant theology, was more inclined to tackle the nineteenth-century issues about the role of history in the development of dogma and the formation of the human person. If the first group was preoccupied with Kantian issues, the second group was more worried about Heideggerian issues. The interest of the Vatican II generation in the theological significance of history entailed a confrontation with the scholastic approaches to doctrinal development and other foundational theological concepts which came to dominate the theological academies after the promulgation of *Aeterni Patris* by Leo XIII in 1879.

Henri de Lubac was a leading protagonist in this confrontation. He was the son of a noble family of the Ardèche, a 'born aristocrat in manner and appearance', a veteran of the First World War and a spiritual collaborator with the French resistance in the Second World War, a *peritus* of the Second Vatican Council, a friend of John Paul II who made him a Cardinal in 1983, an intellectual hero of Benedict XVI, a member of the International Theological Commission, a founder of the theological journal *Communio*, an opponent of interpretations of Vatican II according to a hermeneutic of rupture, and even more famously, an opponent of the dualisms inherent in Baroque-era scholasticism which made him the nemesis of Reginald Garrigou-Lagrange OP, the so-called *monstre sacré* of early twentieth-century neo-scholasticism, now known as Strict Observance or Fundamentalist Thomism.

Specifically, de Lubac and others in his circle were accused by Garrigou-Lagrange of fostering a 'new theology', although de Lubac eschewed the claim and argued that he was simply approaching theology from a perspective typical of the patristic era before the Church's intellectual life got tangled in the conceptual technicalities of late scholasticism. Garrigou-Lagrange's ideas were 'newer' than de Lubac's since it could be demonstrated that concepts such as 'pure nature' and 'supernature' developed late in the Church's history in the sixteenth century. What was certainly true, all polemical labels aside, is that in early twentieth-century French Catholic scholarship there emerged a critical opposition to the whole neo-scholastic project as it had developed during the Leonine and Pian pontificates and that two of the most significant players in this opposition movement were Maurice Blondel and Henri de Lubac. Specifically, de Lubac differed from the neo-scholastics in his approach to (i) the discipline of theology, (ii) the notion of revelation, (iii) the understanding of tradition, (iv) his theological anthropology (including here his understanding of the nature and grace and faith and reason relationships), (v) his analysis of the causes of secularism, (vi) his ecclesiology, and, more particularly in relation to Garrigou-Lagrange, (vii) his stance on the political movement known as *Action française*, and (viii) his opposition to the Vichy government and support for the French resistance. Fergus Kerr has described these differences and the political battles they engendered within the Church as the most bitter theological disputes of the twentieth century.[1]

Strict Observance or Fundamentalist Thomism

Pope Leo XIII sought to revive the thought of St Thomas as a bulwark against various kinds of ideologies which were influential in the late nineteenth century, including the problem of historical relativism. The Thomist tradition thus revived was marketed as offering a 'perennial philosophy' whose chief virtue was its claim to be untouched by historical factors and absolutely rational. It was typical of the Thomism of this period that the philosophical dimensions were extracted from the theological dimensions and then served up to seminarians in handbooks or manuals. The propositions or theses were often cut and pasted from commentaries on the original works of St Thomas prepared in the sixteenth and seventeenth centuries, and no attempt was made to explain how these propositions fitted into the overall structure of the oeuvre of Aquinas or the intellectual and political history of their times or the Church's intellectual treasury considered as a whole. Serge-Thomas Bonino, the current secretary of the International Theological Commission, has described this kind of 'Fundamentalist Thomism' in the following terms:

> This variety of Thomism is easily recognisable on account of its visceral reaction against the historical approach to the Thomistic corpus and is easily irritated by what it considers to be the excessive attention given today to the historical and

---

1. F. Kerr, *After Aquinas: Versions of Thomism* (Oxford: Blackwell, 2002), p. 134.

cultural conditionings of the intellectual life. True, in its aversion to historicism it does have the benefit of defending the trans-historical value of concept and truth, but it does so by forgetting that the absolute of truth is given only in the contingency of history... This position holds up the work of St. Thomas as some sort of timeless Koran, guaranteed by magisterial sanction and containing the definitive expression of theology and philosophical wisdom, formulated once and for all as immutable theses.[2]

The dominant hallmarks of this appropriation of Aquinas are its self-conscious dismissal of the theological significance of history and a kind of lopsided emphasis on intellectual judgement understood in the sense of *ratio* rather than *intellectus* and a corresponding neglect or muting of the 'voice' of other faculties of the human soul. As Robert A. Krieg explained:

Scholastic thought relied on a metaphysics of unchanging substances or essences, a metaphysics that dismissed both the notion of a person as a knowing subject located within a specific time and place, and also the idea of history as a changing reality that shapes human life and thought. Further, the scholastic method required that scholars take up solely the classic or perennial questions in theology and that they answer them by means of fixed categories and the deductive method, derived from Aristotle's *Posterior Analytics*. In this endeavour, they employed propositions or theses that were generated in medieval and baroque theological texts. This method produced a 'theology of conclusions' whose relevance to the Church in the twentieth century remained unclear.[3]

The neo-scholastic aversion to history also fostered an account of tradition which was unhistorical. Here a leading authority was Johannes Baptist Franzelin, a Jesuit Cardinal prominent in the pontificate of Pius IX. He was a papal theologian during the First Vatican Council and in 1870 he published the *Tractatus de divina traditione et scriptura*.[4] Hans Boersma has summarized Franzelin's account of tradition in the following paragraph:

Johann Baptist Franzelin (1816–1886) was one of the most influential neo-Thomist theologians of the time, and he sketched a strictly logical view of the development of doctrine. Franzelin was convinced that revelation had ceased with the death of the last apostles. The fullness of the divine truth revealed to the apostles implied, for Franzelin, that God had provided them with explicit knowledge of whatever doctrine the Church would later define. After the

---

2. S.-T. Bonino, 'To Be a Thomist', *Nova et Vetera* 8:4 (Fall 2010): pp. 763–75 at p. 770.
3. R. A. Krieg, *Theologians in Nazi Germany* (London: Continuum, 2004), p. 17.
4. J. B. Franzelin, *Tractatus de divina traditione et scriptura* (Rome: Collegio Romano, 1860–1864).

death of the apostles, much of this doctrine had been obscured, because the apostles had taught these truths only implicitly. Thus, the later development of doctrine was a slow, but sure, recovery of the teachings that the apostles had known explicitly, but that the Church as a whole now had to re-appropriate subjectively over time. This recovery of the full apostolic doctrine, was, according to Franzelin, a purely logical or syllogistic process.[5]

The last of these principles, the idea that the development of doctrine is a purely logical or syllogistic process, is far removed from the more historically engaged perspective which one finds in works such as John Henry Newman's *Essay on the Development of Christian Doctrine* and Maurice Blondel's *History and Dogma*.[6]

Leo XIII's quite legitimate concern about historical relativism, especially given some of the currents in French and German scholarship of the nineteenth century, was amplified in 1907 in the publication of the encyclical *Pascendi Dominici Gregis* by Pius X. This encyclical condemned a cluster of ideas under the banner of the heresy of 'Modernism'. As Aidan Nichols described the problem 'instead of saying that there is an important place for historical study within theology, history becomes everything'.[7] One of the scholars who helped to draft *Pascendi* was the French Jesuit Cardinal Louis Billot (1846–1931). In 1929 Billot published his own neo-scholastic tract on tradition entitled *De immutabilitate traditonis contra modernam haeresim evolutionismi*. In this work he argued that tradition has no independent existence outside the Church's contemporary teaching. Indeed, he went so far as to assert that 'dogmas have no history'.[8] History and its methods were said to be completely beyond his horizon.[9] Alexander Dru has suggested that the French scholars were particularly inclined towards a static view of tradition because of the psychological effects of the French Revolution (1789–1793). The Revolution was not only directed against the aristocracy, but against the Church and Christianity in general. Dru argues that as a consequence of the Revolution, tradition was henceforth viewed 'in a political light and, regardless of what it was applied to, came to mean the conservation of a heritage, of an object, and

---

5. H. Boersma, *Nouvelle Théologie and Sacramental Ontology: A Return to Mystery* (Oxford: Oxford University Press, 2009), p. 204.

6. For an account of how Newman does not abandon reason or 'institutional Christianity' while pursuing Romantic movement interests, see C. Zaleski, 'Newman for a New Generation', in Francesca Aran Murphy, ed., *The Beauty of God's House: Essays in Honour of Stratford Caldecott* (Eugene: Wipf and Stock, 2014).

7. A. Nichols, *Catholic Thought since the Enlightenment* (Leominster: Gracewing, 1998), p. 84.

8. R. Aubert, in R. van der Gucht and H. Vorgrimler, eds, *Bilan de la théologie du XX siecle* (Paris: Casterman, 1970), p. 431.

9. E. Hocedez, *Histoire de la théologie au XIX siècle, III, La Règne Leon XIII, 1878–1903* (Brussels: L'edition Universelle, 1947), p. 370 quoted in J. Hennesey, 'Leo XIII: Intellectualizing the Combat with Modernity', *U.S. Catholic Historian* 7:4 (Fall 1988): pp. 393–400 at p. 399.

in Christianity of a clearly defined object, the deposit of the faith'. Further, 'the handing down of the "deposit" was looked upon as an impersonal process; the whole emphasis fell on *what* was handed down, and no thought was given to *how* it was handed down'.[10]

Given the extensive political opposition to the Catholic faith in the years of the French Third Republic (1870–1940), it is not surprising that the 'deposit of the faith' was viewed through a political lens. The political realities included the legislation of 1879 which excluded priests from holding administrative positions on the boards of hospitals and charities, the notoriously oppressive Jules Ferry education laws of 1882 which made it an offence to teach the faith in schools and for religious Orders to manage schools, and various initiatives taken during the prime ministership of Emile Combes beginning in 1902. Combes closed down all the parish schools in France and expelled all fifty-four religious Orders with the result that some 20,000 religious were sent into exile to minister to the needs of Catholics in other countries. During these years Combes also worked with members of Masonic lodges to block the career paths of army officers who were faithful Catholics. The Church in France was the subject of a systematic bureaucratic persecution.

One consequence of the persecution was the establishment of the political movement Action française. The movement was founded in 1899 by Charles Maurras (1868–1952) who was at the time an atheist. He died a Catholic but for much of his life his political support for the Church was based on nationalist and utilitarian foundations. He was anti-Jewish and anti-Protestant and referred to Calvinism as a bad Swiss idea. He was strongly in favour of the restoration of the monarchy in a form which would give it more extensive powers than that which is typical in the British Westminster system. The intellectual basis of his movement could be described as a cocktail of Comtean positivism and neo-scholasticism spiced with royalist nostalgia, French nationalism, and a generally negative attitude towards liberal democracy. Its youth branch, known as the *Fédération nationale des Camelots du Roi*, was focused on the promotion of the monarchy. The *Camelots* had a high public profile around the Latin Quarter of Paris and in other centres of French intellectual life where they could often be found distributing royalist literature. They acquired a reputation for getting into scuffles with their opposite numbers in Leftist student organizations and enjoying the sport of baiting liberal academics.

During the pontificate of Pius X (1903–1914), Action française enjoyed the favour of high-ranking curial officials and its members were delighted when in 1920 Pope Benedict XV canonized the French national heroine Joan of Arc. However, the pontificate of Pius XI (1922–1939) was another era. Pope Pius XI wanted a *rapprochement* with the French Republicans and he was inclined to extract the Church from symbiotic relationships with political parties. He did

---

10. A. Dru, Prefatory Note to *Maurice Blondel: History and Dogma* (Grand Rapids: Eerdmans, 1994), p. 214.

not want the spiritual power of the Church to be compromised by entanglements with political power groups bent on harnessing the social power of the Church for nationalist ends. The fact that the movement had as one of its slogans *La politique d'abord* (politics first or the priority of the political) was also something of a red flag to the pope who had taken as his papal motto 'Pax Christi in Regno Christi' (the peace of Christ in the reign of Christ), indicating a certain Christocentric disposition in all things. In 1926 Pius XI was persuaded to place the Action française newspaper on the *Index Librorum Prohibitorum*. The trigger for this was an article published in a journal of the Catholic Association of Belgian Youth (*Cahiers de la Jeunesse Belge*) in July 1925. The journal ran an opinion poll. The question was: 'Among the writers of the last twenty-five years, whom do you consider to be your master?' There were 443 replies, 174 in favour of Charles Maurras who got more votes than Belgium's Cardinal Mercier.

The pastoral result of placing the newspaper on the Index was that Catholics who read it were barred from the sacraments until they had confessed their sin. In one of the standard histories of this event Eugene Weber describes how the decrees of Pius XI and the members of the French episcopacy (who were forced to follow the papal line although many had been strong supporters of Action française prior to 1927), had the effect of dividing the entire Catholic community, including whole families. Supporters of *Action française* were not only prohibited from reading material written by Maurras, but they were also not allowed to receive religious marriages (except *in nigris*), or be buried by Catholic rites if they died unrepentant, or from serving as godparents or participating in Catholic pious associations like a mothers' club or youth group. According to Weber, this led to absurd situations where, for example, a priest was flown over a grave to give his blessing, people included statements in their last will and testimonies declaring their support for *Action française* (in case some pious relative, determined to acquire a Catholic burial for them, might falsely claim that they had repented of their sin), and numerous engaged couples broke up rather than marry since one followed the pope and another continued to support *Action française*.[11] Perhaps most dramatically of all, Cardinal Billot relinquished his red hat. Historians differ on the point of whether this was an act of protest or an act demanded of him by Pius XI. Whatever of that issue, the actions of Pius XI in relation to *Action française* sent shock waves through the French Catholic community which continue to reverberate today almost a century after the event. In this context, it is noteworthy that another high-ranking casualty of the crackdown was Fr Henri Le Floche, the rector of the French seminary in Rome. Le Floche was the major formative influence on the young Marcel Lefebvre who was to become in the 1960s the champion of the traditionalist opposition to the Second Vatican Council.

Before the pontifical intervention of 1926, the *Action française* project was the subject of extensive criticism in the pages of the *Annales de Philosophie*

---

11. E. Weber, *Action française: Royalism and Reaction in Twentieth-Century France* (Stanford: Stanford University Press, 1962), p. 238.

chrétienne, a journal owned by Maurice Blondel (1861–1949). Blondel coined the word 'monophorism' (one-way thinking) to describe both the projects of the Modernists and those of Maurras and his neo-scholastic supporters. Beginning in 1909 he published a series of articles under the pseudonym 'Testis' or witness. In these he went to war against the epistemology of the neo-scholastics, describing it as 'a bad version of Thomas Reid with a taste of false Cartesianism, false Biranism and vague Cousinism'.[12] He also went to war against the neo-scholastic understanding of the relationship between the natural and supernatural order and coined the word 'extrinsicism' to describe the tendency of the neo-scholastics to sharply separate the two. He further argued that this extrinsicist monophorism was retarding the Church's evangelical work. Not surprisingly the 'Testis' series came to the attention of the secret society *Sodalitium pianum* run by Monsignor Umberto Benigni in the Congregation for Extraordinary Ecclesiastical Affairs. The aim of the society was to provide intelligence on the activities of Catholic intellectuals suspected of the heresy of Modernism. Blondel's full-frontal attack on the neo-scholastic constructions of the faith and reason, and nature and supernature relationships ensured his tracking on the *Sodalitium pianum* radar. On 5 May 1913, the *Annales de philosophie chrétienne* was placed on the Index and a month later Fr Lucien Laberthonnière (1860–1932), the Oratorian editor of the journal, was forbidden to publish.

The Seminal Influence of Blondel

Rather than following Franzelin and Billot's account of tradition and the development of doctrine, and the French neo-scholastics' enthusiasm for *Action française*, Henri de Lubac followed in the trajectory of Blondel whose works he read in the years 1920–1923 while a student on the island of Jersey.[13] From 1912 to 1920, one of Blondel's former students, Auguste Valensin (1879–1953), was a philosophy lecturer at Maison Saint-Louis, the Jesuit scholasticate on Jersey. Valensin lost his lecturing post in 1920 because of his appropriation of Blondel's philosophy of action as outlined in *L'Action: Essai d'une critique de la vie et d'une science de la pratique* of 1893. However, by the time the axe fell, Valensin had already started a pro-Blondelian movement by providing copies of Blondel's publications to his students. Henri de Lubac was one of the beneficiaries of this activity.

The practice of distributing underground copies continued well beyond Valensin's time. William Norris Clarke, an American Jesuit who was a student on Jersey in the 1930s, was later to reminisce about sleeping with a smuggled copy

---

12. P. J. Bernardi, *Maurice Blondel, Social Catholicism and Action Française: The Clash Over the Church's Role in Society During the Modernist Era* (Washington, DC: CUA Press, 2009), p. 79.

13. See ASC, p. 18.

of *L'Action* under his pillow. The student practice was to allow one person access to the copy for the duration of a week before passing it on.[14] Valensin's arch-enemy at Maison Saint-Louis was Fr Pedro Descoqs, a passionate Suárezian. De Lubac studied under Descoqs in 1922–1923 and this experience appears to have inoculated him against any empathy for the ideas of Francisco Suárez (1548–1617) for the rest of his life. His antipathy to Suárez was a disposition he was later to share with Joseph Ratzinger. The young Fr Ratzinger famously almost failed his *Habilitationsschrift* because it was critical of the Suárezian account of revelation. Ratzinger was forced to remove the anti-Suárezian section of his dissertation in order to get the document passed by one of his examiners. At the Second Vatican Council de Lubac and Ratzinger both worked on the document *Dei Verbum* which presented revelation as something primarily historical, rather than, as Suárez had it, a handbag of doctrines to top up a rationalist metaphysics. In *Dei Verbum* the Blondelian vision triumphed over the Suárezian, in no small part due to the alliance of Ratzinger, de Lubac, and Karl Rahner. Although the alliance with Rahner was to break down by the 1970s, de Lubac and Ratzinger never had any trouble agreeing with Rahner's judgement that the Suárezian moment in neo-scholasticism represents both the 'original and mortal sin of Jesuit theology'.[15]

In his understanding of tradition Blondel had been influenced by John Henry Newman whose work had been introduced to a French audience by Henri Bremond. In his essay 'History and Dogma' (1903/4) Blondel argued that the *extrinsicism* of certain schools of Thomism and the *historicism* associated with Modernism offered two answers 'each in their own way incomplete, but equally dangerous to the faith'.[16] As R. C. Koerpel has commented: 'extrinsicism tends to emphasize the juridical, abstract, or conceptual nature of dogmatic statements with little or no reference to the concrete and historical circumstances in which they were formulated, while historicism tends to reduce dogmatic statements and texts to the individual, unique, and ascertainable facts of the historical situation from which they arise'.[17]

Blondel sought to overcome the dualism by developing a notion of the incarnation of dogma *within* history and he argued that the synthesis of dogma and history lies 'neither in the facts alone, nor in the ideas alone, but in the Tradition which embraces within it the facts of history, the efforts of reason

---

14. W. N. Clarke, *The Creative Retrieval of Saint Thomas Aquinas: Essays in Thomistic Philosophy, New and Old* (New York: Fordham University Press, 2009), pp. 12–13. Clarke is quoted in E. H. Hendrick-Moser, 'The Auguste Valensin Controversy and the Historiography of *Nouvelle Théologie*', *Ephemerides Theologicae Lovanienses* 90:1 (2014): pp. 41–70.

15. K. Rahner, *Faith in a Wintry Season: Conversations and Interviews with Karl Rahner in the Last Years of His Life* (New York: Crossroad, 1991), p. 49.

16. M. Blondel, *A Letter on Apologetics and History and Dogma* (Grand Rapids: Eerdmans, 1994), p. 225.

17. R. C. Koerpel, 'Tradition, Truth and Time: Remarks on the "Liturgical Action" of the Church', in Craig Hovey and Cyrus P. Olsen, eds, *The Hermeneutics of Tradition: Explorations and Examinations* (Oregan: Cascade, 2013), p. 174.

and the accumulated experience of the faithful'.[18] Yves Congar was later to judge Blondel's approach in the following terms:

> Over against these two opposing caricatures [the hostile to history stance of the Strict Observance Thomists and the historical relativism of the Modernists] Blondel set tradition, in which history and dogma are united by a live current passing in both directions – from the facts to the dogma, and from faith to the facts. To oppose the data of history and the statements of dogma was to make an unwarranted separation between the two elements of a single reality with an essentially religious nature.[19]

In his introduction to the English translation of Blondel's *History and Dogma*, Alexander Dru noted that the very first edition of *Annales de Philosophie Chrétienne* 'pointed to the need to break away from the narrow Latin, Roman and Mediterranean conception of Catholicism by pointing to the relevance of the German Catholic writers of the Romantic period'.[20] This was a reference to the scholars associated with the Tübingen school of Catholic theology such as Johann Sebastian Drey (1777–1853), Johann Adam Möhler (1796–1838), and Johannes Evangelist von Kuhn (1806–1887). While the Tübingen theologians were largely respectful of Magisterial authority and were particularly able defenders of creedal Christianity, they did not share the neo-scholastics' emphasis on dialectical analysis in their approach to the development of tradition. Von Kuhn in fact described the philosophy of Christian revelation as 'the presence of Christ revealed historically, not dialectically'.[21] Möhler argued that 'Christianity does not consist in expressions, formulae, or figures of speech; it is an inner life, a holy power, and all doctrinal concepts and dogmas have value only insofar as they express the inner life that is present within them'.[22] Moreover, Möhler added to this accent on the historical embodiment of dogma, an equally significant emphasis on the organic unity between the contemporary Christian community and Christ, thereby averting the danger of a crude historicism. As Grant Kaplan explained, for Möhler 'the chain of history from nineteenth-century Swabia to first-century

---

18. Blondel, *History and Dogma*, p. 57.
19. Y. Congar, *Tradition and Traditions* (London: Burns and Oates, 1960–1963), pp. 215–16.
20. A. Dru, Introduction to M. Blondel, *A Letter on Apologetics and History and Dogma* (Grand Rapids, MI: Eerdmans, 1994), p. 60.
21. J. E. Kuhn, 'Über den Begriff und das Wesen der speculativen Theologie oder christlichen Philosophie', *Die theologische Quartalschrift* 14 (1832): p. 411. Quoted in T. F. O'Meara, *Romantic Idealism and Roman Catholicism: Schelling and the Theologians* (Notre Dame, IN: University of Notre Dame Press, 1982), p. 154.
22. A. Möhler, *Unity in the Church or The Principle of Catholicism Presented in the Spirit of the Church Fathers of the First Three Centuries,* trans. and ed. Peter C. Erb (Washington, DC: Catholic University of America Press, 1996): p. 111.

Palestine is unbroken. In order to be salvific, the saving truth of Christianity must have been present, even in a truncated form, for every generation of believers'.[23] This is because access to the truth occurs by living the truth.

There is therefore quite a different understanding of tradition underpinning the theology of the neo-scholastics Franzelin and Billot on the one hand, from the works of the more romantically inclined and thus history-friendly Newman, Möhler, and Blondel on the other. De Lubac and his *Communio* colleagues follow in the line of Newman, Möhler, and Blondel, not in the line of Franzelin and Billot.[24]

The Lay Literati

In the first half of the twentieth century, the French Catholic engagement with Romantic movement themes like the significance of history and culture for human formation found expression not only in journals like *Annales de Philosophie Chrétienne*, but also in the publications of the great literary laymen such as Leon Bloy, Charles Péguy, Georges Bernanos, François Mauriac, and Paul Claudel. Mark Bosco has argued that these lay Catholic literati became fashionable in the intellectual salons of Paris between the two World Wars precisely because their Catholicism was 'never served up with triumphant, epistemological certainty or as morally uplifting drama' but rather as 'a place where the mysterious irruptions of grace might shine forth or manifest in profound ways'.[25] These artists created 'a specific vision of French Catholicism, one which was prophetic in denouncing both the rationalism of the state as well as the bourgeois Christianity that made a too-easy concourse with industrial society'.[26] With an emphasis on aesthetic considerations over rational modes of discourse, this vision 'offered both a critique of the modern state and a powerful philosophical and artistic alternative'.[27] It addressed itself to the whole range of human experience, including, but not exclusively, the intellectual. In a work specifically on Claudel, Wallace Fowlie noted that the literary works of the laymen Bloy, Péguy, Bernanos, and Mauriac were laden with attacks on the ideals of the French Catholic bourgeoisie which were 'more moralistic than spiritual', 'far more Jansenistic than purely Christian', 'pursuing an ideal of personal perfection, [and] personal success, rather than a

---

23. G. Kaplan, *Answering the Enlightenment: The Catholic Recovery of Historical Revelation* (New York: Herder and Herder, 2006): p. 104.

24. See, for example, H. De Lubac, 'The Problem of the Development of Dogma', in TH, pp. 248–80. See also R. Voderholzer, 'Dogma and History: Henri de Lubac and the Retrieval of Historicity as a Key to Theological Renewal', *Communio: International Theological Review* 28 (Winter 2001): pp. 648–69.

25. M. Bosco 'Georges Bernanos and Francis Poulenc: Catholic Convergences in Dialogues of the Carmelites', *Logos* 12:2 (Spring 2009): pp. 17–40, at p. 21.

26. Ibid., p. 21.

27. Ibid., p. 22.

love of God and the sensible world'.²⁸ Bernanos famously described the person with bourgeois personality traits as an imbecile. Fowlie suggests that writers like Claudel, far from wanting to defend Christianity by teaching people philosophical theses, preferred to 'illuminate for the contemporary world the mystery of that dogma which is primarily concerned with joy: the mystery of the communion of saints, with its universal solidarity of all the souls who have been born and who will be born'.²⁹ It was this kind of vision which de Lubac was to develop in his ecclesiology as presented in works such as *Corpus Mysticum* (1944) and *Méditations sur l'Eglise* (1953).

Significantly all five of these writers (Charles Péguy, Georges Bernanos, François Mauriac, Paul Claudel, and Leon Bloy) were laymen. Etienne Gilson, another layman (though an intellectual historian and philosopher, rather than an author of fiction), claimed that if he had been constrained by obedience to superiors bent on enforcing Leonine-era neo-scholasticism, he would not have been able to write a hundredth of what he wrote and that he would have been 'crucified'.³⁰ Such a statement was not hyperbolic given the operation of organizations like *Sodalitium Pianum*. Also noteworthy is the fact that within this group of lay writers Bernanos had been a strong supporter of *Action française*, not because of any crude nationalist propensities or out of any attraction to neo-scholasticism, but primarily because of the group's support for the monarchy. The case of Bernanos demonstrates the ambivalent nature of the *Action française*.

A Problematic Anthropology

Blondel and those like de Lubac who followed him were not only dissenting from the neo-scholastic account of doctrinal development (with its underlying ahistorical account of revelation and tradition), but they were also concerned about the understanding of the human person found in neo-scholastic manuals. In this context Blondel complained that the anthropology which was taught in almost all seminaries in the first half of the twentieth century included 'the study neither of religious psychology nor of the subjective facts which convey to the conscience the action of the objective realities whose presence in us Revelation indicates; this ideology only considers as legitimate the examination of what objectively informs us about these realities as designated and defined'.³¹ Blondel further observed:

> Actions are not simply the putting into practice of logically defined ideas and of geometrically shaped theories; and everything is not decided in the domain

---

28. W. Fowlie, *Claudel* (London: Bowes and Bowes, 1957), p. 95.
29. Ibid., p. 96.
30. E. Gilson, *Letters of Etienne Gilson to de Lubac* (San Francisco: Ignatius, 1988), p. 69
31. M. Blondel, as quoted in P. J. Bernardi, 'Maurice Blondel and the Renewal' of the Nature-Grace Relationship', *Communio: International Catholic Review* 26 (Winter 1999): pp. 806–45.

of abstractions, as if human beings were only pure intellects, as if concepts were the adequate substitute of things and the sole motivation of the will, as if we governed ourselves by them and them alone.³²

Speaking of precisely this problem, the Belgian conciliar *peritus*, Albert Dondeyne, was later to argue that the neo-scholastic neglect of the human person's embodiment within the world had exercised a disastrous influence on the ontological interpretation of human existence:

> Thinkers like Newman, Marcel and Jaspers have shown that by eliminating from man's inheritance corporeity as well as the inter-subjectivity and the being-in-history that follow from it, rationalism must end up by emptying human reality of its ontological content and of its intrinsic reference to the Transcendent. To reduce the human person to a bloodless and anonymous spectator is to destroy the very idea of a 'person' and make man a being without soul or destiny, for whom life has neither rhyme nor reason, since there is really nothing he can do. Hence, the importance in metaphysics of Blondel's theme of action...Embodiment contributes to our insertion in being, towards making us participate in...the mystery of being.³³

Stanisław Grygiel recently noted that this problematic was one of the early preoccupations of Karol Wojtyła who found himself contending with neo-scholastics 'who in their metaphysics manuals didn't dare talk of the person, realizing at least the fact that this word was not a universal concept but a name which points at a concrete human being'.³⁴ Grygiel compared those who 'constructed their philosophy on the so-called third grade of abstraction from which quantity had been expelled' as butchers using 'well sharpened knives in a meat-shop with no meat'.³⁵ Similarly, Angelo Scola, Gilfredo Marengo, and Javier Prades López have argued that the extrinsicism between faith and reason (typical of pre-conciliar neo-scholasticism) brought with itself a reduction of the human person to his intellectual capacities, with the consequence that 'the contingent experience of human freedom had to be considered as the merely practical application of universal truth revealed or understood by conceptual means'.³⁶ As de Lubac's friend and confrere Jean Daniélou described the problem,

---

32. Ibid., p. 831.
33. A. Dondyne, *Contemporary European Thought and Christian Faith* (Pittsburg: Duquesne University Press, 1962), p. 83.
34. S. Grygiel, 'Marriage, Family and New Evangelisation', *Humanitas* 2 (2012): pp. 124–29 at p. 124.
35. Ibid., p. 124.
36. A. Scola, G. Marengo and J. Prades López, *La Persona Umana: Antropologia Teologia* (Milano: Jaca, 2000), p. 31.

scholasticism located reality in essences, rather than in subjects, and in so doing ignored the dramatic world of persons.[37]

De Lubac's Alternative Theological Anthropology

In 1938 de Lubac published his first book entitled *Catholicisme: les aspects sociaux du dogme*. Years later in a foreword to the English translation titled *Catholicism: Christ and the Common Destiny of Man*, Joseph Ratzinger described this book as 'an essential milestone on my theological journey' in which de Lubac demonstrated 'how the idea of community and universality, rooted in the Trinitarian concept of God, permeates and shapes all the individual elements of Faith's content'.[38] At the time of its initial publication, however, when Joseph Ratzinger was still wearing Lederhosen, neo-scholastic readers assumed that given the title *Catholicism*, it must be a treatise on ecclesiology and they were concerned to discover that there was not a single chapter on the papacy in this work. Far from offering his readership something juridical, de Lubac's *Catholicism* was focused on the following anthropological theme:

> By revealing the Father and by being revealed by him, Christ completes the revelation of man to himself. By taking possession of man, by seizing hold of him and by penetrating to the very depths of his being Christ makes man go deep down within himself, there to discover in a flash regions hitherto unsuspected. It is through Christ that the person reaches maturity, that man emerges definitely from the universe, and becomes conscious of his own being... through the Christian revelation not only is the scrutiny that man makes of himself made more reaching, but his examination of all about him is at the same time made more comprehensible. Henceforth the idea of human unity is born. The image of God, the image of the Word, which the incarnate Word restores and gives back to its glory is 'I myself', is it also the other, every other.[39]

This particular paragraph is taken up by the authors of *Gaudium et spes* at the Second Vatican Council and condensed in paragraph 22 of that document. During the papacy of John Paul II this paragraph was to be cited more often than any other of all the paragraphs in the conciliar documents. It became the signature tune of the entire pontificate.

Catholicism was followed in 1944 by *The Drama of Atheistic Humanism*. This examined the pathos of atheism as it is presented in the thought of Kierkegaard, Nietzsche, Comte, Dostoevsky, Feuerbach, and Marx. Rather than examining

---

37. J. Daniélou, 'The Conception of History in the Christian Tradition', *Journal of Religion* 30:3 (1950): pp. 171–79.
38. J. Ratzinger, 'Introduction' to de Lubac, C, p. 11.
39. C, p. 339.

atheism as a defect of the intellect, as was typical of neo-scholastic treatments of the problem, de Lubac presented the thought of Nietzsche, Comte, Feuerbach, and Marx as an attempt to offer an alternative humanism to Christian humanism, built strongly upon resentment, a defect of the will. This work was also criticized in neo-scholastic circles for its non-scholastic methodology. Comically, one slip-shod reviewer of the English edition assumed from the book's cover, which featured head-shot images of Marx, Comte, Nietzsche, and Dostoyevsky, that the author was sympathetic to the very ideas he criticized.[40]

Throughout this period of the Second World War de Lubac was a contributor to the *Cahiers du Témoignage chrétien*, an underground publication which stood opposed to collaboration with the Nazis. It was founded in 1941 largely through his efforts and those of Pierre Chaillet.[41] Here again de Lubac found himself in opposition to many of the neo-scholastics and members of the *Action française* who supported Marshal Pétain's Vichy government. Foremost among these was Reginald Garrigou-Lagrange who was of the view that support for the stance of General de Gaulle was not merely a case of backing the wrong team, politically or prudentially speaking, but was actually a mortal sin.[42] De Lubac's friend and confrere Fr Yves de Montcheuil was also a contributor to the *Cahiers du Témoignage chrétien*. De Montcheuil was executed by the Nazis some ten days before the town in which he had been ministering to the spiritual needs of Resistance fighters was liberated.[43] In an essay on de Montcheuil's role in the resistance to Nazism, David Grumett noted that he (de Montcheuil) was one of those Jesuits who had been exposed to the thought of Blondel while living as a student at Maison Saint-Louis, and that he had even assisted Auguste Valensin in the production of a collection of extracts from *L'Action* in 1934.[44] Extracts from the publications of de Montcheuil can be found compiled in de Lubac's *Three Jesuits Speak*.[45]

In the final stages of the war when de Lubac was hiding from the Gestapo, he worked on the manuscript of what was to become his most controversial publication – *Surnaturel: Études historiques*. The work offers an intellectual history of the use of the concept of the supernatural in Catholic theology, along with the concept of 'pure nature'. Themes in this work were later amplified and clarified in *Le mystère du surnaturel* (1965) and *Petite catéchèse sur Nature et Grâce* (1980). Specifically he argued that neither the early Church Fathers nor Thomas Aquinas ever maintained that human persons have a purely natural end attainable by

---

40. ASC, p. 41, n. 19.

41. D. Grumett, 'Yves de Montcheuil: Action, Justice, and the Kingdom in Spiritual Resistance to Nazism', *Theological Studies* 68 (2007): pp. 618–41 at p. 626.

42. J. Komonchak, 'Theology and Culture at Mid-Century: The Example of Henri de Lubac', *Theological Studies* 51 (1990): pp. 579–602 at 601, n. 67.

43. Grumett, 'Yves de Montcheuil: Action, Justice, and the Kingdom in Spiritual Resistance to Nazism', p. 639.

44. Ibid., p. 623.

45. H. de Lubac, *Three Jesuits Speak* (San Francisco: Ignatius, 1987).

their own powers of intellect and will. These ideas he traced back to Denys the Carthusian and the Dominican Cajetan. Joseph Huby in a review of *Surnaturel* summarized the thesis in the following paragraph:

> By supporting the possibility of a substantial natural order, giving satisfaction to the needs and desires of nature, by presenting the latter as a well-closed whole, having the power to achieve its own balance, it made the supernatural order something superfluous, which man was tempted to do without, since this supernatural found no anticipation, no desire, no aspiration in him. This conception of the supernatural as a superstructure coming to rest from outside on an edifice that stands on its own opened the way to a philosophy and a morality that were separate, constituted in complete independence not only of any positive revelation but of any fundamental orientation of the soul to the beatific vision.[46]

The politically explosive nature of *Surnaturel* lay not only in its deviation from the neo-scholastic construction of the orders of nature and grace but moreover in its conclusion that this construction was a contributing factor in the emergence of secularism.

The Period of the 1950s

Surnaturel appeared in 1946 and was quickly criticized by Garrigou-Lagrange in his February 1947 article 'La nouvelle théologie, ou va-t-elle?' published in *Angelicum*.[47] The intensity of the debates which followed were such that in 1950 the Jesuit General ordered de Lubac to stop teaching, and several of his publications, *Surnaturel* included, were withdrawn from the Jesuit libraries. This action was closely followed by the release of Pope Pius XII's encyclical *Humani Generis* which was widely interpreted as a warning shot against de Lubac and his decidedly non-neo-scholastic circle. At the time of its publication de Lubac regarded *Humani Generis*, sub-titled *Concerning Some False Opinions Threatening to Undermine the Foundations of Catholic Doctrine* as being more of a criticism of the neo-scholastic account of grace and nature than his own. He wrote:

---

46. J. Huby, 'Henri de Lubac, *Surnaturel*', *Etudes historiques*, *Etudes* 251 (1946): pp. 265–68. English translation taken from de Lubac, ASC, pp. 205–6. For a comprehensive analysis of the treatment of nature and grace and related anthropological questions in de Lubac, see M. Figura, *Der Anruf der Gnade: Über die Beziehung des Menschen zu Gott nach Henri de Lubac* (Einsiedeln: Johannes Verlag, 1979).

47. R. Garrigou-Lagrange, 'La nouvelle théologie ou va-t-elle?', *Angelicum* 23 (1946): pp. 126–45. For an English translation of this article and other contemporary analyses of the response of Garrigou-Lagrange, see the special edition of the *Josephinum Journal of Theology* 18:1 (Winter/Spring 2011).

> It [*Humani generis*] seems to me to be like many other ecclesiastical documents, unilateral: that is almost the law of the genre; but I have read nothing in it, doctrinally, that affects me. The only passage where I recognize an implicit reference to me is a phrase bearing on the question of the supernatural; now it is rather curious to note that this phrase, intending to recall the true doctrine on this subject, reproduces exactly what I said about it two years earlier in an article in *Recherches de science religieuse*.[48]

De Lubac was also of the view that it was not so much the publication of *Surnaturel* that caused his silencing as his election in 1946 to the General Congregation of the Jesuits. His elevation to such a powerful body required political action by those within the Society hostile to someone so openly critical of the Suárezian system. In de Lubac's words, for the neo-scholastics, '*Surnaturel* came along at a propitious time, allowing the bill of indictment to grow'.[49]

When Pius XII discovered through his (the pope's) confessor Cardinal Bea that Henri de Lubac's works had been removed from the Jesuit libraries and that de Lubac was no longer permitted to teach, the pope sent de Lubac a letter in which he thanked de Lubac for the work accomplished up until then and encouraged him to continue with his research since it 'promised much fruit for the Church'.[50]

Nonetheless, as a consequence of various political interventions by neo-scholastic forces inside the Roman Curia and the Society of Jesus, Henri de Lubac spent much of the decade of the 1950s burdened by the label 'theologically unsound'. He was not, however, without friends and sympathizers and his ideas were far from idiosyncratic among those who approached the study of theology with historical sensibilities. In a 1939 work *Welt und Person* which predated Henri de Lubac's *Surnaturel* by seven years, the Munich-based theologian Romano Guardini had written:

> Seen in the fullness of its energy as Paul proclaimed it and Augustine unfolded it, grace means something that is not added on to the nature of man for his perfection, but rather the form that man definitely is. Of course, this presupposes that we understand by the term 'man' what once again Paul and Augustine mean: not some being artificially let loose in a 'pure nature', but rather that human being whom God intends and of whom Scripture speaks.[51]

Guardini was a mentor of both Joseph Ratzinger and Karl Rahner and he along with other leading German theologians like Gottleib Söhngen (the *Doktor-Vater* of Ratzinger) were working on projects of a more humanist orientation than

---

48. ASC, p. 71. This was a reference to 'Le mystère du surnaturel', *Recherches de science religieuse* 36 (1949): pp. 80–121.
49. ASC, p. 37.
50. D. L. Schindler, 'Introduction' to de Lubac, MS, pp. xxii–xxiii.
51. R. Guardini, *Welt und Person* (Würzburg: Werkbund, 1939), pp. 186–87.

those of the neo-scholastics. Among the French, Etienne Gilson was firmly on the side of de Lubac. The following words come from one of his many letters of consolation to de Lubac, this one composed on the 8th of July 1956:

> People conjure up a Thomism after the manner of the schools, a sort of dull rationalism which panders to the kind of deism that most of them, deep down, really prefer to teach. Our only salvation lies in a return to Saint Thomas himself, before the Thomism of John of Saint Thomas, before that of Cajetan as well – Cajetan, whose famous commentary is in every respect the consummate example of a *corruptorium Thomae*... [Even] in the Order of Friars Preachers, from Hervé Nedellec right up to Cajetan and beyond, so many of them have taken such great pains to camouflage the authentic teaching of the master. Let us say, rather, to emasculate his doctrine and to make of his theology a brew of watered-down *philosophia aristotelico-thomistica* concocted to give off a vague deism fit only for the use of right-thinking candidates for high school diplomas and Arts degrees.[52]

A Personality Conflict between Scholastics and Humanists

In another letter written by Gilson to de Lubac, this one on 1 April 1964, Gilson wrote:

> As a theologian you are tops, but you are also a humanist in the great tradition of humanist theologians. The latter don't care much for the Scholastics, and the Scholastics generally detest them. Why? It's partly, I suppose, because Scholastics understand only propositions that are simple and unequivocal, or which seem so to be. You humanists are more interested in the truth the formula is intended to state, some of which always escapes and will not be imprisoned within the proposition. When the Scholastics don't comprehend it anymore, they get nervous, and since they can't be sure that what is eluding them isn't false, they condemn the principle because it's safer.[53]

Arguably this is one of the most perceptive statements ever made about the conflict between two groups who both claim to have a common enemy in relativism. The so-called new theologians were never trying to defend relativism or undermine Catholic orthodoxy. They regarded their work as a service to the Church in defence of a faith which in their minds was the same in 1930 as it was in the year 33 AD. They did, however, believe that relativism was a popular intellectual disposition that could not be fought in the manner that the neo-scholastics were trying to fight it. As Bernard Lonergan was later to argue, 'until

---

52. Gilson, *Letters of Etienne Gilson to de Lubac*, p. 24.
53. Ibid., p. 68.

we move onto the level of historical dynamics, we shall face our secularist and atheistic opponents as the Red Indians, armed with bows and arrows, faced European muskets'.[54] The fact that this is a fundamental difference between the two groups is clear in a recently published defence of Garrigou-Lagrange by Richard Peddicord. Peddicord claims that the 'scholastic disputation provided Garrigou-Lagrange with a model and method for arriving at the truth', and indeed, 'the disputation ought to be seen as the heuristic key for understanding Garrigou's fundamental style in philosophy and theology'.[55] What Peddicord calls 'scholastic disputation', Dru has called 'syllogistic brillo'.[56] As Fergus Kerr said of Leonine-era neo-scholasticism generally, 'it satisfies some, but repels others'.

Rudolf Voderholzer has described the alternative methodological style of de Lubac in the following terms:

> He [de Lubac] prefers not to regard the faith of the Church as a self-contained block, which originates in a divine decree and which man must therefore accept without any explanation as to what it all has to do with his life. Taking as its points of departure man, as a being that is ordered to the divine transcendence, the kind of apologetics that Henri de Lubac has in mind should demonstrate how the Gospel message addresses the real questions of the human spirit and should finally (to use an expression of Augustine) prove to the pagans, through reason, how unreasonable it is not to believe.[57]

In his own words, de Lubac stated that to do theology 'does not mean simply to "organise truths" and to reduce them to a system or to draw new inferences from the revealed "premises"; it is much rather to demonstrate the "explanatory power" of the truths of the faith ... to do theology means to endeavour to see all things in the mystery of Christ'.[58] Hans Boersma has argued that de Lubac regarded the early medieval shift from an emphasis on symbol to an emphasis on dialectics as regressive.[59]

---

54. B. Lonergan, *Philosophical and Theological Papers: Collected Papers* (1958–1964), ed. by R. C. Croken et al. (Toronto University Press, 1996), pp. 352–83, p. 17. See also A. Kennedy, 'Christopher Dawson's Influence on Bernard Lonergan's Project of "Introducing History into Theology"', *Logos: A Journal of Catholic Thought and Culture* 15:2 (Spring 2012): pp. 138–65 at p. 151.

55. R. Peddicord, *The Sacred Monster of Thomism: An Introduction to the Life and Legacy of Reginald Garrigou-Lagrange* (South Bend, IN: St Augustine's Press, 2005), p. 54.

56. A. Dru, 'From the *Action Française* to the Second Vatican Council: Blondel's "La Semaine sociale de Bordeaux"', *Downside Review* (July 1963): pp. 226–45. Note: Brillo is a trade name for a scouring pad, used for cleaning dishes, and made from steel wool impregnated with soap. The invention was patented in 1913.

57. R. Voderholer, *Meet Henri de Lubac: His Life and Work* (San Francisco: Ignatius, 2008), p. 46.

58. H. de Lubac, *La revelation divine* (Paris: Cerf, 1983), pp. 100–1.

59. H. Boersma, 'Sacramental Ontology: Nature and Supernature in the Ecclesiology of Henri de Lubac', *New Blackfriars* 88:1015 (May 2007): pp. 242–73.

The contrast between those who are satisfied by scholastic disputation and those of a more humanist disposition continues unabated in contemporary Anglophone theological circles. Scholars associated with the *Communio* journal which was founded by Henri de Lubac, Joseph Ratzinger, and Hans Urs von Balthasar in 1972 will often defend the rationality of the faith by mytho-poetic reflections which illustrate the dramatic effects of moral choices upon the formation of the human person. They also engage with Romantic intellectual interests like human freedom and self-formation from a Trinitarian perspective. They do acknowledge a place for doctrine in theological reflection but they do not narrow the discipline of theology down to a systematic presentation of doctrines. John Milbank has described the methodological differences between the Thomists of the Strict Observance and the *Communio* theologians as a conflict between a classical orthodoxy and a romantic orthodoxy. Milbank presents the division in the following terms:

> The 'romantics' think that the collapse of a reason linked to the higher *eros* led to the debasement of scholasticism and then to secular modernity. Resistance to the latter had therefore to oppose rationalism and even to insist more upon the role of the 'erotic' – the passions, the imagination, art, *ethos* etc. [–] than had been the case up till and including Aquinas... The exponents of 'classicism' on the other hand (largely located in the United States) trace secularity simply to a poor use of reason and regard the scholastic legacy, mainly in its 'Thomistic' form, as sustaining a true use of reason to this very day... The conflict between these two parties is therefore one between opposed metanarratives.[60]

The *Communio* scholars trace the current theological crises to dualisms which came to the fore in the post-Tridentine era and issues which were the unfinished business of the Councils of Trent (1545–1563) and Vatican I (1869–1870). The neo-neo-scholastics want to defend baroque-era scholasticism and blame Cardinal de Lubac and his *Communio* colleagues for the current theological crises because they undermined the stable pre-conciliar edifice. What one group reads as 'stable' and 'certain', the other group reads as 'ossified' and 'pastorally ineffectual'. Milbank has suggested that the fact that contemporary proponents of a Strict Observance Thomism are found mostly in the United States may be related to the fact that 'the United States never had a nineteenth century'. By this he means that the intellectual, political, and economic culture of the United States is very much a product of the rationalism of the eighteenth century rather than the romanticism of the nineteenth century. The latter had a seminal

60. J. Milbank, 'The New Divide: Classical versus Romantic Orthodoxy', *Modern Theology* 26 (January 2010): pp. 26–38. Material in this and the following section also appears in ch. 3 of the author's *Catholic Theology* (London: Bloomsbury, 2017) wherein the subject is the methodological difference between *Communio* scholars like de Lubac and contemporary neo-neo-scholastics.

influence on twentieth- and now twenty-first-century European culture but failed to make the Atlantic crossing. The difference in sensibility may also have something to do with different reactions to the First and Second World Wars. After his experience of the First World War, the German theologian Paul Tillich wrote: 'All that horrible, long night I walked along the rows of dying men, and much of my German classical education philosophy broke down that night – the belief that man could master cognitively the essence of his being, the belief in the identity of essence and existence.'[61] Although the American experience of the wars would have been no less traumatic, the reaction was not one of disillusionment with the Enlightenment project. America did not cause either World War. Americans were dragged into a European catastrophe to bring it to an end.

In his *Apocalypse of the German Soul*, completed in 1939, von Balthasar was highly critical of the influence of Kant on the German national culture. The Kantian understanding of rationality kick-started a diabolical separation of faith from reason which taken to its logical extreme ended with the belief that violence could be rational.[62] The link between Kant and nationalistic violence had earlier been made by Vladimir Ern in his famous 1914 Lecture 'From Kant to Krupp'.[63] As Artur Mrówczyński-Van Allen observed, the conclusions of Ern (and one may add von Balthasar) were later echoed in an essay by the Polish philosopher Leszek Kołakowski. Kołakowski described the 'recurrent German philosophical desire as one which consists in the attempt to discover God without God, to find secular and transcendental foundation for moral and epistemological security apart from God'.[64]

The above analyses may help to explain why many of the leading conciliar-generation theologians (who were predominately French, German, and Belgian) regarded an ahistorical neo-scholasticism as completely inadequate to deal with the spiritual trauma of twentieth-century Europeans. For Europeans, reason was tainted. The logic of what Gottfried Benn called 'the lost ego', the person disconnected from God, was life viewed as a nihilistic power trip. Appeals to dialectical rationality were unlikely to be an effective pastoral response to those who had found themselves caught in the conflagration.

---

61. P. Tillich, *Time* 73, 11 (16 March 1959): p. 47. Quoted in Douglas John Hall, 'The Great War and the Theologians', in Gregory Baum, ed., *The Twentieth Century: A Theological Overview* (New York: Orbis, 1999), pp. 3–14 at p. 6.

62. H. U. von Balthasar, *Apokalypse der deutschen Seele: Studien zu einerlehre von letzen Haltunger*, 3 vols (Einsiedeln: Johannes Verlag, 1998).

63. V. Ern, 'Od Kanta do Kruppa', quoted by A. Mrówczynski-Van Allen, *Between the Icon and the Idol* (Oregon: Cascade Publications, 2014), p. 130.

64. L. Kołakowski, 'Reprodukcja kulturalna I zapominanie', in *Czy diabel moze byc zbawiony i 27 innych kazan*, Znak, 2006. Quoted in A. Mrówczynski-Van Allen, *Between the Icon and the Idol*, p. 130.

Paradox and Conceptual Clarity

A contemporary critic of de Lubac from a classically orthodox perspective is Lawrence Feingold.[65] Feingold acknowledges that Aquinas was not clear on the issues which came to be in dispute in the twentieth century, but he prefers the reading of Cajetan to that of de Lubac. Nicholas J. Healy observes that whereas de Lubac interprets St Thomas 'as an authoritative witness to a tradition that preceded him, Feingold begins with Aquinas and then microscopically traces the tradition of commentary on Aquinas's writings'.[66] In other words, one (de Lubac) reads Aquinas forwards through the lens of his patristic antecedents, the other (Feingold) reads Aquinas backwards through the lens of his Thomistic commentators.

More significant however than this genealogical difference is what Aaron Riches has observed to be two distinct approaches to theological perplexity. Riches argues that whereas de Lubac sees theological perplexity as essentially internal to the paradox of the hypostatic union and the mystery of Christology – the very core of Christian thought and practice – Feingold sees perplexity as a problematic failure of reason to understand faith, and thus an aspect of theology in need of resolution in the quest for systematic clarity.[67] For de Lubac a paradox in theology is not in itself a problem since the Incarnation is itself a paradox. Again to quote Riches:

> For de Lubac, the Christological paradox entails that the Church's doctrine will be constituted by 'a comprehensive assembly of opposing aspects', and that these 'opposing aspects' are raised to signify the full depth of the mystery of truth in direct relation to the degree that 'they are mutually supported like flying buttresses (*arc-boutant*), each one braced against the other in the most extreme degrees of tension'. The tensive image of the *arc-boutant* as the soul of orthodoxy suggests the polyphony of the synthesis of theology at the service of the one objective truth.[68]

A further contrast between the two different approaches (the classically and romantically orthodox) has been highlighted by Rudolf Voderholzer. He notes that one of de Lubac's chief concerns is to reunite things that belong together and

---

65. L. Feingold, *The Natural Desire to See God According to St. Thomas and His Interpreters* (Naples, FL: Sapientia Press, 2010). See also S. A. Long, *Natura Pura: On the Recovery of Nature in the Doctrine of Grace* (New York: Fordham University Press, 2010).

66. N. J. Healy, 'Henri de Lubac on Nature and Grace: A Note on Some Recent Contributions to the Debate', *Communio: International Catholic Review* 35 (Winter 2008): p. 557.

67. A. Riches, 'To Rest in the Infinite Altitude of the Divine Substance: A Lubacian Response to the Provocation of Lawrence Feingold and the Resurgent Attack on the Legacy of *Surnaturel*', *Synesis*, vol. 1 (Granada: 2017). Riches was quoting from de Lubac's C, 250.

68. Ibid.

to expose false alternatives.[69] In other words, de Lubac's intellectual orientation was towards synthesis. As Riches and others have argued, 'unity' was his primary transcendental. His motivation was to put pieces of the Christian intellectual jigsaw back together after they had fallen apart in successive intellectual crises beginning with the rise of nominalism in the fourteenth century. He would begin with pastoral problems, analyse their pathology, and as a part of this process he would argue that certain aspects of the Christian kerygma had been overlooked or misunderstood and required re-presentation in a manner accessible to people living today. In contrast, the scholastic orientation is towards conceptual clarification and thus the making of finer and finer distinctions. A scholastic presupposition tends to be that if there is a pastoral problem, the cause is either a defect of the intellect or a defect of the will. Since no amount of intellectual work can fix a defective will, emphasis is placed on fixing the defects of the intellect. De Lubac would agree that problems can be primarily of an intellectual nature. For example, he regarded the social side effects of the neo-scholastic project as a problem that could only be fixed by going back to the roots of the construction of the relationship between nature and grace and intellectually demonstrating the link between this construction and the social marginalism of God. From the perspective of his wider anthropology, however, the neo-scholastic emphasis upon conceptual clarification places rather too many eggs into the basket of a particular type of rationality – in scholastic terms, into the basket of *ratio*. For de Lubac a pastoral crisis could be caused by what Claudel called 'the poverty of a starved imagination' as much as by a breakdown in dialectical rationality. A contemporary joke is that neo-neo-scholastics are people who are strongly left-brain dominant and right-brain weak.

Limbo and the American Dream

Finally, in the context of the issue of different personality dispositions, it is helpful to ask the question, what intellectual or even ideological concerns are driving the preference for one over the other? In an eloquent exposition of the principles undergirding what is sometimes called 'the Cambridge school of ideas', Alasdair MacIntyre advised students that when examining the texts of some scholar, a crucial question is always: Against whom is he writing here? Within what controversy is this or that particular contention to be situated? Scholars 'characteristically invite us not simply to assert p, but to assert p rather than q or r, and we will often only understand the point of asserting p, if we know what q and r are'.[70] At present the state of the debate over *Surnaturel* is focused on the question of whether the

---

69. Voderholzer, *Meet Henri de Lubac*, p. 120.

70. A. MacIntyre, 'Aquinas's Critique of Education: Against his Own Age, Against Ours', in A. O. Rorty, ed., *Philosophers on Education: New Historical Perspectives* (London: Routledge, 1998), p. 96.

natural desire for God is innate or elicited.[71] Applying MacIntyre's interpretive principle, the question becomes: What's at stake here? Why does the difference between 'innate' and 'elicited' matter? Here several scholars have argued that the contemporary attacks on de Lubac are being driven by the desire to defend the concept of limbo (which fits well with the logic of a 'pure nature') and to defend a view of the Incarnation which emphasizes its remedial necessity. Edward T. Oakes has argued, 'there can be no question that Feingold's attack on de Lubac, as well as his defence of the commentary tradition, directly entails, at least for him, the existence of limbo'.[72]

It has also been suggested that an extrinicist account of the grace and nature relationship opens Catholic theology to a comfortable synthesis with the liberal political tradition in a way that de Lubac's account does not, and this fact may help to explain its attraction to Americans. By keeping the secular and the sacred in separate compartments, Catholics who want to baptize the liberal tradition can seek agreement with non-Catholics about public goods on the basis of a shared notion of 'pure nature'. Matters pertaining to the sacred can be privately added on to the philosophically discernible purely natural goods and ends. This became the basis of John Courtney Murray's defence of Americanism, to which the contemporary 'Whig Thomists' (a label proposed by Michael Novak) are the intellectual heirs. The difference that a Lubacian and a neo-scholastic construction of the relationship between nature and grace makes to the way that Catholics approach the realms of politics and economics is well presented in the works of David L. Schindler.[73] In the following paragraphs, he juxtaposes the approach of John Courtney Murray (relying heavily on Suárez) with that of de Lubac:

> According to Murray: faith and grace do not determine the structures and processes of civil society: these are determined by reason, in the light of the lessons of experience... [The Church] does not aim to alter the finality of the state, but to enable the state to achieve its own finality as determined by its own nature. Conversely, for de Lubac, the state occupies no special 'secular' space beyond the operation of the law of the relations between nature and grace. It is from within that grace seizes nature... It is from within that faith transforms reason, that the Church influences the state.

---

71. For an overview of the Status Quaestionis, see D. Braine, 'Henri de Lubac and His Critics', *Nova et Vetera* 6:3 (Summer 2008): pp. 543–91.

72. E. T. Oakes, 'The *Surnaturel* Controversy: A Survey and a Response', *Nova et Vetera* 9:3 (2011): pp. 625–56.

73. In his criticisms of the Americanist project Schindler draws attention to the influence of the Suárezian anthropology on John Courtney Murray's defence of the constitutional framework of the United States. See D. L. Schindler, *Heart of the World, Soul of the Church* (Grand Rapids: Eerdmans, 1996) and *Ordering Love: Liberal Societies and the Memory of God* (Grand Rapids: Eerdmans, 2011). See also D. L. Schindler and N. J. Healy Jnr, *Freedom, Truth and Human Dignity: The Second Vatican Council's Declaration on Religious Freedom* (Grand Rapids: Eerdmans, 2015).

For Murray, grace's influence on nature takes the form of assisting nature to realize its own finality; the ends proper to grace and nature otherwise remain each in its own sphere. For de Lubac, on the contrary, grace's influence takes the form of directing nature from within to serve the end given in grace; the ends proper to grace and nature remain distinct, even as the natural end is placed within, internally subordinated to, the supernatural end. For Murray then, the result is an insistence on a dualism between citizen and believer, and on the sharpness of the distinction between eternal (ultimate) end and temporal (penultimate) ends. For de Lubac, on the contrary, the call to sanctity 'comprehends' the call to citizenship and all the worldly tasks implied by citizenship. The eternal end 'comprehends' the temporal ends.[74]

Vatican II and Subsequent Pontificates

Limbo is not very popular outside of neo-scholastic and traditionalist circles (the two often overlap though not necessarily so). When holding the position of Prefect of the Congregation for the Doctrine of the Faith, Joseph Ratzinger claimed that limbo was never a part of the Church's doctrinal teaching, that it merely enjoyed the status of a hypothesis, and that speaking personally, as a professional theologian, not in his capacity as Prefect, he would abandon it altogether. Statements of John Paul II in *Evangelium Vitae* (1995), to the effect that it is possible to hope for the beatific vision for unborn children, also suggest that John Paul II was more inclined to a Lubacian reading of this issue.[75] Numerous scholars have pointed out the difficulty of aligning limbo with the Trinitarian Christocentrism outlined in the early encyclicals of Wojtyła's papacy, above all *Redemptor Hominis* and *Dives in Misericordia*. The hypothesis of limbo was further politely sidelined by the International Theological Commission in its document *The Hope of Salvation for Infants Who Die Without Being Baptised* (2007). Paragraph 38 of this document also argued that *Auctorem fidei*, a papal bull of Pius VI, should not be construed as a dogmatic endorsement of the doctrine of limbo. As Oakes explains, 'Pius VI did not condemn the Jansenists because they denied limbo, but because they held that the defenders of limbo were guilty of the heresy of Pelagius'.[76]

In general the magisterial teaching of both the pontificates of John Paul II and Benedict XVI was strongly influenced by the theology of de Lubac and others in his circle. The tide in favour of their theological vision began to rise in the

---

74. D. L. Schindler, 'Religious Freedom, Truth and American Liberalism: Another look at John Courtney Murray', in *Heart of the World, Center of the Church: Communio Ecclesiology, Liberalism and Liberation* (Grand Rapids: Eerdmans, 1996), p. 79.

75. For an extensive analysis of the arguments about limbo, see E. T. Oakes, 'Catholic Eschatology and the Development of Doctrine', *Nova et Vetera* 6:2 (Spring 2008): pp. 419–46.

76. Oakes, 'Catholic Eschatology and the Development of Doctrine', p. 426 n. 17.

late 1950s. By 1959 de Lubac was invited by John XXIII to attend the Second Vatican Council as a *peritus*. There he was to have considerable influence on the drafting of the documents *Gaudium et spes* and *Dei Verbum* and his ecclesiology is strongly infused throughout *Lumen Gentium*. *Dei Verbum* significantly undermined the Suárezian account of revelation (in favour of an understanding closer to Newman and the Tübingen scholars) and reframed the relationship between scripture and tradition (in the direction of Blondel rather than Billot). *Dei Verbum* also had the effect of undermining a typically Leonine-era neo-scholastic understanding of the relationship between faith and reason. As Fergus Kerr has argued:

> It remained unsettled at Vatican I whether the natural light by which reason can attain knowledge of God should be equated with the prelapsarian light enjoyed by Adam in the Garden of Eden or the light in which someone in a state of grace might exercise his reasoning powers, or the light which someone might supposedly have independently of the effects of sin and grace.[77]

However, *Dei Verbum* offered a more extensive epistemology embedded within a broader Trinitarian anthropology. (This fact has yet to be recognized by many in neo-scholastic circles where there is a tendency to refer to Vatican I's document *Dei Filius* whenever the subject of the faith and reason relationship is raised and to assume that *Dei Filius* is the last definitive magisterial intervention on the topic, *Dei Verbum* (1965) and *Fides et Ratio* (1998) notwithstanding.)

While *Dei Verbum* offered a theological epistemology, *Gaudium et spes* offered a theological ontology. Although paragraph 22 of *Gaudium et spes* does not specially mention de Lubac, but merely borrows heavily from one of his statements in *Catholicism*, and thus, strictly speaking, one cannot assert that paragraph 22 of *Gaudium et spes* is authority for the magisterial endorsement of de Lubac's specific reading of the grace and nature relationship, numerous authors, including Jarosław Kupczak OP and Cardinals Angelo Scola and Marc Ouellet, read the Trinitarian Christocentrism of the papacy of John Paul II as running on Lubacian grace and nature foundations. As Kupczak explains, for Wojtyła, cognition is linked to the transforming power of the grace of Christ and such grace is 'not presented by Wojtyła as something external or merely added to human nature'. Kupczak concludes that Wojtyła accepted the theory of grace popularized by de Lubac in *Surnaturel*.[78]

De Lubac and Wojtyła became friends at the Second Vatican Council. During a walk through the streets of Rome, de Lubac famously quipped that he was happy for Paul VI to have a long pontificate, but after it was over, Wojtyła was his desired

---

77. F. Kerr, 'Knowing God by Reason Alone: What Vatican I Never Said', *New Blackfriars* 91 (May 2010): p. 222.

78. J. Kupczak, *The Human Person in the Philosophy of Karol Wojtyła/John Paul II: Destined for Liberty* (Washington, DC: Catholic University of America, 2000), pp. 83–84.

successor. At the end of the Council, de Lubac contributed a preface to the French edition of Wojtyła's *Love and Responsibility* and Wojtyła saw to it that de Lubac's essay *Églises particulières et Église universelle* was translated into Polish. In 1970 and 1971, Wojtyła invited de Lubac to Poland but he was unable to accept the offer due to ill health which was a lifelong problem following his head wound received in the Battle of Verdun in the First World War. A decade later during his 1980 papal visit to Paris, Wojtyła, on seeing de Lubac in an audience at the Institut Catholique, remarked: '*Je m'incline devant le Père de Lubac* [I bow my head to Father de Lubac]'. Three years later he made de Lubac a Cardinal. In a similar gesture of homage, Ratzinger wrote that he had never found anyone with such a comprehensive and humanistic education as Hans Urs von Balthasar and von Balthasar's teacher Henri de Lubac. He added, 'I cannot even begin to say how much I owe to my encounter with them'.[79] As Pope, Ratzinger directly cited de Lubac in the 2007 encyclical *Spe Salvi* and Lubacian watermarks are clearly visible in many of his magisterial documents, including *Caritas in Veritate*. In what was to be the final encyclical promulgated under his name, he made the point, strongly evocative of de Lubac's argument in *Atheistic Humanism*, that 'a humanism which excludes God is an inhuman humanism'.

Conclusion

In his *Twentieth-Century Catholic Theologians*, Fergus Kerr makes the point that all the significant Catholic theological figures in the second half of the twentieth century, from the über-liberal Hans Küng to the anti-liberal Joseph Ratzinger, were hostile to Strict Observance scholasticism, and he presented de Lubac as the figure whose work was most successful at discrediting what Bonino has described as the 'timeless Koran' appropriation of the works of St Thomas. Similarly, in his *Theology of Karl Barth*, von Balthasar credited de Lubac's *Catholicism* with 'effecting the breakthrough from the strait-jacket of neo-scholasticism'.[80] In another essay, on the understanding of reason in the thought of Georges Bernanos, von Balthasar referred to a key insight of Bernanos that 'if a priest is supposed to represent the apex of reason, he could not do so merely by mastering a theological system; rather, in keeping with Peter's "all to the Cross" (Jn 21:18) he would have to do it by the radical commitment of his existence'.[81] De Lubac would no doubt agree. In his *Paradoxes of Faith*, he wrote: 'There is nothing more demanding than the taste for mediocrity. Beneath its ever moderate appearance

---

79. J. Ratzinger, *Milestones – Memoirs 1927–1977* (San Francisco: Ignatius, 1998), p. 143.
80. H. U. von Balthasar, *Theology of Karl Barth* (San Francisco: Ignatius Press, 1992), p. 335 n. 37.
81. H. U. von Balthasar, 'Georges Bernanos on Reason: Prophetic, Free and Catholic', *Communio: International Catholic Review* 23 (Summer 1996): pp. 389–418 at p. 417.

there is nothing more intemperate; nothing surer in its instinct; nothing more pitiless in its refusals. It suffers no greatness, shows beauty no mercy.'[82]

De Lubac was not the mediocre type. He was rather what Bernanos would describe as the *honnête homme*, a man of honour, brave enough to serve in a combat position in the First World War and to organize resistance to the Nazis in the Second World War, intelligent enough to identify the problems with trying to fight eighteenth-century rationalism and nineteenth-century nihilist romanticism with a hyper-rationalist neo-scholasticism, and ultimately, urbane enough to stand against the tide of post-conciliar 'clap-trap', as Joseph Ratzinger described some of the 'swinging 60s' pastoral projects that mushroomed in the final decade of the pontificate of Paul VI.

De Lubac died in 1991 at the age of 95, living long enough to see his friend Karol Wojtyła elected to the papacy. Two years later, in his encyclical *Veritatis Splendor* John Paul II wrote, 'Certainly the Church's Magisterium does not intend to impose upon the faithful any particular theological system, still less a philosophical one'.[83]

---

82. PF, p. 137.
83. Para 49 of *Veritatis Splendor* (Sydney: St Paul's, 1992).

Chapter 3

THE INFLUENCE OF MAURICE BLONDEL

Francesca Aran Murphy

This chapter argues that Henri de Lubac was a Blondelian Thomist. 'Paradoxically', as Peter Henrici says, Blondel's 'Jesuit admirers' were drawn by him 'to return to saint Thomas and to reread him in a more accurate historical way than the neo-Scholastic mutilations... in continuity with this rereading, the Jesuits were led to redefine the relation of nature and grace'.[1]

The Twofold Context: Existential Phenomenology and Catholic Theology

Philosophy has often oscillated between an emphasis on the formal, which can overshoot into rationalism, and an emphasis on the experiential, the conscious, and the empirical. Thus, Hume's philosophy is an 'existential' counterpoint to the rationalism and *a priorism* of Clarke and Leibniz. Existentialist philosophies analyse the act of existence as experienced by a subject. Cosmological existentialisms are not oxymorons: they treat nature as a vast subject. In late nineteenth-century France, Comtean positivism was tossed aside by Bergson's vision of the cosmos as the emergent body of a life force which generates novelty.

The philosophy of Maurice Blondel (1861–1949) was focused on the existential subject. But it also attempts a phenomenological study of that subject's conscious relation towards the unknown. Phenomenology studies the character of our relations towards activities or objects; it studies the structures of intentionality. Blondel's existential phenomenology considers how our consciousness is necessarily oriented towards something wider than itself; it examines how human consciousness inevitably projects itself into the unknown, like the grasshopper bounding into the unseen. In his key philosophical text *Action* (1893), Blondel asks: 'Do we not admire how the grasshopper leaps with all its strength, headlong? In giving ourselves to action, do we ever know where we shall come down? And if

---

1. Peter Henrici, 'La descendance blondélienne parmi les jésuites française', in Emmanuel Gabellieri and Pierre de Cointet, eds, *Maurice Blondel et la philosophie française* (Paris: Parole et Silence, 2007), pp. 305–22, p. 220.

we knew clearly where, would we act?'² Writing in 1924, de Lubac, already under the master's spell, asked, 'is the object of the essential will, while remaining only imperfectly revealed to itself, anything other than destiny?' Our Destiny 'is only resolved through the entirety of life', and therefore 'the sense of all things remains constantly mysterious to us; the world cannot be illuminated to our eyes by our own light, and so it must remain hidden from us until we have achieved our end. *Nondum apparuit quid erimus* [what we are is still not apparent to us]'.³ The supreme problem of philosophy, according to Blondel, is that we are *determined* to be *free*, that is, that we *must* go out to meet our destiny, blindly, and yet willingly! *Action* is thus a text in existentialist philosophy.

It's possible for a work to be existentialist without being phenomenological, such as in the writings of Camus. What phenomenology adds is the study of the intentional acts, or intentionalities, which form the core of conscious existence. Moreover, central texts in the phenomenological tradition such as Husserl's *Logical Investigations* ignore existential questions. Phenomenology has no necessary connection with the existential stream of philosophy which reacts against formalism and rationalism. Blondel's *Action* is a founding work in French existential phenomenology because he draws together the two strands, attempting a structural, phenomenological analysis of a pre- or extra-theoretical human orientation, that is, *action*. Back of the great atheist and anti-Catholic writings of Sartre, Camus, and Merleau-Ponty lies Blondel's magisterial work, *Action*.

One could thus find this sentence in many of the French existentialists: 'In question is the whole of man; it is not in thought alone that we must seek him out. It is into action that we shall have to transport the center of philosophy, because there is also to be found the center of life.'⁴ What does Blondel mean when he writes *action*? It does not mean doing something, like walking down the street. It does not mean making something, like cooking a meal. Acting is a prereflexive process which tends towards self-reflection. It is possible to act without thinking (much) about it, but it is not possible to act without seeing oneself doing it. One could almost take Blondel literally at his word: acting is *acting*, as in acting a part. *Action* is *like* acting a part; only a theologian would take him so literally as to mean acting a role in a theodrama! We are *actors* of our lives, as Blondel sees it, and he tries to show phenomenologically, by studying the structure of our intentions, that this presents us with the *existential* dilemma that we can never

---

2. Maurice Blondel, *Action: Essay on a Critique of Life and a Science of Practice* (trans. from the 1893 French version by Oliva Blanchette, University of Notre Dame Press: Notre Dame, 1984), p. 144.

3. De Lubac, 'La philosophie, science de la destinée' (1924), quoted in Georges Chantraine, *Henri de Lubac tome II: Les années de formation (1919–1929)* (Cerf: Paris, 2009), p. 463. De Lubac's juvenilia was 'published' in an in-house magazine called *Quodlibeta*, intended for circulation within the Jesuit philosophy scholasticate. These texts are available as scans from the de Lubac archive in Belgium.

4. Blondel, *Action*, p. 13.

be fully there in what we act. Our efforts to be sincerely *there* fail because the structure of consciousness is such that it projects a part 'too large' for us to fill.

Blondel's notion of action is somewhat amorphous, because it's an operation, not a thing, and an operation which does not have a 'thing' as its intentional correlate. He sees the business of the phenomenologist as studying 'subjectivity', which he calls an 'internal principle of unity, a center of grouping imperceptible to the senses ..., an operation immanent to the diversity of the parts, an organic idea, an original action that escapes positive knowledge'.[5] Subjectivity is an 'idea'; because it is a whole which is greater than the sum of its parts it eludes empirical investigation. When Blondel describes himself as practising a 'method of immanence' we could call that a phenomenological method, a philosophy which finds its mark by tracing the flow of intentionality, the patterns of conscious orientation. As a *phenomenologist* (as distinct from existentialist), Blondel is concerned with the structure of consciousness, whatever the existential status of its objects. In this vein, as a phenomenologist of religion, he tells us that the 'special business' of philosophy

> is to criticize all the phenomena which make up our inner life, ..., to study the connections between them, to show all their implications, to discover what principles are presupposed by thought and by action, to define on what conditions we may ascribe reality to the objects or the means of salvation which are inevitably conceived by us, to study (for example) our idea of God, not just as God, but in so far as it is our necessary and effective thought of God, or again to analyze the conception which we are led to form of revealed beliefs and practices, not just as religious and redemptive Revelation but in so far as we can see them as answering to our needs... Thus the immanent affirmation of the transcendent, even of the supernatural, does not prejudge... the transcendent reality of the immanent affirmations – a radical distinction which... enables us to construct in a scientific manner... the entire phenomenology of thought and action.[6]

An 'immanent affirmation of the transcendent' describes the transcendent as the *target* of our aspirations, not as it is in itself. That is, it describes it phenomenologically.

It sounds as if Blondel were leaning towards inferring God from the immanent orientation of consciousness. Why God? Because God is how immanence rolls. Blondel does not make that move: his argument is that the *idea* of the infinite necessarily appears to an acting agent. He does not affirm that an infinite *being*

---

5. Ibid., p. 94.
6. Blondel's 'Letter on Apologetics', from Maurice Blondel, *The Letter on Apologetics and History and Dogma*, trans., Alexander Dru and Illtyid Trethowan (Grand Rapids, MI: William B. Eerdmans, 1994), pp. 157–58.

exists.[7] It is just this *existential* step which Blondel says cannot be taken by *philosophy*. Philosophy can show there is some awaited presence, an empty chair, but it cannot open the door to let that Elijah in. Philosophy cannot take the *existential* step, because Blondel speaks, not of 'the God of the philosophers', but of the God of Abraham, Isaac, and Jacob: the God of Revelation. Only God can take the existential step of revealing himself:

> We never do anything more than indicate blank spaces which cannot be filled in ... in their reality by any resource of ours. Even when we show that this system of rational requirements rests upon the most concrete living experience, and even when we determine the conditions which seem to us necessary if what we think and will is to *exist*, it is not our philosophy ... which will produce ... being itself, the living truth, the gift which brings salvation. And it is just by the acknowledgement of this impossibility that philosophy is reconciled with theology.[8]

The God who lights Blondel's fire is the Triune God of revelation, the God of Jesus Christ. When we say that philosophy swings between the formalists and the existentialists, think of the *Philosophes* and Pascal.

Blondel's existentialism does not make him anti-metaphysical: it leads him to concentrate the metaphysical in the 'subject', to see the personal as the concentrated essence of the metaphysical. He states, 'Real history is composed of human lives; and human life is metaphysics in act'.[9] God is most 'real' for Blondel when taken as an acting subject, that is, in revelation history. The God of 'natural theology' is relatively unreal, formal, and hypothetical for him.

Were such 'existentialism' to fill the atmosphere of one's thinking, then the notion of a hypothetical 'state of pure nature', which describes what human nature would have been like if it were not for the (historical) fall of Adam and the (historical) redemption of fallen humanity by Christ, would seem, most likely, kind of laughable. Henri de Lubac is Blondel's disciple in his assumption that existential reality is the only reality worth the theologian's time of day. Not all theologians think like this: it is debatable whether a hypothetical state of pure nature is a useful analytic tool. But for de Lubac, because he is a Blondelian, theology is never a matter of analysing aspects of human life in their isolation from the whole acting subject or person. Why were these minority positions among Catholics between 1870 and 1963?

---

7. Oliva Blanchette, *Maurice Blondel: A Philosophical Life* (Grand Rapids, MI: William B. Eerdmans, 2010), p. 67; John J. McNeil, *The Blondelian Synthesis: A Study of the Influence of German Philosophical Sources on the Formation of Blondel's Method and Thought* (Leiden: E. J. Brill, 1966), pp. 20–21.

8. Blondel, 'History and Dogma', from *The Letter on Apologetics*, p. 160.

9. Ibid., p. 237.

In 1870, an ecumenical Council in the Vatican City issued two dogmatic constitutions, one on the Church and the other on the scope and methods of our knowledge of God. The Constitution *Dei Filius* was intended to call out heresies: one was *agnosticism* about our knowledge of God's existence and nature; the other was *rationalism* about our ability to *demonstrate* that God is Triune and has revealed himself. *Dei Filius* teaches that there are two formally distinct means by which we know the one God: one is by reason, which knows from the evidence of the material world that God exists, and the other is by the God-given light of faith, which sees that God is Triune, has revealed himself in Jesus Christ and through the Church. *Dei Filius* teaches the Thomistic doctrine that, although right reason can never contradict faith, since they both know the same God, nonetheless, these ways of knowing God are formally distinct.

The language and content of Vatican I's *Dei Filius* is that of nineteenth-century neo-scholastic Thomism. It put a damper on efforts by some German-speaking Catholics to assimilate Romantic idealism into Catholic theology. Those who had tried to outdo Hegel from within the ramparts of the Church had been condemned as pantheists by *Dei Filius*. In 1879, Pope Leo XIII promulgated *Aeterni Patris*, which instructed the faithful to return to Saint Thomas Aquinas. *Dei Filius* and *Aeterni Patris* reshaped how Catholics articulate their faith.

One practical upshot was that seminarians were first taught an Aristotelian philosophy understood as formally distinct from theology, and then, as the culmination of their formation, they were taught the science of faith. Thomas Aquinas distinguished between philosophical reason and theological faith: late nineteenth-century Catholic pedagogy actively separated the two.

The Modernist Crisis entrenched this rift until the mid-twentieth century. Between 1903 and 1910, men such as Alfred Loisy were condemned as modernists by Pope Pius X. Pius X called Modernism 'the synthesis of all heresies':[10] it was exhibited in historicism, subjectivism, fideism, and immanentism.

The atmosphere of the Modernist Crisis hung over the Church for decades. For the next half century, men were removed from teaching in Catholic institutions, on the grounds of appearing to interiorize the sources of faith (subjectivism), disparaging reason (fideism), conflating reason and faith (fideism), and grounding faith in experience (immanentism). It was not easy to speak of Catholicism as a way of life when eliding faith with reason was denounced as fideism; nor to speak of faith as touching the 'whole man' when relating faith to experience was subjectivism. It was in this context that Blondel wrote his existential phenomenology, and that de Lubac turned this existential phenomenology into theology. Both were punished with accusations ranging from pantheism to fideism, to Modernism, and sometimes all three at once.

Here a minor villain of the piece must take a bow: Charles Maurras enters telling French Catholics, 'just call me Aristotle'. He was a follower of Auguste Comte. For

---

10. Pius X, *Pascendi Dominici Gregis* (1907) #39.

the positivist Comte, 'humanity' is the measure of all other values; for Maurras and for his quasi-political movement the Action française, France and her interests are the measure of all things. Through the Action française, which agitated on behalf of Catholic institutions against secularizing, anti-clerical governments, Maurras convinced Catholics to give their political loyalty to men who regarded France as the good 'that than which no higher can be thought'. How did Maurras convince educated Thomists, Dominicans and Jesuits, and French bishops that his positivist politics could cooperate with their Catholicism?

Maurras did so by treating his atheistic 'positivism', his system of 'natural right', as the formally separable 'bottom half' or foundation of their two-tiered Catholicism: his positivist political philosophy was supposed to be equivalent to their Aristotelian philosophy, while theology was the optional 'upper half', safe behind a moated grange for Catholic believers. *Something* of the vehemence of Blondel and de Lubac's insistence that the compartmentalization of faith and reason is a death blow to reason and to faith flows from antipathy to Maurras's distortion of the Thomistic formal separation of what philosophy and theology can know.

Those who offered social-democratic solutions to France's political problems were accused by Action française supporters of 'social modernism'.[11] Some were silenced, and the most prominent organization, a Catholic youth group called *Sillon*, was shut down by Pius X. Blondel defended Catholic social democracy against Maurras in the journal which he owned, the *Annales de philosophie chrétienne*. Using the pseudonym 'Testis', Blondel assaulted the premise of the strict separation between the natural and political world and the supernatural, upon which Catholic cooperation with the Action française was built. Testis's articles defending the complex interweaving of nature and supernature were published between October 1909 and May 1910.

In December 1910, the Jesuit Pedro Descoqs responded by arguing that Maurras's political system deals solely with this-worldly matters, leaving a believer free to pursue his faith, which is, in any case, formally distinct from the believer's philosophy. The *Annales de philosophie chrétienne* was edited by Blondel's friend Fr Lucien Laberthonnière. Laberthonnière leapt into the breach, and unlike Blondel, this Oratorian Father was an accessible writer. He nailed Descoqs so brilliantly that the case was taken up at Rome. As a result, the *Annales* was shut down, permanently, and Laberthonnière was forbidden to teach or publish for the rest of his life. Taking the supernatural to be intrinsically related to the natural world was political 'heresy' to Maurrasian-Thomists. Blondel used the 'barbarous neologism',[12] 'extrinsicism' to describe the ratification of a material separation

---

11. Michael Sutton, *Nationalism, Positivism and Catholicism: The Politics of Charles Maurras and French Catholics: 1890–1914* (Cambridge: Cambridge University Press, 1982), p. 148.

12. Blondel, 'History and Dogma', in *The Letter on Apologetics*, p. 225.

between supernature and nature, as if the formal distinction between reasoning to God and believing in God by faith were a concordat between the Vatican and a secular state.

Blondel and Henri de Lubac were each the type that Charles Maurras affected to despise, Romantics. Addressing himself in 1903 to the theological problems raised by the modernist Alfred Loisy, Blondel disparaged as 'extrinsicists' those who *don't see that poetic symbolism matters*, and who therefore 'regard the supernatural as a sign or a password' whose miraculous epiphany bears no 'link' to the 'historical event invested with it'. The extrinsicist so scrupulously avoids rooting the supernatural in this world, recoils so expertly from subjectivistic fideism, that he denies that any 'connection can and should be made between the given objective facts' of miracle and supernatural epiphany and 'our thought or our own lives'.[13] So careful is the extrinsicist to avoid the whiff of a suggestion that the supernatural is a *projection* of human desire or volition that he ends up making the supernatural look like an external imposition on a nature which is barricaded against it. According to Blondel, the Modernist Crisis was engineered by two opposite errors: Thomistic extrinsicism, on the one hand, and Loisy's historicism on the other.

Twenty-five years later, in his paper 'Apologetics and Theology', de Lubac would speak of extrinsicism as

> confin[ing] dogma to the far-corners of knowledge in a distant province, believing that in order to remain supernatural, it must be superficial, and that thought becomes more divine in the degree that it is cut off from all human roots. As if the same God could not be the author of nature and grace, and of nature in view of grace! To establish the intimate connection between the two parts of the divine work is not, as people promptly fear, forcibly to relate the second to the first, but rather the reverse.[14]

Our own deepest aspirations come to us from God: they are more intimate to us than we are to ourselves.

Blondel's Key Themes and How De Lubac Assimilated Them

The mainstream phenomenological tradition runs from Brentano to Husserl to Ingarden and Merleau-Ponty. The great founding achievement of Brentano was his recovery of the notion of intentionality. Lacking this scholastic and Aristotelian conception, philosophy had been unable to denote precisely the means by which consciousness relates itself to things. Almost simultaneously, in around 1890, G. E.

---

13. Ibid., p. 227.
14. Henri De Lubac, 'Apologetique et théologie', *Nouvelle revue theologique*, 57:5 (1930): pp. 361–78, p. 374.

Moore and Brentano had reaffirmed the intentionality of consciousness. Maurice Blondel does not speak of intentionality. Writing within the French tradition of the empirical introspection inaugurated by Maine de Biran and drawing on German Romantics like Gottleib Fichte (1762–1814), Blondel uses the notion of 'dynamism' to do the work of 'intentionality'. Both 'intention' and 'dynamism' refer to an exercise of mediation between the agent and its world. Blondel tells us that 'The true science of the subject is the one which, considering the act of consciousness from the beginning as an act, discovers through a continuous progress its inevitable expansion.' As with all the great phenomenologists, Blondel aims to produce a scientific analysis of consciousness; his singularity lies in the ambition to show, scientifically, that the dynamics of consciousness are infinite.

These ideas had flourished in German idealism. Fichte had envisaged the infinite human spirit as needing to commit to action in order to engage finite nature. Fichte believed that 'only a philosophy of action is capable of seizing the real unity of the spirit and of being, because such a unity is realized only in an effective commitment, in a real will-act by means of which the spirit truly descends into the world to carry out an effective action'.[15]

Blondel sees human dynamism as both necessary and free: the human person *necessarily* wills to exist, to do and to act, and yet this volition is 'his own', it fully belongs to the agent as his own free self-expression or self-expansion. The human agent necessarily strives to be itself. Blondel states that:

> I have nothing I have not received; and yet ... everything has to arise from me, even the being that I have received and seems imposed on me. Whatever I do and whatever I undergo, I have to sanction this being and engender it anew, ... by a personal adherence, without my most sincere freedom ever disavowing it. This is the will, the most intimate and the most free, that it is important to find in all my endeavors and to bring finally to its perfect fulfillment.

Blondel writes in the *first person*, not in the sense of confessional writing *per se*, but because his *modus operandi* is introspective analysis. When we act under necessity (as in necessarily willing to live), we do not experience dispossession. The imposed necessity of acting is precisely what results in self-possession: 'There is nothing arbitrary or tyrannical in my destiny.'[16]

One of Blondel's key words is 'disproportion': it has resonances with the anthropological apologetics of Pascal. There is a disproportion between my necessary being and my free acting, because acting transcends being in the direction of the infinite. Think of already-existent things as necessary and as conditioned by a set of finite causes; action stirs the pot, by adding something new to this finite block. In order to act, we must envisage the infinite, that is, we must envisage the next step as transcending the finite and the given: 'the consciousness

---

15. D. Julia, 'Le Savoir Absolut chez Fichte', quoted in McNeil, *Synthesis*, p. 133.
16. Blondel, *Action*, p. 114.

of action implies the notion of infinite; and this notion of infinite explains the consciousness of free action'. What does it mean to act? It means, in the midst of all that determinism, to add something of one's own: 'No one thinks he is acting if he does not attribute to himself the principle of his action and if he does not believe he is someone or something, like an empire within an empire.'[17]

We surpass necessity, by taking the next, new step, and acting, but we never put the whole of ourselves into one, integral action. We cannot make a single integrated action of our lives. To perform a perfectly integrated act would be for us to be simultaneously necessary and free. We cannot make our 'necessary destiny' our own, because to do so seems to be at war with our freedom, experienced by us as self-possession. The opening question of *Action* is, 'Yes or no, does human life make sense, and does man have a destiny?'[18] The conundrum is that having a destiny seems to mean giving up on being free. We cannot act without transcending the necessary conditions of action, without dynamically intending the infinite.

Being impelled dynamically to intend the infinite feels not like a liberation for paradise but like a deadly fate, like the weight of Sisyphus, because we cannot single-mindedly will the infinite, the 'one thing necessary' for us. The human will is divided against itself. It 'splits' under the weight of the infinite dynamism of action into warring factions. Blondel asks: 'What then is this distance from ourselves to ourselves? What keeps our own will from being simple, full and complete? It is the presence within us of hostile desires.'[19]

The way out would be to let the 'infinite' itself take over and will in and with us. Only by volunteering to be the channel of an infinite dynamism can we reconcile what is necessary and what is free in ourselves. Only by agreeing to cooperate with the infinite necessity which is God can we integrate our two wills. Only by consenting to the infinite in ourselves can we cross the 'immense' 'interval' 'from what we are to what we will to be'.[20]

Nothing compels us to take the 'only way'. Idolatry is how we really roll. Idolatry constructs a finite infinite in order to avoid offering oneself to the 'infinite infinite'. One 'fill[s] the immense interval that separates the will from what it wants' with 'Cult', superstition, and artificial religiosity. Since the purpose of this substitution of idols for the infinite God is to avoid renouncing oneself, it is not surprising that the outstanding idol is man himself. The religion of humanity, aimed at maintaining human self-sufficiency and independence, makes an idol of humanity.[21] Auguste Comte's religion of humanity was on Blondel's terms the consequence of his substitution of humanity for God.

---

17. Ibid., p. 123.
18. Ibid, p. 3.
19. Ibid., pp. 165, 141, and 167.
20. Ibid., p. 141.
21. Ibid., pp. 286 and 292.

The argument of *Action* is that human beings are incurably religious. If they will not have the infinite God, they will be forced to take up with finite gods:

> All attempts to bring human action to completion fail; and it is impossible for human action not to seek to complete itself and to be self-sufficient. On the one hand, it is necessary to clear away all stratagems that, starting from man and coming from the most inward sanctuary of his heart, have as their ridiculous and pitiable object to lay hold of the divine. On the other hand, the sense of powerlessness as well as of the need man has for an infinite fulfillment remains incurable. Hence, as much as every natural religion is artificial, the expectation of some religion remains no less natural.[22]

The whole of de Lubac's *The Drama of Atheist Humanism* is in that observation, but before we pass thereto, we need to lay the final stone of Blondel's edifice: as in *Surnaturel*, Blondel's last words are grace and gift.

Human action is brought to its knees by the fact that all action is *infinitely* open-ended: 'in acting we find an infinite disproportion in ourselves' so that the only 'balance' to redress the equation is the infinite. But, infinite perfection cannot be achieved by us: to recognize it is to recognize our own impotence to *be* the infinite to which our actions aspire. We cannot gain or achieve God, the infinitely perfect act: we can only abandon ourselves and admit that our human acting is moved by his gift and grace. The natural human person cannot take a leap of faith into the supernatural and yet it goes against nature for human action to be purely 'natural'. Blondel says that 'Action cannot stay enclosed in the natural order. ... It is not entirely within it. And yet it cannot, of itself, surpass itself.' To be integral, we have to yield, and cooperate with grace, allowing our action not to be a Sisyphean struggle against blind fate but rather a 'necessary *theergy* which integrates the part of the divine in the human operation'; holistic action would be '*theandric* action', action which is 'founded entirely on the divine will' but in which 'the human will remains coextensive' to the divine. So, from the bottom up, as it looks to fallen nature, necessity conditions even the freedom which takes flight from it, but from top down, from the supernatural heights, all of action is 'gift' from God, '[e]ven the élan of the search that brings us to God'.[23]

The core theme of Henri de Lubac's work is the natural desire for supernatural vision. This is a transposition into theological terms of Blondel's anthropology. A theologian begins from different data. Rather than introspective analysis of the dynamism of action yielding the idea of the infinite, de Lubac starts from the divine image in human nature. The divine image is not a static imprint but an *act* or *the acting of self-knowledge* in ourselves, which is simultaneously a knowledge of God. We are always in act, burning with interior light, and that acting is our self-knowing which is illuminated by God's action, that is, God's illumination

22. Ibid., p. 299.
23. Ibid., pp. 224, 345, and 367.

of the soul. God is always drawing us to God, by constantly imaging himself within us:

> God reveals himself continuously to man by imprinting his image upon him. That divine operation constitutes the... center of man. That is what makes him spirit and constitutes his reasonableness.... For if the human soul only knows itself in actual knowledge ..., it possesses nevertheless a certain 'habitual knowledge' of itself... owing to the fact that it is always present to itself; the presence of the soul present to itself, in which it may learn, as in a mirror, the presence of God to the soul. In the same way that the reality of the divine image in the soul is at the center and principle of all rational activity, which should lead it from knowledge of the world to affirmation of God, so... the soul's habitual knowledge of itself can become the principle of an intimate process of reflection, enabling it to recognize its reality as 'image'.[24]

What de Lubac did there was to reposition Blondel's thought within the Christian patristic and medieval tradition. He is finding Blondel in Augustine and Anselm. When we put Blondel's existential terminology like 'destiny' into scholastic language, it becomes 'finality'. Blondel had said that action exhibits an idea of the infinite; de Lubac can simply call the idea of the infinite 'God': 'The primary idea of God in man, or, the natural desire to see God, is the dynamic configuration, the substantial finality proper to the spiritual creature.... It is, in the Aristotelico-Thomistic sense, the "form" of man'.[25] The 'form of man,' or the soul in act, is the divine image, and this image is the hook by which God draws us to himself. This is what it means to be made in the divine image.

Because Blondel bequeathed to de Lubac the principle that the desire for God is intrinsic to human nature, he set him into the field against extrinsicists, and against the theory that human finality is dual: purely natural in itself and supernatural by dint of the extrinsic grace of God. De Lubac will devote many pages to disparaging this basic concept of Baroque Thomists from Cajetan to Desqocs. Aside from the historical argument that the 'double finality' is foreign to patristic and mediaeval tradition, de Lubac's contention is existential: my finality is not something which could be extrinsically changed at will, because it concerns who I am as an individual person. De Lubac writes that:

> It is always within the real world, within a world whose supernatural finality is not hypothetical but a fact, and not by following any supposition that takes us out of the world, that we must seek an explanation of the gratuitousness of the supernatural... But... it completely fails to show.... that I could have had another, more humble, wholly 'natural' destiny.... To convince me that I might really have had this humbler destiny – humbler, but note, also less onerous –

---

24. De Lubac, DG, pp. 12–13.
25. Michel Sales, *L'Être Humaine et la Connaissance Naturelle Qu'il a de Dieu dans la penseé du P. Henri de Lubac* (Paris: Parole et Silence, 2003), p. 44.

you need only show it to me... as something really imprinted upon me, in my nature as it is.... this is... impossible. My destiny is something ontological, and not something I can change as anything else changes its destination.[26]

The divine image makes us who we are, but we nonetheless attempt to flee from it into idolatry. The 'old atheism' of the late nineteenth and early twentieth century drew on genetic reductionism: belief in God is 'really just' animism or fetishism or worship of the dead. *Action* implicitly overturns these claims, and de Lubac makes the reversal explicit, arguing that superstition and idolatry are rife among human beings, because the 'idea of God' is innate in us: the 'gods thus secretly nourished by the idea of God are parasites and prevent the true God from emerging'. Blondel had noted that even the metaphysician's idea of God as 'Being' can become an idol, if he does not realize that God infinitely transcends our concept of God. De Lubac mocks genetic reductionism, but he also uses the notion of the necessary catharsis of religious symbols as a way of 'walking alongside' the atheist's difficulty, his fixation on denying a finite god, 'freeing himself from superstition through atheism'.[27]

Written during the Second World War, *The Drama of Atheist Humanism* takes a darker view of atheistic idolatries. The key figures here are Comte, Feuerbach, and Nietzsche. Each of these has attempted to cure the 'incurable', to excise from the human person its intrinsic orientation towards the divine. Comte and Feuerbach exhort us to substitute love for God with love for humanity. In a more complex way, Nietzsche replaces reverence for the supernatural with veneration of the superman. The result of this idolatrous effort to excise the divine image in us is, de Lubac says, moral 'bankruptcy'.[28] This is the moral and spiritual bankruptcy of National Socialism and of Vichy France, the heir to the Action française. The end result of mid-twentieth-century 'idolatry', as de Lubac shows in *The Drama*, is Maurras's fetishization of nationalism, his reduction of Comte's reduction of God to humanity.

As with Blondel, the heart of de Lubac's claim about the natural desire for the supernatural is that it cannot be achieved by *our acting upon it*. De Lubac argues that the denial of the natural desire is the upshot of idolatrous conceptions of God as a finite being who 'faces' us on the same, natural plane as that on which we look for him, and upon whom we *impose* our 'natural' desire, obliging God to fulfil it, and depriving God of his divine freedom. It's a secret assumption that the being of God is univocal with ours, and not analogous to ours, which leads theologians to deny that we desire him. This is to forget that we desire God because *he* calls us.[29] De Lubac borrows a daring formulation of the principle that God loved us *first* from Maurice Blondel: 'if it is true that man is theocentric throughout all his

---

26. S, p. 80.
27. DG, p. 20.
28. DAH, p. 67.
29. S, p. 485 and 487.

activity, then in recompense God is anthropocentric, and infinitely more than if man had constituted him as a loveable external object which draws him to itself'.[30]

Blondel argues that each of our finite actions wills the infinite, but none of them *is* what it wills: Blondel 'grounded the progressive... expansion of action in the dialectic of human willing which futilely seeks to equate its specific and concrete expressions with its inexhaustible... élan'.[31] We can only come face-to-face with our 'destiny' if we acknowledge that the 'infinite infinite' is the supernatural God acting upon us and cooperate with God's grace. *Surnaturel*, *The Discovery of God*, and *The Drama of Atheist Humanism* are theological representations of this Blondelian idea. De Lubac is a scholastically trained Jesuit theologian. He *sounds* different from Blondel: even 'the natural desire for the supernatural vision' is scholastic speak, not Blondelian lingo (*Deo gratias*). *Surnaturel* reroutes Blondelianism through the patristic and scholastic tradition. Our next step is to show how de Lubac picked up the Blondelian cloak.

Chronology

Blondel went to Paris to study for his PhD in philosophy at the École Normale Superiore in 1881. He formed a friendship with Victor Delbos. Blondel and Delbos were inspired by Emile Boutroux's lectures on Fichte, and Boutroux became their thesis director. Delbos wrote his thesis on Spinoza while Blondel was composing his dissertation on *Action*. Blondel used the history of philosophy strategically, telling Delbos that 'In dealing with the successive forms of dialectical pantheism you ought, then, to consider these doctrines... in so far as they form... the source of your own synthesis.'[32]

Delbos's account of the course of philosophy from Spinoza to Hegel became Blondel's own. Blondel's defence of heteronomous self-abandonment to the infinite, that is, that we cannot will ourselves into happiness and infinite fulfilment, is a deliberate contradiction of Kant's autonomous derivation of moral values, of Spinoza's idea of happiness as union with the absolute, and of Hegel's idea that human thought and action naturally coalesce.[33] Blondel nonetheless 'considered his work as the critical continuation of moral philosophy which had its beginnings in Spinoza's *Ethics* and continued in the works of Kant, Fichte, Schelling and Hegel'.[34] Modern Catholic thought is divided between those

---

30. Henri De Lubac, 'Le motif de la création dans *L'Être et les êtres* de Maurice Blondel', *Nouvelle revue théologique* 65 (1938): pp. 220–25, p. 222. This text in translated in TF, pp. 393–99.

31. Peter J. Bernardi, 'Maurice Blondel and the Renewal of the Nature-Grace Relationship', *Communio* 26 (Winter 1996), pp. 806–45, 808–9.

32. Blondel, *Lettres Philosophiques* (Paris: Aubier, 1961), p. 16, cited in McNeil, *Synthesis*, p. 3.

33. McNeil, *Synthesis*, pp. 110–11.

34. Ibid., p. 9.

who oppose modern secular thought from 'outside of it', as do many schools of Thomism, and those who oppose modern secular thought from within it. Blondel and a squad of Blondelizing Jesuits tried the latter tactic. The critical problem for Blondel is to baptize the principle that human spirit desires and seeks unity with infinite, divine spirit. He needs to flip idolatry into cooperation with grace.

Blondel taught at Aix from 1886 until his retirement, winning many disciples, including most importantly for our story Auguste Valensin (1879–1953). Valensin took Blondel's philosophy courses and was prompted by them to join the Society of Jesus in 1895.[35] He was later to become de Lubac's mentor. Other Catholics who gravitated to Blondel included Laberthonnière, and Joseph Huby S.J. (1878–1948). It was these close contacts in the Catholic world with men of his own generation, created before the Modernist Crisis and refined in its purgatorial fire, that enabled Blondel to form a younger cohort of 'Blondelisante Jesuites',[36] including Jean Daniélou, Gaston Fessard (later a Hegel scholar), Yves de Montcheuil (chaplain to the maquis at Vercors, murdered by the National Socialists in 1944), and Henri de Lubac. The fact that Aix is no great distance from Lyon is of importance for twentieth-century Catholic thought. There is a Jesuit house in Fourvière, a northern suburb of Lyon; Lyon also houses an Institut Catholique, where Jesuits were among the professors. The Jesuit teachers of de Lubac's generation were determined that their charges would not be turned into hollow men by the antimodernist reaction.

Blondel's first sally into the Catholic world of ideas is his 1896 *Lettre sur les exigences de la pensée moderne*, commonly known as his 'Letter on Apologetics'. This piece annoyed neo-Thomists by its assumption that their style of apologetics was unworkable. The presupposition which Blondel proposes for apologetics is that God's revelation addresses our inmost desire. This drew the parry from many Thomists that his thought is Kantian, solipsist, and that he subjectivizes the notion of revelation. The Dominican Marie-Bedoit Schwalm was the first of many Thomists who interpreted Blondel as depriving revelation of objectivity.[37] Schwalm's student Reginald Garrigou-Lagrange took up the cudgels against what he saw as Blondel's voluntarism. In 1896, Blondel was only acquainted with Thomism through modern manuals; he began to study and to teach Thomas himself, and to call neo-Thomism 'extrinsicism'.[38] Blondel's work now turns away from the dialogue with German Romanticism conducted in *Action* to disputation with fellow Catholics.

The Modernist Crisis coincided with the disestablishment of the French Church (1905) and the expulsion of the religious orders from France. It was now

---

35. René Virgoulay, *Philosophie et théologie chez Maurice Blondel* (Paris: Cerf, 2002), p. 181.
36. Henrici, 'La descendance', p. 310.
37. Bernardi, 'Maurice Blondel', pp. 813–16.
38. William L Portier, 'Twentieth-Century Catholic Theology and the Triumph of Maurice Blondel', *Communio* 38 (Spring 2011): pp. 114–15.

that the Action française allied itself to the Church. One of Blondel's Maurrassian-Thomist foes, Jules Fontaine, coined the term 'social modernism' to mean liberal society. Catholic authorities criticized the *Sillon*, the social-democratic youth group run by a former Blondel student, Marc Sangnier. Maurras added fuel to the fire by writing *Le Dilemme de Marc Sangnier* (1905).

Blondel and Descoqs tangled in 1909–1910, Blondel writing as 'Testis' in the *Annales* and Descoqs composing *A travers l'oeuvre de M. Ch. Maurras*. Descoqs seemed to have 'no inkling that the France of Maurras' thought was as much a "Great Being" for Maurras as Humanity had been for Comte; ... no understanding that this France was ... a religious notion insofar as it provided ... a sense of destiny and a principle of community'.[39]

It did not matter to the extrinsicists Fontaine and Descoqs that the Action française lauded an imposed – rather than a chosen – establishment of the Church, because their model for how religious authority works was that of external imposition without the free desire of the subject. 'Social modernism' was liberalism which roots political order in the subject's freedom and interior consent. The Testis articles argue that hostility to 'social Catholicism' followed from a caricature of Thomism which permitted 'no role for subjectivity in the sense of ... inward reflection of the individual conscience': this 'idea of externally imparted faith – for which Blondel coined the neologism *monophorisme extrinséciste* – tended to confound belief with ... compliance to ecclesiastical authority ... Since faith ... was ... inculcated, it was imperative that ecclesiastical authority be able to impose itself upon the unbeliever, and this could be only by way of some special political arrangement or privilege'.[40]

It's hard to imagine a controversy in which the terms of abuse included 'extrinsicist monophorism' and 'social modernist'. To us the debates between Descoqs and Blondel could be a satirical hypothesis invented by Jonathan Swift. But the social-democratic versus royalist-nationalist divide had cut French Catholics apart since the years following the French Revolution. Their dispute would flare again, in 1942–1945, in a three-way civil war between defenders of Vichy France's pact with Germany, Marxist resistance, and social-democratic resistance.

In 1912–1913, Henri de Lubac, already determined to join the Jesuit order, pacified his family by spending a year studying law at the University of Lyon. During this year, he read a book edited by Joseph Huby, containing essays by Huby, C. C. Martindale, and a Thomist who sought to integrate Kantian philosophy, Pierre Rousselot (1861–1915). The book, named *Christus, histoire comparée des religions*, contests the genetic reduction of Christianity to the religions which preceded it by claiming that supernatural religion is hardly likely to be entirely alien to natural religion. Huby's introductory essay claims,

---

39. Michael Sutton, *Nationalism*, p. 112.
40. Ibid., pp. 152–53.

in Catholic doctrine the supernatural order and the natural order are not disparate or contrary, but the one surpasses the other by widening and deepening it, and that the supernatural presupposes radical capacities and virtues in us which it puts into action and perfects. Who would be surprised that one can observe analogies and contacts between these two orders? Sophism consists in concluding from partial coincidences and material similarities to a total and living identity.

Rousselot argues in his chapter that the Thomistic axiom that 'grace does not suppress nature but perfects it' is the key to Catholicism.[41] De Lubac entered the Society in 1913 only to spend 1914–1918 soldiering. He met the Blondelian Huby for the first time in 1915.

The promotion of Blondel and Kant-friendly 'transcendental Thomism' was not welcomed at the Holy Office. In June 1920 Albert Valensin's defensive article on 'Immanence' was ejected from the *Dictionnaire apologétique de la foi catholique* on the orders of Cardinal Merry del Val. It was replaced by Joseph de Tonquédoc's 'Immanence: Critique'. Valensin was not permitted to republish his defence of Blondel's method elsewhere. In July of that year, on del Val's orders, the Jesuit general forbid the teaching of Rousselot's article on 'Les Yeux de foi' in the Society's scholasticates. Huby was extricated from teaching theology and moved into biblical exegesis, where it was hoped he could not incite the young men to 'the eyes of faith'. Albert's brother Auguste Valensin was under a cloud.[42]

De Lubac spent 1920–1923 on Jersey, where the Jesuits had relocated their philosophy scholasticate after the religious orders were expelled from France (1903). Pedro Descoqs became his philosophy professor. De Lubac tells Robert Hamel in 1922 that he

perceived 'more and more that [*Action*] is a master-piece'[43] and he writes to his brother in 1923 that the part of his day which is not devoted to reviewing philosophy for class 'is taken up in the study of Maurice Blondel and some of the countless works which have appeared about his work over the past thirty years. It is extremely interesting but difficult, because every problem in pure philosophy is bound up with theological questions'.[44]

De Lubac read Blondel alongside Auguste Valensin's notes on his professor's thought.

De Lubac recalled that:

During my years of philosophy (1920–1923) on Jersey, I had read with enthusiasm Maurice Blondel's *Action*, *Lettre* (on apologetics) and various other

---

41. Chantraine, *De Lubac II*, pp. 173 and 175.
42. Ibid., pp. 45–46.
43. Ibid., p. 190.
44. Chantraine, *De Lubac II*, p. 161 (23 June 1922).

> studies. Through a praiseworthy exception, some of our masters ..., who were quite strict in what they excluded from our reading, allowed us, though without encouraging us, to study the thought of the philosopher from Aix. Father Robert Hamel (d. 1974) and I read him together. I had heard a lot about him from Father Auguste Valensin. I had visited him for the first time in 1922... Among the contemporaries studied during my formation, I owe a particular debt to Blondel, Maréchal and Rousselot. I did not have the opportunity to know Father Pierre Rousselot personally. He was killed at Eparges, near Verdun, in the spring of 1915... from 1919 on, I had access to all his papers, which had been entrusted ... to Father Auguste Valensin in Lyons.[45]

De Lubac shared his passion for Blondel with his closest friend, Robert Hamel, with Fessard, and with Montcheuil. De Lubac read Blondel's sources, especially Maine de Biran. When asked years later 'Why Biran?' de Lubac answered, 'doubtless partially because of Blondel... I have read him [Biran] closely... and we spoke much of him; he was like a French Hegel'.[46] The Jesuits were wise to Blondel's goal of outdoing idealism from within.

These young men were looking for a different kind of Thomism than that of their teachers, which had been so brilliantly mocked by Blondel in his 'Testis' articles.[47] On a visit to Paris in 1924, de Lubac purchased Joseph Maréchal's first *Cahier, De l'antiquité à la fin du Moyen Âge: La critique de l'ancienne connaissance.* Descoqs saw Rousselot and Maréchal as having 'betray[ed]' Thomas by 'transposing his formulae in an idealist sense'.[48] Descoqs's pupils wanted to read Saint Thomas as a conversation partner with Kant and Hegel.

De Lubac read Blondel alongside Jesuit authors who assisted him in interpreting Thomas Aquinas in a Blondelian light. 1924–1928 were the years of his 'Theologate'. His studies in theology were shared between Hastings (1924–1926) and Fourvière, where the studium relocated in 1926. By 1925 the Blondelizing Thomist is denouncing the Baroque idea of the 'state of pure nature' to Robert Hamel:

> I begin to believe little by little without having read anything or clarified it in my own mind, that 'pure nature' is not only a derivative concept ...; and in fact, the opposition of nature and the supernatural (not that of fallen nature and of grace) is a theological invention of the recent centuries; what obliges us to be prudent on this point is that this rather novel theological doctrine appears to have received an initial consecration from the Magisterium, at the Vatican Council. But P. Huby, whose judgement counts for much, does not see this as an insurmountable difficulty.[49]

---

45. ASC, pp. 18–19.
46. Chantraine, *De Lubac II*, pp. 212–13.
47. Maurice Blondel, 'The Third "Testis" Article', trans. Peter Bernardi, *Communio* 26 (Winter 1999): pp. 846–74; this is from *Annales de philosophie chrétienne* (December 1909).
48. Chantraine, *De Lubac II*, p. 265 and 125.
49. Ibid., pp. 554–55.

Sometime between 1924 and 1925 Huby threw down the gauntlet to de Lubac: was the 'natural desire for the supernatural vision' present in the patristic and mediaeval tradition? Is it in Thomas? At one Sunday gathering of Huby's Blondelian debating club, known derisively to the other Jesuits as 'La Pensée', the squad debated Guy de Broglie's treatment of the 'natural desire for the beatific vision'. As de Lubac later remarked, this subject

> was at the center of the reflection of the masters …: Rousselot, Blondel, Maréchal; we discovered it at the heart of all great Christian thought, whether that of Saint Augustine, Saint Thomas, or Saint Bonaventure… we noted that it was… at the bottom of discussions with modern unbelief, that it formed the crux of the problem of Christian humanism.

And then his teacher challenged him: 'Father Huby, following the line of reflection inaugurated for us by Rousselot, had warmly urged me to verify whether the doctrine of Saint Thomas… was indeed what was claimed by the Thomist school around the sixteenth century, codified in the seventeenth century and asserted with greater emphasis in the twentieth.'[50] De Lubac told Blondel in 1932 that 'It is effectively the study of your work, which I have made for eleven years, which initiated this reflection' on the meaning of a 'state of pure nature' for human persons: the Jesuit had 'remained faithful to this inspiration'.[51]

De Lubac had been claiming since 1926 that French philosophy sees a parting of ways with Descartes, whose extrinsicism hollows out the possibility of faith seeking understanding and of rational apologetics.[52] Étienne Gilson called de-theologized Thomism 'Cartesian-Thomism'. From the second of the six editions of his lifework, *Le thomisme*, Gilson found the 'natural desire' in Saint Thomas's writings. De Lubac often mentions that 1922 edition of *Le thomisme*, kept in a locked cupboard on Jersey and brought out on Feast days and Optional Memoria.[53] For De Lubac, intrinsicism and extrinsicism are foundational premises for considering the relation of faith and reason.

In 1929 and again in March 1931, the leading Thomists in France, Gilson and Jacques Maritain, and the leading rationalists, Brunschvicg and Bréhier, took part in two public debates about whether 'Christian Philosophy' is a reality.[54] Bréhier

---

50. ASC, p. 35.
51. Chantraine, *De Lubac II*, p. 162 (9 April 1932).
52. Henri de Lubac, 'Pascal Anti-Cartésien', 1923, *Quodlibeta*, in the Belgian de Lubac Archive, [Archives Mgr Molette III], p. 61933, 61936, 61945.
53. ASC, p. 19 and 65.
54. Maurice Blondel, et al., 'La querelle de l'athéisme', *Bulletin de la Société française de la philosophie* 28 (1928): pp. 45–95 (Transcript of the meeting of 24 March 1928) and Maurice Blondel, et al., 'La notion de philosophie chrétienne', *Bulletin de la société française de la philosophie* 31 (1931): pp. 37–93 (Transcript of the debate about Christian philosophy, held on 21 March 1931). The only complete translation of the debate has been made by Kenneth Oakes and myself, online at www.illuminatingmodernity.com

was the historian: he maintained that, historically, Western philosophy has never been influenced by revealed religion. Bréhier was publishing a multi-volume *Histoire de la Philosophie* in which Christian thinking makes no substantial contribution. Brunschvicg was a French Hegelian, who had pledged opposition to *Action* at its publication. He claimed that the ascending path of reason has now bypassed the externalities of revealed religion. Some Catholic philosophers agreed that there is no such thing as 'Christian philosophy': one was the Dominican Pierre Mandonnet. Against both the secular and the Catholic rationalists, Gilson argued that it is historically demonstrable that ideas which Christians believe to be revealed, such as free divine creation *ex nihilo*, have guided philosophy to the discovery of truths of which it would otherwise be unaware.

Blondel did not appear on the platform, and never argued his case with the other men in public. He sent in a letter after the event which criticized the rationalists, denigrated Maritain's contribution, and described Gilson as a historicist. Blondel claims that authentic Christian philosophy has yet to be born. Christians will only create a genuine philosophy of religion once they tackle it phenomenologically. Blondel fails to address the 'Bréhier-dynamic' of the debate: has, in fact, revelation influenced the course of philosophy? It is hardly convincing to say it will do one day unless one can persuade people that it already has. Blondel's claim is aimed, rather, at Brunschvicg: yes, the future encounter of religion and philosophy will be not exterior but interior, and that is because Christian revelation is leading philosophy into the study of consciousness.

De Lubac published a description of the Christian philosophy debate in 1936. He claims that Maritain and Gilson could only make their notion of Christian philosophy stick by accepting the definition of this term supplied by Blondel.[55] His paper is a test-case for whether his Blondelian spectacles help or hinder him in interpreting Catholic thinkers. For both Mandonnet and Maritain, reason and faith are formally distinct in the Christian philosopher: in Blondel's terms, both men are extrinsicists, and so de Lubac says their position is really the same. In fact, for Maritain, grace enters the discussion not as engendering ontological novelty, but as affording moral stiffening to the Christian philosopher and thereby helping his reason to preserve its raison d'être. The arguments which bubbled up between Gilson and Maritain over the decades show that de Lubac *was* perceptive in observing the real distance between them. De Lubac is on the ball when he states that 'Gilson's formula that revelation generates reason goes further' than Maritain's claim for the influence of faith on reason.[56] Gilson, who never reneged on his loyalty to Bergson, argued that faith enables reason to attain *new* territory and to see truths which the ancients never envisaged. Maritain denied that claim.[57]

---

55. Henri de Lubac, 'Sur la philosophie chrétienne: Réflexions à la suite d'un débat', *Nouvelle revue théologique* (March 1936): pp. 225–53, 241–43.
56. Ibid., pp. 229–30.
57. I describe the debate in *Art and Intellect in the Philosophy of Étienne Gilson* (Missouri University Press, 2004), Chapter 6. The debates between Gilson and Maritain, about art,

De Lubac felt that Gilson needed completion rather than correction from Blondel. He saw the debate as turning on conceiving faith and reason as intrinsically related (Blondel and Gilson) versus extrinsicism (Maritain and Mandonnet). This helped him see the united front between Gilson and Maritain was rickety, but it also made him typecast all 'extrinsicists' in the same uniform. The vulnerable point in *Surnaturel* will be its hostile stereotyping of all 'Baroque Thomists'.

Blondel mocked the static conceptualism of the Thomists because he recognized that ideas have a dramatic quality. Ideas exist in a political and historical moment, in which someone deploys them. This notion that ideas and the words which express them take their meaning from the historical context in which they are used was the making of de Lubac as an historical theologian. The historical development of the meaning of various 'phrases' is important in de Lubacian texts such as *Corpus Mysticum* (1939, 'corpus mysticum')[58] and *Surnaturel* (1946, 'pure nature'). His juvenilia shows him putting this art to use, arguing that although both Thomas and Descartes distinguish faith and reason, Thomas's distinction means something different in the mouth of 'a seventeenth-century' author who 'wanted to achieve a philosophical revolution on the basis of the tabula rasa of the Cogito'.[59]

In 1929 de Lubac became professor at the Institut Catholic in Lyon: his opening lecture concluded that: 'Catholicism is the true religion because it alone bears the adequate response to human aspirations... and this is its appropriate perfection.'[60] By the early 1930s, in articles about Baius and Jansenius, de Lubac begins to use the optic of 'extrinsicism' and 'intrinsicism' to probe the development of the controversy about the 'natural desire', and to understand how the hypothesis of a 'pure nature' was invented. Antonio Russo shows that this early spadework emerges out of the Jesuit's self-apprenticeship to Blondel.[61] It is easy to forget that considering this development through the optic of 'extrinsicist' versus 'intrinsicist' theologies is a heuristic tool that was invented, by the author of *Surnaturel*, as an effect of Blondel's guidance. By 1931, using this optic, de Lubac argues that extrinsicism distorts the 'Augustinianism' of Baius and Jansenius, He tells Blondel that he is 'more than ever struck by the meeting between the thought of Augustine and your own thinking'.[62] Writing to Blondel in 1932, about the

---

the natural desire for the supernatural, Bergson, the object of perception, and realism are detailed in my biography. See also Henri Bars, 'Gilson et Maritain', *Revue Thomiste* 7 (1979): pp. 237–71.

58. Henri de Lubac, *Corpus mysticum: l'eucharistie et l'église au moyen age* (Paris: Aubier, 1939).

59. De Lubac, 'Pascal Anti-Cartésien', p. 61947. See *Summa Theologiae* I, q. 1, reply obj 1.

60. De Lubac, 'Apologetique et théologie', p. 374.

61. See de Lubac's 'Deux Augustiniens fourvoyés: Baïus et Jansénius', I, Baïus (*Recherches de Science religiuese*, 21, 1931), as discussed by Antonio Russo in *Henri de Lubac: Teologia e dogma nella Storia. L'influsso di Blondel* (Rome: Ediziona Studium, 1989), pp. 155–60.

62. De Lubac to Blondel, 20 January 1931, quoted in Russo, *Henri de Lubac*, p. 165.

nonsensicality of the hypothesis of a pure nature, he tells his philosophy professor that he writes 'with the abandon of a disciple'.[63]

In a 1929 paper responding to handwritten criticisms of Blondel by Rousselot, de Lubac wrote that, following *Action* 'the conditions in which the assertion of being will be legitimate are no longer to be considered as stemming uniquely from the intellectual faculty or from the first empirical act of that faculty. It is necessary to envisage the relationship of the whole human mind with Being. Thus ... moral choice is reintroduced'.[64] Being a realist is a matter of making an adequate response to a reality which is sometimes rather dramatic. The German occupation of France and the response of the Fourvière squad in composing and distributing the *Cahiers du Témoignage chrétien* dramatized the need for an existential, moral, and intellectual engagement with reality. Together with Fessard, Daniélou, and Montcheuil, de Lubac prepared a 'spiritual resistance'.[65]

Thus, between 1938 and 1945 de Lubac publishes his great 'Second World War' tetralogy, *Catholicism* in 1938, *The Drama of Atheist Humanism* in 1944, *De la Connaissance de Dieu* (the original version of *Sur les chemins de Dieu* of 1956), and *Surnaturel* in 1946. It can be doubted whether the Vichy government, which made terms with Hitler, was *all that influenced by the doctrines of Charles Maurras*.[66] What is beyond doubt is that de Lubac believed that the conquering enemy incarnated Maurrasian, extrinsicist principles. It is what men *think* is happening that influences them, and the crucible of the Occupation turned de Lubac's historical surveys and speculations into his own 'spiritual resistance', in four works of apologetic genius, which elaborate Blondelian principles.

France was *already* ungovernably divided in the 1930s, torn in three, between communism, proto-fascism, and social democracy. Once France had been invaded, these violent divisions became a civil war between Petainist collaborators, Marxist insurrectionists, and social-democratic/Catholic resistance.[67] The 'idolatries' that play the role of villains in *The Drama* are, on the one hand, Comtean positivism and Nietzscheanism, and, on the other, Marxist and Feuerbachian 'humanism'.

---

63. De Lubac to Blondel, 3 April 1932, quoted in Ibid., p. 180. The letter is worth reading in full (pp. 178–80).

64. Henri de Lubac, 'Maurice Blondel', in TF, pp. 377–403, p. 387.

65. De Lubac's paper on 'Yves de Montcheuil', in *Three Jesuits Speak*, trans. K.D. Whitehead (Ignatius Press: San Francisco, 1980) is a testimony to the squad's spiritual witness at that time.

66. De Lubac's claim 'The fact that Pétain was at that time surrounded by men from *l'Action francaise* was not ... a coincidence' (CR, pp. 19–20) should be read in the more measured context of, for instance Michèle Cointet, *L'Église sous Vichy, 1940–1945: La repentence en question* (Paris: Librairie Académique Perrin, 1998).

67. For a brief note by a resistance leader on the involvement of Fourvière, and of de Lubac, see Henri Frenay, *The Night Will End*, trans. Dan Hofstadter (New York: McGraw-Hill, 1976), pp. 68–69.

In 1942, de Lubac from Lyon and his confrère Jean Daniélou, in Paris, created a new book series, *Sources chrétiennes*, in which the Greek texts of the Fathers were printed alongside French translations. By 1946, Daniélou had taken over sole editorship, and, as de Lubac charitably but ruefully remarks, he had a series to advertise! Daniélou wrote a 'Blondelizing' promotion piece, in which the dynamic, energetic, and existential 'Fathers' are contrasted with Thomists who come straight out of Blondel's 'Third Testis Article', replete with static, logical solutions to historical problems. Daniélou's article[68] became known as the 'Red Rag to the Roman bull.'

Reginald Garrigou-Lagrange counterattacked with a piece which sealed the fate of the movement which he made known as the 'Nouvelle théologie': 'La nouvelle théologie où va-t-elle?' announces that the movement is marching to Modernism, to the tune of Blondel's *Action*.[69] Like a perennially stopped clock, Garrigou repeated the objection which he had been making against Blondel since 1906, that is, replacing Thomas's definition of truth as the adequation of the mind with reality with his own conception of truth as the adequation of the mind with life (substituting *conformitats mentis et vitae* for *adaequatio rei et intellectus*).[70]

1946 also saw the publication of *Surnaturel*. Pius XII's *Humani Generis* appeared to criticize the notion of the 'natural desire' maintained in that book; his Jesuit superiors therefore silenced de Lubac. Hans Urs von Balthasar said that it was Blondel and Maréchal who gave de Lubac the fortitude to rediscover in Saint Thomas's writings the thesis that the human person is ordained beyond the reach of his own freedom to the grace of the vision of God. But de Lubac's friend and disciple says,

> while Maréchal, threatened by the censors, had to take refuge behind a barbed-wire fence of distinctions and while Blondel, under the permanent terror of being put on the Index, found himself ready for concessions in his late work, de Lubac exposed himself to the attacks of a tutiorist scholastic theology, armed with nothing but the historical and theological truth. Of the three martyrs for truth, he was the most tortured, far beyond the tortures endured by Blondel.... Étienne Gilson... confirmed him the midst of his afflictions with juicy and vigorous letters.[71]

Gilson told de Lubac that if he and Maritain had been clerics, they would have been crucified: 'But I've nothing to teach you on that score, have I? Nonetheless,

---

68. Jean Daniélou, 'Les Orientations présentes de la pensée religieuse', *Études* 251 (April 1946): pp. 5–21.

69. Reginald Garrigou-Lagrange, 'La nouvelle théologie où va-t-elle?', *Angelicum* 23 (July–December 1946): pp. 126–46.

70. Ibid., p. 130.

71. Hans Urs von Balthasar, *The Theology of Henri de Lubac: An Overview*, trans. Roxanne Mei Lum (San Francisco: Ignatius Press, 1991), pp. 12–13.

there will have to be a new edition of *Surnaturel*.'[72] De Lubac had got himself 'crucified' by ascribing the notion of a creaturely intrinsic desire for the beatific vision to the Angelic Doctor.

A Blondelian Thomism

Like the Empress of India, Leo XIII had an extended Victorian family. In de Lubac's lifetime, the Thomist family had numerous branches. There were the teaching-uncles, who repurposed Thomas's thought for pedagogical use, discarding the structure of the *Summas* on the assumption that their perennial message bore scant relation to its historical medium. The Uncles reshaped the 'Perennial Philosophy' to fit contemporary pedagogical goals and pack the seminarian with logic and metaphysics before he was inducted into the Trinity. Their nephew was Jacques Maritain, eager to make Saint Thomas an apostle for modern times. The Transcendental Aunts were disreputable, since they mentioned Kant and Fichte without cursing them, and in polite company, but they were not *that eccentric,* given the relatively a-historical character of the Romanizing Uncles.[73] The transcendental Thomists included Rousselot and Maréchal, who sought to make Thomas *win* in debate with critical philosophy. The Romanists, Maritain, and the transcendental Thomists, all in their diverse ways put Thomas's epistemology at the heart of his doctrine: all were 'modernizing' Thomas's doctrine. Only the country cousins, Étienne Gilson and the Dominicans of Saint Maximin in Toulouse, were Paleo-Thomists, rooting their lineage in the literal texts of Saint Thomas; the *Summa* was the Burke's Peerage of these authentic Thomists, and they were *princes of the blood.*

De Lubac did not understand himself solely as a 'Blondelizing Jesuit' but as a Blondelian *Thomist*. This is carefully put: others may claim Augustine's mantle for de Lubac, or dispute de Lubac's self-ascription to the Thomist family. Our claim is that de Lubac self-identified as a Thomist. De Lubac could have easily shown the heart restless until it rests in God is solid Augustinian tradition. He instead took the combatant route, exposing himself to decades of shellfire by making it the spinal claim of *Surnaturel* that Thomas Aquinas taught that human beings naturally desire the beatific vision.

Those unfamiliar with the history of neo-scholasticism may imagine that 'Suarezian' is a Spanish branch of the family. Suarez's teaching differed from the Angelic Doctor, for instance, in denying the real distinction between essence and existence in creatures. In 1916, Roman Thomists issued 24 Theses for the correct

---

72. Etienne Gilson to Henri de Lubac, 1 April 1964, in Henri de Lubac, ed., *Letters of Étienne Gilson to Henri de Lubac,* trans. Mary Emily Hamilton (San Francisco: Ignatius Press, 1988), p. 69.

73. When Blondel was accused by Roman Thomists of Kantianism, he legitimately 'retorted' that such Thomism was more Kantian than he was (McNeil, *Synthesis,* p. 45).

interpretation of Thomas Aquinas in scholasticates, seminaries, and colleges. The 7th Thesis affirms the real distinction in creatures between essence and existence. In this recondite milieu, 'Suarezian' was not a Spanish branch of Thomism, but non-Thomism. Many early twentieth-century Jesuits were Suarezians, and the fate of Descoqs was to be compelled outwardly to profess Thomism while actually adhering to the doctrines of Domingo Suarez. This must be understood in order to get the point of de Lubac's confession that he was *Thomist instead of a Suarezian*:

> When I left Jersey (I was 27 years old), where a Suarezian spirit still reigned, I had been put down severely as a Thomist (of a Thomism, it is true, revitalized by Maréchal and Rousselot). At that time, this was called 'not holding the doctrines of the Society'. I have never renounced that fundamental orientation. I even believe that I have worked... to lead minds back to the authentic Saint Thomas, as to a master considered ever-current. As for the 'Thomism' of our century, I have often found in it a system that is too rigid and yet at the same time not faithful enough to the Doctor it claims as its authority. I have also seen it raised too often... like a pavilion to cover the most diverse merchandise to be able to take it seriously. I have known a traditionalist Thomism à la Bonald, a Thomism as patron of *l'Action Française*, a Thomism as the inspiration of Christian Democracy,.... and even a neo-Marxist Thomism,... And no salvation outside of each in its turn.... I have... observed a 'Thomism' that was scarcely more than a tool in the hands of the government,... or... the padlock closing the door to all understanding of the thought of others. Even today, despite all the supervening changes, this still makes it difficult for me to be very loud in proclaiming that I am a Thomist.[74]

We may take this bald statement of intent seriously as de Lubac's description of his project. De Lubac thought he drew his understanding of the human mind as a mystery to itself from Saint Thomas. He took it to be Thomistic to contend that

> There is at the bottom of the mind something which the mind itself affirms by its being and its activity, but which it cannot represent to itself: the mystery *of* the mind which is also a mystery *for* the mind, incomprehensible to the mind itself, because it touches in an intrinsic way on the mystery of God, who is Himself incomprehensible.[75]

Robert Hamel felt that Blondel enabled them to put Saint Thomas together with Augustine,[76] to favour Thomas not for his anti-Critical, anti-Copernican 'extroversion' but for his conspectus of the interior life.

---

74. ASC, p. 144.
75. Sales, *L'Être*, p. 39.
76. Chantraine, *De Lubac II*, p. 604.

Thomas's Fourth Way speaks of our arranging goods in hierarchy, and argues that our discovery of degrees of perfection in things, that is, our ability to measure and evaluate things as worse or better, points to a standard of perfection to which our own measurements are held. Calling this the 'telological argument', Maurice Blondel argues that our minds are like a mirror through which absolute perfection is darkly reflected:

> It is not from ourselves... that we draw either the light of our thought or the efficaciousness of our action. An energy hidden in the depth of consciousness, a truth that is more intimate than our own knowledge, a power that at every moment of our development furnishes the force... that is needed, all this is in us without being from us.... The true teleological proof.... Shows that the wisdom of things is not in things, that the wisdom of man is not in man.... it does not take only what is already realized, but also what is incessantly realizing and perfecting itself. It... finds in the relative beauty of things the very principle of all beauty.

As Blondel presents it, the teleological argument argues that my (real) actions cannot attain my mental ideals, nor my mental ideals be made real by my actions:

> There is in me a disproportion between the efficient cause and the final cause; and yet neither the one nor the other can be in me what they already are without the permanent mediation of a perfect thought and a perfect action. All that is beauty and life in things, all that is light and power in man, contains, in its very imperfection and weakness, a sovereign perfection; thus will this triple relation be developed. – It is within us, it is in the real that we discover, as in an imperfect mirror, this inaccessible perfection. And yet, we can neither identify ourselves with it, nor can we identify it with ourselves.[77]

De Lubac used Blondel and Thomas to develop a conception of the primitive *action* of the soul as a preconceptual act of intuition of God. In an essay of 1922–1923, called 'Préciser une notion: (l'intuition)', de Lubac describes intuition as 'the continuous act which engenders human existence'.[78] The 'act' of existence is composite. It is not an act of intuition by itself. 'The intuition', de Lubac says, 'is the intellectual element of an act which is not purely intellectual'. *De Lubac understood Blondel's action as intuition.* So, 'the intuition of freedom is not an act of knowledge by which one grasps oneself as free; it is the free act itself', occurring

---

77. Blondel, *Action*, pp. 319–20.
78. De Lubac, 'Pour Preciser Une Notion: Intuition', *Quodlibeta* XVI (1921–1922). Some of the papers published in *Quodlibeta* were mined for evidence of Blondel's influence by Antonio Russo, in his *Henri de Lubac: Teologia e dogma nella Storia. L'influsso di Blondel*. Chantraine notes with asperity that those who view de Lubac as a pure Blondelian would do well to read this particular text, *De Lubac II*, p. 378: Russo ignores it. Russo shows verbal similarities between some of de Lubac's juvenilia and Blondel's *Action*.

consciously but before it gives rise to the *judgement* and the *concept* 'I am free.' It is true, de Lubac says, that a full mental act proceeds from the intuition to sense things, and thence to conceptual judgement. But without an *immediate* intuition of first principles, sensory facts and their images could not become the material of notions such as 'unity, substance, causality, and finality'. Here de Lubac cites Thomas's *De Veritate*: '*Quaecumque autem sciuntur, proprie accepta scientia, cognoscuntur per resolutionem in prima principia, quae per se praesto sunt intellectu; et sic omnis scientia in visione rei praesentis perficitur*' (Everything which is known, the knowledge is truly received, is known in coming back to first principles, which are themselves immediate for intelligence; and hence all knowledge is achieved in the vision of the present thing).[79]

De Lubac has fused Blondel on *action* with Thomas on the immediacy of our knowledge of first principles. 'Immediacy' with respect to the first principles is the light which guides our mental steps and moves them on their way from truths to Truth. Blondel had said, 'It is not from ourselves... that we draw either the light of our thought', but de Lubac has no intention of saying that precognitive mental life consists in a direct intuition of the divine light. Intuition, our primitive act, the 'a priori condition of all knowledge', as de Lubac calls it, or 'the under basement of the whole of conscious life', is the light from which we infer to the Light which measures and illumines our sight.[80]

The Discovery of God is a reprisal of de Lubac's 1922/1923 reflections on *De Veritate*'s lesson.

> Every human act, whether it is by an act of knowledge or an act of the will, rests secretly upon God, by attributing meaning and solidity to the real upon which it is exercised. For God is the Absolute; and nothing can be thought without positing the Absolute in relating it to that Absolute; nothing can be willed without tending towards the Absolute, nor valued unless weighed in terms of the Absolute.

Here, where one would expect the footnote to take us to Augustine or to Thomas, de Lubac quotes Blondel in feisty form debating Brunschvicg:

> The slightest sensation humanly perceived, the slightest perception directly grasped, the slightest understanding scientifically or metaphysically developed, implies a fundamental affirmation which... surpasses the entire empirical order, the entire conceptual order of our representations. Every act of true understanding, every thought worthy of the name, as elementary as one can imagine,... posits a transcendence of the spirit with regard to the immanent order of things apparently given or experienced. Therefore, before all critical

---

79. De Lubac, 'Intuition', cited in Chantraine *De Lubac II*, pp. 377–78, citing *De Veritate*, XIV, 9.
80. Chantraine, *De Lubac II*, p. 377.

reflection and in order to allow this reflection itself, there is in us the lived assertion of a reality which is beyond or above every act, every self-limiting thought.[81]

The mind itself is a 'moving path' which is pointing to God, not as a signpost would do, to an absent referent, but as the interior condition of its action. We are mysteries to ourselves because our thinking is moved by Mystery personified, by God. Our 'idea' of God is our telos, our innermost final goal, but we cannot 'conceive' the idea of God. It remains mysterious to us. Our certainty that God exists does not, as Kant feared, conflict with our freedom,[82] because God is our innermost desire.

De Lubac made Blondel compatible with Thomas Aquinas by reading Thomas through the eyes of Rousselot. Rousselot's Aquinas is a neo-Platonist for whom intuition (like that of the angels) is a higher mode of knowledge than discursive reasoning. Cognizant of the anti-fideist rationalism of Roman Thomism, Rousselot had argued that Thomas was an 'intellectualist', or prized intellectuality above all other things, only because Thomas held that the beatific vision consists in the intellectual intuition of God. In his 1908 *Intellectualisme de Saint Thomas*, Rousselot had agreed with his Thomist kin that the virtue of Thomism is its realism, but he saw this as a religious, beatifically oriented realism: for Thomas, Rousselot claimed, *'the intelligence is essentially the sense of the real, but it is the sense of the real only because it is the sense of the divine'*. By showing that for Thomas, 'the living God of revelation [i]s the goal of man's spiritual dynamism', Rousselot hoped to show that 'St. Thomas is closer to Blondel than some of his critics believe.'[83] What Gilson most admired in de Lubac is that he does not isolate Saint Thomas from Augustine.[84] De Lubac learned this way of reading Thomas from Rousselot, who 'made it clear' to his rationalizing Uncles that 'his was a Thomism of the Platonic-Augustinian type and that ... the influence of pseudo-Dionysius on the Angelic Doctor should continue to be felt in Thomism'.[85]

As a fellow anti-Suarezian Jesuit, Rousselot was an object of de Lubac's attention from early days. Joseph Maréchal's transcendental Thomism also gave de Lubac pointers for how human mental acts point to God. Maréchal deliberately constructed a modern, post-Kantian Thomism. He accepted the Kantian contention that factual, a posteriori knowledge can never 'accumulate' into an edifice of certain truths: *a posteriori* is separate qualitatively and infinitely from *a priori*. And yet, in every sensible judgement, the mind is driven teleologically

---

81. DG, p. 39 and the footnote on the same page.
82. Ibid., pp. 62 and 48–49.
83. Gerald A. McCool, S.J., *From Unity To Pluralism: The Internal Evolution of Thomism* (New York: Fordham University Press, 1989), p. 49 and pp. 52–53, his italics.
84. 'In Company with Henri de Lubac', Appendix II of *Letters of Gilson to de Lubac*, pp. 180–82.
85. McCool, *Unity*, p. 82.

by the idea of the infinite. Our judgements seek the 'unlimited real' as their teleological measure.[86]

The young de Lubac wondered whether Maréchal tended to 'dissipate the mystery which bathes all of our knowledge'. Did Maréchal swap out seeing indirectly *by the divine Light* for a direct vision of the unconditional Light: 'what I call (without wanting in the least to accuse him of heresy …) his ontologism; he sees too much in the living light against which objects are silhouetted'.[87] Forty years later, in *The Mystery of the Supernatural*, de Lubac is still bothered by Maréchal's borderline 'ontologism'. Nonetheless, he states, the two Jesuit Thomist Aunts were second only to Blondel in their recovery of a true metaphysics:

> Rousselot's thesis, *L'Intellectualisme de saint Thomas*, 1908, and later Maréchal's volumes, *Le Point de départ de la métaphysique*, published between 1922 and 1926, though they contain questionable elements, remain major works which mark a genuine beginning. Rousselot's thesis was, says Gilson, 'the first … of the attempts … to find a Thomist answer to the problems of our time … in an effort to restore its true principles'.[88]

The example of Rousselot and Maréchal made de Lubac's 'Blondelian Thomism' possible.

Blondel: A Minor Key

The 'Prologue' to the Vatican I Constitution *Dei Filius* tells the story of the shipwreck of philosophy, beginning with the Reformation and its principle of private judgement, through the rationalisms of the Enlightenment and on to the materialism of 1870. *Aeterni Patris* includes a narrative in which the summit of 'Christian philosophy' is achieved by Saint Thomas followed by decline: the melancholy ending can, we learn, be reversed by returning to Thomas. Tales about the ascent or descent of philosophy were not the preserve of the Whiggish Enlightenment party. Catholics created them; in addition to Luther, Duns Scotus and Occam were often set among the precursors of Descartes and Kant. Blondel himself offers such a narrative: it is a minor key for Blondel, but enters the substance of de Lubac's philosophy of history.

---

86. Ibid., p. 99.
87. Chantraine, *De Lubac II*, p. 357. Ontologism is the idea that human intellect has a direct intuition of God; it is a misreading of Augustine's idea that God's divine light is that *by which* the human intellect sees. Nineteenth-century Thomist efforts to make a wide berth around this heresy led them to distance Thomas from Augustine. The best explanation of the heresy and its misreading of Augustine by ontologists might be Étienne Gilson's 'The Future of Augustinian Metaphysics' (trans. Edward Bullough, 1930; reprint in *A Monument to St. Augustine*, pp. 289–315. New York: Meridian Books, 1930, 1957).
88. MS, p. 247.

For Blondel, human nature is a 'microcosm' of nature as a whole. De Lubac embraces Blondel's 'microcosm to macrocosm' theme. He claims, for instance, that the evolution from Old Testament to New Testament is recapitulated in the life of every individual.[89]

Blondel's narrative differs from that of a neo-Thomist like Joseph Kleutgen, and falls closer to Idealist philosophies of history in that his external story is an analogue of his internal story of the development and pitfalls of consciousness. For Blondel, the history of philosophy is not a chance series of events, but is itself philosophical, and philosophically significant.

Blondel's history of philosophy has five acts. In the first, ancient Greek philosophy endows natural reason with confidence in its own, independent divinity. In the second act, the period of the 'Christianization' of philosophy, a three-tier hierarchy is constructed, in which reason patrols the lowest 'zone', faith oversees the topmost region, and reason and faith 'mingle' fruitfully in a 'middle zone' which belongs to both of them.[90] The scholastics created an 'unstable equilibrium' of faith and reason, because reason never fully conceded its autonomous rights to divinity. In the third act, therefore, Luther, with his predilection for 'private judgement', creates an 'absolute empire' for reason by destroying the hierarchy of 'zones', and thereby forcing a choice *between* faith and reason. The enforced choice separates reason from faith and turns it into absolute rationalism.[91]

In the period of its cohabitation with faith, reason 'glimpsed' 'immense horizons' which it cannot now unsee.[92] It cannot blind itself to the vistas of interiority which faith had shown it. When Schelling makes the subject the axial principle of philosophy, he is recognizing the new thing which faith has brought. The fourth act could thus initiate the return of the prodigal reason.

But philosophy's 'method of immanence' becomes an idol when it is reified into a 'doctrine of immanence'. Only when philosophy realizes that phenomenological introspection itself shows that immanent consciousness is not immanently self-sufficient will the curtain open on the fifth act. The final act will see a rigorous philosophy of religion and a new, stable alliance of faith and reason, based not in external coercion, but in the analysis of interiority as exhibiting the need for the supernatural.

For Blondel, 'Christian philosophy' does not lie *behind* us, in the Middle Ages, to be recovered and repeated today. It lies in the future of philosophy. The 'Logos', the concealed 'mind' within the wending path of philosophy, has brought about all these five acts, including the apparent missteps into rationalization and

---

89. Cf. SC.
90. Hans Urs von Balthasar's essay 'Regagner Une Philosophie a partir de la théologie', in *Pour une philosophie chrétienne* (Paris: Sycamore, 1983), reprises Blondel's theory of the three zones, with philosophy of religion operating in the middle zone between faith and reason.
91. Blondel, *Letter on Apologetics*, pp. 148–49, 173–76.
92. Ibid., pp. 175–76.

secularization, in order secretly to engineer his own 'ultimate triumph' with the deeper discovery of the meaning of interiority.[93] Narrating this Christocentric history of philosophy will be more important for the theologian de Lubac than even for Blondel.[94]

In de Lubac's own story of how the mind works, reason begins by 'affirming' God, but then stumbles, first into objectifying its concept of God into numerous 'imaginative forms'. It then 'reifies' these imaginative forms, worshipping the forms themselves instead of the deity they denote. Only after a process of purification can reason recover the true God, who is beyond all conceptualizations.[95]

In Blondel's narrative, 'Baroque' scholasticism grows out of the 'unstable equilibrium' of mediaeval scholasticism. The rationalistic theory of 'pure nature', to which so many pages of *Surnaturel* are devoted, is thus a fruit of the transformation of the 'open zone' of reason into the closed, 'absolute empire' of rationalism.

The Drama of Atheist Humanism takes up the fourth act with the warring genii of Occupied France standing in for Spinoza and Schelling. Feuerbach, Marx and Nietzsche represent the serial descent into rationalism, when humanity worships at the shrine of its own projected essence. But the pit of subjectivism into which they dig themselves allows Kierkegaard and Dostoyevsky, the heroes of the drama, to recover genuine subjectivity and, with it, Christian humanism. In the final chapter, de Lubac speaks of a future 'Christian Prometheanism', when the urge to divinize human will power has regained its human face by turning towards the supernatural.

This is why the 'Christian philosophy debate' captured de Lubac's imagination. Both he and Blondel wanted to take over the Idealist or 'Whiggish' claim that the history of ideas matters and cannot be gone back upon, and make it work for Christianity. They argued that once Christianity had 'interiorized' the locus of meaning and value, there is no return. De Lubac saw Blondel's work as leading philosophy forward, through revelation, to a new appreciation of interiority. Through faith, reason has to hand a 'principle of infinite progress': the principle of interiority.[96]

93. Blondel:
Looking, then, to the future, let us descry in these present conflicts the ultimate triumph of the Christ who was humble and hidden in his life and is still humble and hidden in his progress through human history, even leaving to his temporary opponents the apparent initiative for those great inspirations of justice and of reason which have their secret origin in himself.

'The Letter', p. 206.

94. Chantraine:
Thomist in his metaphysics, de Lubac is Augustinian in his analysis of spirit and of its dynamism. He ... desires that philosophy reflect on its own history. ... idealism deserved to be accepted and criticized, accepted, because it is interior to Being and thought; criticized because correlative, with man, ... it is surpassed by the affirmation of God, absolute Being

Henri de Lubac II, p. 392..

96. de Lubac, 'Sur la philosophie chrétienne', p. 248.
95. DG, pp. 104–6.

Conclusion: Drama and Freedom

Writing to Hamel in the academic year 1923–1924, de Lubac claimed that 'philo[sophy] is destiny and nothing is philosophical which does not tackle the problem of destiny. This is the great reason for my love of Blondel'.[97] From its opening line, 'Yes or no, does human life make sense, and does man have a destiny?' *Action* is about an existential question. For the Jesuit theologian too, destiny is *the* critical *aporia*.

The first lesson in the Blondelian Catechism was that the extrinsicism of Descartes had cut natures off from their final ends, leaving an empty platform to be filled by secular, dogmatically immanentist philosophies and science. Many Catholics took Descartes as the magician whose 'Cogito' had disenchanted the modern world. Blondel and de Lubac give credence to this story, up to a point: as de Lubac puts it, it is not Descartes's immanentism which is problematic, but rather, his alliance of methodological immanentism with extrinsicism.[98] Blondel's *Action* closes with reflections on Descartes's notion of the divine 'mark' in human beings.[99] De Lubac's meditations on the divine image are a positive, theological retrieval of Descartes.

Both Blondel and de Lubac make good on Descartes's use of the ontological argument, by dramatizing this most 'immanent' and non-cosmological defence of God's existence. Descartes's countryman Pascal was his counterpart: opposite to him in his intrinsicism, but resembling him in his turn to the subject. Blondel conceives of the human being as struggling to bridge the gap between the infinite ideas which it requires in order to act and the finite means it exercises in every particular action. Fichte's conception of the agent as wrestling with an infinite spirit in a finite, material body found a resonance with the French Blondel, because it is a ponderous, Germanic analogue of Pascal's idea of the human being as a 'thinking reed', torn between 'misery' and 'grandeur'.[100] Blondel and de Lubac in his wake are remaking German 'radical immanentism'[101] in Pascal's Christhaunted image.

The 'natural desire' for God represented an essential 'word' in the dialogue which Blondel and de Lubac undertook with Romanticism. Modern idealism asserted, on the one hand, that the transcendent God of Christianity is a tyrannical monarch, who denies independence to his human colonies, but on the other hand it affirmed that the (immanent) Absolute is our heart's deepest

---

97. Cited in Chantraine, *Henri de Lubac II*, p. 234.

98. De Lubac, 'Pascal Anti-Cartésien', pp. 61934–37. This article, which argues that Pascal is both Cartesian and the anti-Descartes, is a response to Blondel's 'La jansénisme et l'anti-jansénisme de Pascal', *Revue de métaphysique et de morale* 30 (1923): pp. 131–63.

99. Jean Lacroix, *Maurice Blondel: An Introduction to the Man and his Philosophy*, trans. John C. Guinness (New York: Sheed And Ward, 1968), pp. 77–80.

100. Blaise Pascal, *Pensées*, #494 and #526.

101. De Lubac, 'Pascal Anti-Cartésien', p. 61934.

desire. Both in the philosophical forms absorbed by Blondel (Spinoza, Hegel, Schelling) and in the theo-political forms tackled by de Lubac (Marx, Nietzsche), Romantic humanism maintained that human beings desire the 'divine'. It meant that our dream is fulfilled by respecting the divinity present in ourselves, in human nature. Blondel and de Lubac say, '*go with that desire* and it will indeed lead you to paradise; the paradise of the transcendent God, who is no despotic tyrant, blocking your will, but the object of the deepest desire of those born to the glorious liberty of the sons of God'.[102] God is no 'wish-fulfillment' but rather the fulfilment of our deepest wish: for Blondel and for de Lubac, dialogue with modern humanism is between deaf-mutes if we lack the basic 'word', 'natural desire for beatitude'.

What Blondel had called 'determinism' and 'destiny', de Lubac names as 'fate' and 'destiny'. Pre-Christian humanity, de Lubac affirms, is enslaved to Fate, a Fate which is more powerful than the gods, and which strikes down as 'hubris' all human efforts to claim its own legitimate divinity. 'Fate' is the transcendent 'God' as modern anti-theistic humanism conceives it. De Lubac argues that it is from this false god of 'fate', that Christian revelation frees us. Pre-Christian humanity was lacking in hope,

> because the very idea of a *sursum* and a superabundance, the idea of an order incommensurate with nature, the idea of something radically new, something we might call 'an invention in being,' the idea of a gift coming gratuitously from above to raise up that needy nature, at once satisfying its longings and transforming it – such an idea remains wholly foreign to all whose minds have not been touched by the light of revelation.[103]

Revelation shows us that we are born to the purple, ordained not for a dispiriting fate but for a destiny which unshackles the free spirit to be itself. Revelation teaches us that we are made to the image and likeness of God. Through the revealed recognition of the divine image imprinted in us, humanity 'was freed, in his own eyes, from the ontological slavery with which Fate had burdened him'. Human beings could surpass determinism:

> The stars, in their unalterable courses, did not...implacably control our destinies....every man...had a direct link with the Creator, the ruler of the stars...No more *Moira*! No more Fate! Transcendent God...revealed in Jesus, opened for all a way that nothing would ever bar again. Hence that intense feeling of radiant newness in early Christian writing.[104]

102. DAH, pp. 24–25.
103. MS, p. 168.
104. DAH, pp. 22–23.

Both Bergson and Blondel argued that the bogus scientistic claim to total explanation cannot account for new occurrences. De Lubac often points out that historical 'science' could never have predicted the advent of Christ. History-as-science is prepared for the repeated and the statistically normal, but not for the new move which radically alters the scene.[105] Unless the notion that the human person is a free spirit is present, one will not be able to acknowledge that humanity is both predictable and a free initiator of novelty.

What scientism misses is the *drama* of human life. For it is the novel action which is the most dramatic, especially when novelty is the upshot of free *choice*. For Blondel, human life constitutes a drama because it is up to each of us to *decide* between recognizing our impotence to achieve our destiny in God and giving the reins to Him, or continuing in impotent pursuit of the infinite, refusing to relinquish our autonomy:

> the thoughts and actions of each one of us together make up a drama, which cannot reach its conclusion unless the decisive question arises...in the consciousness. Each one of us, simply by using that light which enlightens every man coming into this world, and by the use of his own resources, finds himself called upon to pronounce upon the problem of his destiny. For, in order to make the simplest considered affirmation, about the reality of the objects which make up our thoughts, in order to produce deliberately the most elementary of those acts which enter into the determinism of our wills, we must reach implicitly the point at which the option becomes possible...between the solicitations of the hidden God and those of an egoism.[106]

Blondel puts forward a dramatic anthropology, one which is not fully exposed to theological development until Hans Urs von Balthasar takes it up into his *Theo-Drama*. But de Lubac hints at the theological transpositions which this material merits. He notes that 'Through Christianity, faith in God has promoted the development of consciousness. Man, called by God, has come to know himself by learning to know his vocation. He has become a person forever, to himself.' We learn of this vocation by the inspiring example of the saints, who are, de Lubac asserts,

> the efficacious witnesses of God among us.... When we meet a saint...What we find is a new life, a new sphere of existence...but also with a resonance hitherto unknown to us, and now at last revealed. We are shown a new country, a home we had originally ignored, and as soon as we perceive it we recognize it as older and truer than anything we had known and with claims upon our heart...But in all this we are not left to ourselves, as spectators. It acts upon us as a provocation. It is a summons to choose and to act, unveiling our most

---

105. Ibid., p. 23; HS, pp. 429–66.
106. Blondel, 'Letter', p. 162.

hidden tendencies.... All of a sudden the universe seems different; it is the stage of a vast drama, and we, at its heart, are compelled to play our part.[107]

It is through indications like these that von Balthasar would later put the *actor* into *action*. We are 'compelled' to take roles: the director-God still exercises a 'compulsion', but, on this analysis, one which liberates us to be persons.

'God gave us freedom the day that he gave the soul to itself': this formula of his Jesuit friend Montcheuil delighted de Lubac. This is why he would say, with Montcheuil, that 'God is sufficiently transcendent for us to be immanent' and that the gift of the supernatural is gratuitous, but nature as it now is has a 'positive gap'.[108] In *Surnaturel*, de Lubac distinguishes between the way non-spiritual 'natures' are inherently oriented towards God and how persons are oriented to God: personal beings intend God in a *free choice*.[109] This distinction between 'natures' and 'persons' was developed by de Lubac in early *Quodlibeta* pieces such as 'Liberté de indifférence et concept: Réflexion autour de Bergson'. The young Jesuit argues that 'The restrictive individuation of matter is for man the condition of the individuation which blossoms in freedom: that is to say that he must begin by being nature in order to become spirit. What defines spirit is freedom; that which defines God, is pure freedom.'[110] Blondel ensnared many Jesuits by presenting the Christian way as the road to freedom. His pursuit of a personalist theology of freedom led de Lubac away from de-existentialized theories of 'pure nature', and from conceiving human *being* as 'nature' more than as 'personal'. De Lubac did not so much propound a natural desire for God as a *personal* desire for God, which, as such, lays no compulsion on supernatural freedom[111]: 'Encouraged in this by the tradition present in Blondel, de Lubac affirms God and the person. Without avoiding the world and nature, his philosophy is no longer cosmological but anthropological.'[112]

De Lubac draws from Blondel a dramatic personalism, forged with the intention of retrieving freedom from idealism while reversing its 'primal lie' of human self-sufficiency. For the Pascalian Blondel, the 'primal lie' of rationalists from Kant to Spinoza consists in claiming, 'that man alone can succeed in integrating

---

107. DG, p. 30 and pp. 158–59. See also C, where he writes,
The summons to personal life is a *vocation*, that is, a summons to play an eternal role.... the historical character that we have found in Christianity, as well as the social, emphasizes the reality of this role: since the flow of time is irreversible, nothing occurs in it more than once, so that ... each individual's life is a drama. (331–32)
108. Chantraine, *De Lubac II*, p. 356.
109. S, pp. 197–98.
110. De Lubac, 'Liberté de indifférence et concept: Réflexion autour de Bergson', cited in Chantraine, *De Lubac II*, pp. 493. This piece was printed in *Quodlibeta* in 1922, and revised down to 1926.
111. MS, pp. 145–49.
112. Chantraine, *De Lubac II*, p. 495.

himself into the absolute'.¹¹³ Blondel's anti-Pelagianism is perhaps more absolute than that of his Jesuit disciples, his vision more tragic than de Lubac's. Here we see, maybe, a slight divergence between the two French thinkers. The dramatic moment of each human life, as Blondel presents it, is no exaltation of free choice, but the bleak, Pauline 'To will and not to be able, to be able and not to will, that is the very option that presents itself to freedom: "to love oneself to the contempt of God, to love God to the contempt of self." Not that this tragic opposition is revealed to us with such sharpness and rigor.'¹¹⁴ As philosopher, Blondel views the option from the perspective of fallen nature, while the Jesuit theologian sees it from the perspective of baptismal grace. One does not readily conceive of Blondel celebrating a new 'Christian Prometheanism'. De Lubac's theological hopefulness flows from his study of Saint Thomas: he was the greatest of the Whig Thomists.

As a philosopher, it was Blondel's role to present the 'option' as the human *dilemma*, caught between its infinite desires and its finite means of achieving them. De Lubac's theological stance gives him the distance necessary to present the 'option' as a 'test'. Like the sculptor at Chartres, he can represent man as made to the image of God.¹¹⁵ Following patristic tradition, he claims that man's freedom is exercised in the gap between being 'in the image' and being 'to the likeness' of God. God is his own 'good', and does not choose the good: but creatures must choose between this highest Good and evil; this freedom to *choose* to become the likeness of God is how the creature imitates the perfect freedom of its maker.¹¹⁶

De Lubac claimed that, in Gilson's Christian philosophy, reason would always nibble at faith and absorb it. Maybe, but equally for Blondel, determinism is always one step behind freedom, and ultimately, his philosophical '[f]reedom, emerging out of the determinism of nature, must, in order to achieve its destiny, freely become one with that determinism'.¹¹⁷ For de Lubac, the theologian with a fully fledged dramatic personalism, freedom, divine and creaturely, takes the curtain call.

De Lubac's courage under fire in defending the creaturely, personal desire for the vision of the divine persons was rewarded in *Gaudiam et Spes* which states that 'only in the mystery of the incarnate Word does the mystery of man take on light. For Adam, the first man, was a figure of Him Who was to come, namely Christ the Lord. Christ, the final Adam, by the revelation of the mystery of the Father and His love, fully reveals man to man himself and makes his supreme calling clear'.¹¹⁸

---

113. Maurice Blondel, 'L'Evolution du Spinozisme et l'Accès qu'elle ouvre à la Transcendence', *L'Archivo di filosofia*, Anno XI, Fasc. IV (December, 1932), I-2.3-12; II, 338, cited in McNeil, *Synthesis*, p. 244.

114. Blondel, *Action*, p. 327.

115. DAH, p. 19.

116. S, p. 189.

117. McNeil, *Synthesis*, p. 94.

118. *Pastoral Constitution on the Church in the Modern World: Gaudiam et Spes* (1965), #22.

Chapter 4

RESSOURCEMENT

Jacob W. Wood

Introduction

In 1904, Charles Péguy coined the term *ressource* as part of a *cri d'armes* for a cultural and intellectual revolution:

> A revolution is a call to a more perfect tradition from a less perfect tradition, a call to a deeper tradition from a shallower tradition. It means surpassing tradition in depth by going back, a search for deeper sources; in the literal sense of the word, a *'ressource'*... [A] revolution... cannot succeed unless... it causes a deeper humanity than the humanity of the tradition which it opposes to arise and spring forth ...[1]

It was a noble goal that sparked one of the most important theological movements of the twentieth century. But unfortunately for subsequent scholars seeking to understand the nature of the *ressourcement* movement, while Péguy did describe the general purpose of the revolution to which he was calling his comrades in arms, he did not outline a specific battle plan for the revolution's success.[2] The same is true of most twentieth-century *ressourcement* theologians.

---

1. Charles Péguy, 'Avertissement', in *Cahiers de la quinzaine*, ser. 5, vol. 11 (1 March 1904), p. xxxvii.
2. Péguy was a lay poet and editor, not a priest or theologian. He invented the term *'ressource'* in a preface to a French translation of a rationalist parody of the Presbyterian Westminster Catechism, which he agreed to publish to warn the French about certain 'American' ideas that might soon make their way across the Atlantic: M.M. Mangasarian, *A New Catechism* (Chicago: Open Court, 1902). In the preface to the Catechism, Mangasarian states his intention:
> The old Catechisms which were imposed upon us in our youth – when our intelligence could not defend itself against them – no longer command our respect. They have become mildewed with neglect. The times in which they were conceived and composed are dead – quite dead! A New Catechism to express the thoughts of men and women and children living in these new times is needed.

While it could rightly be said that they generally shared Péguy's vision and even helped to carry out his revolution, few among them wrote specifically about what they thought *ressourcement* was, or reflected on how they thought one ought to engage in it. Henri de Lubac is among those whose silence on the nature and methods of *ressourcement* confronts contemporary scholars with an air of mystery.

When scholars want to understand de Lubac's place in the *ressourcement* movement, they typically look outside the Lubacian *corpus*, turning instead to two of de Lubac's colleagues who did write something about *ressourcement*: Jean Daniélou and Yves Congar. Daniélou wrote one of the few existing articles from the early twentieth century on the methods of *ressourcement*; Congar commented on antecedents to the movement in German theology.

Jean Daniélou (1905–1974) was a Jesuit patrologist who studied theology under de Lubac at the Jesuit faculty at Lyon-Fourvière from 1936 to 1939.[3] In 1942, he and de Lubac agreed to co-edit a collection of patristic writings, *Sources Chrétiennes*, whose object was to bring the Church Fathers into the mainstream of Catholic intellectual life.[4] In 1946, Daniélou published an apology for the series of texts, as well as for the nascent theological movement they were hoping to support by it. According to Daniélou, *ressourcement* is at its heart a 'return to the sources' of theology, 'the Bible, the Fathers...and the liturgy'.[5] Those tropes, 'return to the sources' and 'Bible, Fathers, Liturgy', distinguished a new, historically sensitive approach to the study of theology, rooted in a fresh reading of the primary texts of the theological tradition, from the ahistorical methodology of neo-scholastic Thomism, which arose in the second half of the nineteenth century, which sought in Thomism an inspiration for an ahistorical *philosophia perennis*, and which understood Thomism not in terms of the primary texts of Thomas Aquinas, but rather in terms of the secondary texts of the Thomistic commentators of the sixteenth to eighteenth centuries. On this view, *ressourcement* is purgative of the influence of early modern Thomistic commentators, corrective of the errors in methodology which led them to form an erroneously ahistorical view of theology, and restorative of earlier sources, methods, and conclusions.

Yves Congar (1904–1995) was a Dominican ecclesiologist who did his theological studies at Le Saulchoir in Belgium, and in whose series on

---

3. Bernard Pottier, 'Daniélou and the Twentieth-Century Patristic Renewal', in Gabriel Flynn and Paul Murray, eds, *Ressourcement: A Movement for Renewal in Twentieth-Century Catholic Theology* (New York: Oxford, 2012), 250; Liam Bergin, *O Propheticum Lavacrum* (Rome: Pontifical Gregorian University, 1999), p. 59, n. 76.

4. Pottier, 'Daniélou and the Twentieth-Century Patristic Renewal', pp. 252–53. See also de Lubac, ASC, pp. 30–31.

5. Jean Daniélou, 'Les orientations présentes de la pensée religieuse', *Études* 79 (1946): p. 7. For a neo-scholastic response, see Jean-Paul Labourdette, 'La théologie et ses sources', *Révue Thomiste* 46 (1946): pp. 353–71; Réginald Garrigou-Lagrange, 'La nouvelle théologie, où va-t-elle?' *Angelicum* 23 (1946): pp. 126–45.

ecclesiological renewal, *Unam Sanctam*, de Lubac published his first major work on *ressourcement*.[6] Congar studied with Marie-Dominique Chenu (1895–1990), who introduced him to the method of *ressourcement* by giving him a copy of *Unity in the Church* by Johann Adam Möhler (1796–1838).[7] Möhler's ecclesiology was deeply patristic; its organic focus on communion seemed to contrast with the juridic ecclesiologies of early modern Thomist commentators.[8] The gift inspired Congar to found a series of books to carry forward Möhler's ecclesiological vision,[9] and in this way Congar embraced a mindset with regard to neo-scholasticism and *ressourcement* similar to the one at which Daniélou would later arrive. For this reason, Chenu could observe that a 'liquidation' of early modern theology – the purgation of contemporary theology from the influence of the Thomistic commentarial tradition – began with the Tübingen School,[10] and Congar could confirm that the *ressourcement* movement was at the forefront of that liquidation in the twentieth century.[11]

Given the paucity of other resources for understanding the aims of the *ressourcement* movement and de Lubac's connection to it, it is necessary that we should connect de Lubac's work with the reflections of his colleagues. Moreover, such a comparison is warranted, because de Lubac's work bears significant similarities to that of his colleagues: it is replete with criticisms of early modern and neo-scholastic theologians; it is abundant with references to the Fathers, the liturgy, and the scriptures; it approaches the Christian life in an organic manner similar to that of the Tübingen School, and even makes explicit reference to Möhler. Yet the reception of de Lubac's *ressourcement* is also negatively affected by this method. It does not allow de Lubac to speak for himself, its interpretation of

---

6. *Catholicism: Christ and the Common Destiny of Man*. See Gabriel Flynn, 'Ressourcement, Ecumenism, and Pneumatology: The Contribution Yves Congar to *Nouvelle Theology*', in *Ressourcement*, p. 220.

7. Flynn, 'Ressourcement, Ecumenism, and Pneumatology', pp. 220–21. Chenu documents the historical study of theology at Le Saulchoir in Chenu, *Une école de théologie: Le Saulchoir* (Paris: Cerf, 1985). The text was Johann Adam Möhler, *Einheit in der Kirche oder das Prinzip des Katholizismus* (Tübingen: Heinrrich Laupp, 1825); english translation: *Unity in the Church or the Principle of Catholicism*, trans. Peter Erb (Washington, DC: CUA Press, 1996).

8. Hans Boersma, Nouvelle Théologie *and Sacramental Ontology: A Return to Mystery* (New York: Oxford, 2009), pp. 22–23; Elizabeth Groppe, *Yves Congar's Theology of the Holy Spirit* (New York: Oxford, 2004), pp. 40–43.

9. Flynn, 'Ressourcement, Ecumenism, and Pneumatology', pp. 221–23. Congar tells us that Möhler remained the 'animator' of his thought for the next forty years. See Yves Congar, 'Johann Adam Möhler: 1796–1838', *Theologische Quartalschrift* 150 (1970): pp. 50–51, cited in Flynn, 'Ressourcement, Ecumenism, and Pneumatology', p. 221.

10. Marie-Dominique Chenu, 'La position de la théologie', *Revue des Sciences Philosophiques et Théologiques* 24 (1935): p. 257

11. Yves Congar, *Journal d'un théologien: 1946–1956* (Paris: Cerf, 2001), p. 59; cited in Francesca Murphy, *Art and Intellect in the Philosophy of Étienne Gilson* (Columbia: University of Missouri Press, 2004), p. 227.

de Lubac cannot always be proven with solid evidence from de Lubac's writings, and it locates de Lubac on a side of debates about the reception of the Second Vatican Council that he formally disowned.

Observing the significant influence that Möhler had on Congar and Chenu, some scholars, such as Susan Wood, have sought to connect de Lubac with the broader programme of reform and liquidation in which Congar and Chenu took part.[12] There is a practical problem with this view: De Lubac did not know German, and readily admits that German categories of thought had very little influence on him.[13] When he cites Möhler, it is always or nearly always in the French translation,[14] and sometimes only by means of secondary literature – a particular irony for someone who is famous for his ability to cite primary sources.[15] De Lubac can also be critical of Möhler.[16] While there may be similarities between de Lubac's thought and Möhler's, it would not be entirely accurate to conclude that Möhler was one of the main inspirations for de Lubac's *ressourcement*, even if he was such an inspiration for Chenu's and Congar's.

There is a more significant reason to avoid aligning de Lubac with Möhler, Chenu, and Congar. If we utilize Joseph Ratzinger's distinction between a hermeneutic of rupture and a hermeneutic of continuity and reform in the interpretation of theological developments of the twentieth century,[17] connecting de Lubac with Möhler as Chenu and Congar understood him makes de Lubac one of the protagonists of rupture. While it is true that de Lubac's work precipitated significant paradigm shifts in the areas of anthropology, ecclesiology, and scripture, as we will see below, de Lubac himself gives us reason to question this interpretation of his impact. In protest against all the ways in which he had been held up as a figure of supposed rupture, de Lubac tried, though at times in vain, to present himself as a figure of a broader continuity – continuity with the Fathers, the liturgy, and the scripture to be sure, but also with every other period in the theological tradition.[18]

---

12. See Susan Wood, *Spiritual Exegesis and the Church in the Theology of Henri de Lubac* (Grand Rapids: Eerdmans, 1998), p. 91, n. 58.

13. ASC, 30. De Lubac goes on to admit that he did not really know any other modern European language either. When asked about the possibility of taking up a chair in the history of religions, de Lubac remarks: 'I had the weakness to accept. Without preparation, without books, *without knowledge of any language, European or Asiatic ...*' (emphasis added).

14. At the beginning of his career, see C, p. 41, n. 53. At the end of his career, see ASC, 148. In between, I have not found any instances of de Lubac citing Möhler in German.

15. Cf. C, p. 321, n. 45; SC, 92–93. The latter is more striking. De Lubac devotes an entire page to a discussion of Möhler's importance and influence in ecclesiology without citing Möhler once, all the while reducing some of Möhler's importance to the influence of the French Archbishop, François Fénelon (1651–1715).

16. Cf. de Lubac's remarks on Möhler's understanding of spiritual exegesis in HS, pp. 431–32.

17. Benedict XVI, 'Address to the Roman Curia' (22 December 2005), *Acta Apostolicae Sedis* 98 (2006): 44–45.

18. De Lubac sets forth some of these protestations at the conclusion of BC, pp. 177–290.

I would like to propose that the disconnect between how de Lubac has been received and how de Lubac intended to be received results from reading him against the backdrop of the wrong sort of revolution. De Lubac was not trying to join a revolution of purgative liquidation that supposedly began among nineteenth-century Germans;[19] much to the contrary, he participated in an ongoing attempt among French theologians to establish a deeper vision of humanity and its social vocation in the Church. De Lubac certainly shared in his colleagues' criticisms of early modern Thomistic commentators, as well as their love for the Fathers, for liturgy, and for scripture, but he did not eschew antecedently any one period in the theological tradition; his understanding of the theological tradition as an integral unity prevented him from doing so. Rather, following Péguy's call to a revolution of 'deepening' in preference to a revolution of liquidation, de Lubac retrieved forgotten voices from the whole of the theological tradition, including and especially the early modern Aegidian tradition of the Order of the Hermits of St Augustine. The doctrine of a natural desire for a supernatural end, which he inherited ultimately from this tradition, allowed him to participate in an ongoing French tradition of *ressourcement* which had its origin in the nineteenth century in response to the enlightenment rationalism of the French Revolution. De Lubac argued that this rationalism had taken root in anthropology, ecclesiology, and scripture: in anthropology, by restricting human nature to a naturally achievable act as its end; in ecclesiology, by restricting the progress of the Church to political posturing; in scripture, by reducing the meaning of the sacred text to a narrowly conceived literal sense and an arbitrarily chosen spiritual sense. As an alternative to these anthropological, ecclesial, and scriptural naturalisms, de Lubac proposed that a natural desire for a supernatural end could overcome enlightenment rationalism by bringing to light man's perfection in the vision of God, society's perfection in the Church, and the literal sense's perfection in the spiritual sense.

What follows will be divided into three parts. In the first, I will examine three antecedents to *ressourcement* theology in nineteenth-century France. In the second, I will observe the more immediate context for de Lubac's *ressourcement* in the rise of neo-scholasticism and the controversy over the Dreyfus Affair. In the third, I will trace the form of de Lubac's *ressourcement* in five of his first major works: *Catholicism*, *Corpus Mysticum*, *The Drama of Atheist Humanism*, *Surnaturel*, and *History and Theology*. Owing to reasons of space, I will focus on

---

19. Whether there even was such a revolution among German theologians is a matter which has recently come under dispute. See Grant Kaplan, 'Roman Catholic Perspectives: The Nineteenth Century', in Sarah Coakley and Richard Cross, eds, *The Oxford Handbook of the Reception of Christian Theology* (Oxford: Oxford University Press, forthcoming, 2016). I am grateful to Dr. Kaplan for sharing with me an advance version of this chapter. Kaplan's work, which shows the reliance of the Tübingen School on early modern theologians, necessarily leads to the question of whether the perceived opposition between the Tübingen and the early modern period is perhaps the creation of French theologians looking back upon the Tübingen School, rather than being something intrinsic to the Tübingen School itself.

establishing the pattern according to which de Lubac engaged in *ressourcement* rather than a summary of everything he said when he did. A more complete accounting of de Lubac's contributions to individual fields of theology can be had in the other contributions to this volume. Our task is to illumine the pattern according to which those contributions unfolded.

Responding to the Revolution

When the Revolution of 1789 brought the end of the *ancien régime*, along with the existence in France of the religious orders which had served as mainstays of Catholic life prior to the Revolution, French theologians pondered in what way they could propose the perfection of French society in Christ to a non-Catholic, non-monarchical nation state such as France had become. These efforts were led by people who sought to re-integrate, and in some ways re-envision, the place of Catholicism within mainstream French life. For the purposes of this chapter, we can highlight three such people, each associated with the re-founding and re-introduction of a religious order in post-Revolutionary France: Dom Prosper Guéranger, who re-founded the Benedictine Order in France, sought the social unity of the people in a *monarchical* society marked by a transcendent celebration of the liturgy, which would establish social unity through the worship of God according to one rite; Henri-Dominique Lacordaire, who re-founded the Dominican Order in France, sought the social unity of the people in a *liberal* society, which would achieve social unity through willing submission to the pope; Auguste Gratry, who re-founded the French Oratorians, sought the social unity of the people in a form of *socialism*, which would achieve social unity by transcending the limits of its natural existence in the embrace of the grace necessary to reach the infinite goal of its progress. The efforts of Guéranger and Lacordaire were built upon the philosophy and apologetics of traditionalism, while the efforts of Gratry were built upon responses to it.

The central figures of the traditionalist movement were Joseph Le Maistre (1753–1821) and Louis Gabriel Ambroise de Bonald (1754–1840).[20] Le Maistre, who is widely recognized as the movement's founder, proposed that humanity was given a collective endowment of knowledge by God at Creation. Although the Fall corrupted that knowledge, it did not obliterate it, and so it has been passed down from generation to generation in an unbroken *tradition* since the dawn of time. Tradition may have become admixed with various errors in different societies, but we can identify it if we consider what has been thought 'always, everywhere, and by all'.[21] The knowledge of truth, which is a goal of an individual's human nature, is therefore inherently social. Among the truths that can be known socially is the necessity of absolute sovereignty in order for man to attain to the fullness of truth and to avoid

---

20. Bernard Reardon, *Liberalism and Tradition* (New York: Cambridge University Press, 1975), pp. 20–42.
21. Ibid., p. 33.

anarchy and ignorance.[22] Only the Catholic Church possesses such sovereignty in virtue of the office of the pope; therefore the foundation of true knowledge, true belief, and true society is in the absolute submission of society to the pope.[23]

One of the questions not as thoroughly addressed by Le Maistre was how an individual person ought to recognize as true the idea that there is a need for absolute sovereignty and that this absolute sovereignty is possessed by the Catholic Church. One of Le Maistre's most influential followers, Hugues Felicité Robert de Lamennais (1782–1854), provided the answer.[24] In his *Essay on Religious Indifference* (1817),[25] Lamennais added to Le Maistre's traditionalism on both the psychological and the political levels. On the psychological level, he proposed that there is a faculty of the mind oriented towards giving spontaneous assent to what has been believed always, everywhere, and by all. He called it the 'common sense'.[26] According to this common sense, all people know that God exists, that there is one right way of relating to him, and that such a way requires absolute authority. Anything less than absolute authority is not really authority at all – to the extent that it leaves anything to individual judgement, it does not bring people to true unity.[27] But, since no political system is capable of enforcing the kind of unity that man requires, only a complete, central, and absolute authority, established by grace, can secure the kind of social unity required by human nature – any kind of absolute temporal monarchy would simply stand in the way of that more complete unity.[28]

Lamennais's traditionalism inspired the first of the great nineteenth-century forerunners to *ressourcement*, Dom Prosper Louis Pascal Guéranger, OSB (1805–1875), who re-founded the Benedictine Order in France in 1837.[29] Guéranger observed that the French idea of liturgy in the early nineteenth century was

---

22. Ibid., pp. 33, 41.
23. Ibid., p. 27.
24. For an introduction to the life and works of Lamennais, see ibid., pp. 62–112.
25. Félicité de Lamennais, *Essai sur l'indifférence en matière de religion* (Paris: Leblan, 1817). For a brief summary of its contents, see Reardon, *Liberalism and Tradition*, pp. 68–69. Also see Lamennais's subsequent defence of his work: Félicité de Lamennais, *Défense de l'essai sur l'indifférence en matière de religion* (Paris: Méquignon Fils Aîné, 1821).
26. Reardon, *Liberalism and Tradition*, p. 71. Lamennais's common sense is not the same as the common sense proposed by Thomas Aquinas, whose goal is the synthesis of raw sense data in preparation for the abstraction of its intelligible content. See Thomas Aquinas, *Summa theologiae*, Ia, q. 78, a. 4, in *Opera Omnia*, vol. 5 (Rome: Ex Typographia Polyglotta S.C. de Propaganda Fide, 1889), pp. 255–57.
27. Reardon, *Liberalism and Tradition*, p. 73.
28. On Lamennais's apologetic for Roman authority, see Avery Dulles, *A History of Apologetics* (San Francisco: Ignatius Press, 2005), pp. 230–32. Also see A. Fonck, 'Lamennais', in, Alfred Vacant, E. Mangenot, and Emile Amann, eds, *Dictionnaire de Théologie Catholique* [hereafter '*DTC*'] (Paris: Letouzey et Ané, 1903–1950), p. 8:2479–2480; Reardon, *Liberalism and Tradition*, p. 73.
29. Before entering the Benedictines, Guéranger was an attentive reader of Lamennais. See Kurt Belsole, 'Guéranger, Prosper 1805–1875', in *Encyclopedia of Monasticism*, 2 vols (Chicago: Fitzroy Dearborn, 2000), p. 1:558.

governed by Gallicanism and Jansenism, each of which promoted some form of individualism.[30] Gallicanism led to the hyper-localization of liturgical books among French dioceses, to the point where there was often little correspondence between the books of one diocese and those of another.[31] Jansenism influenced that multiplicity of books such that they generally minimized any element in the liturgy which might direct the participants' attention away from themselves and towards God.[32] For Guéranger, both Gallicanism and Jansenism kept the French people from true unity. Gallicanism proposed the individualism of communities from the Church; Jansenism proposed the individualism of humanity from God.[33]

Influenced by the concerns of Lamennais to bring unity to the French people through submission to Roman authority, Guéranger sought to replace the disparate liturgical books of the dioceses of France with those of the Roman Rite.[34] Breaking

---

30. See Alcuin Reid, *The Organic Development of the Liturgy: Principles for Liturgical Reform* (San Francisco: Ignatius, 2005), p. 50. Cornelius Otto Jansen (often referred to as Jansenius; 1585–1638) sought to retrieve Augustine's teaching on grace in part to oppose Calvin's teaching on Adam's Covenant of Works. In Jansen's chief work, the posthumously published, *Augustinus* 3 vols (Louvain: Jacobus Zegers, 1640), he held that there is a distinction between the gifts of nature and the gifts of grace; the vision of God for which we long by nature is always a gift of grace; even for Adam it has no proportion to our natural actions. Yet even if the beatific vision is a gift of grace, Jansen thought that the grace which brings us to it is owed to Adam's human nature because a desire for it was inscribed upon his heart. Jansen's teaching inspired an ascetical and liturgical movement that took root in France at the convent of Port-Royal, led by Jean du Vergier de Hauranne, the Abbé de Saint-Cyran (1581–1643), and Antoine Arnauld (1612–1694).

In order to oppose condemnations of Jansenism, the French Clergy issued a *Declaration of the Clergy of France* in 1682, proclaiming four points which became accepted as the tenets of Gallicanism: first, that God had given the pope spiritual authority but not temporal authority – *a fortiori* God did not give the pope authority over the temporal affairs of France; second, that there are limits to the spiritual power which the pope has over the Church in France – he cannot simply impose his will, his choices, or his teaching; third, that in addition to those limits, the pope has to observe the laws, customs and constitutions of France, along with the customary modes of interaction between the papacy and France; fourth, that the pope is not infallible, and that therefore his teaching is reformable. See *Documents relatifs aux rapports du clergé avec la royauté de 1682 à 1705*, ed. Léon Mention, 3 vols (Paris: Alphonse Picard et Fils, 1893), pp. 1:26–32. In the late eighteenth and early nineteenth centuries, the four Gallicanist principles were widely received among the French clergy as normative. Consequently, Jansenism – along with Gallicanism – could be found in France even after multiple condemnations. Edgar Hocedez, *Histoire de la théologie au xixe siècle*, 2:149–51, ctd. in Gerald McCool, *Nineteenth-Century Scholasticism: The Search for a Unitary Method* (New York: Fordham University Press, 1989), p. 22.

31. Reid, *The Organic Development of the Liturgy*, p. 58.

32. Ibid., pp. 50–52.

33. Ibid., pp. 51, 55.

34. Ibid., pp. 57–58. Guéranger sets forth his position in Prosper Guéranger, *Institutions liturgiques*, vol. 2 (Le Mans: Fleuriot, 1841). See Cuthbert Johnson, *Prosper Gueranger (1805–1875), A Liturgical Theologian: Introduction to his Liturgical Writings and Work* (Rome: Pontificio Ateneo S. Anselmo, 1984), p. 192.

with Lamennais on the question of monarchy, Guéranger sought in monarchy the natural correlate to Roman authority because he perceived in Lamennais's liberalism a political correlate to Gallicanism.[35] In order to demonstrate the viability of his vision, Guéranger engaged in a form of proto-*ressourcement*: looking backwards to the sources of the liturgy, and forwards towards a more transcendent celebration of it, which would unite its participants in the social worship of God.[36]

A second nineteenth-century French forerunner to *ressourcement* was Jean-Baptiste Henri Lacordaire, OP (known within the Dominican Order as Henri-Dominique Lacordaire; 1802–1861).[37] Like Guéranger, Lacordaire was a priest and theologian who was influenced by Lamennais's traditionalism. Yet although Lacordaire was more sympathetic to Lamennais's liberalism than was Guéranger, Lacordaire agreed to submit to the Roman authorities when Mennaisian liberalism was condemned in 1832 by Gregory XVI in the encyclical *Mirari Vos*,[38] even though this meant a break with Lamennais, who resisted.[39]

After the condemnation of Lamennais, Lacordaire re-envisioned the social unity of the French people in three ways: first, he recast his thought in terms of a re-sourcing of Augustine's *City of God*;[40] second, he tempered Lamennais's appeal to a submission to Roman authority with an observation of the harmony between natural human society and the Church, inspired by the French

---

35. Guéranger expressed these thoughts in the mid-nineteenth century in a protracted debate with the Duc Albert de Broglie. The debate began with the publication of Albert de Broglie, *L'Église et l'Empire romain au IVe siècle* (Paris: Didier, 1857). Guéranger's numerous responses were collected in Prosper Guéranger, *Essais sur le naturalisme contemporain* (Paris: Julien, Lanier, Cosnard, 1858). This debate is outlined in Guillaume Cuchet, 'Comment Dieu est-il acteur de l'histoire?' *Revue des Sciences Philosophiques et Théologiques* 96 (2012): pp. 33–55.

36. See Johnson, *Prosper Gueranger*, pp. 253–60. Guéranger's chief work in this regard was his immensely popular *L'Anné liturgique*. This work was published successively over the course of Guéranger's lifetime, and eventually collected into fifteen volumes (plus an index). Of these the last six were composed posthumously by Lucien Fromage. For an English translation, see *The Liturgical Year*, trans. Laurence Shepherd and the Benedictines of Stanbrook (Westminster, MD: Newman Press, 1948–1950; repr. Loreto Publications, 2013).

37. Lacordaire met Lamennais in May 1830, was won over to Lamennais's idea of a harmony between political liberalism and Roman authority, and even agreed to join with Lamennais in the publication of a journal, *L'Avenir* ('The Future'), in support of these ideas. But Lacordaire was not as committed to the particulars of the project in the same way as Lamennais. See Henri-Dominique Noble, 'Lacordaire', in *DTC*, 8:2394; Reardon, *Liberalism and Tradition*, pp. 92–95.

38. Noble, 'Lacordaire', in *DTC*, 8:2395.

39. Lamennais's resistance was expressed in Félicité de Lamennais, *Les paroles d'un croyant* (Paris: Eugène Renduel, 1833). As a consequence, Gregory XVI published an entire encyclical two years later devoted to condemning Lamennais by name, *Singulari Nos*. Lamennais subsequently broke with the Church and was never reconciled to it. On Lacordaire's break with Lamennais, see Reardon, *Liberalism and Tradition*, 108. Lacordaire subsequently published a criticism of Lamennais's thought: Henri Lacordaire, *Considérations sur le système philosophique de M. de Lamennais* (Paris: Derivaux, 1834).

40. Noble, 'Lacordaire', 8:2399; Reardon, *Liberalism and Tradition*, p. 110. Evidently this aroused suspicion on the part of some of the clergy, who thought him neglectful of scholastic tradition.

Romanticist François-René de Chateaubriand (1768–1848);[41] third, he proposed to spread his approach to unity primarily through preaching rather than through liturgy. For this reason, Lacordaire resolved to enter the Order of Preachers (the Dominicans), and to re-found that order in France in a similar way to that in which Guéranger had re-founded the Benedictines. He even received Guéranger's personal advice and encouragement in the initiative.[42]

Lacordaire entered the Dominican Novitiate in Italy in 1839, and returned to Paris in 1841 to deliver a series of Lenten Conferences at the Cathedral of Notre-Dame de Paris. The first and most famous of these, the 'Discourse on the Vocation of the French Nation',[43] explains Lacordaire's re-sourced Augustinian vision for France. According to Augustine's *City of God*, the world is made up of two cities, an earthly city and a heavenly city,[44] each oriented towards the common object of its love.[45] The City of Man is the association of all those who are bound together by the love of self – its citizens each go wherever their individual desires lead. Since those desires, wounded by concupiscence, do not all lead to the same place, the earthly city tends towards disunity. It is only held together by authoritarian rulers, who exercise their office out of their own disordered lust for power (*cupiditas dominandi*).[46] The citizens of the City of God, by contrast, have their individual desires healed by grace. Consequently, their desires all lead to the same place: the inexhaustible unity of the three trinitarian persons. They are held together not by power but by the sacrificial love of Christ, shown forth by those who rule as servants, not as tyrants.[47]

The way in which Lacordaire engages the two cities is subtly different than the way in which Péguy would later do so.[48] According to Lacordaire, God established

---

41. François-René de Chateaubriand, *Le génie du christianisme* (Paris: Migneret, 1802). On the influence of Chateaubriand on Lacordaire, see Noble, 'Lacordaire', 8:2397–98. On the influence of Chateaubriand on nineteenth-century French theology in general, see Reardon, *Liberalism and Tradition*, pp. 3–8.

42. Noble, 'Lacordaire', 8:2395.

43. Henri Lacordaire, 'Discours sur la vocation de la nation française', *Conférences de Notre-Dame de Paris (Années 1835 à 1843)*, Vol. 1 of *Conférences du Révérend Père Lacordaire des Frères Prêcheurs; précédés d'une notice biographique par P. Lorain*, 2nd ed., ed. Jean Baptiste de Mortier (Brussels: L'Académie Royale de Médicine, 1852), pp. 293–309.

44. Augustine, *De civitate dei* 14.28, in *Corpus Scriptorum Ecclesiasticorum Latinorum* 40.2 (Vienna: F. Tempsky, 1900), pp. 56, 57.

45. Ibid. 19.24.

46. Ibid. 19.6.

47. Ibid.

48. Discouraged by the attenuated state of Catholicism in his day, Péguy could later see how the distinction between the City of God and the City of Man could not be mapped on to the distinction between the Church and the temporal order, or between Catholics and non-Catholics – there are members of the Church who fall prey to self-love, while even those members of the Church who are animated by the spirit of grace are also members of the state by nature. Writing prior to that conflict, Lacordaire still sees the two cities not as representing two forms of love, but rather two forms of life: the temporal life lived out in the state, and spiritual life lived out in the Church.

both the temporal and the spiritual forms of life, but he only gave temporal power to man,[49] because there was a danger that man might abuse spiritual power were it given to him.[50] Nevertheless, man's use of temporal power parallels the development of his spiritual life in its origin, its history, and its purpose: in its origin, because just as God gave moral liberty to mankind at Creation in virtue of the power of free will, so also he gave political liberty to man in virtue of his temporal authority;[51] in its history, because just as man abused his moral liberty at the Fall by turning away from God, so also he abused his political liberty by turning from just authority to domination;[52] in its purpose, because just as Christ transformed humanity personally through his Passion by offering it the grace whereby it might regain true moral freedom in his service, so also he transformed it socially by offering to human persons the grace whereby they might regain true political freedom in the Church.[53]

In France, Lacordaire saw an example of a nation that initially made right use of its liberty and heeded the call to true social unity in the Church.[54] However, he alleges that the French have not always been faithful to this heritage. After withstanding Lutheranism in the sixteenth century, they fell prey to British rationalism and atheism in the eighteenth century.[55] The French Revolution was not the *start* of France's incredulity; it was actually a divine punishment for an incredulity already begun.[56] What changed at the Revolution was not France's Christian heritage or its Christian vocation, only the group of people to whom temporal authority had been given. Whoever wields temporal authority still has to answer the same question as Lamennais had asked: will he/she/they submit their authority to Christ in the Church so that their Christian sentiments can be reunited with and draw new life from the source of their being?[57] Anything less

49. Lacordaire, 'Discours sur la vocation de la nation française', p. 295.
50. Ibid., p. 296.
51. Ibid.
52. Ibid., pp. 296–97.
53. Ibid., p. 296.
54. Ibid., p. 299.
55. Ibid., p. 303. Lacordaire excuses himself for sounding petty in pointing out that rationalism originated in Britain, but it is essential to his argument that he identify rationalism as something inherently 'un-French'.
56. Ibid., p. 297, pp. 303–6. According to Lacordaire, if the French Revolution had been the start of France's incredulity, then one might argue that the best way to restore France to faith would be to restore the *ancien régime*. However, since Lacordaire identifies the Revolution with the providentially arranged consequence of incredulity rather than its inception, he indentifies several remnants of Christianity that continued throughout the Revolution and were even amplified by it: the fact that France's governmental employees are called 'public *servants*', that society has broken down class barriers so that there is no distinction among its citizens, that even Napoleon sought legitimacy for his imperial authority from the papacy. Lacordaire argues that all of this shows that France is Christian in *sentiment*, even if not in *belief*, because its understanding of temporal authority has been permanently transformed by its encounter with the Gospel and its historical relationship to the Church.
57. Lacordaire, 'Discours sur la vocation de la nation française', pp. 294–95.

would be to allow the Christian sentiments of French society to degrade into pre-Christian servitude at the whim of a fallen lust for power.[58]

We can observe in these thoughts of Lacordaire three important advances on Guéranger's proto- *ressourcement*: advances in depth, in scope, and in purpose. In terms of depth and scope, Lacordaire undertakes a more wide-ranging *ressourcement* than Guéranger. Guéranger limited his historical studies to liturgical history; consequently, the renewal he proposed for the Church in France was limited to liturgical theology without necessarily making all the connections that could be made to other areas of theology and life. Lacordaire, by contrast, engaged a broader range of sources in the theological tradition. He sought a more complete renewal in the Church by a more complete rediscovery of the fundamental questions at the heart of theology, especially in his re-sourcing of Augustine's *City of God*.

In terms of purpose, Guéranger's more limited *ressourcement* was also more directly influenced by Lamennais's appeal to Roman authority. Writing after the condemnation of Lamennais, Lacordaire introduced an appeal to the harmonies between human society and the Church alongside the call to the submission of human society to the Church. Although Lamennais's appeal to Roman authority is not therefore absent from Lacordaire's writing, there is more room in Lacordaire's thought for an organic response to the call to unity than that for which Guéranger's writing allows.

Traditionalism as a movement did not long outlast the two condemnations of it in the 1830s. Instead, it gave way to two alternatives, each of which sought to continue the opposition to individualism that traditionalism began: fideism and ontologism.

Fideism was developed by Louis Eugène Marie Bautain (1796–1867).[59] With the advocates of traditionalism, Bautain acknowledged an original revelation to mankind, preserved in a fragmented and corrupted manner among humanity in a fallen state.[60] But he rightfully criticized the way in which access to that revelation was construed among previous traditionalists: since they made human consent the criterion of certainty about the truth, and since they admitted no certain knowledge above that which could be known as true by that consent, they effectively lapsed into rationalism by reducing all truth to that which can be discerned by unaided human reason.[61] It was necessary to recover the place of grace in the act of faith.[62] Bautain's solution was to make

---

58. Ibid., p. 298.

59. His chief work in this regard was Louis Bautain, *De l'enseignement de la philosophie en France au xixe siècle* (Paris: Derivaux, 1833). See Reardon, *Liberalism and Tradition*, p. 121; Aidan Nichols, *From Hermes to Benedict XVI: Faith and Reason in Modern Catholic Thought* (Leominster: Gracewing, 2009), pp. 68–82.

60. Nichols, *From Hermes to Benedict XVI*, pp. 73–74.

61. Reardon, *Liberalism and Tradition*, p. 123. See also p. 75.

62. Bautain was inspired in this by his acquaintance with the mystic, Madelaine-Louise Humann. See Nichols, *From Hermes to Benedict XVI*, pp. 71–73.

grace the sole criterion of certitude in matters pertaining to the truth,[63] and a life of prayer and penance as the means of penetrating that truth more clearly.[64] It is not that he altogether rejected the role of authority in accrediting the truth – he allowed for its *pastoral* importance in helping people arrive at the truth[65] – but certainty about the credibility of the truth could only be had following the act of faith in transcendent truths which can neither be understood nor known outside of faith.[66]

Instead of fideism, some post-traditionalists turned to ontologism. Ontologism had its origin in the theological tradition of the French Oratorians, and in particular Nicholas Malebranche (1638–1715).[67] A devoté of Descartes who accepted a radical Cartesian dualism between the mind and the body, Malebranche isolated the source of all knowledge in a direct, interior encounter between the mind and the forms of things, which he identified with the divine essence. This immediate vision of the divine essence becomes the first cause of the motion of the will, because the will is attracted by the good, and the vision of God is the highest good.[68] In the nineteenth century, ontologism was given its characteristic expression in the Francophone world by Gérard-Casimir Ubaghs (1800–1874).[69] Ubaghs's ontologism was more tempered than that of Malebranche, because it acknowledged at least a degree of difference between the forms seen by the mind and the divine essence, and, similar to traditionalism, identified the forms seen in the mind in part with an original revelation from God.[70] But Ubaghs proposed that each person has these notions immediately impressed upon the intellect by God, as well as a natural inclination to assent to the correspondence of those notions with reality.[71] The assent to that correspondence constitutes the first instance of faith. The assent to revealed truth constitutes a higher mode of that faith.[72]

Neither fideism nor ontologism was completely successful in superseding the rationalist tendencies of traditionalism. The fideism of Bautain collapsed reason into faith, because it made the judgements of reason into acts of faith on a smaller scale, while the ontologism of Ubaghs collapsed faith into reason, because it made all knowledge dependent upon the vision that Christian revelation promises as the reward of grace. A third precursor to French

---

63. Reardon, *Liberalism and Tradition*, p. 127.
64. Nichols, *From Hermes to Benedict XVI*, p. 72, 80.
65. Reardon, *Liberalism and Tradition*, p. 123.
66. Ibid., pp. 129–30, 133.
67. Ibid., p. 159.
68. De Lubac, AMT, p. 50; Jason Skirry, 'Malebranche's Augustinianism and the Mind's Perfection', (PhD diss., University of Pennsylvania, 2010), p. 116.
69. Reardon, *Liberalism and Tradition*, p. 161.
70. Ibid., p. 162.
71. Ibid., pp. 161–62.
72. Ibid., p. 162.

ressourcement, Auguste Joseph Alphonse Gratry (1805–1872), sought to chart a middle course between the two.[73]

In 1852, Gratry asked and obtained from the Holy See permission to re-establish the French Oratorians.[74] Almost immediately he set about publishing a body of work devoted to a re-sourcing of the Augustinian tradition. Yet instead of the Augustinianism of Malebranche, which belonged to the patrimony of his order, he re-sourced a more scholastic Augustinianism, the Aegidian tradition of the Order of the Hermits of Saint Augustine (formerly known in English as the 'Austin Friars').[75] Prior to the nineteenth century, the main proponents of this tradition were Enrico Noris, OESA (Order of the Hermits of St Augustine) (1631–1704), Fulgenzio Bellelli, OESA (1675–1742), and Giovanni Lorenzo Berti, OESA (1696–1766), although it also had representatives in the Francophone world, such as Fulgence Lafosse (1649–1684).[76] Berti gave the classic exposition of their thought in *On the Theological Disciplines*.[77] With the scholastics and against the French Oratorians, Berti affirmed an Aristotelian theory of knowledge, which does not require the vision of God in the mind because it understands the forms of things as abstracted from a sense encounter with the things themselves. Consequently, God's existence is not known immediately; it has to be *demonstrated* by natural reason from his created effects, because the vision of God surpasses all human powers. Nevertheless, Berti argues that from our knowledge of God,

---

73. In history and theology, one may find him referred to by any one of his given names: Auguste Gratry, Joseph Gratry, or Alphonse Gratry. Born to a family of lukewarm faith, Gratry had a conversion experience while studying at the École Polytechnique in Paris, after which he left Paris for Strasbourg in 1828 to study under Bautain and accepted Bautain's emphasis on the role of grace in the act of faith. He was ordained a priest in Strasbourg four years later (1832), and was subsequently appointed chaplain to the École Normale in Paris (1846). A public dispute with the director saw him resign from that post in 1851. See Augustin Largent, 'Gratry', in *DTC*, 6:1755; Reardon, *Liberalism and Tradition*, pp. 192–94.

75. This Augustinianism is often described as 'Aegidian' because its founder was Giles of Rome ('Aegidius Romanus' in Latin; d. 1316).

74. Reardon, *Liberalism and Tradition*, 192; Largent, 'Gratry', 6:1756.

76. Fulgence Lafosse, *Augustinus theologus*, 4 vols (Toulouse: Guillaume Bosc, 1676–1683).

77. Giovanni Berti, *De theologicis disciplinis*, 10 vols (Naples: Gaetano Migliaccio, 1776–1784). This work is a careful, deliberate, and sustained explication of this branch of the Aegidian tradition. The main works of Noris and Bellelli, while still of intellectual value, were composed more as polemical defences than as positive theological syntheses. For Noris, see Enrico Noris, *Vindiciae Augustinianae* (Brussells: Lambert Marchant, 1675). For Bellelli, see Fulgenzio Bellelli, *Mens Augustini de creaturae rationalis ante peccatum* (Lucerne: Anna Felicitas Hauttin, 1711) and *Mens Augustini de modo reparationis humanae naturae post lapsum adversus Baium et Jansenium*, 2 vols (Rome: Bernabò, 1737). For a thorough bibliography of primary sources for this period, including unpublished works, see Winfried Bocxe, *Introduction to the Teaching of the Italian Augustinians of the 18th Century on the Nature of Actual Grace* (Louvain: Augustinian Historical Institute, 1958), pp. 6–10. Bocxe also contains transcriptions of extracts from a number of manuscripts on pp. 55–99.

mediated through creation, arises a desire for the immediate vision of God – our abstractive knowledge of God indicates the possibility of sight.[78]

With the Aegidian tradition, Gratry grounds our knowledge of God's existence in a desire for a God that we do not yet see. He describes this reality in terms of the human soul's being endowed with a capacity for the infinite,[79] which it cannot fulfil by its own power.[80] Gratry thus comes to the conclusion that man cannot reach his perfection without the help of God and that grace is necessary to man for his natural perfection.[81] Having in this way arrived essentially at the Aegidian understanding of man's relationship to God, Gratry attempts an *apologia* for the tradition's great theologians, seeking to show that this Aegidian understanding of man is not only the authentic interpretation of Augustine, but also that of the great scholastic, Thomas Aquinas.[82]

In participation with the ecclesiological renewal of the nineteenth century, Gratry united his concerns about human nature to his concerns about the social unity of people in the Church.[83] In this respect, Gratry describes society as advancing like the individuals that comprise it. Those individuals are compelled in personal progress towards the infinite by a natural desire for the vision of God. As individuals, they cannot reach the goal of that desire without grace, but their nature does not therefore possess any grace before God bestows it.[84] Similarly, human society is compelled in social progress towards the infinite by the collection of individuals seeking it.[85] Evident in the anti-industrial movement towards social justice and the liberation of peoples from forms of economic oppression, that progress, like the natural desire of the human person, reveals the existence of an infinite God not already possessed, who calls humanity through their desire to seek him.[86] The ultimate goal of human social progress is the incarnation of the City of God through the Church.[87]

---

78. Berti, *De theologicis disciplinis*, lib. 3, cap. 1, prop. 1–2 [Naples 1:66–68]. Berti supports this argument on the basis of his understanding of what it means for man to be in the *imago dei*. The *imago dei* is something natural in man. On account of this image man is naturally capable of seeing God, and desires to do so. See Ibid., lib. 12, cap. 7, prop. 2 [Naples 3:31B]; *Additamentum* lib. 12, cap. 2 [Naples 3:78A].

79. Auguste Gratry, *De la connaissance de Dieu* (Paris: C. Douniol, 1853); English translation: *Guide to the Knowledge of God*, trans. Abby Alger (Boston: Roberts Brothers, 1892), pp. 419–20. References will be to the English translation.

80. Ibid., pp. 420–21.

81. Ibid., p. 424.

82. Ibid., p. 418.

83. Auguste Gratry, *La Morale et la loi de l'histoire*, 2 vols (Paris: Charles Douniol, 1968). See Reardon, *Liberalism and Tradition*, pp. 200–3.

84. Reardon, *Liberalism and Tradition*, p. 201.

85. Ibid.

86. Ibid., pp. 201–2. See Gratry, *La Morale et la loi de l'histoire*, p. 1:139. Gratry is particularly critical of the United States.

87. In this way, Gratry espoused a form of Christian utopian socialism. See Reardon, *Liberalism and Tradition*, pp. 200–2.

Neo-Scholasticism and the Dreyfus Affair

Gratry's concern to associate the re-sourced Augustinianism of the Aegidian tradition with the authentic interpretation of Thomas Aquinas foreshadowed the next stage of development in the history of *ressourcement*, in which a primary concern to re-source the Fathers, and in particular Augustine, gave way to an emphasis on the medievals, particularly Aquinas. The major catalyst of a paradigm shift was the publication of Leo XIII's encyclical letter *Aeterni Patris* in 1879,[88] which recommended a renewal of the study of the writings of Thomas Aquinas as the means to overcoming rationalism.[89]

There were three main responses to *Aeterni Patris*. The first was the rise of neo-scholastic Thomism, which sought to improve theology through the use of an exclusively Thomistic philosophy based upon the interpretations of Thomas in the commentarial tradition of the sixteenth to eighteenth centuries. Leo XIII had his own intellectual formation within this movement,[90] and the encyclical helped him to ensure its spread through appointments of its adherents at both the Jesuit College in Rome (the 'Gregorianum') and the Dominican College in Rome (the 'Angelicum').[91] In the period preceding de Lubac's work, the most well-known Jesuit representative of this movement was Pédro Descoqs (1877–1946), who taught metaphysics at the philosophate for the French Jesuits on the Isle of Jersey.[92] The most well-known Dominican representative of this movement was Réginald Garrigou-Lagrange (1877–1964), who taught metaphysics and spiritual theology at the Angelicum.[93]

The second response to *Aeterni Patris* was the development of a re-sourced Thomism, which sought to combine historical studies of Aquinas with an

---

88. Leo XIII, *Aeterni Patris*, in *Acta Sanctae Sedis* [Hereafter *ASS*] 12:97–115.

89. Ibid., p. 24 [*ASS* 12:111].

90. On the beginnings of the movement, see McCool, *Nineteenth-Century Scholasticism*, pp. 135–44. For the relationship of Leo XIII to the movement, see McCool, *Nineteenth-Century Scholasticism*, pp. 226–28.

91. McCool, *Nineteenth-Century Scholasticism*, p. 236.

92. For information about Descoqs's life and career, see Peter Bernardi, *Maurice Blondel, Social Catholicism, and Action Française* (Washington, DC: CUA Press, 2009), pp. 90–94. The French Jesuits followed a different pattern than other religious orders in France. After the suppression of the Society in 1764, they were re-established in 1814 under the Bourbon Restoration. However, in 1880, the Society was expelled from France again, and established a scholasticate in Canterbury, a philosophate on the Isle of Jersey, and a theologate at Hastings. For details of these events, see Cornelius Buckley, *When Jesuits were Giants: Louis-Marie Ruellan, S.J. (1846–1885) and Contemporaries* (San Francisco: Ignatius, 1999).

93. For information about Garrigou-Lagrange's life and career see Aidan Nichols, *Reason with Piety: Garrigou-Lagrange in the Service of Catholic Thought* (Naples, FL: Sapientia Press, 2008); Richard Peddicord, *The Sacred Monster of Thomism: An Introduction to the Life and Legacy of Reginald Garrigou-Lagrange, O.P.* (South Bend, IN: St Augustine's Press, 2005).

application of his work to present questions. In the period preceding de Lubac's work, its most significant representatives were the Dominicans, Ambroise Gardeil (1859-1931), Pierre Mandonnet (1858-1936), and Antonin Sertillanges (1863-1948).[94] In 1904, when the Dominicans were expelled from France, they established a house of formation dedicated to the kind of re-sourced Thomism they proposed to undertake at Le Saulchoir in Belgium.[95]

The third response to *Aeterni Patris* was a continuation of Gratry's scholastic Augustinianism, without as much regard for the call to Thomism. The most significant representative of this tradition was Maurice Blondel (1861-1949). Although Blondel was a layman and studied philosophy outside the scholastic tradition, he was a student of Léon Ollé-Laprune, who was in turn a student of Gratry. Ollé-Laprune mediated Gratry's Aegidianism to Blondel, and the latter's doctoral thesis *L'Action* gives that Aegidian-inspired doctrine of natural desire a turn-of-the-century subjectivist expression, even though explicit references to the Aegidian tradition had been lost in the interim between Gratry and Blondel.[96]

At the turn of the twentieth century, these three methodologies – a neo-scholastic Thomism, a re-sourced Thomism, and a re-sourced Augustinianism inspired by the Aegidian tradition – all flourished among French theologians.[97]

---

94. Guy Mansini, *What is a Dogma?* (Rome: Gregorian University, 1985), p. 239, n. 12.

95. See Flynn, '*Ressourcement*, Ecumenism, and Pneumatology', pp. 220-21. Chenu documents the historical study of theology at Le Saulchoir in Chenu, *Une école de théologie: Le Saulchoir* (Paris: Cerf, 1985). The text was Johann Adam Möhler, *Einheit in der Kirche oder*; english translation: *Unity in the Church or the Principle of Catholicism*, trans. Peter Erb (Washington, DC: CUA Press, 1996).

96. Maurice Blondel, *L'action; Essai d'une critique de la vie et d'une science de la pratique* (1893), 2nd ed. (Paris: Presses Universitaires de France, 1950). For the relationship between Blondel, Ollé-Laprune, and Gratry, see Reardon, *Liberalism and Tradition*, p. 192; McCool, *Nineteenth Century Scholasticism*, p. 272, n. 50; Darrell Jodock, *Catholicism Contending with Modernity: Roman Catholic Modernism and Anti-Modernism in Historical Context* (New York: Cambridge, 2000), pp. 157-58. Although Aquinas was not initially a significant influence on Blondel, Blondel did eventually incorporate Aquinas into his work. See Anna Fabriziani, *Blondel interprete di Tommaso: Tra rinascita del tomismo e condanna del pensiero modernista* (Padua: Antenore, 1984). Blondel's Aegidian insights were eventually brought within the post-Leonine Thomistic revival by Pierre Rousselot (1978-1915) and Joseph Maréchal (1878-1944). Cf. Pierre Rousselot, *L'Intellectualisme de Saint Thomas* (Paris: Félix Alcan, 1908); Joseph Maréchal, *Le point de départ de la métaphysique: Leçons sur le développement historique et théorique du problème de la connaissance, Cahier V: Le Thomisme devant la philosophie critique* (Paris: Félix Alcan, 1926).

97. One even finds healthy, critical interactions among the traditions. For a particularly edifying example, see Gardeil's critical but thoughtful responses to Blondel's *L'Action*: Ambroise Gardeil, 'Les exigences objectives de l'action', *Revue Thomiste* 6 (1898): pp. 125-38, 269-94; 'L'Action: Ses ressources subjectives',*Revue Thomiste* 7 (1899): pp. 23-39; 'Les ressources de vouloir', *Revue Thomiste* 7 (1899): pp. 447-61; 'Les ressources de la raison practique', *Revue Thomiste* 8 (1900): pp. 377-99; 'Ce qu'il y a de vrai dans le néo-Scotisme', *Revue thomiste* 8 (1900): 531-50, *Revue Thomise* 9 (1901): pp. 407-43.

However, it was not long before the first and third of these, the neo-Thomist and the re-sourced Augustinian, were brought into a sharp conflict concerning the social dimension of Christianity. The catalyst of this conflict was the Dreyfus Affair (1894–1906).

In 1894, Alfred Dreyfus, a Jewish army captain, was wrongfully convicted of selling state secrets to the Germans. When the spurious nature of his conviction became known two years later, the army acquitted the true culprit and allowed Dreyfus to remain imprisoned.[98] The political right, the anti-Dreyfusards, supported the army at all costs in the name of preserving national unity and security; the political left, the Dreyfusards, supported the individual rights of Dreyfus and his exoneration. Catholic politicians were mostly to be found among the anti-Dreyfusards.[99] They were led by the fallen-away Catholic-turned-atheist Charles Maurras (1868–1952), who had embraced nineteenth-century traditionalism without its Catholic trappings and turned to Rome as a source of authority and unity. Maurras's embrace of Rome entailed little regard for the need for grace to create and sustain authentic unity in any political endeavour – he was more interested in using Rome as support for the restoration of a monarchy.[100] The locus for this movement was the political organization Action française, whose motto, 'by all means necessary', spoke to its Machiavellian practices.[101]

In the midst of the Dreyfus Affair, Péguy issued his famous call to *ressourcement*. According to Péguy, what made the social aspect of French Catholicism so prone to Maurras's atheist traditionalism was that prominent Catholics had come to equate social progress in the Church with the gaining and preserving of political privileges for it. This was not a new phenomenon. Each of the three nineteenth-century ecclesiologies noted above relied upon some particular political structure. What was different at the turn of the century was the adoption of Machiavellian standards for achieving that political-ecclesial harmony.[102]

Without grace to overcome their Machiavellian scheming, Péguy observed that the French people lacked real unity. He explained this lack of unity in Augustinian terms. Anti-Dreyfusard Catholic politicians claimed that they were building up Augustine's City of God because they supported the political power of the Catholic Church in France, and that the true struggle of the City of God was directed outwards towards anti-Catholic Dreyfusards. On the contrary, the true struggle against the City of Man was *ad intra*, because in spite of their Catholicism,

---

98. On the history of the controversy, see Jean-Denis Bredin, *The Affair: The Case of Alfred Dreyfus*, trans. Jeffrey Mehlman (New York: George Braziller, 1983).

99. See Peter Bernardi, *Maurice Blondel, Social Catholicism, and Action Française: The Clash over the Church's Role in Society during the Modernist Era* (Washington, DC: CUA Press, 2009), pp. 96–97.

100. Ibid., pp. 96–97. We may observe in Maurras's programme the concrete realization of Lamennais's fears.

101. Ibid., p. 98.

102. Péguy, 'Avertissement', xxii, xxvii–xxviii, xxx–xxxi.

anti-Dreyfusards were trying to force the disparate fragments of French society by a Machiavellian lust for power instead of drawing people together by grace.[103] Given the inherent limitations of anti-Dreyfusard Catholicism, Péguy feared that the people might succumb to atheistic socialism. Although socialism would mean a loss of faith, the only true source of unity, socialism had the appearance of unity, because by force it tied together and submitted all the disparate factions of French society to the lust for power as exercised by the State.[104]

To oppose the *apparent* unity of socialism, only a unity born of a more authentic vision of the Catholic faith would suffice. But recovering an authentic sense of unity would require a revolution. Not that Catholics should take up arms in an attempt to restore the *ancien régime* displaced by the French Revolution – that would be the 'arbitrary and academic transfer of power' that Péguy excluded at the outset – rather, Catholics would need to take a revolutionary look at their faith: backwards to the sources of scripture and tradition from which faith wells up, and forwards towards the complete transformation of individuals and of their society by the love that faith inspires.[105] Moreover, this transformation would require men of genius,[106] because men of genius, like grace, bring to life 'the intuition of an unrealized reality'.[107] That true unity was as yet an unrealized vision for the Church in France.

---

103. Ibid., xxvii.

104. Ibid., l–li. Péguy's concern was well-founded in history. Socialists in the early nineteenth century had proposed socialism as a specific replacement for Christianity. As an example of this tendency, see Saint-Simon's *Nouveau Christianisme: Dialogues entre un conservateur et un novateur* (Paris: A. Sautelet, 1825), cited in Carol Harrison, *Romantic Catholics: France's Postrevolutionary Generation in Search of a Modern Faith* (Ithaca: Cornell University Press, 2014), pp. 4–5.

105. In his call to look beyond earthly ambitions, Péguy was prescient. The following year (1905) the French government passed a law establishing the separation of Church and state, and appropriating all Church property for the state. This effectively ended any reasonable hope that the anti-Dreyfusards harboured of successfully restoring the political privileges that the Church lost in the French Revolution.

106. Péguy, 'Avertissement', xliv. Having run out of space in the actual journal, Péguy continued his call for men of vision on the back cover.

Nothing can measure up to an entire life, such as the Christian and in particular the Catholic life, other than the entirety of a new life, the entirety of a revolution (i.e. digging more deeply); the Latins called [revolution] a *res nova*; we call it a *new life*, because a revolution is at its heart digging more deeply into the untapped resources of the interior life; and it is for this reason that the great men of revolutionary action are first of all the great men of a great interior life, the meditative ones, the contemplative ones; people do not start revolutions by an outward motion [*en dehors*]; they start them by an inward one [*en dedans*].

107. Ibid. See also Charles Péguy, 'Supplément aux "Vies parallèles de M. Lanson et de M. Andler,"' *Cahiers de la quinzaine*, ser. 14, vol. 9 (22 April 1913): p. 41. Péguy's association between genius and grace has antecedents in the traditionalism of Joseph de Maistre (1753–1821). See Reardon, *Liberalism and Tradition*, p. 35.

Péguy's call was not immediately heeded. Shortly after the conclusion of the Dreyfus Affair, Pedro Descoqs began a series of articles in defence of Charles Maurras and Action française. Descoqs argued that, although Maurras's atheistic political ideas were not in all ways compatible with the Catholic faith, it would be permissible for Catholics to collaborate with him because his system respected the distinction between the temporal and spiritual orders, could be made to respect the indirect power of the Church in temporal affairs, and could potentially be brought critically to respect the place of the Church in questions of mutual concern.[108]

Blondel was heavily critical of Descoqs's support for Maurras. Blondel made similar arguments against Descoqs as Péguy had made against the whole nineteenth-century French *ressourcement* project: Descoqs wed Catholicism and monarchy together in such a way as to subordinate the Catholic faith to a political agenda and to abandon Catholic morals altogether – he thereby failed to appreciate the transcendent end of man beyond this world, the transcendent end of the Church beyond particular political programmes, and to observe the moral consistency required of Catholics in their practical endeavours.[109] In response, Descoqs attacked the heart of Blondel's ecclesiology by questioning his Aegidian anthropology: man cannot have a natural desire for the vision of God because that compromises the gratuity of grace by proportioning it to nature.[110] Given that the whole of man's nature can be fulfilled in a naturally achievable reality (which grace penetrates and elevates, but which has a completeness to itself), there is no harm in forming a political alliance even with atheists, provided that their conception of political society is sufficiently similar to that which follows properly from the principles of unaided reason.[111]

Blondel responded in turn that Descoqs made grace a purely extrinsic addition to an already complete human nature, and so created a naturalist view of human nature.[112] Blondel's most poignant observation was that Descoqs made conversion into the mere act of submission, just as we have observed above with regard to the nineteenth-century traditionalists.[113] Descoqs responded that, because Blondel made a desire for the beatific vision a constitutive feature of

---

108. For a complete account of Descoqs articles in support of Maurras and Action française, see Bernardi, *Maurice Blondel, Social Catholicism, and Action Française*, pp. 89–118, esp. pp. 107–8.

109. See Bernardi, *Maurice Blondel, Social Catholicism, and Action Française*, pp. 128–38, especially pp. 131–33. Blondel did not hesitate to accuse Descoqs directly of Machiavellianism (p. 135).

110. Bernardi, *Maurice Blondel, Social Catholicism, and Action Française*, p. 151. Descoqs was willing to acknowledge that the alliance between Catholicism and monarchy was contingent on account of political circumstances, not necessary. See ibid., p. 150.

111. Bernardi, *Maurice Blondel, Social Catholicism, and Action Française*, pp. 151–55.

112. Ibid., pp. 167–68.

113. Ibid.

human nature, he compromised the gratuity of grace,[114] the objective character of revelation,[115] and the integrity of the natural order.[116] With these attacks, the nature of post-Reformation Augustinian *ressourcement* hung in the balance. It had been built on man's natural desire to see God, but if that desire could not be maintained, then the early modern Augustinianisms, as well as the nineteenth-century ecclesiologies built on them, would collapse.

De Lubac's Revolution

Prior to the First World War and before entering the Society of Jesus, de Lubac had read 'almost every word of Péguy', including Péguy's call to a revolutionary *ressourcement*.[117] He began to respond to Péguy's call shortly after entering the Society by embracing Blondel's re-sourced Augustinianism.[118] De Lubac did this because he saw in Blondel an authentic representative of a re-sourced theology that connected with the whole of the tradition.[119] One of de Lubac's first writings during his philosophical formation, 'The Desire for God in the Philosophy of Plotinus and of St. Augustine',[120] bears witness to the unity of the tradition as de Lubac perceived it. De Lubac reads Augustine as intimately connected with the theological events of nineteenth and twentieth-century France, interpreting him as holding a doctrine of natural desire nearly identical to the one held by Blondel, which de Lubac claims as a mean between the extremes of the 'proto-Ontologism' of Plotinus and the voluntarism of Protestantism.[121]

At the outset of his publishing career in the 1930s, de Lubac deepened his understanding of the ways in which contemporary concerns of the re-sourced Augustinian tradition related to the broader theological tradition. In one of de Lubac's first articles, 'Two Misguided Augustinians', he rediscovered the Aegidian tradition that had inspired Gratry and that had been mediated to him through Blondel.[122] In a subsequent article, 'Remarks on the History of the Word "Supernatural"' (1934), he applied this discovery to contemporary questions. Garrigou-Lagrange, the foremost Dominican representative of neo-scholasticism,

---

114. Ibid., p. 186.
115. Ibid., p. 191.
116. Ibid., p. 199.
117. Georges Chantraine, *Henri de Lubac*, 2 vols (Paris: Cerf, 2007–2009), pp. 1:82–83, 106, 119, 177, 211. See also de Lubac, ASC, p. 138.
118. Chantraine, *Henri de Lubac*, p. 2:161.
119. Henri de Lubac, *Letter 25 to Yves de Montcheuil*, quoted in ibid., p. 2:535.
120. The manuscript for this conference, known to Chantraine, has unfortunately been lost, along with de Lubac's precise references to passages in the works of Plotinus and Augustine. Fortunately, Chantraine published a summary of its contents together with several extracts of the text in *Henri de Lubac*, pp. 2:392–400.
121. *Henri de Lubac*, pp. 2:396–97.
122. Ibid.

had recently accused the Aegidian tradition of Baianism, a condemned form of misguided Augustinianism, for failing to distinguish between a natural order with a naturally achievable end and a supernatural order with a supernaturally achievable end.[123] De Lubac argues that Garrigou-Lagrange was mistaken: not only had Berti's Aegidianism avoided that critique, but in doing so it gave the authentic interpretation of Thomas Aquinas.[124] Although neo-scholastics accused re-sourced Augustinians of compromising the gratuity of grace, they had missed the theological mark and had lost their patron in the process. They came far closer to Baius than the re-sourced Augustinians had, because the neo-scholastic conception of nature was closed to the vision of God.[125]

Following in the tradition of Péguy and Blondel, de Lubac did not confine his reflections on nature and grace to the case of the individual Christian. In answer to Péguy's call, he sought to find a way to re-source the entirety of the Catholic faith in such a way as to propose a unity for the French people that did not confound progress in the Christian life with progress in a particular form of political life. Inspired in part by his nascent anthropological work, de Lubac's first contribution to this effort was his landmark book, *Catholicism*.

Catholicism utilizes a retrieval of the patristic tradition in order to show how the transcendence of the human person is as social as it is personal. According to de Lubac, this reality is most evident in the Eucharist. The Eucharist is

---

123. Henri de Lubac, 'Remarques sur l'histoire du mot "Surnaturel"', *Nouvelle Revue Théologique* 61 (1934): p. 248, n. 2. Michel de Bay (commonly known as Michael Baius; 1513–1589) was a professor at the University of Louvain in Belgium. Baius had an effectively Calvinist view of Adam: when God made Adam, there was no real distinction between the gifts given to form Adam's nature and the gifts of grace elevating that nature to the beatific vision. Consequently, man's exaltation to the beatific vision was due to the integrity of original nature and its exercise of free will to keep the law. Baius also had an effectively Calvinist view of the Fall: the Fall so wounded human nature that it lost the freedom to perform any virtuous action without grace – all of our actions outside a state of grace are sins. But, in opposition to Calvin, Baius retrieved Augustine's teaching on the freedom of the will as restored by grace. According to Baius, grace heals our wounded nature by enabling us to overcome concupiscence, restoring our free will, and enabling us to keep the law again.

Bainism was condemned as a theological system in 1564 by Pius IV in the Bull, *Ex omnibus afflictionibus* (DH 1847–1850; the full text of the condemnation can be found in DS 1901–1980), a confirmation which was reaffirmed in 1580 by Gregory XIII. See Philip Donnelly, 'Baius and Baianism', in *The New Catholic Encyclopedia*, 2nd ed. (Detroit: Gale, 2003), p. 2:19.

On Baianism in general as it relates to nature and grace, see See Baius, *De meritis operum*, lib. 1, cap. 2, in *Opuscula theologica* (Louvain: Joannes Bogard, 1566), pp. 5–7; Gemma Simmonds, 'Jansenism: An Early *Ressourcement* Movement?' in *Ressourcement*, p. 25. On the dependence of Jansen on Baius, see de Lubac, AMT, p. 36.

124. De Lubac, 'Remarques sur l'histoire du mot "Surnaturel"', p. 248, n. 2.

125. We can detect here an implicit restatement of Blondel's critique of Descoqs, something which de Lubac would have undoubtedly read.

source of social unity because it is the Sacrament of Unity: the eucharistic celebration signifies the unity of the Church and causes it by knitting the members of the Church into the Body of Christ.[126] In this suggestion, de Lubac acknowledges a debt to Guéranger. He quotes a 1912 article which explicitly references Guéranger's most famous work as the proximate source of this idea: 'Contemporary authors do not seem to have attached great importance to this unitive force of the Eucharist. If *The Liturgical Year* and a few rare works on mysticism had not been at pains to revive it, it would have been in our days a forgotten document.' Far from purging himself of the more recent past, de Lubac sees himself as elevating it into a more comprehensive theological synthesis and purifying it of political attachments. He retrieves Guéranger's emphasis on the eucharistic liturgy as the source of our social unity, but purifies it of the need for any particular earthly political goal as the necessary correlate of human unity in the Church.[127]

As the complement to a eucharistic focus in ecclesiology, de Lubac says that an appreciation for patristic ecclesiology requires a return to the spiritual reading of scripture.[128] The spiritual reading of scripture, like the ecclesiology which it undergirds, happens on analogy with an Aegidian anthropology. Just like human nature has a desire for completion by grace, and humanity for completion by the Church, so also the letter of the Old Testament is completed by a spiritual reading enlightened by the New.[129] If we read the Testaments in this manner, then the social nature of salvation comes to light all throughout the persons, nations, and objects of the Old Testament,[130] as well as the parables of the Gospel.[131]

Inasmuch as *Catholicism* articulated an ecclesiological and biblical synthesis inspired by a retrieval of an early nineteenth-century ecclesiology and an early modern anthropology, it also set the course for de Lubac's career of *ressourcement* because it did three things: it mapped out the relationship between de Lubac's *ressourcement* and previous French efforts at *ressourcement*, it mapped out the relationships among all the various theological fields in which de Lubac would engage in *ressourcement*, and it showed how each could contribute to the complete revolution that Péguy called for in the Church.[132] Over the next several decades, de Lubac followed this plan of renewal: he developed his ecclesiology in *Corpus Mysticum* (1944) and *The Drama of Atheist Humanism* (1944), his anthropology in *Surnaturel* (1946), and his biblical studies in *History and Theology* (1950).

---

126. Ibid., p. 89.
127. C, pp. 114-15, 119-21. See Paul McPartlan, *The Eucharist Makes the Church: Henri de Lubac and John Zizioulas in Dialogue* (Edinburgh: T&T Clark, 1993), p. 12.
128. C, 165-216.
129. Ibid., pp. 170-83. See McPartlan, *The Eucharist Makes the Church*, p. 4.
130. C, pp. 183-200.
131. Ibid., pp. 200-16.
132. On the programmatic nature of *Catholicism*, see McPartlan, *The Eucharist Makes the Church*, pp. 3-24.

The necessity of completing the renewal begun by *Catholicism* was made all the more urgent by contemporaneous events in French history. In 1940, Philippe Pétain assumed autocratic control of Vichy France. As de Lubac observed, Pétain was in many ways to Vichy France what Maurras was to the Third Republic: a non-Catholic who valued the Catholic Church for the central authority that it could provide, who was willing to make common cause with Catholics insofar as they supported his political agenda, and who was willing to advance his political aims by any means necessary.[133] Maurras was even said to have remarked that Pétain's appointment was a 'heavenly surprise'.[134] The situation spurred de Lubac into scholarly action.

In 1944, de Lubac published a pair of scholarly works that addressed the situation in Vichy France: *Corpus Mysticum* and *The Drama of Atheist Humanism*. While the two are not ordinarily considered together, the connection between them becomes clear if we consider the parallels between Pétain and Maurras, as well as the pattern according to which de Lubac sought to surpass nineteenth-century ecclesiologies in *Catholicism*. In *Catholicism*, the Eucharist takes the place that particular political structures did in nineteenth-century ecclesiologies. As the focal point of man's temporal unity, it unites human beings by grace into an ecclesial unity. However, in *Corpus Mysticum* de Lubac observes a difficulty in the history of scholastic ecclesiology that threatened the ecclesial synthesis of *Catholicism*: scholastic theologians referred to the Eucharist as the 'real' body of Christ, but to the Church as the 'mystical' body of Christ.[135] By distinguishing mystical from real, these theologians made it seem as though the Church was not really the body of Christ, and that as a 'metaphorical' body it could be replaced or at least imitated by various other mystical bodies.[136] In the *Drama of Atheist Humanism*, de Lubac explores the logic of the various other mystical bodies proposed for mankind as alternate 'churches', especially those with a similarity to Nazi socialism.[137] In this light, *Corpus Mysticum* shows that the Eucharist, as the

---

133. Henri de Lubac, CR, p. 20, n. 12; ctd. in Bernardi, *Maurice Blondel, Social Catholicism, and Action Française*, p. 230, n. 99.

134. While any number of scholars note the comment, Eugen Weber traces its origin to a newspaper article that Maurras published. See Eugen Weber, *Action Française: Royalism and Reaction in Twentieth Century France* (Stanford: Stanford University Press, 1962), pp. 446–47.

135. CM, p. 248.

136. Ibid., p. 249. De Lubac also anticipates his later work on scriptural exegesis by noting that the same real/mystical distinction was mapped onto the distinction between literal and spiritual exegesis. The implication of that set of distinctions was that literal exegesis and the historical critical study of it finds 'real' meaning, while spiritual exegesis does not. '… A temptation developed here, in the case of the Church, precisely as in that of Scripture: the temptation of no longer seeing anything in this metaphor except the metaphor itself, and of considering "mystical" as a watering-down of "real" or of "true."'

137. On the composition of this work, see ASC, p. 40.

one body of Christ, knits those who receive it into an ecclesial body which is just as real, and just as one, as the Eucharist itself.[138]

That de Lubac intended an oblique criticism of atheistic authoritarians such as Maurras and Pétain can be gleaned from an addition which de Lubac included in *Surnaturel: Études historiques* (1946).[139] In that work, which de Lubac used to deepen his anthropology, de Lubac rarely references contemporary events overtly. But at one point he makes an allusion to them which, like his reference to Garrigou-Lagrange in 'Two Misguided Augustinians', shows how he aligns neo-scholastic conceptions of man with traditionalist ones, and how his practice of *ressourcement* is consequently a response to Péguy's call. In a section of *Surnaturel* that reprints 'Two Misguided Augustinians', de Lubac adds a new footnote that explicitly associates traditionalists and Baianists, just as he had previously associated traditionalists and neo-scholastics.[140] Using traditionalism as a middle term with which to connect neo-scholasticism with Baianism makes clear how de Lubac perceived the influence of neo-scholasticism in his day: by separating man from the vision of God, it lapsed into the same sort of enlightenment naturalism which had bound traditionalism as well as the initial nineteenth-century responses to it.

---

138. De Lubac, CM, p. 251. 'Eucharistic realism and ecclesial realism: these two realisms support one another, each is the guarantee of the other ... Today, it is above all our faith in the "real presence," made explicit thanks to centuries of controversy and analysis, that introduces us to faith in the ecclesial body. ...' De Lubac observes that *Corpus Mysticum* was mostly written prior to the Second World War, and came together as his own personal reflections in preparation to be an examiner on a doctoral thesis on Florus of Lyons (d. c. 860). See ASC, p. 29. However, de Lubac himself draws the connections between his work in *Corpus Mysticum* and contemporary events in the conclusion to the work, which was presumably authored more immediately prior to its publication during the War.

To the set of concerns outlined here we can also join those expressed by de Lubac in *The Un-Marxian Socialist: A Study of Proudhon* (London: Sheed and Ward, 1948). The original French, *Proudhon et le christianisme* (Paris: Éditions du Seuil, 1945), was published only a year after *Corpus Mysticum* and the *The Drama of Atheist Humanism*.

139. In that work, de Lubac republished his article on Baius and Jansenius along with three other articles that he had written in the meantime, and a variety of material that he composed while in hiding during the war from the Gestapo. The purpose of this collection was to determine whether or to what extent the early modern Thomistic commentators had faithfully interpreted Aquinas on the question of man's desire for God. The work effectively reiterates the controversy from the 1910s between Descoqs and Blondel, bringing out the anthropology at the heart of ecclesiology, and advocating the Aegidian tradition which Blondel represented. See ASC, pp. 35–36. The articles that went into Surnaturel, in addition to those already referenced, were 'Esprit et Liberté dans la tradition', *Bulletin de Littérature Ecclésiastique* 40 (1939): pp. 121–50, 189–207; 'La rencontre de *superadditum* et *supernaturale* dans la théologie médiévale', *Revue du Moyen Âge Latin* 1 (1945): pp. 27–34.

140. Henri de Lubac, *Surnaturel: Études historiques* (Paris: Aubier, 1946), p. 19, n. 1.

In order to escape naturalism and so to avoid lapsing into its contemporary manifestation in atheist socialism, as de Lubac had warned in *The Drama of Atheist Humanism*, and in order to preserve the ecclesial Augustinian unity-in-charity, such as de Lubac had proposed as an alternative in *Catholicism* and defended in *Corpus Mysticum*, de Lubac offered *Surnaturel* as an anthropological apologetic for the Aegidian doctrine of natural desire upon which his proposal was built. In that work, he calls the Aegidian tradition of the Order of the Hermits of St Augustine 'Augustinianism *par excellence*'; he praises its members for preserving the authentic doctrine of Augustine, the *Doctor Gratiae*, even as they gave the authentic interpretation of Aquinas, the *Doctor Angelicus*.[141] In short, de Lubac exalts the Aegidian tradition as the salve for enlightenment rationalism, and defends it as the basis from which to mount an adequate response.

The last – but by no means the least – piece of the puzzle was scripture. As de Lubac noted in *Catholicism*, the 'deeper' ecclesiology that he was proposing, grounded in the Fathers and revived by Guéranger in the nineteenth-century, could only be built on a reading of scripture that was grounded in the spiritual sense. In order to recover the spiritual reading of scripture, de Lubac re-sourced the spiritual exegesis of Origen – first by an edition of his Homilies on Exodus published as the sixteenth volume of *Sources Chrétiennes* (1947),[142] then as a monograph devoted to the study of Origen, *History and Spirit* (1950).[143] In the latter, he shows how Origen, following the way in which Christ and the authors of the New Testament relate to the Old Testament,[144] provides a pattern for the interpretation of scripture which, without denying the importance of the literal sense,[145] establishes the spiritual sense as the development of the literal sense guided by the analogy of faith.[146] Such a spiritual sense is in every way as 'real' as the literal sense; it is the sense which re-sourced Augustinian anthropology naturally calls forth;[147] and it is the sense which is embodied in the New Testament itself.[148] Yet, just like a re-sourced Augustinian anthropology can only be fully grasped in the analogy of faith, which illumines its object, so likewise can the spiritual sense of scripture only be fully grasped in the analogy of faith in the

---

141. Ibid., pp. 164–65.
142. Origen, *Homelies sur l'Exode*, ed. Henri de Lubac, trans. P. Fortier (Paris: Cerf, 1947).
143. See de Lubac's remarks on Möhler's understanding of spiritual exegesis in HS, pp. 431–32. The conclusion to that work was translated previously in Henri de Lubac, *The Sources of Revelation*, trans. Luke O'Neill (New York: Herder and Herder, 1968), pp. 1–84.
144. HS, pp. 456–67.
145. Ibid., pp. 439–41.
146. Ibid., pp. 446–50.
147. See, for instance, HS, p. 439, n. 26, where de Lubac observes the manner in which the Jansenist Antoine Arnauld, embued with the doctrine of a natural desire for the vision of God, saw the *literal* sense of Old Testament prophecy in its reference to Christ. So also p. 488, n. 191, where he makes a similar comment.
148. Ibid., pp. 456–57.

one who inspires it,[149] and which opens up into the medieval pattern of fourfold exegesis: literal, allegorical, moral, anagogical.[150]

Conclusion

Precisely because de Lubac's *ressourcement* is a revolution inspired by Péguy's deepening and not by Chenu's and Congar's liquidation, a Lubacian *ressourcement* has the potential to bear longer lasting fruit. A revolution of liquidation, which casts aside one period in order to retrieve another, can only happen once; after it locates the object of its search, it can either examine the object ever more closely or it can defend the necessity of having sought it. Those two possibilities can lead to two opposite dangers: those who emphasize defending what has been done face the danger of embattlement; those who emphasize a closer examination of what has been found face the danger of historicism, getting lost in a jungle of obscure historical figures and contexts and losing their way back to the theological tradition which gives those figures life. Not that these dangers are unique to those who engage in *ressourcement* – it is equally possible for those who refuse to engage in *ressourcement* to fall prey to similar dangers: those who emphasize defending what has been achieved in the scholastic commentarial tradition can fall into the same kind of embattlement as those who reject that tradition; those who emphasize an ever closer study of what has been achieved in the scholastic commentarial tradition can fall prey to an obscuritanism which is every bit as disconnected from the unity of tradition as a re-sourced historicism.

Between these extremes of embattlement and historicism/obscuritanism lies de Lubac's virtuous mean: an affirmation of the unity of the theological tradition, the refusal to discount any part of it, and an insistence on maintaining the connection of each part with the whole. In de Lubac's day, Daniélou was not wrong to say that the Fathers, the liturgy, and the scripture were in need of retrieval to be re-integrated into mainstream theological discourse. But in our own day, it may be time to ask whether the theology of the mid-sixteenth to mid-nineteenth centuries awaits a similar *ressourcement*. The renewal of theology in the twentieth century, which owes so much to de Lubac, is indebted to that long period whose theologians de Lubac knew and read, and whose ideas he brought forth into a re-sourced synthesis based upon man's natural desire for the vision of God, the call to society's transformation in the Eucharist, and nourished by the perfection of the Old Testament by the New. That vision of the Catholic faith, which has not been entirely alien to any period in the theological tradition, is what de Lubac offered to the twentieth century; it was casting more light on that vision, not casting off a period where it was hard to find, which formed the heart of de Lubac's *ressourcement*.

149. Ibid., pp. 461–62.
150. Ibid., pp. 467–80.

Chapter 5

HENRI DE LUBAC AND THE SECOND VATICAN COUNCIL

Aaron Riches

'If now we speak [more and more] of *conceptio christiana*, [it is because] we no longer speak of *fides christiana*.'[1] Henri de Lubac made this remark in his diary six months before the close of the Second Vatican Council. With this private, pithy, and brutal judgement, de Lubac summed up, as he saw it, the religious ethos of the bishops and *periti* there gathered. It is not in the Council. It is not a happy judgement.

The whole of de Lubac's relationship to the Council can be summed up in the single provocation of *ressourcement*: return to the true source, which is *fides*

For Professor Tracey Rowland

1. Henri de Lubac, *Carnets du Concile*, 2 vols (Paris: Cerf, 2007), vol. 2, p. 374. For the most part de Lubac's works are cited from the *Oeuvres complètes*, ed. George Chantraine, S.J., et al. (Paris: Cerf, 1999-), in which case the first time I cite the book, the book title is followed by 'OC'. Citations of de Lubac's *Exégèse Médiévale. Les quatre sens de l'écriture* are to the first edition: Paris: Aubier-Montaigne, 1959–1964. In citing de Lubac's works, I have, for convenience sake, included in square brackets page references to the current English editions, when I have had them at hand. On the history of de Lubac and the Council, the invaluable resource on which I have relied is the fourth volume of Chantraine's biography, George Chantraine and Marie-Gabrielle Lemaire, *Henri de Lubac*, vol. 4, *Concile et après-Concile* (1960–1991), *Études Lubaciennes*, vol. 9 (Paris: Cerf, 2013). Additionally, I have used significantly Padre Ricardo Aldana, SDJ's synthesis and commentary on the *Carnets*, 'Las *Notas del Concilio* de Henri de Lubac', *Toletana* 18 (2008), pp. 357–78, in addition to which I benefited from personal conversations with him on the subject. An initial source for me was William L. Portier, 'What Kind of a World of Grace? De Lubac and the Council's Christological Center', *Communio* 39 (2012), pp. 136–51. The literature on the history of Vatican II is massive. The major source is the classic history as told by the so-called Bologna school: Giuseppe Alberigo (ed.), *Storia del Concilio Vaticano II*, 5 vols (Bologna: Il Mulino, 1995–2001). For the English, see Giuseppe Alberigo and Joseph A. Komonchak (eds), *History of Vatican II*, 5 vols (Maryknoll, NY: Orbis, 1995–2006). I have not had access to the English and so have relied on the Spanish edition, see Giuseppe Alberigo (ed.), *Historia del Concilio Vaticano II*, 5 vols (Salamanca: Ediciones Sigueme, 1999–2008). The

christiana. *Ressourcement* was never, for de Lubac, reducible to the retrieval of patristic theology, recovery of a pre-modern construal of the relation of grace and nature, or even the renewal of a Christological hermeneutic of Scriptural interpretation.[2] Particular acts of *ressourcement* are useful only insofar as they provoke the essential return of the human heart to the 'one thing necessary' (cf. Lk 10.42). For de Lubac, the greatest risk to modern theology, and modern Christianity as a whole, was that it would, from within, convert itself into a counterfeit of faith, that it would become a mere *conceptio*, an abstraction that could no longer penetrate the whole life of the human being. And herein lies the deep coherence of de Lubac's critique both of the pre-conciliar theological modus operandi and the post-conciliar theological avant-garde: both tended to reduce the Christian experience to a discourse, a structure of moral or ethical 'values', a system of thought, a cultural agenda, a social project.

For de Lubac, the arid and overly systematized 'orthodoxy' that reigned in the manualism of the Roman schools before the Council typified a certain practice of reducing theology to a dialectic. It did so to the extent that it conceived 'revelation' primarily as a series of supernatural *data* that, now 'revealed', furnished the first principles of the 'system' of theological science. On this scheme, the method of knowing was largely abstracted from the human experience of faith, from the human encounter with Christ. According to de Lubac, after the Council, the obscurantist character of the Roman schools gave way to progressivism, which sought now to 'up-date' Christianity in terms of conceptual paradigms that variously re-conceived theology and the tradition, correcting their supposed deficiencies and developing doctrine in accordance with new ideological paradigms that often attempted to marry the theological virtue of hope with human social betterment. De Lubac understood the malady of the old manualism and the new progressivism as one and the same: the loss of theology's concrete contact with the 'one thing necessary'.

'Bologna school' is not without its serious critiques, and so alongside Alberigo's volumes one should keep at hand Agostino Marchetto, *The Second Vatican Ecumenical Council: A Counterpoint for the History of the Council*, trans. Kenneth D. Whitehead (Chicago, IL: Scranton University Press, 2010). More manageable historical sources include: John W. O'Malley, *What Happened at Vatican II?* (Cambridge, MA: Harvard University Press, 2008); Ralph M. Wiltgen, S.V.D., *The Rhine Flows into the Tiber: A History of Vatican II* (Rockford, IL: Tan Books, 1985); Giuseppe Alberigo, *A Brief History of Vatican II*, trans. Matthew Sherry (Maryknoll, NY: Orbis, 2006); and Roberto de Mattei, *The Second Vatican Council: An Unwritten Story*, trans. Michael M. Miller, et al. (Fitzwilliam, NH: Loreto Publications, 2012). I have also frequently consulted the diary of Yves Congar, *My Journal of the Council*, trans. Mary John Ronayne, O.P., et al. (Collegeville, MI: Liturgical Press, 2012).

2. Hence the limit of Robin Darling Young, 'A Soldier of the Great War: Henri de Lubac and the Patristic Sources for a Premodern Theology', in James L. Heft, S. M. and John O'Malley, S. J. (eds), *After Vatican II: Trajectories and Hermeneutics* (Grand Rapids, MI: Eerdmans, 2012), pp. 134–63.

My purpose in this chapter is to give a preliminary account of the unity of de Lubac's contribution to Vatican II along the foregoing lines. This unity is realized across three broad contributions: (1) the influence of de Lubac's pre-conciliar work; (2) his role as a *peritus*; and (3) his theological response to the post-conciliar crisis. Perhaps the most remarkable – and indeed paradoxical – fact of de Lubac's trifold contribution concerns how in each case his contribution was simultaneously understated and decisive.

De Lubac's Key Pre-Conciliar Provocation

Cardinal Giuseppe Siri, in his trenchant 1980 critique of post-conciliar theology *Getsemani: Riflessioni sul Movimento Teologico Contemporaneo*, singled out a putatively erroneous understanding of the relation of grace and nature as the fundamental error of the post-conciliar theology.[3] The chief source of this theological error, Siri argued, flowed from de Lubac's *Surnaturel* (1946). But if the *Surnaturel* thesis was the font of this putative error, in *Getsemani* Siri focused on the attendant Christocentric anthropology de Lubac proposed already in 1938, in *Catholicisme: Les aspects sociaux du dogme*. Siri writes:

> Father de Lubac says that Christ in revealing the Father and in being revealed by him completes the revelation of man to himself. But what can be the meaning of this statement? Either Christ is only a man, or else man is divine. These conclusions cannot be so tidily expressed; nonetheless they always determine that the notion of the supernatural is implicit in human nature itself. And hence, unwittingly, the door thereby opens to a fundamental anthropocentrism.[4]

One of the towering figures of the so-called conservative minority at the Council and linked to the *Coetus Internationalis Patrum* (which included cardinals Ottaviani and Rufini, as well as Archbishop Marcel Lefebvre), Siri knew well that the Council had made its own these words of de Lubac's *Catholicsme* (1938). *Gaudium et Spes* 22 declares: 'Christ ... in the revelation of the mystery of the Father and His Love, fully reveals man to man himself.'[5] A son of the Church who

---

3. This is also the position of Lawrence Feingold, and is a motor driving his critique of de Lubac in *The Natural Desire to See God According to St. Thomas Aquinas and His Interpreters*, 2nd ed. (Naples, FL: Sapientia Press of Ave Maria University, 2010).

4. Cardinal Giuseppe Siri, *Getsemani: Riflessioni sul Movimento Teologico Contemporaneo* (Roma: Fraternità della Santissima Verginia Maria, 1980), p. 56.

5. *Gaudium et Spes* 22. There are others of the same era who also anticipate this formulation of *Gaudium et Spes* 22, cf.: Étienne Gilson, *Christianisme et philosophie* (Paris: Vrin, 1936), pp. 147–49; Karl Barth, *Church Dogmatics*, III/2, *The Doctrine of Creation*, trans. Harold Knight, et al. (Edinburgh: T&T Clark, 1960), p. 50; and Jean Mouroux, *The Meaning of Man*, trans. A. H. G. Downes (New York: Sheed & Ward, 1952), pp. 134–42. On *Gaudium et Spes* 22 generally, see Francisco A. Castro Pérez, *Cristo y cada hombre: Hermenéutica y recepción de una enseñanza del Concilio Vaticano II* (Rome: Gregorian & Biblical Press, 2011).

would not dare accuse the Council directly, Siri thus took covert aim at it and at a precise point at which the theology of de Lubac was most palpable. The fact that by the end of 1980 the newly elected Pope John Paul II would prominently invoke these words of *Gaudium et Spes* 22 in both of his first two encyclicals could not have boded well in the eyes of the stately Genoese Cardinal.[6]

Catholicisme: Christocentrism and *communio*

Joseph Ratzinger famously described de Lubac's *Catholicsme* (1938) as 'a key reading event' on his own theological trajectory.[7] According to Ratzinger, the book singularly anticipated the theological achievement of the Council, rightly understood,[8] because it broke open a 'narrow-minded individualistic Christianity'.[9] It did so by recovering the centrality of *communio*, the inner unity of difference that is the 'idea of the Catholic, the all-embracing, the inner unity of I and Thou and We', showing that this is not 'one chapter of theology among others', but rather 'is the key that opens the door to the proper understanding of the whole'.[10] At the centre of this vision is the person of Jesus Christ, who makes the Trinitarian love at the source of being 'incarnate', and so is himself the principle of unity who illumines the whole.[11] The core of this vision is summed up in the sentence which provoked the critique of Siri: 'Christ, in revealing the Father and being revealed by him, accomplished the revelation of man to himself.'[12]

If *Catholicisme* refocused the anthropological question on *communio* and the Christocentric heart of what it means to be human, it did so by clarifying the internal relation between anthropology and ecclesiology. The first part of de Lubac's book is, in this regard, most decisive. The key here is the social dynamic of redemption, which implies the recovery of the doctrine of the 'fall' as a fall from unity, from *communio*, into fragmentation and isolation.[13] Redemption

---

6. Cf. John Paul II, '*Dives in misericordia* (1980) 1; *Redemptor hominis* (1979) 8 and 10.

7. Joseph Ratzinger, *Milestones: Memoirs 1927–1977*, trans. Erasmo Leiva-Merikakis (San Francisco: Ignatius Press, 1998), p. 98.

8. Joseph Ratzinger, *Principles of Catholic Theology: Building Stones for a Fundamental Theology*, trans. Sr. Mary Frances McCarthy SND (San Francisco: Ignatius Press, 1987), pp. 48–52. Further on the importance of *Catholicisme* at Vatican II, see Joseph A. Komonchak, 'Interpreting the Council and Its Consequences', in James L. Heft, S. M. and John O'Malley, S. J. (eds), *After Vatican II: Trajectories and Hermeneutics* (Grand Rapids, MI: Eerdmans, 2012), pp. 164–72; 'Theology and Culture at Mid-Century: The example of Henri de Lubac', *Theological Studies* 51 (1990): pp. 579–602; K. Wittstadt, 'En vísperas del Concilio Vaticano II', in *Historia del Concilio Vaticano II*, vol. 1, pp. 373–465, at p. 424; O'Malley, *What Happened at Vatican II?*.

9. Joseph Cardinal Ratzinger, Foreword to de Lubac, C, p. 12.

10. Ibid., p. 11. Cf. Pope Benedict XVI, *Spe salvi*, 13–14.

11. Cf. Adrian J. Walker, 'Original Best: The "Coextensiveness" of Being and Love in Light of *Gaudium et Spes*, 22', *Communio* 39 (2012): pp. 49–65.

12. *Catholicisme*, p. 295 [ET: C, 339].

13. Cf. William T. Cavanaugh, *Theopolitical Imagination: Christian Practices of Space and Time* (New York: T & T Clark, 2002), pp. 10–15.

thus consists in the re-gathering of a broken humanity back into wholeness through the *communio* of the Church, Christ's body. Here it follows that 'if Jesus Christ is the sacrament of God, for us the Church is the sacrament of Christ, she represents him, with all the force of the ancient term: she renders him present in truth'.[14] Just as Christ is the 'sacrament' par excellence of the Father and his Love, so the Church is a 'sacrament' of the unity of humanity. And it is here, in *Catholicisme*, that de Lubac first begins to express the idea that will animate *Corpus Mysticum* (1944), that the Eucharist makes the Church, because the Synaxis of eucharistic gathering makes the *communio* that is the concrete sign in history of the re-gathering of broken humanity.[15] The conclusion of all of this implies a fully Christological and Trinitarian recovery of the theology of *communio* as a correlate of the classical transcendental *unitas* (*unum*). *Catholicisme*, by this turn, set an agenda to accomplish for the transcendental *unitas* what Hans Urs von Balthasar accomplished for the transcendental *pulchrum*.[16] In this context, the theological question of the natural desire of the human being for the supernatural and Christianity as the fundamental *unitas* of the human experience in all of its factors is raised such as it will furnish the basis of *Surnaturel* (1946): 'Outside of Christianity nothing arrives at its End, the only End toward which, without knowing, every human desire, every human endeavour tends: the embrace of God in Christ.'[17]

Surnaturel: *The Unity of Human Experience*

If the key theological impulse of de Lubac's work entails a new theological sensitivity to *communio* and *unitas*, this entailment was nowhere more contentiously articulated than in *Surnaturel*.[18] Reminding us that it was published with an *imprimatur* from 1942, Balthasar describes de Lubac emerging with it as a young David on the field of battle, who has come to make war 'against the Goliath of the modern rationalization and reduction to logic of the Christian mystery'.[19] At the core of this endemic modern reduction, so de Lubac wagers, is an abstract fragmentation of the human experience encapsulated in the neo-

14. C, p. 50 [ET: *Catholicism*, p. 76].
15. C, p. 50 [ET: *Catholicism*, p. 76].
16. Aidan Nichols, O.P., 'Henri de Lubac: Panorama and Proposal', *New Blackfriars* 93 (2012): pp. 1–31, esp. at pp. 29–30.
17. C, p. 186 [ET: *Catholicism*, p. 224].
18. On the current debate, see John Milbank, *The Suspended Middle: Henri de Lubac and the Debate Concerning the Supernatural* (London: SCM, 2005); Serge-Thomas Bonino, O.P. (ed.), *Surnaturel: A Controversy at the Heart of Twentieth-Century Thomistic Thought*, trans. Robert Williams and Matthew Levering (Ave Maria, FL: Sapientia Press, 2009); Nicholas J. Healy III, 'Henri de Lubac on Nature and Grace: A Note on Some Recent Contributions to the Debate', *Communio* 35 (2008): pp. 535–64; David Grumett, 'De Lubac, Grace, and the Pure Nature Debate', *Modern Theology* 31 (2015): pp. 123–46.
19. Hans Urs von Balthasar, *The Theology of Henri de Lubac* (San Francisco: Ignatius Press, 1991), p. 63.

scholastic doctrine of *natura pura*, which breaks Thomas's anthropology from the Augustinian lineage (*Fecisti nos ad te*), resulting in a *théologie séparée*, a theology confined to one side of a *duplex ordo* that no longer penetrates the whole realm of the human experience from its deepest root to its ultimate destiny.

Most Thomist commentators at the time responded negatively to *Surnaturel*. They were hostile both to the accusation that the standard 'Thomist' reading of Thomas was a modern misreading as well as to the theological suggestion that the gratuity of grace could be preserved in any way other than how they had heretofore conceived it. The agonizing debate came to its climax in 1950, with the publication of *Humani Generis*, in which Pius XII set a dogmatic limit against those who 'destroy the gratuity of the supernatural order, since God, they say, cannot (*non posse*) create intellectual beings without ordering and calling them to the beatific vision'.[20]

In his 1985 book-length interview with Angelo Scola, de Lubac insisted not only that he was not the target of the Pian limit but that, to the contrary, the limit in fact paraphrased, at the very point in question, what he himself had written in 'Le Mystère du surnaturel' (1949).[21] Therein, a year before *Humani Generis*, de Lubac clarified that 'if God had so willed it, he need not have given us being, and this being which he has given us he need not have called to vision of himself... God cannot be compelled to give me being, not from anything within or without. Nor can he be compelled by anything to imprint upon my being a supernatural finality'.[22] In his memoirs, de Lubac again claims to have read in the Pian limit only a positive allusion to 'Le Mystère du surnaturel'.[23] This, taken together with the fact that Pius 'avoided any mention of the famous "natura pura", which more than a few highly influential theologians... desired [the Pope] to canonise',[24] meant that, far from 'condemning' the *Surnaturel* thesis, *Humani Generis* realized the opposite. As de Lubac put it: '"Disappointment" does not describe it strongly enough, as a good theologian put it to me at the time, it was for them [the proponents of *natura pura*] a "boomerang"'.[25] It would take another fifteen years before the Magisterium explicitly endorsed the core proposal of de Lubac's thesis: that *hic et nunc* there is no *natura pura* since 'all men are in fact called to one and the same [supernatural] destiny'.[26]

---

20. Pius XII, *Humani Generis*, 26. Cf. Étienne Fouilloux, *Une Église en quête de liberté: La pensée catholique française entre modernisme et Vatican II, 1914–1962* (Paris: Desclée de Brouwer, 1998), pp. 149–310.

21. Henri Cardinal de Lubac [interviewed by Angelo Scola], *Entretien autour de Vatican II: Souvenirs et Réflexions* (Paris: Les Editions du Cerf, 1985), p. 13. Cf. Henri de Lubac, 'Le Mystère du surnaturel', *Recherches de Science Religieuse* 36 (1949): pp. 80–121.

22. De Lubac, 'Le Mystère du surnaturel', p. 104.

23. Henri de Lubac, *Mémoire sur l'occasion de mes écrits* (Paris: Cerf, 2006), p. 72 [ET: ASC, p. 71].

24. De Lubac, *Entretien autour de Vatican II*, p. 13.

25. Ibid., p. 13.

26. *Gaudium et Spes* 22.

De Lubac's Role as Peritus at the Council

The intended target of the Pian limit notwithstanding, the perception at the time was that *Humani Generis* did take aim at *Surnaturel*. From 1950 a cloud of misgiving hung over the theology of de Lubac, who thus was forced to live a 'suspended middle' of fidelity, the experience of a son of the Church suffering under the suspicion that he was her enemy.

On 9 October 1958, Pope Pius XII died. Nineteen days later, on 28 October, Angelo Giuseppe Roncalli was elected Pope John XXIII. Less than four months after his election, on 25 January 1959, the newly elected pope announced his intention to convoke the twenty-first Ecumenical Council, Vatican II. The preparatory commission of the Council was established on 17 May 1959, under the direction of Cardinal Domenico Tardini, to which de Lubac would be subsequently named a *peritus* in 1960.

* * *

In his celebrated eyewitness account of the Council, *The Rhine Flows into the Tiber* (1966), Ralph Wiltgen makes not one single reference to Henri de Lubac. The American journalist and priest, who contributed one of the most important first-hand accounts of the Council, who mentions by name almost all of the important *periti* – including Hans Küng, Joseph Razinger, Karl Rahner, John Courtney Murray, Edward Schillebeeckx, Gérard Philips, Sebastian Tromp, Aloys Grillmeier, and Yves Congar – makes no mention of de Lubac. From the textual evidence of Wiltgen's book, one would be forgiven to conclude that de Lubac was either absent the Council or merely a bit player. This lacuna, however, is not so much a journalistic failure of Wiltgen as it is a witness to the enigma of de Lubac: to the 'spectral' mode by which he was a spiritual protagonist and great presence at the Council.

Unlike Philips, Ratzinger, Murray, or Congar, de Lubac was not one of the great '*periti* redactors'; he did not work significantly on the drafting of texts himself. Unlike Küng, Rahner, or Tromp, de Lubac was not a mouthpiece or advocate for a theological 'party'. Indeed, he was not a primary 'actor at the Council' as George Chantraine puts it; rather he played the role of 'an advisor' – 'he listens and provides assistance to whoever request it'.[27] This readiness to assist, if it was never self-promoted, was also often not taken up by the Council Fathers. Writing during the third session of the Council, in October 1964, Congar attests to the isolation of de Lubac, especially among the French bishops: 'At midday I brought Fr. de Lubac back for lunch. I am astonished and saddened that the bishops no longer approach him and take so little interest in what a man of this quality could tell them.'[28] This isolation was perhaps due in part to de Lubac's refusal to take up and associate with any party or faction. He did not believe in theological 'positions'.

---

27. Chantraine and Lemaire, *Henri de Lubac*, vol. 4, p. 333.
28. Congar, *My Journal*, p. 629.

He recoiled equally from the 'progressivism' of the theologians associated with *Concilium*, as he did the 'integrism' of the Roman theological old guard. Indeed he saw in both the triumph of the same *conceptio christiana*.

But more, for de Lubac the Council was an event in the history of the Word made flesh, driven into the wilderness by the Spirit to be tempted. To be lived well it had to be lived as such. His presence at the Council and his understanding of it are well understood by the later description of the Council by Balthasar:

> The Council has made things harder, not easier. It has been a *Council of the Holy Spirit* like no other Council. For the Spirit proceeds from the Father and the Son; from the Father who created the world and its ordinances and from the Son who redeemed the world through the Cross and through utter renunciation.[29]

The difficulty of the Council, due to its docility to the Spirit who proceeds from the Father and Son, meant a new vulnerability, a riskful openness to temptation for the sake of sanctity. As such the provocation of the Council was not to the anxious pursuit of some self-determined theological 'position', but rather to be open to the same Spirit who lead the Son, and thus to live and judge the Council in the silence of prayerful listening. In the last session of the Council, amidst the noise of much political agitation, de Lubac jotted down a saying of Seraphim of Sarov: 'Keep your heart in peace, and a multitude around you will be saved'.[30] This injunction of the great Russian holy man sums up, on one level, de Lubac's disposition to the Council in session and what he took to be the central meaning and call of his own presence there.

And so he assumed a presence invisible to the daily happenings of the Council, while nevertheless he contributed his person fully, in the form of his pre-conciliar oeuvre and prayerful discernment of spirits guiding the Council in session.[31]

From 'Integrism': The Preparatory Commission

The indispensable source of understanding de Lubac at the Council lies in his *Carnets du Concile*, the personal journal he kept throughout the Council. The first entry is made on 25 July 1960, the day de Lubac received the letter from Cardinal Tardini notifying him of his appointment as a consultant to the Council's Preparatory Theological Commission. The last entry is made on 8 December 1965, the day of the Council's closing.

The inaugural session of the preparatory commission took place in Rome from 11 to 20 November 1960. In the *Carnets* de Lubac laments the reductive

---

29. Hans Urs von Balthasar, 'The Council of the Holy Spirit', in *Explorations in Theology*, vol. 3, *Creator Spirit*, trans. Brian McNeil, C.R.V. (San Francisco: Ignatius, 1993), pp. 245–68, at p. 263.
30. De Lubac, *Carnets*, vol. 2, p. 404.
31. Cf. Chantraine and Lemaire, *Henri de Lubac*, vol. 4, p. 333.

approach taken there regarding 'revelation', as if revelation was nothing more than a set of scholastic theses. 'No feeling of the simple grandeur of the faith of the Church [as something] to proclaim.'[32] De Lubac was impressed by a serious lack of freedom and vision for theology. In Cardinal Alfredo Ottaviani, secretary of the Holy Office, who was charged by the pope with the responsibility of directing the sessions, de Lubac saw 'in general' a 'solid and good sense'.[33] But Ottaviani's theology finally was burdened by an 'always negative and defensive position'.[34] And while Ottaviani attempted to precede from 'a deep attachment to tradition', his sense of tradition was 'too short', as it tended to consist above all in citations of modern papal encyclicals, and as such was 'insufficiently alive with the spirit of the Gospel'.[35]

In the preparatory sessions de Lubac found himself the defender of the orthodoxy for his late confrère, Teilhard de Chardin.[36] Even while de Lubac himself was critical of Teilhard on certain points of doctrine, he was dumbfounded to discover that some of the 'Roman theologians' would have liked to see Teilhard condemned at the upcoming Council.[37] 'Some, as always, have a tendency to think that the motive of a council is that of "specifying" doctrine, that is to say, practically making it more narrow, conceptualising it to the extreme.'[38] De Lubac complains that, among this 'assembly of "theologians"',[39] there is 'a certain superficiality of spirit which confounds me'.[40] 'We are enclosed, not in the liberating ground of faith, but in the narrow hall of a school.'[41] It is finally not only Teilhard that de Lubac had to defend, but also himself.[42] Suspicions of his orthodoxy lingered from the *Humani Generis* affaire.[43] The final episode of de Lubac's defence of his own doctrine is a written letter to the secretary of the commission threatening to hand in his resignation to the Holy Father himself, indicating precisely why.[44] In a letter to Balthasar, de Lubac writes of the preparatory commission as an experience of 'being among wolves'.[45] What was missing, both in the commission and in the documents it was charged to prepare, was any real 'recognition of the Christian Mystery in its profound unity'.[46]

32. De Lubac, *Carnets*, vol. 1, p. 21.
33. Ibid., p. 39.
34. Ibid., p. 39.
35. Ibid., p. 39.
36. Ibid., pp. 25–31.
37. Cf. J. Komonchak, 'La lucha por el Concilio durante la preparación', in *Historia del Concilio Vaticano II*, vol. 1., pp. 155–230, at p. 226.
38. De Lubac, *Carnets*, vol. 1, p. 48.
39. Ibid., p. 41.
40. Ibid., p. 37.
41. Ibid., p. 46.
42. Ibid., p. 41.
43. Chantraine and Lemaire, *Henri de Lubac*, vol. 4, p. 246.
44. De Lubac, *Mémoire sur l'occasion de mes écrits*, p. 118 [ET: ASC, p. 117].
45. Letter to Hans Urs von Balthasar, 24.11.60 (CAÉCHL 5424); as quoted in Chantraine and Lemaire, *Henri de Lubac*, vol. 4, p. 246.
46. De Lubac, *Carnets*, vol. 1, p. 35.

From the Opening to Jerusalem: First Two Sessions

The Council opened on 11 October 1962. Having served on the preparatory commission, de Lubac was appointed by Pope John a *peritus* of the Council. The first principle document treated by the Council Fathers was the schema on revelation, *De Fontibus Revelationis*, which de Lubac judged problematic. De Lubac's basic position against the schema concerned its strong affirmation of a *duplex fons* of revelation, Scripture and tradition. According to de Lubac, the *duplex fons* posits a false dualism that contradicts the Council of Trent, which talks of Jesus as the one source (*fontem*) of Christianity.[47] De Lubac held, thus, there is no *duplex fons* but only the *unus fons* who is the Incarnate Logos.[48]

De Lubac recounts in the *Carnets* the 'historical session' of 14 November 1962, when Ottaviani presented *De Fontibus Revelationis*. Immediately after Ottaviani's presentation, Cardinal Liénart began his intervention: *Hoc schema mihi non placet* (This schema does not please me).[49] In turn Cardinal Frings likewise rose to criticize the document. In response Cardinals Ruffini, Siri, and Quiroga y Palacios defended the schema (even while Siri and Quiroga y Palacios offered that aspects could be revised),[50] declaring: 'the Holy Father sent us the schema so that we should accept it'.[51] But the judgement against the schema could not be stopped: Cardinals Léger, König, Alfring, Suenens, Bea, and patriarch Maximos IV all then rose in turn to denounce the schema as unacceptable. 'It was like a bomb in the nave of Saint Peter's: everyone had expected a council without incident, and now history had begun!'[52]

On 17 November, de Lubac notes happily the constructive intervention of Msgr Paul Joseph Schmitt, bishop of Metz against *De Fontibus Revelationis*.[53] Msgr Schmitt, in line with de Lubac's private judgement, aimed to deconstruct every appeal by the defenders of the schema to Trent and Vatican I, as if evidencing support for the *duplex fons* doctrine. Most decisively, in his intervention Schmitt provided the decisive key of what would later become Dei *Verbum*: 'All revelation consists in the person of Christ, who is Himself the speech of God to men and the revelation of God... [in the] whole of his life, death [and] resurrection.'[54] This moment was decisive: 'Faith does not have to be reduced to ideology [integrist or progressivist]. The church can invite people of today to do nothing but believe in Christ "nobiscum"; [the Church] has

---

47. *Decretum de canonicis Scripturis* (DS 1501).
48. Chantraine and Lemaire, *Henri de Lubac*, vol. 4, p. 262.
49. De Mattei, *The Second Vatican Council*, p. 232.
50. Cf. Wiltgen, *The Rhine Flows into the Tiber*, pp. 46–51; and de Mattei, *The Second Vatican Council*, pp. 232–41.
51. De Lubac, *Carnets*, vol. 1, p. 279.
52. Marce Grelot, *Il rinnovamento biblico nelventesimo secolo: memorie di un protagonist* (Cinisello Balsamo: San Paolo, 1996), p. 172; as quoted in de Mattei, *The Second Vatican Council*, pp. 232–33.
53. de Lubac, *Carnets*, vol. 1, p. 309.
54. Ibid., pp. 309–10.

not "truths" to give [the world] apart from Christ himself, who is the Truth.'[55] Discussion of the document continued until the 20th, when it was put to a vote defeated by the majority of the Council Fathers. To which, on the 21st, the Holy Father responded by having *De Fontibus Revelationis* withdrawn in order to be redrafted by a special committee consisting of members both of the Theological Commission, headed by Cardinal Ottaviani, and the Secretariat for Promoting Christian Unity, headed by Cardinal Augustin Bea.

After 23 November various schemata were presented including *De Beata Vergine Maria*, *De Ecclesia* and the much debated *De Unitate* (on ecumenism). De Lubac was in favour of the opinion that *De Beata Vergine Maria* be integrated into *De Ecclesia*, a theme on which he was consulted by various Council Fathers.[56] On 1 December, Cardinal Ottaviani presented *De Ecclesia*. Significant debate followed, above all concerning the relation of the pastoral to the dogmatic. Msgr Marcel Lefebvre suggested that there ought to be two schemata, one for clerics and teachers, which would be truly dogmatic and scholastic, and another for the lay faithful, which would be more pastoral and less precise.[57] De Lubac was opposed categorically to this logic of *separatio*, of dichotomizing the 'pastoral' and the 'dogmatic'.[58] According to de Lubac, what the schema lacked was a biblical foundation, which would bring to light the true catholicity of the Church, in which the Church could be shown in her life as 'mystery' that receives and reflects the light of Christ, and is thereby discovered as the *communio* in which humanity itself finds its true unity.[59] At the close of the first session, 8 December 1962, the only constitution approved was *De Sacra Liturgia*, what would become known as *Sacrosanctum Concilium*.

* * *

The year between the first two sessions saw the death of John XXIII and the election on 21 June 1963 of Cardinal Giovanni Battista Montini as Pope Paul VI. The latter was known to de Lubac, and had supported his work through the decade of suspicion following *Humani Generis*. Under Cardinal Montini's patronage as archbishop of Milan in 1955, the Italian edition of de Lubac's *Méditation sur l'Eglise* (1953) was published, copies of which the archbishop distributed to his clergy.[60] When the second session opened, on 29 September, de Lubac was not present due to health problems. In the *Carnets* there are no entries until 27 October 1963: 'At the desire of the Fr. Provincial and the Fr. Rector, after recovery and a trip to Toulouse, departure for Rome by car with Father George Haubtmann.'[61]

---

55. Aldana, 'Las *Notas del Concilio* de Henri de Lubac', p. 362.
56. de Lubac, *Carnets*, vol. 1, pp. 410–11.
57. Ibid., p. 435.
58. Cf. de Lubac, *Mémoire sur l'occasion de mes écrits*, p. 343 [ET: ASC, p. 342].
59. Personal note (CAÉCHL 5424). As cited in Chantraine and Lemaire, *Henri de Lubac*, vol. 4, p. 286.
60. De Lubac, *Mémoire sur l'occasion de mes écrits*, p. 75 [ET: ASC, pp. 74–75].
61. de Lubac, *Carnets*, vol. 2, p. 7.

On 8 November, de Lubac notes the now-famous intervention of Cardinal Frings, raising the question of the reform of the Holy Office to which Cardinal Ottaviani responded fulminating.[62] But even as de Lubac notes this, a new and more dangerous threat to the Council was emerging, not around the 'integrism' of the Roman theological old guard, but from the 'progressivism' of the new academic theological vanguard.

On 28 November de Lubac records in the *Carnets* a meeting in Hotel Columbus on the Via della Conciliazione, at which, at the initiative of Karl Rahner and Edward Schillebeeck, a new theology review, *Concilium*, was launched.[63] The idea was to incarnate the 'spirit' of the Council in a joint effort of theologians. Asked to join to the editorial board, de Lubac's first impression was lukewarm: 'The organisation seems serious. The spirit, rather dry, rather "academic"; the language pretends to be very "scientific"; the theologians take themselves rather seriously, etc. Nevertheless the directors [Rahner and Schillebeeckx] seem friendly.'[64] And so de Lubac agreed to join the editorial board.

The second session of the Council ended on 4 December with the approval of *Sacrosanctum Concilium*, the constitution on the liturgy, as well as *Inter Mirifica*. De Lubac was not invested in work on either document, and mentions their approvals only in passing. What occupies his entry is the announcement of the pope's decision to visit Jerusalem. De Lubac was moved by 'the profound significance of this interior gesture of Paul VI', by which he understood the pope to have explained the meaning of the 'decentralization' of the Church, which is in fact an 'ex-centration': the Church going out from herself to follow 'in the footsteps of Jesus Christ, her Saviour and Lord, to draw the sap of her renewal from her first origin'.[65] Hereby the fundamental meaning of the *aggiornamento* to which Pope John XXIII called the Church was clarified:

> Before being carried out in institutions or even in morals, *aggiormamento* has to be carried out interiorly, in what is the heart of everything, in the attitude of faith. In Christianity, it is the gesture of faith that commands everything. This gesture of faith, which Paul VI realises in his pilgrimage 'of prayer, of penance and of spiritual renewal', goes out to adore Jesus Christ in the place where he was born, lived, died and was resurrected. [And by this gesture] ... the Church proclaims that she is the Church of Jesus Christ, that she does not want to be anything else. Far from making herself the centre, she refers everything to Jesus Christ.[66]

62. Ibid., p. 15.
63. Ibid., p. 49.
64. Ibid., p. 49.
65. Ibid., pp. 58–59.
66. Henri de Lubac, 'Paul VI, pèlerin de Jérusalem', *Christus* 41 (January 1964), pp. 97–102; as quoted in Chantraine and Lemaire, *Henri de Lubac*, vol. 4, p. 246.

De Lubac's enthusiasm for Paul VI's gesture is illustratively contrasted with his muted response to the founding of *Concilium*. The former is 'academic', takes itself too seriously, and 'pretends to be very "scientific"'; in a word it tends towards *conceptio christiana*. The latter, by contrast, is a 'gesture of faith' that 'goes out to adore Jesus' and so incarnates *fides christiana*. If no theological 'initiative' can 'save' Christianity, the gesture of a pope who dares to refer 'everything to Jesus Christ' could be the salvation of theology.

Towards an 'Inverse Integrism': The Third Session

On 14 September 1964, the third session of the Council opened. While the Mariological element was now firmly placed in the eighth chapter of *De Ecclesia*, the question of Marian mediation (*mediatrix*) remained in question, as did the issue of collegiality.[67] While in the second session de Lubac had noted his disaccord with the language of *mediatrix* for Mary,[68] the Council Fathers ultimately would decide otherwise, as *Lumen Gentium* would declare her.[69] While in earlier sessions there had been clashes over the schema *De Libertate Religiosa*, in the third session the conflict was raised to a new pitch of intensity.[70] De Lubac lamented: 'A whole series of interventions criticizing religious liberty with more or less brutality: only Catholics have a right to it. Many stupid things have been said, confusion is manifest. Some Spanish [bishops] have demonstrated a total lack of respect for man and a lack [therefore] of Christian spirit. Disconcerting.'[71] One of the key interventions against *De Libertate Religiosa* was that of Msgr Marcel Lefebvre.[72] Lefebvre argued that the basis of *De Libertate Religiosa* was wholly founded in relativism, and so amounted to a betrayal of Catholic faith.[73] While de Lubac could not agree with Lefebvre, the majority of the voices defending the document on religious freedom were imbued with a too ideological and liberal motivation, and so were insufficiently theological. In the midst of this rather bleak debate, de Lubac discerned a glimmer: 'one Polish bishop spoke reasonably and in a Christian manner'.[74] The bishop was Karol Wojtyła.[75]

67. de Lubac, *Carnets*, vol. 2, pp. 118–225, and 127–34.

68. Ibid., pp. 64–69. De Lubac's motivation is based in a concern not to separate Marian theology from Christology and ecclesiology. His penchant for the French School of Pierre de Bérulle and Jean-Jacque Olier, which found its last expression in Louis de Monford, makes impossible any reduction of his position to a so-called Marian minimalism.

69. *Lumen Gentium*, 62.

70. de Lubac, *Carnets*, vol. 2, pp. 131–46.

71. Ibid., p. 137.

72. Ibid., pp. 198–99. The intervention took place 24 September 1964. The next day de Lubac wrote a rejoinder, which was subsequently published, along with de Lubac's French translation of Lefebvre's Latin intervention in *Paradoxes*, OC, vol. 31, pp. 377–82.

73. Cf. Marcel Lefebvre, *Religious Liberty Questioned – The Dubia: my Doubts about the Vatican II Declaration of Religious Liberty* (Kansas City, MO: Angelus Press, 2001).

74. de Lubac, *Carnets*, vol. 2, p. 140.

75. Ibid., p. 320.

On 17 October 1964, with the first issue of *Concilium* not yet published, the question of the theological review arose again, and this time painfully. It concerned de Lubac's judgement of an anti-ecclesial spirit present in a recently published article of Schillebeeckx, titled 'L'Église et le monde'.[76] As de Lubac noted in his journal:

> I wrote to Father Karl Rahner, German college: 'This is a note strictly personal. A reunion of *Concilium* is announced for Friday evening and next Saturday. But since reading a text of Father Schillebeeckx on "The Church and the world", I am struck with a great discomfort. Not only is it impossible for me to be associated with such a theological orientation, but rather, if I had the strength, I believe it would be my duty to combat it. If such an approach it to be that of *Concilium*, it would better that I at once resign from the editorial board.[77]

While Rahner attempted to reassure de Lubac, insisting that Schillebeeckx's article was in no way a programme for *Concilium*,[78] nevertheless the fundamental break between de Lubac and the *Concilium group* was now set, well before the publication of the journal's first issue in 1965.

* * *

De Lubac had from the beginning taken a negative view of the famous schema 13 (previously schema 17), on the Church and the modern world. The schema that became *Gaudium et Spes* had not been part of Pope John XXIII's original vision for the Council. Most histories of the Council credit the genesis of the document to Cardinal Leo Jozef Suenens, who proposed during the first session that *De Ecclesia* should be expanded into two documents: *De Ecclesia ad intra* and *De Ecclesia ad extra*, with the former treating the Church from the point of view of Christians, and the latter treating her in relation to the non-Christian 'modern world'.[79] As much as this bifurcation of *De Eccleisa* is attributed to Suenens, as we have seen, it finds a unique and significant correlate in the earlier proposal of Msgr Lefebvre, who suggested the De Ecclesia should result in two schemata: one dogmatic and scholastic, the other pastoral and less precise.[80]

---

76. Edward Schillebeeckx, 'L'Église et le monde', in *Do-C. Documentatie Centrum Concilie* (French ed.) 3 (1964), nr. 142, reprinted in *Approches théologiques*, vol. 3. *Le monde et l'église* (Bruxelles: Editions du Cep, 1967), pp. 149–67.

77. de Lubac, *Carnets*, vol. 2, pp. 220–21.

78. Ibid., p. 247.

79. O'Malley, *What Happened at Vatican II?*, pp. 157–58; cf. de Mattei, *The Second Vatican Council*, p. 245 and pp. 382–84.

80. de Lubac, *Carnets*, vol. 1, p. 435. In fact from the dates it would appear that the first genesis of the separation of *De Eccleisa* into two discrete documents – *ad intra* (*Lumen Gentium*) and *ad extra* (*Gaudium et Spes*) – came from Lefebvre made his proposal on 1 December, three days before Suenens's suggestion (cf. O'Malley, *What Happened at Vatican II?*, p. 157).

De Lubac gave voice to his grave doubts about the schema in a letter of 23 September to Msgr Antoine Cazaux, bishop of Luçon:

> I wrote to Msgr. Cazaux ... [and] expressed my fear that the redaction of schema 13 is insufficient, that, generally speaking, the desire to 'open to the world', as it is taken up today in the Church, engenders only a confused attitude that no longer permits us to declare with the same assurance and truth of the apostle: 'We do not falter in our ministry, because we have renounced disgraceful and underhanded ways, and we refuse to practice cunning or to tamper with God's Word' (2 Cor. 4.2).[81]

For de Lubac, the Church's relation to the world is constituted by her mission, the divine injunction given her to proclaim the Gospel to the ends of the earth (cf. Mk 16.15). The extent to which her relation to the world is abstracted from this mission – whether due to concerns for natural law, human rights, or 'open' dialogue – 'the more the Church appears as if she exists in and of herself, and not as the messenger of a hope founded in Jesus Christ. The supernatural, in the measure in which we dare to introduce it, takes the form of a super-addition'.[82]

At the core of de Lubac's unease with schema 13 was the singular sense that, at its core, it rested on the dualist presupposition of neo-scholasticism, of a bifurcated view of the world as a 'natura pura' in relation to the Gospel, no longer understood as a revelation that permeates the very depths of the human being, but rather as an external 'super-addition'.[83] The old dualist understanding of the *duplex ordo* had returned: 'An absurdity spreads more and more: to Christians one must speak of the Gospel, but to unbelievers [one must speak] only of natural law'.[84]

De Lubac thus perceived a new theological crisis taking hold within the Church in the later period of the Council. If the reactionary spirit of Roman official theology had, in the preparatory phase and at the first session, threatened the steady gaze of the Council Fathers on the Mystery made flesh, now in the later phase of the Council a secularizing progressivism animated by worldly optimism was threatening the same gaze. The old 'integrism' was being exchanged for an equally abstract and problematic 'inverse integrism'.[85]

While the characteristics of these two 'integrist' theologies are various,[86] in both cases de Lubac discerns how conceptualist reasoning is privileged in a way that abstracts theology from the living source of doctrine, the Mystery Incarnate. While the old neo-scholastic integrism reduced theology to a 'systematisation' of revealed data, the new 'inverse integrism' reduces theology to a quasi-sociology.

---

81. de Lubac, *Carnets*, vol. 2, p. 138.
82. Ibid., p. 141.
83. Cf. ibid., p. 106.
84. Ibid., p. 245.
85. Cf. de Lubac, *Carnets*, vol. 1, pp. 308–9.
86. For what follows, cf. de Lubac, *Carnets*, vol. 2, p. 423.

For both, a conceptual fixation on 'principles' and 'values' distracts our attention away from the life of the spirit, and so reduces Christianity to a moralism. The sense that Christianity is a proposal that concerns the total way of life of the human being sustained in intimate friendship with Jesus Christ is, in both cases, lost from view. If the final result of the old 'integrism' was to justify the modern confessional state, the *nacionalcatolicismo* of Franco's Spain, for example, the new progressivism threatened to exchange the project of constructing a 'confessional state' for the new political goal of 'social justice'. The reduction in both cases, however, remains the same: *fides christiana* is reduced to *conceptio christiana*. The way beyond the temptation to 'inverse integrism' is signalled for de Lubac by the example of Pope Paul's *Ecclesiam Suam*, which addresses the whole of humanity with the Gospel: 'Speaking to all men, one must speak to them in Christian; the Apostles brought Christian hope to men who at first were not Christian … Christianity is a truth of life.'[87]

The closing of the third session was beset by intense drama, which de Lubac judged an unworthy hysteria. It began on Saturday, 14 November, the Saturday of the last week of the session, in what has become known to posterity as *la settimana nera*.[88] In the weeks leading up to the so-called black week, de Lubac complained in his journal that 'from an activist wing that would like to impose itself upon the Council, insinuations against Paul VI are multiplied'.[89] In this suspicious context, on 14 November, the Council Fathers received, 'by the order of the Supreme Authority',[90] a folder containing the text of chapter three of *De Ecclesia* with the famous *Nota explicativa praevia* appended. It had been known beforehand that Pope Paul, through the Secretary of State, had requested the theological commission under the direction of Cardinal Ottaviani to 'interpret' the pronouncement of *De Ecclesia* on collegiality. And such is the *Nota*: a clarification that the college of bishops exercises its authority only with the assent of the pope, such that the traditional primacy and freedom of the papal office were clearly reaffirmed. Not a few Council Fathers and *periti* took the *Nota* as an illegitimate papal interference in the conciliar proceedings. De Lubac, by contrast, took a serene view. In his journal he recalls only that the *Nota* changes nothing fundamental, and 'can be read in a perfectly acceptable sense'.[91]

The *Nota* was not the only cause of agitation of *la settimana nera*. On 19 November, Cardinal Tisserant announced the vote on *De Libertate Religiosa* would be postponed until the final session, disallowing the vote that the Council Fathers

---

87. Ibid., p. 150.
88. On *la settimana nera*, see Luis Antonio G. Tagle, 'La "semana negra" del concilio Vaticano II (14–21 de noviembre de 1964)', in *Historia del Concilio Vaticano II*, vol. 1, pp. 357–416. And cf. O'Malley, *What Happened at Vatican II?*, pp. 240–45; Wiltgen, *The Rhine Flows into the Tiber*, pp. 234–43; and de Mattei, *The Second Vatican Council*, pp. 411–18.
89. De Lubac, *Carnets*, vol. 2, p. 303.
90. De Mattei, *The Second Vatican Council*, p. 411.
91. De Lubac, *Carnets*, vol. 2, p. 320.

were already prepared to take on the document. The reaction among some, again, was one of suspicion. It was feared that the 'postponement' was disingenuous and that a Roman integrist triumph through papal decree was imminent. De Lubac, again, was sanguine. Far from disconcerting him, he was relieved since he judged 'the text they applaud is very mediocre'.[92] Later the same day the drama was heightened by another papal intervention, consisting in nineteen emendations to *De Oecumenismo*. Finally, on the last day of the session, 21 November, Pope Paul named the Blessed Virgin, 'Mater Ecclesiae'. To those who feared an integrist intrigue, the raising of the new Marian title by papal decree was a further and ominous intrusion of papal authority.[93]

Unlike Congar, who took Paul's declaration of Mary 'Mater Ecclesiae' as a reactionary imposition of papal will,[94] de Lubac welcomed the new Marian title. Moreover, he opined that the Pope's motive, far from pandering to an integrist intrigue, had issued from the Holy Father's desire to honour the Polish episcopate who, de Lubac supposed, had requested the new Marian title.[95] Whatever the honour Paul may have sought to pay the Polish bishops, George Chantraine suggests that it is most likely that the Pope 'had in mind the chapter on the Virgin Mary in *Méditation* when he declared Mary "Mother of the Church"'.[96] While the pedigree of the Marian title goes back at least to St Ambrose of Milan, and while the decisive *ressourcement* of the title must be credited to Hugo Rahner,[97] it is a fact that the Marian title does form the basis of the last chapter of de Lubac's *Méditation sur l'Église* (1953),[98] and that the book was highly esteemed by Montini.[99] De Lubac would have never attributed such influence to himself, but he too must have recognized in the elevation of Mary 'Mater Ecclesiae' a vindication of his own Marian impulse:

> At every moment of her existence, Mary speaks and acts in the name of the Church – *figuram in se sanctae Ecclesiae* ['she shows forth the figure of holy Church in herself', as Ambrose of Milan used to say] – ... because she already, as

---

92. Ibid., p. 332.
93. See the comments of Congar, *My Journal*, p. 58. For the 'Marian minimalist' mood of the Council, see de Mattei, *The Second Vatican Council*, pp. 289–99 and Congar, *My Journal*, pp. 15, 54–58, 67, 687, 695–97.
94. Cf. Congar, *My Journal*, pp. 696–97.
95. De Lubac, *Carnets*, vol. 2, p. 320.
96. Chantraine, 'Note Historique', OC, vol. 8, p. xxxi.
97. Hugo Rahner, S.J., *Mater Ecclesia. Lobpreis der Kirche aus dem ersten Jahrtausend* (Einsiedeln: Johannes Verlag, 1944).
98. Cf. Portier, 'What Kind of a World of Grace?', p. 138.
99. Pope Paul cited the book often, see George Chantraine, 'Note Historique', in de Lubac, *Méditation sur l'Église*, OC, vol. 8, pp. xvii–lviii, here at pp. xxix–xxxii. *Méditation* was, moreover, a key source of Paul VI's first encyclical, *Ecclesiam suam*, see Giuseppe Colombo, 'Genesi, storia e significato dell'enciclica "Ecclesiam suam"', in '*Ecclesiam suam' première lettre encyclique de Paul VI. Colloque internationale (Rome 24–25 octobre 1980)* (Rome: Edizioni Studium, 1982), pp. 131–60, at p. 141.

it were, bears and encloses the whole Church within her own person. She is 'the totality of the Church, as [Jean-Jacques] Olier put it.[100]

* * *

On 21 November, the last day of the third session, the Council Fathers approved *De Ecclesia*, the dogmatic constitution on the Church, which henceforth became known as *Lumen Gentium*. The principal redactor of the text, Msgr Gérard Philips, was a theologian with whom de Lubac shared a deep mutual respect. We know for certain that the opening words of the constitution – *Lumen Gentium cum sit Christus* – were authored in their place by Philips. In English the opening sentences of the final document read:

> Christ is the Light of nations. Because this is so, this Sacred Synod gathered together in the Holy Spirit eagerly desires, by proclaiming the Gospel to every creature, to bring the light of Christ to all men, a light brightly visible on the countenance of the Church. Since the Church is in Christ like a sacrament or as a sign and instrument both of a very closely knit union with God and of the unity of the whole human race, it desires now to unfold more fully to the faithful of the Church and to the whole world its own inner nature and universal mission.[101]

The profound Christocentrism of *Lumen Gentium* 1 corresponds to the Lubacian paraphrase in *Gaudium et Spes* 22. Christ is the light of human reality, the spark that illumines and reveals the human to himself, and so illumines every human culture, history, and nation. The Church is so constituted as to reflect this Christological light and gather humanity to it through the *communio sanctorum*. The universality of the Church's mission and the unity of all human beings are here co-constitutive because both are alike rooted in Jesus Christ. The mode by which all of this works is the mode designated by de Lubac in 1938: the 'Church is the sacrament of Christ'.[102]

According to standard theology of the 1930s, the Church was *Societas Perfecta*, the 'perfect society'. By these norms, the language of 'sacrament' applied to the Church would have sounded eclectic and novel. In fact de Lubac's language aimed to do nothing other than deepen the meaning of the *societas* or *communio* of the Church, by clarifying that this communal fact of her being has everything to do with her sacramental economy and so everything to do with the mystery of union (1 Cor. 10.17). De Lubac's motivation, according to Ratzinger, was to respond to the new 'lapse of faith' occurring across Europe, now 'no longer under the aegis of an agnostic philosophy but in the name of humanism'.[103] De Lubac

---

100. De Lubac, *Méditation sur l'Église*, p. 278.
101. *Lumen Gentium*, 1.
102. *Catholicisme*, p. 50.
103. Ratzinger, *Principles of Catholic Theology*, p. 49.

saw how the Church was vulnerable to this new attack to the extent that she understood her sacramental life in a too individualist manner, as something external to her being as *societas*. The task was to propose the Church herself as the true humanism, and the sacramental life as the means of true *communio*. *Lumen Gentium* takes up this theme to such an extent that, in the words of Cardinal Marc Ouellet, it became 'one of the Constitution's fundamental ideas: the *Church as sacrament*'.[104] The sacraments remain seven, but now the deeper mystery of the Church's life is grasped and proclaimed. The *communio sanctorum* is the fruit and source of the sacramental economy and as such the Church is the visible sign of the grace of the 'unity of the whole human race' with God.[105]

A key point in this regard concerns the fact that the 'present-day conditions of the world add [a] greater urgency to this work of the Church'.[106] The human family is 'joined more closely today by various social, technical and cultural ties',[107] and so it is incumbent on the Church to make her proposal all the more that humanity 'might ... attain fuller unity in Christ'.[108] And even while the Church may at times appear a 'little flock', the universality of her mission ensures that the 'whole' abides within her, she is the 'lasting and sure seed of unity, hope and salvation for the whole human race'.[109] This is the case because she is 'Established by Christ as a communion of life, charity and truth' in order that she might be 'used by Him as an instrument for the redemption of all', insofar as she is 'the visible sacrament of this saving unity'.[110]

If the debt of *Lumen Gentium* to de Lubac is signalled in the cluster of *nova* that echoes from *Catholicisme*,[111] this debt is substantiated further by the fact that in the original schema the first chapter was titled 'De natura Ecclesiae militantis', while in its final form it became 'De Ecclesiae Mysterio', echoing the title of the first chapter of de Lubac's *Méditation sur l'Église*, 'L'Église est un mystère'.[112]

Towards the Post-Conciliar Crisis: From the Last Session

Between the third and last sessions, from 29 March to 7 April, de Lubac was in Rome for work on schema 13. De Lubac arrived on 28 March. His diary entry that day consists of a brief comment on an article in the latest issue of *Commonweal*:

---

104. Marc Cardinal Ouellet, *The Relevance and Future of the Second Vatican Council*, Interviews with Father Geoffroy de la Tousche, trans. Michael Donley and Joseph Fessio, S.J. (San Francisco: Ignatius Press, 2013), p. 55.
105. Ouellet, *The Relevance and Future of the Second Vatican Council*, p. 56.
106. *Lumen Gentium*, 1.
107. Ibid., 1.
108. Ibid., 1.
109. Ibid., 9.
110. Ibid., 9.
111. *Catholicisme*, p. 50 [ET: C, p. 76].
112. Chantraine, 'Note Historique', pp. xlix–lii. And cf. O'Malley, *What Happened at Vatican II?*, p. 163 and 188.

'The Council: End or Beginning?'.¹¹³ Written by the Swiss *peritus* Hans Küng, an associate of the *Concilium* journal, the essay suggestively echoes a classic and programmatic 1954 essay of Karl Rahner, 'Chalkedon – Ende oder Anfang?'.¹¹⁴ Ever since the first session when he heard Küng speak on collegiality, de Lubac judged him negatively: a man of 'juvenile audacity'.¹¹⁵ The *Commonweal* article provoked a more bitter response. De Lubac notes in the *Carnets* having read by Küng, 'An incendiary article, superficial and problematic. Very hostile to Paul VI'.¹¹⁶ After a lengthy quote from the article's last section, 'A Standstill is no Longer Possible', which describes the Council as initiating a transitory phase towards a radical new idea of the relationships between the lay and clerical states, de Lubac concludes, 'The article is demagogic, threatening and full of arrogance'.¹¹⁷ The next day, the first day of the meetings on schema 13, de Lubac notes another newly published article: 'L'Église et l'Humanité', written by Schillebeeckx and lately published in the first issue of *Concilium*.¹¹⁸ De Lubac's commentary consists of a single word: 'mauvais'.¹¹⁹

As de Lubac entered the meetings on schema 13 in the spring of 1965, the disheartening direction of the *Concilium* circle was offset by the hopeful surprise of a new friendship:

> Members [Council Fathers] and experts [*periti*], in an improvised room [at St Martha's], often found themselves more or less mixed, such that at some of the meetings I found myself next to Msgr. Wojtyła, and we were able to exchange in a low voice our reflections. It was over the course of these days, when we worked together, that we became better acquainted.¹²⁰

On 31 March de Lubac noted with gratitude an intervention of Wojtyła.¹²¹ When the meeting took a brief recess, de Lubac recalled: 'I took advantage of the pause to thank Wojtyła [for his intervention] and encourage him to persist' with his line of reasoning.¹²² In what must be his own memory of the same event, John

---

113. Hans Küng, 'The Council: End or Beginning?', *Commonweal* 81 (1965): pp. 631–37.

114. Karl Rahner, 'Chalkedon – Ende oder Anfang?', in A. von Grillmeier and H. Bacht (eds), *Das Konzil von Chalkedon*, vol. 3 (Würzburg: Echter Verlag, 1954), pp. 3–49. Written on the 500th anniversary of Council of Chalcedon, the question as to whether Chalcedon is an end or a beginning is answered: that, in matters of Christology, it is both an end and a beginning. For an expanded English version of the essay, see 'Current Problems in Christology', in *Theological Investigations*, vol. 1, trans. Cornelius Ernst, O.P. (Baltimore, MD: Helicon, 1961), pp. 149–200.

115. De Lubac, *Carnets*, vol. 1, p. 305.

116. Ibid., vol. 2, p. 344.

117. Ibid., p. 345.

118. E. Schillebeeckx, 'L'Église et l'Humanité', *Concilium* 1 (1965): pp. 57–78.

119. De Lubac, *Carnets*, vol. 2, p. 345.

120. De Lubac, 'Rencontres avec Msgr. Karol Wojtyła, 1963–1976', in *Paradoxes*, pp. 354–60, at p. 355.

121. De Lubac, *Carnets*, vol. 2, p. 357.

122. Ibid., p. 358.

Paul II later recalled: 'When Schema 13 was being studied (later to become the Pastoral Constitution on the Church in the modern world, *Gaudium et Spes*), and I spoke on personalism, Father de Lubac came to me and said, encouragingly: "Yes, yes, yes, that's the way forward", and this meant a great deal to me, as I was still relatively young.'[123] The feeling was mutual. As de Lubac wrote of Wojtyła in his diary, 'it is clear that he is of a profound Christian sense, without any sclerosis'.[124]

On the question of the schema, de Lubac and Wojtyła were of one mind. They both judged the schema's treatment of atheism to be 'very insufficient', lacking the profundity, for example, of Paul VI's *Ecclesiam Suam*.[125] The problem of atheism had to be considered in its total context, and could not be either reduced and countered, or accepted and accommodated.[126] They both saw that, in fact, the latter (acceptance and accommodation) was the real risk of the schema, the general orientation of which was 'too "humanist", that is to say, secular and naturalistic'.[127] This is seen in the critique Wojtyła offered during the debate on the schema's chapter on culture. As de Lubac recorded, Wojtyła interjected on the question of how 'all culture can be inspired *ab Evangelio, a Verbo Dei*'.[128] Christians must 'participate in human culture', but this is not enough. The task of the Church is *missio*: 'At stake is the active presence of the Church in the World.'[129] The 'immanence of the people of God in the culture is well and good, but [what is needed is the] transcendence of Christian faith'.[130] The task, again, is to to return to *fides christiana* and resist every temptation to reduce the Christian life to mere *conceptio*.

On 7 April, after the last meeting of the working session, de Lubac recorded in his journal: 'Msgr. Wojtyła embraced me. He has sensed our profound union in the faith. I take with me a vivid memory of many of his interventions (he was too little listened to) and our also brief conversations'.[131] The 'difficult birth of the famous schema 13'[132] was in this way bound up for de Lubac with the genesis of a 'profound union in the faith' – what John Paul II referred to as a 'special friendship'.[133]

* * *

123. John Paul II, *Rise, Let Us Be On Our Way*, trans. Walter Ziemba (New York: Warner Books, 2004), p. 165.
124. De Lubac, *Carnets,* vol. 2, p. 358.
125. Ibid., p. 360.
126. Cf. Ibid., p. 391-92.
127. Ibid., p. 374.
128. Ibid., p. 375.
129. Ibid., p. 375.
130. Ibid., p. 375.
131. Ibid., p. 394.
132. De Lubac, *Mémoire sur l'occasion de mes écrits*, p. 175 [ET: ASC, p. 171].
133. John Paul II, *Crossing the Threshold of Hope* (New York: Alfred A. Knopf, 1994), p. 159. Cf. George Weigel, *Witness to Hope: Witness To Hope: The Biography of Pope John Paul II* (New York: HarperCollins, 1999), p. 167. Also, see Karol Wojtyła, *Amour et responsabilité. Étude de morale sexuelle* (Paris: Éditions du Dialogue, 1965), with a preface by de Lubac.

The final session of the Council ran from 14 September to 8 December. While there were quite a few schemata to be voted on, the principal question that animated the council hall concerned schema 13. De Lubac's hopes for the schema were not high. The essential problem with the schema, on his view, concerned 'inverse integrism', the way the schema had absorbed the old dualism of 'natura pura', which it now expressed in a profane and humanist mode.[134] This was typified for de Lubac by the 'disheartening intervention of Msgr. [François] Marty, archbishop of Reims'.[135] According to Msgr Marty, 'we should not see in atheism anything but an occasion for the purification of the faith [of her]…superstitious [qualities]'.[136] Our task in relation to the atheist, Marty contended, does not concern the question of 'belief', but rather our duty to our fellow human, for the sake of whom we must collaborate with 'the atheist in the construction of the world, the human spirit, etc., – distinguishing this clearly from our supernatural [Christian] hope'.[137] The day after Marty's intervention, de Lubac wrote:

> Ever since yesterday morning, I have been thinking of the intervention of Marty: this dualism of hopes: 'human hope' [vs.] 'Christian hope', with no communication between the two; Christian hope relegated to the bottom of the individual soul; and Christians [relegated thereby] to having to follow after an atheism that [now is allowed to] monopolize human hopes [in the public and social realm]…This is exactly what I signalled to (too briefly) in the preface of *Mystère de Surnaturel* as the great peril of today.…[138]

The problematic de Lubac analysed in *Surnaturel* (1946) was now threatening to bear its most bitter fruit, undermining at the root the Christian experience of salvation as *unitas*. If Marty's scheme were to triumph, the supernatural life of the human being in Christ would be cut off from everything social and human, relegated to a pure individualism that would clear the field of universal human experience for secularism, while the concrete experience of 'salvation' in this life risks being reinterpreted in terms of a collaborative project of Christians and non-Christians in 'the construction of the world'.

At the Council de Lubac tried to explain his concern to Marty, unfortunately to the apparent incomprehension of the latter. De Lubac notes in his diary the two concrete issues of which he spoke to Marty: (1) the latter's claim that 'Whatever else the atheist may do, he does not systematically deny God'; and (2) Marty's distinguishing to the point of absolutely dichotomizing a natural human hope

---

134. Cf. Tracey Rowland, *Culture and the Thomist Tradition: After Vatican II* (London: Routledge, 2003), pp. 11–34.
135. De Lubac, *Carnets*, vol. 2, p. 418.
136. Ibid., p. 418.
137. Ibid.
138. Ibid., pp. 420–21. Cf. de Lubac, *Mystère*, OC, vol. 12, pp. 15–16 [ET: MS, pp. xxxv–xxxvi].

from the supernatural hope of the Christian.¹³⁹ The first, de Lubac explained, as a general position, is 'simply false'. Many atheists themselves reject it. Moreover, proposing this posture of the Church in relation to atheism, while celebrating atheism's virtues, is dangerous and overhasty, since clearly certain forms of atheism are predicated on hostility to the Church as such. As regards the second point, de Lubac explains, while it is true that the distinction is valid, the moment the distinction becomes a separation the very basis and meaning of schema 13 is itself negated. Only by virtue of the Church's supernatural mission does she have something to say to humanity and to the world. De Lubac writes:

> The dualism raised by the Marty Intervention amounts to saying: let us join the school of the Marxist atheism (because it is Marxism of which [we speak] when we speak vaguely of 'human hopes') in order to organize the world with [the best] result; we ask only that we be allowed, in the very depths of ourselves, a [little] hope for the hereafter. It is a corruption of Christian hope, and the progressivist illusion of a pure state.....¹⁴⁰

* * *

For most of October, de Lubac was absorbed in the continuing question of atheism in schema 13.¹⁴¹ He recalled, on 16 October, a 'rather vivid argument' between Daniélou and Rahner concerning the question of atheism. He did not elaborate the contents of the disagreement, only that he did 'not understand the path on which Rahner wants to set us'.¹⁴² Work on the schema continued. Some have suggested that in this interval de Lubac was in fact the 'principal redactor' of some sections of schema 13, but this is not in fact the case.¹⁴³ The schema, which as recently as 25 September was described by de Lubac as 'very mediocre and in need of redrafting',¹⁴⁴ had, by 22 October, benefited in his judgement from 'significant improvements'.¹⁴⁵ In the midst of hectic work on schema 13, de Lubac attended a conference of Schillebeeckx at *Domus Mariae*. It provoked a final and decisive response against any association with *Concilium*: 'Fr. Schillebeeckx, O.P., gave a conference at Domus Mariae on the Eucharist. – I have written to Fr. Karl

---

139. De Lubac, *Carnets*, vol. 2, p. 421.

140. Ibid., p. 421.

141. Cf. Congar, *My Journal*, p. 798. It seems that Congar was responsible for arranging this.

142. De Lubac, *Carnets*, vol. 2, p. 440.

143. Jesuit Father, Jean-Yves Calvez, who himself worked in these meeting, told Chantraine that he thought de Lubac was the 'principal redactor' of some paragraphs of *Gaudium et Spes* (19–22). But it is clear from correspondence de Lubac wrote at the time that he was not. See Chantraine and Lemaire, *Henri de Lubac*, vol. 4, pp. 328–529, n. 2.

144. De Lubac, *Carnets*, vol. 2, p. 416.

145. Ibid., p. 445.

Rahner my official letter of resignation from the editorial board of *Concilium*; I sent a copy also to Fr. Vanhengel, O.P., the journal's secretary'.[146]

On 18 November the Council Fathers approved the dogmatic constitution on divine revelation, *Dei Verbum*. While de Lubac did not work directly on *Dei Verbum*,[147] his influence on the text can be seen not the least in the Christocentric overdetermination of the neo-scholastic *duplex fons*.[148] As *Dei Verbum* declares, 'Sacred tradition and Sacred Scripture form one sacred deposit of the word of God.'[149] The text echoes a core claim of de Lubac's *Exégèse médiévale* (1959–1964) according to which Jesus Christ, the *Verbum*, is himself the unity of the Testaments just as he is the unity of the tradition and of exegesis.[150] The sense that de Lubac's pre-conciliar work contributed importantly to *Dei Verbum* has been understood as signalled, moreover, by the invitation of Pope Paul to de Lubac to concelebrate the Mass in honour of the document's approval.[151] He was one of twenty-four concelebrants, of which twelve were *periti*.[152]

As the last weeks of the Council passed, the work on schema 13 did not slacken, neither did disinformation and polemics.[153] More disconcertingly, de Lubac notes 'agitations' from what he now calls the 'para-council', a 'council' of academic theologians positioning themselves as authentic interpreters of the Council, over and against the Magisterium of the Church.[154] In the place of the genuine vocation of Christian theology, de Lubac discerned a 'new ideology ... implanting itself'[155] among theologians who, in the name of 'theology', saw no contradiction between their vocation and relentless 'campaigning against the Pope'.[156] One week before the close of the Council, he wrote:

> In the months and years coming, it will be necessary to resemble the conciliar oeuvre in order to study it seriously, and we will have to know how to take as the hermeneutical centre [*centre de perspective*] the dogmatic constitutions, which are in effect the centre of the whole. This will require knowing how to break with the propaganda and tendentious essays that have already come to light,

---

146. Ibid., p. 455.
147. Chantraine and Lemaire, *Henri de Lubac*, vol. 4, pp. 280–82.
148. Karl Heinz Neufeld, 'Au service du concile. Évêques et théologiens au deuxième concile du Vatican', in René Latourelle (ed.), *Vatican II. Bilan et perspectives. Vingt-cinq ans après*, vol. 1 (Montréal-Paris: Bellarmin-Cerf, 1998), pp. 95–124, at pp. 110–24.
149. *Dei Verbum*, 10.
150. *Exégèse médiévale*, t. I, vol. 1, p. 322.
151. Cf. Rudolf Voderholzer, *Meet Henri de Lubac: His Life and Work* (San Francisco: Ignatius Press, 2008), p. 86; and Tracey Rowland, *Ratzinger's Faith: The Theology of Pope Benedict XVI* (Oxford: OUP, 2008), p. 20.
152. De Lubac, *Carnets*, vol. 2, p. 462.
153. Ibid., p. 466.
154. Ibid., p. 467.
155. Ibid., p. 471.
156. Ibid., p. 472.

and are likely tomorrow to frustrate the reform undertaken and jeopardize the very foundations of the faith.[157]

Against the disconcerting publishing industry of academic theologians and journalists rushing to 'interpret' the Council, de Lubac was conscious that a concrete hermeneutic of legitimate interpretation of the Council would have to be clarified by the Magisterium in order to safeguard the Council's authentic programme of reform.

The closing session of the fourth and final session of the Council was held on 7 December. Schema 13, the pastoral constitution on the Church in the modern world, was approved, and from henceforth would be known as *Gaudium et Spes*. Along with *Gaudium et Spes* and the decrees on missionary activity and the life of priests, the Council Fathers approved the declaration on religious freedom, *Dignitatis Humanae*. The following day, the Feast of the Immaculate Conception, the Council formally closed.

After the Council: Another Provocation of Faith

In 1989 de Lubac gave Georges Chantraine a portfolio of pages, telling him, 'Do with these what you would like'.[158] Among the pages, Chantraine discovered what seemed a manuscript ready for publication, bearing the title *Autres Paradoxes*. These 'other' post-conciliar paradoxes naturally, if not quite formally, form a triptych alongside *Paradoxes* and *Nouveau Paradoxes*, both of which had been published before the Council. As Chantraine published *Autres Paradoxes* in 1994, a petition of Nicholas of Cusa stands as a key aphorism of Chapter 2, 'Concile. Collégialité. Para- et postconcile'.[159] 'O God, if only we could lift up our heads at this time and see our redemption drawing near, because we see that the Church has never fallen so low as it now has.'[160] The judgement is clear: in the crisis of the post-conciliar era, the evidence of our redemption – the fact of our encounter with Jesus Christ – must be verified, neither in nostalgia for an *ancien régime* nor in ideological commitment to some 'new order', but in the depths of the post-conciliar crisis itself, a crisis into which the Spirit had allowed the Church to plunge.

On both the side of integrists and progressivists, the Council came increasingly to be seen as a symbol of rupture with the past. While Msrg. Marcel Lefebvre lamented the 'apostasy' of the Church's 'French Revolution',[161] Karl Rahner celebrated the Council's bringing to an end the 'Pian' order and bringing to birth

---

157. Ibid., p. 483.
158. Chantriane, Présentation to de Lubac, *Paradoxes*, pp. xiv–xv.
159. *Paradoxes*, pp. 191–290, this chapter, pp. 217–40, the quotation of Cusa, at p. 227.
160. Nicholas of Cusa, *De concordantia catholica*, l. 1, c. 12.
161. See Archbishop Marcel Lefebvre, *An Open Letter to Confused Catholics*, trans. Father M. Crowdy (London: Fowler Wright Books, Ltd, 1986).

a new 'world Church'.¹⁶² *Autres Paradoxes*, by contrast, rejects every bifurcation of the life of the Church into that of a 'Church of Vatican II', a 'Church of Trent', of 'Pius X' or 'Paul VI'.¹⁶³ The only legitimate judgement of the Council, according to de Lubac, is one that has learned to embrace the Council within the continuity of the single life of the Church, rooted in the tradition and experience of faith that lies at her apostolic origin: 'councils and the popes, even in the exercise of their authority, are never more than servants of the Christian tradition'.¹⁶⁴ There is 'only one Church, the Church of all time, the Church of Jesus Christ, the Church of the apostles ... which is never renewed except in order to remain herself'.¹⁶⁵ Affirming this continuity, de Lubac rejects outright every hermeneutic of the Council that would posit therein a rupture in the life of the Church, whether celebrated or deplored.

The Council and the Para-Council

Already in 1965, de Lubac wrote to Bruno de Solages that 'what haunts my spirit and pains me more and more, is the state of Catholicism in France. ... It is well the day, now more than ever, to cry out: *Veni, Sancte Spiritus!*'.¹⁶⁶ Out of this cry, de Lubac writes of the 'liquidation of the Gospel' within the Church,¹⁶⁷ complaining that, since the calling of the Council, in France 'the episcopate no longer gives the slightest solid religious instruction'.¹⁶⁸ The failure of bishops to teach the faith occurs in the moment when 'signs of [an] invading atheism ... multiply ... inside of the Church. ... It is from within that we are being ruined, by an opening to a world that is the inverse of what the Gospels calls for'.¹⁶⁹

On 2 August 1965, de Lubac wrote to Georges Villepelet, P.S.S. of his deep 'anxiety about the religious situation in France'.¹⁷⁰ He mentions with grave concern the 'liturgical disorder' provoked by the Council; the broad 'abandonment of tradition'; and a new 'doctrinal and moral laxity', especially in relation to the Eucharist and the traditional 'morality of marriage'.¹⁷¹ These concerns were

162. See Karl Rahner, 'Toward a Fundamental Theological Interpretation of Vatican II', *Theological Studies* 40 (1979): pp. 716–27.
163. *Paradoxes*, p. 218.
164. Ibid., p. 218.
165. Ibid., p. 218.
166. Letter to Bruno de Solages, 06.06.65 (CAÉCHL 3310); as quoted in Chantraine and Lemaire, *Henri de Lubac*, vol. 4, p. 216.
167. CAÉCHL 58495; as quoted in Chantraine and Lemaire, *Henri de Lubac*, vol. 4, p. 216.
168. Letter to André Ravier, 28.12.64 (CAÉCHL 5080); as quoted in Chantraine and Lemaire, *Henri de Lubac*, vol. 4, p. 216.
169. CAÉCHL 5080; as quoted in Chantraine and Lemaire, *Henri de Lubac*, vol. 4, p. 216.
170. CAÉCHL 58507; as quoted in Chantraine and Lemaire, *Henri de Lubac*, vol. 4, p. 216.
171. CAÉCHL 58507; as quoted in Chantraine and Lemaire, *Henri de Lubac*, vol. 4, p. 216.

not new; de Lubac had noted as much already in the *Carnets* and in other correspondence.[172] In a particularly brutal letter of 1964, he grumbled to Solages: 'as far as the liturgy goes, it looks as if the bishops are determined to organize a real mess'.[173] But as deep as his concerns were, in the first years after the Council he remained discrete with his criticism. This changed in 1969.

In 1969, in a lecture at the University of St Louis in Missouri, de Lubac offered a scathing public critique of the one-sided reception of the Council.[174] Published later the same year in an expanded form in French as *L'Église Dans La Crise Actuelle*,[175] de Lubac railed against the post-conciliar ethos: 'While Christian thinkers of the past are dismissed as if they have nothing to say; traditional formulas of faith are presented as ridiculous, in order to hasten their outright replacement; and under the ruse of merely changing the language, the very essence of the faith itself is being evacuated'.[176] The post-conciliar crisis appeared more and more to him as a great and silent apostasy. But not only so: he judged it also a betrayal of the Council itself. Even while the protagonists of the post-conciliar crisis claimed to speak in the name of the Council, they were in fact traducing the Council and the popes who guided it. Accordingly de Lubac was moved to clarify the situation though the contrast he drew between 'the Council and the para-Council'.[177] Chiefly responsible for the latter were academic theologians: 'Just as Vatican II received directives from certain theologians on various points concerning the task it ought to assume, under pain of "disappointing the world", so too the "post-conciliar" Church was immediately and from all sides beset with orders to get in step, not with what the Council had actually said, but what it should have said'.[178] This was the basis of the para-Council mentality: not the documents of the Council, but the 'spirit' of the Council. On this later view the Council was not a doctrinal point of reference as much as a point of progressivist departure. Such an orientation was already clearly indicated in 1965 by Karl Rahner in a lecture given in Munich on 12 December, titled 'Das Konzil – Ein neuer Beginn' (The Council: A new Beginning).[179] Given less than a week after the Council's close, Rahner spoke of the Council not as an end, but as 'the beginning of a beginning'.[180] In this way Rahner spoke of Vatican II in terms reminiscent of his 1954 essay 'Chalkedon –

---

172. De Lubac, *Carnets*, vol. 2, p. 453.
173. Letter to Bruno de Solages, 24.12.64 (CAÉCHL 3290); as quoted in Chantraine and Lemaire, *Henri de Lubac*, vol. 4, p. 219.
174. Henri de Lubac, 'L'Église dan la Crise Actuelle', *Nouvelle Revue Théologique* 91 (1969): pp. 580–96.
175. Ibid., pp. 221–54.
176. Ibid., p. 234.
177. *Petit Catéchèse*, pp. 311–22 [ET: BC, pp. 235–60]. Cf. *Paradoxes*, pp. 217–40.
178. *Petit Catéchèse*, p. 311 [ET: BC, p. 235].
179. Karl Rahner, *Das Konzil. Ein neuer Beginn. Vortrag beim Festakt zum Abschluss des II. vatikanischen Konzils im Herkulessaal der Residenz in München am 12. Dez. 1965* (Freiburg: Herder, 1966).
180. Ibid., pp. 14–15.

Ende oder Anfang?', in which he proposed Chalcedon as 'end' and 'beginning' of a theological programme that would correct the putative 'existential undercurrent of monophysite tendency' that had animated both in the official theology of the Magisterium and the popular piety of devout Catholics.[181] Among the 21 Ecumenical Councils of the Church, Vatican II was thus implicitly given a place of theological pre-eminence alongside Chalcedon while the key to the significance of both Councils, for Rahner, was made to lie, not in what they designated but in what they 'made possible', not in what they declared so much as what they made indeterminable. As such Vatican II was configured primarily as a turning point in the life of the Church that 'makes a new start possible and legitimate'.[182] This attitude was precisely that against which de Lubac took aim in the 1969 address.

After a forceful critique of the post-conciliar situation, de Lubac closed his 1969 University of St Louis lecture with an apology to those who 'might have expected [me to speak], as a scholar'.[183] He conceded that he has not spoken as such, and that in the narrow academic sense his assessment of the post-conciliar crisis was not 'scientific'. Nevertheless, he insisted, he had 'spoken as a theologian'. And it is the responsibility of the theologian, he reminded his audience, that 'when the severity of the moment demands it', he ought to suspend his academic labours 'in order to remember that his entire existence as a theologian, and all the authority his occupation is worth, is based first and foremost on the charge that he has received: to defend and expound the faith of the Church'. The ecclesial vocation of the theologian was thus sharply contrasted against the indulgent 'freedom' of academic theology.

But what had happened to change de Lubac's criticism from discrete to overt between 1965 and 1969? One thing: the year 1968.

De Lubac began the year 1968 examining vernacular translations of the *Novus Ordo* Mass into French. He was not impressed, either with the new Mass to be promulgated in 1969 by Paul VI, much less with the translations from Latin being proposed.[184] In the post-conciliar revision and the French translation of the liturgy de Lubac discerned an intensification of a cavalier attitude towards the tradition he had already deplored during the Council.[185] This proved an omen of the wider crisis of the coming year, and the determination of the French episcopate that year in a decidedly progressivist direction.

On 26 March 1968, Msgr François Marty was transferred from the archdiocese of Reime to Paris. Hardly had the new archbishop arrived in Paris before the city was plunged into the riots and strikes of May 1968, with its slogans: 'Il est interdit

---

181. Karl Rahner, S.J., 'Current Problems in Christology', pp. 151, 158.

182. Karl Rahner, 'The Abiding Significance of Vatican II', in Karl Rahner (ed.), *Concern for the Church*, trans. Edward Quinn (New York: Crossroad, 1981), pp. 90–102, at p. 96.

183. De Lubac, 'L'Église dan la Crise Actuelle', p. 596.

184. Letter to Bruno de Solages, 14.02.68 (CAÉCHL 3391); as quoted in Chantraine and Lemaire, *Henri de Lubac*, vol. 4, pp. 433–34.

185. De Lubac, *Carnets*, vol. 2, p. 356.

d'interdire!' and 'Soyez réaliste, demandez l'impossible!' To the revolutionary slogans of 68 Msgr Marty contributed his own: 'Dieu n'est pas conservateur!'[186] Sometime after the events of May, de Lubac, along with Jean Daniélou and Louis Bouyer, met with the new archbishop. Over the course of the meeting, Daniélou, Bouyer, and de Lubac took the occasion to express their collective anxiety at the state of the French Church, and specifically how the Council was being taken to imply that the Church's tradition was now a *tabula rasa*, to be completely rewritten. Msgr Marty, apparently taken aback, replied: 'After the Council, we thought that it was the beginning of progressivism. Now you now tell me that progressivism doesn't work. Ah fine, let's go back to integrism.'[187] De Lubac returned: 'Monseigneur, it concerns neither progressivism nor integrism, but the truth. – The truth, there is a great word; a theologian's word, my Father!'[188]

As at the Council in session, so again after the Council, de Lubac's witness was lost on Marty. Under Marty, the French Church was set on a course of unswerving progressivism for a generation. Created a cardinal in 1969, as president of the bishops' conference (1966–1975) and as Archbishop of Paris (1968–1981), Marty was the face of post-conciliar Catholicism in France and its most powerful protagonist until the appointment of Jean-Marie Lustiger in 1981. De Lubac judged the depth of the crisis of the Marty era so profound that in 1976, in a letter to Cardinal Renard, he argued that the behaviour of the French episcopate was both provoking and giving every sense of legitimacy to the grievances of those gathering around Marcel Lefebvre's Society of St Pius X at Ecône. Indeed if what was being carried out in France in the name of the Council was in truth mandated by the Council, then the accusation of the Society against the Council would be justified. As the 'affaire d'Ecône' came closer to the ultimate breach of communion with Rome that would in fact occur on 30 June 1988, de Lubac considered that the blame for such a breach would have to be laid, not at the feet of Lefebvre, but at the feet of the French bishops,

> who give every appearance of reason to Msgr. Lefebvre, such that they will be the more real cause of division in the Church and even of veritable schism... When Msgr. Lefebvre writes 'of the radical incompatibility between the Catholic Church and the Conciliar Church' of the 'Conciliar Church with its new dogmas, its new priesthood, its new institutions, its new cult', while he is certainly wrong, nevertheless what is happening in France would seem to give him reason [to justify his claim].[189]

* * *

---

186. On Msgr Marty and May 1968, see Grégory Barrau, *Le Mai 68 des catholiques* (Paris: Les Éditions de l'Atelier, 1998), pp. 52–62.
187. Chantraine and Lemaire, *Henri de Lubac*, vol. 4, p. 438.
188. Ibid., pp. 438–39.
189. Letter to Cardinal Renard, 1976 (CAÉCHL 73057–73063); as quoted in ibid., p. 593.

The crisis of 1968 came to another dramatic head for the Church after the spring events in Paris. Against the backdrop of the publication of *Humanae Vitae* on 25 July, members of the editorial board of *Concilium* drafted a *Déclaration pour la liberté des théologien*. Often referred to as the 'Nijmegen Declaration', the document was meant to protect the supposed 'freedom' of theology, thought to have been won at the Council.[190] Among other things, the *Concilium* group insisted that the teaching office of the pope and bishops 'cannot and must not supersede, hamper and impede the teaching task of theologians as scholars', and that 'the freedom of theologians, and theology in the service of the Church, regained by Vatican II, must not be jeopardized again'.[191] The list of theologians who signed the declaration, 1360, included figures such as Rahner, Küng, Schillebeeckx, Congar, and Chenu, as well as, perhaps more surprisingly, Daniélou and Ratzinger. De Lubac was solicited to sign the document; he categorically refused. On 4 December, he sent a strong letter back to Yves Congar explaining that such a declaration struck him as 'propaganda' aimed to 'intimidate' the Pope, and that in the present crisis the 'freedom of action of the Magisterium of the Church is much more seriously impeded than the free speech of those theologians who demand if for themselves'.[192] To de Solages, de Lubac confided more bluntly: were such a complaint to come from a layman, it would betray a 'bourgeois' and 'violently anticlerical' sensibility; coming from a group of priest-theologians it betrays a self-serving aspiration 'to impose their own dictatorial will on the whole Church'.[193]

Commenting on the Conciliar Texts

Although the whole of de Lubac's post-conciliar oeuvre is animated by commentary on the Council (direct or indirect), in its immediate aftermath he wrote two 'commentaries': *La Révélation Divine* (1968), a commentary on the opening of *Dei Verbum*, and *Athéisme et Sens de l'Homme: une double requête de Gaudium et spes* (1968). In addition to these, one should add the third chapter of *Paradoxes et Mystère de l'Église* (1967), 'La constitution *Lumen gentium* et les Père de l'Église'.

In 'La constitution *Lumen gentium*' de Lubac clarifies that to call the Church a 'mystery',[194] as the constitution does, is precisely to state that she is 'a sacrament ... a sign and instrument ... of ... union with God'.[195] To grasp this properly is to see

---

190. See Hans Küng, *My Struggle for Freedom: Memoirs* (London: Continuum, 2002), pp. 389-91.

191. As quoted in John L. Allen, Jr., *Pope Benedict XVI: A Biography of Joseph Ratzinger* (London: Continuum, 2005), p. 67.

192. A copy of the letter to Congar is included in a letter to Bruno de Solages, 17.01.69 (CAÉCHL 3419); as quoted in Chantraine and Lemaire, *Henri de Lubac*, vol. 4, pp. 441-42.

193. Letter to Bruno de Solages, 22.12.68 (CAÉCHL 3416); as quoted in Chantraine and Lemaire, *Henri de Lubac*, vol. 4, p. 442.

194. *Lumen Gentium*, 5.

195. Ibid., 1. See de Lubac, *Paradoxe et mystère*, p. 72.

how, in patristic fashion, what makes the Church a 'mystery' is nothing she possesses of herself but rather consists in what she makes present: the Mystery of Christ. This is the Christocentric key to the constitution, as it is signalled in its opening declaration, 'Christ is the Light of nations'.[196] Only with this key in mind, de Lubac offers, are we able to grasp the meaning of what is original in the constitution, which consists primarily in the notion of the Church as the 'people of God', on the one hand, and the vocation of the laity within the universal call to holiness on the other.[197] While the first allows us to see the Church as a pilgrim people in historical continuity with the people Israel, the latter highlights how the Church and the call to sanctity are in no way reducible to the hierarchy or to the religious vocation. In both cases, the function and significance of these *nova* are only properly grasped within the great *novum* of understanding the Church herself as the sacrament of Christ, as irreducibly illumined and constituted by making him present in the world. Co-constitutive with the foregoing is the significant inclusion within the constitution of the Council's Mariological doctrine. According to de Lubac, the Council thus recovers a patristic vision of the interrelation of the *figura* of Mary as 'typus Ecclesiae'.[198] And herein we discover a new depth of meaning underpinning the previously noted *nova*: in Mary of Nazareth the holiness of the Church is rooted in the election of Israel, while the higher call to sanctity is not linked so much to a particular 'state' of life, as it is to the fullness of being docile to the initiative of God in Marian fashion (*ecce ancilla Domini*). De Lubac cites Gérard Philips, the key drafter of *Lumen Gentium*, to substantiate this point: 'Mary is not ... the prototype of hierarchical power, but rather the model of spiritual receptivity', and it is as such that she is the *figura* of the Church, the epiphany of its most basic essence.[199]

The provocation of *La Révélation Divine* is again Christological: *Dei Verbum* concerns the 'sacrament' of the divine will in the 'mystery of Christ who, in the unity of his person, is for us the "sacrament" of God. God draws humanity to salvation by Christ and reveals himself to her in Christ'.[200] When we speak thus of revelation and of the Scriptures, de Lubac argues, we are speaking, in both cases, of a person: 'the Word of God is, *par excellence*, and by definition, Christ'.[201] 'He is both the revelation and the one who reveals, the message of the Gospel and the Gospel in person'.[202] According to de Lubac, the Council nowhere better clarified this than when it declared that Jesus is 'both the mediator and the fullness of all revelation'.[203] In this way, according to de Lubac, the whole

---

196. *Lumen Gentium*, 1. See de Lubac, *Paradoxe et mystère*, p. 75.
197. De Lubac, *Paradoxe et mystère*, p. 87.
198. Ibid., p. 105.
199. Ibid., p. 105; quoting Philips.
200. Ibid., p. 63.
201. Henri de Lubac, *Révélation divine*, OC, vol. 4, p. 71.
202. Chantraine and Lemaire, *Henri de Lubac*, vol. 4, p. 447.
203. *Dei Verbum*, 2. Cf. de *Révélation divine*, p. 72.

first chapter of *Dei Verbum* achieves 'what Karl Barth called a Christological concentration'.[204]

The Christological focus of the Scriptures and the Church implies the ultimate Christological meaning of the human person, which is the theme of *Athéisme et Sens de l'Homme*, dedicated to the Constitution on the Church in the Modern Word, *Gaudium et Spes*. The heart of de Lubac's substantive critique of post-conciliar theological culture concerns the question of how the Christian life of grace is present in the world, how Christology illumines the whole fact of human experience in all of its factors.[205] In the post-conciliar context, as we have seen, de Lubac's chief concern involved what he detected as a new form of *conceptio christiana* re-inscribing a *théologie séparée*, now in a distinctly progressivist (as opposed to integrist) guise. Ultimately *théologie séparée*, in whatever form, involves some reduction of the meaning of faith in Christ, as if it were irrelevant to some aspect of the question of what is a 'genuinely human' life. According to Balthasar, this is the central preoccupation of *Athéisme et Sens de l'Homme*, and is signalled when de Lubac clarifies that the section on atheism in *Gaudium et Spes* is the 'punctum saliens' of the whole constitution.[206] The dialogue with atheism, broached in *Gaudium et Spes*, is wrongly understood if the 'mystical dark night of a John of the Cross' is taken as in any way equivalent with 'the night of a Nietzsche'.[207] Every 'death-of-God theology' and every fashionable 'demythologization' of the Christian religion – every 'apocalyticism' that brackets faith or does not arrive at faith – is an epigone that diminishes the essence of Christianity and makes of it a mere *conceptio*. Christianity is not an idea: it is the life that surges from an encounter with the one who alone fully 'reveals man to himself'. In the name of this integral revelation, de Lubac's reading of *Gaudium et Spes* aims to undermine the new *théologie séparée* by insisting that the constitution be read as a whole, that Part 1, 'The Church and Man's Calling', be understood as internally related to Part 2, 'Some Problems of Special Urgency'. The latter is not a pastoral or practical application of the former, rather parts 1 and 2 mutually inform one another such that there is no dichotomy between the 'pastoral' and the 'dogmatic', because the life of the human being is 'one'. The key to this unity is, for de Lubac, a properly Christological understanding of the *vocatio hominis*.[208] Christ illumines the totality of human life or he illumines nothing at all. Accordingly, only a robust rediscovery of the Christological shape of *vocatio hominis* can resist the schemes of various *théologies séparées*, and the attendant 'inferiority complex' of a Church provoked 'to doubt her eternal mission'.[209]

204. *Révélation divine*, p. 74.
205. Portier, 'What Kind of a World of Grace?', p. 142.
206. Henri de Lubac, *Athéisme et sens de l'homme: une double requite de Gaudium et Spes*, OC, vol. 4, p. 413.
207. Balthasar, *The Theology of Henri de Lubac*, p. 47.
208. De Lubac, *Athéisme et sens de l'homme*, p. 629.
209. De Lubac, *Mémoire sur l'occasion de mes écrits*, p. 343 [ET: ASC, p. 342].

The Council and the Continuity of Faith

Even as de Lubac was pained by the reality of the post-conciliar situation, he never confused the crisis with the conciliar documents themselves. He attributed the crisis, rather, to an ignorance of the Council documents, even among bishops.[210] In the course of a few letters to André Ravier written at the end of 1965, de Lubac wrote of the principle constitutions as 'a beautiful doctrinal ensemble',[211] which would in time become 'very beneficial' for the Church.[212] But the key to this beneficial and authentic reception of the Council, de Lubac judged, lay in establishing a proper hermeneutic of the Council, one which would receive it not as a break with the past but in continuity with the wider tradition. As he explained to Angelo Scola in 1985, rightly understood 'Vatican II completed the work initiated by Vatican I... through a solemn teaching that confirms the teaching of the whole Catholic tradition'.[213]

Accordingly, de Lubac opposed every hermeneutic of rupture.[214] There is 'one Church, the Church of all times, the Church of Jesus Christ, the Church of the Apostles... which renews herself only to remain herself'.[215] The hermeneutic of continuity and reform proposed by de Lubac in the 1980s anticipates fully Pope Benedict XVI's famous address to the Roman Curia in December 2005, in which he contrasted two hermeneutics: 'a hermeneutic of discontinuity and rupture', which is a false hermeneutic, and 'the "hermeneutic of reform", of renewal in the continuity of the one subject-Church'.[216] For both Benedict and de Lubac, the unity of the Christian experience requires this. However much the Church is a fact of history, and so a fact subject to the developments and contingencies of historical being, she is also and most fundamentally 'one', rooted in the singular event that constitutes *fides christiana*. As de Lubac put it, 'What we call the development of doctrine is never a relative progress, since the faith that has come from the Apostles was transmitted to the Church "one time for all"'.[217]

If the first and essential hermeneutical lens required for a proper reception of Vatican II concerned for de Lubac a principle of essential continuity with the whole dogmatic tradition of the Church, the second concerned the particular contribution of the Council. Already before the end of the Council, de

---

210. Letter to Msgr. Carlo Colombo, 1982 (CAÉCHL 77157); as quoted in Chantraine and Lemaire, *Henri de Lubac*, vol. 4, p. 491.

211. Letter to André Ravier, 21.10.65 (CAÉCHL 5090); as quoted in Chantraine and Lemaire, *Henri de Lubac*, vol. 4, p. 336.

212. Letter to André Ravier, 27.09.65 (CAÉCHL 5089); as quoted in Chantraine and Lemaire, *Henri de Lubac*, vol. 4, p. 336.

213. De Lubac, *Entretien autour de Vatican II*, p. 58.

214. *Paradoxes*, p. 218.

215. Ibid.

216. Benedict XVI, 'What Has Been the Result of the Council?', in Norman Tanner, S.J. (ed.), *Vatican II: The Essential Texts* (New York: Image, 2012), pp. 3–13, at p. 4.

217. De Lubac, *Entretien autour de Vatican II*, p. 44.

Lubac wrote that the whole of the Council would have to be read through the dogmatic constitutions,[218] and especially *Lumen Gentium*.[219] But if the dogmatic constitutions are the 'keys' to the Council,[220] the content of this concerns how they recover the Christocentric core of the Christian claim and method (cf. 2 Cor 10.5). And thus, according to *Lumen Gentium*, the light that illumines every people and nation is Christ himself.[221] In the same way, according to *Dei Verbum*, the hermeneutical foundation of the Scriptures lies in their Christological unity, the fontem,[222] which is not a *datum* but is 'Christ, who is both the mediator and the fullness of all revelation',[223] so that revelation does not first of all concern a book (or even a tradition) but rather the encounter with the Word made flesh.[224] The Christocentric insistence of the Council is finally given its deepest anthropological expression in the declaration of *Gaudium et Spes*, that Christ reveals the human being to himself.

It is sometimes said that the pontificate of John Paul II should be credited with providing the Church's 'authoritative interpretation of Vatican II'.[225] There is no doubt that he himself saw this as one of the essential tasks of his pontificate. In his first address as pope, John Paul spoke of the 'unceasing importance of the Second Vatican Ecumenical Council' and the 'definite duty of assiduously bringing it into effect'.[226] In this regard the function of the Lubacian paraphrase of *Gaudium et Spes* 22 is decisive; it is quoted in almost every major encyclical of the Pope and has been described as for him the 'most fundamental principle taught at Vatican II',[227] and 'the theological linchpin of the entire Council'.[228] But if John Paul II's pontificate achieved the 'authoritative interpretation' of Vatican II, the central event of the pontificate along this road was the 1985 Extraordinary Synod, on The Twentieth Anniversary of the Conclusion of the Second Vatican Council.

At the solemn inauguration of the Extraordinary Synod, John Paul II invoked the Christocentric texts of *Gaudium et Spes* 22 and *Lumen Gentium* 1 with urgency.[229] In this way he set the course for the proceedings of the Synod to be

---

218. De Lubac, *Carnets*, vol. 2, p. Cf. de Lubac, *Entretien autour de Vatican II*, pp. 41–51.
219. Cf. Henri de Lubac, 'Le cardinal de Lubac nous parle', *France catholique* 203 (19 July 1985): p. 4.
220. De Lubac, *Carnets*, vol. 2, p. 473.
221. *Lumen Gentium*, 1. Cf. de Lubac, *Entretien autour de Vatican II*, p. 25.
222. *Dei Verbum*, 9.
223. Ibid., 2.
224. De Lubac, *Entretien autour de Vatican II*, p. 49.
225. Weigel, *Witness to Hope*, p. 855.
226. See Jarosław Kupczak OP, 'John Paul II's Interpretation of the Second Vatican Council', *Communio* 39 (2012), pp. 152–69, at pp. 163–64.
227. David L. Schindler, Introduction to MS, p. xxvii.
228. Weigel, *Witness to Hope*, p. 224.
229. John Paul II, 'Solemn Inauguration', 6 and 9; in Bernard Cardinal Law (ed.), *The Extraordinary Synod 1985* (Boston: St Paul Editions, 1986), p. 26 and pp. 28–29. Cf. Rowland, *Ratzinger's Faith*, p. 32.

guided by the luminous Christocentrism at the core of the Council's proposal. In this light the *Final Report* of the Synod opined that 'the shadows in the post-conciliar period' are 'in part due to an incomplete understanding and application of the council'.[230] The Synod Fathers, accordingly, recommended a deeper reception of the Council in terms of two fundamental hermeneutical priorities: (1) 'Special attention must be paid to the four major Constitutions of the Council, which contain the interpretative key for the other Decrees and Declarations'.[231] And (2) 'the Council must be understood in continuity with the great tradition of the Church'.[232] As we have seen, de Lubac anticipated these two hermeneutical points. What is more, the *Final Report* went on, beyond these points, to clarify the enduring contribution of Vatican II in terms of a cluster of essential *nova*. Among these it highlighted the sacramental character of the Church (bequeathed from *Lumen Gentium*),[233] as well as the Christological heart of the human being (bequeathed from *Gaudium et Spes* 22).[234] And thus, drawing out the following implications of the Council, the Synod Fathers declared:

> The ecclesiology of communion is the central and fundamental idea of the Council's documents. Koinonia/communion, founded on the Sacred Scripture, have been held in great honor in the early Church and in the Oriental Churches to this day. Thus, much was done by the Second Vatican Council so that the Church as communion might be more clearly understood and concretely incorporated into life. What does the complex word 'communion' mean? Fundamentally it is a matter of communion with God through Jesus Christ, in the Holy Spirit.[235]

Accordingly, the Synod Father in 1985 arrived at the conclusion that the central contribution of Vatican II was precisely what Ratzinger had earlier judged decisive in de Lubac's *Catholicisme*: 'the idea of community and universality, rooted in the trinitarian concept of God, permeates and shapes all the individual elements of Faith's content ... [it] is the key that opens the door to the proper understanding of the whole'.[236]

Conclusion

'O God, if only we could lift up our heads at this time and see our redemption drawing near.' By way of conclusion, I think it is right to read Cusa's prayer and de

---

230. 'Final Report', I.3; Law, *Extraordinary Synod*, p. 39.
231. 'Final Report', I.5; ibid., p. 41.
232. 'Final Report', I.5; ibid., pp. 41–42.
233. 'Final Report', II.A.3; ibid., pp. 46–47.
234. 'Final Report', II.A.2; ibid., pp. 45–46.
235. 'Final Report', II.C.1; ibid., p. 53.
236. Ratzinger, Foreword to C, p. 11.

Lubac's appropriation of it as an intercession, not to avoid the post-conciliar crisis into which the Spirit has allowed the Church to plunge, but rather to allow the crisis to provoke an authentic reawakening of *fides christiana* lived in the midst of the circumstances of concrete history. Catastrophes in the life of the Church are only disasters when they are not lived as portals through which the sign of redemption is understood to shine with new clarity. In this sense, Cusa's prayer is a prayer that the objective reality of a council – which in the case of the Council of Basil did indeed involve an actual para-Council and even an anti-pope – be lived as a provocation to faith, to a deeper certainty of the 'I' in relation to Christ. In this sense, Cusa's prayer is a prayer into the heart of the darkness Pope Paul VI famously lamented on 29 June 1972: 'It was believed that after the Council a day of sun would shine on the history of the Church. But instead there came a day of clouds, storm, darkness, searching and uncertainty.' In the light of prayer, the darkness of Paul VI becomes luminous to the end of redemption, when the sun darkened and the dying Lord, abandoned by his followers, abandoned his own spirit into the loving hands of the Father.

The luminous meaning of darkness in the life of *fides christiana* is clarified when we connect it with another of Cusa's texts, *Reformatio Generalis*, which he wrote more than a decade after the Council of Basel at the request of Pope Pius II. Therein Cusa argues that every reform of the Church is hopeless unless it achieves to conform the inward life of the Church – the 'I' of her collective members – evermore to the *forma* of the Crucified Lord. Cusa writes: 'We, therefore, who wish to reform all Christians, at least, can put forth to them no other form for it than that which we imitate, that of Christ, from whom they receive their name. He is the living law and perfect form according to which judgement is made concerning eternal life and death.'[237]

---

237. Nicholas of Cusa, *Reformatio Generalis*, 6.

Part II

Key Themes in the Theology of Henri de Lubac

Chapter 6

THE MYSTICAL BODY: ECCLESIOLOGY AND SACRAMENTAL THEOLOGY

Gemma Simmonds, CJ

A Sacramental Ecclesiology

Henri de Lubac's famous dictum 'the Eucharist makes the church, and the church makes the Eucharist' is a principle that has become embedded in post-Vatican II ecclesiologies, and came to dominate John Paul II's encyclical of 2003 on the Eucharist in its relationship to the Church, *Ecclesia de Eucharistia*.[1] It lies at the heart of de Lubac's ground-breaking book *Corpus Mysticum,* a study of the Eucharist and the Church in the Middle Ages, written during the difficult years of Nazi occupation in France and first published in 1944. It encapsulates his understanding of the mystery of Christ's indwelling in the community of the faithful, a mystery which calls all who participate in the body of Christ to participate by that same token in the mystical life of union with God and with one another. It is this unifying principle within the Eucharist and the other sacraments that makes them social as well as theological signs. This social aspect of the sacramental life also has in and of itself a transformative dimension within the personal faith life of the individual believer, a faith which must become effective through transforming action in the world. This notion belongs within the definition of the sacrament itself, as a sign which makes real what it signifies. It also evokes its origin within the Ignatian perspective, since, within the *Spiritual Exercises* of St Ignatius, love needs to be translated into deeds as well as words.[2] De Lubac's ecclesiology, as well as his sacramental theology, is ultimately unitive, mystical, and transformative.

De Lubac wrote more about the Church than about Christ himself, and he never elaborated a complete Christology. However, he perceives a seamless dynamic

---

1. SC, p. 134; John Paul II, *Ecclesia de eucharistia*, http://www.vatican.va/holy_father/special_features/encyclicals/documents/hf_jp-ii_enc_20030417_ecclesia_eucharistia_en.html. Accessed 23 January 2017.

2. Ignatius of Loyola, *Spiritual Exercises,* trans. Luis J. Puhl. (Chicago: Loyola University Press, 1952), 230.

between Christ, the Church, and the sacraments whereby Christ is the lord of history, Christ is for us the sacrament of God, and the Church is the sacrament of Christ. For de Lubac the Eucharist and the Church exist in a reciprocal bond whereby the Church has the sanctifying power to make the Eucharist, but the Eucharist also makes the Church by uniting those who gather in Christ into one body which is sanctified in Christ and, in turn, receives the task to sanctify the world. In *Corpus Mysticum* he describes the Church as 'the Eucharist inasmuch as it bears fruit'.[3] He sees the Church sacramentally in terms of a body continually both sanctifying or transforming and being sanctified and transformed. He also sees it as sacramental insofar as it is continually being unified by the Eucharist from which it derives its nature as a body: 'the Eucharist is the mystical principle, permanently at work at the heart of Christian society, which gives concrete form to this miracle [of being made into the body of Christ].'[4]

Thus de Lubac's ecclesiology and Christology are intimately linked. Pius XII's encyclical of 1943, *Mystici Corporis*, identifies the mystical body of Christ with the ecclesial institution of the Church as the visible social body founded by Jesus who is its head and who breathes into it the life of his Spirit.[5] Those not belonging to this visible body nevertheless may have a relationship with the mystical body of Christ through the desire for virtue to which their lives give witness, much as the Church fathers understood the baptisms of blood or desire being attributed to those unbaptized who died during persecution or before they could seal through baptism the lives of virtue they had already embraced.[6] Such a narrow identification of membership of the mystical body with the Roman Catholic Church, whether by full membership or by the conscious or unconscious desire for sacramental or other forms of incorporation into the Church, was seen by many as problematic. This problem was tackled at Vatican II in *Lumen Gentium*'s famous *substitit in*, which allows for different degrees of incorporation.[7] For de Lubac, the relation between ecclesiology and Christology is crucial. Any understanding of de Lubac's sacramental theology must take into account his primary understanding of the Church itself, which must be read in light of his understanding of the relationship of the Church to Christ. Susan K. Wood remarks, 'Within the context of spiritual

---

3. CM, p. 82.
4. Ibid., p. 88.
5. Pius XII, *Mystici Corporis*, http://w2.vatican.va/content/pius-xii/en/encyclicals/documents/hf_p-xii_enc_29061943_mystici-corporis-christi.html.Accessed 23 January 2017, 64, 69. See http://w2.vatican.va/content/pius-xii/en/encyclicals/documents/hf_p-xii_enc_29061943_mystici-corporis-christi.html
6. See Aloys Grillmeier, 'The People of God', in Herbert Vorgrimler, ed., *Commentary on the Documents of Vatican II*, vol. 2 (New York: Herder and Herder, 1967), pp. 168–75, cited by Susan K. Wood, *Spiritual Exegesis and the Church in the Theology of Henri de Lubac* (Edinburgh: T&T Clark, 1998), p. 72 ff.
7. Second Vatican Council, '*Lumen Gentium:* Dogmatic Constitution on the Church', in Austin Flannery, ed., *Vatican Council II: Constitutions, Decrees, Declarations* (New York: Costello Publishing Company, 2007), p. 8.

exegesis Christ and the Eucharist are eschatologically fulfilled or completed in the Church'. The innate significance of the Church 'is both contained within the Eucharist and Christ and, reciprocally, is an objective extension of both'.[8] What makes this view particularly important is de Lubac's understanding, against that of many of his contemporaries, of the fundamental unity of the human race, the eschatological culmination and key point of which is Jesus Christ. His social understanding of the Church lies at the heart of his social understanding of the sacraments. There is some ambivalence about his identification of the Church with the mystical body, however. In some places he clearly identifies the Church with the mystical body but elsewhere he also identifies the mystical body itself, at least potentially, with humanity as a whole: 'Thus the unity of the Mystical Body of Christ, a supernatural unity, supposes a previous natural unity of the human race'.[9]

The danger of identifying the Roman Catholic Church with the mystical body of Christ is twofold. Firstly, it appears to deny that any other baptized person is part of the body of Christ, and secondly it tends to elevate the Church to an undeserved status, given the unfortunate public and repeated lapses from grace within its history, and its undeniably partial fulfilment of its destiny as yet. In *Corpus Mysticum* de Lubac tackles this challenge robustly, pointing out that the patristic and early medieval eras from which he takes much of his material for speaking of the Church as the mystical body of Christ were 'troubled times, eras where disunity and hypocrisy ruled'. He is neither retreating into an idealized past nor building a shelter in some whimsical imaginary future. Nor is he imagining that what makes this mystical body is either the human effort of gathering together or 'the collective exaltation that an appropriate pedagogy succeeds in extracting' from such an effort.[10] It is perhaps for this reason that de Lubac wrote of the Church as both a paradox and a mystery, since in the end one cannot either reduce the mystical body to the contours of the present Roman Catholic Church or fall back on vaguely mystical formulations that are deeply unsatisfactory. De Lubac's own thought in this area develops within his writing from a stance strongly allied with *Mystici Corporis* to one more reflective of *Lumen Gentium*.[11]

Corpus Mysticum itself offers us a better understanding of the relation between de Lubac's ecclesiology and his Christology. He was driven to writing it because the emphasis on the Real Presence that had developed since the Middle Ages had, he believed, obscured the pre-eminent social understanding of the body of Christ. Through the *imago Dei* all humanity is oriented towards a supernatural end and its fulfilment in Christ. Separation of individuals from that primordial unity is what constitutes sin.[12] It is for this reason that he found National Socialist and other doctrines of racism and anti-Semitism so abhorrent. Through the methods

---

8. Wood, *Spiritual Exegesis*, p. 77, 79.
9. C, p. xi.
10. CM, pp. 260–1.
11. Wood, *Spiritual Exegesis*, pp. 84–85.
12. C, p. 8.

of *ressourcement*, he interprets the oldest understanding of the Eucharist, and with it, the Church, through this social understanding. The social and pastoral implications of de Lubac's ecclesiology and sacramental theology as a whole echo the Ignatian spiritual tradition to which the Jesuit de Lubac belonged. In the Ignatian *Spiritual Exercises*, the retreatant is invited into the closest personal union with Jesus as revealed in scripture, in order to join in his mission of transforming the world in concrete terms and building up the community of the faithful. De Lubac's understanding of the relationship between the Eucharist and the ecclesial body of Christ also echoes the work of his mentor, the French philosopher Maurice Blondel, whose insistence on the need for faith to find its truest expression in transformative action in the world can be found in the work of both de Lubac and his contemporary Yves Congar. Echoes of Blondel's social preoccupation can be found in *Corpus Mysticum* (1944), *Catholicism* (1947), and *The Splendour of the Church* (1953). If de Lubac's ecclesiological and sacramental focus and, as it were, his theological understanding of the Church as mystical body can be found within *Lumen Gentium*, then his transformative and social preoccupations are echoed in *Gaudium et Spes*. He avoids seeing the Church as having been formed by believers by his emphasis on the Eucharist as causative of the Church, gathering believers into one body. He also sees the Church, in its social dimension, as embodying grace in the world, which is how he can see those who respond to God's grace while not living full membership of the Roman Catholic Church to be part of that mystical body. By distinguishing the historical Church with the body fulfilled in Christ at the end of time he points to a paradoxical state within the Church as simultaneously united with Christ but yet to achieve completion.

The Unifying Role of the Church: Natural, Supernatural, and the Social Dimension of the Sacraments

De Lubac's life's work was varied and wide-ranging. An historian of theology rather than a systematician, his recourse to patristic sources to flesh out the central contention of his doctrine of the Church and the Eucharist is sometimes overwhelming and not always clearly structured. He himself described the complex and sometimes rambling *Corpus Mysticum* as 'naive', but it provides us, through its exhaustive exploration of early sources, with a deeper understanding of his whole ecclesiology. It also articulates his sense of the dynamic nature of theology itself, dependent as it is on language which is fluid, changeable, and subject to the developments of history. Not only is language fluid, but our very notion of what 'understanding' itself means is subject to change. Thus, for example, static belief in the miracle of transubstantiation in the doctrine of the Real Presence comes to take precedence over the more dynamic contemplation of the mystery of the threefold body of Christ. Though the words 'mystical body' remain the same, the focus of our understanding of these very words becomes so different that it ends up effectively being a different understanding. De Lubac illustrates how this theological shift of perspective came about in the context of controversies against Berengar, dating from the Middle Ages, and then later against the Reformers.[13] For de Lubac the use of the language of substance to explain the nature of the sacrament calls more upon the traditions of science than of theology. The language of sign and symbol is, to him, inadequate, since it fails to make sufficient reference to the sacrament's unifying principle. 'How would the Church really be edified, how would all of her members be assembled into a truly single organism, which must be called ontological, by means of a sacrament which was only a symbol of the One whose body she must become and who alone can unify her?'[14]

De Lubac cannot see reception of the sacraments primarily in the light of the faith and edification of the individual. He sees the more historically recent tendency to lay emphasis on a private, two-way relationship between God and the participant in the sacraments as missing the principal point. *Catholicism*, his first book, already begins by making this clear: 'the unity of the Mystical Body of Christ, a supernatural unity, supposes a previous natural unity, the unity of the human race'. He extends this unity beyond the sacrament of the Eucharist to the Church's sacramental and wider mission of reconciliation, pointing out that 'all infidelity to the divine image that man bears in him, every breach with God, is at the same time a disruption of human unity'.[15]

Any understanding of de Lubac's sacramental theology hangs on his ecclesiology. Any understanding of his ecclesiology is in turn incomplete without an understanding of his conviction, following his philosophical mentor Blondel, that participation in the life of Christ also has a social dimension, requiring participation in transformative action for the good of the world. De Lubac is at pains to show that this is not some 'new' theology, a mere accommodating of the theological tradition to modern understandings of human solidarity. Along with Yves Congar and other *ressourcement* theologians of like mind, his great contribution was to show how such a view is precisely part of the most ancient theological tradition of the Church.

His major critique of neo-scholasticism was not about its methods but about its distortion of Aquinas's teaching on the relationship between grace and nature. His understanding of the union of grace and nature in Christ underlies his whole sacramental theology, which is central to his ecclesiology and vice versa. Grace and nature cannot be set in opposition to one another anymore than our understanding of God's revelation in Christ can be seen as beyond human reason and critical investigation or as having nothing to do with the concrete context in which human beings live. If humanity is to be saved it is to be saved in all aspects of the life it has constructed for itself within society, and those structures must reflect the grace of God revealed in the saving message of Christ. This understanding of the dynamic relationship between God's revelation and human

13. CM, pp. 226–28, 236–38.
14. See TF, p. 74.
15. C, pp. 25, 33.

response in concrete terms, lived out in bonds of unity, is at the heart of de Lubac's sacramental ecclesiology. It is the nature of the Church as saved humanity united in the body of Christ that is pivotal to his thought. Hans Urs von Balthasar, in his book on de Lubac, comments that the Church 'is the real center of his whole life's work: the meeting point of God's descending world and man's world ascending to him'.[16]

For de Lubac not only does the Church as mystical body unite humanity in Christ but it also unites humanity in bonds of brother and sisterhood and unites the natural with the supernatural in a way that refuses a separation of human and divine life into opposing realms. De Lubac read Blondel with enthusiasm as a Jesuit scholastic and knew him personally, editing his correspondence and readily acknowledging his debt to Blondel's work, particularly with regard to the supernatural. He credited Blondel with having dealt the death blow to the dualism within Christian thinking against which he himself fought for so long, opposing both the extrinsicism that considers the supernatural as something external to and separate from human nature and the objective methodologies of intellectual enquiry and the immanentism that reduces it to a purely human construct, thus dispensing with divine revelation. Blondel found in neo-scholasticism a tendency to dispense with historical criticism or rational investigation since it held that divine revelation lives in a sovereign realm far removed from such human considerations. He nevertheless also objected to a tendency he perceived among the modernists to reduce revelation to what human scientific methodologies can make of it. For Blondel each tendency was inimical to true faith.[17] De Lubac's aim, in its turn, is described by one commentator as, 'to make us see […] that Christian thought, within Tradition, unites the gift of God the Creator and the supernatural gift of God the Saviour'.[18]

In this sense the holiness of the Church is to be seen not as something that separates faith and its expression from human reality and the critical awareness of the human mind, but as the corporate and concrete expression, within human reality, of the holiness of God which dwells, by God's free and unmerited grace, within the body of believers. This is both a pledge of God's abiding presence within the Church and a challenge for the Church to be the incarnate and substantial presence of Christ within the world in all its realities. As such it rescues Christians from a prevailing doubt in their own capacity to live lives of grace and sanctification within the world as it is, while challenging them on a daily

---

16. Hans Urs von Balthasar, *The Theology of Henri de Lubac: An Overview* (San Francisco: Ignatius, 1991), p. 105.

17. See Bryan C. Hollon, *Everything is Sacred: Spiritual Exegesis in the Political Theology of Henri de Lubac* (Cambridge: James Clarke and Co, 2010), pp. 98–99.

18. Georges Chantraine, 'The Supernatural: Discernment of Catholic Thought According to Henri de Lubac', in Serge-Thomas Bonino, ed., *Surnaturel: A Controversy at the Heart of Twentieth-Century Thomistic Thought* (Ave Maria, FL: Sapienta Press), pp. 21–40, 22.

basis to lives that speak convincingly even to a cynical and unbelieving world of God's presence within human reality. This has important repercussions for the Church's mission of evangelization. Both Blondel and de Lubac lived in periods of widespread cynicism about and distrust of a Church that was seen by unbelievers to have allied itself too often with the structures of power and privilege for its own protection. For both it was a matter of highest importance to present a faith that is convincing in terms both of its content and of its fruits. In this sense apologetics is not the self-centred monologue of a faith that only speaks to its own adherents but a genuine dialogue with the questions and concerns of unbelievers. It can only be of use when coupled by the active witness of transformative faith.

This was not a matter of reducing faith to a social programme. Blondel was acutely aware of the futile positions taken up by modern philosophy, which accepted nothing that could enter the human spirit but what originated from it and corresponded to its own need for self-expression and self-fulfilment. He was equally aware of a falsity within some contemporary Catholic thought, which saw the supernatural as entirely distinct from human thought and will. He took this further, seeing that the only true and appropriate response to the divine indwelling within humanity was a 'sacramental' action which became to believer and unbeliever alike a sign which made real what it signified. The presence of God in the human soul must find expression in a human compassion and commitment to the truth against all false idolatries and ideologies if faith is to be convincing to those who do not share it. One can see why such notions took hold of the minds of a generation of young Jesuits who were formed in the spirituality of Saint Ignatius, of which this was such a strong echo, and threatened by the toxic atheistic ideologies of the twentieth century which would bring so much death and horror in their wake in the name of human progress and achievement.[19] De Lubac's work challenges not only these ideologies with their mass responses to personal as well as social dilemmas, but also the unbridled enthroning of the self-authenticating ego on which the notion of fascist supremacy was built. An echo of Blaise Pascal's 'the "I" is detestable' is found in de Lubac's objection to 'the swamping of the spiritual life by the detestable "I", the failure to realize that prayer is essentially the prayer of all for all' found in the introduction to *Catholicism*, whose subtitle is, tellingly, *the Social Aspects of Dogma*'.[20] He cites Origen's *ubi peccata, ibi multitudo*, which claimed that individualization and the fragmentation of human social bonds is the result of the fall.[21] This is echoed in Blaise Pascal's *Pensées*: 'Mine, yours. "This dog is mine," said those poor children; "that is my place in the sun". This is how the whole earth began to be

---

19. See Jean-Pierre Wagner, *La Théologie Fondamentale selon Henri de Lubac* (Cerf: Paris, 1997), pp. 38–42. Wagner cites Maurice Blondel, *Lettre sure les Exigences de la Pensée Contemporaine en Matière d'Apologétique* (Paris: PUF, 1956), p. 7.
20. C, p. 16.
21. Ibid., pp. 33–34.

usurped'.[22] In terms of the Church of today this represents a challenge to two streams of contemporary ecclesiology and spirituality. Any tendency to reduce the Church to a this-worldly social programme which ignores the roots of social disorder in personal sin is countered by his insistence on the Church's necessary salvific and eschatological dimensions. Any tendency to focus the spiritual life on a programme of self-help with an eye to personal fulfilment is revealed as narcissistic reductionism in light of the world's urgent need for social, economic, and political transformation as the necessary context for personal salvation. It is small wonder, then, that de Lubac found himself at odds with some post-conciliar developments within spirituality and political theology.

For de Lubac redemption is not only a restoration of the harmony between individuals and their Creator, but a recovery of the lost unity between human beings and one another. This does not only happen as a result of the passion and death of Jesus but as a result of the incarnation itself, since 'Christ from the very first moment of his existence virtually bears all men within himself'. This unity of all human beings in Christ is a mystical reality which results in a 'fraternal charity, a radiant novelty in the midst of a world grown old in its divisions'.[23] This has a considerable bearing on de Lubac's understanding of the nature and role of the sacraments within the Church. The Eucharist is first and foremost the sacrament of unity, both ecclesial and human. De Lubac laments that this is almost a forgotten doctrine in his day, a secondary consideration, not essential to the practice or understanding of the sacrament. For the Fathers the unity of the body of Christ was not subordinate to other doctrinal considerations but was at the very forefront of their thoughts; he cites Cyprian, John Chrysostom, and others emphasizing the merging of Christians in unity with God and among themselves as the whole purpose of the Eucharist.

In the same way de Lubac sees the sacrament of penance not only as the forgiveness of the individual but the sinner's social re-integration. He reminds us of the primitive discipline of the Church, with its elaborate apparatus of public penance and pardon by which the penitent's public reconciliation with the Church was an efficacious sign of reconciliation with God.[24]

Lumen Gentium states, '[The] faithful are by baptism made one body with Christ and are constituted among the People of God; they are in their own way made sharers in the priestly, prophetical, and kingly functions of Christ; and they carry out for their own part the mission of the whole Christian people in the Church and in the world.'[25] Long before the notion became commonplace among post-conciliar Catholics, de Lubac made clear that one of the primary fruits of baptism is humanity's radical incorporation into the priesthood of Christ.

---

22. Blaise Pascal, *Pensées*, V, p. 295, my translation.
23. C, pp. 37, 54.
24. C, p. 87.
25. *Lumen Gentium*, 31.

Through baptism every Christian becomes part of a priestly people whose role is to mediate life and grace to others. He sees the Christian people, as a worshipping community, playing a priestly role as the true 'Israel among the nations' in relation to the rest of humankind, fulfilling a mediatory function as the living image of Christ.[26] This concept of salvation as essentially priestly and social comes from the Jewish tradition found within the Old Testament. Sin is not only a breach with that capacity for union with God planted within each human soul, but also a dramatic disruption of the union of human beings with one another that lies deep within the divine plan:

> all infidelity to the divine image that man bears, every breach with God, is at the same time a disruption of human unity. It cannot eliminate the natural unity of the human race – the image of God, tarnished though it may be, is indestructible – but it ruins that spiritual unity which, according to the Creator's plan, should be so much the closer in proportion as the supernatural union of man with God is the more completely effected.[27]

Thus the mission of the Church is to be the social embodiment of grace, restoring and completing the unity of the whole human race lost by sin. This echoes Augustine's confrontation with the Donatists who sought to divide 'pure' believers from sinners. It is from Augustine that we receive this notion of a universal Church open to all and excluding none.

One author has described de Lubac's *Surnaturel* as 'a question of presenting the Catholic message in a fashion better anchored in tradition (notably by going back to the Fathers of the Church), but at the same time better attuned to the aspirations of the time'.[28] His work, in this sense, is similar to that of the scribe 'trained for the kingdom of heaven' who is described by Jesus as being 'like the master of a household who brings out of his treasure what is new and what is old'.[29] This could as well stand as a description of *Corpus Mysticum* and much of de Lubac's later writing. His insistence on dogma's social aspects was not driven by political ideology, though it found many echoes in the thinking of his non-religious contemporaries. He saw one of the Second Vatican Council's greatest achievements as having broken with the extrinsicism which he believed was the bane of modern Catholicism. In acknowledging the supernatural as being infused within the natural, the Council laid down an understanding of the divine/human relationship in both individuals and the body of the Church which had at its roots de Lubac's sacramental ecclesiology.

---

26. See SC, p. 96.
27. C, p. 33.
28. Étienne Fouilloux, 'Henri de Lubac at the Moment of the Publication of *Surnaturel*', in *Surnaturel: A Controversy at the Heart of Twentieth-Century Thomistic Thought*, pp. 7–8.
29. Matt. 13:52.

Church, Sacraments, and Transformative Action

Through his father de Lubac was influenced by Albert de Mun's Social Catholicism, an attempt to implement Leo XIII's 1981 encyclical *Rerum Novarum* and to bring about social reform through Catholic teaching. His commitment to the French resistance led him, along with several fellow Jesuits, to participate in producing the clandestine *Cahiers du Témoignage Chrétien*, which, in 1941, under the title *France, Prends Garde de Perdre ton Âme*, denounced the anti-Christian nature of Nazism. He sought a theology that would affirm the fundamental goodness of human nature and respond to some of the challenges of modern times. This practical and pastoral application of theological reasoning was the bedrock of his 'sacramental ecclesiology', that is, his desire to see faith as a sign which makes real what it signifies. Despite such intentions this provoked a strong reaction from those who suspected his politics as much as his critique of their interpretation of Aquinas.[30] De Lubac and his contemporaries were painfully aware of the large-scale de-Christianization of parts of France and of French society, notably the working class, largely lost to the Church and the practice of the sacraments. What de Lubac wanted was to ground Catholic social teaching within a solid theological tradition that both responds to urgent human and societal needs and points to the Church and the Eucharist as the true fulfilment of humanity's fundamental orientation towards the divine.[31] This would have implications for de Lubac's writing, as indeed his own actions with regard to Nazism and anti-Semitism, since he could not accept any form of ideology which puts a barrier in the way of the longing for God which he saw as irrevocably linking both Judaism and Christianity. His opposition to Nazism was not born out of political ideology, and he refused on those grounds to join the Free French. He saw it instead as a spiritual resistance in which Christianity and the eucharistic unity at its core was to be defended against the paganism and vile racism which he detected within Nazism and the Vichy regime.[32] Such idolatries were a denial both of the human solidarity at the heart of the Church which could look on no individual or group as hateful in and of itself and of the innate bond of those united in and through Christ to one another, whether by baptism or by their common humanity.

With his friend Yves de Montcheuil, who was executed as a member of the French Resistance in 1944, de Lubac shared an eschatological vision of the Church and of humanity itself. They saw that the total Christian transfiguration

---

30. See Peter J. Bernardi, *Maurice Blondel, Social Catholicism and Action Française: The Clash over the Church's Role in Society during the Modernist Era* (Washington, DC: Catholic University of America Press, 2009).

31. See Raymond Moloney, 'Henri de Lubac on Church and Eucharist', *Irish Theological Quarterly*, 70 (2005): pp. 331–42, at p. 334.

32. See Jacques Prévotat, 'Henri de Lubac et la conscience chrétienne face aux totalitarismes', in *Henri de Lubac et le mystère de l'Église* (Paris: Cerf, 1999), pp. 183–208; Michel Sales, 'La résistance au nazisme du Père de Lubac', *Christus* 47 (2000): pp. 155–61.

of the universe within time is a myth, but they nevertheless believed that human beings are oriented towards a transfiguration in some fundamental sense, and that whatever we achieve in this regard, however partially, remains worthwhile. This is what makes social action in the name of the kingdom valid even if it is always doomed to only partial success. De Lubac saw Montcheuil as a martyr to Christian charity, although in the aftermath of the war he came to fear that the postwar Church was ashamed of such martyrs.[33]

In *Catholicism,* de Lubac offers us a statement which helps to situate his sacramental theology and Christology at the heart of his ecclesiology: 'If Christ is the sacrament of God, the church is for us the sacrament of Christ – she makes him really present [...] she is his very continuation'.[34] All his subsequent reflections on the Church, and in particular *Corpus Mysticum,* are prolonged considerations of the patristic view of the way in which the sacraments, and above all the Eucharist, are the fruit of a redemption and a revelation that work fundamentally at the social rather than the individual level, since grace is conveyed and maintained by the sacraments to the extent to which they join individual believers to the one body in Christ.

> All the sacraments are essentially sacraments of the church. In her alone do they produce their full effect, for in her alone, 'the society of the Spirit', is there, normally speaking, participation in the gift of the Spirit. If we can speak of the sacraments as the means of salvation we must therefore also speak of them as instruments of unity, since, 'as they make real, renew or strengthen man's union with Christ, by that very fact they make real, renew or strengthen his union with the Christian community' [...] it is through his union with the community that the Christian is united to Christ.[35]

In a foretaste of his forensic exploration of patristic and scholastic texts in *Corpus Mysticum* de Lubac quotes Ivo of Chartres' contention that 'the sacraments make the church'. De Lubac contrasts a 'mystical' understanding of the Church as a mystery of faith, which he finds in the early tradition, with the juridical understanding which he sees as emerging from the early middle ages onwards. The mystery of faith proclaimed by Christians is what the Letter to the Ephesians describes as the divine plan, in the fullness of time, to gather up all things earthly and heavenly in Christ, reconciling all creation to God. The culmination of this reconciliation is Christ dwelling within believers as their hope of glory (cf. Eph. 1: 10–12, Col.1:21; 26–27). Paul's doctrine of Christ as head and the Church as body is brought together by de Lubac, following Augustine, in his understanding

---

33. See the dedication to his *Proudhon et le christianisme* and a letter to Jean Danielou cited in Fouilloux, 'Henri de Lubac at the Moment of the Publication of *Surnaturel*', p. 15, n. 66.
34. C, p. 76.
35. Ibid., p. 82.

of the Eucharist as the coming together of the whole body of Christ, living and dead, within the celebrating community, entering by means of the sacrament into a deeper share in the divine life. It is for this reason that he claims that the Eucharist makes the Church.[36] Again de Lubac follows Augustine in a claim that has profound pastoral implications, especially when dealing with those who profess no formal religious faith, since he sees the divine plan as expressing itself in a restlessness and longing for God which, however articulated, is natural to every human being: 'You have made us for yourself, O God, and our hearts are restless until they rest in you.'[37]

De Lubac's 'mystical' view of the Church pertains not only to the Eucharist but to all the sacraments. Beginning with baptism he expresses his understanding of grace as concrete and communal in the patristic notion of the priesthood of all the baptized, whereby all are anointed into the one priesthood of Christ.[38] He sees this priestly role of the body of believers as a whole as mediating the life and grace of God to the whole world.[39] We see this view underlying the theology of the laity found in *Lumen Gentium*:

> Thus it is evident to everyone, that all the faithful of Christ of whatever rank or status, are called to the fullness of the Christian life and to the perfection of charity; by this holiness as such a more human manner of living is promoted in this earthly society [...] The classes and duties of life are many, but holiness is one – that sanctity which is cultivated by all who are moved by the Spirit of God, and who obey the voice of the Father and worship God the Father in spirit and in truth.[40]

De Lubac's understanding of the priesthood of all believers is not merely a function of social benevolence, though it may well have implications that are transformative for society. The consequences of baptism are spiritual and mystical since the Church is not a purely human society. Baptism means incorporation into the mystical body of Christ, so it is a social as well as a salvific sign, implying incorporation into the mystical body, but also what de Lubac terms 'concorporation', mysteriously uniting all humankind in the body of Christ. He lays emphasis on the extent to which this was a commonplace notion in the sermons of the patristic era, though less familiar to his own contemporaries.[41]

Through each baptized person the Church appears as the chief object as well as the chief minister of sacraments. The sacraments, redemption, and revelation,

---

36. CM, pp. 88–89.
37. R. S. Pine-Coffin, ed., *Saint Augustine: Confessions* (London: Penguin, 1961), 1:1–2.
38. SC, p. 93, referring to Augustine, *The City of God,* ed. Boniface Ramsey (New York: New City Press, 2012), 20:10 and Rev. 20:6.
39. Ibid., p. 96.
40. *Lumen Gentium*, 40, 41.
41. C, pp. 37–39, 83–84.

for de Lubac, are all fundamentally social, making real not only our union with Christ but also our union with one another in the Christian community.[42] This derives from Augustine's contention that the Church in this spiritual unity is the true body of Christ.[43] This true body bears within it the fulfilment of God's plan, intended since the beginning and brought to reality in Christ, for the divine and the human to be forever united (Heb. 2:9–10). This is contrasted by de Lubac with the medieval notion of the true body of Christ as the Eucharist, while the term 'mystical body', historically a designation for the sacrament, came to be descriptive instead of the Church.[44] Augustine was concerned not so much with static notions of what later theology called the *sacramentum tantum*, the objective reality of the sacrament, as with the *res sacramenti*, its spiritual fruit within the Church, as gathered body of Christ, which receives it. This is what God designed the Eucharist to bring about.[45]

With patristic writers like Gregory of Nyssa and Hilary of Poitiers he holds that 'he who beholds the Church really beholds Christ'.[46] This may prove problematic for the postmodern believer, who not only lives in an age that is deeply suspicious of public institutions, be they sacred or secular, but has also had to witness recent ecclesial scandals not only at the level of the individual but, far more worryingly, at the level of the institution and its authorities. De Lubac's is not a naive or exalted view of the Church as an institutional reality – he suffered enough at its hands not to be foolishly optimistic in this regard. Instead it is a claim for the presence of Christ in the world, hidden within the life of believers and of all who long for transcendence, and simultaneously for the essentially social nature of the Church in contrast to the rampant individualism of the modern age.

This also has practical implications for how this presence is made visible in transformative action. De Lubac does not claim any monopoly for unitive and transformative desires on the part of the Church. Together with Blondel he recognizes such desires as being present among many non-believers and movements that are not specifically religious. According to de Lubac, 'The unity of the human family as a whole is the subject [...] of some of the deepest yearnings of our age'.[47]

Blondel and Beyond

In the light of all this, it is ironic that, in later life, de Lubac became a critic of liberation theology. Gustavo Gutierrez, one of its founding fathers, nevertheless

---

42. Ibid., pp. 82–83.
43. See Boniface Ramsey, ed., *Saint Augustine: The City of God*, vol. 1 (New York: New City Press, 2012), 7: xii–xxii, p. 483.
44. CM, pp. 105–6.
45. TF, p. 74.
46. C, p. 73.
47. Ibid., p. 353.

cites de Lubac's retrieval of the social and historical aspects of Christian salvation as a source for the development of liberation theology.[48] Liberation theology also inherits the notion of the sacraments as essentially social, unitive, and transformative. De Lubac became hostile to any moves that could be interpreted as diminishing the transcendent character of the Church, but another irony lies in this, since the 'social Catholicism' he espoused was precisely seen as one such attempt by those who opposed him. This seems in one sense to be a revisiting of the old extrinsicism versus immanentism debate, with de Lubac now on the other side of the floor. Yet in much of his writing he sees social concern as being integral to Christian salvation, emphasizing the need for charity to be incarnated in concrete reality.

Despite his later stance, which has been interpreted by some as a move to a more conservative outlook in the aftermath of the Council, it is clear that the bitter quarrel between de Lubac and the Dominican champion of neo-scholasticism, Garrigou-Lagrange, covertly featured political and ideological elements as well as academic and theological ones. Garrigou-Lagrange had favoured the regime of Vichy during the Second World War and, like Marshal Pétain, was enthusiastic in the cause of Maurras's anti-Semitic *Action française* which supported a strong, militaristic, and nationalistic state in which the Church served as an instrument for social order. Despite Pius XI's condemnation of *Action française* in 1926, Garrigou-Lagrange joined many others who blamed 'national apostasy' and the secularism of France's Third Republic for its worst crisis in centuries, considering Pétain to be God's representative in a spiritual renewal of the nation against Bolshevism and freemasonry, and declaring those who opposed him to be in a state of sin. In the name of a sacramental ecclesiology, de Lubac took a different stance. His 'communion ecclesiology' represented an attempt to understand and present the Church concretely in its historical and spiritual dimensions in the face of the challenges of modernity. It brought Catholicism into critical dialogue with the issues of his time and entailed an implicit critique of those forms of ecclesiology and sacramental theology which at best refused to engage with the secular issues and ideologies of the day and at worst colluded with them.[49] De Lubac saw faith as occupying not just the dimension of the spiritual and intellectual, but also that of the social and historical, in which various non-ecclesial elements of human cultures can be seen as preparations for the Gospel.[50]

---

48. Gustavo Gutierrez, *A Theology of Liberation: History, Politics and Salvation* (Maryknoll: Orbis, 1973), p. 70.

49. Dennis M. Doyle, *Communion Ecclesiology: Vision and Versions* (Maryknoll: Orbis, 2000); Michael G. Lawler and Thomas J. Shanahan, *Church: A Spirited Communion* (Collegeville: Liturgical Press, 1995), p. 214.

50. See Joseph Komonchak, 'Theology and Culture at Mid-Century: The Example of Henri de Lubac', *Theological Studies*, 51 (1990): pp. 579–602.

The Church on Earth and in Heaven: Eschatology and Transformation

De Lubac is not naive about the challenges inherent in a view of the visible Church which has a uniting and mediating role but is itself made up of sinners. With St Ambrose he points to the ambiguity of the metaphor of the Church as bride, since she is also a wretched being saved from prostitution at the Incarnation. If the Church is a means of salvation, she is, 'a necessary means, a divine means, but provisional as means always are'.[51] He insists that the hierarchical structures of the Church and even her sacramental character are provisional, necessary in this present time, but destined to pass away at the *eschaton*, where all symbolism will be replaced by naked truth, 'Insofar as she is visible and temporal, the Church is destined to pass away. She is a sign and a sacrament, and it is the peculiar quality of signs and sacraments to be re-absorbed in the reality they signify'.[52]

Despite his robust attitude concerning the temporary nature of the structures of the Church, de Lubac follows St Augustine's claim, echoed by other patristic writers, that the transforming power of the Eucharist changes us, both as individuals and as a faith community, into Christ himself. 'Let us rejoice & give thanks, not only that we have been made Christians, but that we have been made Christ.'[53] He also speaks of unity as the specific property of the Eucharist, whereby, 'By being digested into his body and turned into his members we may be what we receive'.[54] He cites the prayers at the Offertory of the Mass of Paul VI where the priest prays, while pouring a drop of water into the chalice of wine, 'through the mystery of this water and wine may we come to share in the divinity of Christ, who humbled himself to share in our humanity'. He sees this as symbolizing the concrete realization of the infusion of the supernatural with the natural. The priest then washes his hands while praying, 'Lord wash me from my iniquities, cleanse me from my sin'. Just before the highest point of the Mass, where by divine grace the bread and wine are transformed into the body and blood of Christ, we have humanity's acknowledgement of God's redemptive grace and saving action, in response to human sin, which consists in a refusal to share in the divine life at God's invitation.[55]

This sharing is offered to humanity in Christ and the Church of Christ receives the commission to transmit this to all generations for the transformation of the world. Nevertheless, in the aftermath of the Council de Lubac came to resist strongly what he saw as efforts to make this transformative and social aspect of

---

51. C, p. 70. See also CM, pp. 260–1.

52. CPM, p. 53, 74.

53. Augustine, *Tractates on the Gospel of John* (Washington, DC: Catholic University of America Press, 1994), 21:8.

54. Augustine, *The Works of St. Augustine: A Translation for the 21st Century: Sermons 51–94*, trans. Edmund Hill (Brooklyn, NY: New City Press, 1991), 57:7.

55. BC, pp. 168–70.

sacramental ecclesiology part of a secularist and immanentist agenda which, in its utilitarian separation of the natural and supernatural orders, would end up exalting the natural to the destruction of any notion of the supernatural. This led him to a severe critique of Dominican theologian Schillebeeckx's notion of the Church as 'sacrament of the world' (*sacramentum mundi*), which he saw as collapsing human history and salvation history into one and as denying both the world's need for salvation and the Church's mediating role in bringing the light of Christ to the world.[56]

There is a symmetry between de Lubac's eucharistic ecclesiology, his understanding of sacraments as instruments of unity, and his continuing consideration of the relationship between nature and grace. Under the inspiration of his friend and fellow Jesuit Pierre Teilhard de Chardin, he believed that there was a dynamic force within all of creation towards fulfilment and completion in God. The notion of desire is central to the Ignatian understanding of the divine-human relationship as found in the *Spiritual Exercises* and plays a crucial role in de Lubac's understanding of Aquinas's teaching on nature and grace. For de Lubac, God is the creator both of nature and of grace, which are inextricably linked within the human creation. Humankind still needs divine grace and revelation to reach its ultimate end, but nature has an intrinsic tendency towards grace. Humanity's creation in the *imago Dei* means precisely that all human beings have an inherent desire for the vision of God, which de Lubac sees as a free gift, yet also as lying at the root of every soul. It is this *imago Dei* that unites human beings at a fundamental level with one another and with God in Christ when they are gathered together in Christ's body in the Eucharist.

Grace and Transformation

De Lubac's sense of this human and ecclesial unity engendered by the Eucharist is not just an abstract sacramental or ecclesiological consideration but it marries concern for a social and transformative sacramental theology and ecclesiology, sensitive to the concerns of his non-believing contemporaries, with a deep sense of the lost historical patrimony of patristic sources. It was a concern shared by his fellow 'new' theologians and is the pastoral question that lies silently beneath the historical investigations in *Corpus Mysticum*. Taking up these concerns German theologian now turned curial cardinal Walter Kasper speaks of the 'disastrously contracted viewpoint of later development' in theology of the Eucharist and the Word, based on early disputes within the Church. He attributes to the biblical and liturgical renewal for which *nouvelle théologie* was largely responsible the revived awareness of the Church as *communio* and the essential role in forming and sustaining the ecclesial body of Christ played by the Eucharist. This *communio*

---

56. See Hans Boersma, *Nouvelle Théologie and Sacramental Ontology: A Return to Mystery* (Oxford: Oxford University Press, 2009), pp. 257–65. Cf. also CM, p. 261.

is seen as part of the doctrine of the common priesthood of all the baptized which lays stress on the importance of lay participation in worship through word and sacrament. Access to audible liturgy and vernacular text are the tools for encouraging such participation, nurturing the whole life of the Church and finding expression in the *sensus fidelium*.

De Lubac's exaltation of tradition was not rooted in defiance of hierarchy or of modern life, but in a sense of how the division of natural and supernatural, secular and sacred had led to the diminishment both of the religious and of the secular spheres, setting up in both a falsely defensive dualism and isolationism in which dialogue becomes impossible and the full sense of Church and sacrament is lost. This leads to a reduced sense of the full nature and purpose of human living on the one hand and to a disregard for 'worldly' virtues on the other.

By rooting in the Fathers his belief in the unifying power of the Eucharist and its social implications, de Lubac put the force of traditional sources behind his own participation in the struggle against Nazism and anti-Semitism along with fellow Jesuits Fessard, Chaillet, and Montcheuil and their contribution to the journal *Les Cahiers du Témoignage Chrétien*.[57] It is from their writings, along with other sources, that he illustrates his arguments about grace and nature in his *Brief Catechesis on Nature and Grace*, written towards the end of his life. De Lubac is concerned not only with what grace is, but with how it operates within the soul. From this we gain an understanding of how he sees the sacraments as working within the recipient but also within the body of the Church as a transformative power.

We see this transformation in an eschatological sense, in that the supernatural transforms nature at the *parousia*, but we also see it as unfolding already in the here and now, the supernatural transfiguring the natural, according to Teilhard, deepening and bringing to fulfilment our authentic human values. This is not, however, some human utopian dream, a human construct in place of the Church as revealed and instituted by Christ. De Lubac sees humility, and the Christian asceticism of which it is part, as the indispensable condition for realizing the union of God and humanity.[58] Against the totalitarian ideologies that so tragically marked the century which his life spanned, no individual or social structure can ever realize the Christian synthesis. At the same time he is wary of any attempt to pin down one era of human history as being fully and authentically 'Christian', in this sense, since even in the so-called Christian eras human history was corrupt and often contributed to the corruption from within the Church itself. Both the notion of building a human paradise without God and its opposing notion that the Church in some sense is capable of fully realizing the Christian project at

---

57. See James Bernauer, 'A Jesuit Spiritual Insurrection: Resistance to Vichy', in James Bernauer and Robert A. Maryks, eds, *'The Tragic Touple': Encounters between Jews and Jesuits* (Boston: Brill, 2014), pp. 203–18.

58. Again, this is a profoundly Ignatian understanding, echoing the *Spiritual Exercises*. See BC, pp. 82–89.

any point in its history are delusions for de Lubac, who echoes here his friend de Montcheuil's *Le Royaume et ses Exigeances*.[59]

For de Lubac the Church's primary mission is to remind us of our supernatural vocation and to communicate to its members the seed of divine life. This is not just something to which we can look forward at the end of time, but it is being realized already, in the words of the first letter of John, 'Beloved, we are God's children now; what we will be has not yet been revealed. What we do know is this: when he is revealed, we will be like him, for we will see him as he is'.[60] This means not only the transformation of the individual human heart, but also the transformation of history, though this cannot reduce salvation to a this-worldly campaign for societal improvement or reduce the Church to a poor duplication of other benevolent human institutions.[61]

This has a further bearing on de Lubac's understanding of the Church's sacramental ministry of reconciliation. If the incarnation brings about the union of nature and the supernatural, then the union of nature and grace is fully accomplished only through the mystery of redemption as expressed in the forgiveness of sins. De Lubac quotes Pascal's *Memorial* which equates knowledge of God with knowledge of our sinfulness which, through forgiveness and repentance, becomes a source of consolation rather than of desolation.[62] He decries the modern tendency to reject or avoid any mention of the need for pardon and reconciliation, or a reduction of the notion of sin exclusively to the level of collective or social sin. He sees this as the perverse construction of a universe in which evil is 'everywhere denounced, but nowhere admitted'. Against this he claims an integrated and mature faith, entailing an enduring moral and metaphysical responsibility on the part of individual human beings for all their thoughts and acts.[63] No scientific or sociopolitical notion of progress can do away with the reality of sin. Quoting Teilhard he says, 'the *De Profundis* and the *Miserere* remain invulnerable to the best verified results of science; they spring from an experience which science can neither provide nor undermine'.[64] While sharing with Blondel and Teilhard a generally optimistic view of human nature, he rejects the myth of human innocence and its inexorable progress and the false optimism of scientism. Were this myth to be true, it would result in the separation of nature and the supernatural whereby, 'the last word in Christian progress and the entry into adulthood would then appear to consist in total "secularization"

---

59. Yves de Montcheuil, *Le Royaume et ses Exigeances* (Paris: Epi, 1957), p. 91.
60. Jn. 3:2.
61. BC, pp. 111–13.
62. See Pascal's *Memorial* in http://www.users.csbsju.edu/~eknuth/pascal.html. Accessed 23 January 2017. This is also echoed in the Ignatian *Spiritual Exercises*.
63. BC, pp. 131–37.
64. Ibid., p. 147, see also Pierre Teilhard de Chardin, *Le Milieu Divin: Essai de Vie Intérieure* (Paris: Ed. du Seuil, 1957).

which would expel God not merely from the life of society, but from culture and even from personal relationships'.[65]

What de Lubac calls realism is the recognition of the two fundamental human truths of sin and grace. Redemption, in this sense, does not lie in the reduction of salvation to some kind of human liberation or social emancipation but in 'a divine undertaking which comes about in the depths of hearts and is inscribed in eternity'.[66] This takes us back to the enduring theme within his work of the social aspect of Christian belief and practice: 'Our whole religion, in the principal articles of its *Credo*, in its living constitution, in its sacramental system, in the end that it offers to our hope exhibits an eminently social character, which it would be impossible without distortion of our religion to disregard.'[67]

Salvation consists in the pardon of sins and the sinner's joy in receiving God's mercy, experienced not only in the life of the individual but in that of all humanity, united in Christ and with it the whole cosmos. This reflects the cosmic vision of St Paul (cf. Rom.8:18–24), and of Teilhard, for whom, with de Lubac, scientific discoveries pose no threat to Christian dogma, since they drive us to an ever-deeper exploration of the meaning of Christian faith in its concern for the whole of human history and for each member of the human family. The natural desire for human unity which de Lubac detects in human nature will, he believes, lead people of good will to the threshold of Catholicism as it offers a collective transcendent destiny.[68]

De Lubac's sacramental ecclesiology is grounded in paradox, the paradox of the eternal, sinless God being found living within finite, sinful humanity, and that of radical inclusivity, communion, and relationality among human beings despite their sinful tendency towards division, both in the world and within the Church itself, made up as it is of sinners. The mystery of God's presence within the world is worked out concretely within the dynamics of history within the social body of the Church, which bears seeds within traditions and structures not its own.[69] During the Council de Lubac sat on the subcommission which produced the first chapter of *Gaudium et Spes*, which declared that 'The joys and the hopes, the griefs and the anxieties of the men of this age, especially those who are poor or in any way afflicted, these are the joys and hopes, the griefs and anxieties of the followers of Christ. Indeed, nothing genuinely human fails to raise an echo in their hearts.'[70]

Thus the world is seen as the context in which the drama of human salvation is enacted, the Church finding within all that is good in human life and culture echoes of God's saving work. The Church has, from its beginnings, reflected the

---

65. MS, p. xii.
66. BC, pp. 154–59. De Lubac seems to have thought that liberation theology represents one such attempt, in a somewhat pessimistic and less than fair analysis of its theological aims.
67. SC, xii.
68. C, pp. 352–53.
69. Doyle, *Communion Ecclesiology*, p. 211.
70. *Gaudium et Spes*, 1.

full prism of strengths and weaknesses of its human members, but has always held within it the revelation of God's mysterious presence.[71] This is echoed in *Lumen Gentium*: 'While Christ, holy, innocent and undefiled, knew nothing of sin, but came to expiate only the sins of the people, the Church, embracing in its bosom sinners, at the same time holy and always in need of being purified, always follows the way of penance and renewal'.[72]

Conclusion

For de Lubac, membership of the Church is a response to God's invitation to us to share in the life of Trinity, and that Trinitarian relationship is at the core of God's invitation to us to share in the divine life.[73] The Church is the mystical body of Christ because it represents the spiritual and social reunification of the unity of humankind. Susan K. Wood, in her study on de Lubac, raises the crucial question here of an over-identification of the Church with Christ in a way that ignores both the sinful history of the Church itself and the elements of salvation, which de Lubac himself was at pains to show, existed outside the parameters of the Church.[74] She also raises the question of de Lubac's own fluctuating identification of who, concretely, constitutes the Church. In *The Splendour of the Church* he echoes *Mystici Corporis* in its identification of the Church as the Roman Catholic Church, while in *Catholicism* he expresses the more universalist view found in Aquinas and in *Lumen Gentium*.[75] This enables him to find seeds of the Church within Judaism and other non-Christian faiths, as well as in the urge towards human unity and the social aspirations of atheist humanism and other political systems. His Christian humanism has human beings realizing their greatness and their fundamental unity through participation in the divine life. His concept of the supernatural destiny of humanity rests in his understanding of the individual person made in the image of God and the embodiment of that image in the Church of Christ, which in baptism, the celebration of the Eucharist, and penance offers efficacious signs to the world of Christ's indwelling in, but also beyond, human society.

The Church as body of Christ is a sign that awaits completion in the *eschaton*. The Eucharist and other sacraments are a sign of unity, making real our union with Christ and with the Christian community, but also with the rest of society

---

71. CPM, p. 2.
72. *Lumen Gentium*, 8.
73. Henri de Lubac, *La Foi Chrétienne* (Paris: Auber, 1970), pp. 245–49. But see also Susan K. Wood's critique of a certain weakness in this Trinitarian aspect of de Lubac's ecclesiology in *Spiritual Exegesis*, p. 151.
74. Wood, *Spiritual Exegesis and the Church in the theology of Henri de Lubac* (Grand Rapids, MI: William B. Eerdmans, 1998), pp. 132–34, 11–12, 88–95.
75. Ibid., pp. 89–92; *Lumen Gentium*, 8.

which 'hides a divine reality'.[76] The sacraments, as the means of salvation, have a social dimension precisely because they are instruments of unity, strengthening the gathered body of believers for their mission of charity to the world.[77]

De Lubac's sacramental ecclesiology lies at the heart of the most important insights of the Second Vatican Council in terms of the Church's mission to the world and its incorporation, as the mystical body of Christ, in all that is most fully and deeply human, as a sign and symbol of God's saving intention for the world. While in parts it is as impressionistic and partially systematic as the rest of his work, it nevertheless represents a remarkable contribution to our understanding of the rich patristic tradition in terms of both Church and Eucharist as the social embodiment of divine grace within the created order.

---

76. C, p. 35.
77. Ibid., pp. 35–50.

Chapter 7

THE CHRISTIAN MYSTERY OF NATURE AND GRACE

Nicholas J. Healy Jr.

Introduction: The Debate Concerning Nature and Grace

Henri de Lubac's lifelong effort to help Catholic theology return to an understanding of the supernatural at once more traditional, more faithful to the thought of Thomas Aquinas, and more deeply rooted in the mystery of Jesus Christ unfolds on two interrelated levels. His first and most basic concern was to recover the unity of creation and redemption in light of God's plan to recapitulate all things in Christ. By assuming human nature and going to the end of love (cf. Jn 13:1), the Logos 'established himself as the innermost depth of the Father's goodness while also displaying in himself the very goal for which his creatures manifestly received the beginning of their existence'.[1] One of the deepest problems with the modern theory of 'pure nature' is a neglect of the biblical teaching that the cosmos was created in, through, and for Jesus Christ (cf. Col 1:15–20) and that creation itself groans in travail and eager longing for the revelation of the sons of God (cf. Rom 8:19–22). By the same token, the reason why it is necessary to distinguish the gift of nature from the new gift of deifying grace is grounded in the mystery of Christ's Incarnation. And the ground and pattern for the original integrity and ultimate destiny of human nature is the hypostatic union of God and man in Christ. The hidden centre and source for de Lubac's thinking about nature and grace is the mystery of God's love revealed in the Person of Jesus Christ:

> A great deed was done for the world twenty centuries ago: the deed of charity... this deed of love, Jesus, it is you, yourself. Perceptible to man, humble, dying in a corner of Judea, oh!, yes, you are man! Flower of Jesse, you are indeed the fruit of our earth. Born of a woman, truly formed from her substance. You are not some sort of phantom come down from the

---

1. Maximus the Confessor, *Ad Thalassium*, 60, in *The Cosmic Mystery of Jesus Christ: Selected Writings from St Maximus the Confessor*, trans. Paul M. Blowers and Robert Louis Wilken (Crestwood, NY: St Vladimir's Seminary Press, 2003), p. 125.

clouds of heaven. You are deeply rooted in our earth. You were not merely his messenger, you are his living and substantial appearance. Through you, he has not only spoken. Or rather his language is an action, His word is a deed: it is you yourself. *Splendor, verbum et imago Patris.* You, Jesus, on your cross, the act of uniting heaven and earth.[2]

The second level of de Lubac's contribution to the question of nature and grace, which is admittedly more 'technical' and more controversial, involves the interpretation of texts from Thomas Aquinas on the ultimate end of human nature together with related texts on the natural desire to see the essence of God. In his seminal book *Surnaturel, études historiques* (1946), de Lubac showed how certain aspects of Aquinas's thought had been obscured and misrepresented as a result of the early modern theory of 'pure nature', which attributed to human nature an exclusively natural or proportionate ultimate end. This claim requires a brief explanation. According to Saint Thomas, in his divine liberality God created human nature with an ultimate end that is radically beyond the power of human nature. It follows that human beings can only attain their true final end – deifying participation in the very life of God (*consortium divinae naturae*) – through a new gift of grace. Aquinas writes:

> In the very beginning of creation, human nature was ordained to beatitude, not as to an end proper to man by reason of his nature, but given him solely by divine liberality. Therefore, there is no need for the principles of nature to have sufficient power to achieve that end without the aid of special gifts with which God in his generosity supplements them.[3]

Elsewhere, Thomas presents this same teaching more concisely: 'Even though by his nature man is inclined to his ultimate end, he cannot reach it by nature but only by grace, and this owing to the loftiness of that end.'[4] The natural desire to see the essence of God is a sign that human nature has been created for the sake of supernatural communion with God.[5] Human beings are made for, and desire, a fulfilment that can only be attained through the gratuitous gift of God. 'When the

---

2. 'The Light of Christ', in TH, pp. 209–11.
3. Thomas Aquinas, *De Veritate*. In *Sancti Thomae de Aquino opera Omnia*, vol. 22. Leonine Edition. Rome: Editori di San Tommaso, 1975–1976, q. 14, a. 10 ad 2: 'Ad secundum dicendum, quod ab ipsa prima institutione natura humana est ordinata in finem beatitudinis, non quasi in finem debitum homini secundum naturam eius, sed ex sola divina liberalitate. Et ideo non oportet quod principia naturae sufficiant ad finem illum consequendum, nisi fuerint adiuta donis superadditis ex divina liberalitate.'
4. Thomas Aquinas, *In Boethius de Trinitate*, Opera omnia (Rome: Leonine Commission, 1882–), q. 6, a. 4 ad 5: 'homo naturaliter inclinetur in finem ultimum, non tamen potest naturaliter illum consequi, sed solum per gratiam, et hoc est propter eminentiam illius finis'.
5. Cf. Thomas Aquinas, *Summa theologiae* I, q. 12, a. 1; *Summa contra gentiles* III, ch. 51; SCG III, ch. 57; *Comp. theol.*, ch. 104; *In Matth.* 5:8.

end is beyond the capacity of the agent striving to attain it', Aquinas writes, 'it is looked for from another's bestowing'.[6]

In the early modern period, Aquinas's profound and finely balanced teaching on the twofold action of God – the *effectus naturae* and the *effectus gratiae*[7] – was resisted and then reinterpreted on the basis of an overextension of a philosophical axiom. The new idea, which gained currency among Thomists in the sixteenth century, is that the final end of nature must be strictly proportionate to nature.[8] In other words, nature must be able to attain its final end by virtue of its own powers. This idea of proportionality precluded the possibility of a natural

---

6. Aquinas, ST I, q. 62, a. 4: 'quando finis excedit virtutem operantis propter finem, unde expectatur finis ex dono alteriu'.

7. In his book *Aquinas on God: The 'Divine Science' of the Summa Theologiae* (Burlington, VT: Ashgate, 2006), pp. 148–49, Rudi Te Velde offers a lucid summary of St Thomas's teaching on nature and grace:

> Both [nature and grace] refer to God's action with respect to creatures. The *effectus naturae* embraces the work of creation, by which creatures are established in their proper nature. The *effectus gratiae* is something additional, not in itself part of nature. Grace is not in itself a gift of creation but a gift beyond the natural endowment of creatures, enabling the (human) creature to reach for God beyond its natural power ... grace names, in particular, the way God gives himself or communicates his goodness to the human creature, even beyond the divine gift of being ... The gift of grace goes even further [than the relation of creation] and founds a new relationship of (rational) creatures to God. The gift of grace consists in letting the human creature share in the divinity of God ... In this sense grace means deification: by the gift of grace God deifies the human creature, bestowing on him a 'partnership in the divine nature'. (*consortium divinae naturae*)

8. In an essay on 'Nature', in *Philosophische Esssays* (Stuttgart: Reclam, 1993), pp. 25–26, Robert Spaemann notes the shift from a medieval understanding of a natural desire 'that points *in* nature *beyond* nature' to the early modern theory of a wholly immanent desire:

> [According to Thomas Aquinas] on the basis of this '*natura intellectualis*' man has the peculiar trait of being ordered to an end that he nevertheless, because of the '*eminentia*' of the goal, cannot achieve by natural means, but 'only through grace.' And Thomas seeks to draw on no less than the *Nichomachean Ethics* for support of this point: 'That which we are able to do only with divine assistance is not absolutely impossible for us according to the philosopher's observation in the *Nichomachean Ethics*: that which we are able to do through friends we can in a certain way do on our own' [ST I–II, q. 109, a. 4 ad 2]. The later scholastics, however, – precisely the Thomistic ones – in their appeal to Aristotle, gave up the attempt to call something 'natural' that cannot also be achieved universally by the entire species ... All of the Thomists of the 16th century cite Aristotle in this context: 'If nature had given the heavenly bodies the inclination to linear motion, she would also have given them the means for it' [Cf. Aristotle, *De coelo*, II.290a]. The understanding of nature that announces itself here shifts toward the Cartesian-Spinozist definition of substance, as that which can be conceived without the concept of something else. A specifically theological motive operates in the same direction: the thought of a '*desiderium naturale*', which points *in* nature *beyond* nature, would, according to the theologians

desire for something that is radically beyond nature. In the words of Cajetan (1469–1534), '*naturale desiderium non se extendit ultra naturae facultatem*' (natural desire does not extend beyond the capacity of nature).[9] Once this premise was accepted, Thomas's teaching that there is a natural desire for the beatific vision became almost unintelligible. At the same time and for the same reason, Thomas's doctrine that the ultimate end of human nature is supernatural beatitude was reinterpreted to mean that human nature as originally constituted by God has an exclusively natural or proportionate end (*natura pura*). On this reading, the gift of grace modifies nature in the sense of giving it a new end. 'Our supernatural finality', Lawrence Feingold writes, 'is "imprinted on our being" first by sanctifying grace ... [grace is] "supper-added" in the sense of giving us a "new finality."'[10]

In the eyes of de Lubac, the neo-Thomist axiom that the final end of nature and the desire of nature must be strictly proportionate to nature represents an unfortunate departure from the doctrine of Aquinas. The result was a weakening of the organic link between nature and grace, between the order of creation and redemption. It became more difficult to understand how the Christian mystery surpassingly fulfils the deepest desire of the human heart. And it became more difficult to see how and in what sense the mystery of Jesus Christ reveals the original purpose and meaning of creation itself. More subtly, the logic of 'pure nature' entails a questionable understanding of the integrity of nature both as originally created and as transformed by the new gift of grace.

It is undeniable that Henri de Lubac's writings on nature and grace have effected a shift in the entire edifice of Catholic theology.[11] As interpreted and

---

of the sixteenth century, make salvation a right, and grace would cease to be a gift. The consequence of this was that one superimposed a hypothetical purely natural destiny of man, a '*finis naturalis*', onto the actual destiny given in salvation history; and thus the fateful construction of a '*natura pura*' came into being.

9. Cajetan, *Commentaria in primam partem* (Rome: Leonina, 1988–1989), q. 12, a. 1, n. 10.

10. Lawrence Feingold, *The Natural Desire to See God According to St. Thomas Aquinas and His Interpreters* (Rome: Apollinare Studi, 2001), p. 529. See also Bernard Mulcahy, *Aquinas's Notion of Pure Nature and the Christian Integralism of Henri de Lubac: Not Everything is Grace* (New York: Peter Lang, 2011), p. 204 : 'the supernatural end ... is a new and additional finality'.

11. Cf. Guy Mansini, 'The Abiding Theological Significance of Henri de Lubac's *Surnaturel*', *The Thomist* 73 (2009): pp. 593–619, at p. 593: 'The most influential event in Catholic theology of the twentieth century was the appearance of Henri de Lubac's *Surnaturel* in 1946. This is not an especially novel or controversial claim ... By "influential" here I mean "pivotal", an event that makes a watershed, that marks a before and an after.' See also Serge-Thomas Bonino, 'Forward' in *Surnaturel: A Controversy at the Heart of Twentieth-Century Thomistic Thought* (Ave Maria, FL: Sapientia Press, 2009) : '*Surnaturel* contributed not a little to casting suspicion on the Thomism of the schools and to shaking the naïve and instinctive confidence that the neo-Thomists accorded to the commentators,

developed by John Paul II and Benedict XVI (both of whom acknowledge an indebtedness to de Lubac), the Second Vatican Council presents the twofold gift of nature and grace as united without confusion or separation in the Person of Jesus Christ, 'who is the key, the center, and the purpose (*finem*) of the whole of history'.[12] 'Christ the Lord, Christ the new Adam, in the very revelation of the mystery of the Father and his love, fully reveals man to himself and brings to light his high calling'.[13] In other words, Jesus Christ reveals the original purpose and the final end of human nature, 'for the ultimate vocation of man is in fact one and divine'.[14]

More recently, a number of authors have questioned the adequacy of de Lubac's account of nature and grace.[15] The French Jesuit was mindful of the ebb and flow of Catholic thinking. He would not be surprised by the rehabilitation of the theory of 'pure nature'. The resurgence of the idea of pure nature stems in part from a legitimate concern to address the impoverishment of the concept of nature in modernity.[16] In addition, the proponents of pure nature argue that if

---

especially Cajetan. Henceforth, St Thomas will be read more as the inheritor of the great theological tradition that went before him than as the starting point of later Scholasticism.' Already in 1949, Gerard Smith discerned that 'either *Surnaturel* is a most subtly dangerous work or else it is immortal'. ['The Natural End of Man', *Proceedings of the American Catholic Philosophical Association* (1949): pp. 47–61, at 47–48].

12. Pastoral Constitution On The Church In The Modern World – *Gaudium et Spes* Promulgated by Pope Paul VI. [Vatican City]: 1965, 10.

13. *Gaudium et spes*, 22.

14. Ibid.

15. Among the many recent English language publications on the nature-grace debate, see Lawrence Feingold, *The Natural Desire to See God According to St. Thomas Aquinas and His Interpreters* (Ave Maria, FL: Sapientia Press, 2010); Steven A. Long, *Natura Pura: On the Recovery of Nature in the Doctrine of Grace* (New York: Fordham University Press, 2010); Reinhard Hütter, 'Aquinas on the Natural Desire for the Vision of God: A *Relecture* of *Summa Contra Gentiles* III, C. 25 après Henri De Lubac', *The Thomist* 73 (2009): pp. 523–91; Thomas Joseph White, 'The "Pure Nature" of Christology: Human Nature and *Gaudium et Spes* 22', *Nova et Vetera* 8 (2010): pp. 283–322; Christopher J. Malloy, 'De Lubac on Natural Desire: Difficulties and Antitheses', *Nova et Vetera* 9 (2011): pp. 567–624; Andrew Dean Swafford, *Nature and Grace: A New Approach to Thomistic Ressourcement* (Eugene, OR: Pickwick Publications, 2014).

16. Hans Jonas (1903–1993) is an invaluable guide for tracing the evacuation of the ancient and medieval understanding of nature as 'the source or cause of being moved and of being at rest in that to which it belongs primarily, in virtue of itself and not accidentally' (Aristotle, *Physics*, II, 1); see, *inter alia*, 'Seventeenth Century and After: The Meaning of the Scientific and Technological Revolution', in *Philosophical Essays* (New York: Atropos Press, 2010) and 'The Practical Uses of Theory', in *The Phenomenon of Life: Toward a Philosophical Biology* (Evanston, IL: Northwestern University Press, 2001). For an example of the impoverishment of the concept of nature within Catholic thinking, consider the following 'definition of nature' offered by Todd A. Salzman and Michael G. Lawler, *The Sexual Person: Toward a Renewed Catholic Anthropology* (Washington, DC: Georgetown University Press, 2008), pp. 48–49 :

human nature in itself already tends towards the supernatural, then the gratuitous character of grace has been compromised. Henri de Lubac shared these two concerns even as he questioned the provenance and the utility of the modern idea of pure nature.

The unresolved issue at the heart of the contemporary debate over nature and grace is how best to understand and characterize nature's original openness to the new gift of deifying grace. As interpreted by de Lubac, Saint Thomas's analogical understanding of finality serves to hold together the essential difference between nature and grace *and* the unity of God's plan accomplished in Christ. While both de Lubac and Aquinas speak of a 'twofold beatitude' for human nature (one proportionate to nature, the other surpassing nature),[17] the true *finis ultimus* of human nature is supernatural beatitude. Or, to borrow the formulation of Aquinas, although supernatural beatitude is not part of nature (*aliquid naturae*), it is the end of nature (*finis naturae*).[18] The natural desire for an end that is beyond nature (*visio beatifica*) testifies to the unity of God's plan for creation. As aptly stated in the *Catechism of the Catholic Church* § 27, 'the desire for God is written in the human heart, because man is created by God and for God; and God never ceases to draw man to himself'. The neo-Thomist position as formulated by Cajetan and reaffirmed by twentieth-century Thomists such as Reginald Garrigou-Lagrange rejects the possibility that nature as such can desire an end that is beyond nature.[19] Prior to the modification of grace, human nature is 'pure nature' in the sense that its final end and its natural desire are strictly proportionate to nature. For the proponents of pure nature, the original openness of nature is best characterized as a non-repugnance or specific obediential potency to acquiring a new end through the gift of grace.

Given recent criticism and the renewed interest in de Lubac's theology of nature and grace, it may be helpful to restate his basic position, which remained remarkably consistent from his earliest publications on the history of the word *supernaturalis* in the 1930s through his *Brief Catechesis on Nature and Grace*

All we can understand from 'nature' is the naked facticity of a reality, sexuality and sexual intercourse for instance; nothing else. 'Nature' reveals to our attention, understanding, judgment, and decision only its naked facticity, not our moral obligation.... The uninterpreted experience of 'nature', as of every other objective reality, is restricted to its mere facticity and is void of meaning, a quality that does not inhere in 'nature' but is assigned to it by rational beings.

17. Cf. Henri de Lubac, 'Duplex Hominis Beatitudo', *Recherches de science religieuse* 35 (1948): pp. 290–99 [English trans. in *Communio: International Catholic Review* 35 (2008): pp. 598–611].

18. Aquinas, ST I, q. 62, a. 1: '... haec beatitudo non est aliquid naturae, sed naturae finis'. See also ST I, q. 62, a. 4.

19. Cf. Reginald Garrigou-Lagrange, *Grace: Commentary on the Summa Theologica of St. Thomas, Ia IIae, q. 109–114* (St Louis: Herder, 1952); 'Le désir naturel du bonheur prouve-t-il l'existence de Dieu?' *Angelicum* 8 (1931): pp. 129–48.

(1980).[20] Accordingly, Part Two will present de Lubac's position by outlining five theses on the mystery of the supernatural. Where appropriate I will indicate the essential continuity between de Lubac and Thomas Aquinas. One of the difficulties surrounding recent engagements with de Lubac's theology is a certain confusion regarding the concept of 'pure nature'. Part Three will attempt to clarify the current state of the question by considering different senses of *natura pura* as understood by de Lubac and his (Thomist) critics. Finally, a concluding Part Four will attempt a speculative unfolding of de Lubac's theology of nature and grace by way of reflecting on the relationship between the natural institution of marriage and its sacramental character.

Henri de Lubac and Thomas Aquinas on the Supernatural End of Human Nature – Five Theses

In a 'preface' to his 1965 book *The Mystery of the Supernatural*, de Lubac describes the fundamental aim of his various writings on the theme of the supernatural:

> All he [the author] has tried to demonstrate is contained in a single idea. It is to establish or illustrate the one idea that all his arguments are directed, and he would instantly abandon any that turned out in the end to compromise or obscure it ... It is an idea so fundamental that it has been proclaimed, often with total unanimity, in all the ages of Christendom. At the beginning of our own age it seemed for a time to become obscured. Some set it aside with the notion

---

20. In a preface to the 1991 edition of *Surnaturel*, Michel Sales provides a helpful schema of the genetic relations between *Surnaturel* (1946), the articles 'Duplex hominis beatitudo' (1948) and 'Le mystère du surnaturel' (1949), the two books *Augustinisme et théologie moderne* (1965) and *Le mystère du surnaturel* (1965), and finally *Petite catéchèse sur Nature et Grâce* (1980). In his *Mémoire sur l'occasion de mes écrits* (Namur: Culture et Vérité, 1989) [ASC, pp. 34-35] de Lubac recalls the origins of his interest in the question of nature and grace:
> When I was a student in theology ... we gathered each Sunday, under the benevolent and discreet patronage of Father Joseph Huby, to debate a subject chosen and prepared by one of us. This was how the first sketch was born of what would become in 1946 the book entitled *Surnaturel, études historiques*. From then on, the subject was much in discussion. It had just been treated by Father Guy de Broglie...... It was at the center of the reflection of Rousselot, Blondel, Maréchal; we discovered it at the heart of all great Christian thought, whether that of Saint Augustine, Saint Thomas or Stain Bonaventure (for these were our classics par excellence); we noted that it was likewise at the bottom of discussions with modern unbelief, that it formed the crux of the problem of Christian humanism. Father Huby, following the line of reflection inaugurated for us by Rousselot, had warmly urged be to verify whether the doctrine of Saint Thomas on this important point was indeed what was claimed by the Thomist school around the sixteenth century, codified in the seventeenth and asserted with greater emphasis than ever in the twentieth.

that they were simply giving the autonomy of nature and natural philosophy their due. Others did so in the name of a purer orthodoxy: rightly wanting to condemn the excesses which sought to deny something of the Creator's sovereign freedom and the complete gratuitousness of his gift.[21]

What is this single idea or fundamental truth?

Man's relationship with God, who has made us for himself and never ceases to draw us toward him, remains essentially the same. There is always 'in primeval nature just as in nature as developed through history, a depth, a living response, a natural desire, a "force" upon which freely given grace finds something to work. As the Greeks used to say, the incarnate logos gathers the "seeds" planted by the creating logos. The Latins expressed it in different terms: man, as God's image, is fitted to enter into communion with him, in liberty of mind and initiative of love.' This is what we must, if only as a duty to God, continue to clarify with all the means that this age places at our disposal. This is the fundamental truth which we must never allow to be obscured or compromised.[22]

De Lubac's understanding of the fundamental truth of man's relation to God can be unfolded in five interrelated theses.

1st Thesis. As created by God and for God, the ultimate end of human nature is supernatural beatitude. This truth is both ancient and common to the entire Christian tradition. 'For the Fathers of the Church', writes de Lubac, 'man, created in the image of God ... was made in view of his likeness to God, who is the perfection of this image, which is to say that he was destined to live eternally in God, to enter into the inner movement of the trinitarian life.'[23] Augustine's well-known words sum up and express the common faith of the Church: 'You have made us for yourself, and our hearts are restless until they rest in you.'[24] Writing in the twelfth century, Richard of St Victor bears witness to an unbroken tradition of reflection on this theme: 'God, the highest good and immutable good, ... made the rational creature in order to make it a partaker of his beatitude.'[25] In his own time, Thomas Aquinas confirmed this common teaching on the final end of human nature by developing the biblical image of a vision of God: 'The ultimate end of an intellectual creature is the vision of God in His essence.'[26]

---

21. MS, p. xxxiv.
22. MS, p. xxxvi.
23. Henri de Lubac, 'Internal Causes of the Weakening and Disappearance of the Sense of the Sacred', in TH, p. 230.
24. Augustine, *Confessions*, ed. R. S. Pine-Coffin (London, Penguin, 1961), I, 1.
25. Richard of St Victor, *Liber exceptionem*, ed. Châtillon (Paris: Vrin, 1958), p. 104; cited in MS, p. 238.
26. Aquinas, *Comp. theol.*, p. 104: 'est igitur finis ultimus intellectualis creaturae, deum per essentiam videre'.

'Final and perfect beatitude can consist in nothing else than the vision of the divine essence.'[27]

For Augustine, Aquinas, and de Lubac, this supernatural finality is bestowed by God *ab initio*, in the very creation of human beings made in the image of God.[28] In other words, God has inscribed this finality in human nature itself because, as Thomas teaches, 'our intellect is made for the purpose of seeing God.'[29] 'Man was made to see God: for this purpose God made him a rational creature, so that he might participate in his likeness, which consists in seeing him.'[30] Or, in the formulation of de Lubac, 'nature was made for the supernatural.'[31]

Reinhard Hütter aptly summarizes this understanding of human nature as created in the image of God and destined for eternal life: 'Human nature is *capax Dei*, is ontologically ordered towards the beatific vision. There is in the human being a positive fittingness, an opening inscribed in the very core of the nature of the human *intellectus* created *ad imaginem Trinitatis*.'[32] Each of the following four theses can be read as unfolding and safeguarding this foundational claim of Christian anthropology.

2nd Thesis. The ultimate end of human nature is radically beyond nature's innate power or abilities. It follows that human nature can only attain its final end through a new gift of grace. This thesis highlights the transcendent, supernatural, and gratuitous character of Christian beatitude. We must distinguish, de Lubac writes, between 'the first gift of creation and the second, wholly distinct, wholly super-eminent gift – the ontological call to deification which will make of man, if he responds to it, "a new creature."'[33] The abiding difference between nature and grace is grounded in the causal action of God with respect to his creation. The promise of eternal life with God (*visio beatifica*) exceeds the power of nature. 'Man cannot, by his own operation', Aquinas writes, 'attain to his last end, which surpasses the faculty of his natural powers, unless his operation be enabled by the divine power to bring him thereto.'[34] The divine gift that elevates human nature thus allowing nature to attain its supernatural ultimate end is fittingly called 'grace'. Grace is not a constitutive part of human nature; it is, writes de Lubac,

---

27. Aquinas, ST I–II, q. 3, a. 8: '... ultima et perfecta beatitudo non potest esse nisi in visione divinae essentiae'.

28. Cf. Aquinas, ST III, q. 9, a. 2 ad 3: 'Beatific vision and knowledge are to some extent above the nature of the rational soul, inasmuch as it cannot reach them of its own strength; but in another way they are in accordance with its nature, inasmuch as it is capable of them by nature, having been made to the likeness of God.'

29. Aquinas, *De Veritate*, q. 10, a. 11 ad 7: 'intellectus noster quamvis sit factus ad videndum deum'.

30. Aquinas, *De Veritate*, q. 18, a. 1: 'homo factus est ad videndum deum: ad hoc enim deus fecit rationalem creaturam, ut beatitudinis eius particeps esset, quae in eius visione consistit'.

31. TH, p. 231.

32. Hütter, 'Aquinas on the Natural Desire for the Vision of God', pp. 523–91, at p. 588.

33. MS, p. 76.

34. Aquinas, SCG III, p. 147.

'a certain "form", a certain "supernatural perfection" which must be "added over and above human nature" in order that man "may be ordered appropriately to his end."[35] As Thomas argues,

> no created intellect can possibly attain to a vision of the divine substance except by the agency of God who surpasses all creatures… For we have proved that man's happiness consists in seeing God, which is called life everlasting: and we are said to obtain this by God's grace alone, because that vision surpasses the faculty of every creature, and it is impossible to attain thereto except by God's gift; and when such things are obtained by a creature, it is put down to God's grace.[36]

Aquinas was mindful that his teaching that the final end of human nature is beyond the power of nature posed a certain difficulty: 'It would seem that man can attain beatitude by his natural powers. For nature does not fail in necessary things. But nothing is so necessary to man as that by which he attains the last end. Therefore this is not lacking to human nature. Therefore man can attain beatitude by his natural powers.' He responds: 'Nature did not fail man in things necessary, although it gave him not the wherewithal to attain beatitude, since this it could not do. But it did give him free will, with which he can turn to God, that He may make him beatified.'[37] 'For what we do by means of our friends, is done, in a sense, by ourselves.'[38] Human beings are made for an end that we are unable to attain without help from another. This is supremely fitting for creatures who receive their being from another. Ontological humility and gratitude are reflected in the very structure of nature both as created and as elevated in grace to the astonishing gift of participation in the divine nature.

3rd Thesis. There is a natural desire to see the essence of God.[39] The natural desire for beatific knowledge of God is a sign that human nature was created in the

---

35. MS, p. 85.
36. Aquinas, SCG III, p. 52.
37. Aquinas, ST I–II, q. 5, a. 5 ad 1.
38. Aquinas, ST I–II, q. 5, a. 5 ad 2; see also ST I–II, q. 91, a. 4 ad 3; q. 109, a. 4 ad 2; *De Veritate*, q. 8, a. 3 ad 12; q. 24 a. 10 ad 1; and *De Malo*, q. 5, a. 1.
39. See the references in Aquinas, ST I, q. 62, a. 4: 'quando finis excedit virtutem operantis propter finem, unde expectatur finis ex dono alteriu'. In order to understand Thomas Aquinas's teaching on the natural desire to see the essence of God, it is helpful to recall the historical context for his writings on this theme. The specific error or issue that Thomas addresses in these texts is whether or not it is possible for human beings to see the essence of God. In order to show that what has been revealed in the scriptures about man's ultimate end is not contrary to reason, and that perfect beatitude can consist in nothing less than a knowledge or 'vision' of God's essence, Thomas argues that there is a natural desire to know the essence of the cause of any effects that one sees. This natural desire will only come to rest when one attains (through grace) a knowledge of God in his very essence. Although Thomas everywhere assumes the gratuitous character of Christian beatitude, the question of how this natural desire (which cannot be in vain) accords with the gratuity of supernatural beatitude became a pressing concern only in the aftermath of the Reformation and the heresies of Baius and Jansenius.

image of God and destined for eternal blessedness with God (*1st Thesis*). To recall the teaching of the *Catechism* noted above, 'the desire for God is written in the human heart, because man is created by God and for God; and God never ceases to draw man to himself'.[40] The desire for God opens nature from its innermost depths to a mystery that infinitely surpasses nature. What is desired by nature is precisely beyond the reach of what nature can attain by its own powers. Authentic desire is structurally receptive; it is a positive openness to the gratuitous gift of another (*2nd Thesis*).[41] 'When the end is beyond the capacity of the agent striving to attain it', Aquinas argues, 'it is looked for from another's bestowing'.[42]

The natural desire to see the essence of God (*visio beatifica*) provides a crucial point of contact between nature and grace, but it also safeguards the transcendence and gratuity of Christian beatitude. To be created in the image of God with a desire to see God is to desire beatitude only in the context of a friendship that is gratuitous. The human spirit, writes de Lubac, 'desires God as one desires a gift ... the free and gratuitous communication of a personal Being'.[43]

As a sign of the depth and breadth of God's plan for creation, the natural desire for God is essentially mysterious. On the one hand, the desire is truly natural.[44] 'It is', de Lubac writes, 'essentially in nature and expresses the heart of it'.[45] The natural

---

40. *Catechism of the Catholic Church* (Liguori, MO: Liguori Publications, 1994), § 27.

41. In an earlier article, 'Henri de Lubac on Nature and Grace: A Note on Some Recent Contributions to the Debate', *Communio: International Catholic Review* 35 (2008): pp. 535–64, at p. 561, I attempted to express this same point on the receptive character of desire:

If human nature desires a final end that exceeds nature, then the form of nature's desire is receptivity – a receptive desire for the surprising and surpassing gift of friendship and assistance from another. This is supremely fitting for a nature whose very existence is from another. 'What have you that you did not receive?' (1 Cor 4:7). These words from St Paul, which resound like a refrain throughout Augustine's writings, provide a hidden key to the structure of authentic human desire in relation to the novelty of grace. The disproportion between human nature's desire and its power to fulfil it is a kind of created infrastructure that opens nature from within to receive and participate in the new and unimagined gift of deification. This does not mean, however, that grace arrives at the point where nature breaks down. Rather, it means that grace presupposes, activates, and fulfils a receptivity (which involves giving and receiving) that represents human nature at its highest pitch. The archetype of nature's active receptivity is the fiat of Mary.

42. Aquinas ST I, q. 62, a. 4: 'quando finis excedit virtutem operantis propter finem, unde expectatur finis ex dono alteriu'.

43. S, p. 483.

44. Cf. MS, p. 31: 'The fact that the nature of spiritual being, as it actually exists, is not conceived as an order destined to close in finally upon itself, but in a sense open to an inevitably supernatural end, does not mean that it already has in itself, or as part of its basis, the smallest supernatural element'; also MS, p. 85: 'The desire itself ... does not constitute as yet even the slightest positive "ordering" to the supernatural.' The truly natural character of the desire to see God marks one of the essential differences between Henri de Lubac and Karl Rahner's thesis of the 'supernatural existential'.

45. S, p. 487.

desire to see the essence of God is not simply the result of grace modifying nature, although it remains true that grace will transform and elevate this desire.[46] On the other hand, the desire for God is itself a gift from God. Although it is not yet grace, the natural desire for God is a sign that God has created us for Himself and never ceases to draw us towards Himself. Perhaps one could say that the supernatural finality and the desire to see the essence of God are *in* human nature but not *of* human nature.[47]

Jacques Maritain expresses this paradox of a desire that is both rooted in the very depths of nature and a sign of the transcendent and gratuitous promise of God:

> Nothing is more human than for man to desire naturally things impossible to his nature... Such desires... are natural, but one may also call them transnatural. It is thus that we desire to see God... it is thus that we desire beatitude. To say that our intellect naturally desires to see God is to say that it naturally desires a knowledge of which nature itself is incapable... According as it reaches thus for an end which transcends every end proportioned to nature, the desire to see God is an 'inefficacious' desire – a desire which it is not in the power of nature to satisfy, and it is a 'conditional' desire – a desire whose satisfaction is not due to nature. Yet, according as it emanates from nature, it is a natural and necessary desire. It is not a simple velleity, a superadded desire, a desire of supererogation. It is born in the very depths of the thirst of our intellect for being... And because this desire which asks for what is impossible to nature is a desire of nature in its profoundest depths, St. Thomas Aquinas asserts that it cannot issue in an absolute impossibility.[48]

46. Interpreting Aquinas's words, 'eternal life is a good exceeding the proportion of created nature, since it exceeds its knowledge and desire' (ST I-II, q. 114, a. 2), de Lubac writes (MS, p. 220): 'That is the first reason why we need divine revelation and divine grace. But furthermore, even when the natural desire for the vision of God – which we must remember is not the same as an elicited desire – has been recognized, defined and analyzed, its end is still only known "*aliquo modo.*"... Even in the light it gets from God, and at whatever phase one looks at of its intellectual or spiritual life, the believing and hoping soul is ultimately left "facing an intrinsically impenetrable mystery", "what no eye has seen, nor ear heard, nor has the heart of man conceived."'

47. S, 488: 'The desire to see God takes in us the form of duty before taking that of a need... The desire is in us, yes, but it is not of us, since it is satisfied only in mortifying us. Or rather, it is so profoundly in us that it is ourselves, but it is ourselves who do not belong to ourselves: *non sumus nostri*.' In a footnote in MS (p. 102, n. 5), de Lubac expresses his agreement with the words of Timothée Richard: 'It is always in relation to the demands of this beatitude which is assigned to us by God, not by nature, that St. Thomas takes his stand.' De Lubac comments, 'This is how I understand St. Thomas, and how he understood things themselves; with the proviso, however, that in certain circumstances, existing nature can be an indication to us of God's will.'

48. Jacques Maritain, *Approaches to God*, trans. Peter O'Reilly (New York: Macmillan Company, 1965), pp. 98–99.

4th Thesis. God could have created intellectual natures not destined for supernatural beatitude. This is the hypothetical possibility affirmed by Pius XII in *Humani Generis*, 26: 'Others destroy the gratuity of the supernatural order, since God, they say, cannot create intellectual beings without ordering and calling them to the beatific vision.' De Lubac accepts this teaching as true and as consonant with his writings on the supernatural before and after the promulgation of *Humani Generis* in 1950.

The mistaken idea that *Humani Generis* condemned the position of de Lubac has proved surprisingly resilient, despite evidence to the contrary. On several occasions, de Lubac noted not only his fundamental agreement with the encyclical, but the possible dependence of *Humani Generis* on his own 1949 essay 'The Mystery of the Supernatural'. For example, in his annotation of a collection of letters from Étienne Gilson, he writes:

> People thought they saw in the 1965 book [*The Mystery of the Supernatural*] an effort to correct, or at least to defend, the 1946 volume, with a view to making it more conformed to a sentence in the encyclical *Humani Generis* of August 1950. But on the contrary this encyclical was itself demonstrably inspired by my 1949 article, because it avoided invoking the so-called theory of 'pure nature' that a number of theologians wanted the encyclical to validate. (If there had been a first draft, which I am not aware there was, its text would have been closely checked by competent, independent theologians.) Several readers immediately picked up on this; like this author of a letter dated September 25, 1950, who wrote to me: 'The sentence in the encyclical about the supernatural is found word for word in the article in *Recherches*, pointed out as evidently false, because "if God had so willed it, he could have denied us being, and to this being that he did give us, he could have utterly refused the vocation to see him face to face. If this terminology is inadequate, it is not so by reason of the sovereign liberty it recognizes in God. The contrary proposition suggests a double error ... Nothing either from outside him or from within him, could force God to grant me being; furthermore, nothing could make him endow my being with a supernatural character."' Cf. the text of the encyclical: 'Others distort the true concept of the gratuity of the supernatural order when they claim that God could not create beings invested with intelligence without calling and ordaining them to the beatific vision.' I had said that again and again, in the conclusion of this same article in 1949.[49]

Undergirding de Lubac's interpretation of *Humani Generis* is an analogical understanding of nature and finality. The intellectual beings in the hypothetical order of *Humani Generis* would be analogical to human nature as it actually exists, but not the same in every respect. Why? In this providential economy,

---

49. Henri de Lubac, *Letters of Étienne Gilson to Henri de Lubac: Annotated by Father de Lubac* (San Francisco: Ignatius Press 1988), p. 99.

God has in fact created human beings that are destined for eternal life with him. In his divine liberality, God has inscribed this finality in human nature itself, not in the sense that supernatural beatitude is part of nature (*aliquid naturae*), but rather is the end of nature (*finis naturae*).[50] In the providential economy that actually exists, human nature *is* made for or 'inclined' to an end that surpasses nature: '*homo naturaliter inclinetur in finem ultimum, non tamen potest naturaliter illum consequi, sed solum per gratiam, et hoc est propter eminentiam illius finis*'.[51]

5th Thesis. The fact that the ultimate end of human nature is supernatural beatitude (*1st Thesis*), does not entail a denial that nature also has a 'proportionate' natural end. Thomas Aquinas often distinguishes between two types of human happiness or beatitude.[52] The first is a happiness proportionate to human nature's own abilities. The second is the perfect beatitude promised by our Christian faith; it consists in a deifying vision of God's essence. Thomas writes:

> man's happiness is twofold: One is proportionate to human nature, a happiness, to wit, which man can obtain by means of his natural principles. The other is a happiness surpassing man's nature, and which man can obtain by the power of God alone, by a kind of participation of the Godhead, about which it is written that by Christ we are made 'partakers of the Divine nature'. (2 Pt. 1:4)[53]

Concurring with St Thomas's teaching and reviewing the various texts where he speaks of a 'twofold beatitude', de Lubac writes:

> we discover a remarkable continuity of doctrine on our subject [the twofold beatitude of man] – a continuity that stretches from St. Thomas's earliest work to his final writings. These texts reciprocally comment on one another... Each time we hear of a beatitude 'formulated' by the philosophers ... we can conclude that the text refers to the condition of this world. This beatitude is consistently contrasted with that of the 'future life' or of the 'homeland', or to what we await 'after death.' At times, to emphasize its imperfection, St. Thomas insists that it is necessarily mixed, unstable, and transitory. But he can also identify a sort of continuity between the contemplation of the truth the wise man engages in here below and its consummation in the 'beyond', ... This does not keep him from maintaining that no beatitude, however great, that does not entail eternity and

---

50. Aquinas, ST I, q. 62, a. 1: '... haec beatitudo non est aliquid naturae, sed naturae finis'. See also ST I, q. 62, a. 4.

51. Aquinas, *In Boethius de Trinitate*, q. 6, a. 4 ad 5: 'Even though by his nature man is inclined to his ultimate end, he cannot reach it by nature but only by grace, and this owing to the loftiness of that end.'

52. Cf. Aquinas, ST I, q. 62, a. 1; I–II, q. 3, aa. 3–5; q. 5, a. 5; q. 62, a. 1; *De veritate*, q. 14, a. 2; a. 10; *In Boet. de Trinitate*, q. 6, a. 4; and SCG I, c. 5; III, 48; III. 63.

53. Aquinas, ST I–II, q. 62, a. 1.

stability, can be called true; for him, only 'eternal beatitude' is true beatitude (*beatitudo vera*), beatitude itself (*beatitudo per essentiam*), and beatitude tout court... In a word, the first is immanent – at once worldly or temporal and acquired according to internal principles; the second is transcendent – at once heavenly and received according to divine grace. Beatitude is twofold: the first is 'natural', and the second is 'supernatural'.[54]

De Lubac returns to this theme of the twofold beatitude of man in *Augustinianism and Modern Theology*:

in a certain sense it is a question of a man with a twofold end: one, which is proportionate to his created nature and that he can attain by himself; the other which is beyond all proportion and consists in eternal life: 'the understanding of God, most highly loved through direct vision', However for Soto, as for St. Thomas, St. Bonaventure and Scotus, this twofold finality which exists in real man does not in the nature of this man constitute the mark of a possible twofold polarity: it is a real and ordered duality... Coexisting in man as he actually is, in this being which is made in the image of God, in each of us, the two finalities are both to be made real, the one by the other. The first is determined by the laws of prudence and integrity as they had been explained by 'natural philosophers'. It is neither removed nor smothered by the other... but it is subordinate to it. Only the second actually deserves the name of last end.[55]

In light of these texts from de Lubac, it is simply false to claim (as Ralph McInerny does) that 'the rejection of an end proportionate to human nature separates de Lubac more decisively from St. Thomas than anything else, doubtless because this rejection is at the basis of his thought... In de Lubac's account man, no longer has a natural end'.[56]

The question that needs to be explored further is whether this hierarchically structured 'twofold finality' is rooted in nature itself as created by God (de Lubac's position), or whether, as Feingold claims, this twofold finality is instead the result of grace modifying nature because 'our supernatural finality is "imprinted on our being" first by sanctifying grace... [grace is] "supper-added" in the sense of giving us a "new finality."'[57] At the heart of this question is the concept of pure nature.

54. De Lubac 'Duplex hominis beatitudo', pp. 609–12.
55. AMT, pp. 130–31.
56. Ralph McInerny, *Praeambula fidei: Thomism and the God of the Philosophers* (Washington: Catholic University of America Press, 2006), p. 85. McInerny's false accusation against de Lubac has been echoed by several others, including Long (*Natura Pura*, pp. 11–12), who claims that 'a unilateral stress upon certain aspects of St. Thomas's teaching about the natural desire for God led de Lubac to deny the existence of a proportionate natural end as opposed to the supernatural *finis ultimus*'.
57. Feingold, *The Natural Desire to See God According to St. Thomas Aquinas and His Interpreters*, p. 529.

The Unresolved Question – Natura Pura?

Throughout his various writings on the mystery of the supernatural, de Lubac criticized the 'system of pure nature' as a relatively modern and unhelpful development in Catholic theology.[58] It is not surprising that de Lubac's critics have rallied in defence of the concept of *natura pura*. What exactly is meant by 'pure nature'? Consider two representative attempts to explain or define pure nature:

> We first focused our attention on the notion of pure nature itself, that is, on the idea of man *in solis naturalibus constitutus*. Pure nature thus refers to what defines us as human.[59]
>
> [Pure nature is] a concept of nature, and especially human nature, as complete in itself and not dependent for its preservation on divine action ... 'Pure' nature is, moreover, unable to enjoy any form of relation with God, neither in its being nor in its knowledge.[60]

The first of these two citations is presented in the context of a fundamental criticism of de Lubac; the second is taken from a book sympathetic to de Lubac's theology. In my opinion, both of these accounts of 'pure nature' miss the target in a fairly basic way. As understood by de Lubac, the modern idea of pure nature involves a claim about the *final end* of human nature as created by God.[61] The 'system of pure nature' described by de Lubac does not refer to the definitional

---

58. Cf. *Surnaturel*, 101–83; AMT, 145–277. Henri de Lubac, *Athéisme et sens de l'homme: une double requête de Gaudium et Spes*, in vol. 4 of his *Oeuvres Completes* (Paris: Cerf, 2006), pp. 471–500:
> Over the course of the last few centuries, a theory began to gain credence in our classical theology according to which 'nature' and the 'supernatural' each constituted a self-contained 'order', the second being superadded in fact to the first, without any connection between the two other than there existing, in our nature, a vague and general 'obediential potency' for being so to speak 'elevated'. Being and the Christian life thus found themselves on two separate planes ... There is no need to insist on this dualistic conception, the 'two tier' approach, which is familiar to all theologians. It seemed necessary to many people in order to secure the absolute gratuity of the divine gift in the wake of a series of serious errors, from the Baianism of the sixteenth century to the modernist immanentism of the twentieth century. In reality, because of its precedents, this approach proceeded instead on the basis of a break from the traditional dogmatic synthesis, such as the great scholastics, and Thomas Aquinas in particular, had ultimately elaborated it.

59. Mulcahy, *Aquinas's Notion of Pure Nature and the Christian Integralism of Henri de Lubac: Not Everything is Grace*, p. 201.

60. David Grumett, *De Lubac: A Guide for the Perplexed* (London: T & T Clark, 2007), p. 9.

61. Cf. MS, p. 12: '... a pure natural order – remember always that this means a complete order, bearing within it its own final end'. See also BC, p. 24: '... certain systems occurring late in Western theology... These theories, unknown to both the Greek and the Latin

integrity of human nature, i.e. 'what defines us as human'. With the entire Catholic tradition, de Lubac affirms that grace presupposes nature in its integrity. Created nature, he says, has 'its own proper stability and its own definite structure'.[62] De Lubac concurs with the words of Blaise Romeyer: 'Only by taking care not to disregard the relative specific consistency of our nature, and by taking it as a genuine substratum for grace, can we fulfill the requirements either of belief or thought'.[63] What de Lubac finds objectionable in the modern theory of 'pure nature' is not the emphasis given to the integrity and intelligibility of nature in distinction from grace. Instead, his concern is to overcome what he considers to be a one-sided or partial understanding of the finality of human nature. In other words, de Lubac opposes the idea that human nature itself has been created with an exclusively natural final end. Or, to state this same point differently, de Lubac opposes the idea that only with sanctifying grace does human nature acquire 'a new and additional'[64] supernatural finality.

Secondly, the system of pure nature is not identical with the affirmation that God could have created intellectual natures not ordered and called to supernatural beatitude. As noted above (*4th Thesis*), Pius XII, Henri de Lubac, and contemporary neo-Thomists all agree in upholding this hypothetical possibility. 'We know this', writes de Lubac, 'on two counts':

> what we know of God and what we know of creatures. God could never have been constrained or required by anything or anyone, either outside of or himself, to give me being. Nor could he be constrained or required by anything or anyone to imprint on my being a supernatural finality; therefore my nature cannot possess any claim upon it.[65]

In summary, the system of pure nature is organized around the idea that human nature in itself (prior to grace) has an exclusively natural or proportionate final end. Undergirding the theory of pure nature is the philosophical axiom that a nature must be able to attain its final end by virtue of its own power. The corollary of this thesis is that there can be no natural desire for supernatural beatitude. In the words of de Lubac's teacher, Pedro Descoqs, 'desire is natural insofar as the goal to which it aspires is proportionate to nature, in other words, possible to it'.[66]

Fathers, and which began to take shape only at the dawn of modern times, were organized around the idea of "pure nature" conceived of having a "purely natural" end'.

62. MS, p. 31.

63. MS, p. 32.

64. Mulcahy, *Aquinas's Notion of Pure Nature and the Christian Integralism of Henri de Lubac*, p. 204.

65. MS, p. 81.

66. Pedro Descoqs, *Le mystère de notre élévation surnaturelle* (Paris: Beauchesne, 1938), p. 120; cited in MS, p. 151.

In light of the foregoing account of 'pure nature', let me attempt to clarify the current state of the question in the debate between de Lubac and his contemporary Thomist critics. The first step is to identify some significant areas of agreement that are occasionally (mistakenly) put forward as disputed questions. The key issue is not whether or not God could have created an order of pure nature. Again, de Lubac and his neo-Thomist critics agree that a hypothetical order of pure nature is possible. Secondly, both de Lubac and contemporary proponents of *natura pura* affirm the existence of a proportionate natural end that is subordinate to the *finis ultimus*.[67] Thirdly, and more generally, the issue under dispute is not the abiding significance of nature and the natural law within the Christian economy of redemption. De Lubac agrees with the judgement of Marie-Joseph Le Guillou: 'respect for natural values in their own structure is the best measure of our respect for the supernatural in its absolute originality'.[68]

The real issue that continues to divide de Lubac and his neo-Thomist critics is whether or not there is a positive opening *in* nature itself to what is *beyond* nature. Regarding this question, Lawrence Feingold offers a helpful summary of the two basic positions. For the contemporary proponents of pure nature, 'our intrinsic supernatural finality is the result of an accidental form (sanctifying grace), given through Baptism and justification. For de Lubac, our supernatural finality is essential to our ("concrete") nature and given in the creation of nature itself'.[69] In the eyes of de Lubac, by denying that human nature itself is created with an ultimate end that exceeds nature, and that there is thus a truly natural desire for what is beyond nature (*visio beatifica*), the proponents of *natura pura* overlook the hidden depths and the transcendence that belong to nature itself. For de Lubac, the transcendent mystery of God's plan for creation and redemption is not simply on the side of grace (i.e. 'the result of an accidental form ... given through Baptism'); it is reflected in the very structure of created nature itself.

---

67. Cf. Long, *Natura Pura*, p. 23: Commenting on the formulation of Brian Shanley that 'Aquinas holds that man has only one end or telos: the beatific vision of God', Long writes: 'If he had written that for Thomas there is but one *finis ulitimus*, which is beatific vision, or that there are not two "coequal" ends, this would be true. But while there is only one *finis ulitimus*, which is supernatural, this does not rule out an end proportionate to nature.' As noted above, de Lubac says essentially the same thing in his book *Augustinianism and Modern Theology*, trans. Lancelot Sheppard; Introduction by Louis Dupré (New York: Crossroad Publishing Company, 2000), pp. 130-31:

> for St. Thomas ... this twofold finality which exists in real man does not in the nature of this man constitute the mark of a possible twofold polarity: it is a real and ordered duality ... Coexisting in man as he actually is, in this being which is made in the image of God, in each of us, the two finalities are both to be made real, the one by the other. Only the second actually deserves the name of last end.

68. M.-J. Le Guillou, 'Surnaturel', *Revue des sciences philosophiques et théologiques* (1950): pp. 226–43, at p. 238; cited in MS, p. 23.

69. Feingold, *The Natural Desire to See God According to St. Thomas Aquinas and His Interpreters*, p. 336.

In order to support this claim, and hopefully advance the debate, I turn now to consider a particular instance of the relation between nature and grace – the relationship between marriage in the order of creation and marriage as a sacrament.

Implications – Marriage as Nature and Sacrament

In an address to the Roman Rota in 2003, John Paul II suggested that reflection on the relationship between the natural and sacramental dimensions of marriage 'is a fruitful way to investigate more deeply the mystery of the relationship between human nature and grace'.[70]

Guided by these words, my aim in this section is to probe and develop Henri de Lubac's theology of nature and grace by reflecting on the Church's teaching on marriage. There are several reasons why the question of the sacramentality of marriage represents a promising path for a deeper understanding of the mystery of the supernatural. First, marriage has a unique status among the sacraments insofar as the institution of marriage is rooted in the order of creation.[71] As an *officium naturae*, marriage plays a paradigmatic role in safeguarding and disclosing the truth of human nature as created by God. A second reason for thinking about nature and grace in connection with marriage stems from the current crisis of marriage that effects both the natural institution and the sacramental mystery. An adequate response to this crisis requires a renewed understanding of the importance of the natural dimension of marriage coincident with a deeper awareness of how the sacramental mystery of Christ both presupposes and reveals the full truth of marriage.

In order to show the significance and fruitfulness of de Lubac's theology of nature and grace, I will sketch some key aspects of the Church's teaching on the relationship between the natural institution of marriage and its sacramental character. The next step will be to show how this teaching exhibits and illuminates de Lubac's fundamental thesis on nature and grace.

As noted above, marriage has a unique significance among the sacraments insofar as the natural institution of marriage belongs to the order of creation. Hence the difficult question, what is the difference between a natural marriage and a sacramental marriage? What does the grace of the sacrament 'add' to marriage? The answer to this question involves a rich and complicated development of doctrine from Augustine's reflection on the goods of marriage through medieval sacramental theology to post-Tridentine disputes between Church and state over the jurisdiction of marriage. Let me note two points.

---

70. John Paul II, 'Address to the Roman Rota', 30 January 2003.
71. Cf. John Paul II, *Familiaris Consortio*, p. 68: 'The sacrament of Matrimony has this specific element that distinguishes it from all the other sacraments: it is the sacrament of something that was part of the very economy of creation; it is the very conjugal covenant instituted by the Creator "in the beginning."'

First, the newness of a sacramental marriage is given in and through the mystery of Christ himself. Here we can recall the words of Irenaeus: '*Omnem novitatem attulit, semetipsum afferens*.' He brought all newness by bringing himself.[72] The essential difference between a natural marriage and a sacramental marriage is grounded in the gift of grace bestowed in and through the life, death, and Resurrection of Jesus Christ. Because Christ has shared his own life and love, the marriage of two baptized persons is dignified with being a real symbol of his spousal love for the Church. Through the grace of the sacrament of marriage, the reciprocal self-giving of the spouses 'participates in ... the very charity of Christ who gave himself on the cross'.[73]

Secondly, this newness is paradoxical. Christ did not establish a new 'outward sign' or a new form for entering into marriage. Instead, he recalled the original truth of creation: 'he who made them from the beginning made them male and female ... "For this reason a man shall leave his father and mother and be joined to his wife, and the two shall become one" ... therefore what God has joined together let no man put asunder' (Mt 19:4–6). Rather than 'adding' something to marriage from outside, Christ reveals the fullness of God's original plan for marriage and he accomplishes this plan through his death and Resurrection. Henceforth, marriage between baptized represents and participates in Christ's love for the Church.

Holding these two truths together – the pre-existence of the natural institution and the 'elevation' of marriage to a sacrament by Christ – Catholic doctrine affirms the inseparability of the sacrament and the institution (or contract) of marriage. Two texts will serve to illustrate this teaching:

> It is a dogma of faith that marriage has been raised by Our Lord to the dignity of a sacrament. It is a doctrine of the Church that the sacrament is not an adventitious quality superimposed on the contract; it pertains to the essence of marriage itself ... A civil law which supposes that, for Catholics, the sacrament is separable from the marriage contract and on the strength of this supposition dares to regulate the conditions required for validity infringes on the rights of the Church.[74]

> Let no one, then, be deceived by the distinction which some civil jurists have so strongly insisted upon – the distinction, namely, by virtue of which they sever the matrimonial contract from the sacrament, with intent to hand over the contract to the power and will of the rulers of the state, while reserving questions concerning the sacrament of the Church. A distinction, or rather severance, of this kind cannot be approved; for certain it is that in Christian marriage the contract is inseparable from the sacrament, and that, for this reason, the contract cannot be true and legitimate without being a sacrament

---

72. Irenaeus, *Adversus Haereses*, PG 7, pars prior, 1083, IV, 34, i. De Lubac appeals often to this Irenaean axiom: cf. C, p. 239; MS, p. 83.
73. John Paul II, *Familiaris Consortio*, p. 13.
74. Pius IX, 'Letter to the King of Piedmont', 19 September 1852.

as well. For Christ our Lord added to marriage the dignity of a sacrament; but marriage is the contract itself, whenever that contract is lawfully concluded.[75]

The implications of this doctrine of 'inseparability' are endless. The inseparability of sacrament and institution means that the locus of the sacred sign is not the subjective intention of the spouses that their love symbolizes Christ's love for the Church. The sacred sign is the marriage itself. Defending and upholding the natural institution of marriage – with its nature, essential properties, and natural ends – is an inner requirement of the Church's solicitude for the sacrament. At the same time, the novelty of Christ discloses the deepest truth of the original structure and ultimate finality of marriage itself. Precisely as a natural institution, marriage points beyond itself to the mystery of grace concretized in the Person of Christ. Without laying claim to what can only be received as a gratuitous gift, there is a positive opening in marriage itself to the surpassing fulfilment of representing and mediating divine love. 'From the very beginning', writes Leo XIII, 'marriage was a kind of foreshadowing of the Incarnation of the Son; and therefore there abides in it something holy and religious; not extraneous, but innate; not derived from men, but implanted by nature'.[76]

I suggested above that the key issue that continues to divide de Lubac and his contemporary Thomist critics is the question of how to conceive the original openness of nature. The logic of 'pure nature' tends to represent nature's openness as a specific obediential potency to acquiring (through grace) a new and additional finality. De Lubac, on the contrary, thinks of nature as originally and constitutively made for an ultimate end that surpasses nature. Hence the 'natural desire for the supernatural'. Mindful of the limits of analogy, we can transpose these two interpretations of nature to the question of how to think about marriage within the order of creation. The theory of 'pure nature' suggests an account of the natural institution of marriage as having an exclusively natural end. The grace of Christ would bring a 'new and additional finality' to marriage. De Lubac's theology suggests an understanding of marriage as originally and constitutively ordered to something radically beyond itself; namely, the mystery of Christ's love for the Church. For de Lubac, the transcendent supernatural finality of marriage would be an original and structural feature of marriage itself as created by God. The positive openness of natural marriage would represent a kind of prefigurement or foreshadowing of God's plan to recapitulate all things in Christ.

In my opinion, de Lubac's theology of nature and grace provides a more ample foundation for the Church's teaching on the 'inseparability' of institution and sacrament. Precisely because there is a positive opening to the supernatural at the heart of the natural institution of marriage, the natural reality itself can be 'elevated' to signify and participate in the greater mystery of Christ's love. In

---

75. Leo XIII, *Arcanum Divinae Sapientiae*, Encyclical Letter on Christian Marriage. *Acta Sanctae Sedis* 12 (1880): p. 23.

76. Ibid., 19.

one sense, a sacramental marriage is more truly a marriage. At the same time, thinking through de Lubac's thesis in connection with marriage sheds new light on the importance of 'natural ends' that are subordinate to the *finis ultimus*.

The natural end of marriage is the procreation and education of children. This natural end is not displaced or evacuated by the elevation of marriage to the sacramental mystery of a participation in Christ's love. As suggested above, the inseparability of institution and sacrament has implications in both directions. On the one hand, the natural dimension of marriage is constitutively ordered beyond itself and is thus capable of mediating divine love. On the other hand, the sacramental dimension both presupposes and deepens the natural reality of marriage within the order of creation. The natural dimension of marriage opens from within to the supernatural not because it is 'imperfect', but because its natural integrity is itself a sign of the greater mystery of God's plan accomplished in Christ. 'To obscure the natural dimension of marriage', writes John Paul II, '... also entails the implicit denial of its sacramentality. On the contrary, it is precisely the correct understanding of this sacramentality in the Christian life which spurs us to a new estimation of its natural dimension'.[77]

This leads to a final point. An affirmation of the significance of the 'natural end' of marriage suggests a new way of thinking about finality that goes beyond the neo-Thomist axiom of proportionality. If the natural end of marriage is the procreation and education of children, then already at the natural level there is something like a desire for an 'end' that radically transcends the innate power or ability of human nature. 'Parents do not create a child, but pro-create him, which is to say that their own self-transcending activity is a disposal of nature to a causal principle that transcends nature, namely, God's properly creative act.'[78] A child can only be received in truth as a gratuitous gift, yet children remain the proper natural finality of marriage. The principle at the root of the theory of 'pure nature' – the end of nature and the innate desire of nature must be proportionate to nature – is inadequate not only in relation to the supernatural but also within the created order itself.

Conclusion

The enduring achievement of Henri de Lubac consists in opening up and making available the inexhaustible treasures of the Catholic tradition – a tradition which bears witness across the centuries to a 'deep and permanent unity of faith'. Without claiming to offer the last word on the question of nature and grace, de Lubac brought to light an aspect of the tradition that had been neglected in modern scholasticism. At the very heart of nature is a positive opening to the unforeseen

---

77. John Paul II, 'Address to the Roman Rota', 1 February 2001.
78. D. C. Schindler, 'The Natural Supernaturality of Marriage', *Communio: International Catholic Review* (forthcoming).

mystery of God's love. 'The tradition', writes de Lubac, 'presents us with two affirmations at once, not in opposition, but as a totality: man cannot live except by the vision of God – and that vision of God depends totally on God's good pleasure. One has no right to weaken either, even in order to grasp the other more firmly'.[79] Or, in the words of Maurice Blondel, whom de Lubac credits for opening the way to a more traditional understanding of nature and grace:

> What makes the solidarity and beauty of the Catholic thesis on this fundamental point, is this alliance of the two gifts: that of the rational nature, prepared to receive and to taste – and the gift of supernatural grace coming to fulfill in an unforeseen way the expectation of the spiritual nature, without reason by itself ever being able to discover and to attain the term of destiny that renders man 'consors divinae naturae'.[80]
>
> One of the errors in perspective that must be avoided, it seems to me, has to do with the bad habit of considering that the state in which the supernatural vocation places us eliminates the 'state of nature.' No, the latter remains immanent to the divine adoption itself. And it is in this sense that one can, as a philosopher and as a theologian, speak of the essential and indestructible incommensurability of created beings and God, in order better to understand the creations of the divine Charity, the paradoxical ways of transforming union, the metaphysical and properly hyperphysical wonder of our *consortium divinae naturae*.[81]

From the beginning, Christians have been called upon to give an account or defence of our hope for eternal life (cf. 1 Pet 3:15). In our time, in order to account for the truth of Christian hope, it is necessary to first rediscover the intelligibility and goodness of the created order. As Benedict XVI suggests, fidelity to the Word of God includes a responsibility for creation. Perhaps more than ever, a metaphysical understanding of nature is an inner requirement for theologians who seek to interpret and hand on the *depositum fidei*. At the same time, God's revelation in Christ discloses a new depth to nature.

After Henri de Lubac, perhaps the best way to contemplate the mystery of nature and grace is to reflect on the figure of Christ as the living and personal unity of nature and grace. Christ reveals the deepest truth of human nature as a gift that God himself 'presupposes' in the mystery of the Incarnation. Christ's death, Resurrection, and Ascension reveal the supreme eschatological fulfilment of human nature as 'deified' by being included within the Trinitarian exchange of life and love. 'His word', writes de Lubac, 'is a deed ... the act of uniting heaven and earth'.[82]

---

79. MS, p. 179.
80. Maurice Blondel, 'On the Need for a Philosophy of the Christian Spirit', *Communio: International Catholic Review* 38 (2011): p. 172.
81. Maurice Blondel, 'Letter of April 5, 1932' in ASC, p. 186.
82. Henri de Lubac, 'The Light of Christ', in TH, p. 211.

Chapter 8

THE SPIRITUAL INTERPRETATION OF SCRIPTURE

Kevin L. Hughes

Henri de Lubac's role in the typical narrative of modern theology has centred on his controversial thesis about the relationship between the natural and the supernatural; his long discussions of spiritual exegesis have usually found a slightly different audience interested in the history of exegesis and broader ecclesiological and sociopolitical questions.[1] In certain ways, then, apparently clear partitions appear in de Lubac's work, and it may seem rather straightforward to discuss the 'spiritual interpretation of Scripture' in de Lubac. A significant portion of his scholarship is devoted to the question specifically – no less than three long articles on exegesis, a long monograph on Origen's spiritual interpretation, the four-volume *Exégèse medieval,* and two volumes on the 'spiritual posterity' of Joachim of Fiore's exegesis would seem to provide quite enough to occupy an essay such as this one. And I will certainly treat these in turn. But I wish to make a slightly larger argument for the consistent 'capillary' presence[2] of the exegetical framework throughout de Lubac's corpus. Indeed, it lies in the background of even the most controversial theses on nature and the supernatural and on the

---

1. To be fair, historians of exegesis have been interested in de Lubac mostly to discredit what they take to be his historical claims. See, for example, John Contreni's review of the translation of the first volume of *Exégèse médiévale* in *The Medieval Review* (https://scholarworks.iu.edu/dspace/bitstream/handle/2022/4700/99.08.13.html?sequence=1, accessed 1 December 2014), and see Kevin L. Hughes, 'The Fourfold Sense: De Lubac, Blondel, and Contemporary Theology', *The Heythrop Journal* 42:4 (2001): pp. 451–62, for a response. For the ecclesiological and political readings, see, for example, Susan K. Wood, *Spiritual Exegesis and the Church in the Theology of Henri de Lubac* (Grand Rapids: Eerdmans, 1998) and Bryan C. Hollon, *Everything is Sacred: Spiritual Exegesis in the Political Theology of Henri de Lubac* (Eugene, OR: Wipf & Stock, 2009).

2. I borrow this term and its use from Boyd Taylor Coolman, *Knowing God by Experience: The Spiritual Senses in the Theology of William of Auxerre* (Washington, DC: Catholic University of America Press, 2004). Coolman argues for the subtle 'capillary' presence of the doctrine of the spiritual senses in William's theology, such that, even when it is not the focus of reflection, it is present as a method and principle of William's work. I suggest the same is true of de Lubac's understanding of the spiritual interpretation of scripture.

'mystical body of Christ', and it forms the conceptual core of the book he never quite managed to write on Christocentric mysticism. Present at the root of his first book *Catholicism* and in his very last works on Joachim and Pico, the spiritual understanding of scripture simply named for de Lubac the principle and shape of Christian theological hermeneutics as such. That these hermeneutical principles gradually became eclipsed in the later Middle Ages and early modern period lay at the root of much of the theological confusion he found in the discussions of the Eucharist and the desire for God. That we have failed to recognize this capillary presence suggests that he was right.

In this essay I will sketch de Lubac's account of the logic and history of the spiritual understanding of scripture as it develops in his major treatments of the question, proceeding more or less chronologically, both in terms of *its development* over the ages of the Christian millennia and in terms of de Lubac's *own charting of that development* over the course of his long career. I will then indicate several places in de Lubac's other major works – *Corpus mysticum* and *The Mystery of the Supernatural*, in particular, where highlighting the capillary presence of spiritual understanding may add light to our understanding of these controversial works. What connects them all is this conviction: At the very taproot of the *ressourcement* movement, de Lubac aimed to repair Catholic theology and spirituality through the recovery of a deeper patristic biblical perspective. Having described that vital and integral perspective, de Lubac proceeds to chronicle its gradual dissolution and disappearance – a task which occupies most of the second half of his career. Spiritual understanding, for de Lubac, begins to fray or dissolve almost as soon as it takes shape as the rationalization[3] of the theological science gradually – and unintentionally – erodes the paradoxical rationality at the heart and root of patristic spiritual biblical theology. To study de Lubac's spiritual understanding of scripture, then, is to uncover his deeply tragi-comic sense of history and tradition and his hopes for theological renewal.

Against Marcionisms, Ancient and Modern

Henri de Lubac's first shot across the bow in the theological world was *Catholicism* (1937), the book that Hans Urs von Balthasar suggested was 'intended to be and actually became a major breakthrough' in Catholic theology; every other of his major works, says von Balthasar, 'grew from its chapters much like branches from

---

3. I use 'rationalization' in the Weberian sense of the development of institutions and pedagogies of theological education and regulation. This 'scientification' of theology begins in the eleventh and twelfth century, but it becomes normative in theological practice within the universities of the later Middle Ages. For resources on this shift, see Jacques Le Goff, *Intellectuals in the Middle Ages* (London: Wiley-Blackwell, 1993); M.-D. Chenu, *La théologie comme science aux XIIIe siècle* (Paris: Vrin, 1957); William Courtenay, *Parisian Scholars in the Early Fourteenth Century: A Social Portrait* (Cambridge: Cambridge University Press, 1999).

a trunk'.[4] The book is a study of the 'social aspects of dogma', as the original French subtitle claims: Scripture and tradition bear witness to the fundamentally social character of redemption and life in Christ, contrary to the perceived individualism of modern Christian teaching. Fundamental to this social doctrine of salvation was the witness of the Old Testament to the history of God's covenant with the people of Israel, taken up, transformed, and fulfilled by the revelation of God in Christ.[5] Indeed, it is this history that is the *revelatum;* '[it] is a twofold event, a twofold "covenant", a twofold dispensation which unfolds its development through the ages, and which is fixed, one might suppose, by no written account'.[6] Spiritual interpretation does not extract spiritual content from narrative meaning so much as it reads 'historical things spiritually' *and* 'spiritual things historically'.[7] For de Lubac, spiritual exegesis of the Old Testament was constitutive of the Christian understanding of Christ and the Church; the creeping individualism of the modern age was correlated to the gradual distancing of Israel and her scriptures as artefacts long settled in the dust of historical context and unable, therefore, to contribute to Christian self-understanding. The early decision of the Fathers to reject Marcion and cling to the Hebrew scriptures as integral to Christianity had established a fundamental characteristic of Christian faith that the modern age is in danger of forgetting. He suggests that an over-reliance on the literal and historical sense, to the neglect or dismissal of spiritual interpretation, is a kind of new Marcionism that threatens the Church's own self-understanding.

In the years immediately following the publication of *Catholicism*, de Lubac came to see that these new Marcionisms had serious political implications as well, as they threatened the Church's understanding of her intimate and irrevocable relationship to Jews in the present day. He insisted repeatedly that Nazi and Vichy anti-Semitism and their persecution of the Jews were aided and abetted by the modern splitting-off of the Christian Church from its Israelite foundations, of the division between the Old Testament and the New in the name of historical and literal interpretation. Christians found themselves ill-equipped to resist anti-Semitism as it came to be expressed in Christian-cum-Nazi rhetoric, precisely because the vital link between Old Covenant and New

---

4. Hans Urs von Balthasar, *The Theology of Henri de Lubac* (San Francisco: Ignatius Press, 1991), p. 35.

5. De Lubac's chapter on 'The Interpretation of Scripture' is itself structured according to the shape of the 'fourfold sense' of scripture; without calling attention to it, he begins with the '*historia*', the events of God's action in 'the history of the world' (165) as presented in scripture. He then uncovers the 'figures of the Church' and of Christ in the Old Testament – the purview of *allegoria* – and the internalization of this world-historical and theological teaching for the moral and spiritual life of the soul (*moralia*), because 'the law of "spiritual intelligence" is the very law of all spirituality ...' (215). This then points forward to the eschatological (*anagogia*) questions of salvation and predestination in the following chapters.

6. C, 169.

7. Ibid., 165.

had been broken and lost with the disappearance of the spiritual interpretation of scripture.[8] Like the ancient Marcionites and Valentinians, pro-Nazi theologians attempted to separate the Old Testament from the New and dismiss it, a 'Semite Old Testament' stripped off from an 'Aryan New Testament'.[9] To the contrary, de Lubac writes, 'we maintain the indissoluble bond between our two Testaments, always in the final analysis, interpreting the Old by the New, but also always basing the New on the Old. … There is only one single Scripture for us, which, as an entire whole, is sacred to us'.[10] This connection between Scriptural hermeneutics and anti-Semitism helps make sense of de Lubac's own work in the subversive periodical *Les Cahiers du Temoignage chretien* and his simultaneous efforts to edit and publish patristic exegesis and theology in the new *Sources chretiennes* series, even as he evaded the Gestapo in the 1940s. The renewal of theology by patristic exegesis was not just an academic issue but a vital tool of political action, or, as de Lubac preferred, 'spiritual warfare'.[11] Indeed, de Lubac suggests that spiritual exegesis is more than a tool; it is a wellspring of Christian vitality. In de Lubac's view, twentieth-century Christianity's anaemic incapacity to resist its own usurpation or co-optation by Nazi propaganda stemmed from the faithful's amnesiac forgetting of the deepest roots of their own faith. 'A more deeply and integrally lived Christianity, offering less of a hold to the caricatures of the adversary, presupposing perhaps more of reform in our habits and methods, must constitute the sole complete safeguard.'[12]

The Fourfold Sense and the Question of 'Allegory'

It was only after the war ended that de Lubac devoted himself to analysing the spiritual understanding of scripture directly. In a 1948 essay entitled 'On an Old Distich: The Doctrine of the "Fourfold Sense" in Scripture', de Lubac acknowledges that the traditional medieval account of the senses of scripture, captured in the brief mnemonic poem,

---

8. For a more thorough presentation of this argument, see Kevin L. Hughes, '*Ressourcement* and Resistance: *La nouvelle théologie*, the Fathers, and the Bible, against Fascism', in Daniel Wade McClain and Matthew A. Tapie, eds, *Reading the Bible as Political Act* (Minneapolis: Fortress Press, 2015).

9. De Lubac, 'New Religious Front', p. 486. De Lubac is citing the terms of Edmond Picard, *Synthese de l'antisemitisme* (Brussels, 1941). Picard attempted to write the history of Europe since ancient Greece as the war between Aryans and Semites.

10. De Lubac, 'New Religious Front', 486.

11. 'Spiritual Warfare', in TH, pp. 488–501. Originally published in *Cité nouvelle* (1943): pp. 769–83.

12. Henri De Lubac, 'A Letter to My Superiors', in *Theology in History*, trans. Anne Englund Nash (San Francisco: Ignatius Press, 1996), p. 438.

Littera gesta docet, quid credas allegoria,
Moralis quid agas, quo tendas anagogia.[13]

was only one of two major traditions of construing Christian biblical hermeneutics. The other, found in Origen and Cassian and extending throughout the tradition of interpretation, begins from the literal, moves through the moral, and then ends in the allegorical. For de Lubac, this is not just a variation on a theme but a fundamentally different sense of 'moralia'. When authors place the moral sense in front of the allegorical, they tend to draw moral lessons from the text that have little or nothing to do with their specific place in biblical revelation. In this sense, the moral meaning is a kind of 'pre-Christian' or 'pre-spiritual' understanding, the 'milk' in the Pauline sense that prepares for the 'solid food' of Christian spiritual understanding.[14]

The 'fourfold' account, then, articulates the shape and scope of 'spiritual interpretation' rightly understood. It begins from the *littera*, the 'facts' or 'events' of the biblical narrative, which figure the mystery of faith made manifest in Christ and the Church (*allegoria*). *Moralia* then points to the moral sense that is drawn from or ensues from this mystery of faith. It names the way in which the mystery of Christ and the Church elicited through *allegoria* is personally appropriated in the Christian life of discipleship. *Moralia* then culminates in *anagogia*, the eschatological and mystical end of the Church and soul in union with God. De Lubac argues that this fourfold sense gives voice not just to a method of biblical interpretation but to 'a profound logic that contributes a unifying principle to the sacred science'.[15] This profound logic extends from 'the essential fact: the mystery of Christ [*allegoria*], prefigured or rendered present in facts [*littera*], interiorized by the individual soul [*moralia*], and consummated in glory [*anagogia*]'.[16]

Scholars of patristic and medieval exegesis have noted for years that the late-medieval poem is in some sense constructed and artificial. When the fathers and the doctors discuss biblical hermeneutics, one can find a diversity of accounts and rationales for spiritual understanding. Even more, when they interpret scripture in commentaries or homilies, they do not, as a rule, systematically articulate these four senses in an integral way. From Delporte[17] in the early twentieth century to

---

13. 'The letter teaches what took place, the allegory what to believe, the moral what to do, the anagogy where you should be headed'.

14. Henri De Lubac, 'On an Old Distich: The Doctrine of the "Fourfold Sense" in Scripture', in *Theological Fragments*, trans. Rebecca Howell Balinski (San Francisco: Ignatius Press, 1989), pp. 112–13.

15. Ibid., 124.

16. Ibid., 119.

17. L. Delporte, 'Les principes de la typologie biblique', *Ephemerides theologicae lovanienses* 3 (1926): p. 310.

Young[18] and Contreni[19] in the late twentieth and early twenty-first century, scholars have been quick to point to the limited historical evidence for the 'fourfold sense' as a method in the history of exegesis. De Lubac freely admits that the formula is not articulated consistently throughout the tradition, but he argues that it amounts to a proper traditional *distillation* of the fundamental logic of Christian theology as glimpsed in thousands of partial ways over a millennium and more of Christian thought.[20]

Nonetheless, the persistence of the other, threefold sense throughout the tradition points to a complicated and, at times, confusing relationship between Christian exegesis and other non-Christian forms of allegorical and moral reading. For Platonic and Stoic interpreters, e.g., classical mythic forms in Homer or other classical authors served as veils over core philosophical truths about the soul and its conduct. De Lubac labours mightily in several places to distinguish 'Hellenistic allegory' from 'Christian allegory'. Christian allegory, as introduced into the tradition by St Paul's allegorical reading of Hagar and Sarah in his letter to the Galatians (4:21–31), refers to a 'spiritual understanding' that is drawn from the historical and literal sense of the scripture, not to overcome and eliminate the literal, but to fulfil and expand it. 'Christian exegesis was *claiming to discover a spiritual meaning in history* [sic].'[21] Hellenistic philosophical allegory, by contrast, discerns the core philosophical or moral truth beneath the veil of mythic narrative, 'false discourse signifying truth',[22] and then casts the false mythic narrative away. Christian allegory flows integrally from the literal and historical sense, from the *gesta* of the scriptural text, and, in turn, Christian *moralia* flows integrally from the allegorical sense and so is theologically specified by Christian faith.

What complicates this relationship is that Christian writers through the centuries were also good readers of classical and Hellenistic texts, and so one discovers that 'Christian writers never succeeded in any rigorous way in reserving "allegory" for its Pauline significance alone.'[23] One can find a kind of plural use of 'allegory' in Christian writers from Origen through Jerome and Augustine into the Middle Ages. It is this ambiguity of terms that led many early modern critics to dismiss

---

18. Frances Young, *Biblical Interpretation and the Formation of Christian Culture* (Cambridge: Cambridge University Press, 1997).

19. John Contreni, review of Henri de Lubac, *Medieval Exegesis: The Fourfold Sense of Scripture*, vol. 1, in *The Medieval Review* 99.08.13, https://scholarworks.iu.edu/dspace/bitstream/handle/2022/4700/99.08.13.html?sequence=1.

20. For further discussion of the logic of 'tradition' that undergirds this claim, see Kevin L. Hughes, 'The "Fourfold Sense": De Lubac, Blondel, and Contemporary Theology', pp. 451–62.

21. Henri de Lubac, 'Hellenistic Allegory and Christian Allegory', TF, p. 195. This article originally appeared in 1959.

22. Ibid., p. 194.

23. De Lubac, 'Typology and Allegorization', TF, p. 152.

Christian allegorical interpretation as 'a kind of Greek colony of allegorization in Christian territory',[24] a Hellenistic philosophical usurpation of the biblical text. Indeed, these complications led Jean Daniélou, de Lubac's confrére and friend, to distinguish Hellenistic 'allegory' from the Christian practice he preferred to refer to as 'typology'.[25] For Daniélou, the latter term demonstrated the firm grounding of spiritual interpretation in the concrete events of biblical history, while the former was prone to all the confusions and abstractions of Hellenistic interpretation of myth,[26] even in the hands of Origen, arguably its most accomplished Christian practitioner.

De Lubac insisted on maintaining the Pauline usage of allegory for several reasons. First, while both 'type' and 'allegory' are present in scripture and tradition, 'allegory' is by far the dominant term used to describe the breadth of spiritual understanding. But such breadth of allegorization, in the proper Christian sense, is an extension of a root typological interpretation. Daniélou himself admits that 'although Origen is always more likely to follow the mystical and interior interpretation, from which he finds nourishment for his soul, we see that he does so without losing contact with the strictly typological, ecclesiastical, and Christological interpretation that supports it'.[27] So, in practice, Origen's allegorization, though occasionally tainted by the Hellenistic variety, remains rooted in the events of revealed biblical history and its Christological referent. De Lubac thus describes the relationship between the 'typological' and the 'allegorical' is akin to the relationship between theory and practice. Origen's allegory is 'manna, a daily bread, which he distributes to everyone ... Speaking as a simple priest to the baptized who are immersed in daily life ...'[28] In Origen's hands, allegory is thus the more comprehensive and practical term, built around a solid typological theological core. The reality as expressed and practised in patristic and medieval exegesis may be messy and entangled, but de Lubac seeks to defend the fullness of the tradition even in the midst of those entanglements.

---

24. De Lubac, 'Hellenistic Allegory', p. 165, paraphrasing Jean Pépin, *Mythe et allégorie, les origines grecques et les contestations judéo-chrétiennes* (Paris: Aubier, 1958), p. 215.

25. See, for example, Jean Daniélou, *From Shadows to Reality: Studies in the Biblical Typology of the Fathers*, trans. Wulstan Hibberd (London: Burns & Oates, 1960).

26. De Lubac's 'Typology and Allegorization' was actually part of a rather public debate on the subject between the two friends. See Jean Daniélou, 'Traversée de la Mer Rouge et baptême aux premiers siècles', *Recherches Science Religieuse* 33 (1946): pp. 402–30; Henri de Lubac, '"Typologie" et "Allégorisme"', *Recherches Science Religieuse* 34 (1947): pp. 180–226; Jean Daniélou, 'Les divers sens de l'Écriture dans la tradition chrétienne primitive', *Ephemerides Theologicae Lovanienses* 24 (1948): pp. 119–26.

27. De Lubac, 'Typology and Allegorization', p. 160, quoting Daniélou's unpublished manuscript entitled *Isaac, or Passionis figura*, p. 34.

28. Ibid., pp. 160–61.

History and Spirit

De Lubac's interest in defending Origen's exegetical practice yielded a full monograph in 1950, *History and Spirit: The Understanding of Scripture according to Origen*. The book is intended to defend Origen's scriptural theological vision from his many critics, mainly by attending to Origen's exegetical practice rather than his exegetical theory. The latter displays more Hellenistic allegorical tendencies, perhaps in deference to Origen's original audience. The former shows a thinker deeply concerned and engaged with the *historia* of the biblical text. De Lubac's title itself bears witness to the shape of his argument, as he had already indicated in his debate with Daniélou: Origen's exegesis is fundamentally 'an effort to grasp the spirit in history or to undertake the passage from history to spirit'.[29] Here de Lubac draws a conclusion that had been implied in his earlier essays: scripture, properly speaking, has only two senses, the historical and the spiritual;[30] it is this latter dimension that can be split and named in various ways. These two senses are not free-floating parallel semantic fields, but integrally related meanings. That is, spiritual exegesis as it is represented in Origen aims both to understand the typological figures of Christ and the Church in the biblical witness to history and, perhaps even more significant, to allow the passing events of history to pass over into spiritual truth.

To demonstrate this, de Lubac studies Origen's exegetical practice rather than his theory. He suggests that the hermeneutical discussion in the *Peri Archon*, e.g., reflects a younger Origen's view, one more captured (or tempted?) by the Hellenistic spirit of Alexandria. Origen's actual exegesis, stretched over a long career as a scholar and a preacher, reveals a different set of priorities, more grounded in the historical letter of the text, more thoroughly Christological, ecclesial, and sacramental, and more interested in offering allegorical points of connection between the biblical text and the practical 'daily bread' for his congregants. *History and Spirit* is structured topically, and the argument builds, like Origen's exegesis itself, from detailed attention in a long chapter devoted to the literal sense, the 'body' of the Word. 'In his Scripture as in his earthly life, Origen thought, the Logos needs a body; the historical meaning and the spiritual meaning are, between them, like the flesh and divinity of the Logos.'[31] If this is true, then attention to the letter cannot help but consider the spirit, which is always contained within it even as it exceeds it.

> History, in any case, is essentially what passes on. Thus the events recounted in the Bible, whatever they may be, as they were unfolding, all exhausted, so to speak, their historical role at the same time as their factual reality, so as no longer to survive today except as signs and mysteries… Thus, in its entirety,

---

29. HS, p. 317.
30. Ibid., p. 205.
31. Ibid., p. 105.

up to its final event, history is a preparation for something else... The truth to which it introduces us is no longer the order of history. It goes hand in hand with spirit.[32]

In his exhaustive way, De Lubac explores various ways in which Origen treats the historical sense of the text. There are times, de Lubac admits, when Origen seems to leap to allegory in a way that avoids an uncomfortable or unpalatable literal sense; 'here we can speak with some justification of the "escape mechanisms of the allegorical school."'[33] But these instances, says de Lubac, are the exception rather than the rule, and Origen in fact takes advantage of his own theoretical justification to allegorize the odd literal sense less often than he might have.[34] De Lubac gives multiple examples of places where the apparent absurdity of a literal reading of the text might invite allegory, but where Origen maintains a careful attention to the letter nonetheless. Much more often does Origen perceive that the spiritual sense is not opposed to the literal but is the very principle of the letter's coherence. 'If there had not been, beneath the letter, a hidden intention of the Holy Spirit that goes beyond what it says, this letter itself would often be unbelievable... We would be dealing with a mere fable, a bit of gossip.'[35] It is the Spirit which unifies the various books, the various narratives, and all the fine details into a coherent witness of God's work, past, present, and future.

In subsequent chapters, de Lubac focuses on the one spiritual sense of scripture, in its organic movement from figures of Christ and the Church, to the moral formation of the faithful to the mystical and eschatological end. De Lubac, I think, deliberately steps away from what might have been the most obvious structure. There are no chapters per se on *allegoria, moralia* and *anagogia*. Instead, the flow of the chapters follow a kind of order of discovery that demonstrates the movement into deeper spiritual understanding of the scriptures and illustrates the kind of mentality and spirituality that both frames and is informed by spiritual understanding. De Lubac begins his treatment of 'the spiritual sense' with a frank acknowledgement of Origen's debt to the Hellenistic allegory of his Alexandrian predecessor Philo. Acknowledging this debt makes sense of Origen's historical context as a Hellenistic man of letters in the third century, but, even more, it allows the distinct differences between Philo and Origen to emerge more clearly and distinctly. 'We will thus note in Origen many of the elements that come from Philo and from Jewish traditions... But it does not seem to us to be the characteristic fact. The difference here is much more profound than the similarities... Between Philo and Origen, there is the whole Christian mystery.'[36] Origen's specifically Christian spiritual interpretation, then, takes leave

---

32. Ibid., pp. 322–23.
33. Ibid., p. 114.
34. Ibid., p. 116.
35. Ibid., p. 121.
36. Ibid., p. 187.

of Philo and follows 'Jesus himself, who said: "Search the Scriptures... It is they that bear witness to me.... It is Moses [and the prophets] who wrote of me."'[37] The encounter with Christological figures represents the first layer of penetration into spiritual exegesis, and de Lubac traces Origen's discovery of specific Christological themes, converging on the Cross itself, from all the prophets and wisdom of the Old Testament. These Christological themes themselves lead to ecclesial figures: 'The mystery of Christ. But also, *as a consequence*, the "mystery of the Church",'[38] another mystery given ample presence in Origen's exegesis. If scripture reveals to us the mystery of the Church, then we can begin to discern how that mystery comes to bear upon our lives, both in the daily struggles of moral life and in the intimacies of mystical union, the foretaste of heavenly bliss.[39] The line of argument, with the multiplication of examples from Origen's text, performs more than indicates the movement from *allegoria* into *moralia* into *anagogia*.

It is this vision of scripture, animated by the spirit, bearing witness throughout to Christ, nourishing the faithful in great and small ways in their pilgrim journey into God and his Kingdom, that de Lubac finds so essential and worthy of display in Origen. His analysis does not aim to paper over the sorts of allegorization that have excited Origen's critics to reject him, --indeed, he highlights numerous instances. But de Lubac sets these instances in the richer context of Origen's exegesis in practice – a complex, multi-faceted, sometimes idiosyncratic, but fundamentally Christological and sacramental form of deep ecclesial engagement with the scriptures. Once again, de Lubac finds in Origen the fullest expression of the Christian's relation to the scriptures: the historical events of God's covenant with Israel are represented in scripture, fulfilled in Christ, but then not fully understood until they transform the reader of scripture through the reception of the spirit. Spiritual exegesis, then, is not simply a technique but a comprehensive approach to the revelation of God in Christ. De Lubac confesses that, as he studied Origen, his understanding deepened: 'It was no longer even a matter solely of exegesis. It was a whole manner of thinking, a whole new world view that loomed before me... Even more, through this "spiritual understanding" of Scripture, it was Christianity itself that appeared to me.'[40] Defending Origen's exegesis was not simply pursuing an interest in patristic renewal, because this very exegesis bore witness to the 'permanent foundations of Christian thought'.[41]

Henri de Lubac begins the long conclusion to *History and Spirit* with a question and an answer: 'What remains of this vast doctrine, which emerges again before our eyes like a dream palace through the mist of the distant past? Depending on our perspective in approaching it, we would respond: Not much, or, on the contrary: Everything essential.'[42] A work begun in defence of Origen bears fruit

---

37. Ibid., p. 190.
38. Ibid., p. 200 (emphasis mine).
39. Ibid., pp. 204–22.
40. Ibid., p. 11.
41. Ibid., p. 431.
42. Ibid., p. 427.

in a much broader reflection on biblical interpretation and, even wider, on the logic of Christian faith itself. Having endeavoured in the first instance to provide a thick description of Origen's exegetical practice, both in its idiosyncrasies and in its enduring insights, so as to correct the negative judgements, both historical and theological, so often given him, de Lubac in his conclusion begins to ponder what in Origen's particular practice is taken up in the long tradition as a whole, and so what we may continue to receive from it. In so doing, he distinguishes, like Blondel before him, between 'history' and 'tradition'. The former names the *gestalt*, the whole picture of Origen as a man of his time, both as receiver of a legacy and culture and as an innovator. Some of this should be remembered and remembered well, without necessarily desiring to recapture or revive his practice for ourselves. The latter is what is taken up, carried forward, and even transformed. It is also, de Lubac fears, what is or may be lost in a culture grown deaf to the long call of the tradition. At the heart of this tradition's inheritance is Origen's insistence that scripture *has* a spiritual sense at all, not as something added on to the literal, but as the deep sense and meaning of the text. Specifically, the spiritual sense is the deep sense and meaning of the text *as inspired Scripture for the believer*. '[The] spiritual meaning of a mystery is the meaning that one discovers, or rather, into which one enters by living this mystery. Even more fundamentally, the whole process of spiritual understanding is identical in principle to the process of conversion.'[43] De Lubac confesses that it is this process, this movement of the soul, that he attempts to glimpse in and through the spiritual exegesis of Origen, in the hopes that these glimpses might remind us how to perform that same movement: 'Without either a return to archaic forms or servile mimicry, often by totally different methods, it is a spiritual movement we must reproduce above all.'[44] Having attempted this in the book as a whole, he then sketches out what remains to be done, and in this way begins to sketch the outline of what will become his next major project, *Medieval Exegesis*. '[We] have taken things back to their source ... Now it would be necessary to note in detail the transformations introduced one after another in the course of twenty centuries of history, as the essential problems of the Church recur and as the meditation on Scripture comes to respond to new needs or is carried out in new surroundings.'[45] In brief, de Lubac highlights some of the major themes of *Medieval Exegesis*: the spiritual exegesis that had been central to doctrinal development in the Fathers becomes more focused upon the personal mystical experience of the monastic reader. The integral unity of history, doctrine, and spirituality begins to narrow in the early Middle Ages. With the rise of scholasticism, the literal sense is given the sole weight of doctrine, leaving the 'mystical sense' to personal spirituality. The vital unity of the fourfold sense is lost long before the fourfold sense itself ceases to be recognized.

Nor does de Lubac believe that the 'fourfold sense' can or should be recovered for the Church today. 'Spiritual exegesis has long since accomplished an essential

43. Ibid., p. 446.
44. Ibid., p. 450.
45. Ibid., p. 468.

part of its task. It has contributed to the expression of Christian mystery and to the building up of the Church. It could not be reconstructed today in all its fullness. As long as its results are not denied, the damage is not fatal.'[46] So de Lubac ends his long study of Origen with a discussion of precisely what it is we should claim or learn from this tradition. First, he argues that we need to be able to read scripture as opening up a world of divine signification. Where spiritual interpretation sees God communicating through symbolic representation in scripture, modern interpreters are 'anti-symbolic': they tend to read 'God' as a sign of man and heaven as a figure of earth. However we may read scripture, we need hold open the symbolic – one might say sacramental – sensibility. Even more, we must understand that scripture invites the reader to be transformed through deeper and deeper interpretation; this is 'the profound significance' of the traditional doctrine of the spiritual sense ...

> It upholds the idea of a progress of the spiritual life within the Church. It affirms an eschatological mysticism that is no more an eschatology without mysticism than a mysticism without eschatology. It expresses above all in its delicate equilibrium and in its full impact the relationship of the two Testaments.[47]

Whatever form Christian exegesis in the modern age takes, de Lubac implies that it must remain open in an analogous way to this deep engagement in the life of faith, an engagement that is both historical and spiritual, both personal and ecclesial, both mystical and eschatological.

Medieval Exegesis

In 1959, nine years after the publication of *History and Spirit*, de Lubac released the first two volumes of his longest work, *Medieval Exegesis,* with the third volume following in 1962 and the fourth and final volume in 1965. This *magnum opus et arduum*, the fruit of de Lubac's dizzyingly detailed knowledge of Migne's *Patrologia Latina*, fleshes out the brief sketch of the history of exegesis he had provided in the concluding chapter of his work on Origen. Many of the elements of the argument are recognizable: de Lubac again identifies the 'fourfold sense' formula as a later medieval distillation, but he again defends its capacity to capture *in nuce* the tradition of spiritual interpretation that he had documented in Origen. Again he discusses the relationship between the 'threefold' and 'fourfold' formulae, again arguing that they are not necessarily at odds and that the 'fourfold formula' is the more capacious. And once again, de Lubac makes it clear that he thinks some 'restoration' of spiritual exegesis as practised in the Middle Ages neither possible nor desirable. So it seems at first that *Medieval Exegesis* does not

---

46. Ibid., p. 489.
47. Ibid., p. 490.

itself advance or transform de Lubac's argument since its first formulations just after the Second World War.

And yet this patient, exhaustive (and at times exhausting) textual study of medieval exegesis allows certain nuances to emerge more clearly. First, de Lubac explores with great attention the ways in which the 'threefold sense' and the 'fourfold sense' of scripture coexisted and interacted throughout the Middle Ages – sometimes in competition, but more often in parallel or in cooperation, as two modes of expression within the larger horizon of biblical hermeneutics. De Lubac can show that all the various renaissances of the Middle Ages – Carolingian, millennial, twelfth-century – involved a turn or return to the resources of classical grammar in Priscian and Donatus, hand in hand with a *ressourcement* in the biblical and patristic authorities.[48] The influence of Hellenistic grammar and hermeneutics is thus never subtracted or eliminated, but instead, it is continually rediscovered or reapplied. But this ongoing historical influence does not in itself subvert or transform the theological logic of Origenian Christian allegory that is later captured in the brief mnemonic distich of the 'fourfold sense'. De Lubac had said as much in his early articles on allegory, but in *Medieval Exegesis,* he demonstrates this relationship by patiently unfolding example after example from patristic and medieval resources.

But even more significantly, the teeming pages of *Medieval Exegesis* allow de Lubac patiently to unfold a more careful and discriminating account of the gradual unwinding of the spiritual vision that is captured in the 'fourfold sense' in the course of the Middle Ages through the gradual ascent of dialectic as the primary method of theological reflection. De Lubac takes aim at the master narrative that informs the histories of exegesis of scholars such as Beryl Smalley and Ceslaus Spicq, a whiggish account that sniffs out the emergence of 'critical textual scholarship' from the haze of 'subjective allegorism'. Such a narrative begs the argument that it aims to demonstrate – that allegorical interpretation is itself subjectivist interpolations of meaning into the plain literal sense of the text. To the contrary, de Lubac offers example after example where the subjective interpolations to which medieval authors object are interpretations that depart from the kind of orthodox spiritual reading of scripture that harmonizes the Old Testament with the New. 'Deliberately to confine oneself to the "pure letter", even granting that one might do so with exactitude, is exactly what would count as producing a work of "one's own peculiar sense;" that would be to plunge into a subjective interpretation, to "corrupt" Scripture by undermining its integrity.'[49] The shift in exegetical practice cannot be read properly, then, as the rejection of allegory as subjective or arbitrary and the gradual recognition of the superiority of *hebraica veritas*; there must be an alternative narrative. The last two volumes of *Medieval Exegesis* are devoted to a careful telling of that tale. Following this alternative narrative, of the gradual dissolution of the integrity of spiritual interpretation,

---

48. ME, vol. 3, pp. 6–12.
49. Ibid., p. 97.

allows for de Lubac to account for two apparently disparate elements in twelfth-century exegesis as two instances of the same crisis.

On the one hand, de Lubac focuses on the theological legacy of Joachim of Fiore, the monastic 'prophet of Calabria'. The centre of Joachim's intellectual project was exegetical, developing a richly textured symbolic discourse for *intellectus spiritualis*, the spiritual understanding of scripture that, for Joachim, offered the key to the unfolding of history itself. On first examination, Joachim would seem to be an example of monastic spiritual exegesis gone mad, a kind of hypertrophe rather than dissolution of the tradition. If the concordance between the Old Testament and the New is at the root and heart of patristic exegesis, Joachim's writings seem to place such concordances at the centre and to strengthen and expand their scope, even in positing a coming 'third status' of the Holy Spirit, in which the Church herself would be transformed into an *ecclesia spiritualis*, with the wisdom gleaned from the spiritual understanding of scripture as the guiding and animating principle of authority and order. But for de Lubac, Joachim represents a fundamental deformation of the fourfold sense. First, Joachim breaks the unity of Old and New even as he tries to deepen it. In positing a coming 'third status', Joachim envisions a 'profound spiritual transfiguration of the New Testament itself, analogous to that of the Gospel in which the Old Testament had been transfigured'.[50] In particular, he sees in Joachim the prizing apart of the two dimensions of *anagogia*. If the old mnemonic poem had identified *anagogia* as interpretation concerning *quo tendas*, 'where you are headed', the fathers understood this to be both mystical and eschatological. That is, it referred to the ascent of the soul to God into mystical union, and at one and the same time, the movement of the Church, with all creation, towards the coming Reign of God. Joachim's reading, for de Lubac, overdetermines and immanentizes the eschatological, reducing the mystical into the eschatological and so rendering history itself as a dawning eschatological reality. 'Absent critical reflection as well as a certain interiority, he has projected in space and time the symbols that the meditation on Scripture caused to spring up in his heart.'[51] De Lubac would go on to write two volumes on the long and troubling modern legacy of Joachim's immanent eschatology.[52] Joachim and his inheritors represent one particular monastic distortion of the scriptural vision of the earlier tradition; the other most significant shift happens in the schools, in the gradual shift in the understanding of understanding itself. The ascendency of scholastic dialectical rationality begins to alter the meaning of the fourfold sense even as it adopts it.

The School of St Victor holds a prominent place in the narratives of Spicq and Smalley as the centre of a new emphasis on the literal and 'Hebraic' sense of the Old Testament text. In its great master Hugh, these scholars find the birth of a new and more rigorously scientific method of scriptural scholarship. De Lubac argues, to

---

50. Ibid., p. 342.
51. Ibid., p. 419.
52. Henri De Lubac, *La Postérité spirituelle de Joachim de Fiore*, 2 vols (Namur: Culture et Vérité, 1979–1981).

the contrary, that 'far from revolutionizing the principles of exegesis by attacking the old allegorizing routine, Hugh of St Victor is merely trying to consolidate the imperiled tradition'.[53] If Hugh cautions against biblical interpretations that take liberties, he is less concerned with excesses of traditional allegory than with 'indiscreet theological speculation, a rationalistic tendency,... *curiositas*'.[54] 'The principle abuse against which Hugh protested... did not come from an old "routine":... it was rather more the seduction of novelty... Against this seduction, Hugh of St. Victor was driven, in his work of reorganization, to maintain the spirit of past centuries.'[55]

Nevertheless, Hugh does do the work of reorganization, and, in so doing, he does set into motion a gradual change, not yet in the schema of 'spiritual interpretation' as represented by the 'fourfold sense', but rather in the nature of relations among those senses. Hugh's innovation, even if it was intended to conserve the view of the Fathers, was to distinguish between what Chenu called the 'two pieces' of theology, 'the historical reading and the construction of allegory'.[56] By so distinguishing these two modes of theological discourse, Hugh aimed to integrate spiritual interpretation of scripture into a systematic and progressive programme of education. Hugh sought to make the 'habitual framework' of the fourfold sense which, it seems, had to be caught rather than taught, into discreet and teachable skills or practices. As a result, what had been the organic relationship of letter to spirit in Hugh's work became distinct 'orders', two consecutive disciplines, one 'historical' and one 'theological'. Allegory, as a new mode or order, came to have a method and structure separate from *historia*, and so, in practice, from exegesis itself.

> [Historia] will become historical and literal exegesis, free, when the time comes, to change into a veritable 'positive' scholarship;... one day it will be 'criticism'; it will even become, for many, religiously neutral, the exegete leaving to the theologian the burden of doctrinal commitments. At the same time, because of this separation, the second discipline will be free to organize itself more and more as an autonomous system. It will progress in rationality and in abstraction, to become the majestic edifice of the Summas of the great epoch....[57]

Such was not Hugh of St Victor's intent, to be sure; quite to the contrary, he hoped to hold together the patristic wisdom, precisely by integrating it into a system of education that could pass this wisdom on to students of a younger generation. And yet that very systematization set in motion a gradual process of rationalization and separation. In the Victorine legacy, the language of the senses

---

53. ME, vol. 3, p. 222.
54. Ibid., p. 229.
55. Ibid., p. 253.
56. M.-D. Chenu, 'The Symbolist Mentality', *Nature, Man, and Society in the 12th Century*; cited by de Lubac, ME, vol. 3, p. 312.
57. ME, vol. 3, p. 314.

of scripture survives, but it will designate three distinct sciences or disciplines – exegesis, theology, and spirituality – which later masters such as Bonaventure and Thomas would seek to hold together, but in their case almost in spite of, rather than through, the disciplinary modes in which they were trained.[58]

And so the 'dawn of biblical scholarship' celebrated by Smalley in the Victorine school is one of several separated strands to emerge in the wake of the great master Hugh. Richard and Adam of St Victor, Peter Comestor, and Peter Chanter all carry forward a certain mode of separated critical exegesis, while scholastic theology *per se* takes off in earnest in Peter Lombard and the other early scholastic *Summa* authors. And, to round out the equation, the great Victorine Thomas Gallus (of Vercelli) generates a school of spirituality in his mystical readings of Pseudo-Dionysius the Areopagite. While the language of the 'fourfold senses of scripture' would persist well into the later Middle Ages, its signification had changed radically. The fourth and final volume of *Medieval Exegesis* is devoted to teasing out the various ways in which high scholastic exegesis takes up the relationship between spirit and letter, but it is clear that, for de Lubac, the equilibrium of the fourfold sense has been lost. Once again, de Lubac is careful to note that there was a certain necessity in the change: the traditional formula had lost its sap and vigour, and a new mode of engagement was required, a mode more dialectical and scientific in nature. And yet the new modes that arose carried a significant cost – a cost, according to de Lubac, that we continue to pay today.

Rationalization of the theological endeavour in the scholastic movement, then, is the most significant factor that gradually unravels the tightly integrated elements of spiritual exegesis. The very desire to develop scriptural exegesis into an institutional programme of education subtly shifts the orientation of the 'senses' from elements in a spiritual itinerary of deeper and deeper appropriation of the word to distinct areas of interest, spheres of meaning, or subdisciplines. What was intended as a means of transmitting scriptural wisdom to students, says de Lubac, subtly transformed that wisdom into a kind of 'know-how' in a technical field. For de Lubac, this is yet another instance of the way the dominance of dialectic in the medieval schools unintentionally flattened theological discourse. The supple rhetoric of the Fathers that lay at the root of both dogmatic and spiritual theology in the first millennium lost some of its plasticity under the harsh analytic light of dialectic. If this is true in the first instance of spiritual exegesis, de Lubac finds corollary examples in eucharistic theology, ecclesiology, and theological anthropology. Indeed, it is this gradual semantic shift in theological language and practice that lies at the root and core of de Lubac's most famous (or infamous) theological arguments in *Corpus mysticum* and *Surnaturel*.

---

58. Ibid.,, pp. 315–26, but also see volume 4, especially the chapter on St Bonaventure. Volume 4 is currently only available in French: *Exégèse Médiévale*, t. 4 (Paris: Aubier, 1964).

Paradox and Mystery: The Capillary Presence of Spiritual Exegesis in De Lubac

Corpus mysticum is de Lubac's historical and theological study of the shift in eucharistic language in the transition from the first millennium to the second. In the fathers and early medieval theologians, the term '*corpus verum*', the 'true Body of Christ' was understood to be the Church itself, and the Eucharist was the 'sacrament of the body', the mysterious and hidden sacramental sign of that presence, often referred to as the '*corpus mysticum*'. When sceptics like Berengar began to question the presence of Christ within that sacramental sign, theological discourse shifted to defend that real presence in the sacrament, and so tended to focus on sacramental change in the species, etc. To undergird this faith in the sacrament, the presence of the Body of Christ in the elements of the Eucharist came to be affirmed as *corpus verum*, and the Church, in turn, came to be understood as *corpus mysticum*, and this entailed a change in the meaning of both terms. De Lubac's deepest worry in this shift was that the eucharistic presence in the elements of bread and wine could then be understood in isolation from the presence of Christ in the body of the Church. Such a separation may come at the cost of the fundamental mystery at the heart of both, for, as de Lubac famously says, 'the Eucharist makes the Church'. de Lubac is careful not to tell this story as a simple decline narrative; he acknowledges the rational precision which was brought to bear in defence of the real presence of Christ in the sacrament, and he considers that to be a necessary gain. But every gain brings a loss as well, and theological reflection in the second millennium tended to resolve the paradoxical relationship of Church and Sacrament.

De Lubac describes this gain and loss in a chapter entitled 'From Symbolism to Dialectic.' Here de Lubac discerns what he takes to be the deep structure beneath the Berengarian controversy, where, '[more] profoundly, more universally, it was a new mentality that was spreading, a new order of problem that was emerging and catching people's interest, a new way of thinking, the formulation of new categories. Understanding was entering a new era ...'[59] This change was not overt or even intentional, rather it occurred 'further down, in the dark basements of the mind, in that mysterious zone where everything becomes entangled in advance, before seeing the light of day ...'[60] Gradually, almost imperceptibly, 'all the symbolic inclusions [of the earlier tradition] were transformed...into dialectical antitheses',[61] and 'the symbolism in which that faith had expressed itself and flourished was mortally wounded'.[62] Dialectical reason gradually becomes the centre and criterion of theological discourse; the servant becomes the master.

In the hands of Saint Augustine, the relationship between dogmatic truth and mystery was intrinsic. 'Now, if the mystery is essentially obscure to our

---

59. CM, p. 228.
60. Ibid., p. 226.
61. Ibid., p. 226.
62. Ibid., p. 228.

carnal faculties, it is in itself radiant with a secret intelligibility. If it constitutes a challenge to faith, it is at the same time a sign and an appeal. It invites us, and stimulates us to question ... Beneath the letter, we can discern the spirit.'[63] In this last phrase, de Lubac points to the integral relationship between the forms of reasoning and scriptural exegesis. The integral understanding of letter and spirit within the scriptures is of a piece with the symbolic underpinning of the Church's doctrine as it had been carried forward for the first millennium. Indeed, de Lubac argues that the Eucharist and the scripture are 'the two privileged fields open to the exploration of the believer ... In the Eucharist as in the Scripture, [the fathers] thought that everything was full of mystery, that is to say everything is full of reason. The two words were generally offered as synonyms'. What is lost, then, in the shift away from symbolic modes of reasoning, is not just some abstract harmony of affect and intellect, but a wholly different conception of intellectual activity itself, a dynamic and teleological, or, better, *anagogical* understanding of the intellectual life as a life intended towards God. 'For the Fathers, the essential mainspring of thought was not identity, or analogy, but *anagogy*.'[64] But the 'Christian rationalism' that was being born in the eleventh century 'could no longer envisage the understanding of mysteries outside their demonstration'.[65] With the loss of the animating heart of the spiritual interpretation of scripture came the loss of the symbolic and anagogic understanding of doctrine and theology itself.

This same rationalizing dynamic lies at the heart of that other famous and controversial thesis of de Lubac's concerning the 'mystery of the supernatural'. Readers will find more ample discussion of this dimension of de Lubac's work elsewhere in this volume; my only purpose is to point to its convergence with his account of the fate of the spiritual interpretation of scripture. In de Lubac's two-volume sequel to *Surnaturel*, he first sketches the long history of early modern Jansenism and its related figures, highlighting the selective and partial reading of Augustine that these early modern theologians rendered.[66] He then endeavours to sketch a reading of Thomas Aquinas that will place him, according to de Lubac, in the wider stream of the tradition of reflection upon nature and grace. Again, the detailed dimensions of this controversy are beyond our scope; of interest to this essay is that the argument culminates in four chapters on 'Paradox' (ch. 6, 'The Christian Paradox of Man'; ch. 7, 'The Paradox Unknown to the Gentiles'; ch. 8, 'The Paradox Rejected by Common Sense'; and ch. 9, 'The Paradox Overcome by Faith'). For de Lubac, the impasse of arguments over 'pure nature' follows from a level deeper than the arguments themselves, at the level of the logic by which such arguments are imagined. At the heart of the Christian understanding of the human orientation to God lies a paradoxical formulation – we are naturally ordered to a supernatural end; insofar as we have lost our capacity

---

63. Ibid., p. 231.
64. Ibid., p. 235.
65. Ibid., p. 238.
66. Cf. AMT.

for paradox, we will necessarily reduce the paradox into dialectical oppositions seeking determination. Paradox is the mode of reasoning that refuses too-simple resolution, that is patient with unfolding the truth in time, that is preserved and fostered in the patristic tradition of scriptural interpretation. It is a mode of reasoning ordered to *anagogia*. 'For although we cannot yet penetrate the "wall of Paradise", we are not condemned...to keep what the scholastics called the "mode of understanding possible to us"...forever at its lowest level...a defeat forced upon reason may, in some cases, mean a widening...a dilating of it.'[67] Here, in a way less directly than in the case of *Corpus Mysticum,* but in a way no less essential, de Lubac sketches the negative consequences of the collapse of the dynamic, paradoxical, anagogic reasoning that was built into early Christian spiritual understanding.

What, then, does de Lubac propose as a solution? If we see, chronicled in the first instance in the gradual dissolution of the integral, dynamic unity of Christian spiritual exegesis, and echoed in the rifts between Church and Sacrament and between the natural and the supernatural, the ascent of a dialectical mode of reasoning that, on its own, is inadequate to the articulation of the fullness of the faith, are we left sentenced to a modern world of thought wholly alien to and alienated from the 'whole mental universe' of the Fathers?[68] Or, alternatively, should we seek to return to the premodern sensibilities of Origen and Augustine, casting off the scientism of these latter days? De Lubac certainly refuses this latter option: although it is 'quite certain...that the techniques of the science of biblical studies, not to mention those of theology, can no longer accommodate themselves to this ancient form,...to be cool toward the scientific knowledge and the mental habits of our own time would not be a help in retrieving the mental habits of times gone by'.[69] Neither does he settle for the cold despair of lost harmony. Instead, he proposes that we might gain some access to this earlier mentality, paradoxically, in and through the good exercise of modern historical study, so as to succeed 'in restoring in its freshness some ancient form of the life of the mind, a form whose beauty has been lost ...' Indeed, he says, it may even be possible for the Christian historical theologian to succeed 'in conveying a part of this heritage to the present generation, commending to it its understanding, to its esteem, and to its admiration, without hiding from it the weaknesses and decrepit elements that mark it'.[70] So it is a paradoxical solution, in the end, that de Lubac offers to the apparent loss of paradox in modern thought: a *ressourcement* fully modern in its tools and methods that can renew and transfigure this lost premodern past for a postmodern future.

---

67. MS, pp. 173–74.
68. ME, vol. 1, p. xiv.
69. Ibid., p. xix.
70. Ibid., p. xxi.

Chapter 9

AN INHUMAN HUMANISM

Patrick X. Gardner

In his memoir, *At the Service of the Church*, Henri Sonier de Lubac, S.J. (1986–1991) mentions that his first serious reflections were occasioned not by his reading of scripture and the Church Fathers, but by conversations he had with atheists fighting alongside him in the First World War.[1] He later published his notes from these conversations as a modest *apologia* addressed to his unbelieving friends (*De la connaissance de Dieu*, 1945).[2] From then on, the question of atheism would become a central feature of his theological work. When he took up his post on the *Faculté de théologie catholique* at Lyons, he spent much of his time lecturing on the writings of atheists like Pierre Joseph Proudhon and Auguste Comte. During the German occupation in the early 1940s, he presented studies on Ludwig Feuerbach, Karl Marx, and Friedrich Nietzsche at 'semi-clandestine' anti-Nazi conferences – studies which would later form one of his most influential books, *The Drama of Atheist Humanism* (1944).[3] Then in the 1960s, de Lubac served with his friend Jean Daniélou on the newly formed Secretariat for Non-Believers, helping to draft the Second Vatican Council's pronouncements on the topic of atheism (*Gaudim et Spes*, §19–21).[4] It is little wonder, then, that in addition to his many other achievements, de Lubac is remembered as an authority on modern atheism.

Indeed, when one considers the occasions of his writings, it's clear that de Lubac's preoccupation with atheism extends even beyond his works devoted to the topic. It undoubtedly motivated his interest in Maurice Blondel during his philosophical studies in Jersey between 1920 and 1923.[5] His intervention in the Christian philosophy debates of the 1930s ('On Christian Philosophy', 1936) was as much a response to the rationalisms of Émile Bréher and Léon Brunscvig as

---

1. ASC, p. 42.
2. Henri de Lubac, *De la connaissance de Dieu*, 2nd ed. (Paris: Témoignage Chrétien, 1948).
3. ASC, p. 40.
4. Ibid., p. 119. See also Rudolf Voderholzer, *Meet Henri de Lubac: His Life and Work*, trans. Michael J. Miller (San Francisco: Ignatius Press, 2008), p. 85.
5. ASC, p. 19.

it was a response to his fellow Catholics.⁶ His first work of lasting significance, *Catholicism* (1938), was occasioned by criticisms from 'aggressive free thinkers' like Gabriel Séailles, Émile-Auguste Chartier, and Marcel Giron.⁷ His studies on the supernatural (*Surnaturel*, 1946) and the concept of 'pure nature' were, as he says, at the centre of discussions about modern unbelief.⁸ Even his post-conciliar works of theological history, like his volumes on Pico della Mirandola and Joachim of Fiore, address the origins of atheism and the viability of Christian humanism.⁹ As pervasive as the topic of atheism is in his writings, it would seem that among the many themes proposed as the unifying 'center' of his work, this one certainly has a respectable claim to the title.¹⁰

In the essay that follows, I examine the nature of de Lubac's engagement with atheism throughout his scholarly career. The first section is devoted to the context of his writings on atheist humanism and to the thinkers who most influence his interpretation. The second section is devoted to de Lubac's criticisms of the atheist humanists, principally as they are presented in *The Drama of Atheist Humanism*. The final section is devoted to the main features of de Lubac's theological response, including his efforts to foster an authentically Christian humanism.¹¹ Together these points demonstrate how indispensable the question of atheism is for understanding de Lubac's theology as a whole. They also reveal the extent to which de Lubac can still serve as a model for Catholics in the post-conciliar period, responding to the call of *Gaudium et Spes*: the call to detect the hidden causes of atheism in our age and to proclaim Jesus Christ as the true source of human dignity.

---

6. Henri de Lubac, 'On Christian Philosophy', trans. Sharon Mollerus, Susan Clements, *Communio* 19 (1992): pp. 478–506. See also ASC, p. 24.

7. C, p. 15.

8. Cf. *At the Service of the Church*, p. 35. Here de Lubac notes in addition that the question of the supernatural 'formed the crux of the problem of Christian humanism'.

9. De Lubac, *Pic de la Mirandole: études et discussions* (Paris: Aubier-Montaigne, 1974). Henri de Lubac, *La Postérité spirituelle de Joachim de Flore, tome I: de Joachim à Schelling*, Le Sycomore Serie Horizon, 3 (Paris: Éditions Lethielleux, 1979). Henri de Lubac, *La Postérité spirituelle de Joachim de Flore, tome II: De Saint-Simon à nos jours*, Le Sycomore Serie Horizon, 8 (Paris: Éditions Lethielleux, 1981).

10. On identifying the unifying centre of de Lubac's theology, see Hans Urs von Balthasar, *The Theology of Henri de Lubac: An Overview* trans. Susan Clements, Joseph Fessio, and Michael M. Waldstein (San Francisco: Ignatius Press, 1991). Cf. Susan K. Wood, *Spiritual Exegesis and the Church in the Theology of Henri de Lubac* (Grand Rapids: Eerdmans, 1998), p. 129. See also Bernhard Körner, 'Henri de Lubac and Fundamental Theology', trans. Adrian Walker *Communio* 23 (1996): pp. 710–21.

11. De Lubac registers concern that the term 'Christian humanism' could suggest an instrumentalizing of Christianity for the sake of non-Christian humanist ideals. See, DAH, p. 399. Cf. Jordan Hillebert, 'The Death of God and the Dissolution of Humanity', *New Blackfriars* 95 (2014): pp. 674–88, 683–84. However, especially in his post-conciliar writings, de Lubac appears to embrace the term and its variants (ex. 'religious humanism') more explicitly. See de Lubac, *Pic de la Mirandole*, pp. 399–400. Cf. C, p. 368: 'Humanism is not itself Christian. Christian humanism must be a *converted humanism*.'

The Context and Sources of De Lubac's Confrontation

In his essay, 'Christian Explanation of Our Times', de Lubac claims that modern Europe has fallen into a spiritually stifling condition: 'Man is isolated, uprooted, "disconcerted." He is asphyxiated: it is as if emptiness had been formed in him by an air pump ... the consequence is not only a social imbalance. The world itself appears "broken". There is, at the innermost part of consciousness, a metaphysical despair.'[12] Echoing the premonitions of his friend, Teilhard de Chardin (1881–1955), he goes on to characterize this situation as a 'metaphysical crisis', a destabilizing of religious life and of the culture's relationship with the Christian faith.[13] What de Lubac laments in these passages are the effects of an aggressive secularism which had taken hold in his native France. Secularism had ensured that modern societies were now indelibly marked by their rejection of mystery and their 'refusal to see in man any transcendent aspiration'.[14] Most alarming of all, he suggests, is their collective loss of any taste for God, and the exaltation of Man in its place.[15]

Aligned with this sense of loss is what de Lubac calls the *affaisement spirituel*, or spiritual decline among Christians, which he diagnoses in shorter works from the 1940s. Here he speaks of the Church becoming so 'cut off from all its source of nourishment', so 'atrophied', that 'it can no longer see itself except as what an unbelieving world conceives it to be'.[16] This spiritual weakening is a form of amnesia regarding the Church's tradition, rendering it easy prey to every ideology that means to seize and disfigure it.[17] De Lubac notes that while the Christian faith was once thought to be the foundation of human values, it now appears to be disconnected from the exigencies of our nature: a faith with no appeal to the common culture and no power to shape it.

---

12. Henri de Lubac, 'Christian Explanation of Our Times', TH, pp. 440–56, 443.

13. De Lubac, 'Christian Explanation of Our Times', pp. 440, 446. See also Henri de Lubac, 'Teilhard and the Problems of Today', in *The Eternal Feminine: A Study on the Poem by Teilhard de Chardin, Followed by Teilhard and the Problems of Today* trans. René Hague (New York: Harper and Row, 1971), pp. 133–257.

14. Henri de Lubac, *De Lubac: A Theologian Speaks* trans. Stephen Maddux (Los Angeles: Twin Circle Publishing Co, 1985), p. 25.

15. DG, pp. 88–89.

16. De Lubac, 'Teilhard and the Problems of Today', p. 147.

17. De Lubac, *De Lubac: A Theologian Speaks*, pp. 1–2. For de Lubac, the greatest example of this kind of takeover was the acquiescence to Nazism among French Catholics during the occupation. Many of de Lubac's early writings on the theme of 'spiritual crisis' emerge from this context, during which time he – along with fellow Jesuits Pierre Chaillet and Gaston Fessard – began secretly printing the *Cahiers du Témoignage chrétien*: the organ of what de Lubac called his spiritual resistance to Nazism. He saw it as the task of the *Cahiers* to preserve the minds of the French people against the neo-paganism of National Socialism. See ASC, pp. 50–55.

This combined distaste for God and weakening of the faith found its social correlate in what Rudolf Voderholzer refers to as *la séparation*.[18] *La séparation* signifies the complete separation of the ecclesial and political spheres. It is an ideological divide between the French Church's counter-revolutionary heritage and the anti-clerical stance of secular republicans; a divide apparent in the many tensions that overshadowed de Lubac's formation in the Jesuit order. For instance, the closing of Jesuit colleges in 1903, the expulsion of nearly twenty-thousand religious in 1904, and the repeal of the Napoleonic Concordat in 1905, forced de Lubac and other young Jesuits to pursue their novitiate in England.[19] The France in which de Lubac was raised, in other words, was one in which the bitter fruits of the Revolution were still alive and well.

In the intellectual sphere, this division meant that philosophy and theology were being increasingly practised in isolation from one another. On the side of philosophy, what de Lubac calls 'separated philosophy' (*la philosophie séparée*) had been diagnosed a generation earlier by Maurice Blondel (1861–1945) and Victor Delbos (1862–1916), commenting on the irreligion of the French intelligentsia.[20] With the progressive weakening of Catholic culture, French philosophy had begun to value immanence as the sole criterion of rationality. It would countenance, in other words, only what is intrinsic to the structure of human reason or is logically necessitated by it. De Lubac would also refer to this disposition as 'immanentism' throughout his career: the belief that all of the truths necessary for human flourishing are found within the innate powers of human nature, and consequently truths revealed from beyond those powers are deemed to be illegitimate in principle.[21] For de Lubac, then, 'separated philosophy' is not an accident of intellectual history, but rather a construct. He is convinced that reason's natural inclination towards the transcendent had been reshaped in an anti-theological direction not by reason coming of age, but by a set of conscious decisions made by individual thinkers.

The greatest example of this anti-theological construction was undoubtedly the tradition of humanism that would occupy de Lubac's attention throughout the 1940s. In this context, 'humanism' refers to those movements which support the edification of the human being 'into the irreducible, perfectible bearer and guarantor of dignity, equality, and freedom'.[22] As early as the 1910s, *humanisme* had become a major part of the social projects of the Third Republic. Yet it was in the previous century that such social projects were aligned with a vision of human flourishing that rejected any reliance upon God. As de Lubac notes, figures like

---

18. Voderholzer, *Meet Henri de Lubac: His Life and Work*, p. 27.

19. Aiden Nichols, 'Henri de Lubac: Panorama and Proposal', *New Blackfriars* 93 (2012): pp. 3–33, 3–4.

20. Oliva Blanchette, *Maurice Blondel: A Philosophical Life*, Ressourcement: Retrieval and Renewal in Catholic Thought (Grand Rapids and Cambridge: Eerdmans, 2010), pp. 105–17.

21. Cf. MS, p. xxxv.

22. Stefanos Geroulanos, *An Atheism that is Not Humanist Emerges in French Thought* Cultural Memory in the Present (Stanford: Stanford University Press, 2010), pp. 4–5.

Ludwig Feuerbach, Karl Marx, Auguste Comte, and Friedrich Nietzsche were the architects of the kind of unbelief that now characterized twentieth-century Europe. Each gave rise to an atheism that is 'positive' in nature: one no longer content to formulate theoretical arguments against God's existence, but rather presumes to establish the conditions of a well-functioning human society. In France, for instance, Henri de Saint-Simon and Auguste Comte proposed elaborate social systems which mirrored the structure of Catholic institutions. Even Pierre Joseph Proudhon, who exerted a peculiar attraction for de Lubac, sought to realize the liberating kernel hidden within Catholic social teachings, rather than merely convince the world of God's demise. Atheism had managed, in short, to acquire the mantle of humanism, giving rise to the tradition de Lubac labels 'atheist humanism'.

Yet according to de Lubac, atheist humanism could not have claimed exclusive dominion over human flourishing if theology hadn't abandoned its own claim in the first place. A 'separated philosophy' was only made possible by a corresponding 'separated theology' (*la théologie séparée*). A condition of this kind, which de Lubac referred to as 'extrinsicism', ensured that reflection on revealed dogmas was, in practice, disconnected from the most pressing questions facing modern men and women.[23] Partly as a response to the crisis of Modernism and its tendency to conflate Revelation with reason, Catholic theologians isolated theological reflection in an effort to maintain its integrity. However, according to de Lubac, such a 'separated theology' was not in fact preserved from confusion with the dominant currents of the culture. Unable to speak directly to such currents, it was all the more subject to ideological manipulation. Many of de Lubac's Thomist adversaries in the French clergy, for instance, had provided theological support for the Vichy regime and even the Communist Party; telling signs of their intellectual decadence in his eyes.[24] Most importantly, an extrinsicist theology proved unable to demonstrate why Christian doctrines should appeal to human beings at all: 'this small-minded theology makes dogma into a kind of "superstructure" believing that, if dogma is to remain "supernatural", it must be "superficial" and that, by cutting it off from all human roots, it is making dogma all the more divine'.[25]

How then did theology reach this troubled state? Here de Lubac's most infamous work, *Surnaturel: études historiques* (1946), is as much a diagnosis of theology's contemporary problems as it is a study in sixteenth-century Church history.[26] According to de Lubac, extrinsicism was made possible by Neo-Scholasticism's anthropology of 'pure nature'. This account of human nature – 'pure' in the sense of maintaining its integrity apart from the supernatural – reverts back to a pre-Christian definition of nature, one at home

---

23. Here, once more, de Lubac draws his terminology and the outlines of his position from *Maurice Blondel*. Cf. BC, pp. 37–38.
24. ASC, p. 144.
25. Henri de Lubac, 'Apologetics and Theology', TH, pp. 91–104, 94–95.
26. In addition, see de Lubac's developed argument in the companion volumes to *Surnaturel*: *Augustinianism and Modern Theology* and *The Mystery of the Supernatural*.

within an immanent cosmic order. This conception, and the notion of a natural end which it entails, was adopted by theologians in order to resolve disputes over the reception of Augustine's teachings. Yet de Lubac argues that this borrowing represents an enduring tension, always capable of distorting the balance of the Church's doctrine should the intellectual climate allow for it.

Consequently, when the radical Augustinianisms of Michael Baius and Cornelius Jansen arose in the sixteenth century, 'pure nature' was resorted to as a corrective, leading in de Lubac's eyes to a tragic overcompensation. The imbalanced stress on the relative sufficiency of nature led inevitably to the separation of nature and the supernatural. And the more humanity was conceived of as 'a closed and sufficient whole', the more Christian Revelation appeared to be devoid of meaning for humanity. By so exiling the supernatural and baptizing a concept of nature 'that might be acceptable to a deist or an atheist', Catholic intellectuals had succeeded in constructing a theology that could never in principle qualify as a humanism.[27]

Fortunately, the interwar years saw the emergence of Catholic intellectuals in France intent on redressing this error. Along with thinkers like Gabriel Marcel, Emmanuel Mournier, and Jacques Maritain, de Lubac was part of a broadly defined group of theocentric or integral humanists working to recover Catholicism's contact with the exigencies of human nature.[28] These thinkers not only reassert the importance of community, dignity, and personhood within a Christian discourse. More strongly, they demonstrate the necessity of God and the Christian heritage for the coherence of humanist values. Maritain's 1935 treatise, *Integral Humanism*, helped set the agenda for the movement, giving expression to the shared view of bourgeois humanism as self-defeating and intellectually bankrupt.[29] Its atheism, he argues, undermines the very conditions necessary for upholding the values it cherishes. It follows, then, that God and our supernatural destiny cannot be obstacles to human flourishing, as the atheist humanists claim. They are rather the sole guarantors of human flourishing and the only enduring source of our dignity. De Lubac thus echoes Maritain's thesis in his *Catholicism*:

> The first step would be to show to those who have realized that no end short of humanity itself deserves absolutely to be loved and sought... that they are obliged to look higher than the earth in the pursuit of their quest. For a transcendent destiny which presupposes the existence of a transcendent God is essential to the realization of a destiny that is truly collective, that is, to the constitution of this humanity in the concrete.[30]

---

27. MS, p. xxxv.
28. Geroulanos, *An Atheism that is Not Humanist*, pp. 112–13.
29. Jacques Maritain, *Integral Humanism: Temporal and Spiritual Problems of a New Christendom*, trans. Joseph W. Evans (New York: Scribner, 1968).
30. C, p. 353.

For de Lubac, re-establishing Catholicism's contact with humanist values means recovering the unity of nature and the supernatural. As he notes in 1932, theologians can only determine the proper relationship between these principles when they learn how to unite them, not merely distinguish them.[31] And when theologians attend to the traditional Christian view, they can see that it does not permit a separated order of nature apart from the vision of God. Here humanity's supernatural destiny comes first in God's intention, and from the perspective of providence, there can be no separated state of 'pure' nature. On the contrary, de Lubac argues, the tradition speaks of the human as *spirit*, as a being who dynamically exceeds the limitations imposed by its nature. Even more so, it speaks of the human as the 'image of God', a being whose perfection lies in an archetype infinitely beyond its innate capacities. De Lubac, in other words, does not begin with an abstract concept of nature and supplement it with a supernatural dimension. He bases his understanding of the human person on the unity of God's design, evaluating it according to its place in the existing order of salvation history. Nature is created for the supernatural: 'an aptitude for the covenant, a transcendental enabling condition of grace as historically offered to, and accepted by, man'.[32]

This change of perspective explains why de Lubac identifies the image of God and the human spirit with the natural desire for the vision of God (*desiderium naturale visionis Dei*), the impulse within nature for a supernatural end. For de Lubac, this desire is what accounts for nature's capacity to be transformed and perfected by God's grace – something necessary and yet impossible for us to attain on our own. It is even, he says, the Christian mystery within which all the other mysteries are properly understood.[33] In the 1920s, de Lubac's teacher, Joseph Huby, encouraged him to research the natural desire in the writings of St Thomas and his commentators, as a potential solution to the problem of extrinsicism. And as Chad Pecknold and Jacob Wood argue, the fruit of de Lubac's research was in part a revival of the position developed by Giles of Rome (1246–1318) and his Aegidian school, the authoritative reading of St Thomas's teaching within the Augustinian order.[34] Giles attempted to show that the desire of created intellects can only be satisfied by the immediate vision of God – something they must receive as a free gift. As de Lubac himself notes, contemporary advocates of the Aegidian reading, like Gioacchino Sestili (1862–1939) and his fellow Jesuit, Guy de Broglie (1889–1983) had set the terms of his own interpretation years later.[35] De Lubac's version of Thomism was, in short, part of a distinctively Augustinian version of Thomism taking hold in French Catholicism, as a viable alternative to the Neo-Scholastic consensus.

---

31. ASC, p. 185

32. Bruno Forte, 'Nature and Grace in Henri de Lubac: From *Surnaturel* to *Le mystere du surnaturel*', *Communio* 23 (1996): pp. 725–37, 733.

33. MS, p. 167.

34. C. C. Pecknold and Jacob Wood, 'Augustine and Henri de Lubac', in C. C. Pecknold and Tarmo Toom, eds, *T&T Clark Companion to Augustine and Modern Theology* (London and New York: Bloomsbury, T&T Clark, 2013), pp. 196–222, 200–03.

35. MS, p. 188. ASC, p. 35.

In addition, de Lubac's two greatest philosophical influences were also a central part of this Augustinian revival and the renewed interest in the natural desire. As is well known, de Lubac relies heavily upon the thought of Maurice Blondel, having corresponded with him and having studied his *Action* (1893) and *Letter on Apologetics* (1896) during his time as a Jesuit scholastic.[36] Blondel's principal contribution was to demonstrate the dependence of human nature and philosophy on revealed religion. He provides a precedent for de Lubac by analysing the will's desire to transcend every natural limitation as it strives for an object capable of fulfilling it. For Blondel, the human spirit ('action') is in this sense more properly 'transnatural' than it is natural: we can always discern a 'trace' or 'echo' of the supernatural within nature to explain its need for resolution in a higher end (simultaneously necessary yet impossible for it).[37] Blondel's philosophy thus provides some of the theoretical justification for de Lubac's account of the supernatural. He also came to agree with de Lubac and Huby in the 1930s, both of whom identified Augustine's 'restless heart' as the model for his science of action.[38]

Many of Blondel's insights were taken up and developed within Thomism by Pierre Rousselot, S.J. (1878-1915), whom de Lubac credits with defining the intellectual trajectory of the Jesuits at Lyons. De Lubac names Rousselot as his chief influence and even claimed that all of his own efforts were directed towards having Rousselot's insights accepted within Catholic theology.[39] Like de Lubac, Rousselot sought to reform contemporary versions of Thomism which, in practice, treat the human intellect as a 'closed and perfect system'.[40] His thesis was to identify the desire for the beatific vision with the very nature of the intellect. Rousselot thus evaluates every intellectual operation in light of its final, supernatural end. The human mind is a capacity for God (*capax Dei*), but dynamically conceived: a movement that exceeds oppositions as it strives for ever higher levels of intelligibility. De Lubac's writings on the supernatural served mainly as the historical support for this position, arguing that this kind of dynamism is not only an authentic interpretation of St Thomas's teaching, but an authentic interpretation of the Patristic understanding of the human spirit.

What Blondel and Rousselot convey to de Lubac is nowhere more apparent than in his concept of the paradox. If humans are in fact created by God to find fulfilment in an end beyond our natural capacities, then our deepest aspirations will remain frustrated in the pursuit of ends we can attain by the exercise of our natural powers. In addition, human beings will exhibit characteristics that cannot be adequately explained in terms of our nature, tensions that resist comprehension and synthesis. The human condition, de Lubac concludes, is one

36. ASC, p. 183.
37. Blanchette, *Maurice Blondel*, p. 149.
38. De Lubac, 'On Christian Philosophy', p. 483
39. John M. McDermott, 'De Lubac and Rousselot', *Gregorianum* 78 (1997): pp. 735-59, 735.
40. Ibid., p. 737.

of paradox: we exist within what John McDermott calls a 'recurring structure of diversity in unity on various levels', a 'paradoxical oscillation' between dimensions of reality held in an unstable balance. Humans are neither body nor soul, matter nor spirit, essence nor existence, immanence nor transcendence, necessity nor freedom, history nor interiority, individual nor universal, etc.[41] They are rather the very tension between these realities. And when we attempt to resolve these tensions without recourse to the supernatural, de Lubac argues that we are doomed to compromise their balance. In this case, we would achieve only a false synthesis at the expense of reducing the human being to one pole of an antinomy. For de Lubac, however, these tensions are only antinomies in appearance, because they can be and ultimately are resolved in God. In him, our supernatural end, we find perfectly united what can only remain in tension from the perspective of our nature.

In sum, then, if Catholic theology went wrong when Thomism lost sight of the *desiderium naturale*, it is fitting that de Lubac's proposal for a truly humanist theology involves a *ressourcement* of Thomism, with the *desiderium naturale* at its centre. He favours a decidedly Augustinian reading of Thomas's teaching following the lead of scholars like de Broglie, Sestili, and other advocates of the Augustinian school. Finally, he interprets the philosophies of Blondel and Rousselot as modern renditions of this teaching. These thinkers and concepts allow de Lubac to conceive of human beings as *more truly human* to the extent that they embrace God and the mysteries of faith. And from this point an important implication follows. If only God can bring resolution to human antinomies, then de Lubac's framework for criticizing the atheist humanists consists in showing how their attempts to resolve these antinomies without God are doomed to fail.

'The Self-Destruction of Humanism': De Lubac's Critique

De Lubac begins *The Drama of Atheist Humanism*[42] with a title that summarizes his reading of atheism throughout the book: 'a tragic misunderstanding'.[43] For him, what atheism misunderstands so tragically is the image of God in humanity. When it was introduced to the ancient world, the idea of the human as God's image was seen as something liberating, as the source of human dignity and excellence. In the modern age, however, the same idea of the human once welcomed as liberating had come to be experienced as a burden. Now 'Man is getting rid of God in order to regain possession of the human greatness that, it seems to him, is being

---

41. Ibid., p. 753.
42. DAH, p. 65.
43. Ibid., p. 19. De Lubac developed the first part the *Drama* from talks he delivered as part of an organized 'spiritual resistance' to Nazism, which he later published in the journal *Cité nouvelle* and the *Cahiers du Rhône* between 1941 and 1943. The second part of the book adapts his faculty lectures on Auguste Comte, and the third reproduces a series of articles he wrote on Fyodor Dostoevsky.

unwarrantably withheld by another.'[44] De Lubac's basic claim is that this 'immense drift' from one perspective to another – the legacy of atheist humanism – can only end in incoherence.[45] If humans truly are created in God's image, then to reject God is to reject the only principle that establishes human value. All attempts to resolve the paradoxes of the human condition without reference to God will inevitably produce a false and dehumanizing synthesis. Atheism, de Lubac concludes, leads necessarily to the self-destruction of humanism: 'where there is no God, there is no man either'.[46]

As I've noted, the atheism that provoked de Lubac to write the *Drama* involves more than a series of arguments intending to disprove God's existence. It is more properly an '*anti*theism' or 'anti-Christianism', capable of influencing the social as well as the intellectual spheres. De Lubac names three distinct forms of this antitheism, each given shape by its three (or more accurately, four) most influential figures:

> Combining a mystical immanentism with a clear perception of the human trend, [contemporary atheism] has three principal aspects which can be symbolized by three names: Auguste Comte, Ludwig Feuerbach (who must share the honor with his disciple, Karl Marx) and Friedrich Nietzsche ... this inspiration and this logic are very forcibly thrusting mankind away from God and at the same time urging it along the lines of a double bondage, social and spiritual.[47]

De Lubac's main task in the *Drama* is to trace the 'self-destruction of humanism' in each of these representative figures. As Francesca Murphy and Joseph Komonchak have noted, his engagement with these thinkers was part of his effort to reinforce the Catholic Church against threats from both the French political right and the French political left.[48] De Lubac's critique of Comte, for instance, is likewise directed against the positivism of Charles Maurras and *l'Action française*, a movement which de Lubac suspected of infecting Catholics with fascist sympathies.[49] Similarly his studies of Feuerbach and Nietzsche are intended to expose the anti-Christian heritage of Nazi principles. On the left, de Lubac's critique of Marx can be seen as his contribution to the dialogue between the French Communist Party and Catholic intellectuals in the 1930s, both of whom laid claim to the legacy of humanism. In fact, de Lubac's arguments against

---

44. Ibid., pp. 24–25.
45. Ibid., p. 11.
46. Ibid., p. 65.
47. Ibid., pp. 11–13.
48. Francesca A. Murphy, 'De Lubac, Grace, Politics and Paradox', *Studies in Christian Ethics*, 23 (2010): pp. 415–30, 417–18. See also Joseph Komonchak, 'Theology and Culture at Mid-Century: The Example of Henri de Lubac', *Theological Studies* 51 (1990): pp. 579–602, 599.
49. DAH, p. 266.

each strand of atheist humanism served as an archetype for Catholic critiques of humanism throughout the post-war period.

According to de Lubac, Ludwig Feuerbach (1804–1872) is arguably the first great advocate of atheist humanism. Feuerbach's project was to demonstrate that claims made about God refer in reality to human nature (that anthropology is the underlying truth of all theology). For him, God is an unfortunate but necessary 'illusion': a false subject of attributes that properly belong to human beings. In the process of coming to self-understanding, Feuerbach argues, humans must first project their own attributes beyond themselves and encounter them as the attributes of a being they believe to be their antithesis. Human alienation results when we affirm in God what we deny in ourselves, and it is only overcome when we realize that our relation to God is in reality our relation to Humanity in general. Consequently, the promise of atheism, when we deny God and reclaim what has always been rightfully ours, is its ability to reunite us with the attributes that constitute our greatness. In the end the only 'God' to whom we owe allegiance is Man himself: *homo homini Deus* ('man is a God to man').[50]

The tension which de Lubac sees most clearly expressed in Feuerbach's work is that between the absolute and relative aspects of human existence. He grants that religious illusions which emphasize God to the point of alienating humanity are possible. In this sense, de Lubac suggests, Feuerbach can be seen as a modern Xenophanes, purifying the imagination of false forms of the absolute.[51] He notes, however, that it is equally problematic to seek a foundation for human value by denying the absolute altogether – a 'terrestrial illusion'. He insists that the 'God' who seems to be the antithesis of the human is not the Christian God at all. On the contrary, the true Absolute does not squabble with humans over its attributes. It is rather the one thing necessary to instil human nature with absolute value. To deprive the human of its relation to the Absolute does nothing in the end to exalt it, but merely reduces everything in the human to relativity. There can be, in other words, no absolute value to humanity unless there is an Absolute capable of securing it.[52] De Lubac concludes, then, that Feuerbach merely exchanges one form of illusion for another. He does not overcome human alienation, but rather compounds it by alienating humanity from God.[53]

In the *Drama*, the thinker who shares Feuerbach's glory and carries his vision into the practical sphere is Karl Marx. While Marx certainly has his roots in Feuerbach's religion of humanity, he argues that his predecessor erred by treating human nature as a metaphysical constant, 'from all eternity and always the same'. For Marx, on the contrary, Humanity exists 'in the world of men, the state, society', the product of a social order changing in accordance with material needs.[54] Hence,

50. Ibid., pp. 26–30.
51. DG, p. 178.
52. Ibid., p. 181.
53. Ibid., p. 185.
54. DAH, pp. 39–40.

citing Marx's *Theses on Feuerbach*, de Lubac notes that while Feuerbach dissolves the religious being into the human being, Marx dissolves the human being into the social being.[55] Nor then is alienation a matter of misplacing generic attributes. What it signifies is a condition of unjust economic relationships. Religion on this view serves as a symptom of this deeper social alienation: the expression of and protest against the injustices of society. It follows then that atheism means restoring humanity to itself by altering the social arrangements which give rise to belief in God.

As with Feuerbach, de Lubac argues that Marx's presumption to resolve this alienation itself constitutes an illusion, as it is unable to reconcile the personal and the universal dimensions of humanity. While Marx does draw attention to the dehumanizing effects of excessive individualism, according to de Lubac he succeeds only in replacing it with the opposite excess, rather than a true reconciliation. By denying the existence of God and defining humanity entirely in terms of 'a network of social relations',[56] Marx effectively abandons any means of guaranteeing the 'inviolable depths' of the individual person in these relations. De Lubac fears that without such a source of stability, 'exacting universal respect', the individual derives its value entirely from its function in the social whole. There is then nothing in man 'to prevent his being used as a material or as a tool, either for the preparation of some future society or for ensuring, here and now, the dominance of one privileged group'.[57] De Lubac argues, in other words, that in exchange for freeing humanity from economic constraint, Marx has only subjected individual persons to the same kind of exploitation that other individuals exercise on the material world – even to the point of sacrificing the individual at the altar of an impersonal future.[58] De Lubac concludes that Marx's atheism, like Feuerbach's, introduces us in the end to a more damning form of alienation than the one he attempts to overcome: 'For this man has literally been dissolved ... In reality, there is no longer any man because there is no longer anything that is greater than man.'[59]

The second version of anti-theism which de Lubac discusses is that of Auguste Comte (1798–1857), whose thought was so formative in France at the turn of the century that it was 'like the air one breathes'.[60] According to de Lubac, Comte is in many ways an 'ally' to Marx and Feuerbach's counterpart in France, insofar as he too constructs a new religion of Humanity. In his famous law of three states, Comte describes the human race evolving from the primitive condition of belief in God, through metaphysical reasoning, to the 'definitive religion' of positivism, which understands intellectual, moral, and social questions in terms of immanent

---

55. C, p. 358.
56. Ibid., p. 359.
57. DAH, p. 66.
58. C, p. 354.
59. DAH, p. 66. Cf. C, p. 359.
60. DAH, p. 135.

natural laws.⁶¹ Human nature then consists in a social whole: a great organism perfected over time which alone is worthy of our admiration. As a result, theistic religions like Christianity represent a kind of slavery and a principle of division, directing our gaze upward rather than towards union with our fellow humans. Anti-theism, then, means redirecting 'our feelings, our thoughts, and our action around Humanity', the 'new Supreme Being', for the sake of realizing a truly coherent form of society.⁶²

Once more, de Lubac describes Comte's humanism as more illusory than the religion he seeks to replace. According to de Lubac, Comte's position is dehumanizing because he is unable to reconcile our personal and communal aspects; both of which are indispensable to human flourishing. He envisions, in short, a kind of social union that dispenses with the value of persons. Comte is quite clear that valuing the personal is Christianity's great sin against society, and thus the aim of positivism is to replace the personal instinct with a sense of resignation to the greater social whole. Hence it is true to say that for Comte Humanity is glorified at the expense of individual persons. Yet de Lubac contends that it is foolish to think human beings can be perfected by a 'Great Being' who is merely composed of its valueless worshippers.⁶³ He argues, in other words, that Comte cannot achieve an authentic communion if he fails to uphold the value of the individual person. Moreover, he cannot uphold the value of the individual person if he affirms no God apart from Man. Thus de Lubac concludes that despite his ambition to liberate us from our slavery to the divine, Comte only subjects us to 'a double bondage, social and metaphysical', leaving us 'crushed' by society and 'swallowed up' in submission to blind forces: 'the positivist formula spells total tyranny... It refuses man any freedom, any rights, because it refuses him any reality'.⁶⁴

The final version of anti-theism which de Lubac discusses is that of Friedrich Nietzsche. In the preface to his 1950 collection, *Affrontements mystiques*, De Lubac describes Nietzsche's influence as widespread and corrosive, eating away 'like an acid at the consciousness of our contemporaries'.⁶⁵ Like the other atheist humanists, Nietzsche sees God as 'nothing more than the mirror of man': the relinquishing of our greatest qualities into 'another world', denying our existence here below. The idea of God is thus once more an obstacle to human greatness, and atheism is a necessary condition for reclaiming '"those lofty and proud states of the soul" of which we have wrongly despoiled ourselves'.⁶⁶ However, de Lubac gives Nietzsche a measure of credit for acknowledging what neither Feuerbach,

---

61. Ibid., pp. 140–41.
62. Ibid., p. 175.
63. Ibid., pp. 181–82.
64. Ibid., pp. 263–64.
65. Ibid., p. 398. Cf. Henri de Lubac, *Affrontements Mystiques* (Paris: Éditions du Témoignage Chrétien, 1950), p. 12.
66. DAH, p. 44.

nor Comte, nor even Marx were willing to acknowledge. He rightly affirms that this atheism leads inevitably to the dissolution of man. The 'death of God' signals the destruction of every value by which humans have lived. According to Nietzsche, this 'death' allows for the creation of something which genuinely transcends humanity: the Overman (*Übermensch*), a species strong enough to create new values in place of the old ones ('God is dead, long live the Overman').[67]

De Lubac goes on to argue that Nietzsche's ideal of the Overman is intimately bound-up with another one of his fundamental notions, the Eternal Return of the same. On Nietzsche's view, the Overman requires that the Eternal Return fill the void left by God in order to prevent any reversion to the idea of a creator: 'Thus the Eternal Return is imperative as the indispensable substitute for a dead God. It alone can seal up the stone of his tomb …'[68] Nevertheless, on de Lubac's reading these two principles stand in tension with one another; a tension Nietzsche struggles to resolve. In his essay, 'Nietzsche as Mystic' (1950), de Lubac follows scholars like Charles Andler, Daniel Halévy, Armand Quinot, and Lou Salomé, in claiming that Nietzsche attempts to reconcile these ideas by appealing to a kind of mysticism. De Lubac recounts that Nietzsche believed his insights about the Eternal Return and the Overman to be the products of visionary experiences: the first at Sils Maria in 1881, the second at Rapallo in 1882.[69] The ideal of the Eternal Return, that of a repeating cosmos, appears to undermine genuine creativity; while the ideal of the Overman, that of self-determination and the creation of new values, appears to forbid the continual return of the same. Nietzsche proposes to resolve the dilemma by claiming that the Overman rises to participate in, even be identified with, the cosmic force behind the Eternal Return (Fate). By uniting with Fate, freedom and necessity coincide perfectly in oneself, as in God. What from one perspective appears to be an order eternally imposed upon him, the Overman experiences as springing from his own will, to the extent that he becomes an expression of Fate. As de Lubac notes, Nietzsche is only able to utter his famous maxim '*amor Fati*' (love of Fate) because he first utters '*ego Fatum*' (I am Fate).[70]

How then does de Lubac presume to demonstrate Nietzsche's failure in reconciling these ideals? Once again, de Lubac argues, in pronouncing the death of God, Nietzsche pronounces the demise of what gives humanity stability, dignity, and depth. To glorify the Overman in its place may offer the sensation that one has raised oneself to a nobler plane of existence. But it is only a fleeting sensation, a cherished illusion.[71] Far from reconciling creative freedom with a recurring cosmos, Nietzsche's mysticism only enslaves us to 'the old forces of Fate' once exorcized by Christianity. Fate, de Lubac argues, cannot be conquered by the human or even the Overman on his own, so Nietzsche persuades himself that he is

---

67. Ibid., pp. 55–56.
68. Ibid., p. 496.
69. Ibid., p. 474.
70. Ibid., p. 486.
71. Ibid., p. 480.

one with Fate and this is something liberating. However this, according to de Lubac, is Nietzsche's great lie. He sees in Nietzsche the hypocritical adoration of what he knows to be a fiction: '*He pretended to create what he could not help suffering*'.[72] In truth the mystical identification with Fate means abandoning our freedom to the impersonal forces of nature. De Lubac even cites a series of passages from Nietzsche's late correspondence which suggest his melancholy and his misgivings were signs of this terrifying realization. 'Behold', he writes, 'Nietzsche surrounded by the ruins of his thought... the arbitrary decision that changes his pessimism into a cry of triumph is powerless to change anything in the real world... this "mystic" does not need anybody to refute him. He takes care of this task himself.'[73]

Outside of the *Drama*, de Lubac reaffirms his interpretation of atheist humanism: that without appeal to God, humanism is unable to synthesize certain aspects of human existence (the absolute and the relative, the personal and the universal, nature and freedom, etc.), and its attempts to do so entail a more dehumanizing vision than the Christianity it opposes. The same concern is present in de Lubac's early lectures on Pierre Joseph Proudhon (1809–1865), published in 1945 as *Proudhon et le christianisme* (trans. *The Un-Marxian Socialist: A Study of Proudhon*, 1948).[74] As de Lubac describes him, Proudhon remains 'one of the most vigorous representatives of the doctrine of immanence opposed to the Christian faith'.[75] In contrast to the shallower tactics of many freethinking contemporaries, he proposes a more radical anti-theism: 'From religion we are taking everything and assimilating everything, ideas, myths, sentiments, in a word, its soul; we leave the Church only the dead letter, the mummy.'[76] Much like Feuerbach, Proudhon sees Christianity as merely a stage in the development of human thought. It constitutes a kind of allegory for his own version of socialism, identical in substance but more primitive in form. It was once necessary for reason to gain consciousness of itself, but now endures only as a hallucination, deriving its true meaning from the theory of social and economic laws. Hence Proudhon characterizes his philosophy as a 'theology of immanenece', a 'humanitarian theology', and an 'apocalypse of the Revolution'.[77]

What makes Proudhon unique is that unlike the other atheist humanists, he recognizes that the desire for God is a universal and inexorable feature of the human condition. There is then no impulse to replace God with Humanity in Proudhon's writings. He admits that humanity cannot secure its own destiny and that only a transcendent reality could synthesize its many antinomies. He therefore rejects the promise of resolution offered by Hegel's dialectic ('The

---

72. Ibid., p. 503.
73. Ibid., p. 509.
74. Henri de Lubac, *The Un-Marxian Socialist: A Study of Proudhon* trans. R. E. Scantlebury (New York: Sheed & Ward, 1948).
75. ASC, p. 38.
76. De Lubac, *The Un-Marxian Socialist*, p. 234.
77. Ibid., pp. 229, 231, 239–40.

antinomy cannot be resolved') and affirms that our tensions constitute an 'equilibrium'.[78] This equilibrium means that, in the absence of God, we remain in perpetual movement towards more and more perfect realizations of Justice. De Lubac then credits Proudhon with testifying to the paradox of human nature and its longing for the divine, even as he questions whether Proudhon's rejection of God is ultimately in keeping with the trajectory of his own thought.[79] In spite of his often caustic opposition to God and the Church, de Lubac judges that Proudhon's is an atheism with which theologians can enter into genuine dialogue.

In the late 1960s de Lubac was compelled to return to the same figures and themes with renewed interest. Not only had his earlier criticisms of atheist humanism found confirmation among many of his Catholic contemporaries (including Pope Paul VI in his *Ecclesiam Suam*), but they were also echoed in the Second Vatican Council's *Gaudium et Spes* – the teaching of which he helped to formulate. In his *Athéisme et sens de l'homme: une double requéte de Gaudium et spes* (1968), which de Lubac intended as a partial commentary on the Pastoral Constitution, he identifies more precisely the feature that the atheist humanists have in common: their dependence upon, and distortion of, the Christian heritage.[80] What distinguishes them from other atheists is that these thinkers present their arguments as a comprehensive re-interpretation of Christian categories – what de Lubac calls the 'atheistic hermeneutic' of Christianity.[81] They attempt, in other words, to refute the Christian faith by 'comprehending' it, 'appropriating' it, 'developing' it, and finally 'surpassing' it from within.[82] For de Lubac, then, atheist humanism reveals itself to be parasitic upon Christianity, a hermeneutic that 'grafts itself onto its dogma in order to empty it of its kerygmatic contents, all the while conserving it as symbolic'.[83] In his post-conciliar period, then, de Lubac strengthens his claim that the atheisms he criticizes utilize 'laicized ideas', detached from their original place in Christian doctrine.[84]

Already in the pages of *Athéisme et sens de l'homme*, de Lubac suggests that many of these 'laicized ideas' are distortions of 'a tradition that goes back to Joachim of Fiore', the twelfth-century abbot who soon captured de Lubac's attention.[85] De Lubac's earliest writings on Joachim identify him as the source of

78. Ibid., pp. 152–53.
79. Ibid., p. 164.
80. Henri de Lubac, *Athéisme et sens de l'homme: une double requite de Gaudium et spes* (Paris: Les Éditions du Cerf, 1968).
81. Ibid., pp. 23–33.
82. Ibid., pp. 23–24.
83. Ibid., p. 30. Here de Lubac is quoting André Manaranche, *Prêtres à la manière des Apôtres* (Paris: Éditions du Centurion, 1967), p. 66.
84. Here de Lubac is developing more extensively an insight he raises in the 1940s. See de Lubac, 'Christian Explanation of Our Times', p. 442.
85. De Lubac, *Athéisme et sens de l'homme*, pp. 43–44.

questionable exegetical theories and apocalyptic prophecies: in *History and Spirit* (1950) and *Medieval Exegesis* (1961), for instance, de Lubac takes issue with the ways in which Joachim departs from the tradition in his writings on the senses of scripture, the Old and New Testaments, and his alleged spiritual understanding (*intellectus spiritualis*) of salvation history.[86] Soon, however, de Lubac became preoccupied with the figures in succeeding generations who radicalize Joachim's teachings. Here he identifies a 'spiritual line' of Joachim's followers, made up of 'the theologians, the "spirituals", prophets, philosophers, reformers, revolutionaries, and enthusiasts of every kind'.[87] When, therefore, de Lubac published his two-volume study, *La Postérité spirituelle de Joachim de Flore* (1979, 1981), his real concern was that the theologians, philosophers, spirituals, and revolutionaries who claimed Joachim as their inspiration were in fact transforming his ideas in ways that undermine the mysteries of the Catholic faith. This explains why de Lubac sees Joachimism as a great danger to the Church and a theological precedent for secularization:

> Under the various forms it has assumed, I consider Joachimism to be a still-present and even pressing danger. I recognize in it the process of secularization, which, betraying the Gospel, transforms the search for the kingdom of God into social utopias. I see it at work in what was so justly called the 'self-destruction of the Church.' I believe that it can only increase the suffering and bring about the degradation of our humanity.[88]

De Lubac's central claim in *La Postérité* is that Joachim's opinions on a set of important doctrinal topics deviate from the theological tradition so significantly as to lay the foundation for more radical deviations in the modern period. For example, Joachim's theology divides history into three ages or states (*status*), each identified with the distinctive activity of a divine person (Father, Son, or Holy Spirit) and a form of life in the Church (laity, clergy, or religious). These divisions culminate in the third state of the Holy Spirit, with a new spiritual Church, beyond the mediation of signs, letters, or sacraments. This theory, according to de Lubac, involves a dynamic of separation and surpassing (*dépassement*): the Holy Spirit surpassing Christ, and a purely spiritual Church surpassing the Church of Christ, in an age marked by the fullness of human knowledge, peace, and freedom. Here de Lubac finds a pattern for atheists who see themselves surpassing Christianity from within, identifying their philosophy with the true *status* of the Spirit. In the two volumes of *La postérité*, in other words, we find what is arguably de Lubac's most synthetic account of – and final word on – the atheist humanism he criticizes throughout his career.

---

86. HS; see also ME, vol. 3, pp. 327–419.
87. De Lubac, *La Postérité spirituelle de Joachim de Flore, tome I*, p. 13.
88. ASC, pp. 156–57.

God and Man Inseparably: The Christian Hermeneutic

What then is de Lubac's alternative to the errors he identifies with atheist humanism? I've noted that like Blondel, Rousselot, and others, de Lubac argues that our natural desire for the vision of God renders the human being a paradox, with certain tensions that can only be resolved in an end beyond the limits of our nature. I have also noted that de Lubac's fundamental claim about the atheist humanists is that their efforts to resolve these tensions apart from God necessarily fail, belying their humanist credentials. If de Lubac's re-integration of nature and the supernatural was undertaken in order to revive the 'all-embracing humanism' of the Church Fathers, then the task of his theology is to demonstrate how the mysteries of the faith succeed where atheism fails.[89] For if God alone is our end and fulfilment, it follows then that when this God opens his life to creatures and reveals himself in history, he comes and reveals himself as the absolute resolution of our paradoxes: 'Christian revelation ... bears inseparably on God and on man ... it is at the same time and inseparably theology and anthropology.'[90] His mysteries, and the doctrines that formulate them, shed light on the human condition by offering it a coherence it would otherwise lack. Because of this inseparability, de Lubac believes that Catholic doctrines (like the Incarnation, the Trinity, the Mystical Body, etc.) are intrinsically more humanizing than the laicized versions of them found within atheist humanism: they form, he says, a 'higher, richer, more coherent conception of the world and a more comprehensive and fruitful doctrine of life' than those of his adversaries.[91]

This notion that Christian mysteries cast a new 'light' on human nature is present in de Lubac's earliest essay, 'Apologetics and Theology' (1930), which he delivered as his inaugural lecture after joining the *Faculté de théologie catholique* at Lyons in 1929. Here we find de Lubac's proposal for revising the practice of fundamental theology, correcting the Neo-Scholastic manuals which, he says, treat doctrine as 'a block of revealed truth with no relationship whatsoever to natural man.'[92] What de Lubac advocates is a view of apologetics consistent with the Church Fathers, for whom revealed truths penetrate, comprehend, and transform all that is human.[93] We must recall, he claims, that doctrines are not merely concerned with God in himself, but also with the whole of created reality in its relation to God. Theology is then an understanding (of all things) *through* faith and not merely an understanding *of* faith. On these terms, what counts as the strongest evidence for Catholicism are not extrinsic signs like miracles and prophecies, but the 'supernatural brilliance' of the doctrines themselves, that is, their ability to illuminate the human condition and resolve its disparate elements:

---

89. C, p. 321.
90. *The Motherhood of the Church: Followed by Particular Churches in the Universal Church* trans. Sr. Sergia Englund, O.C.D. (San Francisco: Ignatius, 1982), p. 153.
91. De Lubac, 'Apologetics and Theology', p. 98.
92. Ibid., p. 93.
93. David L. Schindler, 'Introduction to the 1998 Edition', MS, pp. xi–xxxi, xv.

And, if one is careful to explain the nature of human aspirations... then it does not seem erroneous or even imprudent to state that Catholicism is the true religion because it alone brings the adequate response to the aspirations of humanity, and, thus, its supreme guarantee of its own perfection.[94]

De Lubac reinforces this claim in his 'On Christian Philosophy' (1936), where he presents it as a response to the 'separated philosophy' of scholars like Emile Bréhier and Léon Brunschvicg. At issue in the 'Christian philosophy' debates (1931-1935) was the possibility of a reason ordered to the Christian faith, and alternatively, of a reason that rationalizes Christian mysteries. In his contribution, de Lubac argues that reason must be considered aspirationally or 'naturally' Christian, since our desire for the supernatural ensures that our antinomies – and thus philosophy itself – can only find resolution in what God reveals of himself.[95] It follows that faith is more than a power to believe truths of a supernatural order. It is simultaneously 'a new power of interpreting the visible world and natural being', what Rousselot calls a 'renaissance of reason'. Revealed mysteries are then shown to expand the human spirit by illuminating its 'unperceived depths', while synthesizing all natural knowledge in the light of faith.[96] Hans Urs von Balthasar is thus correct to locate de Lubac's position in a 'suspended middle', for which philosophy never stands apart from its ultimate transcendence into theology.[97]

In the following decades, in works like *Catholicism* (1938), *De la connaissance de Dieu* (1945), and *The Discovery of God* (1960), de Lubac explains in more detail how particular Christian doctrines contain an answer to the paradoxes of human nature. First, and most simply, he insists that a doctrine of God's transcendence is necessary to reconcile humanity's relative and absolute aspects. Departing from Feuerbach, de Lubac calls for a transcendence that does not diminish immanence, but is the very condition of its possibility.[98] He argues that one cannot establish the absolute value of humanity without affirming the existence of an Absolute in itself, capable of giving humanity value absolutely.[99] The tension in us between the relative and the absolute thus provokes a movement towards a reality in which transcendence and immanence coincide. Only this, de Lubac suggests, can prevent everything in the human from collapsing into relativity, and only something so beyond our nature can free us from 'the doctrines that incarcerate [us] in a nature'. A God who is transcendent, and remains so, unites these values in himself.[100]

---

94. De Lubac, 'Apologetics and Theology', p. 101.
95. De Lubac, 'On Christian Philosophy', p. 487.
96. Ibid., pp. 498-99.
97. Balthasar, *The Theology of Henri de Lubac*, p. 15.
98. C, p. 359. Cf. DG, p. 181.
99. DG, p. 181.
100. Ibid., pp. 184, 187.

Secondly, de Lubac claims that in the Incarnation the synthesis of our antinomies becomes visible. Susan Wood is correct, then, that the hypostatic union serves as the paradigm for our coherence in de Lubac's writings.[101] In Christ, all of the tensions which the natural desire exhibits in us are held together in one being without confusion (absolute and relative, historicity and interiority, personal and universal, etc.). For instance, in him the transcendent and the immanent are not opposed, but exist as a single person: 'in Jesus Christ the transcendent made itself (partially) immanent... for the two elements which we deal with here, nature and the supernatural, have not become an intermixture or confusion but have been joined in intimate union in dependence on and in the image of the two natures in Christ'.[102] So too with the historical and the interior. As man, Christ's actions are genuine human actions, set in history; but being the acts of a divine person, the eternal becomes visible and tangible in them. Thus in revealing himself to humanity, God reveals humanity to itself.[103]

Third, the same reasoning applies to the mystery of the Church, our integration into Christ's body. The central thesis of de Lubac's *Catholicism* is that Christ does not come to save us as individual persons. Nor are his saving acts merely the acts of an individual person. On the contrary, Christ's redemptive action consists in uniting himself with humanity as a whole: 'He assumed in himself the nature of all flesh. Whole and entire he will raise it up from the dead, whole and entire he will save it.'[104] For de Lubac, the mystery of Christ is the mystery of a Whole, of a distinction-in-unity wherein the values of the personal and the universal are no longer antitheses. Christ is a 'concrete universal', a person *become* universal: 'it is the personal which becomes universal, to the degree to which... it realizes more profoundly its own specific character. Universality is the prerogative of the strongest personality'.[105] Christ is himself a concrete individual as well as a universal Whole (the *totus Christus* or Mystical Body). Consequently, de Lubac affirms that it is by incorporation into Christ's Body that we possess a share in Christ's synthesis, which perfects us as persons and as an entire race. We become members of one organism, whose distinction is preserved to the extent that its members are united. 'We are fully persons', he writes, 'only within the Person of the Son...'[106]

Fourth, incorporating us into Christ's Person and enabling us to share in his hypostatic union, is the work of the Holy Spirit. The Spirit is the one who unites the natural desire underlying all human paradoxes with its resolution in Christ, conditioning one for the other. He universalizes what Christ accomplishes as an

---

101. Wood, *Spiritual Exegesis and the Church*, pp. 123–26.
102. BC, p. 85.
103. De Lubac, *Athéisme et sens de l'homme*, p. 42.
104. C, pp. 38–39.
105. De Lubac, *The Eternal Feminine*, p. 95. Cf. Wood, *Spiritual Exegesis and the Church*, p. 100.
106. C, p. 342.

individual, and prepares the human soul to internalize it. He renders the soul capable, in other words, of appropriating the resolution it identifies in Christ. De Lubac describes the Spirit as creating in humanity new depths which harmonize it with the 'depths of God'.[107] He leads us into all truth by communicating Christ, internalizing and universalizing him; and alternatively by integrating the human more deeply into the union Christ reveals and perfects.

Fifth and finally, what Christ and the Spirit offer us is a share in the mystery of the Trinity itself. The supernatural end that fulfils humanity's deepest aspirations is ultimately the very life of the Triune God. The image of God in the human spirit is in the fullest sense an image of the Trinity.[108] Here above all, de Lubac finds the paradigm of human perfection and the final resolution of its paradoxes. In the mystery of the Trinity, we discover on the one hand the 'complete expression of Personality', since the distinctions of the divine Persons are what constitute them entirely. Yet on the other hand we find here the 'consecration of the highest unity', as all three persons exist in one nature. Hence when the Spirit incorporates us into the Body of Christ, we discover our personal and universal aspects perfectly united in God.[109]

Once more, it is when de Lubac returns to these themes in *Athéisme et sens de l'homme* that he summarizes this alternative to atheist humanism most succinctly. In response to the 'atheistic hermeneutic of Christianity', what he advocates is a 'Christian hermeneutic' of atheism.[110] Just as atheist humanism claims to more adequately explain the true meaning of Christian mysteries, so too, de Lubac argues, must Christian humanism present itself as a more comprehensive interpretation of the realities over which atheism claims dominion. To treat Revelation as a 'light' cast on the depths of the human spirit is to treat it as a superior interpretive principle: one that more fully comprehends human nature and its destiny. De Lubac sees clearly that this amounts to the very inversion of Feuerbach's strategy. Rather than reduce theology to anthropology, de Lubac holds that 'a well-ordered anthropology presupposes a theology and is directed to it by an inevitable dialectic ... beginning from our concrete situation, the "social and human drama" finds in the faith its clarification, its real dimensions, and its outcome not in man alone, but in Jesus Christ, the God-man'.[111] In sum, the Christian hermeneutic explains how the mystery of Christ is the 'total expression, the perfect paradigm' of humanity: Christ is the one who 'grounds, transfigures, and eternalizes the being of man and his values'.[112]

---

107. Ibid., p. 339.
108. De Lubac, 'Apologetics and Theology', p. 100.
109. BC, p. 43.
110. De Lubac, *Athéisme et sens de l'homme*, p. 33.
111. Ibid., p. 43.
112. Ibid., pp. 42, 46.

Conclusion

What then can we conclude about de Lubac's confrontation with atheism? First, attention to the context and sources of de Lubac's writings reveals that his theology of the supernatural is inseparable from, and even occasioned by, his encounter with atheist humanism. For him an 'inhuman humanism' was the effect of a separated nature discernible in the crises of European culture. The re-integration of these principles was not merely a matter of theory, therefore, but was undertaken for the sake of re-establishing Catholicism's contact with human values. De Lubac's means of achieving this end was a renewed Augustinian reading of the *desiderium naturale*, supported by his greatest philosophical influences. This approach conveyed to him an understanding of the human as a paradox: a being of tensions only resolved in an end beyond the limits of its nature.

Secondly, de Lubac's understanding of the human sets the conditions for his critique of the atheist humanists. Without recourse to God, all of their attempts to provide a coherent account of human existence result in dehumanizing illusions. The critical phase of de Lubac's theology thus involves demonstrating this failure in the positions of his interlocutors. Finally, de Lubac's approach also conditions his alternative Christian humanism. The positive phase of his theology thus consists in demonstrating how the revealed mysteries of the faith are capable of resolving our antinomies in ways that atheism cannot. Only when the faith is presented in this way – as a 'light' illuminating and elevating the human condition – can theology claim to be a genuine humanism.

In the years following the Second Vatican Council, Karl Rahner called for a new theology capable of dealing seriously with the growing presence of atheism in the modern world: 'No question is more important and topical for the Church today than the question of how to approach the problem of atheism spiritually and pastorally... all questions yield in importance to this one.'[113] De Lubac serves as an enduring model for a theology of this kind, even decades after his death. Indeed, his example is arguably even more pertinent today and his convictions more indispensable. Above all else he shows that the task of theology in our age is not merely to demonstrate the ruin of human values in the absence of God, but even more so to show that the Christian faith embraces everything that ennobles us – and this is the measure of its greatness. Following de Lubac, we must reveal to the men and women of the twenty-first century that 'the deepest part of man will never be understood if it is not illuminated by a ray coming from the unfathomable brightness of Trinitarian life.'[114]

---

113. Karl Rahner, 'Preface', in Karl Rahner, ed., *The Pastoral Approach to Atheism*, Concilium: Theology in the Age of Renewal, 23 (Glen Rock: Paulist Press, 1967), pp. 1–3, 1.

114. De Lubac, 'Apologetics and Theology', p. 100.

Chapter 10

ON RELIGION

David Grumett

Henri de Lubac was both a theological writer and a theological teacher. As a writer, he is best known for the topics covered elsewhere in this book, such as grace, ecclesiology, and scriptural exegesis. However, from September 1929 he was also a teacher, occupying the chair of fundamental theology at the Catholic Theological Faculty in Lyons. Within the Faculty there was no position in the history of religions, so de Lubac was asked to develop and teach a supplementary course on this topic.[1] Although a Faculty member, de Lubac, being a Jesuit, lived in the Jesuit scholasticate on Fourvière, the hill facing the city centre across the River Saône that is dominated by its nineteenth-century basilica. Because he resided at the scholasticate he was also expected, from 1935, to offer a course there, which was also on the history of religions.[2] These duties continued until 1940, when the Vichy government of Marshal Pétain, which had been established with Nazi agreement, assumed control of the southern half of France. As a result of these teaching assignments, de Lubac spent considerable time in the 1930s reflecting on religious origins and the relation of Christianity to other religions. Some of the material amassed through this decade was published at the time, but it also provided the basis for his later writing on religion published during the 1950s and 1960s.

This material has been little read or understood, to the extent that Hans Urs von Balthasar portrayed de Lubac's view of Buddhism as 'Eastern atheism'.[3] This is a significant misinterpretation of the latter's actual assessment of Buddhism, which is all the more striking because it ignores the wider context given by the significant writings on religion that de Lubac published from 1933.[4] I have corrected Balthasar's misreading in an earlier article,[5] so I will not repeat this

---

1. ASC, pp. 31–32.
2. Ibid., pp. 67–68.
3. Hans Urs von Balthasar, *The Theology of Henri de Lubac,* trans. Joseph Fessio and Michael M. Waldstein (San Francisco: Ignatius, 1991), pp. 54–59.
4. TF, pp. 289–307.
5. David Grumett and Thomas Plant, 'De Lubac, Pure Land Buddhism, and Roman Catholicism', *The Journal of Religion* 92 (2012): pp. 58–83.

important discussion here. Rather, in this chapter I shall address de Lubac's understanding of the category of 'religion' in general and his view of the relation of the Christian faith to other religions.

It might be supposed that de Lubac's conception of grace as suffusing the whole of nature – his *surnaturel* thesis – leads him to the view that all religions provide equivalent revelations of divine truth. In fact he opposes such a view, denying that every spiritual or religious manifestation is equally graced. Nevertheless, he is far more accepting of religion as a category, and of specific non-Christian religions, than might be supposed. I shall begin by surveying de Lubac's evaluation of theories about the origin of religion and their archaeological and ethnographic bases. His discussions of monotheism will then be considered, before an exposition of the relation he sees between Christ and Israel. The next topic will be the theology of Christian mission, in both ancient syncretistic and modern global contexts. I shall then show how de Lubac's understanding of Judaism was forged in the crucible of the Nazi persecution of the Jews, and finally consider what de Lubac might offer to Christian–Muslim relations in the present day. In the course of this chapter it will become clear that de Lubac articulates a nuanced theology of religion that is well integrated into elements of his thought that are examined in other chapters.

Religious Origins

Where does the idea of 'religion' come from? In his summary of a course given in 1935, de Lubac begins by excluding four possible illusory origins:

i) Religion cannot be identified with the psychic religious disposition of early humans, because we have scant reliable knowledge of any such disposition.[6] Moreover, although ethnologists might try to understand the past via the present indigenous cultures of Africa and Australia, these do not provide reliable evidence. Prehistorians might draw inferences from ancient artefacts and documents, but even the earliest examples of these, de Lubac reminds his readers, far postdate the dawn of human life.

ii) A picture of religious origins cannot be formed from a synthesis of the religious understandings of diverse indigenous groups into an idea of the 'primitive'.[7] Such syntheses were developed by figures like Auguste Comte, Sir James Frazer, and their successors, who sought to situate distinct cultures within a single developmental trajectory. They were founded on a positivist reduction of religion that was based on speculation and ideology. Their pretext has usually been the notion that true spiritual maturity consists not in religion but in its elimination, which on this view is produced by an original error or an irrational initial principle.

6. TF, pp. 309–11.
7. Ibid., pp. 311–14.

iii) Neither may religion be understood using a methodology that seeks to isolate the purportedly purely religious dimension of every individual manifestation and then to connect these into a developmental trajectory.[8] This, de Lubac asserts, is because religion is always situated within a social and cultural network that changes and evolves as a result of factors that are not themselves purely religious. The notion of 'pure' religion is, paradoxically, a construct of the merely phenomenological terms of scientific determinism.

iv) Religious origins cannot be accounted for by objective facts and method, because these in reality depend on a constructed system that is far from objective.[9] They conflate historical and psychological explanations, ultimately constructing each as a function of philosophy. Moreover, de Lubac avers that purported objectivism treats scientific findings as if they were raw facts, leaving unrecognized the grounding of scientific theory in subjective experience and the need for it always to be interrogated by that experience.

In what amounts to a ground-clearing exercise, de Lubac thereby rejects a series of scientific conceptions of religion, regarding these as outmoded and based on unsupportable assumptions. He then proceeds to a more favourable, and indeed fascinating, discussion of historical conceptions of religious origins. This he opens by refuting the thesis, which was a cornerstone of Leninism, that the earliest phase of human history was irreligious. De Lubac critically discusses how this Leninist view of historical development, which was grounded in ideology rather than research, was nevertheless lent credence by unreliable ethnographic findings.[10] A range of indigenous peoples have often been claimed as atheists, including the Arunta of Central Australia and the Yahgan of Tierra del Fuego, the archipelago at the southern tip of South America. However, following more extensive observation, many such claims have been shown to be ill-founded, with rites and beliefs identified that, although crude, are highly complex. Moreover, de Lubac reports research findings that the earliest significant human remains (dating from the end of the Mousterian period, around 40,000 BCE) evidence a 'care given to burial [that] attests to an order of concerns that is difficult to clarify but that can be called religious, at least in the broad sense'.[11] He also discusses Pygmy culture, to be found in the Congo as well as on islands and in mountain regions from the West African coast to Oceania. This is characterized by the use of wood and bone for tools, the absence of figurative art, dwellings constructed out of tree branches, hunting and gathering, and consequent dependence for food on more agriculturally developed neighbours.[12] It might be inferred from features

---

8. Ibid., pp. 314–15.
9. Ibid., pp. 315–16.
10. Ibid., pp. 318–19.
11. Ibid., p. 319.
12. Ibid., p. 321.

such as these that pygmies lack religious belief. For example, figurative art enables religious representation, while settled agriculture is linked with systems of offering and sacrifice. Nevertheless, observers of pygmy groups have frequently detected elements of animism, magic, mythology, and totemism. These could have spread from neighbours, but the point remains that, contra Marx and Lenin, even basic technological and cultural developments such as the use of stone tools and agriculture, and in some cases fire, are not preconditions for religion. Belief is more deeply rooted in human culture than this and no mere function of material conditions.

De Lubac ends this section with an examination of the less personified *mana* acknowledged by Melanesians and its correlates in other indigenous religions. This may be described as an infinite, impersonal supernatural power 'spread through many diverse objects and absolutely distinct from all material power'.[13] Such a conception, de Lubac suggests, leads the seeker for religious roots into a 'pre-animism' akin to Rudolph Otto's idea of the numinous. It thereby suggestively combines the belief in a unified sacred power immanent in the created order with the sense that this power is supernatural and therefore differentiated from material reality. In Christian context, the notion of a supernatural power diffused through the created order may be combined with a monotheistic concept of God if this power is viewed as the activity, effects, or energy of a single Godhead. De Lubac's exposition of religious origins, while drawing strongly on historical and empirical material, thus includes a clearly theological dimension. Like his better-known theology of the supernatural, it is also grounded in detailed historical research and penetrating theological perception.

The Idea of Monotheism

What more can be said about the form that religious belief might take in less technologically advanced human cultures? It might be assumed that such belief is animist and polytheist, progressing only later to conceptions of the Godhead as simple and transcendent. However, de Lubac positively endorses evidence that monotheism was, in fact, not a late development in human religiosity, embracing the 'primitive monotheism' thesis associated with the Catholic priest and ethnographer Wilhelm Schmidt.[14] De Lubac contends that many indigenous groups with little technological development possess a 'few flashes of the belief in a clearly superior being'.[15] Such a being is named and clearly differentiated from the natural spirits or souls of the dead. This being is the powerful creator

---

13. Ibid., p. 325.
14. For which, see Henryk Zimoń, 'Wilhelm Schmidt's Theory of Primitive Monotheism and Its Critique within the Vienna School of Ethnology', *Anthropos* 81 (1986): pp. 243-60, 246-48; Ernest Brandewie, *Wilhelm Schmidt and the Origin of the Idea of God* (Lanham, MD: University Press of America, 1983), pp. 41-46.
15. TF, p. 322.

of the world, and ruler of life and death. Sometimes the being is good, rendering judgement and watching over the world. Examples of indigenous peoples among whom belief in a single superior being is identifiable include the Pygmies, Arunta and Yahgan, the native American Pawnee, the West African Bantu, and the Jola of Senegal. Confusion has often resulted from the relative invisibility of these 'high gods' in public worship and culture. Nevertheless, in forms such as the Aboriginal 'first Ancestor' and the Native American 'Old Man who never dies', the existence of primitive monotheism brings de Lubac to argue that belief in a single God is not parasitic on religious forms that might be regarded as the product of superstition. This is an important point of defence against critics of modern religion who seek to denigrate it by its association with other religious forms. Monotheism is self-grounding and a perennial feature of the landscape of human belief.

De Lubac is not content to employ 'monotheism' as a univocal category, sharply distinguishing two different types.[16] The first type is a *monotheism of accommodation*. A product of social, political, and intellectual developments, this forms gods in the image of earthly realities. These gods are gradually ordered into a unified hierarchy out of which emerges a God who is supreme. De Lubac identifies this type of monotheism with the privileged imperial religions of Babylon, Persia, Greece, and Rome. However, he contends that the result was either a merely abstract deity or a divinized nature. Monotheisms of accommodation failed to establish a God who truly both transcended the world and was active on and within the world. This is belied by their toleration of polytheistic practices, which were predicated on a tacit acceptance of the limitation of the power of the supreme God.

The second variety of monotheism that de Lubac identifies is an *exclusivist monotheism*. This is grounded in the uncompromising affirmation of divine uniqueness, of a 'Being who is not at all abstract although completely spiritual; an intransigent Being who claims all worship for himself and wishes to be recognized by all; a transcendent Being who extends beyond earthly cities, even the city of the world'.[17] This type of monotheism triumphs over the first, because it succeeds in founding a concept of God as both transcendent *and* all-powerful in the world. In so doing, exclusivist monotheism appropriates to itself the categories and language developed by monotheisms of accommodation for the purposes of expression, conceptualization, and mission. Its pre-Christian roots have been evident in Zoroastrianism (Mazdaism) and in the small and persecuted religion of Israel.

The Gâthâs, which are the sacred poems of the teacher Zoroaster (Zarathustra) that comprise the most sacred texts of the religion named after him, describe a future divine judgement of the world by conflagration. This great event is longed for by the righteous, who receive the title of *saošyant* (benefactor or saviour) and will inaugurate priestly rule on earth. In other Zoroastrian scriptures the role of the supreme Saošyant is emphasized, and world history is divided into four

16. Ibid., pp. 328–29; DG, pp. 26–29.
17. TF, p. 329.

periods each lasting three millennia. The first period is a purely spiritual creation. The second is the formation of the material world, including the primordial man and the primordial bull. The third period opens with the start of the human race and the conflict between Ahura Mazda, the wise Lord, and Aura Mainyu his adversary. The appearance of Zoroaster himself precipitates the fourth and final period, which is composed of three millennial divisions each commencing with the rule of one of his sons. At the end of time the supreme Saošyant arrives on earth flanked by his six assistants in order to destroy evil, complete the world, and resurrect the dead.[18]

Key themes that would become core in Christian theology are here identifiable. These include: a theology of history, with successive epochs of preparation for coming; life, ministry, death, and resurrection on earth; and the post-Ascension mission and preaching of the Church. Also present is a theology of spiritual and material creation, and a final judgement that deploys imagery strikingly similar to that of Revelation.[19] De Lubac appraises Zoroastrianism as offering a broadly optimistic view of history with a positive view of the role of individual agency in bringing the world to its maturity. Nevertheless, he contends that its view of nature was founded on a cosmic eschatology that was at root scientific rather than theological, being an uncritical appropriation of Indo-European conflagration nature-mythology.[20] Religious belief ultimately accommodated itself to existing cosmological boundaries rather than breaking open those boundaries and effecting a radical reorientation of thought and life.

The view of history set forth in the Old Testament and embraced by Israel could not, de Lubac suggests, have been more different. Although cosmological disturbances also occur in the Israelite religious narrative, they are contingent upon human events rather than driving those events, being functions of the drama of the relationship between Israel and Yahweh as history progresses towards its end. For instance, hailstorms or plagues are means of moral and spiritual chastisement. Moreover, although Yahweh is the God of history, He speaks to believers personally.[21] Furthermore, Yahweh's relation with Israel is grounded in covenant. Israel may infringe the terms of this covenant, provoking divine disfavour and judgement, and does not merely perform its role within a narrative of inevitable progress. In general, God acts primarily not in nature but in history, with the principal form of divine judgement being the destruction of empires rather than natural cataclysm.[22] The corollary of this divine judgement is Israel's comprehensive and stubborn Messianic hope. Although they are judged, sometimes with severity, other peoples also experience divine wrath and Yahweh

---

18. C, pp. 158–59.
19. See Anders Hultgård, 'Zoroastrian Influences on Judaism, Christianity and Islam', in Michael Stausberg, ed., *Zarathustra and Zoroastrianism: A Short Introduction* (London: Equinox, 2008), pp. 101–12.
20. C, pp. 160–63.
21. Ibid., pp. 156–57.
22. Ibid., pp. 160–61.

acts in the world with purpose. Despite being a small and marginal group of tribes, Israel exegetes the whole of history, including the catastrophes that bring it to the brink of annihilation, as part of God's plan for his chosen people.

Religions, Christ, and Israel

At the beginning of this chapter it was explained that de Lubac delivered courses in the 'history of religions' (*l'histoire des religions*) at both the Catholic Theological Faculty in Lyons and the Jesuit scholasticate. The comparative approach to religion, based on the supposition that different 'religions' could be neutrally set alongside each other, had been in vogue since the nineteenth century.[23] However, de Lubac had never been satisfied with this methodology, and – notwithstanding his course titles – contested common understandings of the topic by refuting, as was shown, several varieties of psychological, historical, and philosophical reductionism. By the 1960s he questioned the idea of religious pluralism directly. The issue was partly one of language, although not for this reason any less significant. De Lubac asks: 'Does not one speak today, in an empirical sense, of diverse religions, among which there are no scruples about including Christianity – in the class of "universal religions" – all the while affirming that Christianity is the only "true religion"?'[24] Indeed, he observes in a footnote that the standard designation of the subject in Catholic theological faculties has always been *historia religionis*, or 'history of religion', which is singular.

Examples may inevitably be cited from both past history and the present day of spiritual affinity across religious boundaries, especially between mystics. For example, the Sufi may well feel greater commonality with Saint Teresa of Avila, a Zen Buddhist or the Upanishads than with a Shi'ite jurist. Indeed, the mystical inclination is to 'seek a spiritual union of men transcending the walls of specific religious beliefs'.[25] Nevertheless, de Lubac insists that to take the further step of positing a transcendent unity of religions is misguided, giving 'insufficient attention to the qualitative differences' between religions.[26] The nub of the problem is the tendency to view mysticism as the experiential and even epistemological ground of all religions instead of a collection of similar practices identifiable across different religions. Mysticism is not an alternative path to faith that renders the content of belief superfluous. Neither does it provide an entry into a heightened but generic variety of spiritual experience. Rather, mysticism is subsequent to prior concrete faith and dependent upon the content of belief.

So far as the Christian faith is concerned, specifically Christological mysticism is prominent in the New Testament writings of both Paul and John and is taken up

---

23. TF, p. 35.
24. Ibid., p. 40.
25. Ibid., p. 45.
26. Ibid., p. 46.

by early writers including Ignatius of Antioch, Evagrius, and Pseudo-Dionysius.[27] Over time this mysticism has acquired unique characteristics that are not shared with the mysticisms of other religions. It is grounded in a doctrine of likeness, with the divine image present in every person. This does not mean that humans are godlike; indeed, in a religious context it suggests the opposite. Referring to John of the Cross, de Lubac indicates that likeness entails not identity with God but difference from God.[28] For John, this is because creatures are attached to darkness, whereas God is light, and darkness and light are contraries. Quoting Augustine's statement that 'God is whole everywhere, yet he does not dwell in all persons,'[29] de Lubac excludes the possibility allowed by some animistic religions that God is fully present within the created order. For Augustine, God is everywhere by his divine presence although not through the indwelling of his grace, and even his people, who dwell in that grace, remain on an earthly pilgrimage of partial estrangement from him. De Lubac expounds four other distinctive marks of Christian mysticism. It is goal-directed, resisting closure in favour of a hope that will be fulfilled only in God's future time. It is essentially an understanding of Scripture, through the dimensions of allegory (doctrine), tropology (ethics), and anagogy (eschatology). It is established in the loving union of God and the believer, which can be presented as spiritual marriage. It is Trinitarian, and thereby fulfilled in personal Being.[30]

De Lubac judged religion (in the singular) to be a useful constructive category in so far as it aided an understanding of the genesis of Christianity. He unfolds his own understanding of this genesis with breadth and ambition in *Catholicism*, first published in 1938, at the end of a decade during which he had been working extensively on religion. He discusses how Christianity adopts the Jewish historical tropes of sin, captivity, release, and redemption.[31] Just as unfaithful Israel was captive in Egypt until being led out to freedom by Moses, so the sinners chosen by Christ, who awaited his coming, were also set free by him. However, for de Lubac the Old Testament is far more than a source of images to be mined by Christians: the actual history of this Testament is part of Christian history, which embraces and intensifies the historical and social dimensions of the religion of Israel. The reality typified in the Old Testament is 'not merely spiritual, it is incarnate; it is not merely spiritual but historical as well'.[32] De Lubac continues:

What we call nowadays the Old and New Testaments is not primarily a book. It is a twofold event, a twofold 'covenant', a twofold dispensation which unfolds

27. Ibid., pp. 49–51.
28. John of the Cross, *The Ascent of Mount Carmel* 1.4, in Kieran Kavanaugh, ed., *Selected Writings*, (New York: Paulist, 1987), pp. 65–69.
29. Augustine, *Letters* 187.5.16, 4 vols, trans. Roland Teske (New York: New City, 2001–2005), vol. 3, p. 237. Unusually for de Lubac, the references to Augustine and John are reversed by mistake, and the exposition could be clearer.
30. TF, pp. 57–63.
31. C, pp. 154–56.
32. Ibid., p. 169.

its development through the ages, and which is fixed, one might suppose, by no written account. When the Fathers said that God was its author – the one and only author of the Old and New Testaments – they ... saw in him the founder, the lawgiver, the institutor of these two 'instruments' of salvation, these two economies, two dispensations which are described in the Scriptures and which divide between them the history of the world.[33]

This dual covenant, de Lubac continues, is at present incomplete. Many Christian theologians would accept that the Old Testament does not contain a complete literal Christian meaning; however, de Lubac insists that this applies just as much to the New Testament. Each Testament contains a spiritual meaning, which is prophetic. Although truth itself is contained in the New Testament, it is therefore reflected rather than direct. Truth will be fully comprehensible only in an eschatological future, and cannot be accessed in its totality in the present day.

Nevertheless, de Lubac views the New Testament as completing the expository process begun in the Old on the grounds that it contains within itself the principle of its own interpretation. The Old Testament describes a redemption that is still to come, comprising in its later parts a series of prophecies about future events. In contrast, Christ, being himself the truth of whom the New Testament speaks, is equally its interpreter. This Testament is therefore not only chronologically 'newer' in the obvious sense of succeeding the Old but also eternally new by unlocking the key of its own interpretation.[34] For the same reason the New Testament is also the final Testament, lacking nothing necessary for its completion. However, the hermeneutical key that it provides also unlocks the Old Testament, causing Christ to appear 'preceded by the shadows and the figures which he himself had cast on Jewish history'.[35] In Patristic exegesis this idea is expounded in the imagery of the six ages of the world drawn from a reading of the Old Testament through the lens of the parables of Matthew 13, which together 'fashion a sacred history'.[36] The enemy who comes by night to sow weeds among the wheat is allied with Adam and Cain. The mustard seed sown after the Flood grows into the great tree of all peoples. The yeast is the faith of Abraham, which was accepted first in the synagogue but would later spread throughout the world. The buried treasure is the message of the prophets hidden in the field of prophecy. The pearl of great price, which the merchant sells everything in order to purchase, is Christ, who had come to be desired by the Jews in exile. The net thrown into the sea, in which fish of every kind are caught, is the kingdom of heaven.

Thus is presented the harmonious agreement of the Testaments, which together compose a single garment and a single body for the Word. Nonetheless, de Lubac is unafraid to identify a corollary of the New Testament's newness as being the ending of the Old Testament. Christ as the end (*telos*) of the Law

33. Ibid., pp. 169–70.
34. Ibid., pp. 171–72.
35. Ibid., p. 174.
36. Ibid., p. 204.

opens a new scriptural hermeneutic, with an 'outworn literalism... made new in the everlasting newness of the Spirit'.[37] Only Christ can unlock the riddles of the prophets, open the book that has been closed with seven seals, and bring together Jew and Gentile. Only he can provide the body of the Old Testament with its soul. At the moment when Christ died on the Cross, the Temple veil was rent, signifying the 'downfall of the letter of Jewish worship and the manifestation of the mystery foretold in figure by this worship'.[38] Notably, it is through the liturgical texts of the Psalms that Christ continually speaks, whether as saviour, suffering servant, or the community whose body he is.[39]

De Lubac's understanding of the relation of Christian religion and Scripture to those of Israel emerges from his immersion in Patristic texts. For instance, within the long appendix of such texts at the end of *Catholicism* he quotes a passage from William of Auvergne's tract *On the Sacrament of the Eucharist*: 'When God's cult, the true religion, was first established in the world, it existed rather in the manner of a seed or an infant, because the community of mankind itself was immature and unfitted for anything more advanced.'[40] This excerpt effectively illustrates the contradictions and potential ambiguities of the path that de Lubac wished to tread. To designate the faith of Israel as 'true religion' was to afford it a far greater degree of respect than would most contemporary and many present-day theologians. Moreover, in the excerpt humanity is treated collectively across time and space, rather than as successive groupings each possessing progressively superior forms of religion. Nevertheless, simply by employing an allegorical reading of Scripture based on the revelation of Christ, de Lubac is unable to avoid a supersessionist reading of how the Christian religion relates to prior religions, despite the inconsistencies that sometimes seem to be generated by his conflated interpretations of many different Patristic texts in succession. However, it should be made clear that, in de Lubac's exposition, Israel does not serve as a proxy for modern Judaism. The latter became a central concern of his as the Nazi persecution of Jews living in France and elsewhere increased, and will be considered in greater detail later in this chapter.

Religion, Mission, and Salvation

The category of mission can sit uneasily alongside that of religion. For some critics, to accept the validity of the concept of 'religion' is to view differing faith commitments as providing equivalent sets of content that each perform the same function of providing meaning within structurally identical social and cognitive spaces. These different content sets, being dependent on a prior shared structure,

---

37. Ibid., p. 177.
38. Ibid., pp. 179–80.
39. Ibid., pp. 193–95.
40. Ibid., p. 422.

offer narratives that are chosen or refused according to personal preference.⁴¹ Elements of de Lubac's work on the history of religions might seem to lend support to this view of different religions as equivalent. In an essay first published in 1933 he evokes the syncretic religious history of the Gobi Desert, which extends across large swathes of northern China and southern Mongolia.⁴² Traversed by the Silk Road caravan route and later within the Mongol Empire, the desert was a melting pot of interreligious encounter, assimilation, and division. Excited by the discoveries of recent decades in Chinese Turkestan, de Lubac describes how, from around the time of Christ's birth and continuing for almost a millennium, Buddhist missionaries traversed the desert eastward from Turkestan into China while Chinese pilgrims passed westward into India, communicating using the now forgotten common language of Sogdian.⁴³ The Gobi Desert was home to Mahāyāna (Great Vehicle) and Hīnayāna (Smaller Vehicle) Buddhists, Daoists, Zoroastrians, Jews, Manicheans, and Nestorian Christians.⁴⁴ De Lubac describes ancient Jewish trading colonies and Syriac Christian monasteries located in what is now modern China, the latter being the product of the Christian mission that began around the time of the Council of Nicaea.⁴⁵ Having in mind the empires of Greece and Rome, de Lubac depicts the Gobi Desert as an interior Asiatic Sea that, similarly to the Mediterranean Sea, sustained communication between the cultures on its shores and enabled their cross-fertilization.⁴⁶

This spread and transmutation of religions across geographical space did not, however, continue. As Islam in the West and state-sponsored Tang dynasty Buddhism in the East each secured their respective territory, the 'two halves of the world were cut off from each other, and the Gobi fell asleep under its sands'.⁴⁷ Christian missions made little further progress, notwithstanding the continuing presence of small syncretistic communities. Not until Matthew Ricci and the seventeenth-century missionaries who followed him to China by sea would a

---

41. For example, *The Myth of Christian Uniqueness*, eds, John Hick and Paul Knitter (London: SCM, 1987).

42. For the geography, see Ian Gillman and Hans-Joachim Klimkeit, *Christians in Asia before 1500* (Richmond: Curzon, 1999), pp. 205–34, and for a beautifully illustrated wider overview, Valerie Hansen, *The Silk Road: A New History* (Oxford: Oxford University Press, 2012).

43. TF, pp. 296–98, 291.

44. Ibid., p. 300.

45. For the first millennium, including the eighth-century high point, Jean-Pierre Charbonnier, *Christians in China, A.D. 600 to 2000* trans. M. N. L. Couve de Murville (San Francisco: Ignatius, 2007), pp. 19–67; Gillman and Klimkeit, *Christians*, pp. 267–85; Samuel H. Moffett, *A History of Christianity in Asia*, 2nd ed., 2 vols (Maryknoll, NY: Orbis, 1998), vol. 1, pp. 287–323. For the Mongol period of the thirteenth and earlier fourteenth centuries, Charbonnier, *Christians*, pp. 69–90; Gillman and Klimkeit, *Christians*, pp. 234–51, 285–98; Moffett, *History*, pp. 442–56.

46. TF, p. 305.

47. Ibid., p. 307.

new missionary wave break, rekindling memories of a past Christian culture. But this was a very different variety of mission from that which had preceded it. As de Lubac observes, the Christian faith would 'no longer spread from neighbour to neighbour, quite naturally assimilating new human elements at each stage'.[48] Rather, the modern missionary paradigm was established, with mission now understood as a journey from a Christian centre into alien and often hostile territory for the express purpose of making converts.

This concept of mission supposes that belief is grounded in an act of faith by which a person makes a conscious decision to assent to the truth of a specified religion, in this case the religion of Christ. This decision is often termed conversion, especially if the person has previously adhered to a different religion. But may a person who has not converted be saved? Two different possibilities need to be examined: the salvation of the person who has not heard the Gospel message, and the salvation of the person who has heard this message but has not converted.

When considering the salvation of the person to whom the Gospel has not been preached, de Lubac is inspired by Patristic reflection on the salvation of non-Christians. He resists the Jansenist presumption that divine grace is restricted to a small, clearly defined group of faithful Christians. Grace cannot be diluted, and is no less powerful the more lavishly or widely it is bestowed.[49] De Lubac cites the opinion of Irenaeus that, from the beginning of the world, Christ has given some kind of revelation of the Father – even if obscure – to 'all men together, whom from the beginning, according to their capacity, in their generation have both feared and loved God, and practised justice and piety towards their neighbours'.[50] This comprehensive bestowal of revelation results from the universality of Christ's action. Quoting Irenaeus, de Lubac depicts Christ 'universally extended in all the world', encompassing its 'length and breadth and height and depth' and ordering and disposing the whole universe 'in which is crucified the Son of God, inscribed crosswise upon it all'.[51] He cites John Chrysostom's description of grace exerting an attraction upon every soul, 'shed forth upon all, turning itself back neither from Jew, nor Greek, nor Barbarian, nor Scythian ... but admitting all alike, and inviting all with an equal regard'.[52]

De Lubac cites passages suggesting that divine mercy has, through the course of history, been at work among the whole human race and that even non-Christian cultures have hidden saints and prophets.[53] Moreover, in these texts it is made particularly clear that the universality of salvation is the result not of human effort but of God's sovereign action. Neither is the idea of universal

48. Ibid, p. 307.
49. C, pp. 217–18.
50. Irenaeus, *Against Heresies* 4.22.2, in *ANF* vol. 1, eds, Alexander Roberts and James Donaldson (Peabody, MA: Hendrickson, 1994), p. 494.
51. *Irenaeus's Demonstration of the Apostolic Preaching* 34, trans. J. Armitage Robinson, ed. Iain M. MacKenzie (Aldershot: Ashgate, 2002), p. 11.
52. John Chrysostom, Homily on John 1.9, in *NPNF* 1.14, p. 29.
53. C, pp. 218–20.

salvation a concession to liberal theology. Rather, salvation is universal as a result of the divine will that the 'whole race of humankind in all its diversity' will be saved.⁵⁴ In his letter to the priest Deogratias, advising him on how to respond to the pagan question about the status of people who lived before the coming of Christ, Augustine writes that pagans should acknowledge that it 'makes no difference that people worship with different ceremonies in accord with the different requirements of times and places, if what is worshipped is holy.... And the divinity was certainly never lacking to the righteousness and piety of human beings for their salvation'.⁵⁵ This suggests that the power of grace works across religious boundaries. Later in the same letter, Augustine writes of Christ that 'from the beginning of the human race ... he did not cease to speak in prophecies, and there were not lacking those who believed in him, both from Adam up to Moses and in the people of Israel ... as well as in other peoples before Christ came in the flesh'.⁵⁶ The place of non-Jews in God's plan appears again in *The City of God*, in which Augustine avers that 'it is not unacceptable for us to believe that, in other peoples as well as the Jews, there were men to whom this mystery was revealed'. Citing Job, who was not a Jew but an Edomite, he affirms that 'in other nations also there have been some men who belonged, not by earthly but by heavenly fellowship, to the true Israelites, the citizens of the supernal fatherland'.⁵⁷ Similar Old Testament figures include the Moabite widow Ruth, who married Boaz and became the great-grandmother of King David; the Aramean army commander Naaman, whose leprosy Elisha healed; and the Mesopotamian diviner Balaam, who blessed the Israelites and prophesied their destiny.⁵⁸

This generous acceptance of the possibility of the salvation of non-Christians raises an important question, which brings us on to the second possible kind of non-Christian earlier noted: the person who has heard the Gospel message but has not converted. If salvation is possible outside the Church in the shape of an implicit Christianity, why is it necessary for such a person to become a Christian and Church member? De Lubac's initial response is that only those who have encountered the Church are obliged to join it, but he recognizes that more needs to be said because whether a particular person encounters the Church depends on contingent circumstances. Neither can joining the Church be obligated as part of an idea of 'progress' in faith, because this wrongly supposes that faith may be measured by degree.⁵⁹

---

54. Augustine, *Enchiridion* 27, 103, in *On Christian Belief*, trans. Matthew O'Connell (New York: New City, 2005), p. 333.

55. Augustine, *Letters* 102.10, 4 vols, trans. Roland Teske (New York: New City, 2001–2005), vol. 2, pp. 25–26.

56. Augustine, *Letters* 102.15, vol. 2, p. 28.

57. Augustine, *The City of God against the Pagans* 18.47, trans. R. W. Dyson (Cambridge University Press, 1998), p. 893.

58. C, pp. 188–90; Ruth, 2 Kgs 5, Num. 22–24; see also Gerald O'Collins, *Salvation for All: God's Other Peoples* (Oxford: Oxford University Press, 2008), pp. 25–34.

59. C, p. 221.

De Lubac's response to the question is in two parts: a defence of Christian belief, and a defence of the obligation to Church membership. Unlike other religions, he contends, the Christian faith posits a purpose or *telos* to human life. Although any religious believer might gain heightened spiritual awareness or be motivated by a deep love, something is missing in the non-Christian religions. De Lubac writes: 'Outside Christianity nothing attains its end, that only end, toward which, unknowingly, all human desires, all human endeavours, are in movement: the embrace of God in Christ.'[60] This end is linked with the unity of common life, which no other religion or social movement except Christianity is able to provide.[61]

Ultimately, however, to ground a theology of mission in the welfare or salvation of non-Christians is misguided. It is presumptuous, de Lubac suggests, for Christians to suppose that the salvation of non-Christians is secured by the activity of the institutional churches. Rather, mission is a Christian imperative because it is the nature of the Church and the message of Christ. The history of the Church is nothing other than the history of its mission in the world, and the Church remains incomplete in so far as that mission contains gaps. Catholicity imposes upon the Church a 'continual demand'[62] to bring all people to her saving redemption and to the form of Christ.

Nevertheless, even from an ecclesial perspective non-Christians should not be regarded as merely prospective Christians. Their continuing presence in the world serves to remind Christians of the millennia of preparation that were required for the gradual raising up of the social, intellectual, and material life of humankind to the level at which it was ready to receive the Gospel of Christ. De Lubac writes of non-Christians that there might be 'found in their beliefs and consciences a certain groping after the truth, its painful preparation or its partial anticipation, discoveries of the natural reason and tentative solutions'.[63] Moreover, non-Christians who lived before the time of Christ are not like scaffolding, to be discarded once the building of the Christian faith has been constructed. Rather, just as the heavenly Jerusalem is built of living stones, so its scaffolding is also constructed out of living beings. Because all humans share the same eternal destiny, it cannot be the case that some exist, or have in past history existed, only to 'prepare suitable conditions for the development of others'.[64] Although non-Christians 'themselves are not in the normal way of salvation, they will be able nevertheless to obtain this salvation by virtue of those mysterious bonds which unite them to the faithful. In short, they can be saved because they are an integral part of that humanity which is to be saved'.[65] On de Lubac's view, the Church leads towards salvation even those who are not Christians, and indeed must do so in order to be true to its own calling.

60. Ibid., p. 224.
61. Ibid., p. 225.
62. Ibid., p. 229.
63. Ibid., p. 232.
64. Ibid., pp. 232–33.
65. Ibid., p. 233.

Despite taking seriously the possibility that non-Christians will be saved, de Lubac also recognizes the contrary theological axiom, more widely accepted in his day and originating with Cyprian of Carthage, that outside the Church there is no salvation (*extra Ecclesiam nulla salus*).[66] How may these two positions be compatible? The historic formulae that subsequently developed Cyprian's principle, de Lubac immediately adds, excepted the case of invincible ignorance among pagans of good will.[67] So even official Church teaching has been more nuanced than might be supposed. However, from at least the time of Pope Innocent III (1198–1216) the principle of *extra Ecclesiam nulla salus* has been interpreted as excluding the possibility of salvation to Christians in other churches. According to this view, only members of the Roman Catholic Church may be saved.

Viewed positively, Cyprian's principle affirms the power of salvation rather than speculating on damnation. However, despite what de Lubac might have hoped, very many people would not view any Church as the place 'to which a soul amenable to the suggestions of grace spontaneously tends'.[68] Yet in an age where global communications make the message of many churches, including that of the Roman Catholic Church, immediately present across the globe, it is increasingly unrealistic for theologians to posit the existence of a category of person who has had no opportunity to gain any knowledge of that message.

De Lubac concludes his discussion of mission by emphasizing the strong imperative on Christians to engage in missionary work, which is the 'duty of all, normally no doubt the least determined of all duties, but the strictest and the most universal'.[69] By this he means that mission is not, for example, like attending mass, which takes place at specified times according to a set format. Opportunities for mission are varied and frequently unexpected, and must therefore be seized as and when they appear. Through its long preparation, foundation, and expansion the Church was intended for all, so Christians who have been brought within it have no entitlement to enjoy their situation in proud, isolated superiority.[70] On the contrary, Christians have been brought into the Church for the salvation of those outside, in order that all may enjoy their full, God-given humanity. The desire to evangelize, de Lubac insists, cannot be grounded in the supposition that those outside the Church are, or will be, rejected or cursed. Rather, the missionary endeavour entails great respect for the humanity of the person being evangelized, a humanity which they already possess.[71] As will now be seen, however, in the France of de Lubac's day such respect was not afforded to all people.

66. *The Letters of St. Cyprian of Carthage* 73.21.2, 4 vols, trans. G. W. Clarke (New York: Newman, 1984–1989), vol. 4, p. 66.
67. Ignorance was deemed 'invincible' if it could not have been avoided. For instance, a non-Christian living in a region that no missionary had ever visited could be deemed invincibly ignorant of the Christian message and Church, whereas a non-Christian who ignored the preaching of visiting missionaries could not.
68. C, p. 236.
69. Ibid., p. 241.
70. Ibid., p. 243.
71. TF, p. 2.

The Jewish Persecution

On 10 May 1940, the German army invaded France and an armistice was signed just six weeks later. This was effectively a surrender, with the country divided into an occupied northern zone, which included Paris, and a notionally sovereign southern zone, which was governed from the spa town of Vichy and commonly known as the Vichy Republic. Many Parisian intellectuals relocated to Lyons, which was within the southern zone and where de Lubac lived and worked. He concurs with the common assessment that his city became the capital of the Resistance.[72]

In this situation, de Lubac's consideration of the relation of Christianity to other religions was not restricted to abstract academic reflection. He was in demand in the city as a speaker and some of his lectures were published. Nevertheless, the secular and Church media were being manipulated in order to promote Nazi ideology, and de Lubac describes his daily increasing anguish at the degradation of consciences and his own feeling of powerlessness.[73] On 15 April 1941, he wrote to his superiors to protest against the 'anti-Christian revolution' brought about by the Nazi regime and the eight years of religious persecution already suffered in Germany.[74] Roman Catholic schools, associations, theological faculties, religious orders, and media had been closed or rendered ineffectual, sterilization and medical murder had been legalized, concentration camps had been built on French soil, and a culture of political authoritarianism that amounted to a neo-pagan worship of the state had become rapidly engrained in society.

Indissolubly linked with all of this was anti-Semitism. In response, de Lubac repeats Pope Pius XI's 1928 condemnation of 'hatred directed against the people who were once the chosen people of God' and insists that any contravention of the requirements of love and justice, even if not directed against the Church, is an offence to the Church.[75] He writes:

> The anti-Semitism of today was unknown to our fathers; besides its degrading effect on those who abandon themselves to it, it is anti-Christian. It is against the Bible, against the Gospel as well as the Old Testament, against the universalism of the Church, against what is called the 'Roman International'; it is against all that Pius XI, following Saint Paul, claimed as ours the day he cried out: 'Spiritually we are Semites!' It is all the more important to be on our guard, for this anti-Semitism is already gaining ground among the Catholic elite, even in our religious houses. There we have a danger that is only all too real.[76]

72. ASC, p. 48.
73. Henri de Lubac, *Christian Resistance to Anti-Semitism: Memories from 1940–1944*, trans. Anne Englund Nash (San Francisco, CA: Ignatius, 1990, p. 25.
74. TH, pp. 428–39.
75. Ibid., pp. 432, 437.
76. Ibid., pp. 437–38/CR, pp. 26–27. These often-repeated words of Pope Pius XI were spoken to a group of Belgian pilgrims on 6 September 1938. See also TF, pp. 421, 437, 487.

De Lubac's letter was cordially received by his provincial and his rector. Nevertheless, it did not make much wider impact. On 3 June 1941, less than two months later, a law was passed requiring all Jews to register with the authorities. Although just one in a series of over fifty laws, decrees, orders, and rulings directed at the Jews, it was rightly recognized by de Lubac and others as especially pernicious because the list produced could later be used by the occupying German forces for the purposes of internment and deportation.[77] This is exactly what occurred.

Following the passing of the registration law, de Lubac and three colleagues formed a group to produce a 'Draft of a Declaration of the Catholic Theological Faculty of Lyons'. Abbé Joseph Chaine, their convenor, occupied the Old Testament chair and was chaplain for the university parish. Louis Richard, a Sulpician, was professor of dogma and director of the university seminary. Fr Joseph Bonsirven, a Jesuit recently arrived from Belgium, was an expert in ancient Judaism. The group thus brought together Christian theologians and experts in Jewish history and scripture. The key theological statement in their draft declaration read:

> The Church cannot forget that the Israelites are the descendants of the people who were the object of the divine election of which she is the culmination, of those people from whom Christ, our Saviour, the Virgin Mary and the apostles sprang; that they have in common with us the books of the Old Testament, the inspired pages of which we read in our liturgy, the psalms from which we sing to praise God and express our hope for his Kingdom; that, according to the words of Pius XI, we, like they, are sons of Abraham, the father of believers, and that the blessing promised to his descendants is still upon them, to call them to recognize in Jesus the Christ who was promised to them.[78]

The 'Chaine Declaration' was not, however, officially published. No public media would willing to undertake the task, and any attempt to solicit a publisher would probably have attracted official attention and measures such as the closure of the faculty. However, Cardinal Gerlier, the Archbishop of Lyons, authorized clandestine circulation.[79]

De Lubac attributes the document's limited impact to its theological (rather than popular) tone and the absence of a developed distribution network. Nevertheless, the text is important for two reasons. First, it demonstrates how closely bound up de Lubac's theology of religion, especially concerning Judaism, was with concrete events. Second, the proposed clandestine distribution of texts would be achieved far more effectively later that year, when a complex undercover network was established to circulate the *Cahiers du Témoignage chrétien*.[80] These

---

77. CR, pp. 50–56.
78. Ibid., pp. 67–68.
79. Ibid., pp. 61, 71.
80. Ibid., pp. 131–45.

pamphlets pursued similar themes to the Chaine Declaration, but were aimed at a wider readership.[81] De Lubac was one of their most active writers and editors, and his work exposed him to considerable danger.

Theologically, de Lubac's determined defence of the Jewish people was founded on his conviction that, as a believer in Christ, he was a member of a Church that existed in an organic relationship with them. He presents the Old Testament as replete with images of the Church. Job in his trials is the persecuted Church. The Church is Paradise, with Christ the tree of life in its centre; she is Noah's ark, saving her people from death; she is Jerusalem, the city of David and the Temple of Solomon; she is numerous faithful women through whom God works.[82] But de Lubac does not relate the Church to Israel only by means of images. Strikingly, in a lecture delivered and published in 1941 he views the mission of the Church as the continuation of the mission of Israel. The Church has been prepared for its missionary duty by the 'prophets and by the whole history of Israel such as the Holy Books, read and commented on in its assemblies, unfolded to her'.[83] These have given her, even during her past infancy, an extraordinary self-understanding. The Church is the 'heir of the Chosen People and of its hopes'. She is the 'true Israel, Israel according to the spirit, because she alone, thanks to the spiritual revolution of the gospel, can bring to a conclusion the work for which Yahweh has raised up Israel'.

The missionary idea arose in Israel as a result of the prior recognition of the God of the patriarchs and of Moses as unique, exclusive, and single. De Lubac attaches particular importance to the universalist strand within Israel and to those prophets who were 'proclaimers of the New Testament in the midst of the Old', citing Augustine's description of David, who spared his enemy Saul from death, as a 'man in the Old Testament but not of the Old Testament, saved by faith in the future inheritance of Christ'.[84] De Lubac finds this 'summit of prophecy' powerfully present in Deutero-Isaiah (Is. 40–55), in which the foreigners who join themselves to the Lord will be brought to his holy mountain and made joyful, with their burnt offerings and sacrifices accepted on the altar of what has become a house of prayer for all peoples (56.6-8). A key figure in this expansion of Israelite boundaries is the mysterious suffering servant, in whom 'Jewish universalism becomes missionary'.[85] Distant coasts and peoples are to hear his voice, and Israel is to become a light to the nations, so that salvation may extend to the ends of the earth (49.1,6). Teaching will go out from this servant, his justice will be a light for the peoples, and he will deliver salvation (51.4-5). The ambiguity about the identity of the servant, who is

---

81. For more, David Grumett, *De Lubac: A Guide for the Perplexed* (London: T&T Clark, 2007), pp. 40–43.

82. C, pp. 183–88.

83. TH, p. 371.

84. Ibid., p. 373; see *Augustine's Commentary on Galatians* 43, trans. Eric Plumer (Oxford: Oxford University Press, 2003), pp. 204–5.

85. TH, p. 374.

sometimes presented as a particular man but in other places as the personification of Israel collectively, is viewed by de Lubac as profoundly significant, suggesting that the identity of the saviour is inseparable from that of his people.[86] From this missionary perspective even the Babylonian exile may be viewed as providential, as by Tobit in his call to the children of Israel to acknowledge God before the nations 'for he has scattered you among them' (Tob. 13.3). De Lubac repeats the 'sublime' Isaianic vision of the reconciliation that this mission will ultimately achieve: the 'highway from Egypt to Assyria' along which the people of each nation will pass in order to worship together. This will also draw in Israel as a 'blessing in the midst of the earth' (Is. 19.23-5).[87] This imagery is connected with the similarly spectacular vision of Isaiah 60: the nations will walk in the light of Israel, which will receive the abundance of the sea and the wealth of nations, which will fly 'like doves to their windows'.

Islam-Christian Dialogue?

Despite the inspiring visions of Isaiah, harmonious religious convergence is unlikely to occur in present, sinful earthly life. The reality is sometimes interreligious tension and conflict, usually linked with political and social change. This was true of France during the 1960s and 1970s, which saw high levels of Muslim immigration. In 1962, when the French government recognized Algerian independence, *harki* soldiers from Algeria who had been fighting with the French army were allowed to settle in France as citizens, joining many others fleeing the country in response to the instability and French withdrawal. Then in 1976 the French government passed the *regroupement familial* (family regrouping) law. This permitted the families of typically male immigrant workers to come to France, join their husbands and fathers, and gain citizenship. As a result, many children and wives of Muslim immigrants arrived in France to settle. The large majority of these were Maghrebi, including Moroccans and Tunisians as well as Algerians. The numbers were greatest in industrial areas, especially Paris, where de Lubac spent his final years following the closure of the Jesuit scholasticate in Lyons in 1974.

From a Christian perspective, the rise of Islam in France could be viewed negatively, as a consequence of the French state's secular policy of pursuing what has been, at best, a neutral approach to Christianity. However, from a broader religious perspective one can well imagine de Lubac commending the way in which second-generation immigrants have spectacularly challenged the secular terms on which they have been accepted as citizens, and endorsing the resurgence of religion within a historically secular public sphere. In any case, in view of the large-scale social changes that Muslim immigration around him produced, it is

---

86. Ibid., p. 375.
87. Ibid, pp. 391–92.

surprising that de Lubac did not produce an essay on Islam. He did, however, offer disparate reflections in the course of writings on other topics. Because of the importance of Islam in present-day France, this chapter would be incomplete without some attempt to piece together these reflections.

De Lubac recognized that, in the Gobi Desert, Islam had many centuries ago 'invaded' and 'triumphed' over all other religions, and now covered everything with its 'uniform coloring'.[88] However, in its capacity to spread by making large numbers of converts, Islam is by no means unique. When distinguishing his two types of monotheism, de Lubac places Islam in the second, which, he states, is 'charged with an explosive force'.[89] This is an accurate description of the power of Islam today. However, de Lubac goes on to insist that the power of monotheisms of this second type cannot be accounted for by demographics, migration, or global economics, as if properly religious factors were mere epiphenomena of these. Referring to the migration of the Prophet Muhammad and his followers from Mecca to Medina in 622, he writes: 'The Arabs before the Hegira had hardly any unity. We have observed that the idea of God, in its highest as well as most humble appearances, breaks out of and overflows all social as well as mental frameworks.' Nevertheless, within the second, 'explosive' type of monotheism de Lubac also places Christianity, which has witnessed massive numbers of conversions globally and which indisputably remains the world's most successful missionary religion. This suggests that the mission of Islam is analogous to that of Christianity and arguably a radicalization of it.

Alongside this suggested continuity between Christianity and Islam needs to be set a more critical exposition contained within a 1965 preface to a study of mysticism by de Lubac's fellow Jesuit André Ravier. In this, de Lubac critiques the tendency to understand religion and mysticism as if they were two separate things. Rather, he argues, the rules and practices of religion need to be accepted together with the experiential dimension of mysticism, as part of a unified way of believing. De Lubac contends that Islam does not, in practice, usually achieve this. Islam, he argues, takes seriously the root meaning of religion (*religio*, from *relegere*) as a 'feeling of obligation accompanied by fear and scruples toward the superior powers',[90] with the Koran functioning as an exterior and ritualistic code. Drawing on the relatively irenic work of the Roman Catholic priest Louis Massignon, de Lubac correctly recognizes that the Koran leaves some openings for spiritual experience. However, he contends that its interpretive community typically closes these off, and 'condemns as a sacrilege the temerity of anyone who aspires to divine union or believes himself called to it'.[91] Islam does, of course, have mystical traditions, notably Sufism, but de Lubac avers that even these accept a retreat from mysticism in its fullest sense by failing to contest the incommunicability of the

---

88. TF, pp. 300, 305.
89. Ibid., p. 329.
90. Ibid., p. 41.
91. Ibid.

divine message that mainstream Islam supposes. Even the Prophet Muhammad, at his nocturnal ascension, journeyed only as far as the gate of the heavenly city and, unlike Christ, not into the love of God himself. De Lubac writes: 'For the Muslim, the Christian belief in the divine Incarnation and the new order of relations that it established between man and God can only be a blasphemy.' For Muslims, he continues, the 'only possible relationship with God is expressed in the word Islam, which means "submission"'.[92]

On the basis of this exposition it should not be assumed that de Lubac is aggressively hostile to Islam. Rather, he is at pains to comprehend its differences with Christianity, especially its conception of the supernatural as relatively inaccessible. His final attitude is illumined by one of his last written pieces: a 1988 preface to Charles Molette's biography of the Muslim convert Monsignor Paul Mulla-Zadé. De Lubac presents the study as suggestive for what he terms an 'Islamo-Christian dialogue' on the grounds that it examines the 'unfolding of a long drama' in which this dialogue is pursued within a single conscience.[93] Indeed, he here describes Islam and the Christian faith as 'the' two monotheisms. Might they thereby be viewed as providing alternative paths to a truth that exceeds both? Intriguingly, Molette recounts how Mulla's conversion – along with that of another scholar, the Franciscan Jean Mohammed Abdel-Jalil – received impetus from correspondence with Maurice Blondel. This Roman Catholic lay philosopher, who exerted tremendous influence on de Lubac and the whole generation of French Jesuits of which he was part, had laid the philosophical foundations for what would become the latter's doctrine of the supernatural: that is, that all aspects of spiritual and natural life are dependent upon divine grace, and that all are incomplete until they attain in truth the object of the divine union that is present within them by implication. The consequences of this doctrine for an understanding of Islam are ambivalent. Although it suggests that all religious manifestations contain an element of divine truth, its dynamic of ascent and union imply that the Islamic religion is nevertheless exceeded by the Christian fusion of religion with mysticism. De Lubac warms to Mulla-Zadé and Abdel-Jalil because they were converts, while nevertheless praising their 'ever-proclaimed fidelity to the best of what they owed to Islam'.[94]

Conclusion

De Lubac's studies and reflections on religion span his professional academic life of more than fifty years: time teaching in Lyons, spiritual resistance to anti-Semitism, the post-war build-up to the Second Vatican Council, and later writings. Strikingly, most were produced significantly before the Council, which endorsed

---

92. Ibid.
93. TH, p. 575.
94. Ibid., p. 576.

a somewhat more open treatment of the non-Christian religions than that which had preceded it. Some of the studies, including those from his early years, were groundbreaking. His research into Christianity in central Asia anticipates the greatly increased current interest in world Christianity and the slowly growing recognition that Christianity did not originate in Europe. Moreover, his study of religion incorporates the kind of interdisciplinary perspectives that are being promoted in many universities today.[95] His broad acceptance of the concept of 'primitive monotheism' might appear more contentious, in view of many of the critiques of the hypothesis launched from within the Vienna School. Nonetheless, on a careful reading de Lubac did not posit a common primeval revelation underlying different religions, which was the principal and justifiable target of those critiques.[96] Indeed, he later contended that the idea of God confounds the 'laborious syntheses of ethnologists and historians', stating: 'All attempts to find a "genesis" for the idea of God – like the attempts to "reduce" it to something else by explaining its genesis – err in some respect or other. The idea of God is a unique idea, distinct from all others, and it cannot be fitted into any system.'[97]

Living in a constitutionally secular French state and in a Europe that had been ravaged by the anti-Christian politics of both Nazism and Communism, de Lubac focused, in so much of his oeuvre, on apologetics and Christian mission. It is perhaps in relation to these, rather than against abstract theological categories, that his writings on religion should be assessed. In 1980 de Lubac recognized that, in modern society, the rejection of religion as a legitimate category of discourse is often grounded in a similar misunderstanding to that which motivated the rejection of the idea of Christian culture: that to acknowledge the transcendent is to accept an alien and restrictive intrusion into ordinarily natural life.[98] However, he also maintained that religion is an analogous concept, which being such does not refer to structurally identical belief configurations in different contexts.[99] Attacking syncretistic understandings of religion, he protests: 'With no regard to genuine Christianity, today every species of the "sacred" or even every tawdry imitation thereof, every religion, every spirituality, every culture is being exalted, amid total confusion and with no effort at discrimination.'[100] This uncompromising critique provides a suitable note of warning on which to end. De Lubac does not view other religions as equivalent to Christianity, but he does regard them as linked with Christianity as a result of past interactions and contingent structural affinities. Because historical and theoretical dimensions are intrinsic to belief in any form, Christianity cannot be understood or lived out in separation from them or from the connections with non-Christian religions that they bring.

---

95. For instance, on Mousterian religious belief, Graham Ward, *Unbelievable: Why We Believe and Why We Don't* (London: Tauris, 2014), pp. 29–60.
96. For which, Zimoń, 'Wilhelm Schmidt's Theory', pp. 252–55.
97. DG, p. 20.
98. BC, pp. 95–96.
99. Ibid., pp. 96–98.
100. Ibid., p. 99.

Chapter 11

KNOWING GOD

D. Stephen Long

Broad agreement has always existed between Protestants and Catholics as to who God is; prior to the eighteenth century theology proper (who God is) was never a reason for division. God is simple, perfect, immutable, impassible, infinite, eternal, and one, who is revealed in three persons, Father, Son, and Holy Spirit. This foundational understanding of God was pervasive throughout the Christian tradition and united west and east as well as Catholics and Protestants. Since the eighteenth century it has been challenged, but nearly every major Protestant Confession along with the Roman Catholic Catechism endorses it. What has become controversial is how we know that this is who God is. The controversy over theological epistemology not only divides Protestants and Catholics but also Protestants from Protestants and Catholics from Catholics as well as the Orthodox from Catholics. De Lubac's theological epistemology has been at the centre of much of this controversy. It was influenced not only by his Catholic theology but also by his reading in Russian Orthodoxy and to a lesser extent his affirmation of Kierkegaard and Barth.[1]

To understand the significance of Henri de Lubac's theological epistemology and the controversy that attends it, it must first be situated within Catholic debates stemming from Vatican I on theological epistemology. Second, those debates require some knowledge of the distinction in scholastic metaphysics between act and potency and its relation to a teaching on pure nature, along with two important Aristotelian axioms that buttress the doctrine of pure nature. But de Lubac's theological epistemology was not only a matter of metaphysics; he was also concerned with its political and cultural implications. He suspected that a late Medieval and early modern metaphysics colluded unwittingly with secularism in marking out an area of 'pure nature' that contributed to it or at least lacked the resources to stand against it. Only after this fourth point is clear will the importance of de Lubac's theological epistemology come into full view.

---

1. De Lubac affirmed Dostoevsky and Kierkegaard with some reservations in DAH. References to Barth are present from his early to his later works. While unapologetically Catholic, he was an ecumenical theologian.

Situating de Lubac's Theological Epistemology

Henri de Lubac's theological epistemology cannot be properly understood without situating it in terms of arguments stemming from the First Vatican Council, especially the 'dogmatic constitution', *Dei filius*, issued on 24 April 1870. It first stated who God is and then how we know. The first statement should be relatively non-controversial. Nearly every Protestant Confession would agree with Vatican I ...

> that there is one true and living God, Creator and Lord of Heaven and earth ... who, being one, sole, absolutely simple and immutable spiritual substance, is to be declared as really and essentially distinct from the world, of supreme beatitude in and by Himself, and ineffably exalted above all things which, beside Himself, exist or are conceivable.[2]

De Lubac affirmed this statement without challenge. It is the second statement that creates controversy, for Vatican I not only set forth as dogma who God is but also how we know.

> The same Holy, Mother Church holds and teaches that God, the beginning and end of all things, may be known for certain by the natural light of human reason by means of created things, 'for the invisible things of Him from the creation of the world are clearly seen, being understood from the things that are made' (Rom. I, 20); but that it pleased His wisdom and goodness to reveal Himself and the eternal decrees of His will to mankind by another, namely the supernatural way.[3]

Protestant Confessions never explicitly denied such natural knowledge for God; nor did they demand it as a dogmatic statement of faith. Nor is it clear what this theological epistemology requires. Is the natural knowledge of God a knowledge grounded in faith or is it independent of it? It would seem to be the former if the warrant for it is Romans 1:20. Or is it a knowledge grounded upon a realm of pure nature that exists as a second source separated from faith? If it is understood as the former, de Lubac unquestionably affirmed it. If it requires the latter interpretation, de Lubac challenged it. But he, along with many other Catholic theologians who were later made cardinals, never thought it required that narrow interpretation. Catholic theologians continue to debate the theological and philosophical status of this 'natural light of human reason'.

---

2. I am aware that many contemporary theologians challenge this statement. For a defence of it against such challenges, see my 'Does God Have a Future? Theology and the "Future" of God', in Trevor Cairney and David Starling, eds, *Theology and the Future: Evangelical Assertions and Explorations* (London: Bloomsbury T&T Clark, 2014).

3. Quoted in Réginald Garrigou-Lagrange, *God: His Existence and His Nature*, vol. 1, trans. Don Bede Rose (St Louis, MO: Herder Book Co, 1934), pp. 3, 8.

After Vatican I, Roman Catholicism required its adherents to affirm not only the statement on who God is but also the theological epistemology for it. In fact, it became as important if not more so than who God is. The affirmation included an anathema that still accompanied such statements. 'If any one shall say that the one true God, our Creator and Lord, cannot be certainly known by the natural light of human reason through created things; let him be anathema.'[4] The objects of this anathema were 'modernists', which included Catholics who taught that God could only be known by faith, anyone who accepted Kantian criticisms of metaphysics, especially his critiques of the arguments for God's existence, and by implication most Protestants whose teaching on 'total depravity' was supposedly incapable of giving the natural light of reason its due. After Vatican I, the Roman Catholic hierarchy took on 'modernism' by setting Thomas Aquinas' philosophy against it. Four decades later Pius X required all Catholic clergy and religious to take an oath against Modernism. The oath began with the same words found in *Dei filius* from the First Vatican Council:

> I... firmly embrace and accept each and every definition that has been set forth and declared by the unerring teaching authority of the Church, especially those principal truths which are directly opposed to the errors of this day. And first of all, I profess that God, the origin and end of all things, can be known with certainty by the natural light of reason from the created world (see Rom. 1:19), that is, from the visible works of creation, as a cause from its effects, and that, therefore, his existence can also be demonstrated.[5]

The irony of requiring an oath to affirm what should be expected of reason qua reason seemed lost on those most committed to its promulgation.

Like many such required oaths, this one created anxiety that those who were commanded by authority to take it did not properly affirm it by reason. Here is where the story of de Lubac's theological epistemology begins. De Lubac affirmed this teaching.[6] He never wavered from it, and even referred to himself as a 'natural theologian'. But he denied what some neo-scholastics thought, and continue to think, is a necessary entailment of it – a doctrine of pure nature.

Potencies and the Doctrine of Pure Nature

In 1914 Pius X decreed that twenty-four theses set forth Thomas's basic teaching and should be affirmed by all Catholics as a means to combat Modernism. The first thesis drew on Aristotle's distinction between act and potency. It stated, 'Potency

---

4. Garrigou-Lagrange, *God: His Existence and His Nature*, p. 8. Vatican II did not promulgate anathemas.
5. Fergus Kerr, *Twentieth-Century Catholic Theologians: From Neoscholasticism to Nuptial Mysticism* (Malden, MA: Blackwell Publishing, 2007), p. 223.
6. See DG, p. 218.

and act are a complete division of being. Hence, whatever is must be either pure act or a unit composed of potency and act as its primary and intrinsic principles."[7] In the Thomist tradition, potency gets divided between active potency (the 'capacity to bring about an effect') and passive potency (the 'capacity to be affected'). Passive potencies are then further divided based on a distinction between natural and supernatural or obediential passive potencies. Natural passive potencies are actualized by creaturely agents with their 'natural capacities'.[8] Supernatural or obediential passive potencies require something more than natural capacities; they require the elevation of the human person by grace normally acquired in baptism and brought about by divine agency. Thomas Aquinas and the Thomist tradition drew on and developed these Aristotelian metaphysical principles for a theological epistemology, but the interpretation of how they did so is conflicted.

Everyone agrees that Thomas spoke of a 'natural desire for God' present in the human creature. A natural desire is a potency. The debate is what kind of potency this natural desire is. The dominant Thomist tradition distinguished between an innate natural desire that would be equivalent to a natural passive potency and an elicited natural desire that would be an obediential passive potency. For this tradition, the 'natural desire' for the vision of God was understood as 'natural' only as an elicited desire that elevated human nature by grace; it was not innate. Grace elicited the desire, and only grace attained its end – the beatific vision. No one denied that only grace attained the end of the beatific vision, but de Lubac rejected that the natural desire of God was elicited by grace. He thought that made grace too extrinsic to actual human existence and insisted that the natural desire was innate. On Aristotelian grounds innate natural desires had ends God owed to creatures. For this reason, the neo-scholastic tradition, against which de Lubac reacted, rejected an innate natural desire for God that could be attained by grace. If the desire for God were an innate natural desire, so the argument went, God would owe us the beatific vision. De Lubac rejected the Aristotelian axioms that entail innate natural desires can only be achieved through natural means. He interpreted Thomas' natural desire for God as an innate desire attained supernaturally.

For Thomists who affirmed the Aristotelian axioms, the human creature had two ends, one natural and one supernatural. Both ends could make sense of human action, and the natural end became intelligible based on a doctrine of pure nature, a doctrine that was present in Thomas as a hypothetical reality but never an actually existing one. De Lubac found this neo-Thomist tradition subtly influenced by nominalism, where a hypothetical pure nature became an actually existing one. For de Lubac's reading of Thomas, there was only one supernatural end or finality, and it alone rendered human action intelligible in the actually

---

7. Cited in Edward Feser's *Scholastic Metaphysics: A Contemporary Introduction* (Newnkirchen- Seelscheid, Germany: Editiones scholoasticae, 2014), p. 31. Feser provides a clear explanation of the importance of act/potency for scholastic metaphysics as well as its relevance for contemporary philosophy and science, pp. 31–87.

8. See Feser, *Scholastic Metaphysics*, pp. 39–40.

existing creation. Pure human nature – a nature not oriented towards a vision of the Triune God and founded upon creation in, through and for Jesus Christ – never existed.

Even now contemporary neo-scholastic theologians and philosophers question the cardinal's teaching.[9] What is questioned is not the material content of his doctrine of God but its underlying theological epistemology. De Lubac did not affirm 'pure nature', and for some interpretations of Thomas, Thomism, Vatican I, and Catholicism, pure nature is mandatory. It is, according to Lawrence Feingold, a necessary doctrine because without 'pure nature', theology loses grace. Feingold recognizes that de Lubac never taught that our nature has a 'supernatural element' intrinsic to it, and in that sense he 'is in perfect harmony with St. Thomas and with the Catholic tradition ...'. But Feingold rejects that de Lubac can sustain this teaching, because he affirmed 'a supernatural finality imprinted on our nature in creation itself, prior to the reception of grace, determining us to an inevitably supernatural end'. Feingold states that there can only be two responses to such a 'supernatural finality'. It will either have to be understood along the lines of Karl Rahner's 'supernatural existential' or rejected altogether. He thinks the latter option is the only viable one. A natural desire for God should only be understood as the result of 'sanctifying grace', the grace God gives not to a natural potency but an obediential one. 'Clearly the principles of St. Thomas and the Christian tradition', states Feingold, 'demand the latter option'.[10] For Feingold, pure nature is a Catholic and Christian theological necessity that follows from philosophy, theology, and the Church's Magisterium.[11]

De Lubac rejected the claim that the human person had a double finality, one natural and one supernatural, and argued that the Catholic tradition, especially Aquinas, developed theology from the perspective of a supernatural finality that was given to the human person at creation. Neither the anti-modernist oath nor the twenty-four theses explicitly affirmed a doctrine of pure nature and a double finality, but a strict application of two Aristotelian axioms by neo-scholastics inevitably lead to its affirmation and rendered suspect any arguments such as de Lubac's that reject pure nature.

---

9. See Lawrence Feingold, *The Natural Desire to See God According to St. Thomas Aquinas and His Interpreters* (Ave Maria, FL: Sapientia Press, 2010) and Steven A. Long, *Natura Pura: On the Recovery of Nature in the Doctrine of Grace* (New York: Fordham University Press, 2010).

10. Feingold, *The Natural Desire to See God According to St. Thomas Aquinas and His Interpreters*, p. 339.

11. Ibid., 425. 'However, the possibility of a state of pure nature is necessary for both philosophical and theological reasons, and has been taught by the Church's Magisterium. It is philosophically necessary for the coherence of the natural order, and theologically necessary to preserve the full gratuitousness of grace.' He quotes *Humani generis* as the source for the Magisterium's teaching. However, the quote he uses makes no explicit reference to 'pure nature'. See p. 425, n. 109.

Aristotle's Axioms on Natural Desire

The two Aristotelian axioms noted above are these: 'a natural passive potency in a genus never expends beyond the active power of that genus' and 'natural desire is never in vain'.[12] The first axiom stipulates that a *natural* potency will always have a *natural* end and therefore the natural means to attain it. An acorn's potency contains within it an end proportionate to its nature, in its case to be an oak tree. An acorn cannot become a human being. Nor could it become an infinite possibility of entities, for the world would then be rendered unintelligible; reason would not be able to be exercised upon the world as it actually exists. The second axiom, that a natural desire is never in vain, does not mean that an acorn will always attain its end, but that its potency for it must be a possibility it could attain. In that sense, when God created the acorn God 'owed' the acorn all that an acorn naturally is. An acorn may not achieve its proper end, but it has what it needs to do so by virtue of its creation as an acorn.

God does not arbitrarily create potencies that cannot attain their ends without further arbitrary acts of God's power. This Aristotelian teaching allows for nature to have its own integrity. It can be rationally known, and the supernatural virtues of faith, hope, or charity are not necessary either for the nature to be known or for it to attain its natural end. If theology begins with these two axioms, then to affirm that the human creature has a single supernatural finality creates several problems. First, nature loses its integrity. It is no longer self-evident to reason but must be set within the larger drama of the divine economy for its intelligibility. Second, a supernatural finality grounded upon creation rather than given at baptism by sanctifying grace means that the creature has a natural desire for a supernatural end; the end has become disproportionate to the natural potencies and the means to actualize those potencies to attain their end. The logical conclusion will be, if one affirms both Aristotelian axioms, that God owes the human creature the means to its supernatural finality. Such a divine obligation would lack gratuitousness. If God creates natures that have an integrity that allows them to attain their end proportionate to the natures they are, then a supernatural finality imprinted on creatures qua creatures entails God is required to make possible the attainment of that end through their nature; otherwise the natural desire would be in vain. But if God owes the satisfaction of a natural potency to the creature, then universalism would necessarily follow from this innate desire for God.[13] Moreover, unbaptized babies in limbo – who are eternally deprived of their supernatural finality – could not be happy.[14]

---

12. See Feingold, *The Natural Desire to See God According to St. Thomas Aquinas and His Interpreters*, pp. 129–30.

13. For a contemporary criticism along these lines, see Reinhard Hütter's critique of what he refers to as John Milbank's 'radicalized Bulgakovian Lubacianism' that inevitably leads to *apokatastasis* in *Dust Bound for Heaven: Explorations in the Theology of Thomas Aquinas* (Grand Rapids, MI: William B. Eerdmans Publishing Company, 2012), p. 180.

14. Feingold's argument for a doctrine of pure nature draws on Limbo as evidence for its importance if not necessity. See *The Natural Desire to See God According to St. Thomas*

Political and Cultural Implications of the Natural Desire for God

De Lubac's critics are correct *if* the Aristotelian axioms are necessary for theology.[15] De Lubac, like a number of other twentieth-century Catholic theologians such as Hans Urs von Balthasar, Karl Rahner, Bernard Lonergan, and Gustavo Gutiérrez, did not think those axioms should be conceded a foundational position in theology. De Lubac's critics often neglect the historical and political reasons for his theological epistemology.

De Lubac found the emphasis on a logical explication of the knowledge of God by nineteenth- and twentieth-century neo-scholastics incapable of addressing the 'drama of atheist humanism'. He did not seek to be relevant to the modern era, nor to resource modern theology with the patristic era by bypassing scholastic metaphysics. He despised innovation and archaeology. In 1956 he wrote, 'The mania for novelties and for all forms of archeological thought repels me equally, and I know fully well how far they are from the spirit of Catholicism.'[16] Nonetheless, some of those neo-scholastics accused him of innovating. They thought the only way to affirm Vatican I and the twenty-four theses was through a logical explication of God in terms of the Aristotelian axioms that de Lubac challenged.

Réginald Garrigou-Lagrange – an influential Dominican theologian and professor at the Angelicum in Rome – fired the first salvo by tarring the Jesuit house at Fourvière in Lyon, singling out de Lubac in particular, with 'modernism' in a 1947 essay, *La nouvelle théologie ou va-t-elle?*[17] De Lubac had published his controversial *Surnaturel* the previous year. In 1950 Pius XII published *Humani generis*, and many interpreters read it as justifying Garrigou-Lagrange's attack on de Lubac's work as a form of Modernism, 'the sum of all heresies'. The remedy for Modernism was Thomism, so properly interpreting Thomas was essential for warding off what was then construed as the evils of modernity – historicism, relativism, fideism. De Lubac was never explicitly condemned by *Humani generis*, and he never recognized his own work in it or in Garrigou-Lagrange's criticisms. He was silenced not by the Catholic magisterium, but by his own Jesuit order. In 1947 he responded to the accusations to the General of the Jesuits by stating, 'I have to confess that I can find nowhere in my work that I relativize Saint Thomas, ignore truth, disrespect dogma, invent "new principles" or call into existence a heterodox *théologie nouvelle*.'[18] Although never explicitly condemned for his

---

Aquinas and His Interpreters, pp. 371 and 428 among many other places in his argument where Limbo is drawn upon for support of the doctrine of pure nature.

15. Edward Feser has demonstrated how relevant Aristotle's distinction between act and potency is for contemporary philosophy's engagement with science in his *Scholastic Metaphysics*. De Lubac's concerns however remain. Can philosophy alone give us human nature or does it also need theological correction, supplementation, and perfection for it to be understood properly as human nature, taking into account the Incarnation and our creation in the image of the Triune God?

16. DG, p. 208.

17. Jürgen Mettepenningen, *Nouvelle Théologie New Theology: Inheritor of Modernism, Precursor of Vatican II* (London: T&T Clark International, 2010), p. 35.

18. Ibid., p. 107.

teaching, de Lubac's theological epistemology was treated with suspicion. Did it sufficiently affirm the twofold order of knowledge that Vatican I taught and the first of the twenty-four Thomistic theses demanded?

De Lubac did seek to retrieve patristic and biblical teaching through a process of *ressourcement*. However, he never saw this as countering Thomas, for Thomas himself was deeply influenced by the fathers and Scripture. De Lubac's *ressourcement* emerged from the crisis created by the Second World War and manualist Thomists like Garrigou-Lagrange who not only refused to resist Vichy France but also supported it with Thomistic teachings. For de Lubac this failure of Catholic theology was part of a larger failure spelled out in his *Catholicism* and *The Drama of Atheist Humanism*. The error lay in the use of Aristotle noted above. Nature, for de Lubac, had become self-enclosed. If nature has its own ends independent of our supernatural finality in Christ, then the human person could be understood as having a natural destiny that would be sufficient to make him or her happy. It made Catholic theology susceptible of supporting the 'natural' status quo and of colluding unwittingly with secular thought on the political right or left.

For de Lubac, the doctrine of pure nature with its natural destiny appeared similar to the anthropology advocated by Nietzsche, Feuerbach, Comte, and Marx. It could not stand against 'exclusive humanism'. Drawing on such thinkers as Dostoevsky and Kierkegaard, de Lubac insisted that Christ is the 'great disturber' of this exclusive humanism with its innate natural ends. In his preface to *The Drama of Atheist Humanism* de Lubac wrote,'

> Bursting into a world that perpetually tends to close in upon itself, God brings it the possibility of a harmony which is certainly superior, but is to be attained only at the cost of a series of cleavages and struggles coextensive with time itself. 'I came not to bring peace, but a sword.' Christ is first and foremost a great disturber.[19]

Christ disturbs all efforts to conceive of the human creature as if she or he was intended to find 'ultimate repose here below'. Such repose, argued de Lubac, inevitably becomes inhuman by turning the human creature into a means for purely natural or social ends. It neglects her or his 'eternal destiny', which is necessary for a proper humanism.[20]

In *The Drama of Atheist Humanism* (1944), written before *Surnaturel*, de Lubac's cautions about a doctrine of pure nature first come into view. According to de Lubac, the doctrine does not allow for our finality in Christ to have a sufficient role in our understanding of humanity. The fact that he saw how that doctrine contributed to a capitulation to Vichy France only corroborated his concerns. The doctrine of pure nature led to an anthropology that allowed human sociality to be defined as if Christ were not the one in whom, through whom, and for whom all

19. DAH, p. ix.
20. Ibid., p. ix.

things were made; nothing gets disturbed. The Church became less of a visible, social reality and more of a mystical body that facilitated individual conversions by elevating human nature to a supernatural end that then was relegated to a sphere beyond human sociality. Our supernatural finality had little cultural, social, or political consequences.

De Lubac, on the other hand, emphasized the Church's role in culture. His first work in 1938, *Catholicism*, made the argument that Catholicism was essentially a social religion. Its catholicity, or global unity, was the first fruits of God's mission, the mission of unifying humanity. Here too, a double finality of nature and the supernatural was insufficient to assist the Church in its mission. Notice the first two sentences in that great work: 'The supernatural dignity of one who has been baptized rests, we know, on the natural dignity of man, though it surpasses it in an infinite manner.'[21] Supernatural dignity was not a layer added on to an already complete natural dignity; it oriented natural dignity to its supernatural end and consequently ensured natural dignity. De Lubac never intended to evacuate natural dignity but to strengthen it by suspending it from its supernatural finality. All efforts of exclusive humanism to find a natural end immanent in cultural and political realities were incapable of preserving natural human dignity. Humanity's supernatural dignity gave the Church a necessary role in culture and politics, but it was not a theocratic role along the lines of Bellarmine's understanding of the Church.[22] The Church has a mission to facilitate the unity of all God's creatures, thereby preserving their natural dignity as well. De Lubac brings this idea forth in the second sentence of *Catholicism*: 'Thus the unity of the Mystical Body of Christ, a supernatural unity, supposes a previous natural unity, the unity of the human race.'[23]

De Lubac's Theological Epistemology

De Lubac's theological epistemology affirmed Vatican I, but rejected the narrow interpretation of it that demanded more than he thought it required – a doctrine of pure nature and the two Aristotelian axioms that undergird it.[24] He found *Dei*

---

21. C, p. 25.
22. De Lubac wrote, 'Thus we always come back to the Church without ever being able to consider her mystic reality apart from her visible existence in time.' C, p. 217.
23. C, p. 25.
24. De Lubac argues that Cajetan naturalizes the soul.
We have here a further indication of that 'naturalization' or 'materialization' of the soul which we have already seen at work. It is a further application of the principle according to which every being must find its end, corresponding to its natural appetite and natural power, within the limitations of its own nature. The cause of the soul has to be included as a whole in the more general case of the natural being.
AMT, p. 205
As I will note below, this theological epistemology refuses to acknowledge the uniqueness of God as an 'object' of knowledge and the correlative uniqueness of the desire for God by situating it within a univocal, generalized desire for all objects.

filius consistent with a single supernatural finality that drew upon an Augustinian anthropology where the human heart is restless until it rests in God; it was an alternative to an anthropology that posited a nature complete in itself.[25] Given the influence of Augustine on Thomas, de Lubac did not assume that this anthropology required theologians to choose one against the other.

De Lubac was never a theological revisionist. He did not reject what Vatican I affirmed about who God was or how God is known. What he challenged was a theological epistemology that refused to take the uniqueness of God as an object of knowledge into account, a teaching Catholicism affirms. Because God is unique as the 'object' of knowledge, the natural desire for God could not be understood univocally with all other desires. These two axioms – God is a unique object of thought unlike all others; the desire for God must then also be a unique form of desire – form the basis for de Lubac's theological epistemology. It assumes an analogical approach to God consistent with the Fourth Lateran Council where every similarity between God and creatures is marked by an ever-greater dissimilarity. We approach God from our natural desire for the vision of God. The desire is natural and therefore analogous to other desires, but it is at the same time dissimilar because of the uniqueness of God as an object of knowledge. Aristotle can be helpful, but his naturalized potencies have their limits. The natural desire for God can be accomplished only through God's revelation in history, something Aristotle could not have understood. We approach God from the restlessness of a natural desire that can only be satisfied by the mediation of the Church via Word and Sacrament.

Approaching God ...

As an 'object' of thought, God cannot be approached through the same methods by which one would approach other objects, for God is not an object in the world that can be indicated. 'The idea of God', de Lubac stated, 'is a unique idea, distinct from all others, and it cannot be fitted into any system'.[26] The uniqueness of the idea of God placed limitations on univocal approaches to theological epistemology. De Lubac was an early critic of ontotheology. If God is thought in terms of a causality that makes God 'the first link in a chain', then it is not God that is being thought.[27] But the uniqueness of God did not render philosophy suspect or summon forth an end to metaphysics. De Lubac did not challenge ontotheology by rejecting metaphysics or natural theology. His natural theology, however, was grounded on God's gracious act in creation and its similarity to God's act in redemption. He follows Moehler by affirming that God's revelation of himself is twofold. It is both 'natural revelation and supernatural revelation'.[28] These are not two revelations.

---

25. De Lubac wrote, 'the existence of the Augustinian school shows at all events that "pure nature" did not find support everywhere'. AMT, p. 257. For de Lubac, St Thomas, contra Suarez, affirms an Augustinian 'restlessness'. AMT, p. 162, n. 55.
26. DG, p. 20.
27. 'God is not the first link in the chain of being.' Ibid., p. 38.
28. DG, p. 9, n. 15.

They are the same revelation in two different modes, because the Creator is the Redeemer.²⁹ Because the two revelations are the same in different modes, de Lubac can go so far as to state that 'strictly speaking, no other revelation of God is absolutely necessary: that "natural revelation" suffices, quite apart from any supernatural intervention.'³⁰

De Lubac's argument that 'natural revelation suffices' must be properly understood. He is not suggesting that we can read off nature qua nature who God is in God's essence. He does not suggest this because there is no such thing as 'nature qua nature'. His argument assumes a Christological understanding of creation. The Second Person of the Trinity is not only the redeemer whose primary role is soteriological; the Second Person also has a central role in creation. God does not create pure Aristotelian natures that have fixed ends to which Christ as the end is later affixed as a remedy. God creates in God's image, and that image always includes the embrace of the Son by the Father in the Spirit. That image unsettles settled natures, creating longing for God. Because we are created in, through and for the Son, the act of creation and the act of redemption should not be set in opposition to each other.³¹ They are not an identical act. Creation is not redemption and vice versa. But the purpose of both is the same – we are made for communion with God, found in the embrace of the Father with the Son and marked most of all by love. Because this purpose characterizes creation and redemption, no 'pure nature' could possibly exist in God's ordained economy. Such a pure nature could be at most a hypothetical speculation as to what God's absolute power might have been capable of doing.

Although the uniqueness of God as an 'object' of thought placed limits on what logic can accomplish,³² it did not rule out the importance of metaphysics. Rational proofs for the existence of God have their place as long as they do not underwrite a hypothetical speculation of a nature not ordered to God. De Lubac did not think it necessary to revise the simple, perfect, impassible God of Vatican I and Christian tradition. On the one hand, he rejected a common argument among theologians that Nietzsche and the death-of-God theologians who followed in his wake were merely rejecting a metaphysical deity alien to the Christian God. In his *The Drama of Atheist Humanism*, de Lubac explicitly identified and rejected this option. He wrote, 'The God whose death Nietzsche proclaimed and desired is not only the

---

29. C, p. 284. 'The Creator and the Redeemer, the Church adds, are one and the same God.'
30. DG, p. 12.
31. De Lubac develops and defends a single idea he often cites from Chenu:
Man's relationship with God, who has made us for himself and never ceases to draw us towards him, remains essentially the same. ... As the Greeks used to say, the incarnate logos gathers the 'seeds' planted by the creating logos. The Latins expressed it in different terms: man, as God's image, is fitted to enter into communion with him, in liberty of mind and initiative of love.MS, p. xiii
32. See DG, p. 18.

God of metaphysics, but very definitively, the Christian God.'[33] On the other hand, de Lubac was unconcerned to defend metaphysical arguments for and about God that failed to acknowledge God's dynamic interaction with history. A decade later he wrote:

> The God of 'classical ontology' is dead, you say? It may be so; but it does not worry me overmuch. I have no inclination to defend the petrified constructions of Wolff. And if 'classical ontology' disappeared, it was surely because it did not correspond adequately with being. Nor was its idea of God adequate for God. The mind is alive, and so is the God who makes himself known to it.[34]

Of course, the simple, perfect, impassible God of Scholastic metaphysics also had 'life'. De Lubac was not innovating in attributing life to God's being. Thomas Aquinas devoted question 18 of the *Summa Theologiae* to God's life. De Lubac does not reject metaphysics, nor assume that Wolff's ontology is the entirety of it. Like Thomas, he seeks an ontology that 'corresponds adequately with being', and in order to do so being itself is insufficient. It must also include 'life'.

God's life is as a personal agent who acts in history. For this reason an adequate ontology will need to give historical realities their due. In his earliest work, *Catholicism*, de Lubac set forth what would be something of a programme that sought to answer the question of how we know God. He wrote, 'God acts in history and reveals himself through history. ... As a consequence historical realities possess a profound sense and are to be understood in a spiritual manner.'[35] Those historical realities include human creatures and their natural desires. Rather than abstracting from history and seeking God in hypothetical metaphysical arguments, de Lubac supplemented metaphysics with history. Much like Gilson, he was suspicious of any essentialism that abstracted from actual existence.[36] He did not set history and metaphysics against each other; God is to be found in actual existence. That God could be so found did not require abandoning the task of metaphysics. De Lubac unequivocally affirmed that God could be known through reason. He wrote,

> I would affirm, rather [than as a mere matter of opinion] that God is the object of proof. On this point the Catholic Church has expressed herself more than once, helping the reason of those who have confidence in her to regain its self-

---

33. DAH, p. 63.
34. DG, p. 177.
35. C, p. 165.
36. Of course, as de Lubac recognized in his *Augustinianism and Modern Theology*, not all scholastics affirmed such essentialism. For a contemporary scholastic metaphysics that recognizes the problem Gilson identified and provides a defence of Scholastic thought, see Feser, *Scholastic Metaphysics*, p. 212.

confidence, and encouraging reason to face the danger which threatens it in our day: 'the abdication of metaphysics'.[37]

He recognized the legitimacy of proofs for the existence of God, but he did not find them definitive. They were and always will be 'imperfect', because knowledge of God is also a matter of aesthetics.[38] It requires a *sursum*, a lifting up that only occurs through the Church.

... From Natural Desire

The uniqueness of God as an 'object' of thought correlates to the uniqueness of the natural desire for God. For de Lubac, it is unlike other desires. 'Man's longing for God is in a category of its own; we cannot apply univocally to it any of the patterns of thought which we generally use to try to define the relationships between beings in this world.'[39] In order to explain how the natural desire for the vision of God was unique among desires, de Lubac referred to Fénelon's teaching that challenged the assumption that we have a 'being' prior to receiving God's gifts. There is no 'being' prior to the gift God gives us at creation that can receive this gift. Therefore, one should not say, '"God has gratuitously given me being" or "God has impressed a supernatural finality upon by being"' for both would assume a being prior to God's gift.[40] Such expressions divide creation and redemption too thoroughly and make being or nature something other than the gift of being creature.

Natural desire for the vision of God initiates the journey to God because it creates restlessness. No human creature can be satisfied by immanent, material goods alone, not even the goods of family and political society. To be content with them without seeking our 'transcendent destiny' would be to abandon a genuine humanism, because the human being is made for something more. To settle for less would be less than human.[41] For de Lubac a purely natural contentment would be impossible, at most an illusion, for restlessness is implicit in all human thought and desire. He cited Thomas Aquinas to make his point, *Omnis intellectus naturaliter desiderat diviniae substantiae visionem* ('Every intellect naturally desires the vision of the divine substance').[42] This natural desire has several registers. It drives a philosophical and a mystical quest, and both quests must come together in theological epistemology. Evidence for these quests are present

---

37. DG, p. 57.
38. De Lubac stated, 'Metaphysical truths, however rigorously they may have been deduced, do in fact leave the door open to an element of doubt.' DG, p. 42.
39. MS, p. 114.
40. Ibid., p. 100.
41. Feingold is correct that de Lubac would not be able to make sense of Limbo.
42. MS, p. 73. De Lubac cites Thomas Aquinas, *De Veritate*, in *Sancti Thomae de Aquino opera Omnia*, vol. 22. Leonine ed. (Rome: Editori di San Tommaso, 1975–1976), q. 22 a2 ad 1 – 'All knowers know God implicitly in all they know.' DG, p. 35.

in every culture. Knowledge of God requires a merging of the philosophical and mystical, but the unity between them always eludes us. The best we can do before obtaining the beatific vision is approximate it.[43]

The proofs for God's existence are 'ways' that begin one on the journey; they are not themselves the answer to that journey.[44] The proofs are not incorrect; they provide knowledge of God. What is lacking is not in the proof but in the wayfarer. De Lubac states, 'So, in the matter of God, whatever certain people may be tempted to think, it is never the proof which is lacking. What is lacking is taste for God.'[45] Taste for God begins in a natural desire that cannot be satisfied with natural ends. For this reason, Hans Urs von Balthasar referred to de Lubac's theological anthropology as 'the suspended middle'.[46] The human creature is natural. He or she has no innate divinity; de Lubac maintains the traditional Jewish, Christian, and Islamic distinction between Creator and creature. But the creature also has a calling that is more than natural; it is supernatural. Natural desire for God in the human creature is not one desire among other desires anymore than God's existence is one more datum in the universe to be affirmed or denied. The natural desire for God is a desire that changes everything, reordering all other desires.

For de Lubac, and this is a crucial distinction from neo-scholastics who affirm the Aristotelian maxims noted above, nature is understood from the perspective of the supernatural and not vice versa. If the human creature is defined without reference to her or his supernatural finality, then it is not only the supernatural that will be truncated but also the natural itself. This theme also remained consistent throughout his work. He stated it forthrightly in *The Mystery of the Supernatural*: 'It is not the supernatural which is explained by nature, at least as something postulated by it: it is, on the contrary, nature which is explained in the eyes of faith by the supernatural as required for it.'[47] Supernatural finality is 'primordial'.[48]

---

43. De Lubac finds both the philosophical and mystical quest present in Thomas' understanding of the natural desire for the vision of God.
> St. Thomas merges the two points of view which we have just distinguished. The 'desire to see God' which he regards as natural to us, is certainly, at bottom mystical in character.... Nevertheless St. Thomas tries to establish its reality in a purely rational manner, starting from the effects which the intelligence desires to know in their Cause so as to know them fully.

Thomas failed to bring the two together and 'no one will succeed where he has failed'. DG, p. 150.

44. The proofs, suggest de Lubac, are intended to be imperfect because they are 'ways'. Ibid., p. 80.

45. Ibid., p. 83.

46. Hans Urs von Balthasar, *The Theology of Henri de Lubac*, trans. Joseph Fessio, S. J. and Michael M. Waldstein (San Francisco: Ignatius Press, 1991). John Milbank's defence of de Lubac's theology is thus entitled, *The Suspended Middle: Henri de Lubac and the Debate Concerning the Supernatural* (Grand Rapids, MI: William B. Eerdmans Publishing Company, 2005).

47. MS, p. 123.

48. Ibid., p. 124.

Supernatural finality is so present in human nature as it actually exists that to miss it means nothing less than to miss what it means to be human. De Lubac wrote, 'That is why, if I fail to achieve this which is my end, it may be said that I have failed in everything.'[49] Four decades later he made a similar argument in his *Brief Catechesis on Nature and Grace*. If we begin with nature and use it to explain the conditions for the supernatural, theological distortions follow. The Church begins to look too much like the world; theology becomes too secular. Philosophy becomes separate from theology altogether. The supernatural becomes naturalized.[50] Such a theological distortion would fail to recognize the mystical vision that unites nature and the supernatural, which is only found in the Incarnation. It would also fail to bring about the union of nature and grace, which 'can be fully accomplished only though the mystery of the redemption'.[51]

Attaining God through the Mediations of Church and Scripture

The primordial nature of supernatural finality implies that knowledge of God arises not from logic investigating nature but from a lifting up of our nature, a *sursum*. The taste for God occurs liturgically. De Lubac stated, 'God can never really be thought or recognized apart from a *sursum* which no proof can arouse.'[52] The natural desire for the vision of God is an innate desire that drives the human person, but it's fulfilment can only be attained through the Church. The Church is so central to de Lubac's epistemology that it can easily make his work appear triumphalistic. He unequivocally affirms, 'outside the Church there is no salvation'.[53] He is unapologetically Christian in his understanding of how our natural desire for God is fulfilled. 'Outside Christianity nothing attains its end, that only end, towards which, unknowingly, all human desires, all human endeavors, are in movement: the embrace of God in Christ.'[54] The natural desire for the vision of God cannot be naturally satisfied; only the Church satisfies it through the Word and Sacraments entrusted to it by God.

De Lubac's ecclesiology is less triumphalistic than it might at first appear. It does not mean '"outside the Church you are damned", but "it is by the Church and by the Church alone that you will be saved."'[55] The Church is not a theocratic

49. Ibid., p. 73.
50. Every notion which tends to bring down the supernatural order to the level of nature tends, by that very fact, to mistake the Church for the world, to conceive of her after the model of human societies, to expect her to change even in her essential structures and her faith in order to suit the world's changes – and this is what is taking place among a number of our contemporaries. In the past a theocratic temptation may have threatened; today, on the contrary (but because of a similar confusion, and with less excuse, given the historical context), the secularist temptation has come to the fore very strongly. BC, p. 110
51. Ibid., p. 122.
52. DG, p. 158.
53. C, p. 234.
54. Ibid., p. 224.
55. Ibid., p, 236.

political order that should be privileged to rule; nor is it one more sociological ordering that can be understood through secular means. It is the servant who takes up everything good in human culture and lifts it to God. It cannot but affirm whatever good desire is present in any culture. Unlike the neo-scholastics then, de Lubac insists that the Church does not elicit the natural desire through the sacraments; the natural desire for God infuses nature and culture because all things are made in, through and for Jesus Christ. Rather than excluding the desires of other cultures, religions, and peoples, de Lubac's theological epistemology gives them a privileged place, while it affirms the Church (the Roman Catholic Church) as the site for fully recognizing and completing those desires. As de Lubac puts it, 'All men know God "naturally," but they do not always recognize him.'[56] The Church gives form to the desire present in every culture.

The more de Lubac affirmed that outside the Church there is no salvation, the more he could also affirm God was present not only in every human intellect but also in every culture. He critiqued the Reformers for failing to be sufficiently humanist by not finding the good in paganism and preserving it.[57] The Reformers went too far; they moved beyond 'attacking abuses that were only too real' and tried to purify the Church, failing to realize that 'Christianity transformed the old world by absorbing it.' De Lubac affirmed Matteo Ricci's cultural project. 'When Ricci treated Confucius as Ambrose treated Seneca or Cyril Plato, he was on the right path.'[58] The Church's mission is not insular; it is to unite the human race by interpreting revelation and thereby drawing all good and proper human desire to its singular end. 'The human race is one... But salvation for this body, for humanity, consists in its receiving the form of Christ, and that is possible only through the Catholic Church. For is she not the only complete, authoritative interpreter of the Christian revelation?'[59] De Lubac never abandons these early themes in his work.

The natural desire for the vision of God is a starting point, not a settled conclusion. For this reason it always points beyond itself to something more, the more is a transcendent destiny that is neither extrinsic to that natural desire nor identical with it. The Church mediates the satisfaction of that desire because it too is both natural and supernatural. Church and Scripture are visible, material realities that exist in secular culture and history even as they call it beyond itself.

---

56. DG, p. 75.

57. De Lubac's understanding of the Reformers in this regard is certainly lacking. Given that the first generation of the Reformers were often accused of abandoning Scholasticism for Humanism, the story is much more complex than de Lubac indicates. For a good discussion of this point see Erika Rummel, *The Humanist-Scholastic Debate in the Renaissance and Reformation* (Cambridge, MA: Harvard University Press, 1995).

58. C, p. 290. The story of Ricci is also, of course, more complicated than de Lubac suggests. He did not affirm Confucius without at the same time disavowing much in Chinese culture. For the best treatment of Ricci see R. Po-Chi Hsia, *A Jesuit in the Forbidden City* (Oxford: Oxford University Press, 2012).

59. C, p. 223.

De Lubac emphasized the Church's social visibility and feared that the Church was too often understood as a mystical reality that prohibited the exercise of its material form.[60] His work on spiritual exegesis is the retrieval of a form of biblical interpretation that likewise assumes historical realities are properly secular while also infused with a spiritual reality that requires something more, not less, than historical critical studies. They are secular in the sense that God uses ordinary, everyday signs and infuses them with a depth that exceeds their secular intelligibility. To see that depth requires spiritual exegesis.

Any discussion of de Lubac's theological epistemology that does not include his work on spiritual exegesis fails to take into account one of the most important contributions he made to theological epistemology. Bryan C. Hollon rightly notes that interpretations of de Lubac that neglect Scripture miss something essential. 'Spiritual exegesis', he suggests, 'is not, primarily, a speculative academic exercise. Rather, it is social and political to the core since it mediates the Church's ongoing historical engagement with culture'[61] Scripture and Church work in tandem to direct natural and cultural desires to their supernatural finality. Sometimes they do so by perfecting those desires and sometimes by correcting them. Scripture presents a personal God who engages history by fashioning a people as his own. This personal God also calls into questions idols and deities made by human hands. De Lubac does not simply affirm and baptize cultures; he is too careful a biblical exegete for that.

> The God of the Bible is named: he is Yahweh, and affirms his uniqueness by raising up and forming his own people, distinct from all others, by imposing a particular legislation upon them, and through his Prophets he makes a mockery of the gods made by hands. The God of the Gospels is no less personal: he is the heavenly Father, and Christians can only look upon the gods of paganism, if they treat them as having any real existence whatsoever as demons.[62]

De Lubac's spiritual exegesis is significant for many reasons, but a crucial one is his rejection that Christian tradition teaches that there are 'two sources of faith that would have been parallel and radically distinct'.[63] He writes,

> Nobody, though, ever spoke of two 'sources' of faith that would have been parallel and radically distinct – and, whatever authors who read its texts too quickly and superficially may say of it, the Council of Trent did not do so either. It recalls, in utterly evangelical and traditional terms that Christ has commanded the Gospel

---

60. The most interesting development of de Lubac's theology among contemporary theologians can be found in the work of William Cavanaugh, especially his *Torture and Eucharist* (Malden, MA: Wiley-Blackwell, 1998).
61. Bryan C. Hollon, *Everything Is Sacred: Spiritual Exegesis in the Political Theology of Henri de Lubac* (Eugene: OR, Cascade Books, 2009), p. 104.
62. DG, p. 31.
63. ME, vol. 1, p. 25.

to be preached to every creature, inasmuch as it is the *fountainhead (fontem)* of all revealed truth.⁶⁴

He traces a shift, albeit not an opposition, in the interpretation of Scripture by the 'dialectic' that emerged with the 'new questions' that were being asked in the eleventh century which worked against the more allegorical model of Augustinianism.⁶⁵ We see in his critique of the dialecticians a similar criticism to the one he brought against neo-scholasticism. According to those of a more Augustinian persuasion, the dialecticians 'presumed to submit the mysteries of God himself or his action in the world to the laws which rule the nature of things'.⁶⁶ They produced a new conception of faith seeking reason.

In *Medieval Exegesis* de Lubac states that we should not read the dialecticians over and against the allegorists too sharply, or see in their juxtaposition a division between reason and authority on the one side and fideists and free thinkers on the other. Yet in *Corpus Mysticum* de Lubac sets Augustine and Anselm in sharp relief. Anselm's *fides quaerens intellectum*, he writes, was not only an 'innovation, we might also say [it was] a revolution'.⁶⁷ Anselm was not a rationalist, but he did produce a version of 'faith seeking understanding' that differed significantly from Augustine. Anselm was concerned with 'demonstration', whereas Augustine was more interested in contemplation. On the one hand, Anselm did not yet oppose faith and understanding in terms of the bifurcation of the supernatural from the natural, for his 'demonstration itself was the world of a reason whose guiding light is still divine'. Nonetheless, he put into motion changes that would adversely affect theology.

> Anselm's conception of reason had thus not yet been laicized. On the other hand, Anselm's approach was no longer that of Augustine: in its dialectical flavour, in its orientation towards proof, it was the herald of a new era. Anselm was in no way a rationalist – any more than Abelard would be. Nevertheless, Anselm and Abelard were the founders of 'Christian rationalism'.⁶⁸

Once theology becomes divorced from Scripture and takes on a life of its own, independent of the personal actions of God, the fourfold sense of Scripture becomes sidelined. De Lubac writes,

> In the middle of the thirteenth century, the leap is thus made. The break has taken place. 'Dialectic' and its 'questions' have won the day, and the change in methodology is found to have been accelerated by the inroads of an entirely

---

64. Ibid., p. 25.
65. Ibid., p. 62.
66. Ibid., p. 63.
67. CM, p. 237.
68. Ibid., p. 237–38.

new set of contents, that of the philosophy of Aristotle. Teaching no longer has as its framework the triple or quadruple explication of the biblical text.[69]

If Aristotle's philosophy sets the conditions for theology rather than spiritual exegesis, then the God who will be known may not be the God who speaks in Holy Scripture.

Conclusion

De Lubac never set theology against philosophy. Nor did he reject Vatican I's *Dei filius*. He resourced the legacy of nineteenth and twentieth-century Thomism with Augustine, Origen, the history of spiritual exegesis and many other voices from Christian tradition. He opposed exclusive humanism and the secularism it underwrote and sought to distance his theological epistemology from an unwilling collusion with it. His work was holistic; theological epistemology was not an independent activity separate from other theological disciplines. The neo-scholastic tendency to divide objects of knowledge into distinct realms – natural or supernatural, philosophy or theology, nature or grace, reason or faith – and parcel it out by a division of labour produced an inadequate ontology for the living God who revealed himself in creation and Scripture. Any adequate theological epistemology must attend to the living Triune God. God who is known as the beginning and end of all things is of course always at the same time the living Triune God. To divide knowledge up between the living Triune God and God as source and end was to miss God's actual economy. De Lubac witnessed to that actual economy. We approach God through a natural desire that cannot be naturally satisfied but only attained through Christ's body mediated in Word and Sacrament. That approach cannot be logically displayed through an immanent causality that masters its object as it would any other object in the world. It seeks to take the form of the *mystery* of the supernatural.

69. ME, vol. 1, p. 73.

Chapter 12

A THEOLOGY OF HISTORY

Cyril O'Regan

Strictly speaking, for de Lubac, the theology of history is coextensive with the entire breadth of theology in that in the final analysis theology is nothing less than a reflection on the history of revelation and its soteriological and ontological implications. This theological reflection, however, while it intends comprehensiveness, adamantly refuses system, since revelation is at once unanticipatable and incapable even after the fact of being comprehended without remainder.[1] Moreover, theology of this sort can, in de Lubac's view, only be carried on properly in an ecclesial spirit, which puts little value on originality, and refuses to elevate the theologian above the common believer. Such an economy-oriented theology, however, is not intended to disbar all reflection on the ultimate ontological condition or conditions of the economy. Certainly, it is true that the

1. I would like to suggest that this point is axiomatic for de Lubac and is specified through the four different genres of his writing: his specifically theological work, his exegetical work, his exercises in genealogy, and his writings on religious thinkers with which we will deal in this chapter. In the first genre I privilege *The Splendor of the Church*; *A Brief Catechesis on Nature and Grace*, trans. Richard Arnandez (San Francisco: Ignatius Press, 1984); *Catholicism: Christ and the Common Destiny of Man*, trans. Lancelot C. Sheppard and Elizabeth Englund (San Francisco: Ignatius Press, 1988); and *The Christian Faith: An Essay on the Structure of the Apostles' Creed*, trans. Richard Arnandez (San Francisco: Ignatius Press, 1986). For examples of biblical hermeneutics, see *History and Spirit: The Understanding of Scripture According to Origen*, trans. Anne Englund Nash (French) and Juvenal Merriell (Greek and Latin) (San Francisco: Ignatius Press, 2007); *Medieval Exegesis*, vol. 1 (Grand Rapids, MI: William B. Eerdmans Publishing Company, 1998); *Scripture and Tradition*, trans. Luke O'Neill (New York: Crossroads Publishing Co, 2000). In terms of genealogical texts, see *Theology in History*, trans. Anne Englund Nash (San Francisco: Ignatius Press, 1996); *The Drama of Atheist Humanism*, trans. Edith M. Riley, Anne Englund Nash, and Mark Sebanc (San Francisco: Ignatius Press, 1995); *La postérité spirituelle de Joachim de Flore*, 2 vols (Paris: Lethielleux, 1978, 81). For works on individual thinkers, see two works on Teilhard de Chardin, *The Eternal Feminine: A Study on the Poem by Teilhard de Chardin, Followed by Teilhard and the Problems of Today*, trans. René Hague (New York: Harper and Row, 1971); also *The Faith of Teilhard de Chardin and a Note on the Apologetics of Teilhard de Chardin*, trans. by René Hague (London: Burns & Oates, 1965).

economy is the indisputable source of our knowledge of the God who acts in history. Yet it is in and through those actions, constitutive of the economy, that human beings come face to face to the triune God who has loved us into existence, and who is our enduring measure and our ultimate end. God gives Godself truly to us as 'Father', 'Son', and 'Spirit' in an unbreakable unity of love. So before Benedict XVI, and perhaps even before Hans Urs von Balthasar, for de Lubac the fundamental theological proposition is 'God is Love'.[2]

Still de Lubac thinks it right that the economy should be prioritized, and he shows considerable restraint in articulating the relations and modes of relations of the intra-Trinitarian divine.[3] The focus on the economy in turn privileges the Christ event in its full measure of the incarnation, passion, death, and resurrection of Christ. Christ is the Kairos whose entrance into history orders it and provides pattern and direction.[4] Nonetheless, it is not the case that we are dealing with a realized eschatology. True, human being and the world are essentially transformed in the Christ event, and it is equally true that it is this event that gives meaning – indeed absolute meaning – to history and the world. But this meaning is a meaning that requires acceptance, and where there is the possibility of acceptance, there is also the possibility of refusal. History is the site of this yes and no.[5] De Lubac continues to be basically Augustinian in his analysis of the dramatic temper of history and also in his view of the eschaton as a transcendent act of God (SC, 16–18). No less than when he is speaking of the 'Father', 'Son', and 'Spirit' does de Lubac refuse to speak to the person of Christ or pledge anything other than fealty to the Chalcedonian doctrine of one person and two natures. In his view Chalcedon adequately captures the faith of the Christian community in the uniqueness of the figure who saved human beings from death, forgave sin, and healed human beings' alienation from God. Of course, this Christological doctrine, as with the doctrine of Nicaea, is not intended to be an explanation in the strict sense. Doctrines can be no more than the most adequate vehicles of the Christian community's faith in Christ and the God of Jesus Christ.

It is not simply the case that with Christ and the triune God we experience an epistemic limit beyond which our minds cannot go:[6] it is rather that the triune

---

2. For this point, see CF, p. 13; SC, pp. 55–56; BC, p. 41; TH, p. 454.

3. See de Lubac's powerful chapter in CF on the economic Trinity (pp. 85–131), in which he sticks to the economy while insisting that the economic Trinity has ontological import. He does not proceed, however, to articulate the intra-divine conditions of the economy. In this he differs considerably from his most famous pupil Hans Urs von Balthasar and is perhaps closer to the theology of Walter Kasper.

4. This is a point made repeatedly by de Lubac. Cf. SC, pp. 55–56.

5. Once again SC provides evidence of this point (p. 42). De Lubac gives the point real dimension, however, when he recalls Pascal's Augustinian point about the Church being in agony until the end of the world (p. 297). Needless to say, de Lubac cannot be understood to endorse Pascal's Jansenist commitment to the unreality of human freedom. In the end, however, de Lubac is through and through Ignatian. In history human beings decide which banner they follow, that of Christ or the anti-Christ (p. 278).

6. SC, pp. 24–25, 32–34; BC, pp. 65–66.

God and the person of Christ give themselves to us as so superabundantly rich that they encourage both the surrender of language into silent contemplation and symbolic proliferation. From text to text de Lubac can emphasize either. For example, with regard to Christ he often emphasizes how Christ provokes symbolic proliferation. For de Lubac, the Christian tradition is of one voice about the excessive reality upon which concepts and symbols break and the plurality of perspectives with their different emphases that are called forth by Christ as *mysterion* who alone provides the point of their integration.[7] As always in de Lubac, Augustine makes an important contribution, since he can speak to both sides of this complex response of restraint and ecstatic speech, and it is in him also that one finds the Christological bases for the plurality of expressions regarding Christ that otherwise might be thought to introduce fragmentation.[8]

In a truly comprehensive and thus proper treatment of de Lubac's theology of history, his theology of revelation, his Christology, and his view of tradition as reception of mystery would justifiably receive more extensive treatment than I am going to provide here. Each is an integral element of a full analysis of the triune God's gift of self in history. Such, however, would tax a single volume not to mention an article. What I intend to deal with here, however, are de Lubac's view of the Church as simultaneously within and beyond history, and theology of history in the narrow sense of a configuration of revelation which, despite or because of the incarnation, is eschatological through and through, and to gesture to their integration. It is not stretching matters to claim that this integration is fundamentally Augustinian and depends in crucial ways on de Lubac's agreement with *The City of God*'s account of the Church, even if it exceeds it in interesting ways.

Church and Its Eschatological Register

I begin with de Lubac's articulation of the nature and function of the Church, which proved decisive for the articulation of the documents on the Church at Vatican II and especially *Lumen Gentium*. I will briefly discuss in turn de Lubac's interpretation of the Church as mystery, his Augustinian view of the Church as a *corpus permixtum*, and the ways in which inadvertently, desperately, or both, the Church cedes to views which are either intrinsically secular or are capable of secular absorption. I will conclude with a brief reflection on de Lubac's view of the Church as both an event in history and as fundamentally coextensive with and also exceeding it.

---

7. For an implied positive view of the term *mysterion*, see BC, p. 10.
8. Here as elsewhere in de Lubac's oeuvre Augustine is in line with the witness of the entire patristic tradition, and his own articulation of the effect of the mystery of Christ is anticipated in his French predecessors Maurice Blondel and Pierre Rousselot, as well as the reflections of the Tübingen School in general, and Möhler in particular.

Arguably, the *locus classicus* for de Lubac's treatment of the Church as mystery is to be found in chapter 1 of *The Splendor of the Church*.[9] There de Lubac argues that if the Church is the extension of Christ until the eschaton, it follows that, as it shares in the mystery of Christ, in the final analysis the Church too is characterized by mystery. This means, on the one hand, that the Church is not subject without remainder to the categories of sociology (SC, 54; also 48, 101).[10] This is an apologetic move, which insists on a difference between the Church and all other social bodies, something which in the modern world is increasingly refused and deemed to be the worst kind of special pleading. On the other hand, it is not simply the case that the Church is mysterious because it falls outside the categories of the empirical sciences. Rather it is mysterious – here de Lubac is in sync with Louis Bouyer[11] – in the Greek patristic sense of *mysterion*, which originally denoted sacrament. The Church is the sign of the saving action of Christ in the world in general and especially in the sacraments. Needless to say, for de Lubac, the eucharist is the pivotal sacrament, and its communication of this gift is the Church's most fundamental responsibility. But it is also the case that for de Lubac the eucharist is constitutive of the Church (SP, 130–32). There is then a double order: the Church gives the eucharist (CF, 218); it is the eucharist which gives the Church. It is precisely because the Church is the sacrament of Christ that it is the light of the world (SP, 45; CF, 173, 196).[12] This image in due course becomes central in *Lumen Gentium*. In de Lubac's case the image is both biblical and traditional, at once essentially Johannine and an image prominent in Augustine, Pseudo-Dionysius, Aquinas, and Bonaventure. As such it is a theological image in the strict sense, rather than being a juridical or empirical image. It is not a juridical image in that de Lubac is not insisting that the special status of the Church be accepted on authority, which is a point routinely made in neo-scholastic theology; he is rather asking that its specialness be seen. One can characterize de Lubac's fundamental point as aesthetic in that it not only supposes the splendour of the Church but also for precisely this reason its power of attraction. Of course, the splendour of the Church is not her own; it belongs to Christ.

For de Lubac the Church is the light of the world to the extent to which it is, in line with Louis Bouyer and the French School,[13] the school of saints. Still if the Church is the Church of saints (SC, 116), it is equally the school

---

9. See especially SC, pp. 51–83. See also CPM, chs. 1 and 2.

10. De Lubac inveighs against the totalitarian claims of the social sciences (BC, p. 145; also p. 112), and thereby sets the terms for Pope John Paul II in *Fides et Ratio* and also Cardinal Joseph Ratzinger throughout his career.

11. See Bouyer's classic discussion of *mysterion* in 'Mysticism: An Essay in the History of the Word', in *Understanding Mysticism*, ed. Richard Woods (New York: Doubleday, 1980), pp. 42–53.

12. See also C, pp. 88–92. Of course, this point is central to *Corpus Mysticum*.

13. Bouyer is very influenced by the French School of Berulle and Olier. Note de Lubac's citing of Olier: 'If the Church is thus the fullness of Christ, Christ in his eucharist is truly heart of the Church' (SC, p. 161).

of sinners. De Lubac is keenly aware of the fact that the Church throughout history has consistently pointed to itself rather than away from itself to Christ (SC, 66, 76–81). Accordingly, it is guilty of idolatry and,[14] given its involution, on Augustinian grounds, the Church can be presumed to be guilty of sin.[15] For de Lubac the presumption is borne out throughout the history of the Church. In his diagnosis of the constitutive ills of modernity and rehearsal of possible cures in *The Drama of Atheist Humanism*, de Lubac argues trenchantly that neither human being, human reason, nor instinct provide the answer to modern enervation, anomie, and meaninglessness. His answer is the one given by Dostoevsky, the figure of Christ who makes love and humility powerfully luminous and who heals the alienation within and between persons and between persons and God. De Lubac also proscribes immanentist political solutions for what he judges to be spiritual malaise (DAH, 322). According to de Lubac, these would-be solutions can be vehemently secular and totalitarian.[16] But the temptation is also there for the institutional Church to increase its power and to substitute coercion for persuasion.[17] The possibility of confounding the immanent and the transcendent kingdom, however, is basically universal. Ecclesial communities, which experience great powerlessness rather than power, are equally tempted to an intra-mundane solution which substitutes rectification and liberation for salvation which although holistic exceeds history and the world.[18]

The perception of the sinfulness of the Church never leaves de Lubac. This is illustrated well in a post-Vatican II text such as *The Christian Faith*, which worries about power (CF, 181) taking the place of service,[19] which is not only the obligation of the Church, but its very definition. Perhaps more fundamental than everything else is de Lubac's commitment to the biblical and patristic view of the universality of original sin. The very fact that the Church is a post-lapsarian reality necessarily implicates it in sin, just as its constitution in and through Christ's saving act and its inherence in Christ and its inspiration by the Spirit make it immaculate.

---

14. On the Church as guilty of idolatry: cf. BC, p. 225.

15. On the Church as guilty of sin: cf. SC, pp. 89, 113, 282.

16. See SC, p. 173. SC echoes the fully articulated condemnation of Marxism enacted in DAH, pp. 36–42. See especially de Lubac's accusation that Marx has confounded the kingdom of God with the kingdom of man (DAH, pp. 435–37).

17. One can read an intimation of this in de Lubac's reference to the Grand Inquisitor. While he does not deny the historical reference to the Catholic Church, de Lubac believes that in the legend of the Grand Inquisitor Dostoevsky provides us with a spiritual truth that is not exhausted by any particular manifestation in history. In this and in other respects de Lubac interprets Dostoevsky to be articulating a form of Christian apocalyptic which deals with a cultural crisis of the questionability of Christianity and the default (naturalism) and experimental (utopian) alternatives (DAH, p. 322). At points de Lubac expressly connects Dostoevsky's literary opus with the book of Revelation which, he believes, offers a template for Dostoevsky both in terms of what can be said and not said (DAH, pp. 387–91).

18. Thus de Lubac's reservations – no more – about certain forms of Liberation theology. See BC pp. 112–15; also pp. 157–66.

19. See also de Lubac's interesting discussions of witness/martyrdom in SC, p. 191.

Although de Lubac depends on no particular theologian to provide him with this complex bifocal view of the Church, and indeed considers it the teaching of the universal Church, here as elsewhere Augustine seems to be to the fore in terms of the inflection of the Church's paradoxical nature (SC, 89, 113, 289). For de Lubac the Church is also inescapably hierarchical (SC, 121, 133). In this respect it is not a democratic society, nor should it be judged by it. De Lubac enters two hugely important caveats about hierarchy in the Church: first, hierarchy in the Church is more an order of service than power and, second, all distinctions in the Church are of function rather than of kind. Both before and after Vatican II de Lubac resolutely refuses a distinction between lesser Christians (*minores*) and greater Christians (*majors*), and/or between those taught and those teaching. For him elitism in Catholicism is tantamount to Gnosticism.[20] There is one, holy, Catholic and apostolic Church, and instruction in the community goes both ways; the would-be lesser Christians can prove inspiring examples to Christians who have more nearly intellectually appropriated their faith, and those who instruct can in turn be taught by those who are instructed.

Given the primarily pastoral nature of his theology, de Lubac is considerably less exercised by doctrinal error than was the wont in neo-scholasticism, which insisted on formal correctness. If doctrine is crucial for de Lubac, it is because doctrine is a reliable translation of the implicit faith of the Church. Failure on the level of doctrine, and/or systemic failure on the level of theological reflection, is dangerous not only because it corrupts the faith but also because in the modern period it contributes either to modern secularization or barbarism or both. Here I highlight two failures of particular moment for de Lubac. The first is de Lubac's well-known stance on the relationship between nature and grace; the second has to do with his exploration of the relation between the old and new covenants against the all too real backdrop of the holocaust.

Throughout a number of texts, de Lubac addressed the issue of the proper relation between nature and grace.[21] He presumed that the right understanding of the relation between nature and grace was constitutive of Christian self-understanding. If Christians fail to understand the currents of grace cascading in the world through the incarnation and the activity of the Spirit, and construct a two-story universe of nature and supernature,[22] with the former superadded to the putative autonomous functioning of the latter, they do much more than commit a theological error. By dint of an absolute segregation

---

20. The connection of elitism with Gnosticism occurs throughout de Lubac's work. Cf. TH, pp. 461–62.

21. The text that we have privileged in this essay *A Brief Catechesis on Nature and Grace*, which is a late reflection on a position that had been articulated as early as the Second World War. See de Lubac, *Surnaturel: études historiques* (Paris: Éditions Desclée de Brouwer, 1991); *The Mystery of the Supernatural*, trans. Rosemary Sheed. Intro. by David L. Schindler (New York: The Crossroad Publishing Company, 1998); *Augustinianism and Modern Theology*, trans. Lancelot Sheppard; Intro. by Louis Dupré (New York: Crossroad Publishing Company, 2000).

22. See especially BC, pp. 9–55.

they aid the secularist cause by ceding the natural and social worlds to them. Essentially, neo-scholasticism makes Christianity an *adiaphora*, nothing more than a fideistic extra both to the main business of life and to thinking largely defined in instrumental terms.[23] De Lubac contested all aspects of a view that was proposed as apodictically true. Specifically, he challenged the claim that Vatican I supported the two-story view, as well as argued against the neo-scholastic claim that this view was that of Aquinas. Combating this claim made retrieval of the historical Aquinas in principle every bit as necessary as the retrieval of Origen and Augustine. Although he was convinced that Aquinas was being well served by Chenu among others, he saw his task as more nearly genealogical and thus complementary to the renaissance in the retrieval of Aquinas. More specifically, he thought he could and should tell the story of how the consensus Christian view, which received a sophisticated articulation in the texts of Aquinas, gradually unravelled and in the end authorized the very naturalism it would avoid. De Lubac influentially produced an essentially three-stage story of derailment which began with Thomas Cajetan's (1468–1534) notion of *natura pura* (NG, 24–25),[24] proceeded through Francisco Suarez's (1548–1617) wrongheaded interpretation of Aquinas in the Baroque period and culminated in the reactionary neo-scholasticism of the late nineteenth and twentieth centuries.[25] Whatever the simplifications of the genealogical narrative, and whatever the failures to engage neo-scholasticism on its own terms,[26] de Lubac certainly did not fail to offer a compelling account of a fall in which what is lost is an integral vision of Christian thought, praxis, and life.

23. Reginald Garrigou-Lagrange was the most able proponent.

24. The main discussion of 'pure nature' is to be found in the Appendix 1 'The "Supernatural" at Vatican II', pp. 177–90, especially p. 185 where he refers to his early works *Augustinisme et théologie moderne* (Paris: Aubier-Montaigne, 1965) and *Le mystère du surnaturel* (Paris: Aubier, 1965). This is a story that has influenced Radical Orthodoxy. See Milbank's book on de Lubac, *The Suspended Middle*, 2nd ed. (Grand Rapids, MI: William B. Eerdmans, 2014). Of course, since the genealogy of the separation of nature and grace is not central to my theme and is treated elsewhere in this book, I will not go into the complications of de Lubac's genealogy. For instance, Denys the Carthusian precedes Cajetan in separating nature from grace, although he, unlike Cajetan, understands that he has not faithfully represented Aquinas' own position.

25. This is a complex story and has been told by those sympathetic with the nouvelle théologie and those who are not. In whatever story is told the encyclical, *Aeterni Patris* (1879) by Pope Leo XIII, which insisted that Aquinas' thought both sums up and anticipates future Christian thought is central.

26. De Lubac's reading of neo-scholastics such as Cajetan, Suarez, as well as neo-scholastics of his day, such as Garrigou-Lagrange, has been challenge in recent years by Lawrence Feingold and Steven A. Long. For Feingold, see *The Natural Desire to See God According to St. Thomas and His Interpreters* (Washington, DC: CUA Press, 2004); for Long, see *Natura Pura: On the Recovery of Nature in the Doctrine of Grace* (New York: Fordham University Press, 2010). John Milbank mounts a spirited defence of de Lubac's view of the nature-grace relation as well as his reading of neo-scholasticism in *The Suspended Middle: Henri de Lubac and the Debate Concerning the Supernatural* (London: SCM Press, 2005).

Another constitutive theological disorder in the modern period with which the Church has to deal both outside and inside its walls is Marcionism. This is summed up pithily in *The Splendor of the Church*. 'It is an opposition of Jew and Gentile, which is the symbol of all oppositions' (SC, 177). Again, for de Lubac, the Marcionism critiqued by Tertullian and Irenaeus is by no means merely of antiquarian interest. De Lubac is convinced that it is not the canon, but more nearly the separating out of the kerygma from the supposedly Jewish husk of law and ritual that is responsible for nineteenth- and twentieth-century anti-Semitism. De Lubac makes his case in a number of essays, written during and after the Second World War, which are gathered together in part four of *Theology in History*. De Lubac unmasks the unsavoury forms of French and German anti-Semitism but also attacks anti-Semitism's distinguished history in German philosophy from Hegel through Schopenhauer to Nietzsche (TH, 459–62; also 481–82). Denying the intrinsic relation between Christianity and Judaism as given in the Bible clears the way for the ideological monstrosities of a completely Semitic Hebrew scripture and an Aryan New Testament (TH, 486). De Lubac recognizes that such distortions are rhetorically facilitated – although not justified – by a dialectical or Law/Gospel reading of Paul (TH, 429). Against this contemporary cultural and societal calamity, as well as the historical calamity of Jewish-Christian relations, de Lubac insists that the Gospel is the full blossoming of the Bible (TH, 446). Having made what he takes to be an important claim, de Lubac proceeds to write: 'The God of Jesus is the God of the prophets, who concludes by revealing himself. Jesus does not come to reject but to carry out the message of which the people of Israel were the bearer' (TH, 447). For de Lubac, who identified himself above all as an ecclesiologist, this means that the people of Israel are a constituent element of the 'people of God', which is the way that de Lubac commonly identifies the Church well before Vatican II.[27]

As a finite and sinful reality, no more than with regard to any other social body can a Catholic responsibly claim that the Church is the eschatological reality. Not only would such a claim run counter to the empirical experience of the Church as morally flawed, spiritually enervated, and prone to blind spots, it would also run counter to a properly theological understanding of the Church as having only interim status and always being on its way. Throughout *The Splendor of the Church* de Lubac underscores the interim status of the Church (SC, 67), which gives way in the eschaton to the community of saints that no longer requires its mediation of grace (SC, 76–81).[28] The peregrination form of the Church[29] – the Church militant – is obviously linked to the interim status of the Church (SC, 119), while being at the same time analytically separable from it. The Church is always historical, and

---

27. SC provides a good example. See pp. 62, 66, 107, 149, 209. See also de Lubac's discussion of 'people of God' in his chapter on *Lumen Gentium* in CPM, ch. 3, pp. 39–47.

28. It is interesting that these pages involve a reflection on the book of Revelation. The fundamental motif is that of the Heavenly Jerusalem. The modality of this reflection is Augustinian through and through.

29. De Lubac shows his approval of this aspect of Lumen Gentium in CPM, pp. 47–54.

it is at its best when it considers itself as the site of a divinely willed pedagogy. It is true that in terms of the fundamentals, divine pedagogy is closed (SC, 205–9).[30] But the history of the reception of the fundamentals is itself a pedagogical process which is grounded on the revelation of God in Christ and enacted in history through non-competitive agencies of the Holy Spirit and human beings. If de Lubac finds grounds for the first form of pedagogy in both Irenaeus and Origen, perhaps it is the latter who inspires him most with regard to the second.[31] The Church is necessarily always on the way and the realization of what it is for – which paradoxically is its dissolution[32] – does not lie in it, but rather in the triune God. De Lubac feels as comfortable as the Tübingen School in applying organic metaphors to the Church. Importantly, however, while the Church is dynamically oriented towards the future, it is not progressively teleological in the way that an acorn will in due course yield an oak. This too is a Tübingen insight as Möhler, Drey, and Staudenmaier were forced to distinguish the specifically Catholic form of organic,[33] which sets limits to the implied teleology, from its idealist simulacrum. There is the intra-mundane, intra-historical future of the Church and then there is the absolute future of the Church. The temporal future of the Church never rises above history and its chiaroscuro. The Church can never escape the pull of the forces of sin, nor the blandishments that would make it complacently forget its nature and its mission to the world. The absolute future of the Church is the triune God who is the Lord of history and its loving judge.[34] Once again in terms of the theological tradition, de Lubac's view is classical. As it is so, it is also particularly Augustinian, since the 'end' of the Church is the condition of the kingdom in that it gives way to it. But there is also something of an Origenist tincture:[35] the judge is the God of love who loved us utterly into existence, redeemed us on the cross, and accompanied the Church on its long, curving, and interrupted path towards holiness.

In his voluminous laying out of the historical forms of interpretation of the biblical text, it is axiomatic for de Lubac not only that the New Testament represents an exegesis of the Old Testament but also that Scripture in its entirety is a commentary on salvation history that finds its point of maximal concentration in the incarnation and cross of Christ.[36] In a sense Christ enfolds all of history. But again precisely because of this, the same can be said of his

---

30. De Lubac includes here numerous patristic quotations; Augustine is particularly well represented.

31. De Lubac's magisterial *Histoire et Esprit* establishes Origen as the other master patristic theologian besides Augustine.

32. This is a recurring point in de Lubac's work and is laid down as early as *Catholicisme*.

33. For de Lubac the Tübingen theologian is always Möhler.

34. SC, p. 123.

35. This combination of Augustine and Origen or the refusal to harden a contrast into opposition is repeated in Balthasar's works, especially when it comes to the depiction of the triune God and also eschatology.

36. Peter Casarella brings this point out especially well in his useful introduction to *Scripture in the Tradition* (New York: Crossroad, 2000), pp. xi–xxii.

Church. It is true that the Church is in some fundamental respects an event in history in which a group of apostles bear witness to the crucified one.[37] It is equally true, however, that the Church, as the people of God, is inclusive of all of history. This is a point that de Lubac makes in *Catholicism* and which he seems to reinforce throughout his career, and especially in his copious writings on Teilhard de Chardin.[38] Importantly, de Lubac is saying more than that Jews and Christian belong to one history of salvation. This is affirmed, but he also suggests the probity of the figure of Noah's ark and the tree of life in paradise which seems to map the Church with entire humanity making its way through history towards an end that will exceed it. For de Lubac the Church has the plenary form of planned obsolescence built into grace. The Church gives way eschatologically to the unanticipatable enjoyment of the presence of the triune God who transcends history while having entered into it. Only in the eschaton, which is an act of the transcendent Lord of history, is there the full seeing of the length, breadth, and height of the triune God. Only in the eschaton is there the realization of peace and communion. As with Ratzinger who learned so much from him,[39] de Lubac's envisaging of the eschatological state is through and through Augustinian.[40]

Eschatological History and Its Ecclesial Register

Here I examine de Lubac's ecclesially indexed eschatology, which is the complement of his eschatologically indexed ecclesiology examined in Part 1 of this book. Our discussion focuses on a number of interrelated aspects of de Lubac's eschatological reflection, including his opposition to modern secular eschatologies, the essentially Augustinian eschatological model on the basis of which he critiques these eschatologies, his genealogical account of the trajectory of the eschatology of Joachim de Fiore in the modern period, the recycling of secular theologies back into contemporary theology, and finally both the ecclesial and cosmic dimensions of what is essentially an Augustinian eschatology. Similar to Part 1, our textual span is rather wide. What distinguishes Part 2, however, is our focus on a later text of de Lubac, that is, his two-volume genealogical classic, *La postérité spirituelle de Joachim de Fiore* (1979, 1981).

The twentieth-century experiment with Marxism in general, and the enormous intellectual influence of Marxism is post–Second World War France in particular, did not allow de Lubac the luxury of avoiding critical

---

37. In terms of particularity de Lubac has no problem tracing the 'mystical' origin of the Church to the blood flowing from wound on Jesus' side. See SC, p. 54 for a good example.

38. See C, pp. 184–86. For de Lubac's emphasis on these dimensions of de Teilhard's thought, see *The Eternal Feminine: A Study on the Poem by Teilhard de Chardin* (New York: Harper & Row, 1971), pp. 136, 182–83.

39. See Ratzinger, *Eschatlologie: Tod und ewiges Leben* (Regensburg: Pustet, 1978).

40. This is not to deny the equal influence of Origen. Rudolf Voderholzer makes this point well. See his *Meet Henri de Lubac: His Life and Work*, trans. Michael J. Miller (San Francisco: Ignatius, 2008), pp. 207–10.

engagement. De Lubac was not the only French Catholic thinker assessing the phenomenon. There were a number of others, including his fellow Jesuit, the gifted philosopher Gaston Fessard, who had been so important in French resistance to Nazism.[41] Fessard was disturbed by the emergence of Marxism as a kind of default in French high culture in the post-war period, and, similar to de Lubac, attempted a critical engagement which would issue in a theology of history.[42] De Lubac's contribution was his diagnosis that Marxism's attraction lay in its eschatological humanism or humanistic eschatology,[43] which projected the end of alienation within individual human beings and reconciliation between human groups in history. De Lubac took one of the two major sides in the conflict of interpretation about Marxist eschatology. For him it represented a secularization of biblical eschatology rather than an intellectual construction that was in essence a *novum*. Convinced that a Marxist eschatology meant the end of any sustainable notion of transcendence, de Lubac also understood how the Church's lack of conviction, loss of moral and intellectual substance, but above all its imaginative failure, specifically its failure to communicate a vision of the meaning of individual and communal life, provided conditions for its replacement. Here one can clearly see how de Lubac's return to the sources is the complement of his critique of Marxism and other ideologies that come to fill the void created by Christianity in intellectual and public space.

In *The Drama of Atheist Humanism* de Lubac unveils Marxism as a kind of spurious humanism fated to lessen rather than expand the individual human being and her freedom by keeping her within the circle of immanence, and equally fated to destroy the prospect of an authentic community.[44] During this period de Lubac also shows more than a passing interest in non-Marxist ideologies such as those of the positivist Comte and the socialist Proudhon. De Lubac publishes an appreciative book on Proudhon during the same period he writes this famous book on atheism. In it, while he exposes the fervid anti-clericalism of Proudhon, he commends his commitment to justice which has he believes deep – if not fully recognized – roots in the Christian tradition.[45] Comte is a figure who exercised de Lubac greatly in *The Drama of Atheist Humanism*.[46] It would be easy to dismiss

---

41. Fessard and de Lubac were both editors of the anti-Nazi periodical *Cahiers du Témoignage chrétien*.

42. Fessard's forays into articulating a theology of history came to fruition with the publication of *De L'actualité historique* (Paris: Desclée, 1960). The first volume, however, gathered together with new material essays that had been written at the beginning and end of the war. De Lubac had to be aware of these essays.

43. This is not to say, however, that with respect to such a diagnosis he was not also influenced by Fessard.

44. DAH, pp. 36–42, 60–61. Reading Marx as a humanist means among other things reading him as continuing Feuerbach's humanist project by other means. See DAH, pp. 26–35. One finds a similar reading of Marx in *Catholicisme*.

45. The book on Proudhon was written in 1945. The English translation appeared in 1948 as *The Un-Marxian Socialist: A Study of Proudhon*, trans. R. E. Scantlebury (New York: Sheed and Ward, 1948).

46. DAH, pp. 131–267.

de Lubac's treatment of the positivist as itself an exercise in French chauvinism; surely he is dwarfed intellectually by Marx and also by a thinker such as Nietzsche who gave courage to European anti-Semitism?[47] While it is true that de Lubac thinks more highly of Comte than non-French historians of modern European thought, the reason why Comte is important to him is that he offers not only ideological support to the prestige of science and technology in the modern world but also provides an imaginative supplement by telling the story with almost apostolic fervour of the progression of science and the consequent improvement in social mores. Comte is so compelling because he makes a mysticism of science and religiously valorizes its utopian aims. Comte suggests to de Lubac that even should the imaginative appeal of Marxist eschatology fail, there is another eschatological form that could readily take its place.[48]

We noted already how in *The Drama* Dostoevsky is proposed as an alternative to modern secular eschatologies. Surely one legitimate use of Dostoevsky is to avail of him as giving the critical measure between an authentic Christian eschatology and its secularist expressions and secular substitutions. In his wholehearted embrace of the Russian novelist, de Lubac is in excess of Hans Urs von Balthasar who in his *Apokalypse* raised the question whether Dostoevsky's pan-Slavism illustrated another kind of immanent eschatological substitution for a transcendent reality.[49] The kind of appeal to Dostoevsky made by de Lubac was in fact repeated by one of his favourite French writers, Paul Claudel. Perhaps even more than was the case in Balthasar, de Lubac regarded Claudel not only as a great religious poet but also as a Catholic polymath who not only could render what a truly Catholic form of Christianity would look like but also had the learning and intellectual wherewithal to challenge modern ideologies. For Claudel the continuing relevance of the book of Revelation lies in its symbolic power which enables it to read the ideological ferment of the nineteenth and twentieth centuries.[50] For all three thinkers, however, the great modern temptation is to confound the kingdom of God with the kingdom of man. This confusion is of such profound import to de Lubac that it is only with the slightest

---

47. Nietzsche is a figure who is constantly engaged throughout DAH. He is linked with Feuerbach (ch. 1) and Kierkegaard (ch. 2), respectively, in part one, with Dostoevsky in part three (ch. 1), and has a chapter on Nietzsche's mysticism. This chapter was not in the 1944 addition and was added subsequently.

48. Comte may only be a French flavour, but de Lubac's point was that his influence was pervasive enough to have become almost second nature to French intellectuals. He fingered in particular Charles Mauras and *Action française*.

49. Hans urs von Balthasar, *Apokalypse der deutschen Seele. Studien zu einer Lehre von letzten Haltungen*, vols 1–3 (Salzburg: Verlag Anton Pustet, 1937–1939). In volume 2, *Im Zeichen Nietzsches*, pp. 202–312, Balthasar lays down a pattern for de Lubac by treating Dostoevsky and Nietzsche together. For Dostoevsky's panslavism, see *Apokalypse*, vol. 2, pp. 248–51.

50. Paul Claudel, *Interroge L'Apocalypse* (Paris: Gallimard, 1952). If one were to pick out the two most important events of the modern world that comes in for condemnation, it would be the ideologies of the French and the Bolshevik revolutions, respectively.

exaggeration that one can say that it marks all of his post-Vatican II work,[51] and crucially influences at least the work of both Hans Urs von Bathasar and Cardinal Joseph Ratzinger.[52] The distinction, of course, has its foundation in the Gospels and is deepened in the book of Revelation as a kind of book of martyrs. Yet, perhaps more than anything else the distinction is indemnified in *The City of God*, which in some significant respects can be read as a commentary on the book of Revelation.[53] In his opposition to secular eschatologies, this text is never far from de Lubac's mind.

La postérité spirituelle de Joachim de Flore was written in the post-Vatican II period. The level of its achievement impressed Balthasar so much that he thought of it as de Lubac's masterwork.[54] This is a compliment, indeed, when one thinks that the text beaten out by this extraordinarily erudite genealogy is de Lubac's four-volume *L'Éxégèse médiévale*.[55] The compliment may be in equal parts due to the fact that when the book came out in the 1970s, Balthasar is writing *Theodramatik*, one of whose central purposes is tracking the sources of the Hegelian ideas which enjoy such prestige in contemporary theology. It is also true that long before de Lubac in a number of essays,[56] Balthasar had suggested the return of Joachimism in contemporary theology. And, arguably, in his three-volume analysis of apocalypse in the late 1930s, Balthasar offers a description of German high culture which in its emphasis on eschatological temper is analogous at least to the explosion of Joachimism in the medieval period. Still, whatever the background motivations, Bathasar's judgement on the merits of de Lubac's two-volume genealogical text should not be viewed as eccentric. In the range and depth of its genealogy of eschatologically inflected modern discourses *La postérité* exceeds anything produced by Balthasar or any other twentieth-century religious thinker. Over its two volumes it charts a line of influence from

---

51. For a representative example of de Lubac's continuing to be exercised by this confusion, see BC, Appendix 2, 'The Sacrament of the World', pp. 191–234, which is essentially a critique of Schillebeeckx's appropriation of Vatican II. See especially, BC, pp. 222–23, 228, 234.

52. As Balthasar's *Apokalypse* suggests, he had come to this conclusion early on in his career. Still his work in the 1970s owes much to de Lubac. This is even more true of the work of Ratzinger. This distinction is keynoted in the encyclical *Spe Salvi* (2007) by Benedict XVI.

53. Especially books 20–22 of Augustine, *The City of God*, ed. Boniface Ramsey (New York: New City Press, 2012).

54. Hans Urs von Balthasar, *The Theology of Henri de Lubac: An Overview* (San Francisco: Ignatius 1991), pp. 124–26.

55. See *L'Éxégèse médiévale: les quatre sens de l'Écriture*, 4 vols (Paris: Aubier-Montaigne, 1959–1964). Perhaps it is worth pointing out that de Lubac himself considered *La postérité* to be a successor volume to *L'Éxégèse médiévale*.

56. See especially Balthasar's essay 'Improvisations on Spirit and Future', in *Explorations in Theology*. vol. 3. *Creator Spirit*, trans. Brian McNeil, C. R. V (San Francisco: Ignatius, 1991), pp. 135–71. The German volume was published twenty-four years earlier as *Skizzen zur Theologie*. vol. 3, *Creator Spiritus* (Einsiedeln: Johannes Verlag, 1967).

the apocalyptic thought of Joachim de Fiore to contemporary Marxism and contemporary theology. The genre is not that of the history of ideas in which there is a disinterested observation of the transmissions of concepts and symbols. The purpose of the text is resolutely apologetic. For de Lubac, an exacerbated pneumatism and a breathless eschatologism characterize the modern cultural environment, which the Church in turn is in the process of internalizing. The result is the legitimation of disrespect for the authority of the Church, the concomitant relegation of Christ in favour of the Spirit as a free radical, and a nonchalant disregarding of the magisterial tradition and even the theological tradition with both regarded as passé. The genius of de Lubac's text is the deftness with which he shows how the seeds for the most imaginative secular eschatologies are sown in and by the Christian tradition, and specifically the minority Christian tradition which flows from the apocalyptic thought of Joachim de Fiore. In effect de Lubac is arguing that despite the defeat of Joachimism by a more orthodox eschatology with its largely Augustinian frame,[57] Joachimism makes its way into modernity first along a religious track, then a secular track, until ultimately in the twentieth century by a secular and religious blend.

Before *La postérité* de Lubac had commented on the dangers of Joachim's particular mode of exegesis. In *The Four Senses of Scripture*, while praising Joachim's ability to see beyond the literal sense, de Lubac worried about how the mystical or anagogic sense referred to some future condition of human beings rather than the eschatological in the strictest, non-temporal sense.[58] For de Lubac it is a fundamental objection also that the text that is exploited is the book of Revelation, which on his Augustinian view is ultimately a book about the eternal kingdom as that kingdom is intimated in the travails of history. Together with Joachim's suggestion of an eternal Gospel and the rule of the Spirit, de Lubac worried that Joachim's interpretation evinced a fundamental derailment of mainline Christianity.[59] Even if *La postérité* repeats these earlier objections, it also sharpens them. Biblical revelation is relativized, as is the Church, and even Christ, as the Spirit is granted significant autonomy in the periodization of the three persons of the Trinity. De Lubac is not unsympathetic to the motive of the Spirit as providing a critical idiom regarding the institutional Church which is ever in need of reform, and in this sense he is close to Congar.[60] But outright

---

57. For Aquinas and Bonventure's criticism of Joachim, see de Lubac, *La postérité spirituelle de Joachim de Fiore*, vol. 1 (Namur: Culture et Vérité, 1979–81), pp. 123–60. That de Lubac's presentation of these criticisms are essentially accurate is confirmed by Bernard McGinn. See his *The Calabrian Abbot: Joachim de Fiore in the History of Western Thought* (New York: Macmillan, 1985), pp. 209–24.

58. For de Lubac's treatment of Joachim's anagogic-futural exegesis of the biblical text, see Exégèse médiévale, v. 1, pp. 437–558.

59. At the very least, Aquinas and Bonaventure had some reason to worry.

60. One could read the explorations on the Spirit of de Lubac and Yves Congar as complementary, with de Lubac largely focusing on where pneumatology goes wrong and Congar articulating where it goes right in the theological tradition which is under obligation

periodization of the economy and the privilege accorded the Spirit signifies for him a major break with the theological tradition. The characterization of the noetic and existential qualities enjoyed by the community of the Spirit, specifically the fullness of intellect and genuine freedom, absent in the ages of the Father and Son, in turn exacerbates the separation. De Lubac does not believe that his reading of Joachim is in any way tendentious, even if he admits that in Joachim's interpretation of Revelation and his concordance of Old and New Testament one finds material that qualifies the more revolutionary notes struck in his texts. He admits then to orthodox reserves in Joachim's actual texts, and thus would essentially agree with his critics that he has not produced a truly balanced historical portrait.[61] But such a portrait is not precisely the aim of his text. It is sufficient for his interpretation to trace a radical eschatological *Tendenz* in Joachim, even if more traditional forms of exegesis and more nearly orthodox interpretations of the economy also are represented. His real concern, as the very title of the book suggests, is less the pure historical Joachim than the history of effects (*Wirkungsgeschichte*) of Joachim. From his perspective, one can concede that Joachim is not univocally radical, but simply point to the fact that he was read in such a fashion fairly shortly in the Spiritual Franciscans, and ideas that went under the banner of his name were precisely the ones that challenged orthodoxy.[62]

Only the basic outline of de Lubac's grand narrative can be produced here. From the Spiritual Franciscans de Lubac draws a line to Luther and the Reformation in which Joachim is assimilated to the prior history of dissension within the Catholic Church.[63] If the assimilation of Joachimite ideas in Luther and Lutheranism is fairly formal and functions in its self-justification, it is more intense and substantive in figures of the Left-Wing Reformation such as Thomas Muntzer (1489–1525).[64] De Lubac argues that in terms of vision, theological substance, and particular modes of exegesis of scripture, Joachimism is much more substantively actualized in the mystical Lutheran Jacob Boehme (1575–1624).[65] For example, Boehme's first text,

---

to avoid Christomonism. Needless to say, this characterization is only approximate. De Lubac thinks of Origen especially as providing a robust pneumatology that introduces fluidity into the theological tradition. Contrariwise, Congar is critical of a figure such as Joachim. For Congar, see *I Believe in the Holy Spirit*, trans. David Smith (New York: Crossroad, 1999), vol. 1, pp. 126–37.

61. Eminent commentators on Joachim such as Bernard McGinn and Marjorie Reeves have made this point.

62. For de Lubac, John of Parma and Gerard of Borga San Donnino are two of the more important of the many conduits of Joachim's thought in thirteenth century. See de Lubac, *La postérité spirituelle de Joachim de Fiore*, vol. 1, pp. 77–83.

63. Well respected scholars of Joachim such as Marjorie Reeves, Henri Mottu, and Bernard McGinn insist that de Lubac's reading of Joachim might have balanced better the more conservative and radical elements.

64. De Lubac, *La postérité spirituelle de Joachim de Fiore*, vol. 1, p. 177.

65. Ibid., pp. 219–26.

Aurora (1611), is awash with Joachimite Trinitarian periodization and Boehme's eschatology not only is thoroughly pneumatic but also avails of many of Joachim's favourite symbols.[66] De Lubac does not delve into the historiographical issues as to whether Boehme had some knowledge of Joachim's text which were brought to general publication only at the end of the sixteenth century, or what other lines of transmission might have been available to the autodidactic cobbler. And given his general purposes, it probably is sufficient that he can mark the thicker retrieval than that found in the historical Luther. The Boehmian recollection of Joachimism is continued in different ways in Pietism in figures such as Oetinger and Bengel.[67] The latter is especially important in that he takes upon himself the anagogic-futural reading of Revelation and gives a date for the end of history.

It is an important part of de Lubac's narrative to indicate how the radical eschatological thought of Joachim jumps the religious tracks and makes its way into the secular environment. The key figure in this respect is Lessing,[68] who in *The Education of Man* elaborates a periodization of history as a scheme of progress rather a religious belief about the triune God's action in history, and suggests the eternal Gospel as the fruition of the two testaments, although essentially beyond them. Hegel and Schelling are complex sites of transmission, since they not only have Lessing as an ancestor but also Pietism and Jacob Boehme.[69] As one might expect, given his early work, de Lubac underscores the singular importance of Hegel who stands alone as the Joachimite thinker who dares to offer a philosophical justification of an eschatological vision which effectively constitutes history as a theodicy rather than as in Augustine a drama.[70] One of the more fascinating features of de Lubac's masterwork is his coverage of the major social thinkers of the nineteenth century. Long before *La postérité* de Lubac had constructed Marx as an eschatological thinker who had secularized Christian eschatology.[71] *La postérité* repeats and refines the thesis by suggesting that Marx's eschatological lineage can be traced back to the heterodox eschatology of Joachim. Further, there is no problem concerning proximate discourse of transmission, given Marx's dependence on Hegel whatever the changes he rings on German Idealism. Real problems do, however, arise when de Lubac attempts to inscribe the French Socialist movements of the nineteenth century and their discourses of Enlightenment and progress into the Joachimite

---

66. Ibid., pp. 222–23.

67. For de Lubac's treatment of Johann Albrecht Bengel (1687–1752), see ibid., pp. 245–46; for Friedrich Christoph Oetinger (1702–1782), see ibid., vol. 1, pp. 245–49.

68. For G. E. Lessing (1729–1781), see ibid., pp. 277–80.

69. For Hegel, see ibid., pp. 363–78; for Schelling, see ibid., vol. 1, pp. 378–93.

70. Similar point made by Karl Löwith in his *Meaning in History: The Theological Implications of the Philosophy of History* (Chicago, IL: University of Chicago Press, 1957). Although in a sense Löwith's book could be read as a series of portraits of influential views of history, including those of Hegel and Marx, there is a sense in which the book stages a debate between the different theologies of history of Augustine and Joachim.

71. See de Lubac, 'The Search for a New Man', DAH, pp. 399–468.

lineage.⁷² The lines of transmission are hardly self-evident. The Socialist programs of Fourier and Proudhon are relatively endogenous, and both forge socialist paths largely independent of Marx. Still, in the case of Proudhon there is a significant engagement with Hegel.⁷³ De Lubac is on surer ground when he turns to twentieth-century assimilation Marx. Ernst Bloch is the key figure,⁷⁴ since not only does he self-consciously speak of Marxism being within the Joachimite tradition, he essentially baptizes Marxism, thus priming Christian theology to assimilate a prophetic and apocalyptic form of Marxism. As might be expected, Moltmann is the prime figure of such assimilation as he appropriates for Christian purposes Bloch's ontology of the not yet.⁷⁵

One can expect that as with all genealogical narratives, there is simplification. All the major figures display features that do not fit the Joachimite trajectory. I have given the barest examples here. Still de Lubac's treatment of these figures is far more ample than most genealogies provide, and the erudition is astonishing. Still, more important than the absolute vindication of the grand narrative of the continuation of Joachim by secular and Christian means is the apologetic purpose of the text: it aims to show that once again the Church is attracted to eschatologies of great imaginative power which threaten to unmoor it from tradition and institution, relativize its media of grace, and make Christ the occasion for a form of thought that surpasses him. Of course, this will have the effect in the modern world of eclipsing transcendence, dispensing with eternity as a vain dream at best and an alienating force at worst, and issue in removing the distinction between Church and world. As de Lubac understands it, Joachimism in modern theological and secular dress has properties of attraction that the Enlightenment in its unprocessed state does not have. The Enlightenment kills genuine forms of Christian devotion by progressive attenuation and by suggesting that the real life is constituted by the world of *l'homme moyen sensuel*.⁷⁶ One might say that the Enlightenment functions privatively or by subtraction. Modern versions of Joachimism, however, function positively:⁷⁷ they offer a pseudo-religious

---

72. This is especially true of Saint-Simon and the Saint-Simonians.

73. This is a point important enough for de Lubac to devote an entire chapter of his monograph on Proudhon. The engagement, however, is critical through and through, even if from Proudhon's point of view Hegel's social writings are more valuable – because ultimately more empirical based and more respectful of law – than those of Marx.

74. For de Lubac's discussion of Bloch, who he reads as extraordinarily influential in contemporary theology largely if not exclusively through Moltmann, see *La postérité spirituelle de Joachim de Fiore*, vol. 2, pp. 367-73.

75. That Moltmann and contemporary theology is de Lubac's central concern is clear from the very beginning of *La postérité*, Preface, where, opposing Joachim and Augustine, Moltmann sides with Joachim. De Lubac is well aware that this contrast is constitutive of the work of Bloch and provides the backbone of Moltmann's own theology of history as a theology of hope. That Joachimism has made its way back into the churches – not excluding the Catholic Church – is touched on in SC, pp. 205-9.

76. This is a Pascalian trope, but one that he owes to Montaigne.

77. That this is a basic insight to which de Lubac had come fairly early is evinced by his earlier characterization of atheist humanism.

alternative to Christianity in general and to Catholicism in particular by a way of magnifying human being, and community, and by valorizing history.

For de Lubac, true humanism is illustrated by the Church which opens history to the non-historical, the temporal to the eternal, and matter to spirit. While such a *Gestalt* in significant respects hardly amounts to anything more than the Catholic *sensus communis*, it is, nonetheless, comforting from his point of view that it is vouchsafed by all of its magisterial thinkers, for example, Irenaeus, Origen, Augustine, and Aquinas, and in the modern period by the Tübingen School, Newman, Blondel, and Rousselot. For all of these thinkers, scripture, history, and cosmos have a sacramental character, and each of these dimensions mutually supports each other in underscoring how reality is driven towards a reality which is truly eschatological and truly transcendent. This directionality is made possible in and by the incarnation and the working of the Holy Spirit in the world and especially in the Church. One of the generalizations that de Lubac braved was that from the perspective of theological emphasis, the twentieth century was the century of the Church. It was important to him, however, that this emphasis was not a construction, but again a rediscovery of a view that goes back to witnesses in the early Church. Origen is one such important figure. In *Splendor of the Church* he recalls a passage from Origen that he had commented on in Histoire et Esprit (1950), that is, 'the Church is the world of the world' (ho kosmou tou kosmou he ekklesia).[78]

---

78. SP, pp. 231–32. Perhaps it should also be noted how on de Lubac's reading the work of Teilhard supports the picture of the Church – obviously conditioned by the saving action of Christ and the effective work of the Spirit – as being inclusive of all of the cosmos and history and pointing to their transfiguration and its own in the divine milieu. See *The Faith of Teilhard de Chardin*, trans. René Hague (London: Burns & Oates, 1965). See especially Chapters 4 and 5 which reflect on the cosmic Christ.

Chapter 13

MYSTICISM AND MYSTICAL THEOLOGY
Bryan C. Hollon

Introduction

Over the course of his long and prolific career, Henri de Lubac published works of such monumental importance that they continue to shape Roman Catholic identity and mission to this day. Many of the themes treated in his most important works are covered in this book. It should surprise no one familiar with de Lubac's oeuvre to see chapters with titles referencing nature and grace, *ressourcement*, spiritual exegesis, *corpus mysticum*, atheist humanism, and more, since he either edited or authored books, and sometimes a whole series of books, on these subjects. But why a chapter on mysticism in a book such as this, which can't possibly address every obscure matter that de Lubac wrote about at one time or another? After all, he never wrote a book on mysticism. Nor did his work establish mysticism or mystical theology as a central feature in late twentieth and early twenty-first-century Roman Catholic theology. There were no dogmatic constitutions devoted to the subject at Vatican II, and there have been no published manuscripts making an explicit argument that mysticism should be a central dimension of theological work in the contemporary *ressourcement* tradition that de Lubac helped to inaugurate. Certainly, it can be argued that his most important explicit writing on the subject had a rather obscure beginning as a preface to a book published in 1965 by Fr. André Ravier titled *La Mystique et les mystiques*.[1]

Yet, de Lubac had planned a book on mysticism and struggled for years with how to approach the subject. He compiled notes and even wrote the first part of the book that he was envisioning, but he never made use of what he had written. Rather, he determined that the book was beyond his abilities. In fact, as he reflected on the various controversies and circumstances that occasioned his writings, he made this rather remarkable statement:

---

1. ASC, p. 113. This preface was later expanded and published as Henri de Lubac, 'Mysticism and Mystery', TF, pp. 35–69.

> I truly believe that for a rather long time the idea for my book on Mysticism has been my inspiration in everything; I form my judgments on the basis of it, it provides me with the means to classify my ideas in proportion to it.... I have a clear vision of how it is linked together, I can distinguish and more or less situate the problems that should be treated in it, in their nature and in their order, I see the precise direction in which the solution of each of them should be sought – but I am incapable of formulating that solution.... The center always eludes me. What I achieve on paper is only preliminary, banalities, peripheral discussions or scholarly details.[2]

And herein lies the justification for a chapter on mysticism. Henri de Lubac's many works were saturated with mystical theology. Certainly, it is fair to suggest that his *ressourcement* theology was, to a large extent, an effort to infuse the whole of catholic theology and ecclesial life with a mystical dimension. That is, he wanted to see catholic theology and ecclesial life properly ordered to the vision of God's glory, for the sake of the world.

This is the thesis that I will defend in the pages that follow, and given de Lubac's reflections concerning the complexity of the subject, the argument can't be straightforward. The only way that I know to proceed is to consider some of the seemingly more conspicuous themes discussed in other chapters of this book, from the perspective of mystical theology. Accordingly, using the essay 'Mysticism and Mystery' as a primary lens, this chapter will explore some of the major characteristics of Christian mysticism, as de Lubac understood it, through a consideration of his work on the nature of theology, the relationship between nature and grace, and spiritual exegesis. I'll address other issues such as politics, sacramental theology, and ecclesiology along the way, but my comments on these topics will be more incidental in nature. Before I dive into these major themes, however, I will offer a brief clarification about what mysticism is not.

Christian Mysticism Is Not Essentialism

Since de Lubac hoped to see a mystical dimension restored to all catholic theology, it should be stated, from the start, that he was advocating a distinctively Christian and catholic form of mysticism. He admits that the word is easily misunderstood, since it has 'mixed origins'. The same could be said, however, of other words like 'religion' and 'spirituality', and since we must use words, the best we can do is to offer some clarifications. So what does de Lubac intend with the word 'mysticism'?

First, he acknowledges that 'mysticism appears to be a virtually universal occurrence', which is not necessarily confined to those who would call themselves religious. Zen Buddhism, for instance, can hardly be considered religious in its practices and aims, yet it has a mystical dimension. Moreover, there are atheists

---

2. ASC, p. 113.

who claim mysticism for themselves, such as Nietzsche who once said, 'I am a mystic, and I believe in nothing.'[3] Universal occurrences of mysticism, such as these, have been reported in a great variety of contexts outside of the Christian faith and can include 'clairvoyance, stigmata, levitations, visions, moments of extraordinary concentration that break the course of normal life',[4] and much more. Experiences like these, however, fall outside the scope of de Lubac's use of the word.

In de Lubac's thinking, mysticism always takes a distinctive shape and is contextualized by the various cultures and religious traditions within which it exists. He certainly does not advocate an 'essentialism' that is basic to all people and constitutes a shared experience among all the world's religions. Essentialism, he argues, is 'based on a superficial examination of the texts, lifted out of the spiritual milieu in which they are shrouded, and on insufficient attention to the qualitative differences of the religions in which the described experiences occur'.[5] Although mysticism is common to all humans, the particularities of human experience and the distinctiveness of various religious traditions shape mystical experience in different ways. 'All mysticism is not "ignorant" in the same way, nor is it "learned" in the same way.'[6] Mysticism, de Lubac insists, 'is never without an a priori.'[7] Nor is all mysticism true in the sense that it constitutes experience in union with the one true God. According to de Lubac, 'the God whom we adore and who wants us to be united with him is not faceless: he has a superior form, an "infinitely determined form"'.[8] When he speaks of Christian mysticism, de Lubac has in mind something that will always involve participation in the life of the Trinity through a union with Jesus Christ given in grace. It is worth quoting him at length on this issue:

> In Jesus Christ we have had the perfect and definitive revelation of the human being as a personal being. God's revelation to man was at the same time the revelation of a relationship between man and God. What applies to one revelation, however, applies to the other: as God reveals himself in his tripersonal Being, intervening in our humanity, he also reveals us to ourselves as personal beings capable through grace of responding to him in love. What the Catholic Church calls mysticism is only the conscious actualization of this gift of God.[9]

3. De Lubac, 'Mysticism and Mystery', p. 42.
4. Ibid., p. 44.
5. He writes that
Many observers of mystical experiences are convinced of the unity of mysticism. 'I have just read successively', wrote René Daumal, 'some texts on bhakti, some citations from Hasidic authors, and a passage from St. Francis of Assisi. I add a few Buddhist words, and I am once again struck by how close they come to being the *same thing*'... Simone Weil reflected that 'mystics of almost all religious traditions are almost identical'. (Ibid., p. 46)
6. Ibid., p. 45.
7. Ibid., p. 39.
8. Quoting Hans Urs von Balthasar, Ibid., p. 63.
9. De Lubac, 'Mysticism and Mystery'.

There is thus a true and distinctively Christian form of mystical experience, and its distinctiveness comes from the distinctiveness of God Himself. 'If mystical life at its summit consists of an actual union with the Divinity', argues de Lubac, 'such a union could be possible only through a supernatural grace whose normal setting is the Church and whose normal conditions are the life of faith and the sacraments... it is only in the Church that a "true mysticism" can be found; outside of the Church, no mysticism'.[10] Indeed, de Lubac insists 'Christian mysticism is necessarily an ecclesial mysticism, since the incarnation achieves first of all in the Church the marriage of the Word and humanity.'[11] This marriage is mediated, of course, by the eucharistic mystery, which 'makes the Church'.[12] Christian mysticism is, essentially, the internalization of this mystery in believers.

When de Lubac writes of Christian mysticism, he is not thinking of one particular sort of Christian experience that can be separated from other sorts of experience. Instead, he has in mind nothing more than a spiritual understanding characteristic of the life of faith shared by all believers. In a beautiful statement offered during a lecture given in 1942, de Lubac describes the whole of creation as a 'vast and diverse symbol across which the Face of God is mysteriously reflected. A man is religious to the very degree that he recognizes everywhere these reflections of the divine Face, that is, that he lives in a sacred atmosphere'.[13] Christian mysticism, as an internalization of the Christian mystery, entails the deciphering of symbols and thus a graced capacity and participatory[14] endeavour of 'knowing' the God who made and is signified by these symbols.

> Now, basically, this world is not by itself either sacred or secular, for it receives its significance only through man. It can become one or the other according to the way in which man behaves in its regard. This world is for man like a first and immense sacrament, the great natural sacrament that was, in the state of innocence, to lead us as if effortlessly to the unique Source of all that is sacred, which is to say, to God, and which even now, in our state as redeemed sinners, is to rediscover all its meaning and all its sacral value thanks to another great sacrament, more mysterious still and more intimate, more intrinsically sacred:

10. Ibid., p. 43.
11. Ibid., p. 62.
12. Cf. CM. Although I won't give sustained attention to de Lubac's eucharistic theology here, I have addressed that issue within the context of his larger project, and especially his non-juridical approach to ecclesiology in Bryan C. Hollon, *Everything Is Sacred: Spiritual Exegesis in the Political Theology of Henri de Lubac*, Theopolitical Visions (Eugene, OR: Cascade Books, 2009), pp. 39–71. See also Susan K. Wood, *Spiritual Exegesis and the Church in the Theology of Henri de Lubac* (Grand Rapids, MI: Eerdmans, 1998).
13. De Lubac, 'Internal Causes of the Weakening and Disappearance of the Sense of the Sacred', in *Theology in History*, trans. Anne Englund Nash (San Francisco: Ignatius Press, 1996), p. 231.
14. 'All, in one measure and for reasons that can vary much but that are never negligible, all is sacred by destination and must therefore begin by being so through participation' (ibid.).

the supernatural sacrament, the wholly divine mystery in which all the others are summed up: *Sacramentum Christi, Mysterium Christi*.[15]

Christian mysticism is thus to read the signs and share in the vision of God's glory reflected in all things.

As already mentioned, this graced and participatory way of knowing has a Trinitarian shape and finds its normal setting in the Church and the life of faith. This kind of mysticism is especially 'conspicuous' in the New Testament in the Pauline epistles, the Johannine literature,[16] and, of course, throughout the Church's long history.[17]

Contra Extrincisim: A Mystical Theology

Just as he rejects essentialism, de Lubac opposes any form of 'extrincisim' that conceives God, in nominalist fashion, as one being among others (albeit of greater power and proportion) and, as a corollary, any form of theology disconnected from lived experience. As other chapters in this book have noted, de Lubac began his service to the Church during an especially tumultuous time in the history of Europe. He fought in the First World War at the great Battle of Verdun and sustained an injury there that would plague him for the rest of his life. Several of his most significant works were written during the Second World War when he was in hiding from the Nazi occupation of France. De Lubac was acutely aware of the cultural forces at play during the nineteenth and twentieth centuries, and he saw his own struggle as a theologian as a struggle for the soul of the Church whose vision of human flourishing was increasingly challenged by aggressive forms of atheism and more subtle, though equally problematic, forms of secularism.[18]

At the time of his priestly formation, neo-scholastic theology held a firm grip on the mind of the Church and on its engagement, or lack thereof, with an increasingly secular European culture. De Lubac was especially critical of neo-scholastic theology because, by his account, it had far too little to offer a Church struggling to bear witness to the good news of Christ risen and victorious. He argued that the 'masses' were turning from the Catholic faith because they had

---

15. De Lubac, 'Internal Causes', pp. 232–33.
16. Impressive is the 'christological mysticism' in the writings of St Paul. One of its effects is to give us 'a more complete awareness of the depths and heights of the spiritual life on earth …' The Pauline doctrine of the union of the believer with Christ, on the presence and action of the Spirit in the Christian community, is quite clear.... As for the mysticism of St. John, it is, if possible, even more evident. (De de Lubac, 'Mysticism and Mystery', p. 50)
17. De de Lubac, 'Mysticism and Mystery', p. 49. For a more detailed engagement of the mystical tradition, see TH, pp. 117–240.
18. For his brilliant refutation of Atheist humanism, see DAH.

'lost in so large a proportion the sense of the Sacred'. Rhetorically, he asks, 'Is it not first of all because we have not known how to maintain it in them, to protect it against other influences? Much more, is it not because we have more or less lost this sense ourselves'?[19]

The sense of the sacred, or rather, the mysticism entailed in a proper reading of signs, was lost when the Church's own theologians embraced a form of dualism that separated nature from its proper context in supernatural grace. For too long, neo-scholastic theologians had been focused on epistemological justifications of their own Thomist system of thought, and this, according to de Lubac, resulted in the captivity of Roman Catholic theology to a suffocating form of rationalism. The problem with neo-scholastic theology, he suggests, is 'conceiving of dogma as a kind of "thing in itself", as a block of revealed truth with no relationship whatsoever to natural man'.[20] De Lubac believes that such an approach is nothing less than an evasion of a theologian's true vocation,[21] so he derides those who

> stroll about theology somewhat as if in a museum of which we are the curators, a museum where we have inventoried, arranged and labeled everything; we know how to define all the terms, we have an answer for all objections, we supply the desired distinctions at just the right moment. Everything in it is obscure for the secular, but for us, everything is clear, everything is explained. If there is still a mystery, at least we know exactly where it is to be placed, and we point to this precisely defined site. ... Thus, for us, theology is a science a bit like the others, with this sole essential difference: its first principles were received through revelation instead of having been acquired through experience or through the work of reason.[22]

In contrast to the stale and extrinsic rationalism of neo-scholasticism, de Lubac believed that theology must maintain an apologetic stance and always confront reigning secular ideologies in order to shed a critical and explanatory light upon them, making the world more comprehensible, offering hope, and calling the Church to faithfulness. In his commentary on Vatican II's *Dei Verbum*, de Lubac explains that

---

19. De Lubac, 'Internal Causes', p. 224.
20. Henri de Lubac, 'Apologetics and Theology', in TF, p. 93.
21. 'The fault is often that of an indifference on the part of theologians who, refusing to face squarely the problems they nevertheless have a mission in the Church to study' ('Internal Causes', p. 226). Also, 'There was, as it were, an unconscious conspiracy between the movement that led to laicism and a certain theology, and while the supernatural found itself exiled and proscribed, it happened that some among us thought that the supernatural was placed outside the reach of nature, in the domain where it was to reign' (ibid., p. 232).
22. De Lubac, 'Internal Causes', p. 233. For a recent essay describing the historical context of the struggle between *nouvelle théologie* and the neo-Scholastics, see Aidan Nichols, 'Thomism and the Nouvelle Théologie', *The Thomist* 64 (2000): pp. 1–19. See also Hollon, *Everything Is Sacred*, p. 35, n. 89.

To reflect in Christ or, as one says, 'to do theology', does not only mean to 'organize truths', to systematize them or draw new conclusions from the revealed 'premises'; it is more to 'demonstrate the explanatory power' of the truths of faith in relation to the changing context of the world. It is to strive to understand the world and man, his nature, his destiny and his history, in the most diverse situations, in the light of those same truths. It is to attempt to see all things in the mystery of Christ. For the mystery of Christ is an illuminating mystery, and in considering it in this way, one really deepens it without removing its mysterious character. Thus, the enterprise of a 'theology of history' must not be considered as a merely marginal phenomenon; every theologian must be, more or less, a 'theologian of history'. In no way does all of this mean, however, that history as such is the medium of revelation or salvation: on the contrary. Whether it is a matter of secular history or the history of the Church: by themselves, historical events bring us no increase in supernatural revelation. They remain always 'ambiguous' and come 'in anticipation', and it is they that must be illuminated for us by the light that comes from the Gospel.[23]

In contrast, neo-scholastic theology tended to focus on truth in the abstract, and secular ideologies and political movements, such as *Action française*, too easily seduced its practitioners. Importantly, some of de Lubac's neo-scholastic theological opponents were also his political opponents during the Second World War. They supported the fascist Vichy regime in France even as de Lubac and others were forced into hiding for their opposition to Nazism.[24]

Consequently, a major debate between the Dominican neo-scholastics and the Jesuit proponents of *ressourcement* erupted just after the Second World War. Jean Danielou, a friend and collaborator of de Lubac, published an essay in 1946 titled *Les Orientations Présentes de La Pensée Religieuse*, which took aim at the neo-scholastics and argued for an illuminating theology engaged with human affairs rather than a theology concerned only with a disconnected, extrinsic, and abstracted interpretation of truth.[25] Like de Lubac, Danielou advocated a return to the sources and an approach to theology akin to the great patristic works, which were a 'vast commentary on Holy Scripture'.[26]

Neo-scholastic theologians received Danielou's essay as a dangerous subversion, heralding a new and obfuscating approach to theology. Mockingly, they

---

23. Henri de Lubac, *La Révélation Divine* (Paris, France: Editions du Cerf, 1983), pp. 100–1 (author's translation).

24. For more on these political tensions, see Hollon, *Everything Is Sacred*, pp. 11–71. One of de Lubac's earliest published writings offers great insight into the conflicting perspectives concerning the Church's earthly mission held by the neo-scholastics and the proponents of what would come to be called, *Nouvelle Théologie*. See de Lubac, 'The Authority of the Church in Temporal Matters', TF, pp. 199–233.

25. J. Daniélou, 'Les Orientations Présentes de La Pensée Religieuse', *Études* 249 (1946): pp. 5–21.

26. Ibid., p. 9.

referred to the *ressourcement* movement as *la nouvelle théologie*.[27] Marie-Michel Labourdette, one of the leading Dominican scholars of the era and editor of the *Revue Thomiste*, responded to Danielou with an essay titled *La Théologie et Ses Sources*.[28] Labourdette articulated the primary concern when he wrote, 'what we can never accept is the complete evacuation, in a perspective like this, of the idea of speculative truth'. Additionally, 'we understand by "truth" the conformity of the knowing intelligence with a reality which for it is a "given", "never a construct"'.[29]

Labourdette's essay elicited a strong response from the Jesuits in the form of an essay titled simply, *La Théologie et Ses Sources: Réponse*.[30] Although de Lubac was the primary author, the essay was published anonymously with input from Jean Daniélou, Henri Bouillard, Gaston Fessard, and Hans Urs von Balthasar, all Jesuits.[31] The Jesuits took an offensive, rather than defensive, approach and accused the neo-scholastics of hijacking theology in order to promote their own very disconnected perspective rather than true orthodoxy.[32] True orthodoxy, the Jesuits would insist in

---

27. The same phrase had, of course, been used to describe Martin Luther's theological innovations during the reformation.

28. Marie-Michel Labourdette, 'La Théologie et Ses Sources', *Revue Thomiste* 46:2 (1946): pp. 353–71. For more on the debate between the neo-scholastics and proponents of ressourcement, see D.L. Greenstock, 'Thomism and the New Theology', *The Thomist* 13 (1950): pp. 567–96. See also Brian Daley, 'The Nouvelle Théologie and the Patristic Revival: Sources, Symbols and the Science of Theology', *International Journal of Systematic Theology* 7:4 (November 2005): pp. 362–82. Also, Nichols, 'Thomism and the Nouvelle Théologie'.

29. Labourdette, 'La Thélogie et Ses Sources'. Cited and translated in Daley, 'The Nouvelle Théologie and the Patristic Revival', pp. 367–69.

30. Anonymous, 'La Theologie et Ses Sources: Réponse', *Reserches de Science Religieuses* 33 (1946): pp. 385–401.

31. Marie Dominic Chenu was an important Dominican ally, and his views on the nature of theology sound much like de Lubac's:

> many theological studies treat faith only as a matter of juridical assent ... [since they provide] basic facts, and on these are built a structure of arguments, syllogisms and theses. This is hollow speculation which, in all truth and in the very strongest sense, *lacks the light (lumen sub quo)*, since the faith is taken merely as the source of propositions and not as an interior perfection which endows the spirit with a pleasing understanding of things divine ... This is a regrettable separation of theological study from the spiritual life.

Marie-Dominique Chenu, 'The Eyes of Faith', in *Faith and Theology* (New York: The Macmillan Company, 1968), p. 13, n. 7.

32. In his recently translated and published notebooks from the Second Vatican Council, de Lubac makes consistent and often scathing remarks about neo-scholasticism, which was still very much dominant at the time. In a note concerning the much-maligned Cardinal Ottaviani from October 1962, for instance, he describes the neo-scholastic tendency to defend 'diminished truths'. He says the neo-scholastics prefer

> the 'God of nature' to the Christian God; an abstract idea of revelation to the revelation of Christ; they teach that God reveals himself to us 'in order that we might serve him', not in order that we might become his children; sin, original or actual, is nothing other than an infraction of the law, not the refusal of our divine vocation, etc.

the totality of their works, is always engaged with the historical times and likewise provides an illuminating light – an ability to read the signs and see the Face of God mysteriously reflected in them. Looking back at the controversy, one historian described it as 'the only theological debate of any importance at least in France, between the condemnation of modernism and the Second Vatican Council'.[33] The debate was important, indeed, and it focused on a central issue around which de Lubac's various works are gathered – a more 'mystical' form of theology.

I mention all of this to underscore the fact that, for de Lubac, the nature and scope of a theologian's ecclesial vocation is serious business; there was much at stake then as there is now and always will be. Accordingly, his appeal for a more 'mystical' approach to theology stems from his desire to see theology remain grounded in the transcendent 'mysteries of Christ' yet always attuned to and engaged with the real word – the unfolding of history.

De Lubac's endorsement of mysticism is thus a commendation of theology grounded in the mysteries of faith that avoids the extrincisit, ahistorical metaphysics of neo-scholasticism and embraces a participatory understanding of the relationship between God and his people. Theology cannot remain in the abstract, allowing the Church's leaders to embrace secular ideologies and political movements. Rather, the Church's theological vocation is to bear witness to the light of Christ, which illumines all.[34]

Moreover, argues de Lubac, the neo-scholastics embrace 'human theories, most often ones that are rather recent, puerile, or outdated, to which they are just as much if not more attached than to dogma, on which they dig in their heels, and which make them forget the essential part of the Christian mystery' (*Vatican Council Notebooks*, vol. I [San Francisco, CA: Ignatius Press, 2015], p. 149).

33. Translated and cited in Nichols, 'Thomism and the Nouvelle Théologie', pp. 1–19, 2.

34.

Whatever might be the future progress of our race, whatever the enlargement of its knowledge or the refinement of its ideal, we will not be taken unawares. The coming of Christ has marked the fullness of time. No fullness, no depth will ever exhaust the Deed of Calvary. That is why, peaceful about the past, we also look to the future without fear.... Sure that our faith will never mislead us, we go ahead of the excavations of history and the research of science. Ahead too, of human progress – and we know too well that all progress of the world will not obtain the least beginning of salvation! Ahead of the new values to which history gives birth through its crises. Man can vary and perfect his culture without end. He can discover and exploit new potentialities in it. The very Universe can grow immeasurably, and distant stars can one day reveal a humanity more numerous, more civilized – more miserable – than our own: the Deed of Christ would still take it in. It embraces all worlds, just as it shines above time. For all equally, for each one of us and at all times, for those who believe in many and for those who despair of him, its rays are those of Eternal Life. 'He has come, the Christ of God, the Leader of the Promises! And without any doubt he has been, he alone, to the exclusion of all those who preceded him – and I have the audacity to say, he is to the exclusion of all those who follow him – the one awaited by the Nations'. (de Lubac, 'The Light f Christ', in TH, pp. 219–20)

A Mysticism of Likeness

We should recall that, in 'Mysticism and Mystery', de Lubac insists that Christian mysticism entails a union with God 'whose normal setting is the Church and whose normal conditions are the life of faith and the sacraments'.[35] For de Lubac, the Church and the sacraments are the context within which human participation in the Triune life takes place. But what are the distinctive characteristics of this participatory form of life?

First, it entails a 'mysticism of likeness'. Whereas all people are made in God's image, only those who are conformed to the likeness of God can be said to achieve union with God. Another way of expressing this would be to say that all persons are made in God's image, with a natural desire for God, but only the supernatural grace of God will satisfy this natural desire. Being made in God's image offers no guarantee that a person will be conformed to God's likeness. We see this theme throughout de Lubac's corpus. Consider the following from his first book, *Catholicism*:

> Christ completes the revelation of man to himself. By taking possession of man, by seizing hold of him and by penetrating to the very depths of his being Christ makes man go deep down within himself, there to discover in a flash regions hitherto unsuspected. It is through Christ that the person reaches maturity, that man emerges definitively from the universe, and becomes conscious of his own being... for through the Christian revelation not only is the scrutiny that man makes of himself made more searching, but his examination of all about him is at the same time made more comprehensive. Henceforth, the idea of human unity is born. That image of God, the image of the Word, which the incarnate Word restores and gives back to its glory, is 'I myself'; it is also the other, every other. It is that aspect of me in which I coincide with every other man, it is the hallmark of our common origin and the summons to our common destiny. It is our very unity with God.[36]

A Christian mysticism of likeness is always 'directed toward a goal, toward God who calls to us and beckons us to meet him at the end of the road'.[37] We are not oriented towards a natural but rather a supernatural end. The neo-scholastic position asserted too great a separation between nature and grace and approached the supernatural as a static given. De Lubac argues that, for his theological opponents,

> The supernatural gift... appeared as a super-imposed reality, as an artificial and arbitrary superstructure. The unbeliever found it easy to withdraw into his indifference in the very name of what theology was telling him: if my very

---

35. de Lubac, 'Mysticism and Mystery', p. 43.
36. C, pp. 339–40.
37. de Lubac, 'Mysticism and Mystery', p. 57.

nature as a man truly has its end in itself, what should oblige or even arouse me to scrutinize history in the quest for some other vocation perhaps to be found there? Why should I listen to a Church which bears a message having no relation to the aspirations of my nature?[38]

It is no surprise, therefore, that de Lubac's notorious *Surnaturel* (1946), which addressed the relationship between nature and grace, became the central focus in the debate between the neo-scholastics and proponents of the so-called *nouvelle théologie* – de Lubac and his Jesuit co-conspirators.

There is no need, in this chapter, to review the long and difficult controversy over nature and grace that led de Lubac into so much controversy, since other contributors have taken up that subject.[39] However, I would like to offer a few comments about the implications of that debate for Christian mysticism. I have already suggested that, for de Lubac and others, theology must illumine the contemporary situation – enabling Christians to examine not only themselves but also all things in the light of Christ.

In his various works on nature and grace, de Lubac suggests that persons, created in God's image, have an innate natural desire to be transformed into God's likeness by the vision of His glory. In other words, the vocation of theology to provide illumination – the vision of God's glory reflected in all things – is a vocation that facilitates the graced fulfilment of an innate natural desire for the supernatural that is shared by all people. Christian mysticism, in de Lubac's mind, is thus a gift of grace that fulfils a natural desire; it is 'an "infused" gift of "passive contemplation"'[40] entailing the vision of God's glory reflected in all things. Elsewhere, de Lubac refers to this contemplative vision as 'spiritual understanding' and suggests that it is 'in its principle, identical to the process of conversion. It is its luminous aspect. *Intellectus spiritualis credentem salvum facit* (Spiritual understanding saves the believer)'.[41]

For de Lubac's neo-scholastic opponents the position outlined above was fraught with problems. Namely, they did not believe that persons could be endowed with a 'natural desire' for something that can be received only by supernatural grace, since, in order to desire something, one must already possess an idea of that thing. How can a person desire, in a meaningful sense, something that they do not already comprehend and cannot even imagine? For the neo-scholastics, humans have a natural desire for a natural end only yet a capacity (obediential potency) for the infusion of this desire for a supernatural end. De Lubac found this *duplex ordo* highly problematic because, as we have already seen, it separated theology from

---

38. Henri de Lubac, 'Nature and Grace', in *The Word in History*, ed. Patrick Burke (New York: Sheed and Ward, 1966), p. 32.
39. For my own treatment of the controversy, see Hollon, *Everything Is Sacred*, Ch. 4.
40. de Lubac, 'Mysticism and Mystery', p. 39.
41. Henri de Lubac, *Scripture in the Tradition* (New York: Crossroad, 2000), p. 21.

philosophy and politics from the supernatural grace of God.[42] This separation led to an extrinsic form of theology that failed to maintain an apologetic stance, and it led many Catholics to assume that the natural order could operate self-sufficiently in its pursuit of natural ends, apart from the supernatural grace of God. This, in de Lubac's mind, explained the neo-scholastic embrace of secular political movements like *Action française*. His thesis on nature and grace was thus a way of avoiding these dualisms and challenging those who embraced them.

However laudable his efforts to avoid the dualism and extrinsicism that characterized neo-scholasticism, de Lubac's thesis sometimes appears to collapse the orders of nature and grace in an unacceptable way.[43] Recently, the neo-scholastic position has received renewed attention, and de Lubac's position has received renewed scrutiny. Steven A. Long's criticisms are characteristic. He believes that de Lubac assumes too great a continuity between nature and grace so that, in the end, nature is dissolved into grace, and the whole scheme diverges from classical Christology with its stress on the two natures of Christ. Long writes,

> a teaching that renders human nature to be a vacuole or pure nought lacking proportionate created integrity and unknowable apart from the beatific vision seems to make the doctrine of Nicea unintelligible. For what is assumed in the Word is defined in precision from the datum of its assumption. One does not say, 'The Person of the Word' assumed the nature that is defined by its being assumed by 'The Person of the Word' – for that would render the hypostatic union a necessary function of finite human nature.[44]

Yet, the neo-scholastic emphasis on two distinct orders with two distinct ends (the *duplex ordo*) is hardly satisfying, as it leads to an unacceptable dualism and a false sense that the order of nature can be, in some way, self-sufficient.

Importantly, in his essay on mysticism, de Lubac emphasizes the discontinuity between nature and grace: 'If it is possible... to speak of a Christian mysticism, it can only be a converted mysticism. For that reason, its effect on the religion within which it appears seems to be the inverse of the effect mysticism generally seems to have elsewhere.'[45] That is, in other religions, mysticism seems to be a natural capacity whereas, for the Christian, it is always a gift of grace. Further, he

---

42. R.F. Gotcher, *Henri de Lubac and Communio: The Significance of His Theology of the Supernatural for an Interpretation of Gaudium et Spes* (PhD dissertation: Marquette University, 2002), p. 113.

43. Others have noted that de Lubac's treatment of this issue developed over time and that his later treatments of the subject placed more emphasis on a discontinuity between the orders of nature and grace. See Susan K. Wood, 'The Nature-Grace Problematic within Henri de Lubac's Christological Paradox', *Communio (US)* 19 (Fall 1992): pp. 389–403.

44. Steven A. Long, 'On the Loss, and the Recovery, of Nature as a Theonomic Principle: Reflections on the Nature/Grace Controversy', *Nova et Vetera* 5:1 (2007): pp. 133–84, 151.

45. de Lubac, 'Mysticism and Mystery', p. 64.

suggests the 'mystical life is *not directed toward an experience desired as an end*, but toward a blossoming of Christian life. It is defined primarily by its triple and unique relationship to the mystery that is realized in faith, hope, and love'.[46]

In the sentence quoted above, de Lubac seems to have changed his position on nature and grace in relation to his earlier works. He now emphasizes a necessary discontinuity between nature and grace, and he suggests the impossibility of 'desiring' the vision of God's glory 'as an end'. The change in emphasis suggests that De Lubac needed clearer philosophical language to deal with the subject. One wonders whether both the neo-scholastics and de Lubac were limited in that they conceived the relationship between nature and grace in exclusively univocal terms, whereas Thomas Aquinas spoke of two different orders, the order of nature and the order of grace, with the same ultimate end since they enjoy an analogical relationship to one another.[47] To clarify, we might say that all persons are naturally ordered to truth, justice, peace, and other ends proportionate to human nature. Indeed, we see that people everywhere, regardless of cultural and religious context, desire these good ends. We can affirm that this constitutes a natural desire for proximate natural ends and at the same time a natural desire for God in whom these goods find their ultimate ground and meaning, their ultimate end. Insofar as a person desires justice or peace or love in the natural order, they ultimately desire the God in whom alone perfect justice, peace, and love are found. This is a natural desire for God in an analogical rather than a univocal sense, however. [48]

Yet, because of sin, this natural desire is corrupted, and all people remain frustrated and incapable of achieving even a proximate, natural beatitude without the grace of God lifting them and making them participants in the transcendent, supernatural order of salvation. In an Augustinian sense, our created nature may entail, for instance, a good and natural desire 'to love and be loved', but sin has

---

46. Ibid., pp. 68–69, emphasis added.
47. For a helpful essay making this point, see Kevin M. Staley, 'Happiness: The Natural End of Man?', *The Thomist* 53:2 (April 1989): pp. 215–34. For my own discussion of this issue, see the footnotes in Hollon, *Everything Is Sacred*, pp. 81–94.
48. For a more technical discussion of problems in de Lubac's thesis on nature and grace and the potential of the doctrine of analogy to offer a solution, see the footnotes in Hollon, *Everything Is Sacred*, pp. 86–91. For Thomas Aquinas' treatment of the issue, a good place to begin is in *Summa Theologiæ*, I-II, q. 109, a. 4. In the following quotation, Aquinas clearly distinguishes between proximate and ultimate ends. He asks 'whether Man can love God above all things by his natural powers' and answers that

> each thing acts as it is made fit to act [i.e. desires an end proportionate to its own nature], as is said in *2 Physics*, text 78. Now it is clear that the good of the part is for the sake of the good of the whole. It follows that every particular thing, by its own natural desire or love, loves its own peculiar good for the sake of the common good of the whole universe, which is God.

Then, in a later paragraph, he adds, 'charity loves God above all things more eminently than does nature. Nature loves God above all things because he is the beginning and the end of the good of nature. Charity loves God because he is the object of beatitude, and because man has spiritual fellowship with him'.

disordered our loves and keeps us from actually desiring or finding rest in these proximate ends.[49] And of course, apart from grace, sin keeps us from desiring or resting in the vision of God, our ultimate end.

A Mysticism of the Word

Even if de Lubac's work on nature and grace could have been strengthened by an appeal to the doctrine of analogy, his rejection of neo-scholastic dualism was surely warranted. Both his politics and his entire *ressourcement* project infused the Church with a much clearer understanding of Her own nature and mission in the world. Certainly, in focusing much of his scholarship on ecclesiology, sacramental theology, and spiritual exegesis, de Lubac forged a path that would enable the Church to reaffirm the vitality of the classic means of grace, which had become tangled in the confusion of historicist and extrincisit conceptions of the faith. His voluminous work on spiritual exegesis, for example, shows that sacred Scripture is a gift of grace, which mediates the vision of God's glory and, through a process of conversion, fulfils a natural desire shared by all persons.

Like the Church Fathers, de Lubac believed that theology must remain thoroughly exegetical since 'knowledge of the faith [is essentially] knowledge of Scripture'.[50] He wrote more pages on spiritual exegesis than on any other topic and, in the process, offered a profound apology for patristic and medieval exegesis. He showed that spiritual exegesis provides a Christological mediation so that the order of nature can find rest in supernatural grace as readers are repeatedly converted and drawn deeper into the mystery of Christ and thus into a participatory knowledge of God. This mediation is the logic undergirding the four senses (the literal, allegorical, tropological, and anagogical) whose meaning is summarized in an ancient adage: 'the letter teaches what took place, the allegory what to believe, the moral what to do, the anagogy what goal to strive for'.[51] 'The mystical or spiritual understanding of Scripture', insists de Lubac, 'and the mystical or spiritual life are, in the end, one and the same. Christian mysticism is that understanding pushed to its most fruitful phase by its four traditional dimensions – history, "allegory" or doctrine, ethics or "tropology" and anagogy – each of which is absorbed by the following one'.[52]

---

49. If it is true, however, that we have an innate desire for proximate natural ends such as love and justice, and sin corrupts these desires, then it is equally true that our inability to attain these proximate ends leads to a profound 'restlessness', and disorientation, which is only satisfied with the supernatural grace of God – our ultimate end. In this sense, supernatural grace satisfies the natural desire for God who is our ultimate end and ground of all proximate ends. This, incidentally, is characteristic of the relationship between nature and grace found in Augustine's *Confessions*.

50. MS, p. 28, n. 1.

51. Henri de Lubac, 'On an Old Distich: The Doctrine of the "Fourfold Sense" in Scripture', TF, p. 109.

52. De Lubac, 'Mysticism and Mystery', p. 58.

The literal sense is fundamental and begins the process of conversion. Although patristic and medieval exegetes are often criticized for their supposed disinterest in authorial intent, they were actually well aware of the dangers of eisegesis.[53] Indeed, ancient readers of Scripture believed that the goal of sacred reading is assimilation to God and that the process of assimilation requires attentiveness to what the bible actually has to say about Jesus Christ. In an essay on figural readings of Scripture, John David Dawson remarks that 'Christianity demands respect for the letter of the spirit, respect for the grammars of difference that constitute identity. Christians choose to identify themselves with one who has already identified himself with each person.'[54] Attention to the literal sense of Scripture thus begins the process of conversion as readers are confronted with a story and a truth that draws them outside of themselves and focuses attention on the Saviour who came to fulfil the hope of Israel.

The literal is often misunderstood because it can refer either to a historical event narrated in Scripture or to a figurative event, such as the stories narrated in the first chapters of the book of Genesis.[55] The Fathers understood even these figurative stories as historical because they communicate a kind of historical truth, for example, God created the earth and considered it good; humankind fell from grace, and so on. The literal sense always presupposes a *telos* or an end that gives history its meaning. It would be a mistake, therefore, to study the literal sense from a historicist perspective, 'which reconstructs the past without paying any attention to what the past was pregnant with'.[56]

The literal sense does not imply a positivistic understanding of history but anticipates its transformation in the spiritual sense and remains incomplete without it. The facts of history, de Lubac writes, do 'not yet give us and cannot give us anything but an exterior and distant view of what we too quickly take to be the "Face of God". Only the order of the spirit founded upon history and disengaged from history, will finally allow us to say, with Saint Gregory: *In his Scripture we look, as it were, upon his face*'.[57]

---

53. Beryl Smalley, *The Study of the Bible in the Middle Ages* (Notre Dame, IN: University of Notre Dame Press, 1964), pp. 87–97.

54. John David Dawson, 'Figural Reading and the Fashioning of Christian Identity in Boyarin, Auerbach and Frei', *Modern Theology* 14:2 (April 1998): pp. 181–96, 194.

55. Regarding potential misunderstandings of the literal sense, de Lubac explains that it has been said that a literal reading is not identical to a historical one; in many passages, even in entire books, it can offer no historical meaning: this is true for parables, proverbs, commandments, etc. It cannot be said of it: *gesta docet*. But – without considering that in this case a terminology used until the thirteenth century would have resulted in a denial that there was still a literal meaning – here we are dealing with the 'letter' of the Scripture taken as a whole. Nevertheless, is it not essential for Scripture to recount a history, the history of redemptive events? Is that not, even for the unbelieving observer, the characteristic that most markedly differentiates the Bible from so many other sacred Scriptures? Again, it has been said that, even if allegory has a certain value, it alone does not provide the doctrine to be believed. Is not the doctrine often expressed by the literal reading? (Ibid., pp. 122–23)

56. De Lubac, *Scripture in the Tradition*, p. 39.

57. ME, vol. 2, p. 82.

The second sense – the allegorical – instructs Christians in 'what to believe'. According to de Lubac, the '"other thing" that a literal reading suggests and that allegory gives us is doctrine, the very object of faith. It is the "mystery" that immediately follows the history. They are the *sanctae fidei sacramenta*, that is, the totality of truths concerning Christ and his Church, prefigured throughout the Old Testament and present in the New'.[58] The most important aspect of the allegorical sense is that its object is Christ and the Church. When Christ is united with the Church as head to a body, then we have the fullness of Christ. The allegorical sense points to the fullness of Christ.

Notably, the allegorical sense of Scripture is to be located in historical events rather than in the text.[59] De Lubac explains that when the Church Fathers used the allegorical method, they 'felt that, rather than giving a commentary on a text or solving a verbal puzzle, they were interpreting history'. He goes on to explain that 'history, just like nature ... was a language to them. It was the word of God. Now throughout this history they encountered a mystery which was to be fulfilled, to be accomplished historically and socially, though always in a spiritual manner: the mystery of Christ and his Church'.[60] The Fathers believed that the sacred history narrated in Scripture was animated by the Spirit of God and that their task as interpreters was to 'understand the spirit of history without impairing historical reality. For there is a spiritual force in history ...; by reason of their finality the very facts have an inner significance; although in time, they are yet pregnant with an eternal value'.[61] Thus, the Fathers interpreted Old Testament events, such as the Jewish Passover, as though they were pregnant with a meaning that was only fully revealed in Christ – the true Passover lamb.[62] It was, for the Fathers, as though 'the shadow [existed] before the body' and the 'copy [came] before the original'.[63] Together, because they provide us with a vision of Christ as the hope of Israel

---

58. De Lubac, 'On an Old Distich', p. 114.
59. Ibid., p. 432.
60. C, p. 170.
61. Ibid., p. 168. De Lubac notes the difference between Christian and pagan allegory. Whereas early Christian allegory offered a means for discovering the depths of history, Hellenistic allegory tended to neglect history altogether.

> The idea of a spiritual Reality becoming incarnate in the realm of sense, needing time for its accomplishment, that without prejudice to its spiritual significance should be prepared, come to pass, and mature socially in history – such a notion is entirely alien to these philosophers. Confronted with it, they find it a stumbling-block and foolishness... Even Philo in trying to derive a spiritual teaching from the Bible denudes it somewhat of its historical significance. (C, pp. 166–67)

For an essay devoted entirely to the differences between Christian and Hellenistic allegory, see Henri de Lubac, 'Hellenistic Allegory and Christian Allegory', TF, pp. 165–96. It seems that de Lubac may overstate the differences between early Christian and pagan allegory, since patristic allegory did not always seek to 'discover the depths of history'. See, for example, Ambrose' *On Naoboth*.

62. The same can be said of Jesus (as depicted in the gospels) and of the Apostle Paul.
63. C, p. 17.

and as the saviour of our own souls, the literal and the allegorical senses call us to repentance and prepare us for continued conversion.

The tropological sense carries the reader forward in conversion as a person comes 'to know himself with his misery and his sin while getting to know the perfection for which God destines and calls him'.[64] An important conversion takes place in tropology as disordered loves find a new and supernatural orientation. Through the light of Christ, we come to see ourselves anew as we identify with the apostasy of Israel, the foolishness of the disciples, and the struggles of the apostles. The biblical drama becomes our story, and the coming of Christ becomes good news for us. According to one commentator, tropology 'is essentially, then, a reproduction or an interiorization of Christ's Mystery in the life of individual Christians'.[65] In *Life Together*, Dietrich Bonhoeffer urges Christians to read with attention to the whole sweep of redemptive history, and, perhaps inadvertently, describes a tropological reading of Scripture:

> Forgetting and losing ourselves, we, too, pass through the Red Sea, through the desert, across the Jordan into the promised land. With Israel we fall into doubt and unbelief and through punishment and repentance experience again God's help and faithfulness. All this is not mere reverie but holy, godly, reality. We are torn out of our own existence and set down in the midst of the holy history of God on earth.... It is not that God is the spectator and sharer of our present life, however important that is; but rather that we are the reverent listeners and participants in God's action in the sacred story, the history of the Christ on earth. And only in so far as we are *there*, is God with us today also.[66]

With Bonhoeffer's words in mind, it should not surprise us that the tropological sense is, in de Lubac's view, 'mystical'. It entails the gift of a vision of God's glory shedding light on our own existence even as it illumines all things. Thus, the chapter in the second volume of *Medieval Exegesis* that deals with tropology is titled 'Mystical Tropology'.[67] De Lubac believes that the mystery of Christ can be 'interiorized in man in such a way as to bear its fruit within him'.[68] He quotes St John of the Cross:

> When we speak of the union of the soul with God, we are not referring to the union that already exists between God and all his creatures, but to the union of the soul with God and its transformation by his love. This transformation takes place, however, only when the soul, through love, resembles that of the Creator. That is why union is called supernatural. It takes place when two wills, that of

64. De Lubac, 'On an Old Distich', p. 115.
65. Marcellino D'Ambrosio, *Henri de Lubac and the Recovery of the Traditional Hermeneutic* (Washington, DC: Catholic University of America, 1991), p. 199.
66. Dietrich Bonhoeffer, *Life Together: The Classic Exploration of Faith in Community* (San Francisco, CA: Harper San Francisco, 1954), pp. 53-54.
67. ME, vol. 2, pp. 127-77.
68. ME, vol. 1, p. xvi.

the soul and that of God, are in agreement, and one has nothing that repels the other. Thus, when the soul completely rejects all that is repugnant or does not conform to the will of God, it is transformed into God through love.[69]

The tropological sense facilitates a conversion of the believer that leads to a union with God, though this union is not to be mistaken for 'an identification', since 'between the human soul and God, as in the marriage of the Church and the Lamb, there is always union, not absorption'.[70] Christian mysticism can thus be understood through the 'symbolism of spiritual marriage'.[71]

Finally, the anagogical sense is eschatological in nature since it looks ahead to the consummation of all things in Christ. The anagogical sense shows the Church 'what goal to strive for',[72] and it enables a mystical unification between the Church in the present and the fullness of Christ to come. The anagogical interpretation of Scripture enables the Church to experience the eschatological consummation as both now and not yet:

> In traditional eschatology...the doctrine of the four senses is achieved and finds its unity. For Christianity is a fulfillment, but in this very fulfillment it is a promised hope. Mystical or doctrinal, taught or lived, true anagogy is therefore always eschatological. It stirs up the desire for eternity in us. This is also why the fourth sense is forced to be the last. No more than it could really lack the three others could it be followed by a fifth. Neither is hope ever lacking nor, in our earthly condition, is it ever surpassed even if it already encroaches upon its term.[73]

The anagogical sense, more than any of the others, means that the revelation of God can never be the 'given' demanded by de Lubac's neo-scholastic opponents. Instead, the anagogical sense stresses that readers must remain ever open to the coming of Christ and the vision of his glory, a coming that can be experienced in time though its fullness will entail the consummation of time. This vision cannot be a 'given' anymore than God can be an object, limited in nature. In the words of Augustine, 'however high anagogy leads, it always leaves something to look for and always with greater fervor, because it still does not uncover the Face of God'.[74]

Conclusion

Lest we misunderstand de Lubac's enthusiasm for the traditional senses of scripture, it may be helpful to remember that he did not advocate a strict return

---

69. de Lubac, 'Mysticism and Mystery', p. 62.
70. Ibid., pp. 60–61.
71. Ibid., p. 60.
72. De Lubac, 'On an Old Distich', p. 115.
73. Translated and cited in ME, vol. 2, p. 197.
74. ME, vol. 2, p. 193.

to an ancient methodology.[75] Even for the ancients, the four senses were less a methodology and more an aid to contemplation.[76] The ongoing value of de Lubac's work on the four senses is in his demonstration and endorsement of the participatory, assimilative, and ultimately mystical nature of all theology and especially of spiritual exegesis, theology's deep source and greatest fruit. He believed that these qualities enabled ancient interpreters to conform themselves and the Church to the Catholic and orthodox faith in a far deeper way than many modern interpreters do.[77] These qualities, he suggests, are enduring and necessary even if their use in a contemporary context informed by critical scholarship will look quite different than it did in an ancient context. Modern interpreters 'must approach matters with greater freedom if we hope to recapture anything of the spiritual interpretation of Scripture, as it existed during the first centuries of the Church. We must, above all else, reproduce a spiritual movement, often through completely different methods, while avoiding a retreat into the archaic or into slavish imitation.'[78]

In summary, de Lubac wanted to see Christians engage in theological work and read Sacred Scripture in more participatory, assimilative, and mystical ways, as our ancestors did, because he hoped to see the Church grounded in the mystery of Christ and able to offer true witness to a culture in need of the vision of God's glory, as every culture is. His long and prolific career was characterized by a tremendous and often controversial effort to challenge the obstinate metaphysical dualism separating theology from life and the Church from her true political witness. While challenging the reigning metaphysical dualism of neo-scholastic theology, his work in ecclesiology, eucharistic theology, and spiritual exegesis sought to reconceive, in mystical fashion, the means of grace by which the vision of God's glory is realized.

---

75. For a helpful discussion of the four senses and exegetical 'methodology', see Ibid., pp. 207–16.

76. For a discussion of the question of the four senses and exegetical methodology, see Bryan C. Hollon, 'Knowledge of God as Assimilation and Participation: An Essay on Theological Pedagogy in the Light of Biblical Epistemology', *Perspectives in Religious Studies* 38:1 (Spring 2011): pp. 85–106, 93, n. 35.

77. When I suggest that ancient interpreters were able to 'conform themselves and the Church to the catholic and orthodox faith', I have in mind Sarah Coakley's description of an 'assimilated orthodoxy' that cannot be disentangled from prayer, worship, ethics, politics, and so on. According to Coakley, '"Orthodoxy" as mere propositional assent needs to be carefully distinguished from "orthodoxy" as a demanding, and ongoing, spiritual project, in which the language of the creeds is personally and progressively assimilated' (Sarah Coakley, *God, Sexuality, and the Self: An Essay "On the Trinity"* (Cambridge: Cambridge University Press, 2013), p. 5).

78. De Lubac, *Scripture in the Tradition*, p. 24.

Chapter 14

AN EMERGING CHRISTOLOGY

Noel O'Sullivan

In Search of the Christology of Henri de Lubac

The title of this chapter is intended to alert the reader to the fact that there is not a systematic Christology in the works of Henri de Lubac. He does not use the term and, furthermore, by his own admission, he always hesitated at the prospect of writing a book on Jesus Christ:

> I cannot help thinking that it is a certain spiritual superficiality rather than the feeling of my intellectual deficiencies or even than the conviction that I am far too unequal to such a subject to dare ever to approach it head-on, that has always made me postpone undertaking that work on Jesus Christ that would have been dearer to me than all the others, and in view of which I did much reading and recorded many reflections but which I never really attacked.[1]

This is surprising because Christ is ever-present in his prodigious output. His confession of 'a certain spiritual superficiality' should surely read 'a profound appreciation of the mystery of Christ', which would better explain his hesitation at the prospect of a work on Jesus Christ.

This chapter will attempt to glean from the author's corpus what the outline of 'that work on Jesus Christ' might look like. Obviously our choice is inevitably limited because of the constraints of a mere chapter on such a major subject.[2] I will focus on the emerging Christology that we find in his publications on the question of the *surnaturel* and, in particular, on lesser known articles, including

---

1. ASC, p. 147.
2. For a full treatment of de Lubac's Christology see, Noel O'Sullivan, *Christ and Creation: Christology as the Key to Interpreting the Theology of Creation in the Works of Henri de Lubac* (Oxford: Peter Lang, 2009).

some unpublished material from the 'Archives Chantraine' in Namur, Belgium.[3] Some of de Lubac's other published works will also offer material helpful to our subject.

De Lubac's Christological concerns are soteriological rather than ontological and, while he does not settle for a functional Christology, his underlying concern is the human relationship with God. It is this question that leads him into the minefield of the debate on the supernatural, which will be the first leg of our reflection. We will then move to his more explicit Christological writings, both published and unpublished. These will consider major issues like the purpose of the Incarnation, the freedom and sinlessness of Christ, the possibility of growth in consciousness, the Trinitarian nature of de Lubac's Christology, and the prominence he gives to the binary image and likeness.

The Emerging Christology of Henri de Lubac in the Surnaturel *Debate*

The word *surnaturel* is in a certain sense the term most associated with Henri de Lubac and one that evokes the pain he suffered as theologian and churchman. A trenchant criticism of two different and erroneous interpretations of St Augustine's understanding of grace by Baius and Jansenius, published in 1931,[4] marks the beginning of his public involvement in the question of the supernatural. His interest, however, goes back to his student days at Ore Place in Hastings (1924–1926) when he was part of a research group that consisted of twelve students under the direction of Joseph Huby (1878–1948). It was Fr Huby who encouraged de Lubac, as part of his research task, to verify if the neo-scholastic understanding of the supernatural really represented the thought of Saint Thomas Aquinas.[5] This experience showed him that what had been filtered to him in the textbooks was not reliable. The exposition he gave on the fruit of his research formed the basis of a dossier that eventually led to the publication of *Surnaturel: Etudes historiques,* in 1946.[6] Three years later he published an

---

3. Georges Chantraine S.J. (1933–2010) was a close friend of Henri de Lubac and was archivist of his works and unpublished papers in Namur. He published two volumes of a biography on de Lubac before his unexpected death in 2010. Georges Chantraine, *Henri de Lubac, t. I: De la naissance à la demobilisation 1896–1919* (Paris: Cerf, 2007); *Henri de Lubac tome II: Les années de Formation 1919–1929* (Paris: Cerf, 2009). I am indebted to Fr Chantraine and the Jesuits in Namur for giving me access to the unpublished writings of Cardinal de Lubac.

4. Henri de Lubac, 'Deux Augustiniens Fourvoyés', *Recherches de Science Religieuse* 21 (1931): pp. 422–43, 513–40.

5. ASC, p. 35.

6. My references to this work will be from the original French edition as I do not have access to an official English translation.

article entitled: 'Le mystère du surnaturel',[7] where he clarified some of the issues raised by his earlier work. Then in 1965 came two further works: *Augustinisme et théologie moderne*[8] and *Le mystère du surnaturel*.[9] Of considerable interest also is the publication in 1980 of *Petite catéchèse sur nature et grâce*.[10]

The relevance of the supernatural debate to our purposes here is the Christological impoverishment of that debate, a lacuna recognized by Lubac, and the gradual emergence of Christological categories in his works over a twenty-year period. We shall illustrate this by juxtaposing some quotations from *Surnaturel* (1946) and *Augustinisme et théologie moderne* (1965). De Lubac regrets not making clear from the beginning that the debate presupposed a basic abstraction, which explained 'a nearly total absence of any consideration of historic revelation or of creation in Christ and for Christ'.[11] He failed to free himself fully from the confining categories of the neo-scholastic tradition.[12] In this regard he refers to the more concrete and synthetic way of proceeding as outlined by his colleague Henri Bouillard, who substituted the more existentialist title 'the Christian mystery' for that of 'the supernatural order'.[13] It was largely within the categories of natural/supernatural that de Lubac began to arouse a rigid theological world to a new way of thinking, one that would eventually cause what was presumed to be an impenetrable neo-scholastic bastion to implode.

De Lubac's acute awareness of the Christological limitations of his contribution to the supernatural debate is evident long before his *Mémoire sur l'occasion de mes écrits*, published in 1989, a limitation which he tries to correct as he entered more deeply into the question of the supernatural. A comparison of *Surnaturel* (1946) and *Augustinisme et théologie moderne* (1965) gives an indication of the author's desire to make his theology of grace Christologically explicit. For example, in the later work he includes the two chapters on Baius and Jansenius, with only minimal changes to what had been published in the earlier work. We will refer to two such changes – though there are others in similar vein – which highlight

---

7. Henri de Lubac, 'Le mystère du surnaturel', *Recherches de Science Religieuse* 36 (1949), published in *Théologie dans l'histoire* II (Paris: Declée de Brouwer, 1990), pp. 71–107. English translation: 'The Mystery of the Supernatural', TH, pp. 281–316.

8. Henri de Lubac, *Augustinisme et théologie moderne* (Paris: Aubier-Montaigne, 1965). English translation: AMT.

9. Henri de Lubac, *Le mystère du surnaturel* (Paris: Aubier-Montaigne, 1965). English translation: MS.

10. Henri de Lubac, *Petite catéchèse sur nature et grâce* (Paris: Fayard, 1980). English translation: BC.

11. ASC, p. 199.

12. It is important to distinguish between the terms 'scholastic' and 'neo-scholastic'. The scholastic tradition which developed in the twelfth and through the thirteenth centuries under the influence of Aristotelian philosophy is of immense value, whereas the neo-scholasticism, which consisted of commentaries on the *Summae*, led to a certain sclerosis of theology. It tended to neglect the writings of the Fathers. Much of de Lubac's contribution to theology was in rediscovering the true teaching of the Scholastics.

13. ASC, p. 199.

the Christological character of grace. In the first instance, he comments on the non-opposition between nature and grace in the theology of Saint Augustine. The following juxtaposition reveals a simple but most significant change between the two works (the emphasis is mine):

1946	1965
'*Grace* becomes holy desire in order the better to overcome the other (evil desire) and is not for all that the direct opposite of nature.'[14]	'*The grace of Christ* becomes holy desire in order the better to overcome the other (evil desire) and is not for all that the direct opposite of nature.'[15]

Grace is referred to as *the grace of Christ* in the later work. Grace is seen here not as obliterating nature, but as enabling nature to become what it can be at its best. Christ is the Mediator of this perfection. The significance of this change in the two texts brings out the personal – the Christological – aspect of grace. An understanding of grace which is divorced from the self-communication of God in love runs the risk of being reified.

De Lubac's concern to bring out the Christological dimension of grace is more fully appreciated when we consider the second instance, where the earlier text is considerably amplified in the later work. Commenting on the relationship between grace and the human will, as understood by Augustine, de Lubac corrects Jansenius' misguided interpretation whereby he obliterated the will and replaced it with grace, whereas Augustine saw grace as informing and enabling the will but not replacing it:

1946	1965
'Grace enables the will to overcome concupiscence, the spirit to overcome the flesh. Grace is liberating.'[16]	'This grace enables the human will to overcome concupiscence, free will to overcome sin, the spirit to overcome the flesh. "Victory by which sin is overcome is nothing other than a gift of God, aiding free will in that struggle." On our own we shall be vanquished in the struggle; but when we are helped by *the grace of God, by Jesus Christ our Lord*, the strength of health returns to us and the attraction of righteousness is in us the victor over everything that leads us to sin (…). *The grace of Jesus Christ, which must never on any account be thought of apart from the Incarnation itself, is therefore liberating.*'[17]

14. S, p. 70.
15. AMT, p. 54; de Lubac, *Augustinisme et théologie moderne*, p. 92.
16. S, p. 72.
17. AMT, p. 81; de Lubac, *Augustinisme et théologie moderne*, p. 96. The quotation from St Augustine is cited in Latin in the original French edition and is from *De gratia et libero arbitrio* I, IV, p. 8, PL 44, p. 887.

The 1965 text is explicitly Christological and contrasts starkly with the 1946 work. In de Lubac's view the autonomy of the human person is respected; the will does not become the pawn of a power coming from outside itself. Grace is not a reified commodity; it is rather the power of God which is active internally 'through Jesus Christ our Lord'. It is significant that de Lubac highlights the connection between the grace of Christ and the Incarnation. The gift of God, which frees the human will to act in accordance with its higher nature, is none other than Jesus Christ who is known through the historical event of the Incarnation. It is the decisive event at the heart of de Lubac's Christology. The 1965 quotation is a considerable advance on the 1946 work which did not relate the liberating gift of God to the person of Christ. Much could be made of the fact that grace is linked here to the God incarnate and not to the Redemptive act of the Cross. However, for de Lubac the Incarnation is redemptive. He makes this explicit in the note on the *De correptione et gratia* of Augustine, which he adds to the third chapter of *Augustinianism and Modern Theology*, where he writes: 'This grace comes from the redemptive Incarnation by which God lowered himself to the level of our wretchedness.'[18]

We retain two important points from this analysis of the relationship between the 1946 text, *Surnaturel,* and the 1965 text, *Augustinisme et théologie moderne.* First, grace is explicitly defined as the grace of Christ in the later text. De Lubac is obviously aware of the Christological limitation of the earlier work. This grace of Christ comes from the redemptive Incarnation. Thus the redemptive act of the Incarnate One is the source of grace. Second, it is clear that de Lubac does not separate Incarnation and Redemption, a point whose import is extensive. In particular, it addresses the question of the reason for the Incarnation; whether it was to complete God's revelation or whether it was uniquely redemptive. We find that the reasons for the Incarnation were both revelatory and redemptive in de Lubac's Christology. The primary purpose of Christ's coming was to reveal the fullness of God's love: his redemptive role is secondary. The Incarnation was not contingent upon man's sin. In this interpretation de Lubac finds himself in the Scotist tradition rather than in the satisfaction theology of Anselm and, to a lesser extent, that of Thomas Aquinas, as we will illustrate presently.

The Newness and Transcendence of Christ

A significant and explicitly Christological publication is an article entitled 'The Light of Christ'[19] which gives an outline of de Lubac's Christological vision and is worthy of close attention. It is paradigmatic for his Christology. It first appeared as a pamphlet in 1941 and was distributed in the churches. It was subsequently

---

18. AMT, p. 93; de Lubac, *Augustinisme et théologie moderne,* p. 109.

19. Henri de Lubac, *La Lumière du Christ* (Le Puy: Mappus, 1941), republished in *Affrontements mystiques* (Paris: Témoignage chrétien, 1950), pp. 185-213, and *Théologie dans l'Histoire* I (Paris: Desclée de Brouwer, 1990), pp. 203-22. English translation: 'The Light of Christ', TH, pp. 201-20.

published in *Affrontements mystiques* in 1950 and in *Théologie dans l'histoire* in 1990. De Lubac describes it as a 'kind of meditation on "The Light of Christ"'.[20] It outlines the major Christological concerns of the author though none of them is fully developed. Of considerable importance are the issues raised and the manner of doing so in a relatively short article. It puts into focus the following critical themes: the newness and transcendence of Christianity; the radical originality of Christ; the revelatory function of Christ; the Father as the God who is Love; Calvary as the apogee of Love revealed; the role of the Spirit in the Incarnation; the Trinitarian dimension of de Lubac's Christology. Throughout the article there is a concern to show the importance of dogma and the manner in which the Christological dogmas, in particular, were quarried from the pit of human concepts and language. It is in this article too that the author articulates the revelatory and redemptive roles of Christ.

For de Lubac Christianity is not the superlative of nature: 'The *supernatural* is not a higher, more beautiful or more fruitful nature (…). It is the irruption of a wholly different principle.'[21] It is not a super addition (*superadditus*) onto nature: it of a different order. Salvation is not of the same order as human progress: 'We know too well that all progress of the world will not obtain the least beginning of salvation!'[22] Although God is actively present in all of history, the Incarnation is not just one moment in a continuum. As de Lubac wrote in his first published work (1938): 'Christianity … brought something absolutely new into the world.'[23] The coming of Christ was anticipated and, in that sense, the Incarnation is in continuity with the Old Testament. While acknowledging that, de Lubac stresses the rupture, the complete unexpected nature of what happened in the Incarnation. His is a Christology from above: it is not a synthesis arising from a continuum in history. He explains his position by contrasting extrinsic and intrinsic transcendence, rejecting the former in favour of the latter. Extrinsic transcendence amounts to a Hegelian-type emergence of Christ from the history that preceded him. De Lubac rejects extrinsic transcendence. Intrinsic transcendence, on the other hand, is of a different order and cannot be explained by an evolutionary understanding of history.

Though not opposed to continuity with what preceded it,[24] intrinsic transcendence is not just a synthesis of what came before, or of what is contemporaneous with a given reality. It surpasses all existing elements and is more than a new combination of these elements. It is a transformation of everything brought about by a certain 'revival from within'.[25] Applied to Christianity, this intrinsic transcendence means that something totally new comes about. Though

---

20. ASC, p. 58.
21. Henri de Lubac, 'The Search for a New Man', DAH, pp. 399–468, 466.
22. 'The Light of Christ', TH, pp. 219–20.
23. C, p. 137.
24. 'The Light of Christ', TH, p. 205, n. 4.
25. Ibid., p. 205.

it is in continuity with the past and is its fulfilment, nevertheless it is much more. The origin of this newness is the Spirit of God.

De Lubac expresses the newness of Christianity thus: 'He has stolen in with gentleness, and he has burst in with power. He has penetrated human history, and all has been transformed.'[26] He then elaborates further:

> The Spirit of Christ has founded a wholly new thing, the religion of Christ, and this religion of Christ, for which all human history had prepared, for which all human thought had slowly woven the fabric, suddenly rises up, in the midst of men; '*sine patre, sine matre, sine genealogia*'. Pure creation, pure miracle.[27]

Two points need to be highlighted from this quotation. One is the dialectic transcendence/history; the other is the pneumatological character of the Incarnation. On the first point, it is important to emphasize that while the coming of Christ transcends history, it takes place in history. This quotation encapsulates at once the preparation, the continuity but also the rupture that is the Christ event. And yet, this 'pure miracle' takes place 'in the midst of humanity', in history. God acts in history, though history alone cannot explain it. While rejecting an extrinsic transcendence as inadequate, whereby the Incarnation could be explained as a synthesis within history, de Lubac's insistence on the historical nature of that event is all the more significant.

From his first published work, *Catholicisme*, he stressed the historical nature of Christianity and dogma:

> For if the salvation offered by God is in fact the salvation of the human race, since this human race lives and develops in time, any account of this salvation will naturally take a historical form: it will be the history of the penetration of humanity by Christ.[28]

This quotation brings together the Economy and Theology, to evoke the traditional binary. God communicates himself in an Economy. At the same time this Economy opens up the Being of God to us: there we discover the Theology. This brings us to the second point highlighted in the above quotation from 'The Light of Christ' on the pneumatological nature of de Lubac's Christology.

Here we see the place attributed to the Spirit in the creation of something new in history. One senses an allusion here to the creation of the world, when 'God's spirit hovered over the water.'[29] He makes this explicit: 'Like the creative Deed, which does not cease to maintain being and life everywhere, the Deed of Charity is pursued over the world. The second Genesis, henceforth, as permanent as the first and, like it, infinitely fruitful.'[30] The Spirit brings about a new creation:

---

26. Ibid., p. 206.
27. Ibid.
28. C, p. 141.
29. Genesis 1: 2.
30. 'The Light of Christ', TH, p. 210.

'Pure creation, pure miracle.' The new era is a time of grace: 'It is a wholly new order that begins (…). A dyke has been broken, which lets the flow of Love pass through.'[31]

The transcendence of Christianity is not just relative to other and earlier events; it is not only superior to them: it is an absolute transcendence and is totally new. Invoking the phrase of St Irenaeus, de Lubac emphasizes that this is the transcendence, the newness that comes from Christ. The quotation from Irenaeus is as follows: 'He brought total newness by bringing himself, who had been announced.'[32] De Lubac uses this quotation from Irenaeus on two occasions in the article. In the context of the absolute transcendence of Christianity, he quotes the first part of the phrase: *Omnem novitiatem attulit*. Then when he refers explicitly to the Person of Christ, he continues the quotation to include the important words: *semetipsum afferens*. What is absolutely new about Christianity is Christ himself. The final part of Irenaeus's quotation – *qui fuerat annuntiatus* – though not quoted by de Lubac, is certainly implied by him, given the emphasis he puts on the Christ event as the fulfilment of the scriptures. Interestingly, Michel Sales introduces his Foreword to *Théologie dans l'histoire* by giving the full quotation from Irenaeus.

The intrinsic transcendence of Christianity lies in the irruption of the Spirit of Christ into a world where he had been announced but the radical nature of the event had not been anticipated. Transcendence and newness are of a pair: its transcendence lies in its radical newness which has its origin in the Spirit of Christ; its newness is absolutely transcendent, in that it comes from the Spirit of Christ and is not the result of some evolutionary process within history. De Lubac summarizes: 'There is no absolute newness, no revelation properly speaking, no true transcendence outside of the unique reality of his Person.'[33] Turning this quotation about, we can retain three significant things about de Lubac's understanding of Jesus Christ: the God Incarnate is 'absolute newness'; he is 'revelation properly so-called'; he is 'true transcendence'.

The uniqueness of Christ is also underlined here. This quotation is taken from the end of a paragraph where the author has been summarizing the relationship between the dogmas of the faith and Christ: 'If the articles of faith are numbered, the Object of Faith is marvellously one. If the former are formed of abstract propositions, the Latter is marvellously Living!'[34] Recognizing the necessity of concepts of whatever philosophical provenance, these can only channel 'a part' of the divine revelation. Even then, they do so only when related to 'that same revelation, to the living Center, to the divine Center from which all radiates and to which all must lead us: to Jesus Christ'.[35] He is unique 'because in Him dwells

---

31. Ibid., p. 207.
32. 'Omnem novitatem attulit, semetipsum afferens, qui fuerat annuntiatus', Saint Irenaeus, *Adversus Haereses* IV, pp. 34, 1.
33. 'The Light of Christ', TH, pp. 217–18.
34. Ibid., p. 217.
35. Ibid.

the fullness of divinity.'³⁶ Thus 'the unique reality of his Person' refers primarily to his divinity. It is because Jesus Christ is divine that we have 'absolute newness', 'revelation properly so-called', and 'true transcendence'. The divinity of Christ is essential to his function as Mediator as, of course, is his humanity.³⁷

The Christological Dogmas: Hypostatic Union

De Lubac inherits the theological tradition; therefore he does not have to invent the Christological wheel, as it were. This means that we find an acceptance rather than an attempt at a speculative reinterpretation of the Christological dogmas. In this he differs from theologians like Rahner, Pannenberg, and Moingt. However, at times he does refer to these dogmas, but it is with the intent of highlighting a particular issue which he is treating. For example, in *Catholicisme,* he invokes the monophysite heresy in Christology to caution against monophysite tendencies in ecclesiology. In 'The Light of Christ', he stresses the radicalness of the two natures, human and divine, while avoiding any sense of separation. We will show here his purpose in doing so. It is in this section that we will elaborate the problematic of the unpublished article, 'Sur la liberté du Christ',³⁸ because it concerns the two natures and the unity of Christ.

Regarding the human nature, for example, Jesus is not a phantom from heaven but is of the same substance as the woman from whom he was formed. In emphasizing the humanity of Jesus, one expects de Lubac to proceed immediately to the question of redemption. But this is not the logic of the article 'The Light of Christ.' The humanity of Jesus Christ is stressed because otherwise God would not be able to communicate with humanity in the way that he does in the Word made flesh. If the Son of Man is not incarnate, then Jesus is a mere intermediary and not the Mediator. This is how de Lubac argues: 'How would God give himself to man if he remained a stranger to him? And how would his Word penetrate him if it were not also to become a human word?'³⁹ The emphasis of the author here is on the Incarnation as revelation of God. There is no mention of sin and redemption, at least not here. Towards the end of the article de Lubac – in a footnote – says that revelation and redemption cannot be separated: 'One risks minimising revelation if one does not see that it is at the same time Redemption, personal transformation, and efficacious grace.'⁴⁰ This comment is reminiscent of what the author had already stressed in his first published work: 'Revelation and redemption are linked and the Church is their only Tabernacle.'⁴¹

---

36. Ibid.
37. *Quod non est assumptum non est sanatum,* St Gregory Nazianzus, *Ep.* 101 *ad Cledon.* PG 37, 181C–184A.
38. 'Sur la liberté du Christ', Archives Chantraine no. 2338.
39. 'The Light of Christ', TH, p. 206.
40. Ibid., p. 218, n. 39.
41. C, p. 226.

De Lubac sees the Incarnation as primarily motivated by the desire on God's part to reveal himself to humanity. The thrust of 'The Light of Christ' is to emphasize that Christ is the Revelation of God who is Love. In him, God communicates with humanity and invites the human person to share this Love with others. It does not mean that sin is denied; it is presumed as part of the background to the article, but is not the primary concern.

Likewise the author underlines the radical originality of Jesus by the way in which he describes his divinity. He does so from the perspective of a Jewish monotheist for whom belief in the divinity of a man would indeed be folly, especially when faced with the crucifixion of the divine person. De Lubac's quotation from Clement of Alexandria is worth recalling. We give a slightly extended version from an English translation: 'For those who in their own estimation are wise consider it fabulous that the Son of God should speak by man and that God should have a Son, and especially that that Son should have suffered.'[42] The impact of this way of approaching the question of divinity is to underline the radicalness of the self-communication of God to humanity.

We turn to *Catholicism* (Chapter VI), to complete the author's emphasis on the unity of Christ. Here he deals with the relationship between the pre-existent Son of God and the historical Jesus. In a section on the interpretation of Scripture, he surveys the figures in the Old Testament who preceded the Incarnation and then poses the question as to how the figures, or types, could precede the One who existed before them and through whom they were created. He asserts: 'Christ, in so far as transcendent and pre-existing before all things, is anterior to his figures, yet as a historical being, coming in the flesh, he appears after them.'[43] This is the truth perceived by John the Baptist.[44] Christ is one in the meeting of the Eternal and the temporal: 'Christ existing before all things cannot be separated from Christ born of the woman, who died and rose again.'[45] Thus we find in his first published work that the author clearly highlights the unity of the person in two natures.

One of the underlying questions is the possibility of finding in the works of de Lubac a systematic Christology. We have pointed out from the beginning – on the basis of de Lubac's own words – that he did not undertake a systematization. However, a patient sifting through the texts reaps rich rewards by way of diverse comments and references that enable us to piece together an outline of his Christology. In the two texts referred to above, we find the Christological dogma of the two natures and their unity in the one person: the unity of the pre-existent Son of God and the humanity of Jesus of Nazareth; the coming together in Christ of the Eternal and the historical. Now we turn to the article, 'Sur la liberté du Christ,' where the author treats of a core Christological issue.

---

42. Clement of Alexandria, *Stromates*, Book 1, Chapter XVIII. English translation: Alexander Roberts and James Donaldson, *Ante-Nicene Fathers* 2 (Massachusetts: Hendrickson, 1999), p. 320.
43. C, p. 174.
44. John 1: 30.
45. C, p. 174.

Sinlessness and Freedom of Christ

'Sur la liberté du Christ' is concerned with the question of the sinlessness and freedom of Christ. As Mediator, Christ needs to act in total freedom but, if his mission is given him by his Father, is he not obliged to carry out that command? Otherwise would he not be sinless? How can the mission necessitated by the Father be reconciled with true freedom? This is the problematic as presented by de Lubac in this unpublished article. His manner of dealing with it is based on the understanding of the two wills in Christ, a question which was the subject of the Third Council of Constantinople (680/1), though the author does not refer to this Council by name.

De Lubac emphasizes the importance of understanding 'precept,' 'obligation,' and 'obedience' analogically in relation to Christ. God is not a human leader with Christ as his subaltern. The initiative of our salvation and the manner of its execution belong to the Word just as it does to the Father. Thus the Son is not the object of a precept that has been imposed on him externally and which he is obliged to obey (in an external way). In an extended note at the end of the article, de Lubac points out that the redemption is an initiative of the Son, a spontaneous act of love towards us: 'Jesus is the manifestation of the divine Charity.'[46] In the same note, the author asserts that in the work of our redemption there is neither a human initiative on the part of Jesus nor is there a precept of the Father, in the strict sense of the term. He quotes St Bernard: 'God did not require the blood of the Son, but accepted what was offered.'[47] And what was offered was love. This is a critical point in relation to the satisfaction theory of St Anselm, for example. It is not the death of Christ as such which brings about our salvation but it is his obedience to the point of dying out of love for humanity: it is not a case of 'blood for blood'. We are here concerned with the economy of grace and of pure love.

We need to tease out a little further what de Lubac means when he claims that the work of redemption is neither a human initiative on Jesus' part nor a precept of the Father. First, it is the initiative of the Eternal Son of God and not just an obligation that Jesus discovered in the course of his human life. Second, the sense of obligation to obey a precept is the mark of a human being whose freedom is imperfect. De Lubac writes:

> Where there is true freedom, perfect freedom, there is no 'obligation' properly so-called, obligation being a liberating constraint, the condition necessary for reaching perfect freedom. So, precept and a feeling of obligation are correlatives. Obligation is interiorised (and loses the quality which gives it this name) to the extent that perfection grows, since perfection means union with God and unity of being. So, in Christ we cannot conceive of a sense of obligation. Nevertheless,

---

46. 'Sur la liberté du Christ', Archives Chantraine no. 2338, note 4.
47. 'Deus Filii sanguinem non requisivit, sed acceptavit oblatum', St Bernard, quoted in 'Sur la liberté du Christ', no. 23387, without reference.

in relation to him, we can speak of a most perfect obedience, because that is an objective view.[48]

What de Lubac is at pains to emphasize in this consideration of the relationship between sinlessness and freedom is the unity of Christ. In him it is the divine person who is deciding and acting. He believes that other attempts to deal with this question fail because their starting point is human – and therefore imperfect – freedom which, inevitably, conflicts with the divine will. He explains this as an 'indifferent freedom',[49] which is an existential 'power' to choose between good and evil. This is the condition of the human being: through a series of choices, under grace, we gradually arrive at a state of full freedom in the Beatific Vision. For de Lubac, freedom is being (*esse*) itself in its state of excellence. Through the mediation of Christ this movement towards total freedom is possible.

In Christ there is no imperfection, no sin and, therefore, in him is perfect freedom. He chooses to love unconditionally in total obedience to his Father, without feeling a sense of obligation. De Lubac prefers to speak of an absence of indifference in Christ rather than a sense of necessity, because it is difficult to avoid an interpretation of external obligation in the popular use of the term necessity. He suggests that necessity and freedom can coexist without contradiction or opposition. Absolute objective necessity is the form in which absolute subjective freedom is represented to the observer, using the idea of Rahner that the body is the form being takes so that being can be seen by another.[50] Similarly, necessity is the body of freedom, according to de Lubac.[51] An absence of indifference means that Christ was free of the capacity for sin. In this we can also say that he was fully human, understanding human in its state of perfection, the capacity for sin being a limitation of the human and not part of its definition. Sinlessness and freedom, far from being contradictory, are coextensive: one is the inverse of the other.

This brings us to the question of the relationship between the two wills in Christ and the unity of his Person. De Lubac rightly asserts that the will is a function of the nature, while freedom is the function of the person. Thus, in the case of Christ, there are two wills – human and divine – or principles of free operations, but there are not two principles of freedom: this would amount to two

---

48. 'Sur la liberté du Christ', no. 23407f. This is a note (4) accompanying the text (no. 23390).

49. Ibid., no. 23390. See also St Thomas Aquinas, STh III, q. 18, art. 3–4.

50. 'That the body can and may be considered as the symbol, that is, as the symbolic reality of man, follows at once from the Thomist doctrine that the soul is the substantial form of the body.' Karl Rahner, 'The Theology of Symbol', *Theological Investigations* IV, trans. Kevin Smyth (Baltimore, MD: Helicon Press, London: Darton, Longman & Todd, 1966), p. 246.

51. Ibid., no. 23399.

persons.⁵² Freedom is an initiative of the person, or subject, not of the will. There is, therefore, one freedom in Christ which reverts to his person. Thanks to the hypostatic union, this freedom is perfect. For de Lubac, the relationship between the natures is expressed in terms of Christ's freedom because 'it is the very core of the spirit'.⁵³

Consciousness of Christ

The underlying question which presents itself throughout the foregoing is the possibility of development in Jesus Christ. If his human nature is perfect from the moment of his conception in the womb of Mary and if he is born in a state of complete freedom, how is it possible to consider growth in consciousness, development of the human will, and a life lived like ours in time and space? This is the question which de Lubac considers more pertinent than the more traditional one concerning the union of two natures in one being, in the unity of the person of the Word. His answer lies in the idea of paradox. Evoking the Fathers of the Church in his work, *Paradoxes*, de Lubac describes the Incarnation as the 'Paradox of paradoxes'.⁵⁴ In the article we are considering here, 'Sur la liberté du Christ', he describes it as the mystery of mysteries and the miracle of miracles, evoking Origen and Bonaventure. He continues in that article to explain the use of the term paradox in relation to the Incarnation: 'But doesn't every great truth appear at first sight to the senses and even to reason as paradoxical and wonderful, all the more so the greater it is?'⁵⁵ As he affirms in *Surnaturel*: 'Paradox is a necessary sign of truth.'⁵⁶ De Lubac employs the idea of paradox to the *desiderium naturale videndi Deum*; he does so in relation to the Church and he applies it to the Incarnation. 'Paradox' enables the author to hold in tension what appears as impossible. The question which arises, then, is the adequacy of the idea of paradox for expressing the apparent divergence between the sinlessness, freedom, and perfection of Christ on the one hand, and the possibility of human development in Jesus Christ on the other.

---

52. What de Lubac is guarding against here is the danger of Monoenergism and Monothelitism, both of which were rejected at the Third Council of Constantinople (681). Monoenergism was the belief that there was only one energy or one principle of activity in Christ: the human is subsumed in the divine. In similar vein, Monothelitism proposed that there was only one will in Christ. In both these heterodox positions the human principles of operations (activity and will) would be redundant, an aberration reminiscent of Apollinarianism. The orthodox position, in contrast, respects the human and divine principles of activity and will in Christ, thereby respecting the two natures. The person of Christ takes into account these two principles of operations when exercising his freedom.

53. Ibid., no. 23401.

54. *Paradoxes, suivi de Nouveaux paradoxes* (Paris: Seuil, 1959); republished under the new title, *Paradoxes* (Paris: Cerf, 1999), 8.

55. 'Sur la liberté du Christ', no. 23402.

56. S, p. 484.

We have seen that de Lubac's primary emphasis is on the unity of Christ, which has its source in the hypostatic union: it is the Person of the Son who is human and divine. He is the pre-existent Son of God made man, his humanity is perfect and his freedom is total. The question de Lubac raises about the possibility of development in the personality and self-consciousness of Jesus is very apt and pertinent in contemporary Christology. His response is unfortunately truncated. He answers the question by restating it in different terms. To describe the Incarnation as the mystery of mysteries, the miracle of miracles, and the paradox of paradoxes does not attempt to face the very real Christological issue which he legitimately raises. Before attempting a response on our part to this issue as presented by de Lubac, we need to elaborate somewhat how we understand the question. We begin by referring to some scriptural evidence to support the interpretation that Jesus experienced some of the limitations of human existence.

For example, if the temptations were real for Jesus then there must have been some sense in which, at a human level, he hesitated, was afraid, and simply didn't know. In a note entitled 'La Liberté du Christ,' which follows the article, 'Sur la Liberté du Christ,' de Lubac writes: 'As there is no ignorance in him, he always knows what is best and he does it.'[57] How do we reconcile the perfection of Christ with the lived experience of the Nazarean? For example, in Mark's Gospel, Jesus says no one knows the day or the hour of the coming of the Son of Man, not even the Son knows it (Mk 13: 32). Can this be taken as evidence of ignorance on the part of Jesus? On a less important level, the Gospels give ample testimony that Jesus used the accepted wisdom of his contemporaries on issues like the Davidic authorship of the psalms (Mk 12: 35–37), or the popular understanding of epilepsy, which was treated as a case of demonic possession (Mk 9: 14–29). We believe that some progress can be made in regard to these questions if we refer to the commentary of Jean-Pierre Torrell on the question of the freedom of Christ in the *Summa theologiae*.[58]

Fr Torrell's comments on the distinction between the terms *comprehensor* and *viator*, in relation to Christ, form a useful background for our interpretation of de Lubac's position. In his relation to the first term he writes:

> In his quality as *comprehensor*, Christ couldn't choose a good other than God, not because he would have lost his power of choice, but because a good greater than God does not exist. It is unthinkable that the One who already possesses the supreme good could turn away from it towards an inferior good.[59]

---

57. 'La Liberté du Christ', Archives Chantraine no. 23422.
58. The comment occurs in relation to STh III q. 18, art. 4, ad tertium. See also ST III, q. 15, art. 10.
59. St Thomas Aquinas, *Somme théologique. Le Verbe incarné* III, Questions 16–20, Jean-Pierre Torrell (Ed.) (Paris: Cerf, 2002), p. 321.

As for the second, the Dominican affirms:

> In his quality as *viator*, Christ had to act in time; so he had the opportunity to choose between different goods or different options to do with the fulfilment of his mission, as they appeared to him to be more or less fitting in the service of the intermediary objectives and the final good which he had set himself as an end.[60]

The import of this distinction is to recognize, on the one hand, the freedom of Christ to choose the ultimate good and nothing other than this and, on the other hand, the manner in which this was lived in time and space. While Torrell, following St Thomas, on whose work he is commenting, does not compromise the sinlessness or obedience of Christ, still he recognizes, in a concrete way, that decision was part of Jesus' life and there were moments of indecision and lack of clarity regarding the future. Aquinas himself referred to the struggle of Jesus in the face of evil: 'Although Christ did not have to put up with interior struggles caused by the sinful condition, he endured the exterior attacks of the world and the devil.'[61] This distinction is critical: Aquinas admits of the possibility of temptation, but not of sin. Bernard Sesboüé, for his part, insists that freedom of choice is constitutive of being human and, therefore, to exclude it in the case of Christ is to compromise his humanity: 'He (Christ) couldn't, without ceasing to be a man, escape from the destiny of freedom of choice, which is part of man.'[62] Do these comments, then, suggest that de Lubac does not give adequate recognition to the humanity of Christ? We will make two remarks.

First, it is important to point out that de Lubac does not exclude the aspect of *viator* from the person of Christ. In fact his appellation of paradox suggests, on the contrary, that he recognizes this quality. Otherwise there would be no paradox. In his note entitled 'La Liberté du Christ' – to be distinguished from the article 'Sur la Liberté du Christ' – de Lubac acknowledges the human element in freedom. While recognizing that freedom is a function of the person rather than of the nature, the fact that it is exercised in a human nature means that we can speak of human freedom. Otherwise, says de Lubac, 'the divine Person would only be manipulating an automaton with a human appearance.'[63] The assertion is, of course, valid, but the author does not pursue the issue any further. He does not enter into the issue of the psychology or consciousness of Christ.

Second, de Lubac's assertion that Jesus enjoyed perfect freedom because of the hypostatic union is not at variance with the views of St Thomas which we have just quoted. Aquinas' point is that Jesus struggled with the world and the devil, but in an external way: his inner decision was always intact because he

---

60. Ibid.
61. 'Et licet non sustinuit impugnationem interiorem ex parte fomitis, sustinuerit tamen exteriorem impugnationem ex parte mundi et diaboli', St Thomas Aquinas, *Summa Theologiae*, III, q. 15, art. 2, ad tertium.
62. Bernard Sesboüé, *Jésus-Christ dans la tradition de l'Eglise* (Paris: Desclée, 1982, 2000), p. 127.
63. 'La Liberté du Christ', Archives Chantraine no. 23422.

was sinless. Though he had to choose – in a human way – between different 'goods', and different possibilities for accomplishing his mission, he did not have to choose between good and evil: his freedom was not indifferent, to recall de Lubac's distinction. In the note entitled 'La Liberté du Christ', he clarifies further this point when he affirms that freedom should not be looked at primarily in terms of a particular act, but in terms of adhesion to the final end, which is the reason for each particular act. In the case of Christ, his adhesion to the ultimate good and the final end being perfect, there is no question of his particular acts being compromised.[64]

In summation, then, the articles on freedom which we find in the archival material of the author distinguish between the knowledge and freedom of Christ in regard to the ultimate good and the final end. There is no question of error or the possibility of sin in this regard. What remains to be clarified is the process that Jesus of Nazareth went through in his ordinary life, as he wrestled with the consequences of his decisions in obedience to his Father. This evokes all that is implied by the question of the self-consciousness of Christ. De Lubac does not treat of this issue.

Ontological and Functional Christology

Two works, in particular, treat of the relationship between ontological and functional Christology, and they do so from different perspectives: *La Révélation divine* (1983)[65] and *La Foi chrétienne* (1969).[66] In his commentary on *Dei Verbum*, de Lubac traces the development of the document in relation to the understanding of faith that would be agreed by the Fathers of the Second Vatican Council. The issue was the difficulty of agreeing on a wording that would do justice to the two aspects of faith, cognitive and personalist. On the one hand, it was necessary to maintain the tradition of faith as an intellectual assent to truth and, on the other hand, to give adequate expression to faith as the existential, subjective experience of the believer.

The search for this equilibrium in the redaction of the Council document provides de Lubac with the opportunity to make some pertinent points on the relationship between faith and dogma. For example, in relation to the Scriptures, he makes the distinction between the Old Testament, where faith in the revealing and saving God is primarily an adherence of trust in God's promises in the context of the Covenant, and the New Testament, which gives added weight to the cognitive aspect of faith. It is the Act of Christ[67] and all that this involves

---

64. Ibid.
65. *La Révélation divine* ('Unam Sanctam', 1968); *Œuvres complètes* IV (Paris: Cerf, 2006), pp. 35 231.
66. *La Foi chrétienne, Essai sur la structure du symbole des Apôtres* (Paris: Aubier-Montaigne, 1969). English translation: CF.
67. *La Révélation divine*, p. 114.

which demands a clearer cognitive element than was required previously. As de Lubac summarizes: 'A certain pre-eminence of the intellectual aspect coincides with the "christocentricism" of the New Testament.'[68] As well as being a response to the Logos, to the Truth, adherence to Christ is also profoundly personal and existential. The earlier work, on the structure of the Creed, provides a rich source for probing the thought of the author on the relationship between faith and dogma.

In *The Christian Faith*, de Lubac treats of some extreme – Protestant – positions whereby experience is exalted to such a peak that the dogmas of the faith are reduced in importance. Recognizing that some writings of Luther (1483–1546) and Melanchthon (1497–1560) have been used to reduce the person of Jesus Christ to his work, de Lubac asserts that both Reformers are grounded in the Christological and Trinitarian dogmas. But he admits that neither Luther nor Melanchthon nor Calvin (1509–1564) pauses to analyse the *being* of the Son of God. By this he means, for example, that they do not concern themselves with the ontological Christ but proceed directly to explain the redemptive work of Christ: 'Their entire perspective remains soteriological.'[69] He quotes Melanchthon: 'To know Christ is to know his benefits, not to consider his natures and the modalities of his Incarnation.'[70] A Christology reduced to a *pro me/pro nobis* attitude can degenerate into a purely subjective existential preoccupation, where God just becomes what I consider him to be for me in the contingencies of my own life. What should be objective and independent of the human subject becomes subjective and unrecognizable apart from the human subject. De Lubac summarizes: 'For Catholicism, the dogmatic affirmation, without constituting by itself alone the act of faith, is essential in order to nourish and orient the latter. It always maintains the primacy of objective being over personal meanings and appropriations.'[71] The insights we gain from de Lubac's analysis of the relationship between dogma and faith in the Reformed tradition enable us to gain some deeper appreciation of how he himself understands Christology. We can signal two important points.

First, his trenchant criticism of reducing dogmatic Christology to functional Christology in some Protestant circles permits us to discern his own Christology. It may have been evident that de Lubac's is a soteriological Christology but, in the light of the foregoing, we need to emphasize that this in no way diminishes the centrality of the Christological dogmas in his system. It is because of who Christ is that he can be the effective Mediator, enabling the human person to grow from image to likeness in the internal movement of the Trinity. The significance of the acts of Christ, in his life and in his death, depends on the nature of his Being.

---

68. Ibid.
69. CF, p. 100.
70. 'Hoc est Christum cognoscere beneficia eius cognoscere, non, quod isti docent, eius naturas, modos incarnationis contueri', Philip Melanchthon, *Loci communes theologici*, 1521 (1), Gütersloh: Strupperich, 1952, 7. De Lubac quotes this dictum in French without reference: CF, p. 99.
71. CF, p. 102.

The action of Jesus is significant because of the pre-existent Logos whose action it is. De Lubac quotes André Feuillet to underline the pre-eminence of *being* over *action*: 'In the fourth Gospel the understanding of the Logos' saving intervention depends on the understanding of the mystery of his origin and of his nature, and so of the very mystery of God.'[72]

Now we turn to the second insight we can glean from de Lubac's affirmations on the importance of dogma in relation to faith in Christ. It concerns the centrality attributed throughout the author's work to the Incarnation as the revelation of God. The significant reference occurs in *The Christian Faith*, in the context of his criticism of the truncated views of some Protestant interpretations of redemption: 'If one begins with an experience in which the person of Christ tends to disappear behind his gifts, if the Incarnation is looked upon as a simple prelude to the redemption, it is quite natural to find oneself being carried away to a more and more subjective theology.'[73] The context here is the very subjective perspective of some Christians, often preoccupied with their own sinfulness, whose only interest is to be freed of their burdens. In such a context the pardon of the sinner is uppermost and, often, exclusively so. Thus the wider and primary purpose of the Incarnation, which is the revelation of the triune God, fades into the background. The importance of this insight from the point of view of this chapter is critical. De Lubac does not accept that the Incarnation is just a prelude to redemption. Though intrinsically connected with the redemptive act of the Son of God, the Incarnation has another significance which is that of revelation.

In *Surnaturel* (1946) de Lubac draws attention to the reductionism of the revelatory role of Christ in the theology of Baius. He reiterates this criticism in *Augustinisme et théologie moderne* (1965): 'According to this idea Christ is only a "restorer." As his role is much reduced so his revelation is very much restricted.'[74] We find an even more explicit comment, as follows: 'Beyond redemption properly so-called, understood as atonement for sin and freedom from evil, the Word of God came, by taking our humanity, to unite it to the divinity.'[75] In this way humanity is raised to a new level, one which can never be claimed by right: we are children of God by adoption. In the language of 'image' and 'likeness', the Word of God came, not just to restore the image of God in us, but to create something new whereby we would be like him. Likeness, or divinization, is the ultimate purpose of the Incarnation and the Cross. In this lies the end or goal of revelation. Whatever the theological context, de Lubac is insistent that Christ is the revelation of God and not simply the restorer of lost innocence.

---

72. André Feuillet, *Le Prologue du quatrième Evangile* (Paris: Desclée de Brouwer, 1968), p. 117, quoted in CF, p. 104, n. 1. Pope Benedict describes Christology as a discourse 'concerning God's presence in his (Christ's) own action and being'. Pope Benedict, *Jesus of Nazareth* (London: Bloomsbury, 2007), p. 63.
73. CF, p. 101.
74. S, p. 25.
75. *La Révélation divine*, p. 29.

We retain from this second insight, which emerges from the author's reflection on the relationship between dogmatic Christology and soteriology, that the Incarnation is not just a response to a sinful humanity. Foreseen in the divine plan from all eternity, the Word became flesh to reveal his divine origin and nature, and so – to evoke the words of André Feuillet quoted above – 'the very mystery of God'.

De Lubac's primary concern is with the implications of the Christological dogmas for the living faith of his audience rather than with a speculative reinterpretation of the dogmas. But here he is at pains to create the realization that these dogmas were not dictated from heaven, knowing that an appreciation of the cut and thrust of the theological process is essential for a fuller understanding of its conclusions. He quotes the wonderful passage from Paul Claudel where the poet evokes the human effort behind each of the articles of the Creed as he hears the *Credo* sung – badly – in his village Church! He thrills with an inner enthusiasm as he has the feeling of being present at the creation of the world.[76]

A Trinitarian Christology

It is the Trinitarian thrust of de Lubac's Christology that merits its greatest interest. In his commentary on *Dei Verbum,* de Lubac lauds the 'christological concentration'[77] of the document while, at the same time, insisting that this is not pure Christocentricism. Revelation is not an amalgam of diverse mysteries, but rather finds its unity in Christ, the Mediator and fullness of revelation. In this lies the 'christological concentration' of the understanding proposed by the document. Similarly, de Lubac points out that *Dei Verbum* rightly avoids 'christomonism': all the persons of the Trinity are involved in revelation and redemption. Acknowledging the 'christological concentration' on the one hand, but on the other, cautioning against a pure 'christocentricism' and 'christomonism' is a nuance of considerable importance.[78] These subtle distinctions make sense in the context of a Trinitarian Christology. The gaze of Jesus is turned towards the Father; similarly with the Spirit. De Lubac makes this important pneumatological point in *La Révélation divine,* when he writes: 'finally, the Spirit has only one movement: the same movement of Jesus towards the Father'.[79] This is the Trinitarian Christology of Henri de Lubac. It is here that we find the core of his Christology and, by implication, of his theology of the Church and of creation. Christ cannot be understood in isolation from the community of the Trinity; neither can the Church nor creation, for that matter. Christ reveals God as the

---

76. 'The Light of Christ', TH, p. 213, n. 27.
77. *La Révélation divine,* p. 46.
78. Ibid., p. 47.
79. Ibid., p. 104.

internal movement of love. The Church, and through her, all of humanity, is called to participate in this community. But the process in which this comes about is also Trinitarian in character: it is through Christ, in the Spirit, towards the Father.[80] Thus the history of salvation is Trinitarian.

Christ is the Mediator, not the term. It is the Father rather than the Son who is the term and centre. The revelation which finds its apogee in Christ is turned towards the Father.[81] Jesus Christ is the Word, but the Word of the *Father*. His work is the work of the Father.[82] He is the Son who does not speak on his own behalf but in obedience to the Father who sent him.[83] His mission is to make the Father's name known.[84] The Father is the beginning and the end of all things; these exist through the Son and in the Spirit. Jesus came from the Father and returns to him, but he does not return alone. He brings all things with him, an idea summarized by de Lubac as follows:

> For the Fathers of the Church, man, created in the image of God, that is to say, with those divine prerogatives of reason, freedom, immortality and dominion by right over nature, was made in view of his resemblance to God, who is the perfection of this image, which is to say, that he was destined to live eternally in God, to enter into the inner movement of the trinitarian Life and to bring all creation along with him.[85]

De Lubac's anthropology finds its clearest expression in the binary of image and likeness. Image is given to the human person at creation and can never be lost. Likeness, on the other hand, is a potential that is present from the beginning and develops through time, leading finally to the *visio Dei*. 'Likeness' is an eschatological category in that it implies all that the human person can become in the fullness of time. However, it is also a reality which is partly realized in time. What we can emphasize here, on the basis of the writings under consideration, is that 'likeness' is not an individualistic condition but is communitarian in essence. The basis for this lies in de Lubac's understanding of 'person', and, more fundamentally, the Trinitarian nature of 'likeness', where the human person is destined 'to live eternally in God, to enter into the internal movement of the Trinitarian Life and to bring all creation along with him'.

---

80. In this regard, *Dei Verbum* § 2 makes appropriate references to Ephesians 2: 18 and 2 Peter 1: 4.
81. The sense of being turned towards the Father is the literal meaning of the first verse of St John's Gospel: *pros* is more correctly translated by the preposition 'towards' rather than 'with', as is usually the case.
82. John 10: 25, 32, 37; 17: 4.
83. John 12: 49f.
84. John 17: 26.
85. Henri de Lubac, 'Internal Causes of the Weakening and Disappearance of the Sense of the Sacred', TH, pp. 223–40, 230.

Conclusion

We are now in a position to make some concluding remarks about the Christological outline we have found in the literature surveyed in this chapter. De Lubac sees the role of Christ as being primarily revelatory. Christ came not as restorer of lost innocence but to reveal *and be* Love incarnate. We proposed the article 'The Light of Christ' as possibly providing the structure for a Lubacian Christology. This intuition turned out to be well founded, but we constantly found the need to flesh out the main currents of that article with material from other works by the author. In short, then, we found that the Christology of Henri de Lubac is centred on the Incarnation, with the emphasis on the transcendent newness of that event, one which highlights the revelatory role of Christ. The Word made flesh reveals the Father as Love, a love which shows its power in the weakness of the Cross; the Act of Love reaches its apogee in the Act of Calvary. This is not an external act performed on our behalf to make satisfaction for our sins; it is rather one which transforms us from within through love. Revelation and redemption are not separated in this perspective. Despite our utter helplessness where our salvation is concerned, God does not treat us as objects whom he redeems; rather, he invites us into a personal relationship of Love in which he reveals himself. There is but one mystery of Christ which is at once both redemptive and revelatory.

The transcendent newness of Jesus Christ enables image to become likeness. On the basis of the article, 'The Light of Christ', likeness can be understood as growth in love. The Love revealed and made present in Christ shows the heights to which the human person is called. The article 'Sur la Liberté du Christ' enables us to propose likeness as freedom, which is 'the very core of the spirit'.[86] As a quality of the spirit, freedom is rightly identified with image rather than with likeness. However, because of sin, man is not born with perfect freedom. The only perfect freedom is in Christ: in his life on earth he was unreservedly orientated to the final good and so could only choose the good. Instead of being a limitation, this manifested his total freedom. From that perspective, freedom and obedience merge. The freedom to which the human person is called is to attain to the freedom of Christ in whose image he is created. In that he grows in likeness.

The Christology of Henri de Lubac is a descending Christology,[87] which takes the Incarnation as its starting point. His concern is to interpret it in all its radicalness and transcendent newness. We have seen above in the quotation

---

86. 'Sur la Liberté du Christ', no. 23401.
87. The New Testament provides several instances of a descending Christology: Galatians 4: 4–7; I Corinthians 8: 6; Ephesians 1: 3–11; Colossians 1: 15–20; John 1: 1–18; 3: 34–36; 16: 28.

from *Catholicism* that he uses a term like 'pre-existence'[88] without hesitation. He presupposes the Christological dogmas, and his concern is to highlight the salvific significance of Christ, which we have interpreted throughout as a restoring of lost unity and growth towards the supernatural end for which man was created, which he describes as 'likeness'. He does not concern himself with the relationship between the natures in Christ: his emphasis is on the person of Christ and His place in the Trinity. This is the provenance from which God is revealed and humanity is redeemed. The soteriological dimension of de Lubac's Christology must be taken in tandem with the revelatory function of Christ. It is as revelation of the Father and, ultimately, as revelation of the Trinity that de Lubac's Christology is seen in its full blossoming and originality.

---

88. Though not a New Testament term, 'pre-existence' can be traced back to the second century in St Justin's dialogue with the Jew, Trypho (c. 135 CE). The New Testament, however, makes several references to the expression 'from the foundation of the world', or 'before the foundation of the world': Mt 13: 34ff; 25: 34. Lk 11: 49f. Jn 1: 14; 17: 24; Eph 1: 4; Heb 4: 3f; 9: 24–28. 1 Pt 1: 17–20.

Part III

A Theological Legacy

Chapter 15

HENRI DE LUBAC AND A DESIRE BEYOND CLAIM

Jean-Yves Lacoste

(Translation by Oliver O'Donovan)

Could God have created man without ordering him to the end described in Western theology as 'the beatific vision'? Would such a hypothetical human have been capable, nevertheless, of some kind of beatitude? And does the exploration of this unreal possibility help us to think more clearly about what we actually are? These three questions summarize the theory in reaction to which Henri de Lubac wrote his works on the 'supernatural' and its 'mystery' between 1947 and 1965, the theory of 'pure nature'. Lubac's objections to it are distilled in the well-known theological proposition he defended and illustrated. Against the tendency of this theory to duplicate final ends theology's only coherent defence of its intellectual project is a paradox: the assertion of 'a natural desire for the beatific vision' – that is to say, a natural desire for a supernatural end.

Discussion of what God in his *potentia absoluta* might have done but did not do could go on for ever. Theology speaks of what is real, what God has done in his *potentia ordinata*. And within the terms of this reality there is one end, and only one, which deserves to be called a 'final end'. There is one eschatology, one eternal happiness that demands our consideration, corresponding as it does to an impulse deep within our being, and that is the vision of God. Lubac's plea for actuality against the counterfactual, his plea for historical human experience against a hypothesis that cannot be framed in terms of existence, but only in abstract ontic terms, won the argument (unsurprisingly, in my view) hands down over a theology that strikes us immediately as decadent. The concept of 'pure nature' died, in all probability, from Lubac's refutation. But does that mean it is of interest only as an episode in the history of nonsense theology? Must we resign ourselves to learning nothing from what can teach us nothing? I do not think so. I suggest we shall never grasp what Lubac had to say, nor why he is rather more than a jouneyman defender of traditional doctrines, until we come to grips with the very real attractions of the double eschaton in the theory of 'pure nature'. Only by locating what is at stake, implicitly or explicitly, shall we avoid agreeing with Lubac too quickly, and perhaps missing the real thrust of his argument. At any rate, the following pages are written in the hope of throwing a line around them both.

What, then, *is actually said* by the hypothesis (found in Cajetan's or Charles Boyer's pages) of a 'creatable' human being that might have existed, but never, they are careful to add, did exist, without the possibility of a supernatural end? And what *is it meant to say*? Those two questions by no means come to the same thing! The intention that generates and sustains the hypothesis is quite clear; a couple of brief reminders will make it clear. It does not need much theological science to know that a definition of what man is begins by referring to him as a *creature*. It does not need much more to know that a definition of what I am in my existence here and now adds a reference to *a breach with my origin*. Mankind's absolute beginning is open to speculative reflection upon 'Adam', a name that is quite simply that of the human race. At the beginning there was innocence, but I am born a sinner. At the beginning there was immortality, but I am mortal. Between Adam and myself (or, rather, between Adam's Eden-morning and the hour of his exclusion) there is fracture, the first sin (*Ursünde*), a reality persisting as 'original' or 'inherited' sin (*Erbsünde*). Must this breach be understood as the loss of all that made Adam man? Is 'human nature' limited to the absolute beginning, so that under the shadow of death and sin we have to do solely with a de-natured ex-humanity? Some theologians have answered that question affirmatively. We need not concern ourselves with the history of this answer, since, because it was Luther's answer, Catholic theology, in its orthodox streams at least, rejects it outright, unsurprisingly. It was not of Adam's nature or his birthright, the counterargument ran, that he could not die and could not sin. He possessed these powers by grace, like other gifts conferred over and above the bare created nature of his being.

The logic of beginnings ('protology'), then, is in fact a logic of duplication: there is creation, and there is elevation. Within the terms of his creation Adam is born mortal and liable to concupiscence; within the terms of his elevation he is called to immortality and to master concupiscence with a 'power not to sin' (*posse non peccare*). My death, in short, is perfectly natural; so is the fact that my body, affections, and desires are out of control. But Adam had graces as well as nature, and by reason of his sin his graces were withdrawn, from himself and from all mankind thereafter. Human nature, on the other hand, remains intact. If we must grant that there is in me a tendency to sin that cannot be laid at the door of human nature in its pure created reality, we posit instead a 'debility', the result of sin, which affects nature only extrinsically, depriving it of *auxilia*, or 'aids' that would have been granted Adam if his creation were not immediately accompanied by elevation: 'the removal of grace does not detract from the essential integrity of nature'.[1] So much, heavy with consequences, by way of reminder.

In this modern guise it is obvious enough that the doctrinal treatise on creation and elevation can offer the most generous hospitality to a hypothesis of natural existence without grace. There have been plenty of authors, Bonaventure

---

1. Charles Boyer, *Tractatus de Deo creante et elevante* (Rome: Aedes Universitatis Gregorianae, 1933), p. 423: *ablatio gratuiti non impedit quominus naturalia sint integra intrinsece*.

at their head, who assumed that time elapsed between the day when man was created (*in naturalibus*) and when he received his supernatural vocation. But this point is inessential. Boyer, who lacks Bonaventure's breadth as a theologian but has the advantage of knowingly defending a thesis Bonaventure never heard of, denies such a lapse of time. Everyone will agree that God did not *in fact* leave man to his own 'natural' devices. The reason for maintaining in theory a right corresponding to no actual fact is not wrapped in any great obscurity. We can state it in a single sentence, which we shall then go on to elaborate: instead of understanding 'nature' and 'grace' as correlative terms, it understands them as mutually exclusive.[2]

From a theological point of view, it is admirable, this concern to conceive of the supernatural order as the object of no natural claim whatever. It is, in any case, a theological platitude, an elementary point in the grammar of theological concepts: grace is gratuitous; a gift is not due. To be sure, what I am by nature, and what Adam was by nature, is already evidence of an original gift. But that first gift is worlds apart from the subsequent offer of an absolute future far in excess of the limits of flesh and 'being-towards-death'. Adam does not exist *for* death before he is offered the grace of God, but he undeniably exists *towards* death, since his nature is a mortal one. It makes no difference that natural existence and supernatural vocation could have been granted both at once in a single moment. As they were both granted Adam, so they are both granted me. But God who grants them both could just as easily have granted one and not the other. Had he done so, he would not have diminished humanity in any respect. He would have made a possible human destined to enjoy a possible beatitude, undiminished by any lack. The concern to uphold the gratuity of supernatural gift, to think of an order of grace uncontaminated by nature, leads by strictly logical steps to the thought of a nature uncontaminated by grace.

The idea of 'pure nature', in sum, comes into existence by extending a point. It 'fixes' a clean distinction between creation and elevation and then transforms that into a possible condition of affairs, like projecting an object into an imaginary further dimension. There remains, however, a question that cannot be put off for ever: what precisely is understood by the 'nature' of man? One among Boyer's numerous definitions of 'pure nature' gives us the materials for an answer, or, at least, for a helpful reformulation of the question: 'the state of "pure nature" referred to is one in which everything resulting from the constitutive principles of nature, or required to effect the end of nature, is granted, but no gift beyond the constitution or requirement of nature'. What, then, are the ends and requirements of nature? The text continues by indicating what they are not: 'Concretely it is a state in which man is not destined to the end of intuitive vision, enjoys no

2. In 1980 Lubac maintained their correlativity again (Petite catéchèse sur nature et grâce, [Paris, 1980], p. 12; English translation: BC, 13). That did not stop him observing a little later that 'the pair natural-supernatural ... must be conceived initially as a relation of opposition, *i.e.* of spiritual difference and infinite distance, but that if man is open to it, it is resolved in a relation of intimate union' (p. 37; English translation: BC, p. 49).

immunity from concupiscence or the necessity of death, nor any of the privileges connected with these, and yet has everything he needs to attain his natural end, whether within his own nature or from God's help beyond it.'³ The 'natural', then, is what *has the wherewithal to attain its end*, an entelechy. By simple conceptual equivalence the 'natural' is what has the wherewithal to attain its proper good, allowing the *a priori* inference of *bene esse* from *esse*. If we pursue the foundational philosophy developed elsewhere by this same author, we shall end up with this deceptively commonplace conclusion: 'The beatitude of man is God alone, possessed by acts of will and intellect.'⁴

Deceptively commonplace we call it – not, in the first instance, because it is a *commonplace* – which it is, though the number of philosophers subscribing to it as it stands is not high – but because it is a *philosophical* commonplace, and we have therefore shifted ground from an exclusively *doctrinal* problem to a thesis which contains the name of God but proposes no theological argument. This slippage is no accident. Neither is it accidental that we introduce a very precise distinction between theology and philosophy which could hardly pass muster as a serious interpretation of any high scholastic text. In a manual of theology reissued in 1964, one year before the publication of *The Mystery of the Supernatural* and with a *nihil obstat* from that very same Charles Boyer, the point is made luminously clear:

> It is a *theological* certainty that man could have been created by God without a vocation and without elevation to the intuitive vision of God... Beyond that the question – about nature, its end and its natural powers – seems to be a *philosophical* one. From which it follows that the positive possibility of pure human nature must be said to be a philosophical certainty.⁵

It would be impossible to state more clearly what is fundamentally at stake in the question of 'pure' nature. The purity is that of a philosophical object, accounted for by philosophy alone. The theologian has nothing to do but countersign the conclusions philosophy has reached.

---

3. Boyer, *Tractatus de Deo creante et elevante*, p. 327. *Status naturae purae ille est in quo omnia quidem bona conceduntur quae ex principiis constitutivis naturae resultant vel ad finem naturae exiguntur, sed nullum donum habetur quod ultra naturae constitutiones vel exigentias procedat. In concreto est status in quo homo nec destinaretur ad finem visionis intuitivae, nec gauderet immunitate sive a concupiscentia sive a necessitate moriendi, nec privilegia his connexa possideret; sed omnia haberet sive in sua natura intrinsece manentia sive auxilio divino reposita quibus finem suam naturalem attingere valeret.*

4. *Cursus philosophiae ad usum seminariorum, vol. II* (Paris: Desclée De Brouwer, 1937), p. 453. *Beatitudo hominis est solus Deus, actibus voluntatis et intellectus possidendus.*

5. J.-M. Hervé and C. Larnicol, *Manuale Theologiae Dogmaticae*, vol. II (Paris: Apud Berche et Pagis, 1964), p. 341: *Theologice certum est hominem potuisse creari a Deo sine vocatione et elevatione ad visionem Dei intuitivam... Ulterius quaestio videtur esse philosophica, nempe de natura eiusque fine et viribus naturalibus. Hinc possibilitas positiva naturae humanae purae dicenda videtur philosophice certa.*

There are several things to be said of this philosophy, whose rights the theologians seem so anxious to protect, and its corollaries. But they can be said only if we first identify the wholly *modern* character of a proposal that appeals so fallaciously to such an ahistorical 'certainty'. It is probably no simple chronological coincidence that the redundant idea of a 'pure' nature enclosed in its own perfections acquires its status with Cajetan in the century that saw the condemnation of Pomponazzi by the Fifth Lateran Council. Catholicism encountered modernity with the most solemn affirmation possible of the unity of truth and of the illicitness of philosophical conclusions contravening the science of faith: 'We declare completely false every assertion that contradicts the truth of revealed faith.'[6] The Council's canon is in no way innovatory, but the circumstances of its promulgation were new. The history of medieval theology is in large measure a history of philosophical influences, Greek, Roman, and Arabic, upon a *doctrina sacra* elaborated in cathedral or monastic schools and later in universities officially designated for the service of the sacred science. This history is a history of struggles as well as of successful alliances between the thinking of faith and rationalities with no inherent relation to Christianity. But for all the explosive episodes provoked by Latin Averroism and its condemnation at Paris and Oxford, this history of struggles posed no direct threat to an organization of knowledge which made theological arguments more or less unchallengeably trumps. It is a history, then, of debates that were in the first place internal to Faculties of Theology, or other institutions occupying the same role.

The question of neo-Aristotelianism at Padua, however, demonstrates a change that can be described in a phrase to be penned by Kant in 1798. There is a 'strife of the faculties', a strife between the Faculty of Theology and the Faculty of Philosophy, which will always thereafter be a possibility. Our present discussion is not concerned with debates between Catholic theology and modern or contemporary philosophy. But the problem with which we are concerned cannot be understood without appreciating the terms of those debates. 'Nature' and 'grace' are, classically, correlative terms connected by a strictly theological grammar. It would be pointless to rehearse the formal proof of this – that the concept of grace is a purely theological concept, but it is certainly necessary to throw in that there is no real univocity between the 'nature' that theologians like Augustine and Thomas Aquinas refer to and the *phusis* or *natura rerum* spoken of in ancient philosophy. However, we have just said that when the idea of 'pure' nature arises, it is as though theology ends up with the philosophical idea *par excellence*, an idea which, logically enough, requires no theological interpretation. Of course, this paradox requires the theologian to know in advance how the philosopher will have to account for his object. But because it is a matter of interpreting a 'natural' order, closed in upon itself by definition, the exercise of 'natural' reason must be enough to achieve a right reading of it. Individual

---

6. Pope Leo X, *Apostolici Regiminis*, in H. Denzinger, ed., *Enchiridion symbolorum et declarationum* (Freiburg i. Breisgau: Herder, 1964), no. 1441: *omnem assertionem veritati illuminatae fidei contrariam omnino falsam esse definimus.*

philosophers may go wrong, but in principle philosophy is always mistress in her own house. Her discourse is in principle autonomous. Here one sees the emergence of an ideal, yet highly unstable, arrangement. Because man is always in possession of his nature, even without certain 'aids' that would have been forthcoming had Adam not sinned, and because the good use of reason is one aspect of that nature, man can take cognisance of what he is. And what applies to our 'natural' aptitude for the moral life (it is as a fact of our present condition that grace is needed for persistent obedience to God's commands) applies, doubtless, to reason, too. Though the possibility of misunderstanding remains, I have the resources to know myself dogmatically guaranteed. And because theology *always already knows* what philosophy can and should say, the identification of misunderstanding remains theology's privilege. The theses maintained by philosophers such as Pompanazzi (that the soul is naturally mortal, that there is only one soul, etc.) are philosophical errors demanding philosophical refutation, but the philosophical critique of philosophical nonsense is duplicated by theological critique. The verdict of the Faculty of Philosophy and the verdict of the Faculty of Theology should be in line. And if they are not, it proves that philosophy has erred in interpreting its own object. The duty of theology then, if the expression may be allowed, is to restore philosophy to its right mind.

A brief survey of the corpus of modern Catholic theologians would serve to demonstrate the fragility of such a way of organizing the hierarchy of knowledge. After the sixteenth century the right to philosophical certainty, underwritten by theology, cannot be saved from running up against the hard fact that philosophers refused to hold the discussions that they ought to have held. The history of modern and contemporary philosophy, as traced through the manuals of neo-scholastic theology and already a matter of comment in the innumerable polemical engagements of baroque scholasticism, is a history of *philosophical errors,* a history of the incapacity of philosophers to grasp the object – the humanity of man – which unaided natural reason ought in principle to have allowed them to grasp. The idea of pure nature and its train of epistemological implications is a *modern* idea, which could only be formed in an age where theology and philosophy represented two quite separate courts of appeal. And it is an idea of modern *theology* which rules from its fastness of doctrine every conflict that might arise between the two faculties. It is, however, an idea doomed to run into the ground. At the end of the day the only philosophies to fulfil correctly the programme theology set for them would be philosophies composed by theologians themselves, or under their supervision. It is no accident, certainly, that in taking the measure of the idea of pure nature we have looked first at a theological treatise and then at a philosophical manual by one and the same Professor of Theology!

Situating the texts within their context gives us a better view of what they are saying, whether or not they meant to say it. The definition of beatitude put forward by Boyer is supposed, we must repeat, to be a philosophical definition, and also, we must repeat again, to confirm, with the authority of a professional theologian, what can be called 'double beatitude'. The beatitude spoken of, while wearing the philosopher's cloak, is not for philosophers alone, to be sure. Yet it is difficult to read it as other than a proposal for the philosophical life. The proposition is partly rhetorical, of course, a definition in a manual for apprentice theologians, not one of whom, we may guess, ever thought himself destined to 'possess God by acts of intellect and will' and discover insurpassable beatitude in the process! But rhetorical or not, there the proposition is, and it speaks of nothing if not a right to the *vita philosophica*, still surviving intact after all that Christianity and its theology are supposed to have said about the happy life. In freeing up the field of philosophical knowledge, the theology of pure nature used the language of 'right' to conceal a *fait accompli*. Modern philosophy had no more need of this 'right' to exist than it suffered real damage when Luther set about denying all the claims of reason. But it does not follow from the existence of philosophy, which cannot be denied, that it must include conditions for 'the', or 'a', happy life. Even less does it follow that theology should acknowledge philosophy's command of these conditions. Of a connexion between the practice of philosophy and the quest for happiness we need raise no serious doubt. Though we are not aware of any philosophy today that presents itself as an 'art of living', or claims a privileged place in the actual living of life – when did Logical Positivism, for example, make such a claim? – most of them do claim to have some principles of welfare in their repertoire. And even if this welfare can no longer be expressed in terms of 'nearness to God', even if philosophy thinks God dead or absent, it does not cease, for all that, to take an interest in my happiness: Heidegger's 'serenity', as we see, offers a very good example. But does that mean that the philosophers actually pursue the discussion of happiness which the theologians have assigned them as their task? Are the various happinesses of which they speak in their various languages fit for inclusion in a logic of beatitude? That is far from clear.

Obviously, our example is carefully targeted. The chronological irony is that Boyer's philosophy course was published in 1936, the very year of Heidegger's first course on Nietzsche in Freiburg. The history of philosophy does not belong exclusively to the great; it is composed, too, of ideas from works of very minor importance, and that is entirely the case here. Nothing apart from chronology, it might seem, could connect the evolution of Heidegger's meditations with the dying philosophical posturings of Roman neo-scholasticism. But is that so certain? The modernity of the theoretical preoccupations giving birth to 'pure nature', that is an impressive fact. That the philosophy supposed to examine human nature in its pure state never existed outside the philosophical texts of theologians with theological intentions: one might also think that fact to be impressive. Yet there is room for suspicion about this modern way of giving philosophy its rights, the right to an independent faculty to which theology will allow the responsibility for an account of human nature and assure it of the resources it needs. Does this theory of 'pure nature' not actually serve as an unconscious warning of the whole fate in store for man's humanity in the modern period? Of course, no theology, not even decadent theology, can be blamed for all the misfortunes of the West. Yet we may be allowed a suggestion: however pious the fairies that watched over its cradle, the idea of pure nature was in fact bound to deprive man of hope, leaving him unarmed before the disturbing reality of nihilism.

One piece of terminology will be enough to shore up our suggestion, the *finis ultimus*, 'final end'. The concept of 'end' appears in Boyer's philosophy textbook with three applications. An end may be said to be 'intemediary': the seminarist for whom the book is intended makes it his end to pass his exams, the qualification for admission to the priesthood. An end may be said to be *ultimus secundum quid*, 'relatively final': admission to the priesthood is such an end for the seminarist. And an end may be said to be *ultimus simpliciter*, 'absolutely final': the seminarist makes it his final end to serve God.[7] Words are not things, and we need not doubt that this otherwise conventional author believes in the difference between what may be called a 'final' end in an argument labelled as philosophy and what Christian faith speaks of as 'final ends'. Mishaps of language are, however, revealing. It is not to be taken for granted that an order of ends which lies wholly under the shadow of death (even if it makes reference to a relation to God) can have anything to do with 'ultimacy'. Within the limits of verification, the last word certainly rests with death. But the first word spoken by Christian faith rejects an eschatology within the confines of verification. 'Ultimacy', with its strictly eschatological note, cannot dignify any reality of which the Kingdom of God does not hold the conceptual key, or for which the resurrection of the flesh (and, in Western theology, the 'beatific vision') is not the hermeneutical principle. With even a smattering of theological coherence, then, we will notice that no other end, however desirable or admirable, can pretend to more than penultimate status.

Nothing contained within this world is eschatological without qualification. And if there is one job that theology seems competent to do well, and without too much difficulty, it must surely be to demolish eschatologies within the limits of being-in-the-world. To imagine a teleological order which was ultimate and this-worldly, except, perhaps, as a result of sheer absent-mindedness, would appear to part company with theological reasoning pretty conclusively. Not terribly alarming, perhaps, if it remains possible to claim to be speaking two different languages, so that an end called 'ultimate' in a 'purely' philosophical exposition may be demoted to 'penultimate' when one gets to theological discussion. But can this double language be sustained consistently? And in sustaining it, does one not run the risk of letting philosophy adopt an eschatology where no further 'beyond' can be conceived? Worse, does one not run the risk of giving birth to eschatologies *meant* to be theological, weaned on theological notions at least, but incapable of swallowing anything 'beyond' the 'natural' conditions of beatitude? A brief reflection upon Hegel may help us see what a reply involves, and allow us to return the volley.

Hegel's philosophy is an organization of whatever can be thought, that is of all reality, on eschatological principles. That is hardly open to doubt. Never disavowed, though extensively re-written for other maps, the journey of consciousness in the *Phenomenology of Mind* is one towards the advent of the definitive. The essential,

---

7. *Cursus philosophiae*, p. 435.

the permanent, makes its entry at the end, in the experience of man reconciled with the Absolute in the historical event of Good Friday, the man who knows today, and only today, how to draw the consequences from that reconciliation and attain to absolute knowledge. This is familiar, and there is no need to spend long over it. One may linger a while, however, over a most surprising affinity. The Hegelian problematic is mostly about the 'provisional' and the 'definitive'. Something is 'definitive' in two respects: in overcoming the provisional and, at the same time, in recalling it to memory. The question of the definitive is raised in terms that are not exactly philosophical – not, at any rate, in a philosophy that maintains studied ignorance of theological discussions. Nothing could be more distant from the Hegelian project than a 'pure nature', hypothetically projected and independent of the concrete history in which the only end conceivable for man to attain is at once and inseparably theological and philosophical. Yet whatever the distance, it remains the case that Hegelian eschatology leads us back to the heart of our problem, for it confronts us with the satisfaction in the present of every real need to be met by a fully human existence.

The logic of need is expressed by theorists of pure nature in the language of 'claim', or 'exigence'. 'Things without which nature cannot attain its proportionate end, the end commensurate with its natural powers, belong to nature. This may be expressed by saying: *what nature claims is natural*.'[8] The highest claim of nature is already included in Boyer's definition of beatitude as *possessing God* 'in acts of intellect and will'. It would not be pressing texts and contexts too aggressively to suggest that Hegel's absolute knowledge achieves concretely what is here suggested abstractly. Let us read Boyer a little further: beatitude lives by means of possession, 'the object that makes us happy must be possessed to be enjoyed'.[9] 'Natural beatitude' is not the highest experience of God there is, but an 'imperfect act of possession' in which there is still 'desire' (the sole concession made to this reality) 'for the intuitive vision'. But – and here the text becomes really fascinating – 'the existence of a desire whose fulfilment would be known to exceed nature's due, would neither disturb the mind nor restrict the joy derived from less-than-perfect knowledge of God'.[10] One could hardly find a more effective way of announcing the supremacy of discursive knowledge. And all we have to do is replace 'natural

---

8. Boyer, *Tractatus De Deo creante et elevante*, p. 243: *Pertinent ad naturam ea sine quibus natura non posset pertingere ad finem ad quem proportionem habet, ad finem nempe mensuratum per suas potentias naturales. Quod etiam exprimitur dicendo: naturalia sunt ea quae a natura exiguntur.* We must admit that there are neo-scholastic texts of greater subtlety than this. While J. de Finance concludes his *Éthique générale* (Rome: Presses de l'Université Grégorienne, 1967) with an analysis somewhat embarrassed by the relation of 'natural beatitude' to 'supernatural beatitude', he does not deny himself an observation that would hardly be out of place in Lubac: 'There we see the paradox of spiritual being: a capacity and a desire that exceeds the proportion of its power and its rights' (§311, p. 431).

9. *Cursus philosophiae*, p. 454. *Objectum quod beatos facit non habetur nisi possideatur.*

10. Ibid., p. 456. *Existentia autem huius desiderii, cuius adimpletio cognoscetur ut naturae non debita, mentem non turbaret neque gaudium ex cognitione Dei minus perfecta hauriendum impediret.*

knowledge' of God with the Christian faith as Hegel understands it in elevating it to the level of 'concept', and we shall see in Hegel's 'absolute knowledge' something like a completion of what first got going in and around Cajetan.

The difference between Cajetan and Hegel is the difference between possibility and reality. We do not suggest that the possibility of the one inspired the reality of the other directly; yet we can maintain that no one can take the measure of that possibility without observing that it could be realized – even (who knows?) that it was the fate of modern philosophy to realize it. Hegel, of course, says nothing of any other eschatology beyond absolute knowledge; he never makes room in his logical sequence for Christian hope. We should not conclude that he never secretly cherished the hope that Christianity professes openly; it is simply that there is no room for it within the constraints of his system. The idea of something over and above absolute knowledge 'does not disturb' (in Boyer's words) whoever attains that knowledge. Enjoyment is unqualified. To say that is to say a great deal, and it forges a remarkable link connecting the destiny of this knowledge that transcends confessional boundaries, historical intervals, and a thousand differences we need not go into here, to that of a 'natural beatitude' whose rights were supposed to be guaranteed in a modernity that still thought of itself as Christian.

Hegel conceived the advent of the definitive. Hardly more than a century since the philosophy of history first appeared in Vico and Voltaire, Hegel's philosophy radically disenchanted history by conceiving the parousia of the definitive, the apocalypse of meaning. That is a curious fact. Yet there is no contradiction between the two. The thought that history is not, after all, a realm of brute contingency where nothing is essential, that historical coming-to-be and passing-away are indispensable revelations of the meaning of being and *à fortiori* the genesis of the essential, may be a newcomer to philosophy, but it is a very ancient presence in theology. Christianity, for its part, having encountered as one of its earliest theoretical obstacles the apparent scandal of the non-realization of the eschaton (the 'delayed parousia'), and having learned to deal with this without raising new messianic expectations for the future, is perfectly equipped to teach men how to exist undramatically in a realized history without ontophanic and ontopoetic promises. It is not absurd, though it is paradoxical, to say that in a certain sense Hegelian philosophy mastered the logic of history solely in order to do away with history, to reach a human nature that would be an eschatological reality.

It is not out of order, then, that the name of Hegel should crop up in a discussion of texts which say nothing about him, and that its inclusion should allow us to add some real density to the theological hypothesis of natural beatitude. Hegel makes no distinction between the order of nature and the order of grace. On the one hand absolute knowledge can be understood as a present 'possessing' of God, 'undisturbed' by any thought of a more elevated proximity; on the other, absolute knowledge is the fact of a man reconciled to God, a man to whom the Trinitarian secret of divine existence is revealed – two features that might qualify absolute knowledge as 'supernatural'. That said, the secret connivances go deeper than the differences. Hegel knows more than any 'natural' knowledge of God can know, to be sure, but he knows it at the climax of a history in which man has become what he is. The happiness of knowing still presents itself as the last word of experience within the terms of being-towards-death. Hegel would not call absolute knowledge an 'imperfect act of possession', certainly; more importantly, however, the conception he proposes is one of an entirely *this-worldly* realized eschatology. In each case – in the accomplishment of reason bringing the content of faith to concept, as in the triumph of 'natural' reason – we must ask, how can the supposition that God is known *beyond* the present conditions of experience in the beatific vision count for anything at all, if we allow that failure to possess it is no burden on our present happiness?

One question remains to be put, however. Under one name or another the idea of a natural beatitude with a relation to God at its core may in fact be conceived, and has been. The thought that man survives the end of history, or lives in a history which has exhausted what it has to 'say' or 'reveal', is not foolish. If, on the other hand, we accept that Hegel cannot have the last word in philosophy, the fate of philosophy after Hegel ought to alarm us. Without taking too seriously Löwith's caption for the history of philosophy in the decades between Hegel and Nietzsche, 'the destruction of reason', we may yet still think that only after the route from Hegel to Nietzsche has been traversed can we take the measure of Hegel's eschatology. What happens in Nietzsche may be one possible consequence of Hegelianism, and a radical alternative to Hegel himself. It is worth asking that question, at any rate.

Nietzsche demands a hearing at this point because he connected two events, the death of God and what we presume to call 'the death of history'. The connexion does not appear strictly necessary. Atheism, beginning with the Hegelian Left, fits in very well with the material side of a conception of history, which may even be fitted out with an eschatology. Nietzsche, for his part, cannot be bothered with Hegel's 'Swabian piety' and 'gothic titanism', and to all appearances he never read much of him.[11] Yet it is possible to think that the thesis he set most store by, the 'eternal return of the same', is his reply to Hegel. The mythological connotations of the words should not deceive us as to their conceptual freight. Is there still room for a history when God is no more? *A fortiori* when the Christian God is no more, whose promises gave history intelligibility and who tied his fate to that of the Crucified at a precise moment in history? The atheist Hegelians try to persuade us that nothing has changed, and to make us forget, what Nietzsche knew well enough, that Hegel was a theologian.[12] Hegel conceived the reign of the definitive as a supreme experience of knowledge; they propose to postpone the eschaton to the precise moment when we shall know how to produce it ourselves with our own hands. Hope has lost its rationality in Hegel's system; it has recovered it in these 'left-wing Hegelian' ideas of a mankind giving itself its own reasons for

---

11. Nietzsche, *Werke: Kritische Gesamtausgabe* (hereafter *KGW*) (Berlin: De Gruyter, 1967–Present day), 7/2, 251.

12. Ibid., 7/2, 150.

hope. But that is precisely what Nietzsche refuses to do, and his refusal is what makes his relation to Hegel more important by far than that of Marx or Bloch.

The eternal return of the same, and the constellation of concepts to which it belongs (nihilism, the will to power, the appearance of the superhuman), do not suggest the impression merely of hope in retreat. The 'superman' is a figure by which man's future (evidently) is discussed, or, more precisely, the future of the being that is to emerge out of man. With the will to power, again, it is the future that is in question: the intensified affirmation of life, the perpetual will to live more, stops us supposing that it is all a matter of repetition, pure and simple. Nihilism, the arrival of which Nietzsche announced in 1884, is a 'desert' we must want to get out of. A certain history, and a very clear reading of history, remain at the heart of a conceptual and experiential framework in which other criteria prevail than those of historical explanation. Yet an interpretation, or an interpretative programme, which stopped at that point would conceal what is really in play in the period between Hegel and Nietzsche. Left-Hegelianism notwithstanding, the death of history and the death of God are strictly coordinated. Hegel disenchants the future so that the present can accommodate the fullness of time and the fullness of man's relation with God; and with that it is goodbye to history – goodbye, at any rate, to history's pretensions to carry ontophanic and ontopoetic responsibilities. What follows next, if God does not exist? The straightforward answer is that history floats free of the theological underwriting of its meaning, and that experience in Hegelianism is not, after all, eschatological, though it contains a few valuable hints on promoting the reign of the definitive for ourselves. Nietzsche's answer is more forceful. The death of God, the death of supreme value, leaves life willing its own survival, and with the aid of a will-to-power that can make new values, survive it will. But – and this is what requires reticence in our use of the language of hope – the task of willing power is infinite. It has no closure, no end in view; eternally and circuitously it folds back on itself. The will-to-power never speaks a final word. It will never lead to a final experience. It must affirm itself exultantly, we must accept it as the deepest secret of existence, we must know that it gives us a future. But it leads us to no Kingdom; it neither can nor will do that. The truth of being reigns in it here and now, and that must be enough. Nothing is owed us but what we are. The will to power calls in no promises, and issues no promissory notes to hope.

Is it totally absurd to suggest that none of this could be said till after Hegel, after the most grandiose theological effort ever made to allow man to attain his ends in their entirety this side of death? Is it totally absurd to say that every theory that houses an eschatology this side of death, a beatitude this side of death and beyond reach of the challenges of hope, whatever theological accreditation it may lay claim to, places the God who gives no ground for hope in danger of death? Is it totally absurd to say that eschatologies made by human hands, supposed to give grounds for hope after the death of God, can never escape being undermined by nihilism? And is it absurd to say that nothing, after that, is more difficult to think of, or recover the thought of, than beatitude?

It is left for Heidegger, whose thinking is done in the midst of nihilism and knows it, to offer us the conditions of possible happiness on an earth unprotected by God and abandoned by the gods. Theology used to speak of beatitude; so did the philosophers, but it rather seems as though the word has become unpronounceable since then. So it is 'serenity' which, in the later texts of Heidegger, stands for the well-being of the mortal who harbours no hope but interacts with earth, sky, and the enigmatic company of 'divinities', a relation almost impossible to describe in detail without invoking some Eden-like features.[13] These features are pagan, to be sure. But it is striking that this paganism has affinities to the natural beatitude (and natural religion) which some of Heidegger's non-pagan contemporaries were still ready to defend. The right to natural beatitude is nothing but the right to the philosophical life, understood from one side as the highest human experience, from the other as a self-enclosed experience where man enjoys what is due to him, and nothing in excess of his 'ontological claims' will ever trouble him.

'Serenity' may perhaps be interpreted as an aspect of this beatitude (basically, the only aspect it can wear in a nihilistic age), untroubled by the omnipresent certainty of death and by such 'nods' (*Winke*) as the divinities direct towards mortals. In a course of 1951–1952 on the meaning of thinking a citation from Nietzsche's *Zarathustra* serves as the Leitmotiv: 'the desert grows – woe to him who harbours deserts in himself!' The growth of the desert must be met by thought. But what is thinking? Texts of the period connect thinking with building and dwelling. They connect thinking with man's physical contact with the country paths he treads in his meditations. They explain how things reveal to anyone with eyes to see the meeting of sky and earth, mortal and divinity. None of which, however, provides a basis for hope. Divinities make no promises to mortals. Mortals may await the coming, or return, of the true God, but expect no more than grace to live better here and now. If it is possible to speak of 'salvation' still, in a Sibylline manner, we must be careful not to take this to imply anything beyond the world (or, in this context, 'the earth'.) 'Serenity' knows no beyond.

Heidegger has nothing to say about human 'nature', a point which we can hardly hold against him. The complicated interest he once displayed in Protestant theology could permit the suggestion that the paganism of mortals is not man's 'nature' but his fallen, denatured state – perhaps! That would not constitute a great objection. Talk of the Fall, not absent from Heidegger's work, appeared in *Being and Time* only to undergo a thorough de-theologization. More importantly, it is no longer of Fall and non-domiciliation that the later texts speak, but of autochthony, of earthly existence as being-at-home. And when in these texts the philosopher wonders what we are, in whichever way he approaches the question, serenity becomes the new 'fundamental tonality' of experience in which man – the mortal – says exactly who he is, and how he must live to be true to what he

---

13. ['Serenity' follows the author's French translation of Heidegger's *Gelassenheit*, sometimes rendered by his English translators with the term of art, 'releasement'. 'Divinities' are *die Göttliche*, in French *les divins*.]

is; who he is, and how he must live to survive the threat that nihilism brings to bear upon his being. Hope is not passed over wholly in silence. Heidegger never returns to his critique of the 'vulgar' concept of temporality, so the present of experience remains dependent on the future. But death is still the only seal to hold this dependence in place. Serenity, then, takes precedence over hope, not least because it is thought through, while hope is not. It does not dispel the nihilist shadows that cover the world, yet for one who knows how to think, it defeats the grip in which nihilism holds mortal existence. And that, to all appearances, is enough. We may wish for more, but we cannot claim more. Who would there be, in any case, to press our claim on?

Hegel's God died, perhaps, from not having permitted man to hope. The eschatologies that survive the death of God offer no resistance to the infinite claims of will-for-power. The present-day commerce of mortals with the divinities can be spoken of without mention of hope. Natural beatitude is enclosed in its present. These four observations are all connected with each other.

The supremely important thing about Henri de Lubac's work on the supernatural is that it was focussed on the seam between the middle ages and modernity, and the thesis he recovered from the oblivion of a corrupt intellectual tradition, the natural desire for the supernatural, was as remote from the thought of modern times as it was possible for it to be – or nearly. The modern logic of experience is not defined in terms of despair, evidently. Modern man, if he was Christian, had a nodding acquaintance with such terms as 'vision of God' and 'beatific vision', and professed to await 'the resurrection of the dead and the life of the world to come'. What made him modern was not that he supposed, expressly or by implication, that there was a yawning gap between earthly happiness and eschatological beatitude, between the natural ends of man and the supernatural ends. It was that, expressly or by implication, he understood his *nature* as a *power* to obtain his ends. He therefore forbade himself to hope 'naturally' for what he could not claim, though he felt the lack of it and felt diminished by the lack. The logic of modern existence may be characterized, then, as a kind of logic of satiety. Man naturally desires to know; this desire can be accommodated, since he lives in an intelligible world. Man naturally desires well-being; nothing in the nature of things prevents his attaining it. If it should happen to be the case that the present conditions of experience – my own, or those of my social class or my epoch – are *not* conducive to well-being, my desire for happiness, though frustrated by the facts today, has right on its side. Nothing in the nature of things forbids me to claim that this right should be respected. All of which has a corollary: I *ought* to satisfy myself, and enforce my right.

Yet does the power to achieve my ends *define* me, straightforwardly? In an Aristotelian universe, such as formed the background to the concept of finality from which the concept of pure nature was forged, that could certainly be the case. It is certainly the case in the modern logic of existence, where the end is the end I assign myself and take steps to attain. An end out of reach, beyond claim but not beyond desire, falls outside the conceptual horizon of modernity; such desire has no place in modern man's self-experience. But the limits and risks of this conceptual horizon and experience are strikingly clear. It is basically because we *will* to attain our ends that we assert our power to do so. The form of 'willing' that engenders power has a name: will-for-power. The absolute future to which will-for-power leads (if one may speak of 'absolute future' in the horizon of Eternal Return) also has a name: the superman, the only final end that the will-to-power could promise. From this 'eschatology' that is supposed to lie within our grasp we know that we have more to fear, in all probability, than to hope. To be the artificer of the definitive, indeed, is not an enviable position. We can do what we will. We will what will endure. 'To imprint on the future the character of being' – is that not the highest ambition of the will-for-power?[14] But what endures is nothing more than the impersonal affirmation of life by life – within the impervious horizon of death.

This, then, is the appropriate point to explore the logic of the desire that outreaches claim. It means, in the first place, thinking in terms of 'the provisional', and thinking how human nature can be among the 'provisional' realities. When we speak of man, we are evidently not speaking of something quite inaccessible. There are questions about man, which is enough to show that man is not wholly evident to us, as we are not evident to ourselves, but there are answers, too. It is a philosophical commonplace that man is the strangest of beings, yet this 'strangeness' is something more than simple enigma, and we can have an informed discussion about what we are here and now. In talk of 'provisionality' we are concerned with something different: the dependency of present reality upon an absolute future, exposed to its measure and critique. This dependency is by no means a matter of course. Whether we think of man's essence as having a history or think of it as always the same, everywhere and for all; whether we think that man's end is in his beginning, or regard the two as distinct, our thought takes one or the other of these routes with a certain end in view, an end we imagine we have the power to accomplish, to account in thought for what we really are. The conditions of fully human life, we suppose, converge upon today – today *at last*, or today *as always* – and it is possible here and now to have an experience in which our identity is reviewed without remainder. Even if there is a gap between the possibility and its realization, there is no real hiatus to divide our present thought and experience from the future in which all humankind will achieve an existence fully worthy of it. There are other things we may think of beside the definitive, of course, yet we seem doomed to assume a certain presence of the definitive when we think about these other things, whether they are abstractions like the laws of natural beatitude or concrete events like the coming of beatitude at the end of history. This definitive presence, however, is just what must be denied.

It is denied when we affirm that nature is a relative concept, the sense of which is partly undetermined if its correlation with the idea of the supernatural is not taken into account. It is denied when we affirm that the only real end of man, the only absolute future that can make him happy, is something over and beyond present experience, to which Western theology gives the name 'beatific vision'.

14. Nietzsche, *KGW*, 8/1.320.

What lies beyond death is intelligible to the extent that it is real. The reality may surely be a commerce between man and God from which man will derive true joy. Meanwhile, however, it is the provisional that gives a purchase for thought. We are told only that this intelligibility and reality are a beginning, a beginning that lays no claim upon an end, but which we could never mistake for an end or a fulfilment. The final word, the final experience remain at a distance. The present cannot accommodate an eschatology. Our sense of the present is dependent on a future beyond our control, but not beyond our desire, which is why we cannot enclose our being within its immanent teleologies.

What kind of experience is appropriately situated to register this dependence? At this point we must not let ourselves be taken in by words. We use the word 'desire', as Lubac does, because we cannot find another translation for the Latin *desiderium*. The paradox we are exploring, that of a 'natural' desire for a beatitude no one owes us, claims to be the ultimate truth of our being, a truth capable of appearing to consciousness. No desire can be thought of, it would seem, which is incapable of coming to consciousness. Yet who has ever really become conscious of an eros that lifts us beyond our nature and demonstrates that nature is made for something more than itself? The connexion between desire and the depths of the affective life permit us to recognize its ambiguity and non-transparency. I am not master of my desires; what I desire I do not truly know. I might even say, in a manner of speaking, that there is something that desires *within* me, rather than that 'I' desire for myself. In the confusion of my desires I would be at a loss to identify a clear and distinct witness to pure eschatological tension, such as medieval thinkers and Lubac call *desiderium*. Lubac acknowledges this clearly in his own words:

> It hardly matters that in the actual circumstances of this existence, immersed as I am in material things and unaware of myself, I do not recognise this desire objectively in its full reality and force; I shall do so without fail on the day I see my nature at last as what it fundamentally is – if it is ever destined to appear to me that way.[15]

On this basis the question may be asked without diffidence: if desire for the eschaton were wholly self-aware, would it not itself turn out to be an eschatological event? In conditions of experience dictated by being-in-the-world, is it the destiny of *desiderium* to slip past us unrecognized?

This question, and the admission that provoked it, draw attention to a problem it would be perilous to sidestep. We speak of 'the world' in a phenomenological sense, and thus of what we are in fact, our own facticity. But our worldly existence is atheistic first and foremost, one on which death alone has the last word. Within the limits of the world no consistent protest is ever raised against the eschatological rights of death. One may adjust the coordinates, following the line

---

15. *The Mystery of the Supernatural*, trans. Rosemary Sheed (London: Geoffrey Chapman, 1967), p. 70.

of Heidegger's own reflections, and substitute the concept of 'earth', inhabited in a certain proximity to the sacred, for 'the world'. But in either case, whether in *a priori* atheism or in *a priori* paganism, the reign of death and its control over the logic of existence is inexorable. Theology knows grounds of hope; theology knows of the end of man. It does not follow that the end has a hold over the *a priori* laws governing our relations to one another and to things; it does not follow that hope has a transcendental reality. A theological account of what we are, with its correlation of nature and supernature, may elicit the admission that our native conditions of experience are no more than a provisional incarnation; yet it cannot enforce the conviction that the definitive can trouble the waters of the provisional in our experience right now. It is paradoxical, but the *theologoumenon* Lubac rehabilitated through his intellectual labours between 1947 and 1965 may actually leave the Heideggerian hermeneutic of facticity in place. He never purported to describe the 'actual conditions of our existence', and so his theoretical concerns suffer no damage from it.

But need we settle for this? Are the facticity of human existence and its vocation simply unrelated to each other, so that theology can leave the right and responsibility for the former to a procedure called 'philosophy', with only the reservation that 'the facts' should be acknowledged to be provisional? Not a negligible reservation, perhaps, that allows us to demystify any eschatology that confines itself to the condition of *Dasein,* or 'mortal', or, elsewhere, 'superman'. Yet the suggestion it makes terms with presents us with a difficulty. It forces us in effect to deny transcendental reality to hope, and advances the disturbing idea that man is entirely cut off from his true end by the his *a priori* conditions of existence. This idea is not incoherent; indeed, it can produce theological letters of credit: in the Epistle to the Ephesians one and the same verse links the worldly reality of existence, atheism, and the lack of hope.[16] We must admit, besides, that it has considerable descriptive power. But does the logic of the *a priori* (the logic of the existential) fall wholly under the hammer of this description? In what follows, I shall explain why I am not convinced it does.

We turn to speak, then, of *restlessness* and of *the heart*. These two terms, it is well known, go together in the Augustinian tradition, and we can expect them to crop up wherever there is a loss of conviction in the claim that the world (or earth) contains happiness no future can disturb. The world (or earth) does not *stand in the way* of happiness; that much can easily be agreed on. Even in *Being and Time,* where anxiety is stipulated to be the crucial test which demonstrates our finitude, the laws of being there do not deny finitude all possible happiness. In Heidegger's later texts, where death is even more insistently present than earlier, serenity is a possible name, or a possible form, of happiness. But does our talk about happiness and experience of it mean that we can talk in the same way about beatitude? Is beatitude an end that lies within our powers? When Lubac in a footnote attacks the definition of natural beatitude proposed by Boyer ('God alone, possessed by acts of will and intellect'), his polemical edge is not, we may

---

16. Eph. 2:12.

suppose, turned against the identification of the happy life and union with God. On the contrary, we may be sure it is turned against the idea of a beatitude that man is capable of securing for himself, to the point of 'possessing' it, indeed! (Metaphor is never innocent!) Though capable of happiness in the formal sense – well-being, serenity, or whatever – may we not discover, even in exercising this capability, that we are incapable of winning ourselves beatitude? Does experience of happiness not have a reverse side? Does it not unfold inexorably as experience of non-beatitude? That is what the idea of *restlessness* permits us to express.

Restlessness does not render our joys inauthentic; it does not actually stop us enjoying 'repose' in the world, a happiness of the present moment. But it does suggest that there can be no enclosing of the present within its joys. That is impracticable, except, perhaps, as a parenthetic interlude. The present moment of conscious life can really be 'saturated' by experience of joy. Yet only a little philosophy, and only a little experience of joy, will teach us how unstable this saturation is, how illusory the experience it gives us. Whether it marks an achievement we set our heart on, or a happy chance we never looked for, a 'gift of grace' as we call it (another metaphor!) beyond our asking or deserving, in either case the occasion of joy shows us how impotent we are to *institute* joy, to make it the perpetual tone of our experience. Beatitude must be the permanent institution of joy; we must know nothing but happiness. But because the present tense of joy cannot shake off the grip of the future on the present, we cannot know any truly carefree joy. No joy can extinguish the conditions that produce anxiety. No enjoyment we take in our being can silence the insistent claims of nothingness.

The menacing pressure of anxiety on our joys is one thing, the critical reflection that restlessness provokes is something else. Anxiety and restlessness agree in declaring that present joy is not beatitude; to identify happiness with beatitude is to make a mistake about our own identity. But restlessness, as it is understood in the tradition of Augustine (which is too theological to admit of any secularization), has rather more to say. Anxiety pronounces a negative judgement: beatitude is not achievable within the world. Restlessness can tell of the conditions which make it possible still to think of beatitude: that the present hangs upon an absolute future. We can never bring such a future about, we can never lay claim on it, we cannot even represent it adequately. Yet it is the only thing that can put an end to the logic of instability that governs every joy within the world, not excepting *true* joys, as when one senses the nearness of God here and now.

This last point carries the whole weight of the discussion we have been sketching out. We can enjoy the present without appealing to the Absolute; we can assert that knowledge of God promises the greatest happiness imaginable. But given the way our knowledge is effected within time, how can we ever speak of beatitude? One thing alone is enough to block our way: the unyielding bond that ties the pure joy of knowing to the claims of what we have to call 'the heart'. This is clear enough, and easy to illustrate from a disagreement between Hegel and Schleiermacher, in which we know what one said and the other replied, but do not know what response may have been made to the reply. In brief, man wants a God accessible to *affective knowledge*, claims Schleiermacher. Not so, replies Hegel, for affect (*Gefühl*) is not an organ of knowledge, and Schleiermacher is not speaking in cognitive terms. If God has revealed himself, it is for human reason to take note of that revelation; for reason, though it does not abolish feeling, simply as a matter of definition *knows* more than feeling ever can. Within the limited terms of this debate (which does not ask what affects are for, and how much they can know) Hegel is right beyond doubt, if only because Schleiermacher has overlooked the intrinsic *ambiguity* of feeling. Feeling is in its element within the immanence of life to itself, and within the pressure that the world (or other human beings, or God) exerts on the self. Feeling 'suffers itself' in suffering the other, and with 'religious' feeling it is practically impossible to distinguish auto-affection from hetero-affection. But granted all this, and without denying the theoretical vulnerability of a position in which absolutely the last word belongs to unaided knowledge, the demands which Schleiermacher (and others with him) voiced cannot be ignored. These demands, we may say, reach our ears like inarticulate cries. Feeling can only express itself in borrowed words of discursive rationality, and so must fend for itself on alien ground. Its theoretical insecurity should hardly surprise us. Yet we ought not to condemn the reasons of the heart to remain dumb. Though we may have nothing but words to attend to, we can hardly fail to notice that this voice is first and foremost that of the *body*: 'desire for the beatific *vision*', 'heart', and so on. What it tells us is that it wants no part in any eschatology, any beatitude, from which the body is excluded.

It is not surprising that this voice makes itself heard at this point. The idea of natural beatitude was the brainchild of theology, a face-saving retreat before the claims of philosophy. When everybody knew that philosophy was no longer theology's handmaid, it could safely be conceded an autonomous regime. Assisting at the birth of the brainchild was a bevy of tacit theoretical assumptions: philosophy knows that man is spiritual; philosophy knows that spirit finds its joy only in knowing God; philosophy can conceive of an eschatology of unhindered intellectual joy within the limits of the world. There have been plenty of philosophers who thought of such joy, whatever substitute they may have found for the name of God. But, then, there had already been plenty of philosophers who thought of it before Christianity gave currency to the notion of a redemption of the flesh, as well as of the spirit, plenty of philosophers who ignored the cry of the body doomed to death. Yet it is obvious that we have not the slightest philosophical reason to ignore it. And of theology, at least, we have a right to expect that it should not forget that it always heard that cry in the past. It should not forget that it was interested in the future of the body, from one point of view, before it was interested in a hypothetically or provisionally disembodied spirit.[17]

---

17. Latin theology has also deployed the concept of 'beatific vision' to think the future of the human soul between death and resurrection (as in Benedict XII's constitution *Benedictus Deus*). It is undeniable that the Absolute Future of the body became marginalized; but this does not detract from the interpretative force of our observations.

Actually, it was not Lubac's ambition to connect the desire for beatitude, whatever form it might take, with a theology of bodily existence. It is the spirit as such that his writings on the supernatural declare incapable of finding satisfaction, or 'rest', in possession of the Absolute by intellect and will. But what precisely is it about the spirit, the human spirit, that is, that *essentially* precludes such possession from giving peace? It does no violence to the thread of his argument to suggest that there is only one acceptable answer: the bond that links the absolute future of spirit with an absolute future of the body. Our affections draw on the inextricably interwoven life of spirit and body. When we speak of 'the heart', the symbolism draws attention to their inseparability in a way we cannot avoid. The restlessness of the heart hovers over and beyond philosophical distinctions that would disentangle the future of the body from that of the soul. Restlessness brings us back in this way to an archaeology of desire, to a hypostatic union of wants which seals the marriage of a reason in quest of supreme knowledge to an affection in quest of a *summum amabile,* and even (who knows?) a *Summus Amans.* The heart wants what it cannot claim. That is why it hopes, casting off the logic of what is 'due'. Faced with all that pure reason offers with or without the endorsement of theology, the heart's desire appears irrationally insatiable. It wants what is clearly beyond its means; it wants what it is clearly unfit for. It wants altogether too much. But might this weakness not be its greatest stroke of fortune? Let us leave that on the table as our last hypothesis.

We still lack the resources to write a complete history either of nihilism or of metaphysics, or to display their intelligibility as a whole. Heidegger defines metaphysics as a way of organizing the realm of thought that identifies essence with presence, *to ontôs on* with *to paron.* 'Pure nature', on these terms, is an eminently metaphysical notion. Does man appear as he is? Is it on the basis of his present experience of self and God that we predict for him an absolute future? Can we project a logic of the eschaton in which the word 'end' conforms to the terms dictated by the present? The theory that flowered in the century after Cajetan thought that all these questions could be answered positively. But one product of metaphysics is nihilism, and any theology tying its fortunes too closely to the one was bound to encounter the other. The link between theology and metaphysics goes back before the sixteenth century, of course, a fact that deserves very careful study for its impact on the questions we have been concerned with. The double eschaton of the theorists of pure nature arose, perhaps, out of a pious desire to preserve the gratuity of the divine gift, but it showed a surprising eagerness to sign a treaty with modernity before modernity had said and done all that it had to say and do, and this latter motive counted for more than the former. The conflict of the faculties was settled in anticipation; the anticipation was not matched by the reality, which was to see natural beatitude come to power in the form of absolute knowledge, surviving the era of the death of God under the guise of a serenity to which all hope was foreign – 'only a God can save us' notwithstanding. It was also to see the theology faculty wholly marginalized, a guardian of the supernatural order with no purchase on the nature of things, above all, on the nature of man. It is not foolish to say that God 'died' because men ceased to hope, before he 'died' of men's unbelief. Nor is it foolish to say that the Faculty of Theology carries a heavy weight of responsibility for the crisis of Christian hope.

To want too much is not the best way to secure one's due. Yet may we not *have* to want too much if we are to discover what it is we really want? Is there any other way to learn whether the will has a higher object than a perpetually engrossing affirmation of life for its own sake, or the serenity of one from whom God turns his face away, who must be contented with his commerce with 'divinities'? Henri de Lubac, who knew the reality of nihilism as we all do, certainly had no interest in what Heidegger calls 'metaphysics'. His arguments are theological, and one may, of course, refuse to pay attention to them. Yet we must ask ourselves: did this theology, in simple faithfulness to primary intuitions, have what it takes to escape the 'metaphysical' idea of man? Did a historian's modesty, in short, allow Lubac to take that small step back that precedes every great leap forward, and may even constitute the leap itself?

Chapter 16

HENRI DE LUBAC AND PROTESTANTISM

Kenneth Oakes

Introduction

There are three different ways of handling the topic of Henri de Lubac and Protestantism. One could examine Henri de Lubac's reception among Protestants and detail and evaluate which elements of his thought are adopted and the uses to which they are put. Another possible route would be a doctrinal interrogation of de Lubac's work from the perspective of Protestant commitments. De Lubac's contention that 'Eucharist makes the Church' could be countered by the claim that 'mission makes the church', or the charge could be made that de Lubac, despite his best intentions, finally subsumes grace within nature, lacking as he does a Protestant emphasis upon grace's critical moment.[1] Finally, one could mine de Lubac's texts in an attempt to uncover his understanding of and engagement with Protestant figures, texts, and traditions. It is this third way which will be pursued in what follows and thus this chapter will primarily be descriptive.

There are some difficulties to flag at the beginning. First, Henri de Lubac's works cover a heady range of themes: from the history of the fourfold sense of Scripture, the Eucharist, and the relationship between nature and grace; to reflections on somewhat eccentric figures such as Origen, Giovanni Pico della Mirandola, and Teilhard de Chardin; to paradoxical aphorisms and occasional essays; to studies of Pure Land Buddhism, interreligious dialogue, atheism, and Christian resistance to Nazism; and to works on the Catholic doctrine of the Church or the history of the Apostle's Creed. While this breadth constitutes a challenge for anyone approaching de Lubac's thought, those attempting to detail his engagement with Protestantism find themselves before a vast, exotic, and decidedly Catholic panorama. Second, de Lubac's more technical writings tend to be loosely historical, with evaluations and constructive proposals embedded within the projects themselves and coming to the surface only at varying times. The adjective 'loosely' indicates that de Lubac's historiography heavily leans

---

1. Joshua B. Davis, *Waiting and Being: Creation, Freedom, and Grace in Western Theology* (Minneapolis: Fortress Press, 2013).

upon the history of texts rather than social history. Third, and more serious for the present task, Protestant theologies, history, texts, and figures are typically and only intermittently enfolded within wider narratives involving Catholicism. Protestants and Protestantism, then, stand almost entirely as epiphenomenal realities in de Lubac's project of *ressourcement* and renewal in the Catholic Church and then in the Church Catholic. There is a contrast developed here between Catholic Church and church catholic.

Given the nature of de Lubac's work and his handling of Protestantism, the following chapter consists of two parts. The first outlines de Lubac's understanding of Protestantism through his casual or infrequent asides while the second handles Protestantism's place within de Lubac's four genealogies of the sacramental and ecclesial bodies (*Corpus Mysticum*), nature and grace (*Surnaturel inter alia*), exegesis (*Medieval Exegesis*), and Franciscan apocalypticism (*La postérité spirituelle de Joachim de Flore*).

Catholic Fullness and Protestant Partialism

When it comes to de Lubac's understanding of Protestantism, there are three overlapping levels to consider: his most general asides to Protestantism, his brief comparisons of Catholic and Protestant doctrinal positions, and his remarks on individual Protestant figures. De Lubac's approach tends to be critical when he deals with Protestantism at a highly abstract level and when comparing particular doctrines. However, when dealing with individual figures de Lubac can show warm appreciation for their convergence with Catholicism and for the salutary reminders they can offer to it.

Baldly put, de Lubac's formal understanding of Protestantism can be understood as a combination of John Henry Cardinal Newman's vision of Catholicism as harmonious fullness with Johann Adam Möhler's characterization of Protestantism as a tradition which favours opposition, antitheses, pessimism, and one-sidedness. Such a combination is natural given that Newman's and Möhler's views are mirror images of each other and differ only in accent. The invocation of the names of Newman and Möhler is not merely heuristic but should also flag de Lubac's nineteenth-century predecessors and the traditional nature of this Roman Catholic characterization of Catholicism and Protestantism. De Lubac himself realizes that he is following a standard line here: 'It has also very often been noted that the various Protestantisms were religions of antitheses: the Catholic fullness always offers a synthetic character.'[2]

Examples of such depictions of Catholicism and Protestantism can be found throughout de Lubac's works. In his programmatic 1938 *Catholicism* de Lubac speaks of the 'fullness of the Catholic spirit, a spirit, that is to say, of the broadest

---

2. TH, p. 308.

universality coupled with the strictest unity'.³ A substantial part of this work is dedicated to demonstrating that the Catholic Church is an organic, historical, and synthetic community which is simultaneously visible and spiritual. That there is a clear lineage to Newman should be evident inasmuch as de Lubac includes a lengthy portion of Newman's response to Anglican historian Henry Hart Milman – the most famous line of which is 'They are ever hunting for a fabulous primitive simplicity; we repose in Catholic fullness' – under the heading 'Catholic fullness' as part of the appendix of quotations in *Catholicism*.⁴ In contrast to this vision of Catholicism, 'Protestantism, whether primitive or modern, Lutheran or Calvinist, orthodox or liberal, generally occurs as a religion of antitheses. Either rites or morals, authority or liberty, faith or works, nature or grace, prayer or sacrifice, bible or pope, Christ the savior or Christ the judge, sacraments or the religion of the spirit, mysticism or prophecy.'⁵ Such a view of Catholicism, and its implicit corresponding judgement upon Protestantism, reappears in *The Christian Faith* (1969): 'Catholic theology, better balanced as a rule because of its knowledge of and respect for a long tradition, is wary of overly radical antitheses, even when seeking to reestablish a neglected truth to its full worth; and its language makes less frequent use of dialectic and paradox.'⁶ As is common at this broadest level of description, no specific Protestant movements, doctrines, or figures are invoked to support this contrast. De Lubac does, however, at times admit that nuances would have to be made to these portrayals and that he is only keeping 'to the most general characteristics'⁷ of Catholic and Protestant thought.

This broadest view of Catholicism and Protestantism reappears when de Lubac discusses particular Catholic and Protestant doctrinal differences, and yet it is at this level that nuances begin to be offered. In the unfinished essay 'Tripartite Anthropology' de Lubac compares the relationship between 'religion, morality, and

---

3. C, p. 79. In his *Unity in the Church* Möhler offers a similar definition of 'Catholic': 'As the term "heresy" describes a separation from unity, so *ekklēsia katholikē* [Catholic Church] describes unity in diversity in such a way that it cannot be dissolved without the parts that make up the whole being destroyed by such dissolution.' Johann Adam Möhler, *Unity in the Church or The Principle of Catholicism Presented in the Spirit of the Church Fathers of the First Three Centuries*, trans. Peter C. Erb (Washington, DC: The Catholic University of America Press, 1996), pp. 277–78.

4. For Newman's response to Milman, see John Henry Cardinal Newman, 'Milman's View of Christianity (1871)', in *Essays Critical and Historical*, vol. 2 (London: Longmans, Green and Co, 1907), pp. 231–33; de Lubac, C, pp. 431–33. On de Lubac's characterization of Catholic theology as 'both/and' and Protestant theology as 'either/or', see Hans Urs von Balthasar, *The Theology of Henri de Lubac: An Overview*, trans. S. J. Joseph Fessio, Michael M. Waldstein, and Susan Clements (San Francisco: Ignatius Press, 1991), pp. 28–29; and Rudolf Voderholzer, *Meet Henri de Lubac: His Life and Work*, trans. Michael J. Miller (San Francisco: Ignatius Press, 2008), p. 120.

5. C, p. 315.
6. CF, p. 158.
7. TH, p. 187.

mysticism' within Catholicism and Protestantism.[8] He states, 'it is characteristic of the Catholic Church to assure the equilibrium between the three components (religion, morality, mysticism), an equilibrium necessary to the integrity of the human being. Faithful in everything to her spirit of synthesis, she maintains all three in solidarity'.[9] By contrast, 'The various Protestant confessions place more emphasis on contrasts and clashes'.[10] The lineage to Möhler is made clear when de Lubac invokes a passage from Möhler's *Symbolik* in this regard: Catholicism

> considers religion and morality as inwardly one and the same, and both equally eternal; while the Protestant Church represents the two as essentially distinct – the former having an eternal, the latter a temporal value. Luther, in numberless passages of his writings, insists on keeping both principles, the religious and the ethical, as far apart, nay, further apart, than heaven and earth.[11]

For de Lubac, as for Möhler, Luther represents the separation of 'the religious' and 'the ethical', which in turn deforms all three. De Lubac is aware of the presence of mysticism within the Lutheran traditions but argues that the depreciation of all moral activity mutates mysticism into quietism and truncates the religious. The moral, however, will not be content with its exile, and 'as a repercussion, when morality reclaims its place, in other authors of Protestant inspiration, it sometimes absorbs religion and dries up mysticism by incarcerating all spiritual life "within the limits of reason"'.[12] Beside the allusion to Kant, no other modern Protestant theologians are named as representative of this position, although one suspects that Ritschl might be lurking in the background. If Luther and Lutheranism represent the separation of the religious and the mystic from 'the ethical', Calvin is offered as an example of the separation of mysticism from religion and morality. De Lubac notes this only in passing and no indication is given of the venerable presence of the motif of union with Christ or emphases upon the experiential and the affective in either Calvin's writings or in the Reformed traditions more broadly.[13]

---

8. Henri de Lubac, 'Tripartite Anthropology', TH, pp. 117–200.
9. Ibid., p. 187.
10. Ibid.
11. Within this context, de Lubac also quotes from Johann Adam Möhler, *Symbolism: Exposition of the Doctrinal Differences between Catholics and Protestants as Evidenced by Their Symbolical Writings*, trans. James Burton Roberston (New York: Crossroads, 1997), §25, p. 184. §25 contains what Möhler calls 'the culminating point of inquiry' between his investigation of Catholic and Protestant views. A similar allusion to Möhler can be found in TH, p. 282.
12. TH, p. 188.
13. In 'Mystique et Mystère' de Lubac also argues that Protestantism has tended to place 'a radical opposition between all mysticism and the Christian faith'. Representatives of this tendency include Karl Barth, Roger Mehl, Calvin, and his followers, and 'numerous Lutherans'. Henri de Lubac, 'Mystique et Mystère', in *Théologies d'occasion* (Paris: Desclée de Brouwer, 1984), pp. 37–76, 51.

The doctrinal issue for which de Lubac reserves his most pointed criticisms of Protestantism concerns the visibility and invisibility of the church. In *Catholicism* de Lubac notes that the church is not 'a transcendent hypostasis', nor 'a mere federation of assemblies', nor a 'simple gathering' of individual believers, nor an 'external organism' subsequently formed or adopted by believers.[14] The 'vain endeavor of most Protestant theology', and here de Lubac references Theodore Beza, Edmond Schérer, and Emil Brunner, has been attempting, and failing, to hold together these 'two extreme theses' regarding the invisibility and visibility of the Church. Another standard Catholic trope emerges when de Lubac notes that the loss of ecclesial visibility means the handing over of the Church to the patronage of the state:

> If necessary, the experience of Protestantism should serve us as sufficient warning. Having stripped it of all its mystical attributes, it acknowledged in the visible Church a mere secular institution; as a matter of course it abandoned it to the patronage of the state and sought a refuge for the spiritual life in an invisible Church, its concept of which had evaporated into an abstract ideal.[15]

In the later *The Splendor of the Church* (1953) de Lubac reemphasizes 'the two aspects of the one church', its simultaneous visibility and invisibility; invokes Luther, Calvin, and Leibniz on the Church in rapid succession; and ominously notes to an imagined interlocutor, 'You are not only opening the door to general doctrinal anarchy, as Melanchthon was rapidly obliged to admit and to deplore; you are shutting out all understanding of the "eternal purpose" which God "made in Christ Jesus Our Lord". You are denying all Scripture for the sake of human consideration.'[16] The question de Lubac poses is whether Protestant ecclesiologies conflict with Protestant commitments to Christ and to Scripture. A note of sarcasm can even emerge when discussing Protestant ecclesiologies, as when de Lubac speaks of 'the great "Reformers"' and contends that 'all the very diverse Protestant ecclesiologies are human inventions, invented according to circumstances, in order to justify and to make viable de facto situations'.[17]

As mentioned, at this level of doctrinal comparison and difference de Lubac can note convergence. Such is true even of ecclesiology. In *Catholicism* there are positive references to Barth's remarks on the unity, visibility, and invisibility of the Church, and a nod is given to the beginning of book four of Calvin's *Institutes*.[18]

14. C, pp. 62–63.
15. Ibid., pp. 75–76. In *The Christian Faith* de Lubac wonders whether the twentieth century in particular shows the deleterious consequences of this handing over of the Church to the patronage of the state; CF, p. 335. Notice also the allusions to Barth and Bouillard.
16. SC, p. 86.
17. MP, p. 123.
18. C, p. 67; allusions are, presumably, to Karl Barth, *The Church and the Churches* (Grand Rapids, MI: Eerdmans, 2005), pp. 19–20; and John Calvin, *Institutes of the Christian Religion*, vol. 2, ed. John T. McNeil, trans. Ford Lewis Battles (Louisville, KY: Westminster John Knox Press, 2006), IV.1.3–4, pp. 1014–16.

When speaking of the 'motherhood of the church' in *The Christian Faith*, de Lubac approvingly notes the continuation of this metaphor and motif in Luther, Bucer, and Calvin.[19] Although the references are few, Calvin's ecclesiology fares well in this work and positive allusions are made to Calvin, Barth, and Bonhoeffer.[20] Calvin and Barth are in venerable company when explaining why the Apostles' Creed says *credo ecclesiam* and not *credo in ecclesiam*, for we do not believe 'in' the Church as we believe 'in' the Father, Son, and Holy Spirit.[21] Barth 'speaks in witness to the most Catholic tradition when he tells us that Christian faith is "a *credere in*" ... it has God himself for its object, the God of the gospel, Father, Son, and Holy Spirit."[22] Barth himself even provides the necessary affirmative complement to this negation surrounding belief 'in' Church, for it is actually the whole Church who believes.[23] Nevertheless, 'I believe in the Spirit' must be followed by 'I believe the Church,' something which Barth understands as well.[24] Protestants can even offer reminders regarding the mission of the Church: 'As Karl Barth has pointed out, if the Church has no end other than service of herself, she carries upon her the stigmata of death; and every Catholic will agree with him.'[25] Finally, while de Lubac can criticize 'the first Lutheran ecclesiology' as being without visible and tangible structure, something which 'even Protestants' would find objectionable,[26] he can also admit, 'For the Reformed churches also, *ecclesia* is first of all the *congregatio fidelium*, as we read in the Augsburg Confession, and this similarity of language, pointed out by Karl Barth, shows that there is no total and across-the-board opposition between the Protestant and Catholic ecclesiologies in the post-Tridentine period.'[27]

The topics of 'religion' and mission also illustrate Protestantism's tendency to relish in opposition as well as de Lubac's practice of recognizing convergence between Catholicism and Protestantism. When discussing Protestants on religion, de Lubac typically refers to Barth and Bonhoeffer, both to defend them against potential mischaracterizations and to note that Catholicism views other religions differently due to its views of nature and tradition and its allergy to antitheses, dialectics, and paradox. Despite these differences, however, 'on the main point in question here, the thinking does converge', for Barth and Bonhoeffer, no less than Catholic doctrine, seek to highlight the objective, transcendent, and personal character of Christian revelation in the face of immanentism.[28] As for mission,

---

19. CF, p. 199.
20. Cf. Ibid., pp. 215–16. Bonhoeffer's *Communio Sanctorum* is also singled out for praise on p. 183.
21. CF, pp. 179–80.
22. Ibid., pp. 169–70.
23. Ibid., pp. 186–87.
24. SC, p. 41.
25. Ibid., p. 225.
26. MC, p. 178.
27. CF, p. 173.
28. Ibid., p. 157.

in a long essay entitled 'The Theological Foundation of the Missions' (1941, 1946), de Lubac briefly traces missionary activity among the early Lutherans and Reformed. When first invoking Luther and Calvin, de Lubac notes,

> Is there any need to say that we will not recall them in a spirit of polemics? Lutherans as well as Calvinists have, since then, recovered the Christian tradition on the missionary duty with enough eagerness for there to be no longer a question of anything but emulation of them. Their historians, moreover, are the first to recognize the deficiencies that we must note on this point in the first generations of the Reformation.[29]

As for more recent work in missiology, de Lubac notes that in distinction to the 'thesis inspired by Barthian theology', the 'Catholic thesis' for missionary work realizes that the treasure of the Church, its deposit of revelation, serves to purify, vivify, deepen, and bring to 'a successful conclusion' the diversity of human culture and religion just as these cultures play 'their part in bringing out the full value of her own treasure'.[30] In an appendix to this essay, de Lubac discusses the Dutch missiologist Hendrik Kraemer, who represents the voice of dialectical theology within theology of religions. While Kraemer is able to resist the psychologizing and naturalism of Protestant liberalism, de Lubac thinks that his affirmations are postulated on an indictment, not on contemplation. Catholic doctrine and practice are opposed both to Protestant liberalism and to anthropological pessimism.[31]

If the level of doctrinal engagement contains the nuance de Lubac mentioned in his most formal pronouncements, the most positive references to Protestants and Protestantism occur in de Lubac's offhand remarks on individual figures. The list of figures and topics here is long and varied. He positively references Gerhard Ebeling on the continuity of the faith of the Old and New Testaments and that, when properly ordered, the doctrine of God and the doctrine of salvation are identical.[32] He appreciates the efforts of Luther, Melanchthon, and Calvin to reemphasize faith as heartfelt trust and denies that they should be held responsible for the 'immanentism of liberalism'.[33] There are positive references to Bultmann on the continued vitality of faith[34] even if Bultmann sets up an ultimately untenable opposition between revelation outside and inside us.[35] There are also positive references to Paul Tillich,[36] George Lindbeck (in his guise as

---

29. TH, p. 395.
30. See also ibid., p. 405.
31. Ibid., p. 423.
32. CF, pp. 285, 91.
33. Ibid., p. 310.
34. Ibid., p. 249.
35. Ibid., p. 93.
36. Ibid., p. 167.

ecumenical Lutheran),[37] T.F. Torrance,[38] and even an endorsement of Harnack's statement that the Church must continually renew itself.[39]

While most of de Lubac's writings on Protestants are occasional or couched within his grand narratives, he does devote a chapter to Søren Kierkegaard and Friedrich Nietzsche in his *The Drama of Atheist Humanism* (1944).[40] Nietzsche and Kierkegaard are both enlisted as opponents of Hegelian rationalism and historicism. De Lubac thinks that Kierkegaard 'restores faith to its towering height and he brings man back into genuine contact with God';[41] that he is both 'the philosopher of transcendence' and 'the theologian of objectivity', and that his emphasis upon inwardness should not be interpreted as subjectivism:[42] that he is best taken as a tonic, in moderation, such that he does not become a toxin;[43] and that where Kierkegaard speaks of 'paradox' and the 'improbable' de Lubac would say 'mystery' and 'marvelous'.[44] Nevertheless, de Lubac offers high praise to the melancholy Dane, claiming that he 'was the witness chosen by God to compel a world that increasingly disowned it to contemplate the greatness of faith; that in a century carried away by immanentism, he was the herald of transcendence'.[45]

Similarly to other Catholic *ressourcement* figures, de Lubac consistently held Barth in high regard. There is even a brief interpersonal history between the two. Both de Lubac and Barth were present at Henri Bouillard's dissertation defence at the Sorbonne in Paris. Bouillard, also a French Jesuit, had written a three-volume interpretative summary of Barth's works.[46] De Lubac describes his encounter with Barth in this way: 'Barth came to be present at the defense of this thesis (June 16, 1956); full of good humor, he led us afterwards to sample from shark-fin soup in a little Chinese restaurant; from all tables, people turned toward him to hear his animated discussion on justification; he also complained to us about the tragic turn of events in the Church in the time of Luther, which he did not like.'[47] Barth was also present at Hans Küng's defence of his licentiate thesis (1957), which also dealt with Barth and which was heralded as a breakthrough in Protestant and Catholic dialogue regarding the doctrine of justification.[48]

---

37. Henri de Lubac quotes George Lindbeck in his 'The Total Meaning of Man and the World', *Communio* 35 (Winter 2008): pp. 613–41, 637, 640.
38. CF, pp. 93, 101, 191.
39. SC, p. 275.
40. DAH, pp. 73–111.
41. Ibid., p. 100.
42. Ibid., p 103.
43. Ibid., p. 109.
44. Ibid., p. 110.
45. Ibid., p. 111.
46. Henri Bouillard, *Karl Barth*, 3 vols (Paris: Aubier, 1957).
47. ASC, p. 70.
48. Hans Küng, *Justification: The Doctrine of Karl Barth and a Catholic Reflection*, trans. Thomas Collins, Edmund E. Tolk, and David Granskou (Louisville, KY: Westminster John Knox Press, 2004). Hans Küng's description of these events can be found in his *My Struggle for Freedom: Memoirs*, trans. John Bowden (Grand Rapids, MI: Eerdmans, 2003), p. 129.

When Küng in turn attacked Bouillard's study of Barth by arguing that it was too critical and bad for ecumenicism,[49] de Lubac stepped in to defend Bouillard.[50] In this short defence, de Lubac spends time addressing specific complaints Küng levelled at Bouillard before turning to Bouillard's reading of Barth on justification in *Church Dogmatics* IV. With Bouillard and against Küng, de Lubac contends that Barth's doctrine of justification is not so easily reconciled with that of the Roman Catholic Church, especially as elaborated at the Council of Trent, and argues that the honourable cause of ecumenical dialogue is not furthered by easy *rapprochement* but by acknowledging genuine and irreducible differences when they are present. Given that de Lubac's goal is to defend Bouillard against Küng rather than to criticize Barth, his worries and critiques of Barth's doctrine of justification are gentle and few, although significant. They primarily deal with the cognitive register of Barth's account of justification and how this register then (mis)construes what faith is and how one relates the objective and subjective moments of reconciliation. Many years after these events, de Lubac notes that 'to judge from the reception that he continued to afford me after this, Barth was not displeased with this clarification'.[51]

Consistent with his treatment of other Protestant figures (save Kierkegaard), de Lubac's references to Barth are casual and mainly positive. For instance, de Lubac maintains that Barth knows that to disdain the Church and tradition means becoming a slave to current times;[52] that Mariology is indeed the 'crucial' dogma of Catholicism;[53] that the Second Vatican Council did not start the process of secularization;[54] and that Jesus is indeed God's only Son, a truth which German Protestantism would do well to remember.[55] As should already be clear from the topic of 'religion', de Lubac was also not without his criticisms of Barth. He does not, for instance, agree with Barth's argument regarding the problematic nature of the term 'person' in the doctrine of the Trinity,[56] and he wonders whether Barth may have been unfair to Schleiermacher.[57] No less than with Kierkegaard, de Lubac appreciates Barth's emphasis upon the objective, transcendent, and glorious nature of God's revelation to humanity and the concrete forms of human faith and obedience which the gospel inspires.

Catholicism as a tradition of harmonious fullness and Protestantism as a tradition of opposition which at times can converge with and remind Catholic

---

49. Hans Küng, 'Dialog mit Karl Barth', *Dokumente: Zeitschrift für übernationale Zusammenarbeit* 14:3 (1958): pp. 236-37.

50. Henri de Lubac, 'Zum katholische Dialog mit Karl Barth', *Dokumente: Zeitschrift für übernationale Zusammenarbeit* 14:6 (1958): pp. 448-54.

51. ASC, pp. 70-71, n. 20.

52. BC, p. 70.

53. SC, p. 317.

54. MP, p. 46.

55. CF, p. 154; de Lubac, *More Paradoxes*, p. 90.

56. CF, p. 82.

57. Ibid., p. 154.

theology of the best elements of its own tradition: these are the prevailing trajectories of de Lubac's engagement with Protestantism. There are, however, some cautionary notes to sound about this harmonious fullness. First, de Lubac emphasizes that *the* Christian synthesis has never been realized; 'in no individual, no given social structure, no century, has the Christian synthesis ever been fully realized, nor will it ever be. Perfect harmony can never be achieved'.[58] Second, Catholicism cannot be lured by Protestantism's penchant for antithesis and dialectic into becoming merely a kind of anti-Protestantism:

> But Catholicism does not accept these dichotomies and refuses to be merely Protestantism turned inside out. The splendid name of Catholic, that has been so fittingly translated as 'comprehensive', a term 'as full of welcome as outstretched arms, far-reaching like the works of God, a term of wonderful richness, filled with echoes of the infinite', has not always been perfectly grasped even by the church's own children. Instead of signifying, in addition to a watchful orthodoxy, the expansion of Christianity and the fullness of the Christian spirit, it came to represent, for some, a sort of preserve, a system of limitations; the profession of Catholicism became linked with a distrustful and factious sectarian spirit.[59]

The 'narrowing effects of controversy' can impact Catholicism no less than Protestantism.[60] De Lubac tells his fellow Catholics that 'We have learned our catechism too much against Luther, against Baius or even against Loisy. For a long time after Luther's desecration of it no one dared even to mention "Christian liberty."'[61] It is not a matter of combating one specific Protestant or Catholic error by reemphasizing its antithesis and thus becoming embroiled in a dialectical tit-for-tat. The goal is to recover as far as possible 'the whole treasure of revelation' and thus order and surpass the sheer opposition of Protestant thesis and Catholic antithesis.[62] Such a goal is consonant with de Lubac's overall desire to recover (or at least encourage) the fullness of Catholic thought and practice itself, and Protestantism and Protestants function as helpmates to this goal inasmuch as Protestantism itself emphasizes and recalls salutary elements of revelation and the Christian tradition.

Protestantism in de Lubac's Four Genealogies

Protestantism also participates in the changes and malformations which de Lubac detects in Roman Catholicism as traced in his four grand stories: *Corpus*

---

58. BC, p. 88.
59. C, pp. 315–16.
60. Ibid., p. 317.
61. ibid., p. 310.
62. TH, p. 228.

Mysticum, *Surnaturel*, *Medieval Exegesis*, and *La postérité spirituelle de Joachim de Flore*. Each of these stories is, in some sense, a declension narrative, and the distortions within Catholicism which de Lubac detects and describes were in germ long before the various Reformations and continue long beyond them.

Corpus Mysticum (1944)

Protestantism makes a minor yet dramatic appearance in de Lubac's *Corpus Mysticum* (1944), his first major work after *Catholicism*. Simply put, *Corpus Mysticum* mines a massive number of patristic and medieval texts for semantic shifts which in turn are suggestive of theological shifts. As is well known, de Lubac notes that *corpus mysticum* originally referred to the single yet threefold sacramental body, ecclesial body, and body of Christ, while *verum corpus* referred to the Church. These significations, however, were later both reversed and constricted such that *verum corpus* became the eucharistic body and *corpus mysticum* the Church. For de Lubac, these semantic shifts suggest a wider dissolution of the primitive unity of these three bodies; a shift within the Church from being a sacramental body to a juridical and political reality; and the rise, following Berengar of Tours, of a rationalistic dialectic between 'true' and 'mystical' such that they become competitive rather than compatible qualifiers.

Although the text is ostensibly concerned with tracking changes in sacramentology and ecclesiology in the early Middle Ages, de Lubac clearly has his sights set on contemporary Catholic thought and practice, especially the deviations he had already outlined in *Catholicism*. Given this overall context, it is not surprising that Protestantism only makes two brief appearances. If Berengar is the inaugurator and representative of the opposition between 'true' and 'mystical', John Calvin briefly appears as a cipher for the tendency of ecclesiological and eucharistic 'realism' to be watered down simultaneously.[63] For de Lubac, 'virtual presence' describes well Calvin's understanding of Christ's presence in both the sacrament and in believers. This reference to Calvin, though, is only made in passing. More striking is the appearance of Protestantism at the conclusion of the first half of the book. In these few pages de Lubac drastically switches from his meticulous study of texts to some of the social implications of these changes in sacramentology and ecclesiology. With an eye towards the relationship between Church and state and the contestations between 'papal theologians' and 'royal theologians', de Lubac notes the various responses given by the royal theologians to strong papal claims to temporal power in the Middle Ages. Some of these royal theologians countered that Christ alone is the head of the Church, an idea which would eventually gain prominence in the various Reformations, and 'What started off as the simple articulation of a power struggle, once it had begun to dissolve the social edifice of Christendom, finally played a role in the breaking up of the Church itself.'[64] De Lubac admits that there had been 'an exaggerated

63. CM, p. 252.
64. Ibid., p. 116.

attempt' to reduce the mystical body to the visible body for the sake of temporal authority and power. He notes, 'This lack of prudence would exact a heavy price. Beyond any of these abuses, the objections of the lies of Wycliffe, Jan Huss, Luther or Calvin would assail Catholicism itself, and the inverted excesses of their "spiritualist" reaction would lead to the total dissociation of the mystical body of Christ from the visible body of the Church.'[65] In this grand story, Protestantism appears as an understandable, even if lamentable and unnecessary, reaction to a constellation of developments within the Middle Ages.

Nature and Grace (1930s–1980)

Protestants are largely absent from de Lubac's main writings on nature and grace: *Surnaturel* (1946), *Augustinianism and Modern Theology* (1965), *The Mystery of the Supernatural* (1965), and *A Brief Catechesis on Nature and Grace* (1980). These works track the relationship between nature and grace mainly through the interpretation and reception history of Augustine and Thomas Aquinas. The main figures are almost exclusively Roman Catholic: Baius, Jansen, Cajetan, Molina, Suárez, and a cadre of lesser known Augustinians and Thomists. The topics and controversies discussed involve minute and technical distinctions: the pure nature hypothesis; the natural desire for the supernatural; humanity's original state and final end; and justification, merit, and predestination. While Protestantism has its own traditions of Augustine and Thomas interpretation, and the above issues have their Protestant parallels, the discussion remains decidedly intra-Catholic.

As is often the case when Catholics deal with the legacy of the hyper-Augustinianism of Baius and Jansen, comparisons to Protestants quickly follow. De Lubac's own comparisons are often occasional asides without much textural support or in-depth analysis. De Lubac thinks, for instance, that Luther, Calvin, and Baius subjected the supernatural to 'dialectical abuses';[66] that Baius and trenchant Calvinism 'argued as if the Old Testament had given us definitive light on the primitive state of man and his destiny';[67] that Baius sounds like Luther when dealing with sin's corruption of humanity;[68] and more generally that 'Luther did not understand St Paul, nor did Baius really understand St Augustine. Through Baius the Augustinian theory of merit without grace was to be falsified in the same way that through Luther the Pauline theory of faith without works came to be falsified.'[69] Nevertheless, the extremes which de Lubac sees in Baius and Jansen stem from trajectories within the history of Catholicism rather than being an import from Protestantism.

Interestingly, de Lubac is also aware of the exegesis and use of Augustine within Protestant theology and historiography. He references in passing Calvin's use of

65. Ibid.
66. AMT, p. 231.
67. Ibid., p. 14.
68. Ibid., p. 232.
69. Ibid., p. 11.

Augustine's distinction between *adiutorium sine quo non* (aid without which something does not come to pass) and *adiutorium quo* (aid by which something comes to pass) in his 1547 'Acts of the Council of Trent with the Antidote'.[70] He is aware that some Protestants (e.g. Harnack and Melchior Leydecker) view the 1566 *Catechismus Romanus* as the 'last manifestation of Augustinianism within the Catholic Church'[71] and locate the return of the Catholic Church to Pelagianism in Pius V's condemnation of seventy-five propositions of Michael Baius in 1667. For de Lubac, however, these Protestant accounts and uses of Augustine on nature, grace, and justification are just as one-sided and erroneous as those of Baius and Jansen.

De Lubac's account of shifts in the interpretations of Thomas regarding the state of pure nature and the natural desire for the supernatural is also an intra-Catholic affair. When Cajetan and his followers offered a novel and problematic reading of Aquinas on humanity's final end they were responding to developments within Catholic theology itself, or at least to a more general situation of increasing cultural and theological disintegration. De Lubac can state, then, 'Nor does it appear, as some have thought, that concern to oppose Lutheranism played a leading part in the development of this exegesis'[72] and that the theology and exegesis of the Reformers 'injected no new elements' into Catholic controversies surrounding nature and grace. In fact, de Lubac notes Ferdinand Christian Baur's criticism of a strict distinction between nature and grace such that nature becomes largely self-sufficient and grace an extrinsic addendum. In his tussle with Möhler, Baur offered the keen insight that once a 'separate theology' and a 'separate philosophy' have developed, grace becomes a superficial afterthought and Christianity a mere *opus supererogationis*.[73] Regardless of the intuitions behind Baur's objection, de Lubac notes that it was valid 'of a certain school of theology' and that 'Moehler had no time even to seek to remedy it'.[74]

In *A Brief Catechesis on Nature and Grace* (1980), his last statement on nature and grace, de Lubac states that both extreme Lutheranism and Jansenism pit nature and grace against one another and mistakenly kill one for the sake of the other.[75] In contrast to Luther, Calvin, and Protestant theology more generally, 'which seems to delight in antithesis',[76] the best of Catholic theology maintains

---

70. Ibid., p. 40. This distinction appears in chs. 11 and 12 of *De correptione et gratia*.

71. Ibid., pp. 132–33. For Harnack, the *Catechismus Romanus* was the 'last official document' of Augustinianism within Roman Catholicism, while its demise as a movement was somewhat later; 'The feeble Pope, Clement XI., issued the "Constitution Unigenitus (1713)", in which Romanism repudiated for ever its Augustinian past.' Adolf von Harnack, *History of Dogma*, vol. VII, trans. Neil Buchanan (New York: Dover, 1961), p. 96.

72. AMT, p. 214.

73. Ibid., p. 263; F. C. Baur, *Die christliche Lehre von der Versöhnung in ihrer geschichtlichen Entwicklung von der ältesten Zeit bis auf die neuste* (Tübingen: Osiander, 1838), p. 185.

74. AMT, p. 263.

75. BC, p. 34.

76. Ibid., p. 96.

that freedom, and by implication nature, was 'wounded but not destroyed'[77] by Adam's Fall. Grace comes to a wounded nature, but to nature nonetheless, and thus grace judges and condemns sinful nature but for the sake of healing and elevating nature. Both Catholic and Protestant theologies have not always appreciated this twofold aspect of grace. One of reasons de Lubac offers for this under-appreciation contains an interesting parallel to *Corpus Mysticum*. Speaking of the nature and grace controversies as a whole, de Lubac laments that 'on both sides these discussions were inspired by an attempt to rationalize the problems, with too little respect for the mystery'.[78]

The History of Exegesis (1950s–1964)

In *Historie et Espirit* (1950) de Lubac discusses Origen's doctrine and exegesis of Scripture and gives particular attention to Origen's use of the literal and spiritual sense of Scripture. In the conclusion to the work de Lubac briefly outlines the differences between Catholic and Protestant interpretations of Scripture. He admits that Luther levelled justified criticisms against the abuse of allegorical interpretations and that from quite early on Luther gave up interpreting Scripture according to its fourfold sense.[79] He goes on to say, however, that Luther 'nonetheless retained the essence of spiritual interpretation, following Saint Paul and Saint Augustine. For him, Christ was truly the key to all the Scriptures'.[80] Luther's dialectic of law and gospel, however, proves disruptive to 'traditional thought' and risks consigning Scripture to the category of 'law'. De Lubac thinks that later liberal and critical theologians did indeed succumb to this tendency, which becomes full grown in Harnack. Calvin and his own tradition reach the inverse conclusion, for they do not abandon the Old Testament but were concerned with 'increasing its value',[81] or 'reasserting its worth [*le revaloriser*]',[82] as can be seen in Calvin's 'City-Church' and the history of Puritanism. De Lubac thinks that Catholic theologies have avoided both tendencies but that he does not wish to dwell on the disagreements, especially 'as portions of our common heritage are returning to us today from Protestant hands'.[83] Calvin's convergence with Catholic theology on matters of exegesis is acknowledged and de Lubac notes that 'The

---

77. Ibid., p. 122.
78. Ibid.
79. HS, p. 498. Elsewhere, however, de Lubac can be critical of Luther's harsh judgement on the previous traditions of exegesis while also noting 'his more reasonable moments'; SC, p. 354. De Lubac also thinks that most of Protestantism followed Luther in rejecting the fourfold sense of Scripture; ME, vol. 1, p. 9.
80. HS, p. 498.
81. Ibid., p. 499.
82. Henri de Lubac, *Historie et Espirit: L'intelligence de l'Écriture d'après Origène*, Œuvres complètes XVI (Paris: Cerf, 2002), p. 439.
83. Using here the translation from Henri de Lubac, *Scripture in the Tradition*, trans. Luke O'Neill (New York: Crossroad, 2000), p. 77; HS, p. 500.

exegesis of someone like Karl Barth, Roland de Pury, Wilhelm Vischer, recalls in many ways the exegesis of the ancient Fathers.'[84] On the final pages of the work de Lubac provides quotations from Barth, Pury, and Vischer (all Swiss Protestants), in which there appears an appropriate relationship between the Old and New Testaments, and thus between the literal and spiritual sense of Scripture.[85]

In his four-volume *Medieval Exegesis* (1959–1964) de Lubac shifts his attention to the history of exegesis from Christian antiquity to the early modern period more broadly. This work is a flowing historical and theological meditation on the fourfold sense of Scripture (the literal, the allegorical, the tropological, and the anagogical senses) and by implication on the perennial couplets of 'letter' and 'spirit' and exegesis and theology. Couched within these historical meditations is a declension narrative of the disintegration of the fourfold sense and thus along with it of spirit and letter and theology and exegesis, which occurred primarily in the fourteenth century. The two main culprits in this disintegration are Joachim of Fiore (here de Lubac's criticisms of Joachim and his followers presage his last great work[86]) and the Franciscan Nicholas of Lyra (1270–1349) and his highly influential *Postilla super totam bibliam*.

For de Lubac, Joachim is the inaugurator of a new Scriptural hermeneutic, one which emphasizes the literal-prophetic sense and marginalizes the other spiritual senses, offers a novel theology of history, and harbours immanentist, millenarian, and historicist tendencies. De Lubac maintains, controversially so, that this style of exegesis was further popularized by Nicholas of Lyra,[87] who was perhaps Luther's favourite medieval exegete. De Lubac claims that Joachim's hermeneutic is as foreign to the spirit of the Reformers as it was to traditional Catholic exegesis, albeit for different reasons: 'The Reformers of the sixteenth century will be turning toward the most ancient past. Joachim himself, however, had turned to the future.'[88] De Lubac does not spend much time dealing with the exegesis of the Reformers in the fourth volume of *Medieval Exegesis*. He briefly discusses Luther, but does so in the context of a discussion of Erasmus and the emergence of humanism and for the sake of largely absolving Erasmus of any responsibility for the Reformation. Erasmus's influence was diffuse, de Lubac argues, and he was more of a precursor for the Catholic Reformation than for the Protestant.[89]

---

84. HS, p. 501.
85. Ibid., pp. 505–6.
86. ME, vol. 3, pp. 327–419.
87. For a rebuttal to de Lubac's genealogy, see Ryan McDermott, 'Henri de Lubac's Genealogy of Modern Exegesis and Nicholas of Lyra's Literal Sense of Scripture', *Modern Theology* 29:1 (January 2013): pp. 124–56.
88. ME, vol. 3, p. 344.
89. Henri de Lubac, *Exégèse médiéval: les quatre sens de l'Écriture*, vol. 4 (Paris: Aubier, 1964), p. 459.

Joachim and Franciscan Apocalypticism (1979–1981)

De Lubac opens the Preface of his last great work *La postérité spirituelle de Joachim de Flore* (1979–1981) by recounting a short exchange between Barth and Jürgen Moltmann:

> On 17 November 1964, from his hospital bed in Basel, Karl Barth wrote to Jürgen Moltmann: 'To put it pointedly, does your theology of hope really differ at all from the baptized *principle* of hope of Mr. Bloch?' On 4 April 1965, Moltmann responded to Barth from Bonn: 'In recent times the doctrine of the Holy Spirit has come to have a wholly enthusiastic and chiliastic stamp. *Joachim is more alive today than Augustine.* Thus some depict direct knowledge as a transcending of faith and others depict faith as a transcending of the Christ event.'[90]

De Lubac remarks, 'These words, the question and the response, characterize fairly well the following study.' The discussion between Barth and Moltmann will return only some 800 pages later. In the meantime de Lubac returns to Joachim's exegesis, apocalypticism, and eternal gospel and tracks their influence upon Western theology and philosophy up until the present day, with one chapter devoted to Russia. Protestant theologians and philosophers occupy a good portion of the book but are often dealt with in the space of a couple of pages or paragraphs, which is not surprising given the sweeping task which de Lubac is undertaking.

Despite the attempt of some to link Joachim to the Reformers either as a matter of condemnation or approbation, Lubac detects a fundamental disagreement in orientation between Joachim and the Reformers. De Lubac repeats his judgement that Joachim's vision is decidedly fixed upon the future, while the Reformers wanted to return to the origin and to the sources.[91] Luther's conservative and pessimistic temperament rendered him hostile to rampant innovation and excess while Calvin's penchant for the Old Testament would make repugnant to him any purely spiritual Church. Luther and Calvin are, then, unable to incorporate Joachimism within their respective theologies. Nevertheless, de Lubac comments that the 'absolute individual freedom in Biblical interpretation' proclaimed by Luther would 'provoke apocalyptic fevers' which would then turn against Luther himself, most notably in the figure of Thomas Müntzer.[92]

Not all of the followers of Luther and Calvin, however, were immune to Joachim. De Lubac spends several pages detailing 'the curious mixture of two extremes: the Joachimite and the Protestant, each pushed to the extreme and reunited under the

---

90. Henri de Lubac, *La postérité spirituelle de Joachim de Flore*, Œuvres complètes XXVII–XXVIII (Paris: Cerf, 2014), p. 7. Ernst Bloch discusses Joachim in his *The Principle of Hope*, vol. 2, trans. Neville Plaice, Stephen Plaice, Paul Knight (Cambridge, MA: MIT Press, 1995), pp. 509–15.
91. *La postérité spirituelle*, pp. 175, 268.
92. Ibid., p. 177.

sign of an old immanentism and by virtue of a growing rationalism.'[93] Elements of Joachimism appear soon after the onset of the various Reformations in some Lutheran mystics, Quintin Thiery and the Spiritual Libertines, and Swedenborg, Lessing, and Herder are called 'the three great Neo-Joachimites'.[94] Joachimism really gathers pace, however, with the highly influential Lutheran visionary Jacob Böhme (1575–1625).[95] Friedrich Schlegel and Novalis are designated 'the two main converts' to Böhme, but de Lubac notes the sweeping influence of Böhme, along with Oetinger and Saint-Martin, over a host of figures from German Romanticism and Idealism more broadly: Baader, Fichte, Schelling, and Hegel. Schleiermacher, on the other hand, emerges mostly unscathed, as his Christology and ecclesiology do not allow for the absorption of Joachimism.[96] Generally speaking, de Lubac is aware of the differences between Luther himself and these more exotic strands of Lutheranism, just as he is aware of the differences between Luther and nineteenth-century modern Lutherans.[97] The mysticism which 'developed at the fringes of the Lutheran confession' and which was tempted at times to abandon Scripture runs 'against Luther's biblicism'.[98] Likewise, there is certainly a Lutheran resonance when Swedenborg speaks of 'the Word' but this Word is different from that described by the Reformer.[99] As for Hegel, de Lubac references Hegel's letter to the great Pietist August Tholuck: 'I am Lutheran, and by philosophy, entirely anchored in Lutheranism.'[100] Yet de Lubac's own sense is that Hegel's 'anti-catholic Luther is, in fact, and profoundly so, the authentic Luther',[101] but doubts that Hegel's 'libertarian Luther' is the legitimate Luther. Within Hegel's philosophy there is a great deal of Lutheran teaching present, but it has been 'philosophically interpreted and encircled in the luxuriant surroundings of Joachimism'.[102]

De Lubac concludes the book by discussing 'contemporary Neo-Joachimites' and the discussion returns to Barth and Moltmann. While de Lubac does not explicitly state it, it is strongly implied that Moltmann numbers among the 'contemporary Neo-Joachimites'. He spends some time on Moltmann's *Theology*

---

93. Ibid., p. 182.
94. Ibid., p. 287.
95. Ibid., p. 218.
96. Ibid., p. 329.
97. For instance, de Lubac maintains that Ritschl and Harnack wrongly appeal to Luther in order to justify their Christianity without dogmas, even if Luther's emphasis on *pro me* gives Hegel, Ritschl, Harnack, and Bultmann some justification when identifying Luther as their predecessors and warrant; CF, p. 98. Generally speaking, de Lubac had little time for liberal Protestantism, which he understood as an attempt to rid Christian revelation and theology of its object; CF, p. 321.
98. *La postérité spirituelle*, p. 255.
99. Ibid., p. 257.
100. Letter from Hegel to August Tholuck from 3 July 1826; A. Chapelle, *Hegel et la religion* (Paris: Paris-Bruxelles, 1963), p. 8, as cited by de Lubac, *La postérité spirituelle*, p. 364.
101. *La postérité spirituelle*, p. 364.
102. Ibid., p. 365.

of Hope, especially the critical appropriation of Bloch, and *The Crucified God*, focusing here on the doctrine of the Trinity. He thinks that Moltmann has been less than successful in his attempt to Christianize Bloch and cites H.G. Meyer's worry that Moltmann 'reduces the constitutive character of the history of Jesus Christ to a pure accident of the Old Testament history of revelation', and Heinrich Fries's criticism that 'One cannot simply spell and conjugate the Credo and its contents in the future tense.'[103] He notes in passing that Barth's Christocentricism and Newman's concept of tradition prevent construing the relationship between Christ, the Spirit, and the Church in Joachimite terms, such that the Spirit effectively replaces the revelation of Christ and the Church's tradition.[104] In response to Joachimite tendencies, de Lubac claims that the relationships between Jesus Christ and the Holy Spirit, and of the Church to the Holy Spirit, always remain the same even if they are always renewed.[105] He ends the work by saying that 'The constantly necessary turning towards the God of the Gospel is without doubt the always upright desire to rediscover without break in the church the undivided truth of the gift of God.'[106]

Conclusion

The above has focused on de Lubac's depictions of Protestantism in relationship to Catholicism more generally and in his four main genealogies. Responding both to his portrayal of Protestantism as well as his constructive projects is complicated by several facts. First, de Lubac's work consists of exegesis of obscure figures coupled with sweeping historical narratives and his positive prescriptions for a renewed Church are often tacitly built into the questions and projects themselves. There is thus a deep indirectness or self-effacing quality to his works despite their audacious aims and scope. Second, de Lubac's concern was first and foremost for the health and vitality of Catholic thought and practice. Within the overarching task of *ressourcement*, engagement with Protestantism and Protestants could exhibit the best characteristics of Catholicism and remind the Catholic Church of the riches of its own traditions. This tactical use of Protestantism means, however, that Protestantism is rarely addressed or considered on its own merits or at length. Nonetheless, de Lubac's works and claims have raised some issues worth exploring further.

First, there is de Lubac's portrayal of Protestantism. Protestantism is an embodied tradition of worship, exegesis, and mission just as rich, varied, and full as Catholicism itself, and so there always remains the issue of the selection of figures in any historical or systematic undertaking. We might say that de Lubac's selection of figures from within Protestantism was wide and multifaceted – from

---

103. Ibid., p. 832.
104. Ibid.
105. Ibid., p. 837.
106. Ibid., p. 838.

the Reformers to Lutheran mystics to Schleiermacher and the German idealists to Harnack, Barth, Bultmann, and Moltmann – and yet the depth of analysis was seldom very deep. That being said, it is still a statement to a basal level of generosity and perceptiveness that he can refer positively to the Reformers themselves, even attempting at times to save their intuitions against their later followers; positively quote Luther, Calvin, Harnack, and Bultmann; point to Kierkegaard's and Barth's contributions to the church catholic; and explicitly note that the various malaises he is diagnosing originated and developed within Roman Catholicism itself, long before the Reformations and independently of them.

Second, there is the matter of the common Catholic trope and self-description of its tendency to be 'both–and' while Protestantism is 'either–or'. There is, of course, some ironies in using such an inclusive and all-encompassing description as a matter of self-definition over and against Protestantism. It is, admittedly, a highly abstract way of characterizing diverse commitments across a range of doctrines and so it is best thought of as a programme or guideline to be qualified as needed. The obvious ironies and abstract qualities aside, the 'both–and' self-identification can be helpful as regards de Lubac's own goal of unity or establishing an intimate relationship between a variety of bifurcations he believed to be occurring in Catholicism past and present. The divisions which he lamented were many: between Scripture and tradition, faith and reason, faith and works, Word and Spirit, the Old Testament and the New, authority and freedom, nature and the supernatural, theology and spirituality, theology and exegesis, and the visibility and invisibility of the Church. These dissolutions should also be of concern for Protestant theologians. Each pair would require its own type of reparative therapy and it should be admitted that in some cases (particularly those of spirituality and theology and theology and exegesis) this therapy would first be a matter of performance, praxis, and practical reasoning rather than theory. Equally, the best traditions and trajectories of Protestantism have seldom advanced an agenda of 'either–or' when dealing with these pairs, but have instead offered their own accounts of the internal relations in each couplet. In some cases, where Catholicism might be concerned to maintain a 'both–and', Protestant theology would rather speak of a 'first–then': first Christ then Scripture; first Scripture then Church and tradition; first faith then works; and so on. This relation would be one of material and logical rather than chronological priority; it would be an internal relation with absolute priority given to one of the elements within the pair. Even Karl Barth, when fighting against the 'both–and' not of Roman Catholicism, but of nineteenth-century Protestant theology in his fiery and strident 'The First Commandment as Theological Axiom' (1933), argued for placing earth in the light of heaven, and reason and experience in the light of revelation, but in such a way that the First Commandment remained the criterion of theological thought and existence.[107] There are also many readily imaginable instances, whether practical

---

107. Karl Barth, 'The First Commandment as an Axion of Theology', in H.-M. Rumscheidt, ed., *The Way of Theology in Karl Barth: Essays and Comments* (Allison Park, PA: Pickwick, 1986), pp. 63–78.

or theoretical, in which Protestantism would be happy and grateful to reserve the possibility or even the necessity of being 'either–or' (as Barth was keenly aware of as well) or note that a dichotomy being placed before us is only an apparent one (as in authority and freedom).

Third, and most broadly, we might ask what Protestant theologians can and should take away from de Lubac's work for their own (assumedly Protestant) theological ends. There is a proviso that should be registered at the start. As has already been noted, many of de Lubac's constructive or reparative suggestions took the form of sweeping historical portraits and dealt primarily with intra-Catholic debates. This observation should not be taken as discouragement but as a reminder of the wider ecclesial and academic contexts in which these debates and practices took place. For instance, the type of Scriptural exegesis and interpretation traced and described in *Medieval Exegesis* had a host of ecclesial and material presuppositions as well as forms of life formed over the course of centuries as its spiritual and intellectual context. Equally, the debates regarding nature and grace had their initial home in protracted and controverted traditions of minute and specialized exegesis of texts from Augustine and Aquinas in which whole schools of theologians and even various religious orders participated. It is undeniable, however, that there is still much for Protestants to learn from de Lubac in terms of doctrine and the traditions of the Church. This learning will occur by way of negative example (as de Lubac's account of Joachim and his descendants skilfully provides a swathe of theological errors to be avoided), by way of general theological programme and outlook (as wide an adoption of theological voices and traditions as possible; a comfortability with paradox and mystery), by way of questions asked (the enduring issue of nature and grace), and by positive contribution (Christ as the unity of Scripture; the necessity of holding theology and spirituality in close contact). These different avenues from and by which Protestant theologians still have much to learn from de Lubac's works and example can only be flagged at this point, as each would require the kind of patient elaboration and development, curiosity, spiritual maturity, and gentleness of spirit which de Lubac himself embodied.

Chapter 17

HENRI DE LUBAC AND RADICAL ORTHODOXY

Simon Oliver

The theological sensibility known as Radical Orthodoxy emerged in the 1990s among a group of theologians in the University of Cambridge. It quickly became one of the most influential and widely discussed strands in contemporary Christian theology, offering a bold new confidence (some would say hubris) in the face of the supposed decline of religion and the apparent hegemony of secular discourse. From its beginnings, Radical Orthodoxy understood itself as a variety of *ressourcement* theology, seeking to recover the riches of patristic and high medieval Christian orthodoxy in order to address contemporary theological, philosophical, political, and cultural concerns. Although Radical Orthodoxy's roots lie to some degree in the tradition of catholic Anglicanism, it is not an attempt to resource any particular Church or denomination. One of Radical Orthodoxy's most significant but easily overlooked achievements is the considerable attention it has drawn from a wide range of theological traditions, including Roman Catholicism, Orthodoxy, and Reformed Protestantism. Add to this the significant conversations between Radical Orthodoxy and other disciplines and philosophical traditions, and one quickly realizes its important contribution to our recent intellectual culture.

Radical Orthodoxy has found natural allies among theologians and philosophers seeking to challenge the priorities and assumptions that are characteristic of modern and late modern thought. Among twentieth- and twenty-first-century figures, one might include Charles Péguy, Maurice Blondel, Karl Barth, Hans Urs von Balthasar, Louis Bouyer, Alasdair McIntyre, and Charles Taylor. Most importantly, the perspective of Radical Orthodoxy is 'in profound continuity with the French *nouvelle théologie*' and none of the figures associated with that movement is more important than Henri de Lubac.[1] He is the only modern thinker who has been the subject of a book-length treatment under the Radical Orthodoxy banner, namely John Milbank's *The Suspended Middle: Henri de Lubac*

---

1. John Milbank, Catherine Pickstock, and Graham Ward, eds, *Radical Orthodoxy: A New Theology* (London: Routledge, 1999), p. 2.

*and the Debate Concerning the Supernatural.*² In an essay on the programme of Radical Orthodoxy, Milbank writes,

> Radical Orthodoxy considers that Henri de Lubac was a greater theological revolutionary than Karl Barth, because in questioning the hierarchical duality of grace and nature as discrete stages, he transcended, unlike Barth, the shared background assumption of all modern theology. In this way one could say, anachronistically, that he inaugurated a postmodern theology.³

De Lubac has a pervasive influence in so many writings in the Radical Orthodoxy genre and the defence of de Lubac's position on nature and grace has proved central to the various debates in which Radical Orthodoxy is most invested.

In order to assess de Lubac's considerable influence on Radical Orthodoxy, I will first offer a brief description of its key priorities and claims. This will include Radical Orthodoxy's genealogy of the secular and its account of the tradition of patristic and Thomist theology which gave way to modernity. Having briefly established Radical Orthodoxy's basic contours, this chapter will focus particularly on the debate concerning grace and nature. This is the arena in which Radical Orthodoxy has thus far engaged most thoroughly with de Lubac's thought. Included within this grace-nature discussion will be fundamental contemporary themes, particularly the nature of the secular, theology of gift, the centrality of paradox, and the structure of teleology.

What Is Radical Orthodoxy?

While its concerns and claims have expanded and developed over twenty years, Radical Orthodoxy⁴ arguably began with the publication in 1990 of John

---

2. John Milbank, *The Suspended Middle: Henri de Lubac and the Debate Concerning the Supernatural*, 2nd ed. (Grand Rapids, MI: Eerdmans Publishing Company, 2014). In a substantial review of Milbank's book, Edward Oakes comments,

Milbank's admiration for de Lubac seems ultimately grounded, at least as I read his text, in his insistence that de Lubac was really the first advocate, *avant la lettre*, of Radical Orthodoxy: 'In effect, the *surnaturel* thesis *deconstructs* the possibility of dogmatical theology as previously understood in modern times, just as it equally deconstructs the possibility of philosophical theology or even of a clearly autonomous philosophy *tout court*.'

See Edward T. Oakes, S. J., 'The Paradox of Nature and Grace: On John Milbank's *The Suspended Middle: Henri de Lubac and the Debate Concerning the Supernatural*', *Nova et Vetera* 4:3 (2006): pp. 66796, here quoting p. 682. Oakes is quoting Milbank, *The Suspended Middle*, page 11 of the first edition and page 12 of the second edition. All further references to *The Suspended Middle* are to the second edition (2014).

3. John Milbank, 'The Programme of Radical Orthodoxy', in Laurence Paul Hemming, ed., *Radical Orthodoxy? – A Catholic Enquiry* (Aldershot: Ashgate, 2000), p. 35.

4. For a more detailed introduction, see Simon Oliver, 'Introducing Radical Orthodoxy: From Participation to Late Modernity', in Simon Oliver and John Milbank, eds, *The Radical*

Milbank's groundbreaking and provocative *Theology and Social Theology: Beyond Secular Reason*.[5] In this work, Milbank offers a stunning theological challenge to the standard thesis of secularization in the West that began around the sixteenth century. The standard thesis understands the secular to be a sphere of neutral and autonomous reason that developed through the simultaneous retreat of religion and theology, hence the common association of secularization with *de*sacralization. So the clutter of theology and religion in antiquity and the Middle Ages was swept aside to reveal the cool, clear air of natural and autonomous reason. In this new secular world the question of humanity's (or creation's) ultimate origin and purpose is largely sidelined in favour of questions that concern the more immediate and immanent workings and functions of human beings and nature. Questions about the facts of nature were now divorced from questions of value or purpose. Desacralization sees the secular as the result of clearing away the debris of superstition, ritual, and tradition that we imagine dominated medieval Europe in order to open new possibilities directed by the neutral hand of reason expressed most particularly in the natural sciences. The advent of the secular is therefore seen as the result of the inevitable progress of human knowledge and thinking. Moreover, desacralization is a negative thesis with its own theological assumptions because it assumes that what is real consists in an indifferent natural order to which is *added* a sense of the sacred. Therefore, sociology tends to regard Christianity not as the discernment of reality, but the *addition* of the sacred to an essentially neutral bedrock. The sacred is not intrinsic to the natural order and is a superfluous addition; desacralization is the process of its removal.[6] We will see below that Radical Orthodoxy points to a direct connection between modernity's invention of an autonomous secular sphere of the natural and a supposed *natura pura* to which is added divine grace.

Milbank rejects this view of the emergence of the secular from the ruins of the medieval consensus. The secular is not simply that which is left behind once we have rid ourselves of religion and theology. Neither is it a neutral, dispassionate, or objective view of the world and ourselves; it had to be created as a positive ideology. The secular view holds its own assumptions and prejudices concerning human society and nature that are no more objective or justifiable than those of the ancient and medieval philosophers and theologians. It had to be instituted and imagined through theology, philosophy, politics, and the arts. So Milbank's crucial point is that the secular is not simply the rolling back of a theological consensus to

---

Orthodoxy Reader (London: Routledge, 2009), pp. 3–27; James K. A. Smith, *Introducing Radical Orthodoxy: Mapping a Post-Secular Theology* (Grand Rapids, MI: Baker Academic, 2004).

5. John Milbank, *Theology and Social Theory: Beyond Secular Reason*, 2nd ed. (Oxford: Wiley-Blackwell, 2006).

6. Ibid., p. 9. In important respects, Milbank's thesis is in agreement with Charles Taylor's seminal *A Secular Age* (Cambridge, MA: The Belknap Press of Harvard University Press, 2007).

reveal a neutral territory where we all become equal players, but the replacement of a certain view of God and creation with a different view which still makes theological claims, that is, claims about origins, purpose, and transcendence. The problem is that this 'pseudo-theology' is bad theology. Secularism is, quite literally, a Christian heresy – an ideological distortion of theology.

The void opened by the advent of the secular is filled with many ideologies and philosophies that attempt to provide new metanarratives. The Enlightenment pursuit of neutral and objective reason, eventually distilled in modern philosophy and the natural sciences, is perhaps the most familiar, accompanied by the characteristic modern suspicion of tradition, practice, and history and its devotion to 'progress' through the overcoming of the past. The late decades of the nineteenth century saw the pursuit of reason devoid of tradition and community begin to founder on the rocks of suspicion and scepticism. The logic of modernity finally reveals itself in the postmodern disavowal of the reality of truth and the reduction of philosophy and theology to the play of cultural and linguistic forces (hence Radical Orthodoxy's tendency to refer to 'late' rather than 'post' modernity). In the midst of the remains of the so-called Enlightenment project and the contorted knots of postmodern philosophy and critical theory, Radical Orthodoxy detects an opportunity for theology. While not a movement of reactionary nostalgia, Radical Orthodoxy seeks to recover the riches of ancient and high medieval Christian thought in order to confront the ideologies and confusions of late modernity. As such, it is in profound continuity with *ressourcement* writings of the twentieth century and, one might add, the earlier Anglican Tractarian movement of the nineteenth century. At the instigation of figures such as John Keble, E.B. Pusey, and John Henry Newman, the Tractarian renewal first returned the Church to the sources of orthodox patristic theology through a host of new translations of ancient texts. This was paralleled in de Lubac's establishment, with Jean Daniélou and Claude Mondésert, of the *Sources chrétiennes* series in the early 1940s. In short, the Church was to recover itself by recovering its *proper* theology and philosophy, and its understanding of the dynamic inheritance of faith.

In returning to the riches of Christian thought prior to modernity, Radical Orthodoxy's method lies between the genealogical approach of late modern philosophy and the *ressourcement* theology of de Lubac and his *confrères*. The realization that concepts are not fixed and timeless but have complex histories and contexts informed the various genealogical methods of nineteenth- and twentieth-century philosophers, notably Nietzsche and Foucault. The method of genealogy – tracing the origins and fluctuating histories of concepts – has become characteristic of Radical Orthodoxy, with writings focused on topics and discourses beyond the restricted purview of modern theology: nihilism, repetition, the city, motion, music, work, and the gift, to name but a few. This approach refuses to accept the fixed disciplinary boundaries of modern academic discourse and reflects the traditional Thomist view that theology does not have a strictly defined subject matter, but is about all things in relation to God.⁷ De Lubac's *ressourcement* was similarly concerned with tracing the history of theological concepts in opposition to the ossifying tendencies of neo-scholasticism. Uncovering shifts in the understanding of nature and grace, the interpretation of scripture, and the meaning of *corpus mysticum* and *corpus verum* are three obvious examples. Nevertheless, as some commentators have pointed out, Radical Orthodoxy's *ressourcement* extends beyond the immediate concerns of the Church's self-understanding and is an extension of the project of *la nouvelle théologie*. As Milbank writes,

> Is *ressourcement* enough? Is it enough to recover, after de Lubac, and many others, an authentic paleo-Christianity? Clearly not, and clearly the thinkers of the *nouvelle théologie* thought of *ressourcement* as but the prelude to a new speculative and constructive effort. It is, in a sense, the task of this 'next phase' which Radical Orthodoxy has sought to take up, though in a wider ecumenical context.⁸

Radical Orthodoxy's return to the sources is focused on the recovery of a particular Christian ontology: the metaphysics of participation.⁹ It is the loss of the centrality and meaning of creation's participation in God in the late Middle Ages that inaugurated the rise of the secular and the notion of an autonomous sphere of existence standing alongside God that would eventually become the *natura pura*. What is meant by 'participation'?

The metaphysics of participation is more fundamental than a vague notion of 'joining in' or 'taking part'; it is the doctrine of creation that enables the clear elucidation of the *communio* ecclesiology characteristic of *la nouvelle théologie*. The nature of participation in Christian theology can be explained through

---

7. It has been noted that Radical Orthodoxy has extended the application of Christian ontology well beyond de Lubac's concerns. See, for example, Bryan C. Hollon, *Everything Is Sacred: Spiritual Exegesis in the Political Theology of Henri de Lubac* (Eugene, OR: Cascade Books, 2008), chs. 6 and 7.

8. John Milbank, 'The Grandeur of Reason and the Perversity of Rationalism: Radical Orthodoxy's first decade', in *The Radical Orthodoxy Reader*, p. 373.

9. See Milbank, Pickstock and Ward, *Radical Orthodoxy*, p. 3: 'The central theological framework of radical orthodoxy is "participation" as developed by Plato and reworked by Christianity, because any alternative configuration perforce reserves a territory independent of God.' Catherine Pickstock's recent discussion of repetition includes a crucial and complex analysis of the paradoxical Platonic notion of participation in the Same and the Different. A detailed discussion of this book is beyond the scope of the present chapter, except to remark on the depth of Pickstock's new reflections on the metaphysics of participation. For example, creatures are both the same as themselves and yet, in constantly exceeding (or non-identically repeating) themselves in the dynamism of their existence, they are different. This participation in the Same and the Different (concepts traceable to Plato's *Timaeus*) is, in a sense, the bedrock of time's participation in eternity. See Catherine Pickstock, *Repetition and Identity* (Oxford: Oxford University Press, 2013), pp. 51–53.

Aquinas's distinction between existence that is *per essentiam* and existence that is *per participationem* – by essence or by participation.[10] Whereas God exists in himself essentially, all that is not God – everything from angels to stones – exists only by participation in God. Aquinas writes:

> Every thing, furthermore, exists because it has being. Consequently, a thing whose essence is not its being is not *through its essence*, but *by participation* in something, namely, being itself. But that which is through participation in something cannot be the first being, because prior to it is the being in which it participates in order to be. But God is the first being, with nothing prior to Him. The essence of God, therefore, is His own being.[11]

What this amounts to is a crucial claim: there is only one real existent, and that is God.[12] When God creates, there are not suddenly two foci of being or two 'things', God plus creation. Creation does not stand alongside God or even 'outside' God. Crucially, in no sense is creation autonomous because creation is, at every moment, *ex nihilo*. It is suspended over the *nihil*, held in existence by participating in existence itself. So creation has no existence that is self-standing and properly its own. Rather, it receives its being at every moment from an infinite and gratuitous divinity. Creation's existence is, in this sense, 'improper'. Yet even the very participation of creation in God is 'improper' to creation; it does not belong to creation by right or power, but is always the gratuitous gift of God.

There is an important corollary of this metaphysics of participation: the difference between God and creatures is not like the difference *between* creatures. Whereas my difference from the table at which I am sat belongs both to the table and me because we have material natures that define the respective boundaries of our spatial existence, the difference between a creature and God is instantiated purely by God's gratuity. To put the matter another way, God grants creation its own autonomy – its own otherness from God's being – yet paradoxically this is no autonomy at all. To put the matter another way, God 'holds' creation as other than himself. This ontological difference is a sheer difference that Aquinas expresses in terms of the simplicity of divine being (essence and existence are one and the same) and the structure or composition of created being (essence and existence are united but really distinct). Moreover, the nature of this participation is analogical in the sense that all creatures are held together by their relation to a common focus in God, even amidst their countless and immeasurable differences.

---

10. Thomas Aquinas, *Summa Theologiae*, eds and trans., Thomas Gilby, et al. (New York: McGraw-Hill, 1964–1981. Reprinted by Cambridge: Cambridge University Press, 2008), 1a.3.4.*responsio*; *Summa Theologiae*, 1a.4.3.ad 3.

11. Aquinas, *Summa Contra Gentiles*, 4 vols, trans. A. Pegis, J. Anderson, V. J. Burke, and C. J. O'Neil (Garden City: Doubleday, 1955–1956), I.22.9 (my emphases). Unless otherwise indicated, translations of Aquinas are my own.

12. Of course, this is directly traceable to Plato's allegory of the sun in *Republic* VI: everything exists by participation in the Good.

Another important consequence of the metaphysics of participation that will become important in the discussion of de Lubac's view of nature and grace concerns causation. Just as there can be no 'competition' or 'contrast' between divine existence and creaturely existence because they are fundamentally different, so there can be no 'competition' between divine causation and creaturely causation. The *Liber de Causis* ('The Book of Causes'), a neoplatonic work upon which Aquinas wrote an important commentary, begins by stating that 'Every primary cause infuses its effect more powerfully than does a universal second cause.'[13] This means that God, as first cause, is the very foundation of all causation within creation. Within creation, we can delineate a hierarchy of causes for any event. For example, what causes the football team to win a match? The players? The coach? The fans? The club's owner? In a sense, they are all causes, but in different ways.[14] There is, however, a fundamental difference between creaturely or 'secondary' causation and divine or 'primary' causation: the primary cause is universal, the origin of existence, the source of all other causes and therefore infuses itself most deeply in things.[15] To put the matter simply, God is not a cause among causes, one agent among many, but the very basis of all causation. Crucially, because divine primary causation and creaturely secondary causation are of a completely different order, they do not compete with or displace each other. Rather, the latter participates in the former.[16] An action need not be God's *or* mine; it can truly be both. So participation in God's primary causation does not render secondary causes purely instrumental or determined. Secondary causes within creation are real and potent.[17] As we will see, the blending of primary and secondary causes is also the blending of grace and nature. This has the important implication that grace is not a miracle.[18] A miracle occurs when secondary causes – that is, natural causes – are removed to leave only the divine primary cause. Grace, on the

---

13. Thomas Aquinas, *Commentary on the Book of Causes* trans. Vincent A. Guagliardo, O. P., Charles R. Hess, O. P., and Richard C. Taylor (Washington, DC: The Catholic University Press of America, 1996), p. 5. All references are to the page numbers in this edition.

14. See Aquinas, *Summa Contra Gentiles*, III.70.

15. Aquinas, *Commentary on the Book of Causes*, 8: 'But the activity by which the second cause causes an effect is caused by the first cause, *for the first cause aids the second cause*, making it to act. Therefore, *the first cause* is more a cause than the second cause of that *activity* in virtue of which an *effect* is produced by *the second cause*.'

16. Aquinas, *Commentary on the Book of Causes*, 132:
Now, whatever abundantly participates a characteristic proper to something becomes like it not only in form but also in action.... Because form is the principle of action, everything that acquires its action from an abundant participation of the infusion of a higher agent must have two actions: one according to its proper form, another according to a form *participated from the higher agent*, as a heated knife cuts according to its proper form but burns insofar as it is heated. (my emphasis)

17. For Aquinas's account of providence and divine causation, see *Summa Theologiae* 1a.22.

18. Milbank, *The Suspended Middle*, p. 25.

other hand, involves the blending of causes both divine and natural; they are not mutually exclusive. Jacob Schmutz, in an important essay on the changing views of causation beginning in the fourteenth century and the concomitant rise of the concept of *natura pura*, points to the paradoxical nature of Aquinas's position, focusing simultaneously on autonomy and dependence:

> Aquinas could indicate both the dependence and the autonomy of the creature's being and action in relation to the Creator, on the one hand, by distinguishing them, through the doctrine of analogy, and on the other, by indicating the dependence by means of the doctrine of the essential participation of the secondary cause in relation to the first cause. Creatures can provoke movement or change, but they are not the adequate cause of them inasmuch as God is the immediate, active agent and giver of being... The first cause gives being, the secondary causes only determine it. ....[19]

This means that, for Aquinas, the primary cause acts *in* the secondary cause by means of *influentia* or 'influx' into the secondary cause. This will become very important for understanding the blending of nature and the supernatural.

Having sketched the basic lineaments of Radical Orthodoxy's vision, we now turn to the key debate where its main proponents have found most consonance with de Lubac's work, the relationship between grace and nature.

Grace and Nature: The Paradox of Creation

As Henri de Lubac observed, the debate concerning grace and nature that so dominated mid-twentieth century Catholic theology, while frequently focusing on the interpretation of Thomas Aquinas and the Thomist legacy, touched every aspect of Christian theology. Radical Orthodoxy has diagnosed with de Lubac the inherent dangers of separating existence into dual realms that stand over and against each other on a univocal plane, hence the desire to articulate the blended but distinct spheres of grace and nature.[20] The wider debate concerning the supernatural is discussed in detail elsewhere in this book. Our focus here is Radical Orthodoxy's particular contribution.

---

19. Jacob Schmutz, 'The Medieval Doctrine of Causality and the Theology of Pure Nature (13th to 17th Centuries)', in Serge-Thomas Bonino, O. P., ed., *Surnaturel: A Controversy at the Heart of Twentieth-Century Thomstic Thought* trans. Robert Williams (Ave Maria, FL: Sapientia Press, 2009), pp. 20350, here citing pp. 209–10.

20. Conor Cunningham, '*Natura Pura*, The Invention of the Anti-Christ: A Week with No Sabbath', *Communio* 37 (Summer 2010): pp. 24354, here citing p. 244. 'There is a perennial temptation that haunts all thought, a temptation that is dangerous for most discourse, but terminal for theology, namely, to parse existence in terms of dualisms: transcendence/ immanence; natural/ supernatural; sacred/ profane; philosophy/ theology, and so on.' Cunningham argues that only God could be a 'pure nature'.

For de Lubac, the heart of the Christian mystery is paradoxical. While it is possible that humanity could have a purely natural end, it is the case that humanity is created with a natural desire for the supernatural vision of God.[21] Humanity's natural ends are simply intermediate ends which are enfolded in our final end.[22] It is this final end which defines human nature. De Lubac writes:

> For this desire is not some 'accident' in me. It does not result from some peculiarity, possibly alterable, of my individual being, or from some historical contingency whose effects are more or less transitory... My finality, which is expressed by this desire, is inscribed upon my very being as it has been put into this universe by God. And, by God's will, I now have no other genuine end, no end really assigned to my nature or presented for my free acceptance under any guise, except that of 'seeing God'.[23]

De Lubac sees that humanity's desire for the supernatural, in not being accidental, is constitutive of human nature. Of course, the vision of God is connatural only to God and cannot be achieved by humanity's natural power, even though the *desire* for that ultimate end is apparently natural. Following Aquinas, de Lubac insists that a natural desire of any creature cannot be frustrated without twisting and contorting that nature. So to frustrate humanity's desire for the *visio dei* would be to confine humanity to an endless suffering. So it seems that God is obliged to realize the beatific vision because the desire for that vision is innate in humanity's nature and, in being innate, it must be fulfilled.

But how could God's realization of humanity's natural desire for the supernatural be a matter of grace – that is, a free gift – and, at the same time, of obligation? Milbank's answer to this conundrum reaches to the heart of Radical Orthodoxy's appropriation of de Lubac and the Thomist vision he espouses:

> the traditional account of grace and the supernatural [that of Aquinas prior to his sixteenth-century commentators] is *ontologically revisionary*. The natural desire cannot be frustrated, yet it cannot be of itself fulfilled. Human nature in its self-exceeding seems in justice to require a gift – yet the gift of grace remains beyond all justice and requirement. The paradox is for de Lubac only to be entertained because one must remember that the just requirement for the gift in humanity is itself a created gift.[24]

21. Following Aquinas, for example in *Summa Contra Gentiles*, III.57.4: 'Besides, it was proved above that every intellect naturally desires the vision of the divine substance, but natural desire cannot be incapable of fulfilment. Therefore, any created intellect whatever can attain to the vision of the divine substance, and the inferiority of its nature is no impediment.' See also *Summa Contra Gentiles* III.59.1. However, de Lubac does not resort to arguments from authority. He is not interested in the possibility of a purely finite natural end of man (a possibility he readily admits), but the actual openness of human desire towards the infinite – the 'restlessness' of St Augustine.
22. Milbank, *The Suspended Middle*, p. 25.
23. MS, pp. 54–55. See below for a more detailed discussion of teleology.
24. Milbank, *The Suspended Middle*, p. 35.

Maintaining the paradox of grace and nature in this way is part of Radical Orthodoxy's commitment both to creation as *the* gift *ex nihilo* and also to the metaphysics of participation. How? We saw above that the difference between God and creation is not like the difference between creatures; it is not symmetrical. God establishes creation as other than himself. The difference between God and creation is itself a gift. Importantly, creation's participation in God is not proper to creation; God grants to creation a participation in his own substantiality. So it is not the case that creation establishes itself as 'other' than God and then becomes the subject of God's gratuity because creation is, in itself, nothing. To put the matter another way, creation's ability to receive the gifts of God is itself a gift. There is nothing that stands outside this economy of divine gratuity. What creation has is genuinely its own, but what belongs to creation is always a gift. To return to the matter of grace and nature, for Milbank, following de Lubac, the innate and natural desire of humanity for the beatific vision does not constitute an obligation which is external to God, lying outside the divine economy of gratuitous creation, because that desire also finds its ultimate source in God. Of course, that natural desire for the supernatural is genuinely the creature's own, but its ultimate first cause is God. Humanity's just requirement for the genuinely new *second* gift of grace which will bring humanity to the beatific vision must be understood as 'beyond all justice and requirement' because that just requirement emerges from a natural desire for the supernatural, which is God's *first* gift in creation. Put more simply, humanity renounces any claim upon God because its primary nature is receptivity to the divine gift, first of 'being' and second of 'beatitude': 'For who sees anything different in you? What do you have that you did not receive? And if you received it, why do you boast as if it were not a gift?' (1 Corinthians 4.7).

The view that the natural desire for the supernatural is a gift of God, however, carries with it an obvious danger: it seems to turn everything into a matter of grace and rids human nature of any integrity. Of course, this is precisely the concern of those who maintain the need for a *natura pura*, namely the preservation of the gratuity of grace. Yet Radical Orthodoxy holds fast to the paradox of the natural desire for the supernatural. As we have seen, creation is the first gift of an existence that is other than God, while grace is the second and wholly new gift of deification in which humanity is united to God without losing creaturely integrity. The natural desire for the supernatural is 'the gift of the bond' between the first and second gifts, 'negotiated by the spirit's freedom'.[25] So the natural desire for the supernatural is a 'suspended middle' (to coin von Balthasar's phrase which is in turn borrowed from Erich Przywara[26]) that indicates the unity-in-distinction of the orders of grace and nature. It rests in a double paradox: creation is autonomous

25. Ibid., p. 44.
26. Hans Urs von Balthasar, *The Theology of Henri de Lubac: An Overview*, trans. Joseph Fessio and Susan Clements (San Francisco: Ignatius Press, 1991), pp. 14–15; Erich Przywara, *Analogia Entis: Metaphysics: Original Structure and Universal Rhythm*, trans. John R. Betz and David Bentley Hart (Grand Rapids, MI: Eerdmans Publishing Company, 2014), 290ff.

being and yet heteronomous gift while grace is the raising of human spirit, as human spirit, to be beyond human spirit.

In a now-famous letter to Maurice Blondel written in 1932, de Lubac asks, 'This concept of a pure nature runs into great difficulties, the principal one of which seems to me to be the following: how can a conscious spirit be anything other than an absolute desire for God?'[27] It is conscious spirit that stands in a suspended middle that cannot be simply a part of nature or purely a matter of grace. So what is 'conscious spirit'? It is something natural and supernatural, human and divine. Following de Lubac, Milbank answers this question through a category that has been central to Radical Orthodoxy's engagement with wider theology and philosophy, namely gift.[28] Spirit is conscious of continuously receiving itself as gift. This is more than a feeling of absolute dependence; it is the drive to know the source of what we are as recipient spirits who cannot fully command what is received because a gift must always 'flow', continually giving itself anew. The response is gratitude towards the mysterious and unfathomable source of an infinite gift. This establishes an important characteristic of the gift for Radical Orthodoxy, and Milbank in particular: reciprocity. While Derrida theorizes a pure one-way gift in which no return is possible lest the giver be tainted by self-interest, Milbank insists that for a gift truly to be gift it must be acknowledged as such. This acknowledgement takes the form of gratitude. The recipient offers a return gift: thanksgiving. So whereas, for Derrida, for a gift to be truly a gift it must be only one way – from giver to recipient – and thereby totally selfless or purely altruistic, for Milbank the gift requires reciprocal exchange because the gift must be acknowledged as such. The recipient acknowledges the gift and reciprocates with gratitude to the giver. So gift, for Milbank, establishes relationship through reciprocity.

Moreover, following the logic of de Lubac's position, Milbank argues that *natura pura* fails to guarantee the absolute gratuity of grace because it conceives of grace in a way that is univocal with gifts *within* the created order. Donation within creation implies the gift of something to an already established recipient. Similarly, *natura pura* implies a recipient standing in purity outside the economy of gift prior to the receipt of any gift. How, asks Milbank, does this 'pure nature' receive this gift? Does it do so purely of its own volition, recognizing and thereby receiving the gift by virtue of its own wilful power, a power kept in reserve beyond the gift? Indeed, if a pure nature is understood to stand outside the economy of gift in this way, it establishes an autonomy for the created order and a distance

---

27. Henri de Lubac, *Mémoire sur l'occasion de mes écrits*, ed. Georges Chantraine and Fabienne Clinquart (Oeuvres complètes, 33) (Paris: Cerf, 2001), p. 188.

28. Milbank, *The Suspended Middle*, pp. 49–52. Milbank's interventions in the philosophical and theological debates concerning the gift have been crucial. See in particular *Being Reconciled: Ontology and Pardon* (London: Routledge, 2003); 'The Soul of Reciprocity Part One: Reciprocity Refused', *Modern Theology* 17 (2001): pp. 335–91; 'The Soul of Reciprocity Part Two: Reciprocity Granted', *Modern Theology* 17 (2001): pp. 485–507. See also Graham Ward, *Christ and Culture* (Oxford: Blackwell, 2005), especially ch. 2.

from God whereby humanity can wilfully *require* of God the gift of beatitude on the basis of its self-standing 'pure nature'. According to de Lubac, this reduces to Pelagianism.[29] Crucially, for grace to be truly gratuitous it must presume nothing, 'not even creation'.[30] This is why creation *ex nihilo* is not the establishment of a *natura pura* to which grace is later added, but the expression of an eternal gratuity into which nature is always drawn, even from the moment of its being spoken into existence by God. This is what Milbank refers to as 'gift without contrast'. There are modes or distinctions of gift and always the possibility of the genuinely new gift, but there is nothing lying outside the economy of divine gratuity against which it can be contrasted.

Milbank gives de Lubac's understanding of the gratuity of grace an even more radical reading. As we have seen, Aquinas's neoplatonic understanding of causation involved the in-flowing, or *influentia*, of divine causal power into secondary causes in such a way that God is not simply one cause among others.[31] This has the crucial consequence that creation is not an object upon which God acts by means of the delivery of grace, but is the very instantiation of causation or 'influence'. So rather than God acting *on* something through the delivery of grace, Milbank proposes that the correct Thomist view as followed by de Lubac is that the act of creation is at one and the same time 'a gift of a gift to a gift'.[32] God's creation establishes a threefold order of gratuity: the recipient of the gift, the gift itself, and the donation of one to the other. This seems to establish, however, a radically unilateral gift: God simply gives everything.

So does this fatally compromise the gratuity of grace and the proper autonomy of the creature? Quite the contrary: this is the only way of preserving the sovereignty of God and the gratuity of grace. To understand why this is the case, we must recall that the difference between God and creation is not like the difference between creatures. Whereas the difference between creatures (for example, between two people) belongs properly to creatures because of their separate and autonomous substantial natures, the difference between a creature and God is itself a gift of God. In itself, the creature is nothing; it does not instantiate itself as other than God and thereby exert its own causal influence or claim. It is God who, in the act of creation, gives existence to that which is other, holding creation at a distance so that it can be creation. The nature of creation's autonomy from God is therefore paradoxical: on the one hand, creation is autonomous because it is not God, while on the other hand this is no autonomy at all because creation's 'otherness' is always due to God and his act of creation *ex nihilo*.

29. Milbank, *The Suspended Middle*, p. 50; De Lubac, MS, p. 48.
30. Milbank, *The Suspended Middle*, 50.
31. Schmutz, 'The Medieval Doctrine of Causality', pp. 215–30. Schmutz describes the shift in the understanding of *influentia* away from the influx of primary causes *into* secondary causes towards an understanding of primary causes acting *with* or *alongside* secondary causes. The distinction is subtle but the latter understanding leads to a more flattened view of 'causes among causes' rather than a hierarchical view of causation in which the higher causes inhere in the lower causes and act not *with* them but *in and through* them.
32. Milbank, *The Suspended Middle*, p. 96.

Having received itself as the unilateral and all-encompassing gift of God *ex nihilo*, creation's only response is to return itself in gratitude to the source of its being. A creature's expression of its nature in its very existence is its return to, or desire for, God. Yet God does not receive anything because whatever God receives, God has already donated. So Milbank proposes a most profound paradox at the heart of the Christian doctrine of creation: 'unilateral exchange'.[33] While there can only be genuine reciprocity in the Trinity or between creatures, the apparently reciprocal exchange between God and creation is only ever a matter of God's *influentia* by which creation is given the power of responding and returning to God. This guarantees the gratuity of grace because it refuses any pure natural autonomy that can be the basis of a claim by creation on God's gratuity. In short, there is nothing outside the gift and no position from which creation can assert itself over and against God. On this view, grace is the genuinely new (yet always inchoately anticipated) gift arising from within the primordial gift of creation by means of God's *influentia*.

Throughout Radical Orthodoxy's appropriation of de Lubac's understanding of grace and nature, the paradoxical structure of Christian theology is made evident. Indeed, Aaron Riches sees this as the heart of the dispute with neo-scholastic theologians such as Lawrence Feingold who defend the concept of *natura pura*.[34] For many modern theologians, paradox is a sign of incoherence and confusion and must therefore be resolved. Something must belong either to the realm of nature or the realm of grace. As nature is relinquished, it gives way to supernature in a kind of 'zero-sum game' – we have one or the other. For de Lubac, Christian theology is paradoxical in the sense that it is structured around both/and, not either/or. Creation is *both* other than God *and* nothing; Christ is *both* divine *and* human; spiritual creatures are *both* natural *and* intrinsically orientated to the supernatural; grace is *both* innately desired by nature *and* a wholly new gift. Paradox is not a logical contradiction to be overcome or a mystery that will be clarified on the far side of the *eschaton*. It is not a fog that will clear once

---

33. This paradox is expressed in the Church of England's eucharistic liturgy with the use at the offertory of King David's prayer dedicating the people's gifts for the building of the Temple: 'For all things come from you, and of your own have we given you' (1 Chronicles 29.14).

34. Aaron Riches, 'To Rest in the Infinite Altitude of the Divine Substance: A Lubacian response to the provocation of Lawrence Feingold and the resurgent attack on the legacy of *Surnaturel* (1946) – Part One', unpublished essay provided by the author, p. 32:

> In this regard, the divide between de Lubac and Feingold concerns two distinct approaches to theological perplexity: the one sees theological perplexity as essentially internal to the paradox of the hypostatic union and the mystery of Christology – the very core of Christian thought and practice – while the other sees perplexity as a problematical failure of reason fully to understand faith, and thus an aspect of theology in need of resolution in the quest for systematic clarity.

See also Part Two, 8ff. See Lawrence Feingold, *The Natural Desire to See God According to St. Thomas Aquinas and His Interpreters*, 2nd ed. (Ave Maria: Ave Maria University, Sapientia Press, 2010).

further investigation has been undertaken or the concepts clarified. Paradox is not simply a function of language that could be resolved if only we sorted out our conceptual schemata, but is part of the highest reaches of metaphysics. The tension of paradox is itself (paradoxically) revealing. So it is only by holding together divine and human, grace and nature, faith and reason, sacred and secular, that the non-competitive and blended structure of these concepts becomes apparent and each reveals the other.[35] Milbank sees the paradoxical nature of metaphysics and theology as contrasted with modern dialectics that is associated particularly with the philosophy of Georg Wilhelm Friedrich Hegel (1770–1831).[36] Put very simply, dialectical thought works through the proposal of thesis and antithesis that are resolved into synthesis. In short, dialectics overcomes all tension and resolves into a unity, whereas paradox requires the maintenance of tension as intrinsic to the depths of created being.

The importance of paradox for de Lubac and Radical Orthodoxy can be understood in relation to the central paradox of Christian theology, the incarnation.[37] Christ is fully divine and fully human, yet one person. How can the infinite dwell with the finite in one person? How can Jesus Christ be both God and man, and one person? Attempts to resolve this paradox – to decide that Christ is really divine *or* human – were rejected by the ecumenical councils of the Church. Asserting Christ's essential divinity is known as Docetism while opting exclusively for his created, albeit exalted, nature is associated with the followers of Arius. At the same time, resolving the paradox by mixing or synthesizing the divine and human natures of Christ results only in a hybrid whereby Christ is a separate third entity, neither human nor divine. All of these attempts at resolution fail because they do not do justice to the theological insight that only a single divine humanity can bring salvation. One the one hand, we are only saved by God's grace; on the other hand, it must be a human sacrificial action that reconciles us to God because it is humanity that has estranged itself. So Christ must stand in a 'suspended middle' between divine and human, finite and infinite, by being *both* divine *and* human. Because these are not mutually exclusive univocal natures (they do not, as it were, compete

---

35. See Rowan Williams's recent reflections on the wider implications of paradox in *The Edge of Words: God and the Habits of Language* (London: Bloomsbury, 2014), ch. 5: 'Advances in understanding come when both theoreticians and experimenters identify the oddity within "normal" discourse and press its tensions a bit further – not with the aim of removing all tension but in order to find ways of holding it in a larger structure and discovering new tension at that level which in turn will generate further fruitful crises' (p. 130).

36. John Milbank, 'The Double Glory, or Paradox versus Dialectics: On Not Quite Agreeing with Slavoj Žižek', in Creston Davis, John Milbank, and Slavoj Žižek, eds, *The Monstrosity of Christ: Paradox or Dialectic?* (Cambridge, MA: The MIT Press, 2009), pp. 111–233.

37. The connection between Christological disputes concerning the relation between divine and human natures and the debate concerning nature and grace is drawn by Aaron Riches, 'Christology and *duplex hominis beatitudo*: Re-sketching the Supernatural Again', *International Journal of Systematic Theology* 14 (2012): pp. 44–69.

for space in Christ), Christ is fully both. This paradoxical relationship between infinite and finite is mirrored in the paradoxical relationship between Christ's body, the Church, and the world, as well as between the grace which Christ offers and the nature which always intrinsically desires that grace. The paradox of Christ, which seeks no synthesis or resolution, reveals implications beyond Christology in the paradoxical nature of metaphysics itself in which tensions give rise to tensions and there cannot be any final and complete analysis outside God in whom all opposites coincide.[38] Whereas modern thought seeks mastery and control in terms of resolution, the philosophy and theology of antiquity and the Middle Ages understood paradoxical mystery to lie at the head of a symbolically created reality which points, paradoxically, to a creator who lies beyond all image and symbol.[39]

Grace and Nature: Some Implications

For de Lubac, the debate concerning grace and nature had significant implications for the relation between faith and reason, the sacred and secular, and the Church and state. Likewise, Radical Orthodoxy has proposed the always blended but distinct realms of theology and philosophy as well as faith and reason.[40] The neo-scholastic concept of grace standing alongside a realm of *natura pura* mirrors an understanding of the Church standing outside the worldly and autonomous domain of the secular, delivering grace from outside according to the mechanism of its sacraments. The notion of a *natura pura* is coterminous with the modern establishment of the secular as a desacralized, autonomous and neutral order to which the sacred is added as an extrinsic addition.[41] By contrast, for de Lubac

---

38. The term 'coincidence of opposites' belongs to the fifteenth-century Cardinal, philosopher, mathematician and theologian Nicholas of Cusa (1401–1464). See especially his treatise *De Docta Ignorantia* (On Learned Ignorance) in Nicholas of Cusa, trans. H. Lawrence Bond, *Selected Spiritual Writings* (New York: Paulist Press, 1997).

39. The most sophisticated account of the metaphysical implications of paradox in the Radical Orthodoxy genre can be found in Johannes Hoff, *The Analogical Turn: Rethinking Modernity with Nicholas of Cusa* (London: SCM Press, 2013). Hoff's outstanding analysis focuses particularly on the mystagogy of Nicholas of Cusa and his notion of the coincidence of opposites.

40. See, for example, John Milbank, *Beyond Secular Order: The Representation of Being and the Representation of the People* (Oxford: Wiley-Blackwell, 2013), ch. 1; Pickstock, *Repetition and Identity*. For an account suitable for students, see Andrew Davison, *The Love of Wisdom: An Introduction to Philosophy for Theologians* (London: SCM Press, 2013) and Andrew Davison, ed., *Imaginative Apologetics: Theology, Philosophy and the Catholic Tradition* (London: SCM Press, 2011). For a very closely related understanding of the relation between theology and philosophy, see D. C. Schindler, *The Catholicity of Reason* (Grand Rapids, MI: Eerdmans Publishing Company, 2013).

41. See, for example, Henri de Lubac, DAH; TH, Part 2 section III. See also Adrian Pabst, *Metaphysics: The Creation of Hierarchy* (Grand Rapids, MI: Eerdmans Publishing Company, 2012), pp. 311 12.

grace is not an extrinsic power applied to autonomous nature. The natural desire for the supernatural means that grace works by the divine *influentia* in nature. De Lubac outlines the implications of this vision in an early essay:

> In general, the law of the relationships between nature and grace is the same everywhere. Grace seizes nature from the inside and, far from lowering it, lifts it up to have it serve its ends. It is from the interior that faith transforms reason, that the Church influences the State. The Church is the messenger of Christ, not the guardian of the State. The Church ennobles the State, inspiring it to be a Christian State... and, thus, a more human one.[42]

The understanding of grace grasping nature from within is a clear rejection of what de Lubac calls the 'extrincist' understanding of grace that can be seen in the writings of early modern thinkers such as Michael Baius (1513–1589) and Cornelius Jansenius (1585–1638) and brought to fruition in the theology of neo-scholasticism.[43] The idea that grace is an extrinsic addition to an autonomous natural realm issues in an understanding of the Church as an institution standing outside the world, shoring up its own boundaries and becoming one influence among other institutional influences over an autonomous 'pure' secular domain.[44] Following Aquinas, for whom grace is not 'extraneous', de Lubac sees that faith transforms reason from within while the Church is not an agency external to secular civic society which delivers grace from without. Rather, it builds up true society from within. For Milbank, viewing the Church as the extraneous source of grace leads to a sense that it is just another locus of power wielded within and over the world rather than the means of pointing to, orientating and perfecting an already present natural and created drive towards transcendence.[45]

This approach to nature and grace has further implications for the understanding of theology's relation to other modes of intellectual enquiry and investigation. Does theology wield a kind of extraneous power over other disciplines somewhat analogous to an extrinsicist view of grace? It is often assumed that Radical Orthodoxy has a triumphalist attitude to disciplines beyond the boundaries of theology that entails the extraneous judgement or 'placement' of non-theological modes of reason. We might even think that, in the end, all intellectual pursuits should be regarded as different modes of theology, answering to the external power of its canons of authority and reason. This, however, is certainly not Radical Orthodoxy's position and this can be shown through its appropriation of de Lubac's

---

42. 'The Authority of the Church in Temporal Matters', TF, p. 212.
43. See Henri de Lubac, AMT, chs. 1–3.
44. For a helpful and succinct account of de Lubac's rejection of 'political Augustinianism', which radically separated Church from state, see David Grumett, 'Henri de Lubac: Looking for Books to Read the World', in Gabriel Flynn and Paul D. Murray, eds, *Ressourcement: A Movement for Renewal in Twentieth-Century Catholic Theology* (Oxford: Oxford University Press, 2012), pp. 23649.
45. Milbank, *The Suspended Middle*, p. 23.

basic theological sensibility. If one regards nature as intrinsically orientated to the divine and human nature (including its various modes of intellectual enquiry) as innately desirous of the vision of eternal truth, this implies that all modes of human investigation harbour an intrinsic thrust towards the knowledge of God via the particular knowledge of other things. This is why Aquinas can appropriate pagan Aristotelian metaphysics and natural philosophy to produce a synthesis with the Neoplatonic tradition, all under the interpretative authority and orientation of the Church's holy teaching. Just as grace perfects nature, so Christian theology turns the water of pagan philosophical learning into the wine of Christian theology.[46] It is not that theology acts extraneously as just another mode of intellectual enquiry that must be victorious over other disciplines in a battle for superiority. Rather, theology operates as that mode of reason orientated always towards transcendence and yet lacking any specific subject matter. It works, as it were, within human enquiry to perfect our investigations in pointing to the ultimate goal of all enquiry in a singular and transcendent source of truth. Theology might also identify erroneous theologies or metaphysics lying behind certain disciplines, and this has certainly been one of Radical Orthodoxy's defining tasks.[47] So human investigation of the created order by means of natural philosophy (later becoming the natural sciences) is prompted by the sense that new discoveries orientate us towards a transcendent truth. This is why de Lubac could take a very positive approach to theological dialogue with science, including (with Teilhard de Chardin) the exploration of evolutionary theory.[48] Nevertheless, following the Thomist tradition, we cannot understand such wonder and exploration as simply a matter of epistemological curiosity; as Milbank makes clear, it is part of creation's basic *ontological* orientation to a divine end in which every creature is united to God after the manner of its own nature.[49]

Grace and Nature: The Final End

As we have seen, much of the debate surrounding grace and nature concerns the relation of divine action, creaturely causation, and humanity's ultimate end. According to Radical Orthodoxy, the idea of a purely natural end only arises once teleology is eclipsed in early modernity.[50] More specifically, a shift occurs in the

---

46. Aquinas, *Summa Theologiae*, 1a.1.8 and Thomas Aquinas, *Faith, Reason and Theology: Questions I-IV of his Commentary on the De Trinitate of Boethius* (Toronto: Pontifical Institute of Mediaeval Studies, 1987), 2.3. ad 5.
47. Aside from Milbank's critique of the social sciences in *Theology and Social Theory* and Pickstock's theological consummation of philosophy in *After Writing*, see Michael Hanby, *No God? No Science?* (Oxford: Wiley-Blackwell, 2013) and Conor Cunningham, *Darwin's Pious Idea: Why the Creationists and Ultra-Darwinists Both Get It Wrong* (Grand Rapids, MI: Eerdmans Publishing Company, 2013).
48. Milbank, *The Suspended Middle*, p. 24.
49. Ibid., pp. 26–27; see Aquinas, *Summa Contra Gentiles*, III.25.
50. Milbank, *The Suspended Middle*, p. 21.

way that teleology is understood. So what is teleology and how does this affect the debate concerning grace and nature that so embroiled de Lubac?[51]

Teleology refers to the study of final causes – the purpose or goal of a particular action or event. Typically, a teleological description will use phrases such as 'in order to' or 'for the sake of'. For example, I go to the shop to buy a drink in order to quench my thirst. What causes me to go to the shop is the *telos* of quenching my thirst. For ancient and medieval philosophers and theologians, the whole of nature is teleologically ordered.[52] The bird has wings in order to fly. The man runs in order to get fit. The child prays in order to become closer to God. In the modern period, however, the notion of final causes came under significant attack, particularly from natural philosophers such as Francis Bacon (1561–1626) and René Descartes (1596–1650). It was clear, they thought, that teleological orientation, if there is such a thing, belongs only to human beings because human action is intentional and purposive. A person can deliberate and plan so that certain goals are achieved, whereas wider nature works by efficient causation and mechanism. To the extent that artefacts and human systems (chairs, cars, the postal system) are the outcome of human intentional planning, they too are orientated towards certain ends and might therefore be classified as teleological. However, the teleological orientation of something like a chair is not intrinsic. It does not belong to the chair *per se* as a material object. Rather, the teleological orientation of the chair (the act of sitting) emerges from the chair's designer and the person who uses it. In other words, the teleological orientation of the chair is extrinsic – it lies outside the chair, in its designer or user.

So we arrive at an important distinction in the modern understanding of teleology: an end can be intrinsic or extrinsic. Insofar as the goal of a creature is an expression of that creature's intrinsic nature – or, to put it in more precise Aristotelian terms, its blend of form and matter – the goal is intrinsic or innate. When the goal does not belong to a creature but is applied from elsewhere, for example by the designer of an artefact such as a table, it is extrinsic. The rejection of 'real natures' or 'form' in the increasingly mechanistic natural philosophy of the seventeenth century suggested that there were no genuinely intrinsic ends, except perhaps in the case of human intention. Matter came to be understood as passive and something to which one could subsequently *add* a goal or purpose.[53] So just as the teleology of a car is extrinsic and donated to the material by a human

---

51. For a more detailed account of this shift in the understanding of teleology, see Simon Oliver, 'Aquinas and Aristotle's Teleology', *Nova et Vetera* 11 (2013): pp. 84970.

52. For example, Aquinas, *Summa Theologiae* 1a.44.4.*responsio*: 'Every agent acts for an end: otherwise one thing would not follow more than another from the action of the agent, unless it were by chance. … Therefore, the divine goodness is the end of all things.'

53. For a clear and succinct account of the understanding of matter as passive, see Gary Deason, 'Reformation Theology and the Mechanistic Conception of Nature', in David Lindberg and Ronald Numbers, eds, *God and Nature: Historical Essays on the Encounter between Christianity and Science* (Los Angeles: University of California Press, 1986), pp. 16791.

designer, similarly the teleological orientation of nature was first and foremost extrinsic, being granted by God the creator. God comes to be understood as a designer according to an analogy with human designers of artefacts, hence the growing popularity of the design argument for God's existence based on the concept of extrinsic teleology. Meanwhile, any attribution of intrinsic teleology to the natural realm, and particularly to inanimate objects, is merely a case of anthropomorphic projection. We only see purposiveness in nature because we humans are (uniquely) purposive creatures who are apparently less restricted by irrational animal instinct. In fact, there is no intrinsic purpose in nature; it works by simple material mechanisms orientated towards certain functional ends given by the divine designer. Modernity therefore marks the rejection, first and foremost, of intrinsic teleology. Extrinsic teleology, in which purposes are layered on top of a passive material nature according to a design, is preserved insofar as it is consistent with a more fundamental mechanistic cosmology.

How does this compare with pre-modern understandings of final causation? For Aristotle there is no dualism of intrinsic and extrinsic teleology. Human intentionality is just another instance of the wider intrinsic thrust of all things towards their particular ends or goals, and eventually towards the Good. For Aristotle, the end or goal of something is already given by its form; he says clearly 'the form is the final cause'. To be a heavy object is simply to be orientated towards a low place in the cosmos. To be a bird simply is to be orientated towards flight. To be an acorn is to be orientated towards becoming an oak. To be a human being simply is to be orientated towards God. The form contains potentially that which is fully actualized in the achievement of something's *telos*. For example, the oak tree is contained *potentially* within the acorn. Crucially, the motion from potency to act in the achievement of a *telos* is the creature's own. Yet blended with this intrinsic orientation is a creature's continual striving to exceed its current state in moving towards a yet-to-be-achieved goal that lies as yet out of reach. As Aquinas puts it, 'To desire or have appetency is nothing else but to strive for something, to stretch, as it were, toward something which is destined for oneself.'[54] The creature, being receptive to the external actualizing power of others, achieves its goal. So the intrinsic and extrinsic aspects of teleological orientation are always blended. Even in material human artefacts, the matter (for example, the marble of a sculpture) is not entirely passive and the teleology is not wholly extrinsic. By virtue of its substantial form, the matter is intrinsically orientated towards certain ends and not others – one can make a statue out of marble but not a coat.

Returning now to the relationship between grace and nature, it is possible to see that the neo-scholastic position opposed by de Lubac requires a strict distinction between intrinsic and extrinsic teleology. A *natura pura* has an intrinsic orientation towards certain natural ends that are largely concerned with self-sufficiency and self-regulation and hence come to be intelligible in

---

54. Thomas Aquinas, *De Veritate*, in *Sancti Thomae de Aquino opera Omnia*, vol. 22. Leonine ed. (Rome: Editori di San Tommaso, 1975–1976), 22.1.

mechanistic terms.⁵⁵ To this is added a desire for the supernatural that is 'elicited' and is therefore extrinsic in origin, even though it comes to reside in nature. Thus there are two ends that run parallel, one intrinsic and purely natural (the things that are proportionate to human nature such as making dwellings and supplying food) and the other extrinsic and supernatural (the vision of God).⁵⁶ Yet it is not clear how, if at all, these dual orders relate. This means that the extrinsic supernatural end can be seen as an arbitrary and unintelligible addition to the purely natural and self-sufficient ends of humanity. The supernatural end becomes a focus for superstition and it leaves behind a largely autonomous 'secular' realm of the purely natural.⁵⁷

For de Lubac, humanity's orientation towards the supernatural is natural in the sense of being an intrinsic or innate *desire*; it is extrinsic because it is an orientation to what is transcendent that is achieved only through the second gift of grace. It is by grace that God enables the human creature to be moved and to move towards a supernatural end. In other words, the teleological motion towards God is both God's and genuinely the creature's own, made 'sweet and delightful', as Aquinas puts it, by God's grace.⁵⁸ For de Lubac and Radical Orthodoxy, the very form of humanity is always a teleological orientation towards the beatific vision: 'My finality, which is expressed by this desire [for the vision of God], is inscribed upon my very being as it has been put into this universe by God.'⁵⁹ The key point of dispute concerns the more exclusively extrinsic nature of human teleology conceived by neo-scholasticism. For Reinhard Hütter, for example, the second gift of grace begins by *initially* ordering the first gift of created human nature to a supernatural end (an end it did not previously have in any guise) *and then* perfecting that nature in beatitude.⁶⁰ So both acts are, as it were, extrinsically ordering human nature to a supernatural end in such a way that humanity becomes passive and its beatitude a matter of 'design'. According to

---

55. See Milbank, *The Suspended Middle*, p. 22.

56. See, for example, Feingold, *The Natural Desire to See God According to St. Thomas and His Interpreters*, pp. 230–42.

57. Of course, contemporary defenders of *natura pura* according to the tradition of Francisco Suárez (1548–1617) and against de Lubac completely reject this accusation. It is beyond the scope of this chapter to engage their intricate arguments in detail. See Feingold, *The Natural Desire to See God According to St. Thomas and His Interpreters*, pp. 339–43 and 431–35; Steven A. Long, *Natura Pura: On the Recovery of Nature in the Doctrine of Grace* (New York: Fordham University Press, 2010), ch. 1.

58. See Simon Oliver, 'The Sweet Delight of Virtue and Grace in Aquinas's Ethics', *International Journal of Systematic Theology* 7 (2005): pp. 52–71.

59. MS, p. 55.

60. Reinhard Hütter, '*Desiderium Naturale Visionis Dei – Est autem duplex hominis beatitudo sive felicitas*: Some Observations about Lawrence Feingold's and John Milbank's Recent Interventions in the Debate over the Natural Desire to See God', *Nova et Vetera* 5 (2007): pp. 133–83. See especially pp. 102–3.

Radical Orthodoxy's appropriation of de Lubac, the first gift of created human nature is *always* teleologically ordered to a supernatural end that is, paradoxically, beyond all proportion to human nature.[61] Blended with this intrinsic teleological orientation is the second gift of grace that brings that desire to fruition. As Aquinas puts it, 'when [an] end is beyond the capacity of the agent striving to attain it ... it is looked for from another's bestowing'.[62]

This emphasis on 'form' is open to an important objection articulated by Lawrence Feingold, whose position on the relationship between grace and nature is squarely opposed to that of de Lubac and Radical Orthodoxy. If the form is indeed the final cause, this implies that the addition of a new form known as 'grace' will also bring with it a new final *telos*. Feingold states:

> we cannot conclude that because God has destined man for an end that is above his nature, such an end must therefore be a finality 'imprinted on the nature' itself, or an 'intrinsic' or 'ontological' end, or an 'essential finality'. All that we can conclude is that if God has eternally destined us to a supernatural end, it is fitting that he give a new form, 'added on' to our nature, by which we are suitably ordered to that supernatural end. This new accidental form, which is sanctifying grace, must necessarily be above our nature, so as to make us proportionate to an end above our nature, connatural only to God.[63]

Nicholas Healy points out that the texts to which Feingold appeals (*Summa Contra Gentiles* III.150 and *Summa Theologaie* 1a2ae.62.1) do not support the view that the addition of the form of grace provides humanity with a new final end.[64] In the passage from the *Summa Contra Gentiles*, Aquinas is particularly concerned to argue that 'sanctifying grace is a form and perfection remaining in man even when he is not acting'. In other words, sanctifying grace is not simply a force acting externally on the human person; it is a power that becomes the person's own and in which the person is settled through a transformed nature, not merely transformed activity. Form, for Aquinas, is complex and may be qualified or added to. The addition of the new form of grace perfects natural form, it does

---

61. The standard neo-scholastic argument that over-extends the Aristotelian principle that 'the end of nature must be proportionate to that nature' seems to suggest that grace is a gift that renders nature proportionate to its supernatural end. It is not clear, however, that a created nature could *ever* be proportionate to the vision of God. The supernatural end is, rather, the deification of humanity that is a deepening participation in the divine life, not by proportion but by attribution.

62. Aquinas, *Summa Theologiae*, 1a.62.4. *responsio*.

63. Feingold, *The Natural Desire to See God According to St. Thomas Aquinas and His Interpreters*, p. 321. See also p. 318.

64. Nicholas J. Healy, 'Henri de Lubac on Nature and Grace: A Note on Some Recent Contributions to the Debate', *Communio: International Catholic Review* 35 (2008): pp. 53564, especially pp. 56061.

not destroy it or supplant it. The basic natural orientation of humanity to its final end is qualified by the addition of a genuinely new form called grace: humanity is now able to move and be moved to its final end in response to its natural formal desire for that end.

Healy and Riches, clarifying further the basic contours of Radical Orthodoxy's appropriation of de Lubac, trace much of the dispute concerning grace and nature to different deployments of Aristotle's maxim that 'the end of nature must be proportionate to nature'.[65] For neo-scholastic theologians, this maxim applies both to the desire for an end and the power to achieve that end. Yet crucially Aquinas's views of providence and grace include two elements: first, degrees of potency to a given end and, second, a hierarchy of ends in which the lower participate in the higher. So while there is a sense in which humanity is in potency to beatitude as its final end, that potency is radical (a passive potency) because it takes the form of a desire that cannot be fulfilled except by God's grace.[66] Yet at no point is humanity neutral or indifferent with respect to the vision of God. Therefore, it cannot be neutral or indifferent to the means of achieving that vision, namely grace. Meanwhile, humanity has two ends, one natural and another ultimate or supernatural. These ends are not parallel or separate. Rather, they are non-contrastive in the sense that humanity's natural end is enfolded in the ultimate end of beatitude.[67] For de Lubac, expounding a text from Aquinas's *Summa Theologiae*,[68] humanity's beatitude is twofold (*duplex*

---

65. Ibid., and Aaron Riches, 'Christology and *duplex hominis beatitudo*.' While Healy is not in agreement with Milbank's position concerning de Lubac's response to *Humani generis* (see p. 552, n. 41 of his 'Henri de Lubac on Nature and Grace') his view on the debate concerning the supernatural compliments very effectively the arguments of those who identify themselves explicitly with Radical Orthodoxy.

66. Aquinas, *Summa Theologiae*, III.9.2.*responsio*:
What is in potentiality is reduced to act by what is in act; for that whereby things are heated must itself be hot. Now man is in potentiality to the knowledge of the blessed, which consists in the vision of God; and is ordained to it as to an end; since the rational creature is capable of that blessed knowledge, inasmuch as he is made in the image of God. Now men are brought to this end of beatitude by the humanity of Christ, according to Heb. 2:10: 'For it became Him, for Whom are all things, and by Whom are all things, Who had brought many children unto glory, to perfect the author of their salvation by His passion.'

67. Aquinas, *Super Boethium De Trinitate*, q.6. a.4 ad 5: 'We are endowed with principles by which we can prepare for that perfect knowledge of separate substances but not with principles by which to reach it. For even though by his nature man is inclined to his ultimate end, he cannot reach it by nature but only by grace, and this owing to the loftiness of that end.'

68. Aquinas, *Summa Theologiae* 1a2ae.62.1:
Now man's happiness is twofold, as was also stated above (q. 5, a. 5). One is proportionate to human nature, a happiness, to wit, which man can obtain by means of his natural principles. The other is a happiness surpassing man's nature, and which man can obtain by the power of God alone, by a kind of participation of the Godhead, about which it is written (2 Pet. 1:4) that by Christ we are made 'partakers of the Divine nature'.

beatitudo).⁶⁹ First, we have an imperfect beatitude that belongs to this world. Second, we have a true and perfect beatitude that is the vision of God obtained only by grace even though that perfect beatitude is desired by nature. According to Aquinas, the first beatitude is associated with the contemplation of divine things that we find in ancient philosophy that indicates a desire for the vision of God possessed by the blessed that comes only by the grace of God in Christ. The desire that leads to the contemplative life is fulfilled – not supplanted – only in the vision of the First Truth, namely God.⁷⁰

For Healy, a key implication of de Lubac's position on nature and grace is that the primary form of humanity is receptivity (following 1 Corinthians 4.7). 'If human nature desires a final end that exceeds nature, then the form of nature's desire is receptivity – a receptive desire for the surprising and surpassing gift of friendship and assistance from another. This is supremely fitting for a nature whose very existence is from another.'⁷¹ The exemplary instance of this receptivity is Mary's fiat in the incarnation. As Riches points out, this is also an affirmation of the doctrine of creation *ex nihilo* in which the first gift of created reality – the reception of being – is consummated in receptivity to *theosis*.⁷² The natural desire for the supernatural is therefore a recognition that the creature, in itself, is nothing and receives its being at every moment. This leads to the renunciation of any demand on God. It is not, however, a passive receptivity because it is also a positive yearning for the utterly gratuitous and unmerited friendship of God.⁷³ With an emphasis on receptivity as well as donation, this view supplements very effectively Milbank's appropriation of de Lubac focussed on gift as a fundamental theological category. Milbank offers a more radical extension of de Lubac's theology because the gift of grace and the receptivity of nature do not constitute only a theological anthropology and soteriology but also a doctrine of creation.⁷⁴ Insofar as nature is teleologically ordered to the human person in such a way that creation is made for the intellectual spirit, the ends of all creatures are gathered up in the supernatural *finis ultimus* of humanity's vision of God.

---

69. See Henri de Lubac, '*Duplex Hominis Beatitudo* (Saint Thomas, Ia 2ae, q. 62, a. I)', *Recherches de science religieuse* 35 (1948): pp. 290–99 translated by Aaron Riches and Peter M. Candler, Jr. in *Communio: International Catholic Review* 35 (2008): pp. 599–612.

70. Aquinas, *Summa Contra Gentiles*, III.63.2 and 10.

71. Healy, 'Henri de Lubac on Nature and Grace', 561.

72. Riches, 'Christology and *duplex hominis beatitudo*', 56. See also Healy, 'Henri de Lubac on Nature and Grace', 547.

73. Healy, 'Henri de Lubac on Nature and Grace', 548.

74. Lewis Ayres is right that what de Lubac (mostly) treats as matter of theological anthropology, Milbank extends to a doctrine of creation centred on gift. See Lewis Ayres, 'The Soul and the Reading of Scripture: A Note on Henri de Lubac', *Scottish Journal of Theology* 61 (2008): 17390, here citing 183, n. 23.

Conclusion

The extent of Henri de Lubac's importance and influence over contemporary theology is demonstrated by Radical Orthodoxy's thorough appropriation of his work. This is particularly the case with respect to the crucial debate concerning grace and nature that has been the focus of this chapter. More could be said about the importance of de Lubac's *Corpus Mysticum* for Radical Orthodoxy and the centrality of the Eucharist for ecclesiology and language.[75] A more thorough absorption by Radical Orthodoxy of de Lubac's work on the theology of history and biblical exegesis remains in the future.

It would be a misunderstanding, however, to think that Radical Orthodoxy simply picks up what de Lubac says about grace and nature in isolation. The alignment with de Lubac is possible because of more fundamental and basic agreements concerning the importance of *ressourcement* (particularly, for Radical Orthodoxy, the neoplatonic legacy), the interpretation of Thomas Aquinas, the understanding of philosophy's relation to theology, and the basic structure of creation *ex nihilo* centred on the metaphysics of participation. It is clear that Radical Orthodoxy is not merely repeating de Lubac but regards his legacy as unfulfilled.

> For some time now I have contended that Roman Catholic intellectual culture finds it very difficult, for institutional reasons, altogether to negate a false Tridentine legacy, and to pursue all the consequences of de Lubac's theological revolution (a subversion as real as it was stealthy). An enterprise of 'natural theology'... is perpetuated, along with a parallel discourse of 'natural law' considered in an unThomistic way, apart from the law of charity.[76]

For Milbank, there is still a tendency to delineate a realm of 'nature' lying beyond theology and the Church that remains ostensibly indifferent to a transcendent finality. In particular, he has pressed the political implications of de Lubac's vision through an insistence that there is no 'pure nature' lying outside the economy of reciprocal gift and charity, an economy that can only be understood theologically on the basis of creation as gift. This means that worldly politics and economics, while tragically necessary in a fallen world, are only possible because of a more fundamental ontology of gift exchange. The postulation of a *natura pura* in any guise will simply perpetuate the violent power play of modernity because there will be a contest (into which the Church is inevitably drawn) for control of that supposedly neutral sphere.

---

75. See, for example, Catherine Pickstock's use of de Lubac's *Corpus Mysticum* in her *After Writing: On the Liturgical Consummation of Philosophy* (Oxford: Blackwell, 1998), pp. 158–66.

76. Milbank, *Being Reconciled: Ontology and Pardon*, p. 117.

Also, Radical Orthodoxy's appropriation of de Lubac has implications for the understanding of the task of theology. With no *natura pura*, there is no sphere to which theology is indifferent. This means that de Lubac's vision deconstructs the notion of an autonomous and self-enclosed Christian dogmatics that is focussed on a clearly delineated subject matter known as 'revelation'.[77] As a wholly independent natural theology is also rejected, so too is a purely autonomous philosophy. While theology and philosophy remain distinct for Radical Orthodoxy (and strictly speaking not conflated as a 'philosophical theology'), theology requires philosophy's original speculative structure and philosophy in turn is ordered to, and consummated by, theology. As von Balthasar states, 'De Lubac soon realized that his position moved into a suspended middle in which he could not practice any philosophy without its transcendence into theology, but also any theology without its essential inner structure of philosophy.'[78] With no strictly delineated subject matter such as the modern concept of 'revelation', theology *looks* different; it will always involve speaking about God by speaking about other things and in continual conversation with other modes of human enquiry that nevertheless enjoy their distinct subject matters and modes of enquiry.

Central to Radical Orthodoxy's speculative extension of de Lubac's work, however, is the view that there is no pure nature lying outside gift. That gift, grounded in the doctrine of creation *ex nihilo*, is taken to a wholly new and unimaginable pitch in the deliverance of grace through Christ. The radical implications of this claim are explored in conversation with the Christian orthodoxy so beautifully expounded by de Lubac.

---

77. Milbank, *The Suspended Middle*, p. 12. For an excellent account of the origins of the modern concept of revelation in the work of Francisco Suárez, see John Montag, S. J., 'Revelation: The False Legacy of Suárez', in Milbank, Pickstock and Ward, eds, *Radical Orthodoxy: A New Theology* (London: Routledge, 1999): pp. 38–63.

78. Von Balthasar, *The Theology of Henri de Lubac*, p. 15 quoted in Milbank, *The Suspended Middle*, p. 13, n. 17.

Chapter 18

HENRI DE LUBAC AND POLITICAL THEOLOGY

Joseph S. Flipper

The political, broadly construed, is nowhere and everywhere in Henri de Lubac's writings. On the one hand, de Lubac rarely thematized the political in his theological writings, unlike his friend Gaston Fessard, SJ. On the other hand, the political events and social conditions of twentieth-century France seep into his writings, producing an account of the social and political world and its relationship to the eternal. Despite the ubiquity of social and political themes in his writings, his lack of systematic integration allows his insights to pass by unnoticed.

De Lubac's early career and writings corresponded with the rise of *social Catholicism* of the 1920s–1930s. *Social Catholicism* names the renewal of theological and pastoral efforts aimed at the reconstruction of Christianity as a visible form of life.[1] At the fin de siècle, European Catholicism was challenged to re-envision its place in civil society due to the loss of political power as well as rapidly changing economic and social development. Catholics closely associated God's providence over the world with the Catholic Church's control over territory. When Italy captured the Papal States in 1870, the entire temporal framework had to be re-envisioned. Beginning in 1879, the government of the French Third Republic began to expel Catholic religious congregations and created a secular system of public education. In most Catholic European countries, the Catholic Church experienced increasing marginalization and loss of its traditional exercise of political power. Responding to these challenges, the papacy became the centre of production of Catholic thought through the deployment of neothomism in theological education and the dissemination of Catholic social doctrine through papal encyclicals. In 1891, Pope Leo XIII disseminated the encyclical *Rerum*

---

1. See Jean-Yves Calvez, 'The French Catholic Contribution to Social and Political Thinking in the 1930s', *Ethical Perspectives: Journal of the European Ethics Network* 7:4 (December 2000): pp. 312–15; Jean-Yves Calvez, *Chrétiens, penseurs du social*, Histoire de la morale (Paris: Éditions du Cerf, 2008). See also Peter J. Bernardi, *Maurice Blondel, Social Catholicism, and Action française: The Clash Over the Church's Role in Society During the Modernist Era* (Washington, DC: Catholic University of America Press, 2009).

novarum, which raised the social question, that is, how Christianity is to be lived amidst urbanization, capitalism, and secularization.

During the fin de siècle, many Catholics envisioned a return to an imagined medieval unity of faith and social life. This ideal influenced writers, philosophers, and converts to Catholicism, including Léon Bloy, Paul Claudel, Charles Péguy, Georges Bernanos, and Jacques and Raïssa Maritain. Taking advantage of support for this ideal of social unity and popular resentment towards French *laïcité* (secularization), Action française, a nationalist party that repudiated the French revolutionary legacy and sought a return to monarchy and social hierarchy, captured the allegiance of the majority of French Catholics from 1910 to 1920. A principal figure in Action française, Charles Maurras, though he was agnostic, sought the restoration of Catholicism as a state religion. Maurras believed that Catholicism was requisite for the establishment of a unity of state, culture, and race, a unity that he called *intégrisme*. In 1926 Pope Pius XI condemned Action française for making religion a mere means of political ends. This condemnation promulgated the Catholic search for another model for the social embodiment of faith. Pius XI disseminated the encyclical *Quadragisimo anno* (1931), which returned to the 'social question' raised forty years earlier by *Rerum novarum*. In the 1930s, a number of theologians and philosophers engaged the question of the relationship between the Church and the sociopolitical order, including Emmanuel Mounier, Jacques Maritain, Gaston Fessard, and Henri de Lubac.

Although the writings of de Lubac that directly address the political order are few, the entirety of his theological production revolves around the issue of the relationship between lived human experience and salvation. He produced an account of salvation as essentially a social reality, lived historically as a sacrament of the eternal. De Lubac's efforts in the spiritual resistance to anti-Semitism, his writings on the supernatural, and his ecclesiology all contribute to understanding the political. Nevertheless, de Lubac did not fully form an account of political order. His writing on the political is less concerned with establishing clear and applicable theoretical constructs or with practical solutions, as it is concerned with the discernment of the present situation and the Church's calling in light of God's revelation and plan.

The following examines the broad contours of Henri de Lubac's political theology. Part I briefly examines de Lubac's theology of human unity in *Catholicism* and his writings during the Second World War. Part II considers de Lubac's theology of the supernatural as a source for a political theology. Part III examines contemporary Lubacian theo-political trajectories. Part IV examines de Lubac's ecclesiology for his understanding of the Church's political role.

The Unity of Humanity and Spiritual Resistance

Henri de Lubac's first book, *Catholicism* (1938), contains in seed practically all the themes that he would unpack during his long career. In it, he responds to the charge by critics of Christianity that Christians await life in heaven but lack interest in improving the conditions of our terrestrial existence. His chief insight concerns the social nature of Christianity: 'Catholicism is essentially social. It is social in the deepest sense of the word: not merely in its applications in the field of natural institutions but first and foremost in itself, in the heart of its mystery, in the essence of its dogma.'[2] In *Catholicism* de Lubac argues that Christianity is not only a sociological phenomenon, but is also social *in nature*. Christianity is essentially concerned with the temporal order and the future of human life. According to de Lubac, history is meaningful to the Christian because salvation is experienced in history. He writes, 'if salvation is social in its essence it follows that history is the necessary interpreter between God and man'.[3] Christianity, unlike Platonism, regards the historical world as the locus of encounter with God rather than as something to be escaped. History possesses an 'ontological density'.[4]

This account of Christianity responded to what de Lubac called one of the 'deepest yearnings of our age', namely how to engender human unity. Marxism and fascism similarly seek the unity of humanity by 'dissolving' the human into the social order. Seeking to overcome human estrangement, Marxism compounds this estrangement by cutting off the human from its transcendent destiny.[5] Christianity, on the other hand, unites a transcendent destiny with social salvation. According to de Lubac, salvation is experienced socially because humanity is itself essentially social. The early Church, he claims, saw sin as a fragmentation of the original unity of the human race. It is the orientation towards the transcendent that provides the basis for human unity: 'The same mysterious participation in God which causes the soul to exist effects at one and the same time the unity of spirits among themselves.'[6] In the Christian vision, the social unity of humanity converges on and is completed only in the transcendent goal, that is, humanity's eschatological union with Christ. The temporal order itself yearns for completion in the transcendent. For de Lubac, the key theological paradox is that salvation is worked out on the temporal plane, yet salvation remains fundamentally incomplete within the bounds of time.

During the German occupation of France (1940–1944) in the Second World War, the vision of the unity of humanity developed in de Lubac's *Catholicism* became vitally important to his role in the spiritual resistance against Nazism. In 1940 Germany invaded the north of France and exercised authority over the

---

2. C, p. 15.

3. Ibid.

4. Ibid., p. 142. See also Joseph S. Flipper, *Between Apocalypse and Eschaton: History and Eternity in Henri de Lubac* (Minneapolis, MN: Fortress, 2015), pp. 91–127; Omar César Albado, 'La reflexión sobre la temporalidad en la teología de Henri de Lubac', *Teología* 100 (2009): pp. 465–80.

5. In *Catholicism*, de Lubac confronted primarily the social anthropology of Marxism. It is a strange omission that he treats fascism only briefly in the footnotes. See *Catholicism*, 361n15, 16. In Germany, the National Socialists had long been in power, and by 1934 Adolf Hitler had been given emergency powers and become dictator. Benito Mussolini had been Prime Minister of Italy and *Il Duce* of the National Fascist Party since 1922.

6. C, p. 29.

Vichy government in southern France. During this time, de Lubac lived in Lyon, in the *Zone Libre* controlled by the Vichy government. His efforts in Lyon during the German occupation were primarily literary and pastoral. His participation in the resistance against Nazism was spiritual precisely because it was unarmed. Yet his writings during this period should not be thought of as passive responses to political events. Publishing during the occupation was highly curtailed. Anything published officially had to be sent to censors. In addition to publishing censored material, de Lubac also published abroad and contributed to clandestine publications, including the journal Cahiers *du Témoignage chrétien* (Christian Witness Notebooks). The clandestine literature published during the occupation was referred to as *témoignage* (witness). *Témoignage* was not seen as merely an account of events but intentional, active participations in the events described and a testimony to the truth silenced by the Vichy and German authorities.[7] De Lubac's writings from 1940 to 1944 should be thought of as instances of *témoignage chrétien*, the active witness to the truth of Christianity that resists the current regime.[8]

De Lubac's response to anti-Semitism was principally theological, a plea to Catholic Christians to reject an ideology that was not only anti-Jewish but also anti-Christian. In a letter dated 25 April 1941, de Lubac wrote to his superiors in the Jesuit order. In it he claimed that Hitler's war is first of all an 'anti-Christian revolution', the 'brutal return to instinct' of neopaganism.[9] In addition to describing a worsening human calamity and the appearance of concentration camps in France, he described a slow imposition of the 'cult of the state', leading to a 'collective apostasy'.[10] The occupiers were waging both a propaganda campaign of anti-Semitism influencing lay Catholics and a campaign to dissuade religious superiors and bishops from speaking out. Religious leaders were pressured to avoid 'political Catholicism', that is, inserting the Church into the political sphere. De Lubac accused the French Church, particularly the clergy, of passively accepting the anti-Semitism of the Vichy government. This is why de Lubac presented anti-Semitism as an essentially spiritual and religious problem. He writes, 'The anti-Semitism of today was unknown to our fathers; besides its degrading effect on those who abandon themselves to it, it is anti-Christian. It is against the Bible, against the Gospel as well as the Old Testament.'[11] De Lubac's plea to resist anti-Semitism is set theologically within the Christian's baptismal call to resist the 'tricks of the adversary'.[12] The war was not merely political, for de Lubac; it was being waged over the soul of the French Church.

---

7. See Margaret Atack, *Literature and the French Resistance: Cultural Politics and Narrative Forms, 1940–1950* (New York: St Martin's Press, 1989), pp. 16–29.

8. Cf. CR.

9. Henri de Lubac, 'Letter to My Superiors (Lyons, 25 April 1941)', TH, p. 429.

10. Ibid., p. 432.

11. Ibid., p. 437.

12. Ibid., p. 436.

In *Catholicism*, de Lubac appealed to the vision of the unity of humanity to elaborate the theological basis for anti-racism in the contemporary context. In a two-part lecture delivered in Lyon in January 1941 entitled 'The Theological Foundation of the Missions', de Lubac rooted the universal mission of the Church in the universal vocation of Israel. Israel was called by God as the servant to the nations, to bring God's reign to all the earth. Like Israel, the Church is not Catholic because of its universal territorial extent, but because she is called to facilitate the unity of humanity: 'Her catholicity is her vocation, which is mingled with her being.'[13] Even while the Church is the 'means of salvation', the Church is also the 'end', that is, the spiritual unity that constitutes salvation. As a result, the promises of God to Israel are being fulfilled now in the Church, but in a union of humanity that will not be complete until the end. He writes, 'There is no work more necessary or greater than to work, through all the chaos and all the heartbreak of this world, to construct this City.'[14] The unity of humanity is constituted by its supernatural destiny that begins and takes place through time, beginning with God's call to the people of Israel.

The second lecture, censored and unpublished until 1946, was more provocative. In it, de Lubac interprets Nazism religiously and theologically as anti-Christian at its very root. Racism, he claims, constitutes the contemporary heresy fundamentally opposed to the common supernatural destiny of humanity. Nazi racial hierarchies in Adolf Hitler's *Mein Kampf* and the work of Alfred Rosenberg, the Nazi propagandist of race – with blacks occupying the bottom and Nordic groups at the top – constitute a fundamental opposition to the unity of humanity described in the Judeo-Christian tradition. The rise of racism concerns the worship of power and blood that is in fundamental opposition to Christian universalism: 'When we speak of "neopaganism," that is not a polemical expression. In a renewed form, it is indeed the ancient pagan ideal that is waking to reject Christ.'[15] Moreover, de Lubac diagnoses racism as the principal symptom of the rejection of the God of the Bible in modernity. The hatred towards Judaism in humanist atheism – including that of Auguste Comte, l'Action française, Louis Ménard in France, and Hegel, Schopenhauer, Wagner, and Alfred Rosenberg – is principally an attack on the idea of God: 'What it blames [Judaism] for, then, is what is most incontestable as well as most spiritual in the Bible. For its very transcendence.'[16] They object to a Judaism and Christianity that have dispelled the ancient myths and for the notion of the divine transcending the universe. For de Lubac, European anti-Semitism is fundamentally theological, for its chief

---

13. 'The Theological Foundation of the Missions', 381 in *Theology in History* (San Francisco: Ignatius Press, 1996).
14. Ibid., p. 394.
15. Ibid., p. 418.
16. 'A New Religious "Front"', p. 485. Similarly, de Lubac's article 'Spiritual Warfare' (1942) claims that contemporary atheism seeks to assault the very heart of Christianity. De Lubac, 'Spiritual Warfare', TH, pp. 488–501.

characteristic is the rejection of the God of the Jews. Racist anti-Semitism, he argues, 'is nothing less than the definitive apostasy of Europe'.[17] Thus, de Lubac characterizes racism as the principal heresy opposing the Christian message and as the principal symptom of a return to neopaganism in modern culture.

During the occupation, de Lubac's theological analysis motivated his actions aimed at emboldening the Church to resist the Vichy government. In the summer of 1941, de Lubac participated with Abbé Joseph Chaine, Louis Richard, and Joseph Bonsirven, SJ, in drafting the Chaine Declaration, a response to the anti-Semitic statutes passed by the Vichy government on June 2. The statutes banned Jews from public service and limited the number of Jews in certain professions. Moreover, it widened the biological definition of Jew so that more people were subject to the statutes on Jews. In the Chaine Declaration, the authors argued that these statutes contrasted with a French precedent of non-discrimination on the basis of religion. They voiced their objection not only on legal precedent but also on religious grounds: 'The blessing promised to [Abraham's] descendants is still upon them.'[18] Disseminated on 16 June, the Chaine Declaration influenced the French Assembly of Cardinals and Archbishops to issue their own statement on 24 July. At stake was not only the perception of the faithful but also the Vichy use of Church baptismal and marriage records in the identification of Jews.

De Lubac's writings during the occupation aimed at a spiritual interpretation of the present time for a diagnosis of the spiritual pathologies affecting Europe. In a 1941 lecture, published as 'Vocation de la France' (1942) and 'Explication chrétienne de notre temps' (1942), given at École des cadres d'Uriage, near Grenoble, de Lubac addressed the spiritual dimension of the current crisis, which he calls the 'essential factor'.[19] He explains that the social dimension of the Church, as a 'fraternal community', was gradually eroded. Fundamental Christian social ideals – 'liberty, equality, brotherhood', 'nationality', 'progress', and 'social justice' – were detached from their Christian roots and became ideologies.[20] Without an embodied faith, human beings have fallen into despair:

> Man is isolated, uprooted, 'disconcerted'. He is asphyxiated: it is as if emptiness had been formed in him by an air pump ... The consequence is not only a social imbalance. The world itself appears 'broken'. There is, at the innermost part of his consciousness, a metaphysical despair. It was of this hunger and this thirst that the prophet Amos once spoke: absolute hunger and thirst. Hunger and thirst that, in

---

17. Henri de Lubac, 'Pour le Christ et la Bible', part 1, *La Vie spirituelle* 66 (1942): p. 549.
18. CR, p. 68.
19. École des cadres d'Uriage was founded in 1940 under the Vichy government as a school for the education of an elite class for a French renewal. The original founders were loyal to the Vichy government. However, the school was only ambivalently supportive of the Vichy government. As France succumbed to collaborationist policies with the Germans, many instructors and administrators were openly critical of the government and many had ties to the French resistance movements.
20. 'Christian Explanation of Our Times', TH, p. 442.

many cases, do not even know themselves to be such but that leave on the deepest palate a taste of death.... substitute faiths... fill this tragic void... Inevitably something like a great call for air is produced in his inner void, which opens him to the invasion of new positive forces, whatever they might be.[21]

For de Lubac, just as the moral void in France led to its subsequent weakness to invading German forces, the spiritual void in human beings led to their subsequent receptivity to dangerous new faiths which fill the void. The contemporary return to neopaganism flows directly from the loss of Christianity as a social reality.

In opposition to ideologies of race, de Lubac appealed to French universalism – the French claim that their culture is not limited by the particularities of time and space – as an ideal fundamentally rooted in a Christian understanding of humanity. 'French nationalism is never turned in on itself... Through a kind of expansive generosity, it is always, by the same stroke, in some way a universalism.'[22] Thus, the French universalist spirit embodies the spirit of Catholicism itself, the *kath'oulou* (universal) spiritual unity of all human beings, a unity not primarily of geographical expansion, but of which point of origin is the transcendent. By grounding the French universalist spirit in the catholic spirit, de Lubac tried to sever French nationalism from the forms of racist nationalism of the 1940s. De Lubac neglected to consider that French universalism served as a vehicle of reproducing racial otherness in France. Just as universal French identity contrasted with a particular Jewish identity in the 1940s, an abstract model of French identity was employed to justify French colonial occupation in Africa, the Middle East, and Southeast Asia.[23]

De Lubac's wartime writing also contributed to diagnosing the spiritual undercurrents of modern atheism. *The Drama of Atheist Humanism* appeared in 1944 and examined Auguste Comte, Ludwig Feuerbach, and Friedrich Nietzsche. In concert with his previous writings, *The Drama of Atheist Humanism* explored atheism as not only a negation of the divine but also as a 'mystical immanentism' joined to a philosophy of history.[24] Modern atheism, he says, is part of the story of a new 'awakening' to the human being as a locus of agency and dignity that triggered modern aspirations for arbitrating one's destiny and for creating one's social and economic world. This new perception of the human, de Lubac argued, also gave way to the desire to liberate humanity from the forces of nature and from God. Modern atheism seeks to liberate humanity from an oppressive supernatural and by freeing the human from the laws of providence. But for de Lubac, the annihilation of the transcendent results in the 'annihilation of

---

21. Ibid., p. 443.
22. Ibid., p. 449.
23. For an account of difference as an obstacle to French identity, see Joan Wallach Scott, *Parité!: Sexual Equality and the Crisis of French Universalism*, Chicago Studies in Practices of Meaning (Chicago: University of Chicago Press, 2005).
24. DAH, p. 11.

the human person'.[25] For de Lubac, atheist humanism was founded on a tragic misunderstanding, namely that the preservation of human dignity, agency, and social unity demands a form of historical immanentism and requires the loss of the supernatural.

Following the war, de Lubac remained concerned to preserve the tension between the social form of Christianity and the transcendence of grace. This tension is found especially in de Lubac's evaluations of communism after the war, a period during which French society was undergoing significant transition. There had been a tactical alliance between communists and Catholics during the German occupation. In the post-war period, the question of whether there could be a strategic alliance, albeit partial, was widely debated. In Paris in 1947, at the *Semaine Sociale*, an annual conference of lay people devoted to understanding and applying Catholic social thought, Jean Lacroix called for collaboration between Christians and communists. Appearing at the same event, de Lubac was more cautious. His lecture, entitled 'The Search for a New Man', contains his reflections on the value of the temporal as well as its fundamental incompleteness:

> Such confrontations [relating doctrine to life] are legitimate, they are even often necessary, if it is true that the great problems of our temporal life can be resolved only in the light of our total destiny and that Christianity, on the other hand, is really lived only on condition of being, as they say today, fully incarnated. It is nonetheless true that these confrontations are always in danger (as we have had occasion to imply above) of misleading and blurring somewhat in minds the distinction between the plane of nature and that of the supernatural.... On the one side, the temptation of a new naturalism, which Christian hope, diverted from its goal, still feeds with its ardor; on the other, it is a forgetfulness of our true condition, a failure to recognize the earthly tasks through which the salvation of creation is to be worked out.[26]

For de Lubac, authentic Christianity is a living, historical reality *incarnated* in social life, taking a visible form. Yet, to speak of the visible *incarnation* of Christianity risks confusing limited human efforts, political programs, and social structures with the supernatural. The Christian, says de Lubac, must work to better the world, yet recognize that the supernatural transfiguration of this world cannot occur in full within the bounds of time.

Although de Lubac affirmed the authenticity of the desire for a better world in Marxism, he warned of Marxism's lack of transcendence. Concerning communism, de Lubac and his good friend Gaston Fessard disagreed. Frédéric Louzeau explains that Fessard and de Lubac held different interpretations of 'the historical present' (*l'actualité historique*) because they engaged different

---

25. Ibid., p. 12.
26. Ibid., pp. 464–65.

"'instruments" to observe and decrypt it'.[27] Fessard maintained the strict parallel between the two forms of totalitarianism and spoke of the danger of Christians collaborating with communism. Fessard recognized in both communism and Nazism elements of a Hegelian dialectic in which Christian religion is surpassed and overcome. De Lubac responded that the situation with regard to Nazism and communism was entirely different since France was not under an occupying force. Moreover, he states, communism contains 'a number of elements on which religion has nothing to say, or which it can and must approve'.[28] Although de Lubac did not deny the danger of Marx's worldview and its secularism, he believed that the social aspiration of communists was something affirmed in Christianity.

Henri de Lubac's writing during and shortly after the Second World War is both illustrative of his theological approach and the seedbed for political themes in his work. De Lubac's overarching theo-political concern was to discern the vocation of the Church in present history in light of the ultimate calling of humanity. De Lubac's linking of Judaism and Christianity was clearly a rhetorical polemic to convince Christians of their duty to resist. Yet it was also a spiritual interpretation of historical events, events that formed part of the confrontation between God and the forces of evil. De Lubac recognized the spiritual root of anti-Semitism as a return to idolatry. The God of Israel was the obstacle to the emergence of the gods of nation and blood. Although his post-war intervention in the debate concerning communism did not contain the same urgent apocalypticism as his wartime writings on Nazism, he recognized that both ideologies contained the same suffocating *terrestréité*.

De Lubac's early work and resistance writings place in tension his quest to articulate a temporal form of Christian life as a lived, incarnate reality, while at the same time maintaining the absolute alterity of grace. His subsequent writings on the supernatural and ecclesiology would explore and deepen this tension without ever entirely resolving it.

The Politics of the Supernatural

Henri de Lubac's book *Surnaturel: Études historiques* (1946) appeared soon after *Le Drame de l'humanisme athée* (1944). The concerns in both books were similar, namely the rise of a historical immanentism that turns into an exclusive humanism. *Surnaturel* consists of a series of studies on the nature-supernatural dichotomy in the Middle Ages and its transmission to modern theology. While de Lubac's focus in *Surnaturel* was historical, his thesis was explosive. Rejecting a theory of pure nature that arose in the late Middle Ages, de Lubac defended an

---

27. Frédéric Louzeau, 'Gaston Fessard et Henri de Lubac: leur différend sur la question du communisme et du progressisme chrétien (1945–1950)', *Revue des sciences religieuses* 84:4 (2010): p. 537.
28. 'Letter to Gaston Fessard (12 August 1945)', in ibid., p. 521.

Augustinian account of the natural desire for God. He argued that the concept of nature transmitted by modern neo-scholastics – that is, nature as a discrete locus of properties and powers strictly delimited to an immanent teleology – did not correspond to that concept of nature in Thomas Aquinas. According to de Lubac, Thomas Aquinas incorporated Aristotle's concept of nature into a Christian anthropology inspired by scripture and Augustine, yet did not endanger the supernatural finality of the human being. However, de Lubac accused Thomas' neo-scholastic followers of expunging the core of Thomas' anthropology in which the 'natural desire for the supernatural' is prominent. De Lubac claims that the innate desire for God, implicit in all human activity, constitutes what it means for the human being to be created in God's image. De Lubac's theology of the supernatural has been appealed to as presenting a uniquely Christian ontology and anthropology and, as a consequence, as a formulation of a distinctly Christian political and social practice.[29]

De Lubac rejected the system of *pure nature*, a theological construct designed to preserve the gratuity of grace, as it developed in the neo-scholastic commentary tradition from Thomas Cajetan, Domingo Báñez, and Francisco Suárez. *Pure nature* was the concept of a human nature that could attain its end by its own powers, within its own order, apart from grace. Pure nature preserved an Aristotelian account of nature in which the finality of a being is proportionate to its powers. Thus, human beings have an entirely natural end proportionate to their constitution and a supernatural end elicited by God's grace. De Lubac admitted that the concept of pure nature was useful for safeguarding God's freedom in a philosophical milieu in which the ontological difference between God's being and the being of creation was already compromised.[30] However, pure nature became an entire system of thinking about the order of creation as something independent of a supernatural end, not dissimilar to an Enlightenment account of the natural order as a self-enclosed system. De Lubac argued that the idea of the system of nature transmitted in modern Catholic theology contributed to the construction of a world picture in which the supernatural is superfluous to human fulfilment. Essentially, he suggests that modern scholasticism was in part responsible for contributing to the secularism that it had been organized to combat.

In his theology of the supernatural, de Lubac presents the human being as a creature paradoxically destined to a goal that transcends it. De Lubac argued that the Judeo-Christian notion of God as creator and human beings as the image of God significantly changed a Hellenistic view of nature and the human. Humanity can find fulfilment, not itself and through its own power, but only

---

29. See Bryan C. Hollon, *Everything Is Sacred: Spiritual Exegesis in the Political Theology of Henri de Lubac* (Eugene, OR: Cascade Books, 2009); John Milbank, *The Suspended Middle: Henri de Lubac and the Debate Concerning the Supernatural* (Grand Rapids, MI: William B. Eerdmans, 2005); David L. Schindler, *Heart of the World, Center of the Church: Communio Ecclesiology, Liberalism, and Liberation* (Grand Rapids, MI: William B. Eerdmans, 1996).

30. AMT, p. 275.

through the elevation to a supernatural reality categorically different. Human beings have a single, supernatural finality, that is, nothing short of the vision of God can suffice for their fulfilment, possessing a concomitant 'natural desire for the supernatural'. Consequently, the human being is a paradox: God calls humanity to a supernatural end, yet humanity lacks the equipment to attain that end under its own agency. He writes, 'The supernatural end of man, his only end, is "eternal life" (Jn 6:27; Rom 5:21, etc.), which is poured out by the Holy Spirit into the depths of the human heart but cannot flower fully save in circumstances wholly other than those of space and time.'[31] De Lubac's anthropology is intensely eschatological insofar as human nature seeks a reality that cannot be had within the bounds of history and that the significance of human life in all of its aspects can be understood only in light of this eschatological goal.

The earliest assessments of de Lubac's *Surnaturel* accused him of possessing an inadequate account of the relative autonomy of the natural order. In a critical review of de Lubac's *Surnaturel*, Phillip Donnelly, SJ, explains, 'the importance of Aristotle consists in having aided his disciple of the middle ages to take carefully in account the entire natural order – human, moral, and cosmic – and, thereby, to disencumber himself in a great part from the exaggerated Platonic tendencies of Augustinianism'.[32] Donnelly criticizes de Lubac for a thin account of nature in which nature is 'not a center of properties and a source of activity strictly limited and enclosed in its own order'. It is 'un néant dont le Créateur peut tout tirer à son gré' ('a nothingness that the Creator could draw at will').[33] A recent commentator, Reinhard Hütter, writes, 'the relative integrity of the principle (or the order) of nature is the necessary condition for the possibility of differentiating properly between the realities of creation, creation *sub conditione peccati*, and redemption'.[34] This integrity of nature is required for establishing the goodness of creation even in its fallen state in contrast to Calvinistic accounts of human nature and also to establish the inherent limitations of human nature in contrast to Pelagian tendencies of post-Enlightenment thought. At stake is whether de Lubac's theology of the supernatural can support ethics based on natural law or a natural cognizance of political goods. The classic Thomist charge against

---

31. BC, p. 100.
32. Phillip Donnelly, 'Discussions on the Supernatural Order', *Theological Studies*, 9:2 (1948): p. 226.
33. Ibid., p. 238. Quotation from Henri de Lubac, *Surnaturel*, Theologie 8 (Paris: Aubier-Montaigne, 1946), p. 435. Donnelly, following Boyer, quotes de Lubac out of context. De Lubac is not proposing 'a nothingness that the creator could draw at will' as an adequate description of human nature. He is instead contrasting this 'nothingness' that he attributes to the patristic concept of *image of God* with the Aristotelian concept of *nature*. Thomas Aquinas, he states, blends these two concepts, though not without ambiguity.
34. Reinhard Hütter, 'Desiderium Naturale Visionis Dei – Est Autem Duplex Hominis Beatitudo Sive Felicitas: Some Observations about Lawrence Feingold's and John Milbank's Recent Interventions in the Debate over the Natural Desire to See God', *Nova et Vetera*, English Edition 5:1 (2007): p. 102.

Augustinianism is that it similarly fails to recognize natural human and political goods.

De Lubac was aware that his conception of the single supernatural end and the innate human desire for the supernatural had political implications. Augustine had been accused of depreciating the relative integrity of the natural order and, as a consequence, depreciating the autonomy of human government in the natural order. De Lubac addressed the thesis of Msgr. Arquillière that 'St. Augustine's tendency to "absorb the natural order into the supernatural one" was bound to lead him to "absorb the natural law of the State into supernatural justice and ecclesial law."'[35] According to this position, Augustine's *City of God* harshly critiques the pagan political structure and corruption of the Roman Empire. Failing to conceive of justice in the Earthly City, Augustine presents justice as the exclusive domain of the City of God, thereby contributing the theoretical foundation for theocracy. *Political Augustinianism* refers to a theocratic strain of theology ascribed to the followers of Augustine. In contrast, the medieval appropriation of Aristotle enabled a more coherent establishment of two distinct orders – the natural and the supernatural – and their corresponding 'spheres of action'. De Lubac recognized that the critique of Augustine is also a critique of his own theology. The systematic question is whether an Augustinian anthropology like de Lubac's can sufficiently support a distinction between the natural and the supernatural orders, thus supporting the relative autonomy of the temporal. (And this in turn impacts whether you can be both Catholic and a republican.)

De Lubac's response to the charge against Augustine is twofold. First, he argued, the theory of political power referred to as political Augustinianism is not authentically Augustinian.[36] Political Augustinianism reaches an apex in Giles of Rome's *De Ecclesiastica potestate*, which claims the *plenitudo potestatis* (the fullness of [temporal] power) for the Pope. The followers of Giles united a theory of matter and form from an Averroistic interpretation of Aristotle and a Dionysian hierarchical vision of the relationship between the lower bodies and higher bodies: 'They provided theocracy, which had just attained its summit with Innocent IV, with entirely new principles: those of Averroistic Aristotelianism, which the Latin West had just discovered, and that a not negligible part of its elite had already adopted.'[37] Their political theology owed almost nothing to Augustine.

---

35. Henri de Lubac, '"Political Augustinism"?', TF, p. 256. Quoting Arquillière, *Réflexions sur l'essence de l'Augustinism politique* (Paris: Études Augustiniennes, 1954), vol. 2, pp. 991–1001.

36. de Lubac, '"Political Augustinism"?', p. 237. De Lubac notes that this essay was written in the 1930s, revised and presented in the 1954, and revised subsequently.

37. Ibid., p. 281. Moreover, the anti-theocratic theories of political power that emerged in the late medieval period in Jean of Jandun and Marsilius of Padua were indebted to the theoretical foundations laid by Giles. The fourteenth century marks the contestation over two theories of political power – one that hands the totality of power to the prince, and another that hands it Pope. Both depend upon a cosmology filtered through Averroistic interpretation of Aristotle.

In contrast with the tradition of political Augustinianism, Augustine's dualism of the two cities is biblical: it is based on the Johannine dualism of darkness and light, the Pauline flesh and the spirit, the old Adam and the new Adam. It goes back to Jesus's call to 'Render unto Caesar the things that are Caesar's and to God the things that are God's.' This dualism does not, however, function for Augustine as a political category or as a theory of governance. It is primarily a theology of history. De Lubac argues, the 'authentic culmination of the thought (or at least the "tendency") found in the *City of God* ... [is] the *Spiritual Exercises* of St. Ignatius of Loyola'.[38] In sum, the tradition of political Augustinianism is not really Augustinian.

Second, de Lubac attacks the implication that the incorporation of an Aristotelian philosophy of nature established the relative autonomy of nature and a differentiated harmony between Church and state. Instead, he claims, the incorporation of Aristotle's vision of human nature was a problematic turning point in the Christian theo-political tradition, one that encouraged theologians to place nature and the supernatural in the same system, and eventually into the same genre. Aristotle inspired a new account of nature as a self-enclosed centre of properties and powers, an account that generated a radically new anthropology. Scholastic theologians proposed theories of double finality in which there exists a natural end proportionate to human nature and a supernatural end superadded by the reception of grace. Modern theology, de Lubac says, separated and juxtaposed the two: 'It sees nature and supernature as in some sense juxtaposed, and in spite of every intention to the contrary, as contained in the same genus, of which they form as it were two species. The two were like two complete organisms; too perfectly separated to be really differentiated, they have unfolded parallel to each other, fatally similar in kind.'[39] In de Lubac's assessment, the integration of an Aristotelian account of nature into Christian theology eroded, rather than established, the ontological difference between nature and the supernatural. This ontological homogeneity between the natural and supernatural present in Catholic theology in modernity supported viewing the transcendent as superfluous to human fulfilment.

Although de Lubac's *Surnaturel* was a historical study of theological anthropology, its broader purpose was to trace the emergence of secularism in Western culture, specifically an intellectual genealogy of the emergence of a world in which the supernatural was no longer necessary. His theology of the supernatural filled in the gaps by explaining the emergence of atheist humanism, in which the transcendent God in Christianity and Judaism is seen as the obstacle to human agency and dignity. It is in this light that de Lubac read political ideologies of historical immanence in Marxism and the return of paganism in Nazi Germany and Vichy France. For de Lubac, recovering a conception of the supernatural – not only as transcendent other but also as the essential goal of human life – is essential to ordering ourselves and our lives in the world.

38. Ibid., p. 266.
39. MS, p. 37.

Lubacian Theo-Political Trajectories

Given the Augustinian features of de Lubac's theology of the supernatural, his theology of the supernatural is resonant with the notion that the Church constitutes a participation in the City of God in opposition to the Earthly City, a political 'counter-society'.[40] Today, theologians appeal to de Lubac's theology of the supernatural as the basis for a political theology, or at least, as the theological justification for a distinctly ecclesial social and political practice. David L. Schindler, John Milbank, and Byran C. Hollon differ in their interpretation of his theology of the supernatural yet agree remarkably in their assessment of its political significance for a distinctly ecclesial practice.

David L. Schindler applies de Lubac's thinking to the constellation of anthropology, economics, and politics in post-Vatican II Catholic social thought. Schindler's *Heart of the World, Center of the Church* (1996) argued against the compatibility of political liberalism and Christian anthropology, appealing to the Vatican II document *Gaudiam et spes*, the constitution on the Church and the modern world.[41] At stake for Schindler is whether *Gaudiam et spes* and, more broadly, the Second Vatican Council and papal teaching following the council embrace the political liberalism of the United States and Europe. He says, inherent in the principles of America's founding is the rejection of a Christian vision of liberty and the prioritization of an enlightenment account of human freedom.[42] For Schindler, de Lubac offers an account of the relationship between nature and grace, and Church and world, which preserves a tradition of Catholic social thought on the nature of political liberty.

Schindler's critique revolves around a paradox of political liberalism. On the one hand, liberal political theorists claim neutrality with regard to any account

---

40. Bernd Wannenwetsch, 'Liturgy', in Peter Scott and William T. Cavanaugh, eds, *The Blackwell Companion to Political Theology* (Malden, MA: Blackwell, 2007), pp. 86–87.

41. Schindler, *Heart of the World, Center of the Church*. See also Nicholas J. Healy, 'Henri de Lubac on Nature and Grace: A Note on Some Recent Contributions to the Debate', *Communio* 35:4 (2008): pp. 535–64; Robert Franklin Gotcher, 'Henri de Lubac and Communio: The Significance of His Theology of the Supernatural for an Interpretation of Gaudium et Spes' (PhD diss., Marquette University, 2002).

42. Schindler challenges the belief on the part of Catholic neo-Conservatives like Robert Novak and George Weigel that there exists an essential harmony between the principles of the American founding and Catholicism. See Michael Novak, *The Catholic Ethic and the Spirit of Capitalism* (New York: Free Press, 1993). Schindler develops his position in response to John Courtney Murray, SJ (1904–1967), the apologist for the compatibility of the American liberal tradition and Catholicism. Murray claimed that, unlike continental liberalism that characterized human freedom as excluding transcendent ends, American liberalism embodied an openness to transcendent ends. The religion clauses of the First Amendment were 'articles of peace' and the religious freedom provided therein is best understood for purposes of political order as immunity from coercion. It does not imply an anterior rejection of transcendent ends for the human being. Therefore, Murray argued, the American emphasis on individual freedom to choose one's religion is not inherently in conflict with a Catholic account of the human good.

of the ultimate good. Liberal societies are only committed to formal-juridical procedures that provide freedom for each individual to decide for their ultimate ends. In this sense, liberalism claims to be compatible with any account of truth. However, Schindler states, those formal-juridical procedures already saturate the terms of the dialogue, covertly constituting an account of human freedom that prioritizes the individual's power to choose as the ultimate political good. Freedom becomes an absolute value prior to any direction for that freedom. Liberalism draws us into a deception as to the status of metaphysics. Although it endorses only a formal-juridical structure, it carries with it the implication that individual liberty is absolute. Implicit in its anthropology – liberty is prior to truth – is a rejection of a Christian world view in which liberty has a finality for transcendent truth. Liberalism, Schindler claims, works only on the assumption of the complete autonomy of human nature and the state (and formal-juridical procedures) from ultimate human ends. Human nature, and therefore the state, possesses its own ends independent from God's grace. As an implication, the supernatural end is distinct and fundamentally inconsequential to the natural ends. This is why, according to Schindler, the American notion of freedom underwrites anti-Christian ideology that prioritizes individual liberty in spheres of economics and family life, thus requiring consumerism and abortion as its products.

Schindler contrasts the metaphysics implicit in European and American liberalism with the metaphysics implicit in *Gaudium et spes* and explicit in the work of de Lubac. He explains, for de Lubac, the temporal end is always already *within* the supernatural. He explains:

> To be sure, there is a distinction between the orders of creation and redemption: no responsible Catholic would deny this. But the issue raised by de Lubac and others is precisely that of the relation between these order, and thus the issue of whether man is created with a single – supernatural – end... De Lubac saw nature, and all of its penultimate ends, as ordered internally and from its creation toward the God revealed in Jesus Christ. De Lubac did not thereby deny the distinctness of nature; on the contrary, he simply placed that distinctness from the beginning within a prior unity (of natural and supernatural orders).[43]

The key for Schindler is whether the natural and supernatural orders are conceived as 'first within or first outside or juxtaposed to each other; whether any resulting unity between them therefore comes about by way of "integration" or, contrarily, by way of addition.'[44] Schindler argues that de Lubac's anthropology, in which human nature is ordained to a single supernatural end, implies an account of human freedom, political institutions, and law intrinsically ordered to the transcendent. The world – including its human society and political structures –

---

43. Schindler, *Heart of the World, Center of the Church*, pp. 77–78.
44. Ibid., pp. 79–80.

has a finality for the supernatural. At the same time, the political world and the Church remain distinct.

According to Schindler, de Lubac's theology of the supernatural provides the basis for a political theology that can avoid the perils of secularism, which detaches the ultimate end from the temporal ends, and integralism, which fails to distinguish between the state and the ecclesial communion. For Schindler, de Lubac's anthropology supports an alternative to that of Western liberalism, offering a way of seeing political, economic, and social reality as essentially theological because they are comprehended by God's intention for humanity. Schindler maintains the formal distinction between nature and the supernatural, though one must view political realities as essentially theological because of our supernatural finality. There is no political sphere insulated from the theological.

John Milbank and the Radical Orthodoxy movement have contributed to another influential interpretation of de Lubac, one which significantly contrasts with Schindler's.[45] According to Milbank, de Lubac's theology of the supernatural founds a distinctly Christian politics by dismantling the formal distinction between nature and grace and, as a consequence, by dismantling the notion of a secular realm autonomous from divine ends. De Lubac's theology of the supernatural contributes to what Milbank calls the 'integralist revolution', that is, 'the view that in concrete, historical humanity there is no such thing as a state of "pure nature": rather, every person has always already been worked upon by divine grace, with the consequence that one cannot analytically separate "natural" and "supernatural" contributions to this integral unity'.[46]

Milbank identifies two Roman Catholic streams of integralism: a French version that stems from Maurice Blondel and Henri de Lubac, and a German version indebted to Karl Rahner and influential in Latin American liberation theologies. The latter, he claims, reworks the nature-supernatural dichotomy in neo-scholasticism to preserve the gratuity of the supernatural. His accusation is

---

45. Radical Orthodoxy is certainly not a homogeneous group. For the purposes of this chapter, I will limit myself to commenting on Milbank. For the main sources in Milbank's interpretation of de Lubac, see John Milbank, *Theology and Social Theory: Beyond Secular Reason*, 2nd ed. (Malden, MA: Blackwell Publishing, 2006); John Milbank, 'Henri de Lubac', in David F. Ford, ed., *The Modern Theologians: An Introduction to Modern Theology since 1918* (Malden, MA: Blackwell, 2005); Milbank, *The Suspended Middle*. Others have developed these themes in response and opposition to Milbank. See Sean Larsen, 'The Politics of Desire: Two Readings of Henri de Lubac on Nature and Grace', *Modern Theology* 29:3 (2013): pp. 279–310; Hollon, *Everything Is Sacred: Spiritual Exegesis in the Political Theology of Henri de Lubac*; Hütter, 'Desiderium Naturale Visionis Dei'.

46. Milbank, *Theology and Social Theory*, p. 206. Milbank clarifies that *integralism* is not *integrism* (*intégrisme*), referring to Catholic anti-modernists in France who sought to subordinate the state to the Catholic Church and to return to an integral unity of faith and society. This could be a point of confusion since most scholars use the term *integralism* to refer to forms of Catholic nationalism.

that, for Rahner, the historical events that constitute Christian revelation only make supernatural grace explicit. In this version of integralism, the supernatural is already universally available; historical events become merely signs of grace.[47] Milbank fears that, by implication, historical-ecclesial praxis becomes merely an accessory to the individual's self-transcendence. Only the former, the French stream of integralism, can ground an authentic political theology: 'Only the French version truly abandons hierarchies and geographies in theological anthropology, because it refuses even to "formally distinguish" a realm of pure nature in concrete humanity.'[48] The natural is not segregated to an ontologically delimited realm. The supernatural is not delimited to a 'permanent "area" of human life'.[49] Therefore, the political and social practice of the Church is open to becoming the locus of transcendence.

Although, for Milbank, de Lubac does not develop a social or political theology, he does provide the theological rationale for one. De Lubac conceives of salvation as essentially social, as the incorporation into the body of Christ beginning in time. Milbank claims de Lubac 'is open to recognizing structural elements of emplotment', that is, he recognizes that salvation takes place concretely and through one's participation in the action of the Church.[50] This implies that the concrete community of salvation is a visible and historical reality. However, Milbank claims, de Lubac does not follow through with his insight because he carefully insulates the Church from secular concerns and political action. Despite this limitation, de Lubac's integralism provides the basis for differentiating between ecclesial practice and secular practice, that is the 'difference of supernatural charity as the historical, though incomplete insertion of a different community, and a different ethical practice'.[51] In de Lubac's formulation of the supernatural, the Church and, by extension, ecclesial practices (political, social, economic) constitute the sites of grace. Milbank does not deny the neo-scholastic accusation that de Lubac fails to ground a theory of natural law, ethics, or politics. Instead, Milbank claims, this failure is de Lubac's strength.

---

47. Milbank's reading is unsympathetic and unfair to Rahner, whose theology is presented in terms of that of Paul Tillich. However, Milbank has a legitimate concern, namely that the Church could become secondary to an individualistic spirituality.

48. Milbank, *Theology and Social Theory*, pp. 208–9. Milbank repeatedly asserts that de Lubac 'supernaturalizes the natural', a phrase that he admits could be misleading. Ibid., p. 207. Milbank eliminates any formal distinction between the natural and supernatural in de Lubac's theology of the supernatural. As a result, he overlooks the tension that drives de Lubac's theology as a whole, namely the tension between God's complete revelation in history (and the Christian's lived corporate embrace of the supernatural life) and the fundamental incompleteness of human history (and society, and institutions). Despite this deficiency, Milbank grasps the possibilities in de Lubac's theology for presenting salvation as a living reality with temporal visibility and extension.

49. Ibid., p. 209.
50. Ibid., p. 228.
51. Ibid., p. 235.

By dismantling the partition between nature and grace, de Lubac dismantles the partition between ecclesial action and transcendence, allowing for us to imagine a different community shaped by charity.

Like Milbank, Bryan C. Hollon discovers in de Lubac the basis for a distinctly Christian political practice. In contrast with Milbank, Hollon recognizes that the generative force for this distinctive politics is grounded in the practice of reading scripture.[52] De Lubac's retrieval of pre-modern biblical interpretation, he argues, escapes the pitfalls of postliberal theology and Radical Orthodoxy. He argues that while postliberal theologians emphasize the literal biblical narrative as the basis for Christian identity, they do not adequately account for how the Bible 'absorbs the world', that is, how the story engenders 'a new "mode of being"'.[53] He also criticizes Radical Orthodoxy for failing to show how Christians can derive their social identities and practices from the scriptures: 'Radical Orthodoxy deconstructs secular social theory but makes no concrete suggestions as to how Christians are to inhabit the space created by deconstruction.'[54] De Lubac, Hollon claims, provides a framework for uniting the biblical narrative with concrete ecclesial social practice.

De Lubac's *Exégèse médiévale* (1959–1964) recovered not only a pre-modern interpretation of the scriptures, but also the means for imagining the Christian social life *inside* the scriptures. *Exégèse médiévale* elaborated the fourfold sense of scripture – the literal, allegorical, tropological, and anagogical – employed in the Patristic and medieval periods. The literal sense constitutes the historical meaning described in the Bible. The allegorical, tropological, and anagogical are the *spiritual senses*, the depth dimension of the letter. The spiritual senses are not, however, esoteric meanings. They describe the unfolding of the mystery of God in the economy of salvation. Allegory is the Christological meaning: since all things in the economy have their fulfilment in Christ, he is the referent of the events of salvation. Tropology constitutes the mystical and ecclesial interiorization of the events recorded in scripture. Thus, the Church and its practices discover their identity only within the biblical narrative. Anagogy points to the continual ascent of the Church to its eschatological goal. For Hollon, de Lubac's recovery of spiritual interpretation forms the basis for Christological mysticism, that is, the historical participation of the Church in the salvific actions of Christ.

In Hollon's interpretation, de Lubac's recovery of the fourfold sense bridges ecclesiology and soteriology, intimately relating human action and divine action. The fourfold sense relates God's actions narrated in the Bible and our present historical experience as part of the same history of salvation. As a result, we can locate the Church's political and social practice *within* the salvific actions of

---

52. Hollon, *Everything Is Sacred: Spiritual Exegesis in the Political Theology of Henri de Lubac*.
53. Ibid., p. 131.
54. Ibid., p. 141.

Christ. In this way, Hollon claims, de Lubac's theology suggests that the reading of scripture can mediate a distinctive ecclesial politics and social practice.

Although these interpretations differ in their construal of the relationship between sociopolitical practice and supernatural grace, each draws from de Lubac's theology of the supernatural an account of Christian life as a social reality that embodies a distinct practice. Hollon helps to break down the wall between soteriology and ecclesiology, a wall especially prominent in Reformed traditions, by showing how reading scripture suggests an ecclesial participation in the actions of Christ. Building from Hollon, it is of critical importance to recognize that the Church is still sinful in its historical state and action, and to reject forms of political triumphalism or Constantinianism. For Milbank, the lack of formal distinction between nature and the supernatural grounds an essentially theological politics, a social practice that embodies the supernatural. His interpretation of de Lubac is difficult to support exegetically, given the nearly ubiquitous affirmation in de Lubac's work of the absolute difference between nature and the supernatural. However, Milbank grasps the political consequences of de Lubac's theology, that is, the Church's visible, social life as the site of salvation. Schindler's interpretation of de Lubac's theology of the supernatural is accurate, though it is ambiguous on the question of how the Church itself possesses political dimensions.

The Body of Christ and the Form of the Social

For de Lubac, the Church itself constitutes, in the phrase of Susan K. Wood, the 'social embodiment of grace'.[55] The Church is the social embodiment of grace primarily insofar as sacramental practice mediates the visible, historical Church's participation in its invisible, eschatological fulfilment.[56] The ecclesial communion becomes the visible site of God's ongoing activity. But to what extent can we speak of structures of social existence and political actions of the Church as social embodiments of grace? In other words, what visible form does the embodiment of grace take? De Lubac's answer to this question is not easily resolved. On the one hand, de Lubac affirmed the eternal's presence in the historical order and the visibility of the Church as the social site of the embodiment of grace. On the other hand, he was reticent to identify any particular temporal or political development, order, or practice as definitively embodying the supernatural.

The idea that God's grace is embodied socially and historically constitutes one of the major themes of de Lubac's writings. In *Catholicism*, de Lubac wrote, 'It is the Eternal found at the heart of all temporal development which gives it life and

---

55. Susan K. Wood, 'The Church as the Social Embodiment of Grace in the Ecclesiology of Henri de Lubac' (Ph.D. diss., Marquette University, 1986).

56. Susan K. Wood, *Spiritual Exegesis and the Church in the Theology of Henri de Lubac* (Grand Rapids, MI: William B. Eerdmans, 1998).

direction.'⁵⁷ In a broader sense, de Lubac envisioned all of history as an anticipation of its eternal goal. More precisely, de Lubac located the eternal ecclesially. The Church is a living, organic body, with features that are both 'institutional and mystical, hierarchical and communal'.⁵⁸ It is precisely the visible, institutional, and hierarchical elements of the Church that constitute the sacramental means to the invisible, the mystical, and the communal: 'Communion is the objective – an objective which, from the first instant, does not cease to be realized in the invisible; the institution is the means for it – a means which even now does not cease to ensure a visible communion.'⁵⁹ The ecclesial communion is constituted horizontally and vertically, so to speak, by the social constitution of the Church and by the invisible union with God in the body of Christ. Apart from the essential hierarchical structure of the Church, de Lubac says, discernment is required to recognize which communities and structures are elements of the 'real "communion" toward which the force of the Spirit of God tends to direct us within the great Church'.⁶⁰ The lines are fuzzy between those communions and communities that make visible the Spirit and those that do not.

De Lubac more clearly identifies the visible characteristics of the absence of communion than the visible characteristics of its presence. In *The Motherhood of the Church* (1971), de Lubac described the impersonal society emerging in the post-war world as spiritually similar to the totalitarianisms of the twentieth century. Combining a preoccupation with efficiency, bureaucratic capitalism, social planning, and rationalism, this new world delivers people into 'anonymity' and 'solitude'.⁶¹ Modern technology and industry, he claimed, brought about a society 'being constructed on the model of the machine and the number, extending its anonymous tyranny over all citizens'.⁶² De Lubac's critique becomes concrete when he speaks of urban housing development contributing to a process whereby communities become '"fragmented and agglomerated" at one and the same time'.⁶³ Thus, the spatial and economic dimensions of human life contain and signify spiritual features. These are the features, he believed, of a world closed to the divine initiative. This post-Vatican II diagnosis is similar to that of his *The Drama of Atheist Humanism*: a world whose horizon is only terrestrial becomes a dehumanizing world.

Despite his emphasis on social and historical embodiment, de Lubac did not positively identify the structural and political features of ecclesial communion because he sought to avoid reducing the supernatural to any particular elements of the world. He did not speak of the Church as a counter-society comparable

57. C, p. 362.
58. MC, p. 34.
59. Ibid., p. 35.
60. Ibid., p. 163.
61. Ibid., p. 148.
62. Ibid., pp. 144–45. Quoting Carl Jung, *Présent et avenir* (Paris: Buchet/Chastel, 1962), 178, Bertrand Russell, *Ma Conception du Monde*, Collection Idées 17 (Paris: Gallimard, 1962), 172.
63. MC, p. 146.

to civil society, and he expressly denied that the Church should possess power in the temporal order. Moreover, he denied that progress in the temporal order constitutes a means to the coming kingdom. These negations, however, are situated in a broader affirmation of the Church's embrace of all of human life, including the political.

The Power of the Church in the Temporal Order

De Lubac did not identify the Church as a counter-society or counter-politics in a sense that the Church possesses jurisdiction, power, or coercive force analogous to the state. In an essay entitled 'The Authority of the Church in Temporal Matters', de Lubac denied that the Church normatively possessed coercive power. The Catholic Church had a longstanding jurisdictional claim expressed forcefully in Pope Boniface XIII's papal bull *Unam sanctam* (1302), which declared papal supremacy over the Church and the hierarchical supremacy of the spiritual over the temporal order. Giles of Rome's *De Ecclesiastica potestate* (1302) interpreted this position as *direct power over the temporal*. Robert Bellarmine's *On the Temporal Power of the Pope* (1610) presented a more moderate theory of *indirect temporal power*. De Lubac was not convinced of the difference between the two, arguing that both claim jurisdiction and thereby diminish the difference between spiritual and temporal power: 'Believing that they are justified in spreading her empire, they are ready to expose her (if that were possible) to the loss of sacred authority – to the rank of the powers of the world.'[64] In these theories, the authority claimed by the Church is homologous to that of the state.

De Lubac's opposition to theories of direct and indirect temporal power is based not only on his opposition to associating the Church with coercive force, but more fundamentally on the lack of differentiation between the temporal and spiritual. The claim of ecclesial jurisdiction over civil authority is based on confusion over the natural and the supernatural. Instead, the distinction between nature and grace affirms the role of the Church as a leaven for the world. He explains,

> Grace seizes nature from the inside and, far from lowering it, lifts it up to have it serve its ends. It is from the interior that faith transforms reason, that the Church influences the State. The Church is a messenger of Christ, not the guardian of the State. The Church ennobles the State, inspiring it to be a Christian State (one sees in what sense) and, thus, a more human one.[65]

The categorical difference between nature and grace requires the differentiation between state and Church.

---

64. Henri de Lubac, 'The Authority of the Church in Temporal Matters', TF, p. 210.
65. Ibid., p. 212.

De Lubac weaved a pathway between the claims of temporal authority of the Church (by lay and clerical French Catholics who opposed laicization) and the French laicization that would offer the Church only the ability to give counsel to its members.[66] The authority of the Church, he says, 'is entirely spiritual... limited to the individual conscience'.[67] Yet this is not a limitation of domain. He explains that the power of the Church is not 'power over the temporal' but rather 'power in *temporal matters*'. *Temporal matters* constitute an expansive category encompassing 'all domains of activity that are specifically human or natural, either theoretical or practical: philosophy, the arts, even the sciences, as well as politics, the economy, and diverse forms of social organization'.[68] The domain of the Church is virtually limitless since it concerns the entirety of human life and existence.

> Christianity is universal not only in the sense that all men have their Savior in Jesus Christ but also in the sense that all of man has salvation in Jesus Christ. Since the destinies of Christianity were placed in the hands of the Church, the Church is catholic – that is, universal – in that nothing human can remain alien to her. And it is hard to see why 'politics' should be an exception to this principle.[69]

Christianity concerns humanity in its entirety and its destiny. The authority of the Church is not limited to a spatial domain precisely because of its universality. In this sense, by refusing to grant the Church jurisdiction, he grants it an unlimited sphere of action. De Lubac's de-spatialization of ecclesial authority evidences a powerful political theology, notwithstanding the absence of concrete recommendations for action.[70]

Temporal Progress and the Kingdom

According to de Lubac, the Church constitutes the means to and proleptic anticipation of the Kingdom of God. The ecclesial communion is a visible and social reality. It exists in history and has temporal extension. In its very historical visibility, the Church is a sacrament of the eschatological fullness. So, do social structures and political actions connected to the visible communion of the Church

---

66. Ibid., p. 228.
67. Ibid., p. 211.
68. Ibid., p. 214.
69. Ibid., p. 230. Echoes of this statement are found in the first lines of *Gaudium et spes*: 'The joys and the hopes, the griefs and the anxieties of the men of this age, especially those who are poor or in any way afflicted, these are the joys and hopes, the griefs and anxieties of the followers of Christ. Indeed, nothing genuinely human fails to raise an echo in their hearts.'
70. I am indebted to Justin Klassen for this observation.

participate in the Church's anticipation of the Kingdom? On this question, de Lubac is ambivalent.

In *A Brief Catechesis on Nature and Grace*, de Lubac argues that social organization and political policies and the reign of God belong to 'different orders of reality'.[71] Progress is made by an effort of organizing the world, technical advancement, deploying new systems. Temporal progress – 'justice, liberation, and social advancement' – are products of human efforts alone. Progress is not salvation:

> Salvation is a gift of God; it is entry into the Kingdom... 'One cannot,' whether for oneself or for the world, 'plan for it, organize it, build it, construct it'; one cannot even 'imagine it or get any idea of it; for it is something given, a bequest; we can only inherit it. The coming of God's Kingdom is a miracle and action of God'. In its social meaning liberation of every kind belongs to time; salvation is for eternity, and for that reason always anticipates time.[72]

De Lubac affirms two distinct goals, that of terrestrial improvement and that of heaven. The first goal, he says, is not the 'indispensable preparation for the second'.[73] It is always possible that social and political advancement may sometimes lead people away from God. Conversely, the experience of terrible conditions may open human hearts to the Gospel. Human progress in the temporal order remains ambivalent with regard to salvation. Political progress cannot in any way be perceived as a necessary precondition to the coming of God's reign. Although there is no 'separation' between the two in history, there remains a categorical distinction between the liberation of humanity and the reign of God.

De Lubac does, however, provide for another way of thinking about the matter when discussing *Gaudium et spes*, which both relates and distinguishes earthly progress from the Kingdom. *Gaudium et spes* states, 'Although we must be careful to distinguish earthly progress from the increase of the kingdom of Christ, such progress is of vital concern to the kingdom of God, insofar as it can contribute to the better ordering of human society.'[74] As de Lubac explains, *progress* has an equivocal meaning. For much of *Brief Catechesis* de Lubac considers political and social progress as merely objective results – mere procedures – abstracted from the spiritual dimensions of human life.

According to de Lubac, however, insofar as the Kingdom of God is 'already present on this earth', it may be considered '"mysteriously"... in the depths of men's

---

71. BC, p. 102.

72. Ibid., pp. 106–7. Quoting Walter Kasper, *Jésus le Christ*, trans. J. Désignaux and A. Liefooghe (Paris: Cerf, 1976), pp. 116–17.

73. BC, p. 107.

74. *Gaudium et spes* in Austin Flannery, O.P., ed., *Vatican Council II: The Conciliar and Postconciliar Documents*, Revised (Northport, NY: Costello Publishing Company, 1996), para. 39, p. 398.

hearts, in that holiness which the Church must promote through the fruits of the Spirit who dwells in her and through the external, observable results, measurable in human terms, of the progress of society'.[75] This latter meaning of progress considers more than the exterior result or juridical form, but the visible qualities of concrete communions of people. It is the human element of liberation that de Lubac does not sufficiently explore in his writings, though his ecclesiology and theology of the supernatural develop the resources for its exploration.

The theo-political tensions present in de Lubac's work mirror the tensions present in *Gaudium et spes*. On the one hand, the document speaks of the rightful autonomy of earthly affairs: 'For by the very nature of creation, material being is endowed with its own stability, truth, and excellence, its own order and laws.'[76] At the same time, *Gaudium et spes* indicates that this earthly, human autonomy is understood only by the light of God's revelation in Christ:

> In reality it is only in the mystery of the Word made flesh that the mystery of man truly becomes clear. For Adam, the first man, was a type of him who was to come, Christ the Lord, Christ the new Adam, in the very revelation of the mystery of the Father and of his love, fully reveals man to himself and brings to light his most high calling.[77]

This latter statement echoes de Lubac's earliest book, *Catholicism*: 'By revealing the Father and by being revealed by him, Christ completes the revelation of man to himself.'[78]

For Henri de Lubac, salvation is essentially social and takes a historical and embodied form in the Church. The ecclesial communion, and, by extension, its historical and social life, is sacramental insofar as God's action within it makes it meaningful and a means to its eschatological fulfilment. If the visible Church is the social embodiment of salvation, or alternatively the 'incarnation of Christian life', then can its social and political practices also embody that salvation? De Lubac did not make explicit the political and social implications of his theology of the supernatural and his ecclesiology. The categorical distinction he made between the natural and the supernatural orders implies that the natural order, including human political life, requires transformation and conversion. But this distinction is in no form a temporal or spatial partition. The visible characteristics of the Church – its sacraments, hierarchy, social life, and political intervention – are part of that transformation. De Lubac did not envision the Church as a counter-society, a competitor to a secular civil society. Instead, he envisioned the Christian life as incarnate in society, part of the dense set of relationships difficult to untangle and interpret. Our human history and human lives are part of the unfolding history of salvation, part of the human and divine drama.

75. BC, pp. 228–29.
76. *Gaudium et spes*, para. 36, p. 935.
77. Ibid., para. 22, p. 922.
78. C, p. 339.

In the wake of upheaval in the role of Christianity in twentieth-century Europe, de Lubac's writings explored the sacramental relationship between the temporal and the eternal. Perhaps, like Augustine, de Lubac's attention was on the human yearning for the supernatural such that he did not sufficiently attend to the political and social order. Yet, much of his historical theology sought to understand our terrestrial history as a spiritual autobiography. He sought to interrogate philosophical, theological, and political movements for their spiritual core. His political theology consists of less an articulation of principles for ordering human life and more of a discernment of the human spiritual condition in light of God's revelation. In this sense, de Lubac's political theology is a discernment of God's presence and intention for humanity within the fabric of the human story.

Chapter 19

HENRI DE LUBAC AND THE CHRISTIAN LIFE

Nicholas M. Healy

For Henri de Lubac, 'the Christian life' – or its equivalent, 'the spiritual life' – refers to living in relation to Jesus Christ by the Holy Spirit within the Church. Since only Christians seek to follow Christ, Christian lives should be different in significant respects from the lives of non-Christians. However, de Lubac is not especially interested in sorting out the details of what Christians are to do and not do, nor does he dwell particularly on how what they do makes them visibly different from other people. Rather, his concern is with the theological issues pertaining to the account of what makes the Christian life both possible and actual. In other words, de Lubac does not approach the topic in the way a modern moral theologian is likely to do, perhaps by sorting out moral quandaries, developing a theory about Christian virtues, or distinguishing Christian practices from those of other traditions. Instead, his understanding of the Christian life is the product of extensive historical and systematic theological inquiry centred largely on the doctrines of God, the Church, and the person.

We will not review these doctrines since they are amply treated in other chapters of this book. But we do need to touch on de Lubac's theology of the person, since it directly informs so much of what he writes about the Christian life. This is not to suggest de Lubac takes an individualistic approach; quite the contrary. His anthropology is thoroughly relational and social and, on that account, personal. To be a person is necessarily to be in relation to other persons; we become and can remain Christian persons only as faithful members of the Church; and everything depends upon the fundamental doctrine that the person – any person, not only the Christian – is intrinsically and concretely always in relation to the triune God. De Lubac's retrieval of a more traditional anthropology to counter contemporary extrinsicism thus bears directly upon his description of the Christian life.

Rather than approach the topic by way of the nature and supernature issue or de Lubac's concept of the image of God, we will draw upon an essay of his entitled 'Tripartite Anthropology',[1] which develops a set of terms that have a

---

1. TH, pp. 117–200. This is part of a somewhat larger unfinished piece, the other part of which has been translated as 'Mysticism and Mystery', in TF, pp. 35–69.

direct bearing upon the Christian life. One aim of the essay is to show the relative inadequacy of the bipartite anthropology popular in neo-scholastic theology and in modern Catholicism generally, according to which the person is constituted by two elements: body and soul. The soul is that part of us, which determines whether a person lives according to the flesh (*sarx*) or the spirit (*pneuma*), as St Paul puts it (e.g. Gal. 5.16-26). De Lubac argues that, while this bipartite view is not exactly wrong as far as it goes, it is inadequate, for it suggests that all we are is our nature, our body and soul, and thereby makes it difficult to address the question as to how grace works within us without falling into extrinsicism and historicism.

De Lubac therefore draws upon St Paul and traditional exegesis to retrieve a tripartite anthropology. The main biblical text for this is 1 Thessalonians 5.23, where Paul writes that we are 'entirely, spirit and soul and body', which could be taken to indicate that a person is spirit in addition to soul and body. What Paul means by the word 'spirit' has, of course, been interpreted in different ways. De Lubac rejects any reading that dissolves spirit into body and soul and thereby renders Paul's anthropology bipartite.[2] He also rejects Platonic interpretations that take the spirit to be *nous*, the superior aspect of ourselves that is part of our nature, since this would render it as susceptible to extrinsicism as the bipartite anthropology. He much prefers Karl Barth's view, that the spirit in each person is not the person's spirit at all – for it cannot be part of our nature – but is God's spirit working within each of us. Barth goes a bit too far, though, for de Lubac, because Barth rejects the idea that the spirit is in any sense who we are concretely.[3] While de Lubac agrees with Barth that the spirit is not the spirit of the person, he does want to say that it 'is certainly not the Holy Spirit' either. To maintain this vital ambiguity he appeals to 1 Corinthians 2.11-13. There, he argues, 'after having said "the spirit of the man", Paul corrects himself in a way by saying: "the spirit who is in him."' This is 'a nuance of capital importance',[4] for the spirit is intrinsic to each of us as an inherent element of our concrete identity as a person, yet it is not part of our nature.

It is this 'spirit' – with this necessarily ambiguous meaning – that fruitfully complexifies any properly theological discussion of the Christian life and, indeed, of any theological topic. For it follows that if we are body, soul, *and spirit*, there is a depth to each of us that not only cannot be captured by psychology or sociology but also cannot be described by flat-footed rationalistic theology either.[5] As tripartite persons, each one of us is revealed to be 'mystery' in that the spirit dwelling in us transforms our concrete identity into something more than natural.[6] Indeed, each one of us is 'a living paradox'.[7] Accordingly, theological language, following the Gospel, must often employ paradoxical language to point to the mystery.

2. TH, pp. 118–19.
3. Ibid., p. 128.
4. Ibid., p. 129.
5. See also the discussion of human mystery and paradox in MS, pp. 101–84.
6. BC, p. 81.
7. PF, p. 8.

Such language is both 'more realist and more modest', since it 'specifies, above all ... the things themselves, not [merely] the way of saying them'.[8] Theological matters, including the theology of the Christian life, cannot be approached by straightforward language. As he notes himself, it is not by coincidence that what is probably de Lubac's most direct discussion of the Christian life is found in his two books of paradoxes.[9]

It follows that who each of us is as a person must be understood not as our achievement, but as gift. Our personal, concrete identity is such that we both construct it and receive it as we lead our lives, for we are both moved in the spirit and it is *our* spirit that moves. Accordingly, de Lubac stresses 'the importance of humility in the Christian life'.[10] Humility is not merely a moral virtue acquired through repeated practice, as it is for Thomas Aquinas. It is that, too, but it is more of a basic stance, 'a *passive* virtue',[11] and is therefore 'a fundamental disposition upon which the entire edifice rests'.[12] Existential humility is integral to the Christian life and, as we will see, has nothing to do with diffidence or subservience. It is something like a cardinal principle: 'Forget ... your greatness and confess your dependence ... Do not neglect the light that is given to you, but do not attribute the source to yourself. Try to discover your reality as a mirror and as an image. Know yourself by knowing your God.'[13]

The tripartite anthropology thus supports de Lubac's affirmation of Augustine's description of the Christian life – indeed, of any human life – as inherently restless until we rest finally in God. The spirit within us, strangely part of our identity yet not of our nature, disturbs us and pushes us towards God. It is the source of the dynamic that is at the heart of living as a Christian, and is at work in all persons, irrespective of their sinfulness and whether they are members of the Church or not.[14]

The Three Domains of the Christian Life

The Christian life, then, is rightly called 'the spiritual life', because it takes the form of a movement, prompted by 'our' indwelling spirit, ever further into the mystery that is the triune God. This movement is traditionally understood to have a three-part pattern of ascesis, transformation, and synthesis, which parallels the body,

---

8. Ibid., 10.
9. De Lubac rejected dialectic as an alternative to paradox, but he had in mind the progressive dialectic that resolved into a synthetic view of the whole, as in Hegel and Marx. Karl Barth's understanding of dialectic is arguably much closer to de Lubac's paradox.
10. BC, p. 55.
11. Citing Paul VI; BC, p. 62.
12. Ibid., p. 55.
13. DG, p. 13.
14. See the discussion in C, pp. 217–40.

soul, and spirit of the tripartite anthropology.[15] A third parallel pattern is what de Lubac calls the 'three domains' (or 'denominations') of the Christian life within which this movement occurs: religion, morality, and mysticism or spirituality.[16] These triple patterns or schemas and the spiritual movement they reflect can be found 'across the diversity of vocabularies and in very diverse cultural milieux' within the tradition.[17]

Thus an initial sketch of the Christian life within the Church would be something like the following. It begins with the Church teaching the child or the convert what to believe and what to do as a member of the Christian 'religion'. Here the 'body' is trained by schooling in behaviour (ascesis). The Church is the authority, rightly demanding our obedience to its dogmatic and moral definitions and its practices. As the Christian learns more and becomes more proficient within the religious domain, the soul develops and is to some degree 'transformed', acquiring Christian virtues. One's soul begins to turn towards the spirit and away from the flesh.[18] For example, one cares for others not because one is told to, but because one has become the kind of person who is lovingly disposed towards those who need care. At this second level, then, one begins to interiorize what one has learned so as to live more fully in charity and become more of a faithful, rather than merely obedient, member of the Church. And as one moves further into the spiritual domain, *fides ex auditu* – the faith acquired through the Church's teaching and practices – 'deepens and interiorizes my relationship with the Church, in proportion as the Church's faith penetrates me more deeply and becomes more interiorly mine'.[19] It is this movement towards greater interiorization and 'synthesis' that characterizes the spiritual domain.

Unfortunately, 'the three denominations of religion, morality and mysticism are often presented as independent or even opposed to each other',[20] leading to their distortion and with serious consequences for the Christian life. Sometimes they are even thought of as the three 'faculties' of the person, which the 'tripartition of the human being' does not at all intend.[21] So we will go through each of the three domains in a little more detail to see how de Lubac uses them to describe the proper form of the Christian life and rule out distortions.

The Religious Domain

De Lubac uses the word 'religion' in various ways, but as one of the domains of the Christian life it refers specifically to our active obedience to the Church's order

---

15. Cf. BC, p. 81.
16. 'Spirituality' replaces the third term here 'in those instances where "mysticism" would seem to be too strong a word' (TF, p. 42).
17. TH, p. 117.
18. In Paul's sense of flesh (*sarx*); one never leaves the body (*soma*) behind.
19. CF, pp. 194–95.
20. TH, p. 155.
21. Ibid., p. 166.

and its doctrinal and moral teachings, and our to participation in the Church's sacramental and other practices. During de Lubac's time, there were two critiques of religion, one from within the Church, the other over against it. The external critique was rather similar to the contemporary rejection of religion that is often cast in terms of a distinction between 'organized religion' and 'spirituality'. Religion is portrayed as oppressive, dogmatic, thoughtless, and conformist, while spirituality is its opposite: life-affirming, giving wings to the deepest and richest elements of one's self.[22] (This sense of 'spirituality' has, of course, little in common with de Lubac's use of the word.) The internal, theologically orientated critique viewed religion as a kind of humanism developed in opposition to genuine faith. So, for example, for the early Barth, religion is a form of hubristic human striving towards the divine that fails to trust in the *extra nos* and *pro me* of the Cross. As such it is riddled with worldly and sinful elements that include a contractual relation to God and an overly comfortable relation to worldly society.[23]

In response, de Lubac notes how the mature Barth affirms the necessity and the goodness of religion, rightly understood and practiced. Barth must do so because the Christian life is at root a relation between God and the person, and this relation begins, as it can only begin, within the religious domain, for it is religion that 'establishes a link between man and the Divinity'.[24] Thus religion and faith are mutually necessary and, though different, are never opposed. It is of course true that the Christian religion, like all religions, is a human construction. It is true, too, that Christianity has drawn upon many elements of earlier religions to construct its own religious response to Jesus Christ. But de Lubac contends there could be no alternative to doing so, given that the Christian religion is our communal attempt to respond in the spirit. Religious obedience to the authority of the Church's teaching is therefore an absolute necessity for the Christian life because it is both a product of, and produces, the Christian faith.

Any 'purism of the faith' – the idea that faith must be free from religion and its doctrines and obligations – is therefore nothing but an 'intellectual fiction'.[25] Because the 'revelation of the trinitarian mystery turned the world upside down', faith must be dogmatically informed.[26] If we were to reject the Christian religion's authoritative teaching in favour either of what we might now call a 'personal spirituality' or of a faith that is sheer trust without dogma and Church practices, we would make the 'passage from transcendence to immanence', and thus 'from Christian faith to atheism'.[27] Not incidentally, this is the problem with so-called natural religion, in which the absence of dogma gives it 'a strangely secular appearance'.[28]

22. The external critique is discussed in more detail below.
23. BC, pp. 92–99.
24. CF, p. 151.
25. Ibid., p. 160.
26. Ibid., p. 12.
27. Ibid., p. 197.
28. TH, p. 232.

That said, de Lubac draws a clear distinction between Christian faith and Christian belief. Faith 'is something completely different from a simple conviction' that the Church's system of beliefs is true. Rather, faith 'is an essentially personal act which, if rightly understood,... gives a definite orientation to one's entire being'.[29] My faith is my own response to my relation with God in the spirit, even though it is a relation which cannot be maintained without beliefs about God that can only be acquired within the religious domain. Accordingly, 'religion' and 'faith' cannot be generic terms of which Christian religion and faith are specific forms, for they are in fact far too specific. The religions are very diverse, and Christianity is unique in what it means by 'faith'.[30] So we must reject any tendency to 'oppose religion in the name of faith' or in the name of a supposedly religionless 'spirituality'. For the opposition to make any sense at all, 'we would have to begin by giving religion a narrow and pejorative definition; this definition would be arbitrary and tendentious, would contradict the constant usage of Christian tradition from the beginning and would not be justified either by the most correct etymological explanation'.[31]

So although the Christian life is a spiritual movement through the three domains, we can never move beyond religion into some religion-free higher plane, nor should we ever try to. One cannot transcend the body or get to a mystical level where religious obedience in doctrine and practice are no longer necessary. The 'Christian's entire spiritual life, rooted in faith, is a sharing in the life of the Church... The Christian soul... is essentially an *anima ecclesiastica*'.[32] For 'Catholicism is essentially social', 'not merely' in the sociological sense of a society or community, but at the heart of its reality: 'the expression "social Catholicism" [is] pleonastic'.[33] If mystical heights are ever attained, they can only be the heights of a dogmatically formed Catholic faith.

On the other hand, there has never been a perfect form of Christianity, whether as a religion or as a Christian civilization.[34] The religious domain is often distorted, most commonly by its overemphasis at the expense of the moral and especially the spiritual domains. Genuine orthodoxy is destroyed when it is turned into a 'religious purism' that identifies faith with sheer obedience. For de Lubac, 'a conformist "orthology" cannot suffice for a true believer'.[35] 'If the spirit should be lacking, dogma becomes no more than a myth and the Church no more than a party' or, as we might say now, no more than an association of opinionated like-minded.[36] 'When we are right without praying, without loving, our "right" bears but the fruits of death. To be right against everyone else is too cheap a thing

---

29. CF, pp. 145–46.
30. Ibid., p. 161.
31. Ibid., p. 151.
32. Ibid., pp. 223–24.
33. C, p. 15.
34. BC, p. 88.
35. PF, p. 20.
36. Ibid.

and often also too seductive.'[37] More broadly, 'Credulity, sectarianism, and sloth are three natural tendencies of man. Too often he canonizes them under nobler names.'[38] Thus an overemphasis upon the religious domain may prompt the Church to give way to 'what can be called her "permanent temptation", that of self-idolatry'.[39] For the Church sometimes forgets that Christian faith must conform to Peter's confession of Jesus as the Christ. It cannot be faith in Peter himself, nor in his descendants, neither can the Church itself be an object of faith.[40]

To avoid the reduction of the Christian life to mere obedience or to slothful group-thinking, the Church must acknowledge in practice as well as theory that there is no antithesis between genuine religion and genuine faith.[41] For 'it is precisely authentic, logical and interiorly lived faith that preserves one from all fanaticism'.[42] The religious requirement that each of us obediently follow the Church's teachings 'neither prevents us nor dispenses us from receiving these within ourselves so as to express them through ourselves. We escape this interpreter [i.e., each one of us] only to fall into banality and verbalism'.[43]

The Moral Domain

Christians visibly express and begin to 'interpret' (or 'synthesize') the Church's faith within the moral domain, and more fully as they develop within the spiritual domain. We noted at the outset that de Lubac's treatment of morality is not like that of a modern moral theologian. He is not interested in discussing difficult moral issues nor, in spite of remarks about the errors of secular society, does he devote much space to emphasizing how the Christian way of life is different from ways of life outside the Church. Rather, his primary effort in this area – and quite possibly the primary concern of his work overall – is the reform of the Church by means of a constructive retrieval of traditional theological insights. He uses such insights to engage errors in the Church's thought and practice, in order that Christians may be moved to live more truthfully, lovingly, and spiritually in relation with the triune God and one another. Accordingly, the moral life must be treated as one of the three domains of the Christian life rather than as a more or less independent area of theology or as the basis for an ecclesial apologetics that asserts the superiority of the Church's practices over those of the world. It is not that de Lubac is against either activities in principle. But when they are independent of a properly theological treatment of the Christian life, they are likely to fail to reckon sufficiently with the paradoxical aspects of life in the 'spirit'.

---

37. Ibid., p. 167.
38. Ibid., p. 21.
39. CF, p. 182.
40. Cf. ibid., pp. 174, 191.
41. Ibid., p. 159.
42. PF, p. 168.
43. Ibid., p. 17.

De Lubac's account of the moral domain is governed by his doctrine of God. God is not primarily a law-giver, to whose will each of us must respond obediently if we are to secure our salvation. 'We are not to obey God because God is "Master"'. On the contrary, we 'owe God the free gift of ourselves. We owe him an intimate assent, a love, which is justified or even made possible only if God is Love and has loved us first'.[44] God is not to be thought of as 'the cause of moral obligation or the sanction of duty'.[45] Rather, our relation to God in the moral domain should be determined by the revelation of the triune God in Jesus Christ, where God is revealed to be 'the very substance of Good'.[46] The moral domain is thus the place of the loving encounter between God and the person, between Christ and his Church, and between persons in charity.

In loving our neighbour we already begin to enter into eternal life. 'By charity we start eternity right here below. *Manet caritas*' – 'charity persists'.[47] The moral domain cannot be transcended, even by the achievement of solitary union with God, for love of God is necessarily also love for others. 'The Christian virtues, proposed for the practice of all, are not simply means of freeing oneself; their exercise is not simply something transitory: in their substance, they are already something of the end itself'. This is because, in Jesus Christ, we see 'the true God, revealing himself as God of Charity'.[48] Thus the spiritual domain is not 'higher' than the moral domain, but rather a different and deeper perspective on it and thus a more complete fulfilment of it.

As with the religious domain, in which our obedience is but the way towards genuine fidelity to the Church, so, too, within the moral domain our obedience to the moral teachings of the Church is of itself neither sufficient nor even the primary concern. 'To fulfil the prescriptions of religious authority faithfully, strictly, without any omission, is good. But if you are satisfied with that, you have not begun to *obey*. You take for an end what is still only a means, for an act what is only its condition. You violate the idea of Catholicism.'[49] It is therefore a mistake to think of sin as a disobedient thought, word or deed that goes against God's law and the Church's teaching. It is far worse than that, because sin is nothing less than 'a refusal of God's invitation to share his life'.[50] If we are slaves to sin, we must become liberated from ourselves, for life with God.[51] Our stance of humility in this domain should take the form of an ongoing attempt to interiorize our knowledge that the 'basic sin' is to believe in our personal innocence and – just as bad – the innocence of humanity.[52] The Christian life is therefore one of repentance,

---

44. Ibid., p. 25.
45. Ibid., p. 24.
46. Ibid., p. 24.
47. Ibid.
48. Ibid.
49. Ibid., p. 27.
50. BC, p. 169.
51. Ibid., p. 160.
52. Ibid., pp. 140–41.

reconciliation, and renewal: 'the full realization of what sin is does not exist in the sinful Christian, however lucid he may be, but only in the repentant Christian'.[53] Sin is fundamentally personal and cannot be excused as merely a product of social sin.[54]

There are other ways the moral domain may be distorted. Our moral life may be too free from the religious domain, losing dogma and faith to become a humanist ethic where, perhaps, Jesus is portrayed as merely a great moral teacher. Or the moral domain may be insufficiently oriented towards the spiritual life. De Lubac remarks how 'the gift of self goes astray into aimless activism if it is not the overflow of an inner life'.[55]

The Spiritual Domain

The spiritual domain includes both mysticism, in the sense of a life dedicated to a quest for union with God, as well as the less specific forms of spirituality that should be practiced by every Christian whatever their vocation. De Lubac's treatment of both is guided by 'the first principle of Augustinian mysticism: *inter animam et Deum nulla natura interposita.*[56] Each individual needs the *mediation* of all, but no one is kept at a distance by any intermediary'.[57] The gospel of St John teaches that 'Life came and dwelt among men and that, by his Spirit, Life dwells in men's hearts.' Consequently we may say that there has been 'a Christian interiority' from the very beginning.[58]

With regard specifically to mysticism, de Lubac is sympathetic to the quest for union. He warns those with 'a certain spiritual aestheticism and for amateurs of psychological analysis' that the mystical quest is likely to be harmful, but it is only such 'parasites' whom it injures.[59] For those whose faith is genuine, it 'restores to the soul its strength and energy'. Moreover, having mystics among its members is good for the health of the Church community: 'In the end it is an ever more real and more widespread spiritual society that must be rediscovered in the deepest, most abandoned interior silence.'[60]

However, de Lubac is by no means uncritical. He shares St John of the Cross's concerns regarding visions and delightful emotions.[61] He notes, too, that even St Bernard's 'fervent piety' was 'not without its traces of individualism', and drifted a little too free from the Church.[62] A truly Christian mysticism can never detach

53. Ibid., p. 131.
54. Ibid., pp. 136–37.
55. CF, p. 14.
56. 'Nothing of a created nature can come between the soul and God'. This is reflected in de Lubac's understanding of the third 'part' of the person, the paradoxical 'spirit'.
57. C, p. 334.
58. TF, p. 51.
59. C, p. 347.
60. Ibid., p. 349.
61. PF, pp. 208–9.
62. C, p. 128.

itself from Christianity as a 'concrete form of religion'. If it does, though 'sometimes sublime', it will be 'incompatible with the Faith'.[63] In the mysticisms of other religions, he finds little more than 'individualistic doctrines of escape' that, despite all other differences, have in common the doctrine that 'the world from which escape must be sought is meaningless, and the humanity that must be outstripped is without a history'.[64] For Christianity, on the contrary, humanity is social and as such has a genuine history that must remain 'the necessary interpreter between God and man'.[65]

With regard to Christian spirituality more broadly, de Lubac is critical of much of the piety developed within the modern era. The romanticism of the nineteenth century in particular encouraged pious practices in which 'Religiosity outstripped religion', so that 'the Catholic renaissance became sentimental and feminine'.[66] He condemns the 'selfish piety, the narrow religious outlook, the neglect of ordinary duties in the multiplication of "devotions" [and] the failure to realize that prayer is essentially the prayer of all for all'.[67] This impoverishment of the spiritual domain was due in part to the shift in theological inquiry away from modes proper to the mystery of faith. An early symptom of this was Aquinas's view that faith is necessary only for the present life and will be transcended in the next by the comprehension of vision. The earlier tradition by contrast understood faith to be an unending and ever deeper penetration of mystery. The theological intellectualism that developed after Aquinas described faith not as that which opens 'up a path to contemplative understanding' but rather as 'an obstacle, set up by God himself, to cut across the appetite for rational speculation'.[68]

To address these various developments, the Christian life needs to be 'more firmly established in the heart of religion, whereas it was established, on the contrary, in a climate as unfavourable as possible to the flowering of the sense of the sacred':

> between the abstract theology, or the spirituality for specialists, and the at times mediocre quality of popularized piety, where, for a long time now, has been the place of religion itself, simple, concrete, human, virile, profound religion? On the one hand, we have a hypertrophy of piety particularly for the use of women, and on the other hand, we created, for example, a social morality or other, more indifferent things.[69]

The Christian understanding of the sacred is complex, for although it is reasonable to distinguish between the secular and the sacred, the distinction 'is in one sense

---

63. TF, p. 48.
64. C, p. 139.
65. Ibid., p. 166.
66. TH, p. 348.
67. C, p. 16.
68. CM, p. 240.
69. TH, p. 348.

an abstraction. For in reality, nothing is purely "in itself"'. This we learn from the most concrete form of the sacred, which 'for us' is none other than 'Christ, God and Man'. It is only by our focus upon Jesus Christ in faith that we can avoid 'the twofold peril of slipping into the secular and of a sacrilegious surrender to a "sacred" usurper'.[70] With Jesus Christ in view we realize how life is inherently oriented towards the sacred, and that it takes the form of a corporeal spirituality, as it were. Our bodiliness is inherent not only in the religious and the moral domains but, of necessity, in the spiritual domain, too. Our desire for God is and can only remain an embodied spiritual desire. Accordingly, de Lubac rejects what he considers to be the overly sharp distinction between *eros* and *agape* made by Anders Nygren.[71] Our love for God in the spirit is a 'transformed desire'. It cannot become pure *agape*, since it is as persons that we want and need God.

More generally, de Lubac rejects any suggestion that spiritual growth enables any of us to transcend the supposedly lower elements of our humanity, whether by Stoicism or some other kind of a mental imperviousness achieved through meditative practices or by a stance of superiority vis-à-vis this world. He remarks: 'A lofty soul bears contempt, insult, or slander easily enough. The only risk is that it may transmute them into pride.'[72] Christian humility requires us to accept our full humanity, not as something to move beyond, but as the gift that is who we are before God.

De Lubac sharpens this point by discussing how we are to suffer as Christians. 'In the order of the spirit, a method of painless birth will never be found.'[73] Certainly, we should not go looking for suffering, nor love it 'for its own sake'.[74] But we can be truly happy only if we are not 'ignorant of suffering'; so we should not 'run away from it' by various devices, but 'accept the transfiguration it brings'.[75] This transfiguration is not at all a matter of learning how to be heroic and splendid, for: 'When we suffer, we always suffer badly.'[76] 'No real suffering, at the moment it is experienced, is noble.'[77] De Lubac's advice – presumably learned from personal experience – is that when 'pain is at its height, to escape the poison it distils, look at yourself now and again with a humorous eye'.[78] If we are to 'welcome suffering', then, it is not in order 'to take pleasure in it. It is not love of suffering for its own sake. It is consent to one's humiliation by it. ... There is an art in suffering – but it must not be confused either with the art of cultivating suffering or with the art of avoiding it'.[79] Again, this is directly linked to Jesus Christ: 'The person who suffers

70. Ibid., p. 240.
71. Anders Nygren, *Eros and Agape*. First published in 1938, the French translation was reviewed by de Lubac in 1945: *TF* pp. 85–89.
72. PF, p. 184.
73. Ibid., p. 186.
74. Ibid., p. 172.
75. Ibid., p. 173.
76. Ibid., p. 175.
77. Ibid., p. 177.
78. Ibid., p. 174.
79. Ibid., p. 172.

has the finest opportunity of bringing the law of Christian life into effect: let him not be ashamed of resembling and having recourse to the Man of Sorrows.'[80]

For de Lubac, then, the Christian life is a never-ending movement ever further into the reality of God's love revealed to us in Christ Jesus. He offers this summary:

> God's revelation in Christ comes to meet man, not to set him in motion, but to orient and correct his steps. It shows him the way, teaches him to sacrifice the desires of flesh and blood in order to begin loving as God loves. This necessary turning is at the same time an accomplishment for man. For in the depths of human nature, beyond the aberrations of man's conscience and of his free will, there exists a deep longing, a combined desire for what is good and for happiness which always remains ready to recognize its goal in the disinterestedness of divine love.[81]

Concretely, however, the Christian life is difficult and costly. 'We are too desirous of being set at ease, and we do not consent to being taken out of our usual element. That is why we make a petty religion for ourselves and seek a petty salvation of our own petty proportions.' So the Christian must be restless, always attempting 'self-criticism, self-renewal, constant self-adaptation, without letting anything in one die'.[82] For the 'permanent danger of all spiritual life' is 'gradually settling down in the vantage point one occupies, the good conscience one enjoys'.[83] We might say, perhaps – though he does not use the word – that the Christian life is something like an 'adventure'. If so, it is the most exciting and all-consuming adventure possible, not least, but not only, because it never ends.

Contemporary Significance

Late in life, Henri de Lubac wrote: 'The problematics, in the kinds of subjects I approached in turn, has changed too profoundly in recent times for any of my books to maintain any lasting timeliness.'[84] We can agree there have been significant changes since his day. Neo-scholastic theology and philosophy have lost their dominance within the Church, due in large part to the influence of de Lubac's work. Their decline had already begun by 1938, when de Lubac – choosing his words carefully – could report: 'Many are already growing impatient with the new scholasticism, the mixture of abstractions and metaphors in which it tends to be entangled. Others are anxious, not perhaps without some semblance at least of

---

80. Ibid., p. 177.
81. CF, p. 301.
82. PF, p. 15.
83. Ibid., p. 14.
84. ASC, p. 157.

reason, at the vague mysticism and the unsystematic speculation that are in some instances the price of its success.'[85] Beyond that, the developments occurring with Vatican II, the theologies of liberation and identity, and broad shifts in social assumptions and practices have indeed all raised new questions.

Yet de Lubac's self-assessment of his work is rather too sweeping, for there is much that is of lasting significance, and not least with regard to the contemporary *problematique* of the Christian life. His diagnosis of the central issue is arguably still very relevant: 'The religious problem, everywhere and always, is essentially a problem of the spiritual order.'[86] And his retrieval and contemporary application of a more traditional understanding of the Christian life is an achievement that can point towards ways to address the Church's current problems. To support these judgements an argument could be made along the following lines.

The Roman Catholic Church continues to suffer steep declines in its membership in many parts of the world.[87] Whether this is a good thing or not – and one could with reason argue either way, perhaps – it may be that some responsibility for the decline lies with the Church, rather than it being due simply the Gospel's lack of appeal for modern people. It could be argued that the Church has not sufficiently overcome extrinsicist elements in its theology and has not addressed the distortions of Church teaching and culture to which those elements give rise. The persistence of the bipartite understanding of the person has made it difficult to acknowledge and address positively the consequences of the Pauline 'spirit' (or its equivalent in other terms). There remains a heavy emphasis upon the religious and moral domains at the expense of the spiritual domain, with the clergy sometimes seeming nervous about encouraging the latter in the faithful. Consequently, those people who are searching for a way to bring themselves into a closer relation to God, and who might have been attracted to a contemporary version of the traditional, well-rounded Christian life de Lubac describes, may find themselves distanced from the Church, and may feel it necessary to look elsewhere for their spiritual needs.

Without trying to argue that de Lubac himself would necessarily agree with this suggestion, let us consider it a little further in relation to two topics, beginning with religious authority. The Church has been generally unable constructively to address shifts in dominant contemporary cultural forms that undermine acceptance of what is rather too easily taken to be the traditional notion of religious authority. Its leaders and pastors tend to condemn the rejection of their doctrinal and moral teaching as if it were nothing more than sinful disobedience. When they try to understand some of the complex cultural forces affecting many Christians, they often condemn those forces, sometimes in starkly dualistic terms. To be sure, such reactions are not entirely unreasonable.

---

85. C, p. 324,
86. PF, p. 70.
87. I focus on the Roman Catholic Church in Europe and North America. Africa and Asia do not face decline but have different problems for which de Lubac's work could perhaps also help, though I cannot make that argument here.

The religious domain, as such, does indeed require obedience if one is to progress in the moral and spiritual domains. And the cultural forces that undermine authority and obedience in the Church have their own, often less visible but equally rigorous demands, which are frequently incompatible with any faithful form of the Christian life.

However, the result may be that the Church leadership can appear more authoritarian than authoritative, especially in the moral domain. For rather than portraying the moral domain as the stage, as it were, upon which each of us builds and lives out our spiritual life, the Church has tended to treat it as if it were more or less independent of the spiritual domain. As a result, its moral teachings can appear to be imposed upon us extrinsically. Put another way, the moral domain seems too dominated by the religious domain, with its focus upon ascesis and obedience, and is separated from the spiritual, so that the latter – where one develops one's personal relation to God within the Church – can seem like an optional extra suitable only for the especially devout. The demand for obedience to moral teachings then may appear inauthentic and oppressive, and its rules largely irrelevant and often wrong, even when they are very relevant and correct. And so people leave what they believe is an authoritarian Church. Those who leave are not only those who simply disagree with the Church's moral teaching, but also those who take it seriously and – whether rightly or wrongly – find it wanting in depth. Were moral teaching informed more by due consideration of the spiritual domain, these misunderstandings could conceivably be addressed.

What seems often missing in the Church's response to modern cultures, then, is a clear acknowledgement of and support for the Lubacian idea that the Christian life should move through simple obedience to mature fidelity, by ascesis and transformation, interiorization and synthesis, and that this movement will increase both the Christian's personal relation to God *and* her or his fidelity to the Church. Because of this omission and the distortion it causes, de Lubac's criticism is still pertinent:

> Nothing less adequately expresses the truth than the extrinsicist doctrines which maintain in the Church only a unity resulting from constraint – unless it be a unity resulting from indifference, having no other link than a visible transmission and a visible authority. They transform the obedience of faith into a faith which is mere obedience. Totally oblivious of the Spirit of Christ, they suffocate Christian liberty; then, rejected sooner or later as an intolerable yoke, they soon give way to spiritual anarchy.[88]

Here the 'they' de Lubac writes about are extrinsicist doctrines, not the Church leaders, and the latter are not, of course, oblivious of the Spirit of Christ. But de Lubac's point applies in a certain way to them, too, for it is they who are charged with teaching doctrines and practices correctly and appropriately so that those they teach may live well as mature Christians. Even the new *Catechism of the Catholic*

---

88. CF, p. 197.

Church seems not adequately to reflect de Lubac's concerns. Its emphasis is clearly on Church doctrines and practices, and on moral guidance; it offers relatively very little directly concerning the spiritual domain.[89] We can certainly point to leaders and pastors who exemplify and teach the Christian life as described by de Lubac, and who are accordingly not at all authoritarian. But they are relatively uncommon and as a result, the Church's authoritative teaching is presented in an unnuanced and unspiritual way, with the result that it is too often misunderstood by Christians, clerical as well as lay, and by those looking on from outside the Church. It may well be, then, that a persistent 'extrinsicist mentality' still attempts 'to insure the perfect unity of the faith at too cheap a price'. It is 'not sufficiently respectful of the Christian's dignity, [and] not sufficiently concerned about the Holy Spirit's action in souls'.[90]

The argument could therefore be made that, if de Lubac is correct in his reading of the tradition, the Church's response to challenges to its authority is not merely sometimes inadequate and misguided. It is also the product of a distortion of its own tradition that has left its religious and moral authority dangerously misunderstood and undermined, and – a great loss – its spiritual authority too often unexercised. The Church may have put itself in a position where it has little alternative other than to demand simple obedience from its members, rather as if it were a merely 'natural' institution under threat, and not the Body of Christ and Temple of the Holy Spirit. Again, we can understand how this came about over the course of some very difficult centuries for the Church. To point this out is not at all to cast blame. The point is intended constructively: de Lubac helps us diagnose the problem and indicates a possible way of addressing it.

The second issue concerns the popularity of quests for an authentic 'spirituality' outside the Church, another reason why people are leaving. Here, again, the Church's lack of interest in encouraging genuine Christian spiritualities among all its members may well be a contributing cause. A related factor may be the Church's emphasis upon community and family at the expense of the person. Pope Benedict XVI decried this 'sociological levelling down' in which the sacraments 'are often seen merely as celebrations of the community where there is no more room for the personal dialogue between God and the soul – something many greet with condescending ridicule'.[91] That ridicule may also be partly to do with the kind of practices the Church makes available for the devout, some of which border on the heterodox and are – as de Lubac points out – often rather sentimental or in dubious taste. Within the parishes there is usually little

---

89. *Catechism of the Catholic Church* (Liguori, MO: Liguori Publications, 1994). The third part, headed 'Life in Christ' is largely taken up with moral guidance. The spiritual life is discussed briefly in the smallest part, entitled 'Christian Prayer', where the Lord's Prayer is given less space than the Ten Commandments are in the third part, and only three pages are devoted to contemplative prayer.
90. Ibid., p. 229.
91. C, p. 12.

alternative to these unless one looks hard to find them. By contrast, one never needs to go looking for the Church's moral teaching.

Because the Church is not perceived to be as concerned or even willing to foster a genuine Christian spirituality among its membership, people inside and outside the Church are not altogether unreasonable in thinking that Roman Catholicism is an 'organized religion' standing in opposition to the 'spirituality' they prefer. To be sure, the spirituality chosen by those rejecting the Church may often be vacuous and self-serving; where, in the words of Nicholas Lash, 'the "spiritual" floats free from fact and calculation and responsibility, massaging in fantasies of feeling the bruised narcissism of well-heeled individualists'.[92] But while this may be an accurate description of the spiritualities of some of the more self-involved, the desire on the part of many who have left the church for a richer interior life cannot be dismissed as mere vanity.

With the benefit of hindsight, we might venture to suggest that the Church's worries and controversies over individualism and secularism have prevented it from taking up the opportunity this not uncommon spiritual searching affords, namely to describe and exemplify how the Christian life, properly lived in the 'spirit', is in fact just the sort of thing such people are looking for. It is as personal as any other, yet it is also thoroughly communal, thus satisfying another contemporary desideratum. It is 'organized', but the organization is there to help each of us develop our response to God, to others, and to the world. The Church is not a support group, but it can be a little bit like one. The Christian life, when understood along the lines indicated by de Lubac, can be as challenging, exciting, and maturing as any other, and in fact far more so, once undertaken, not least because it never ends, unlike any other way of life whatsoever.

The discipline of the Christian life, conceived as a movement into God that transforms the person, has secular parallels that are attractive to many people. The disciplines of the military, for example, though often decried by well-heeled liberals, can give meaning and maturity to those who would otherwise be trapped in poverty. Learning a musical instrument or excelling in a sport requires some rather similar movements to those indicated by the three triple schemas of the traditional Christian life. Certainly, there are all kinds of radical differences and contradictions between such secular disciplined lives and the Christian life. But the fact that many take up such disciplines indicates that not all those who reject the Church's requirement of ascesis and transformation should be dismissed as self-indulgent or well-heeled slackers. Rather, the problem may also be the Church's lack of clarity about the intended outcome of its discipline: a mature Christian who is on that account a more self-directed person, rather than merely an obedient and docile follower of what seems to be something all too arbitrary.

De Lubac insists that a 'personal religion and interior life are by no means synonymous with individualism and religious subjectivism'.[93]

---

92. Nicholas Lash, *Holiness, Speech and Silence* (Aldershot: Ashgate, 2004), p. 34.
93. C, p. 346.

Just as the act of faith is the freest of all acts, so the expression of faith is the most personal of all expressions. Submissiveness to revealed truth and the supernatural neither prevents us nor dispenses us from receiving these within ourselves so as to express them through ourselves. We escape this interpreter only to fall into banality and verbalism.[94]

Critical Questions

While de Lubac offers some critical insights into problems within the contemporary Church, we can also ask some critical questions with regard to his own work. In a recent book the Christian ethicist, Luke Bretherton, rightly takes it as axiomatic that any 'account of the Christian life has to reckon with the dual problematic of Christian political thought: that we are called to seek first the kingdom of God but also to seek the welfare of the city even though it be Babylon (Jer. 29.7)'.[95] Because it may seem to lie so much within the Church, we might wonder whether de Lubac's account of the Christian life says enough about how it necessarily involves action within and for the world. Furthermore, in some of his later work, he has some critical things to say of at least some forms of theology that are explicitly concerned with social and political justice. So should we conclude that his conception of the Christian life and the theology that undergirds it may be to some extent antagonistic to, or at least rather dismissive of, such activity?

Perhaps the first thing to note in response is de Lubac's own active political engagement in the form of his 'spiritual resistance' to Nazism in France during the Second World War (briefly described in *ASC*, pp. 46–55). Although he does not always stress it explicitly, de Lubac manifestly held that seeking the welfare of society beyond the Church is indeed a necessary aspect of the Christian life. However, in the course of showing us why such activity is required, he adds something of vital importance that is sometimes overlooked. Thus he insists: 'Without concern for its social and temporal consequences, the spiritual life is distorted.'[96] But he is concerned about those dialectical theories, usually derived from Marxism, that require suffering in the present in order to achieve the utopian future. Any theological appropriation of such theories would be suspect for de Lubac, not least because there is a vast difference between the kingdom of heaven and any this-worldly utopia. But more directly at issue is the inadequacy of any comprehensive theory or metanarrative of human betterment.

To counter such 'ideologies', de Lubac sought to keep our focus on what is fundamentally at stake, which is not following a theory of how to achieve human

---

94. PF, p. 17.
95. Luke Bretherton, *Christianity and Contemporary Politics: The Conditions and Possibilities of Faithful Witness* (Chichester, UK: Wiley-Blackwell, 2010), p. 189.
96. PF, p. 93.

betterment, but following Jesus Christ: 'When we choose the poor, we can always be sure of not going wrong. When we choose an ideology, we can never be sure of not being at least partly wrong.' What makes us always right about the central matter is that when we choose the poor, we 'have chosen like Jesus. And we have chosen Jesus'.[97] So he will write:

> It has been and still is indispensable, in opposition to the falsely supernatural illusions of an airy apostolate, as well as the pharisaism of the privileged, to insist upon the economic and social conditions without which it would be vain to preach the practice of Christian virtues to the masses. More profoundly, it is good to react against certain social structures which, being dehumanizing, are the natural enemies of any faith.

But he immediately adds a warning: 'But do not go thinking that faith and Christian virtues would flourish automatically in a society where these obstacles would have been removed.'[98] As with the Church, so with the world: his concern is primarily for the liberation that comes with the life of the spirit. That is the gift Christians should bring whenever they work, as of course they should, for social justice.

In sum, de Lubac's response to such developments would be to remind us that even though it is certainly true the Christian life is distorted without due 'concern for its social and temporal consequences', it is also the case – as is perhaps more obvious now than when he wrote – that 'without a deepening of spirituality all social progress remains unworthy of man and can finally turn against him. God, for whom man is made, can only be reached by their convergence.'[99]

A rather different way to discuss the relation between the Church and the world has developed since de Lubac's time, in relation to which his account of the Christian life is also pertinent. Bretherton's book was written after the advent not only of political and liberation theologies, but after 'what might be called the "ecclesial turn" in theological reflection upon political life'.[100] With this turn, the Church is itself understood to be a distinctive politics or social ethics, and leading figures of this movement (mostly within Protestant churches)[101] argue that the Church should live in visible contrast to the politics and societies of the world. The Church's alternative politics and the distinctively Christian lives of its members are the primary forms of our witness to Jesus Christ in the world.

97. Ibid., p. 135.
98. PF, p. 69.
99. Ibid., p. 93.
100. Bretherton, *Christianity and Contemporary Politics*, p. 189. Bretherton does not make the moves of the ecclesial turn outlined in this and the following paragraph. With his Augustinian leanings, he may be closer to de Lubac in significant ways.
101. See, for example, the work of Stanley Hauerwas and John Howard Yoder. The Christian life is an area where specific denominational histories and cultures must be allowed to factor in any attempts at reform, however. The ecclesial turn makes a great deal of sense within some Protestant churches since it is arguably a necessary attempt to recover

While it is quite possible that de Lubac would have been sympathetic with some aspects of the ecclesial turn, he might not have been altogether content with it. To be sure, the Church has developed a set of practices and beliefs that others do not share, so we do live somewhat differently. But perhaps de Lubac would point out in response that in a real and concrete way Catholicism encompasses all humankind: the tripartite anthropology is common to us all; the Holy Spirit is at work as our 'spirit' everywhere. We are all united to God, whether we know it or not, and this relation has its effects everywhere, even if they go mostly unnoticed. Furthermore, some versions of the ecclesial turn place a strong emphasis on the religious and the moral domains, upon obedience in belief and practice, and the acquisition of virtues. The result can be a tendency to construe the Church as a system of practices and beliefs formally similar to the systems of other sociopolitical groups, with which it is therefore in competition. For de Lubac, Christianity is not merely a religion or a morality or a politics. It is all three, but unless they are understood in light of the 'spirit' and thus brought within, and reshaped by, the spiritual and personal domain, the ecclesial turn can issue in a form of extrinsicism and an overly sharp distinction from other kinds of life.

A perhaps more substantive criticism of de Lubac's retrieval of the traditional account of the Christian life is its possible elitism. That is, it may seem to require the retrieval of the traditional division within the Church between the few devout spirituals and the vast majority. Each group had its own form of the Christian life, one of which was the proper one, for example the *status perfectionis* of the Middle Ages, while the other was but a making-do. People in the latter group were unlikely to enter the spiritual domain. They were to remain in the religious domain and in the moral to some extent, through their obedience to their spiritual superiors. The most recent version of this division is the description – in another three-part schema (albeit sardonic) – of the ordinary Catholic's way of life as: 'pray, pay and obey'.

It seems unlikely that de Lubac thought along such lines. We can note, to begin with, how he makes it clear that a mature Christian life is not at all contingent upon social standing or education:

> the best Christians, the most genuine and most living, are not necessarily or even generally counted among the learned or the clever; among the intellectuals or the politically-minded; among the custodians of power or wealth; among the 'social authorities'. Consequently their voices rarely resound in the squares and in the press, their actions usually make no noise and do not take the public eye… It is

---

– in the terms of de Lubac's useful schema – the significance of the religious domain within Church cultures whose members are well developed within the spiritual domain, but in a way that is distorted by modernity. For an enlightening account of this problem within the Baptist churches, and a turn rather more to 'catholicity' than simply to the Church as an alternative to the world – and thus more in line with de Lubac – see Curtis W. Freeman, *Contesting Catholicity: Theology for Other Baptists* (Waco, TX: Baylor University Press, 2014).

nevertheless they who contribute more than anyone else to the difference that this earth of ours has from hell.[102]

Anyone of any class and circumstances may have a deep spiritual life, so there are 'many saints' who, 'even after their death, remain unknown'.[103] But that said, de Lubac's account of the Christian life may seem so demanding that only especially devout Christians who also have enough spare time would be able to practice it properly. So one might conclude that the division in the Church would result, since those who, for example, have to work long hours at minimum wage to support young families cannot spare the time nor are likely to have the energy after their busy days to do more than say a few prayers before falling into an exhausted sleep.

Although de Lubac does not address this issue head-on, and perhaps could have said rather more about it, four major Lubacian concepts undermine such a conclusion: faith, Church, vocation, and the 'spirit'. 'Whatever their level of culture, whatever their role in the drama of history, all true believers ... share, objectively, in the same faith.'[104] Faith, we recall, is not simply a set of beliefs in various objects or articles, but is an active and very personal response to God in the 'spirit'. This is faith 'in the primary meaning' of the term, 'the very faith of the Church herself, which is, precisely, "divine faith."'[105] As such, it is the same in form and quality in all Christians. It is true, of course, that there are varying degrees of a 'conceptual grasp of the faith', and many 'involuntary errors', but that applies to very devout as well. Because we all live within the Church, everyone is 'one in proportion as they participate in a single faith, which is the faith of the Church. All of them have received the same basic instruction, the unique Christian initiation'.[106] Even if this is very basic, it is sufficient for living the Christian life.[107]

De Lubac contends that 'even the humblest movement of faith secretly introduces us to this end that knows no end'.[108] If this is so, if follows that faith brings us into all three domains at the outset of the Christian life. We should not think of the schemas as describing a step-by-step movement from the religious through the moral to the spiritual domain as if it occurs necessarily *seriatim*. Not only can one never leave behind the two earlier domains, the faith of the Church brings each of us already into the spiritual domain, if only in an initially limited way. Anyone with faith is already living the Christian life in all its dimensions.

There are, of course, significant and often obvious differences among Christians. But these do not necessarily indicate that some are more sinful or not living in the 'spirit'. Rather, the difference may well reflect a person's vocation, her or his relation with God that calls the Christian to live in a particular way.

---

102. PF, p. 198.
103. Ibid.
104. CF, p. 239.
105. Ibid., p. 229.
106. Ibid., p. 234.
107. Ibid., p. 227.
108. C, p. 316.

'The summons to personal life is a *vocation*, that is, a summons to play an eternal role.'[109] Only a few people are called to the religious life, or to the priesthood, or to a job that is in some obvious way related to Christianity. The rest of us are called to be Christian each in our own way, which does not mean that we choose that way so much as have it given us, a gift that is also the gift of ourselves. 'Sincerity is fidelity. Man's perfection is a must be. He does not merely *have*, he *is* a vocation. Sincerity is fidelity to one's vocation since it is fidelity to oneself.'[110] Perfection, then, lies in the living of the life given to each one of us. Thus one can lead a good Christian life in obscurity, without explicitly seeking perfection, merely by responding to one's call and without giving any significant external indication that one is actually doing so. For the primary thing is always the 'encounter':

> A new idea of God, a new idea of man, a new idea of the relationships between man and God: this is what was latent in the first act of Christian faith. ... [which] in its newness, was not an idea but reality. It dealt with an encounter, with *the* encounter... A personal challenge addressed to man by God, revelation calls forth from man an equally personal response: that is what faith is. Thus, a relationship is established which must be called reciprocal... [and] 'interpersonal'.[111]

In all its various forms and aspects, this encounter is for Henri de Lubac the centre of the Christian life and what it fundamentally is all about.

---

109. Ibid., p. 331.
110. PF, p. 59.
111. CF, p. 282.

BIBLIOGRAPHY

Works by Henri de Lubac

de Lubac, Henri. *Affrontements Mystiques*. Paris: Éditions du Témoignage chrétien, 1950.
de Lubac, Henri. *Amida*. Paris: Editions du Seuil, 1955.
de Lubac, Henri. 'Apologetics and Theology'. In *Theological Fragments*, pp. 91–104. San Francisco: Ignatius Press, 1989.
de Lubac, Henri. 'Apologétique et Théologie', *Nouvelle Revue Théologique* 57 (1930): pp. 361–78.
de Lubac, Henri. *Aspects of Buddhism*. London: Sheed & Ward, 1953.
de Lubac, Henri. *Athéisme et sens de l'homme: une double requite de Gaudium et Spes*. Paris: Éditions du Cerf, 1968.
de Lubac, Henri. *At the Service of the Church: Henri De Lubac Reflects on the Circumstances that Occasioned His Writings*. Translated by Anne Elizabeth Englund. San Francisco: Communio Books, 1993.
de Lubac, Henri. *Augustinianism and Modern Theology*. Translated by Lancelot Sheppard; Introduction by Louis Dupré. New York: Crossroad Publishing Company, 2000.
de Lubac, Henri. *Augustinisme et théologie moderne*. Paris: Aubier, 1965.
de Lubac, Henri. *A Brief Catechesis on Nature and Grace*. Translated by Richard Arnandez. San Francisco: Ignatius Press, 1984.
de Lubac, Henri. *Carnets du Concile*, 2 vols. Paris: Cerf, 2007.
de Lubac, Henri. *Catholicism: Christ and the Common Destiny of Man*. Translated by Lancelot C. Sheppard and Elizabeth Englund. San Francisco: Ignatius Press, 1988.
de Lubac, Henri. 'Christian Community and Sacramental Communion'. In *Theological Fragments*, pp. 71–76. Translated by Rebecca Howell Balinkski. San Francisco: Ignatius Press, 1989.
de Lubac, Henri. 'Christian Explanation of Our Times'. In *Theology in History*, pp. 440–56. Translated by Anne Englund Nash. San Francisco: Ignatius Press, 1996.
de Lubac, Henri. *The Christian Faith: An Essay on the Structure of the Apostle's Creed*. Translated by Richard Arnandez. San Francisco: Ignatius Press, 1986.
de Lubac, Henri. *Christian Resistance to Anti-Semitism: Memories from 1940–1944*. Translated by Elizabeth Englund. San Francisco: Ignatius Press, 1990.
de Lubac, Henri. *The Church: Paradox and Mystery*. Translated by James R. Dunne. Staten Island, NY: Alba House, 1969.
de Lubac, Henri. 'Le combat spirituel', *Cité nouvelle* (1943): pp. 769–83.
de Lubac, Henri. 'The Conditions of Ontological Affirmation as Set Forth in *L'Action* by Maurice Blondel (1899)'. In *Theological Fragments*, pp. 377–92. Translated by Rebecca Howell Balinski. San Francisco: Ignatius Press, 1989.
de Lubac, Henri. *Corpus Mysticum: The Eucharist and the Church in the Middle Ages*. Translated by Gemma Simmonds, Richard Price, and Christopher Stephens; Edited by Laurence Paul Hemming and Susan Frank Parsons. Indiana: University of Notre Dame Press, 2007.

de Lubac, Henri. *De la connaissance de Dieu*. Paris: Editions du Témoignage Chrétien, 1945.
de Lubac, Henri. 'Deux augustiniens fourvoyés'. *Recherches de science religieuse* 21 (1931): pp. 422–43, 513–40.
de Lubac, Henri. *The Discovery of God*. Translated by Alexander Dru; Footnotes translated by Mark Sebanc and Cassian Fulsom. Edinburgh: T&T Clark, 1996.
de Lubac, Henri. *The Drama of Atheist Humanism*. Translated by Edith M. Riley, Anne Englund Nash, and Mark Sebanc. San Francisco: Ignatius Press, 1995.
de Lubac, Henri. 'Duplex Hominis Beatitudo', *Communio* 25 (Winter 2008): pp. 599–612.
de Lubac, Henri. 'Duplex Hominis Beatitudo'. *Recherches de science religieuse* 35 (1948): pp. 290–99.
de Lubac, Henri. 'L'Église dan la Crise Actuelle', *Nouvelle Revue Theologique* 91 (1969): pp. 580–96.
de Lubac, Henri. 'Esprit et liberté dans la tradition théologique'. *Bulletin de literature ecclésiastique* 40 (1939): pp. 121–50, 189–207.
de Lubac, Henri. *The Eternal Feminine: A Study on the Poem by Teilhard de Chardin, Followed by Teilhard and the Problems of Today*. Translated by René Hague. New York: Harper and Row, 1971.
de Lubac, Henri. *Exégèse Médiévale. Les quatre sens de l'écriture*, 4 vols. Paris: Aubier-Montaigne, 1959–1964.
de Lubac, Henri. *The Faith of Teilhard de Chardin*. Translated by René Hague. London: Burns & Oates, 1965.
de Lubac, Henri. *History and Spirit: The Understanding of Scripture According to Origen*. Translation from French by Anne Englund Nash; Greek and Latin translation by Juvenal Merriell. San Francisco: Ignatius Press, 2007.
de Lubac, Henri. 'L'idée chrétien de l'homme et la recherche d'un homme nouvea', *Etudes*, October, November (1947): pp. 1–25, 145–69.
de Lubac, Henri. 'Internal Causes of the Weakening and Disappearance of the Sense of the Sacred'. In *Theology in History*, pp. 223–40. Translated by Anne Englund Nash. San Francisco: Ignatius Press, 1996.
de Lubac, Henri. 'The Light of Christ'. In *Theology in History*, pp. 201–20. Translated by Anne Englund Nash. San Francisco: Ignatius Press, 1996.
de Lubac, Henri. *Letters of Étienne Gilson to Henri de Lubac*. Translated by Mary Emily Hamilton. San Francisco: Ignatius Press, 1988.
de Lubac, Henri. 'Letter to My Superiors'. In *Theology in History*, pp. 428–39. Translated by Anne Englund Nash. San Francisco: Ignatius Press, 1996.
de Lubac, Henri. *Lettres de M. Étienne Gilson adressées au P. Henri de Lubac et commentées par celui-ci*. Paris: Cerf, 1986.
de Lubac, Henri. *Medieval Exegesis*, 3 vols. Grand Rapids, MI: William B. Eerdmans Publishing Company, 1998, 2000, 2009.
de Lubac, Henri. *Mémoire sur l'occasion de mes écrits*. Paris: Cerf, 2006.
de Lubac, Henri. 'Le motif de la création dans *L'Être et les êtres* de Maurice Blondel', *Nouvelle revue théologique* 65 (1938): pp. 220–25.
de Lubac, Henri. *The Motherhood of the Church: Followed by Particular Churches in the Universal Church*. Translated by Sr. Sergia Englund. San Francisco: Ignatius Press, 1982.
de Lubac, Henri. 'Le mystère du surnaturel', *Recherches de Science Religieuse* 36 (1949): pp. 80–121.
de Lubac, Henri. *Le Mystère du Surnaturel*. Paris: Aubier, 1965.

de Lubac, Henri. 'The Mystery of the Supernatural'. In *Theology in History*, pp. 281–316. Translated by Anne Englund Nash. San Francisco: Ignatius Press, 1996.

de Lubac, Henri. *The Mystery of the Supernatural*. Translated by Rosemary Sheed. Introduction by David L. Schindler. New York: The Crossroad Publishing Company, 1998.

de Lubac, Henri. 'Mysticism and Mystery'. In *Theological Fragments*, pp. 35–69. Translated by Rebecca Howell Balinkski. San Francisco: Ignatius Press, 1989.

de Lubac, Henri. 'Nature and Grace'. In *The Word in History*, pp. 24–40. Edited by T. Patrick Burke. New York: Sheed and Ward, 1966.

de Lubac, Henri. 'The New Man: The Marxist and the Christian View', *Dublin Review* 442 (1948): pp. 5–35.

de Lubac, Henri. 'On an Old Distich: The Doctrine of the "Fourfold Sense" in Scripture'. In *Theological Fragments*, pp. 109–38. Translated by Rebecca Howell Balinski. San Francisco: Ignatius Press, 1989.

de Lubac, Henri. 'On Christian Philosophy', *Communio* 19, no. 3 (1992): pp. 478–506.

de Lubac, Henri. 'The Origin of Religion'. In *Theological Fragments*, pp. 309–32. Translated by Rebecca Howell Balinski. San Francisco: Ignatius Press, 1989.

de Lubac, Henri. *Paradoxes of Faith*. San Francisco: Ignatius Press, 1987.

de Lubac, Henri. 'Paul VI, pèlerin de Jérusalem', *Christus* 41 (January 1964): pp. 97–102.

de Lubac, Henri. 'Petite catéchèse sur la "nature" et la "grace"', *Revue international Communio II*, no. 4 (1977): pp. 11–23.

de Lubac, Henri. *Petite catéchèse sur nature et grace*. Paris: Fayard, 1980.

de Lubac, Henri. *Pic de La Mirandole: Études et discussions*. Aubier-Montaigne, 1974.

de Lubac, Henri. *La Postérité spirituelle de Joachim de Flore*, 2 vols. Paris: Lethielleux, 1978, 1981.

de Lubac, Henri. 'The Problem of the Development of Dogma'. In *Theology in History*, pp. 248–80. Translated by Anne Englund Nash. San Francisco: Ignatius Press, 1996.

de Lubac, Henri. 'À propos de la conception medieval de l'ordre surnaturel (Échange de vues avec J. De Blic)', *Melanges de science religieuse* 4 (1947): pp. 365–73.

de Lubac, Henri. *Proudhon et le christianisme*. Paris: Éditions de Seuil, 1945.

de Lubac, Henri. 'La recontre de "superadditum" et de "supernatural" dans la théologie medieval'. *Revue du Moyen Âge Latin* 1 (1945): pp. 27–34.

de Lubac, Henri. *La recontré du Buddhisme et de l'Occident*. Paris: Aubier, 1952.

de Lubac, Henri. 'Remarques sur l'histoire du mot "surnaturel"', *Nouvelle Revue théologique* 61 (1934): pp. 225–49, 350–70.

de Lubac, Henri. *La Révélation divine*. In *Révélation divine; Affrontements mystiques; Athéisme et sens de l'homme*, 36–230. Paris: Cerf, 2006.

de Lubac, Henri. 'Saint Thomas: *Compendium theologiae*, c. 104'. *Recherches de science religieuse* 36 (1949): pp. 300–5.

de Lubac, Henri. 'Sanctorum Communio'. In *Theological Fragments*, pp. 11–34. Translated by Rebecca Howell Balinski. San Francisco: Ignatius Press, 1989.

de Lubac, Henri. 'The Search for a New Man'. In *The Drama of Atheist Humanism*, pp. 399–468. Translated by Edith M. Riley, Anne Englund Nash, and Mark Sebanc. San Francisco: Ignatius Press, 1995.

de Lubac, Henri. *The Sources of Revelation*. Translated by Luke O'Neill. New York: Herder and Herder, 1968.

de Lubac, Henri. 'Spiritual Warfare'. In *Theology in History*, pp. 488–501. Translated by Anne Englund Nash. San Francisco: Ignatius Press, 1996.

de Lubac, Henri. *The Splendor of the Church*. Translated by Michael Mason. San Francisco: Ignatius Press, 1986.
de Lubac, Henri. 'The "Supernatural" at Vatican II'. In *A Brief Catechesis on Nature and Grace*, pp. 177–90. Translated by Richard Arnandez. San Francisco: Ignatius Press, 1984.
de Lubac, Henri. 'Sur la philosophie chrétienne: Réflexions à la suite d'un débat', *Nouvelle revue théologique* (March 1936): pp. 225–53.
de Lubac, Henri. *Sur les chemins de Dieu*. Paris: Aubier, 1956.
de Lubac, Henri. *Surnaturel: Études historiques*. Paris: Éditions Desclée de Brouwer, 1991.
de Lubac, Henri. 'The Theological Foundation of the Missions'. In *Theology in History*, pp. 367–427. Translated by Anne Englund Nash. San Francisco: Ignatius Press, 1996.
de Lubac, Henri. *Theological Fragments*. Translated by Rebecca Howell Balinski. San Francisco: Ignatius Press, 1989.
de Lubac, Henri. *Theology in History*. Translated by Anne Englund Nash. San Francisco: Ignatius Press, 1996.
de Lubac, Henri. *Three Jesuits Speak*. San Francisco: Ignatius, 1987.
de Lubac, Henri. 'The Total Meaning of Man and the World', *Communio* Winter 35 (2008): pp. 613–41.
de Lubac, Henri. '"Typologie" et "Allégorisme"', *Recherches Science Religieuse* 34 (1947): pp. 180–226.
de Lubac, Henri. *Universal Church and an Interview Conducted by Gwendoline Jarczyk*. San Francisco: Ignatius Press, 1982.
de Lubac, Henri. *The Un-Marxian Socialist: A Study of Proudhon*. Translated by R. E. Scantlebury. New York: Sheed & Ward, 1948.
de Lubac, Henri. *Vatican Council Notebooks*, vol. I. San Francisco, CA: Ignatius Press, 2015.
de Lubac, Henri. 'Zum katholische Dialog mit Karl Barth', *Dokumente:Zeitschrift für übernationale Zusammenarbeit* 14, no. 6 (1958): pp. 448–54.
de Lubac, Henri and Angelo Scola. *De Lubac: A Theologian Speaks*. Los Angeles, CA: Twin Circles Publishing Company, 1985.

Ecclesial Documents

Council of Trent. '*Decretum de canonicis Scripturis*'. In Heinrich Denzinger, ed., *Enchiridion symbolorum et declarationum*, p. 1501. Freiburg: Herder, 2001.
Pope Benedict XVI. 'Address to the Roman Curia (22 December 2005)', *Acta Apostolicae Sedis* 98 (2006): pp. 44–45.
Pope Benedict XVI. '*Spe salvi*. Encyclical Letter on Christian Hope', *Acta Apostolici Sedis* 99 (2007): pp. 985–1027.
Pope John Paul II. *Catechism of the Catholic Church*. Liguori, MO: Liguori Publications, 1994.
Pope John Paul II. '*Dives in misericordia*', Encyclical Letter on the Revelation of Mercy, *Acta Apostolici Sedis* 72 (30 November 1980): pp. 1177–232.
Pope John Paul II. '*Familiaris Consortio*. Apostolic Exhortation on the Role of the Christian Family in the Modern World (22 November 1981)', *Acta Apostolici Sedis* 74: (1982): pp. 91–92.

Pope John Paul II. '*Redemptor hominis*', *Acta Apostolici Sedis* 71 (4 March 1979): pp. 257–324.
Pope Leo X. '*Apostolici Regiminis*'. In Heinrich Denzinger, ed., *Enchiridion symbolorum et declarationum*, p. 1440. Freiburg: Herder, 2001.
Pope Leo XIII. '*Aeterni Patris*: Encyclical Letter on the Restoration of Christian Philosophy', *Acta Sanctae Sedis* 12 (4 August 1879): pp. 97–115.
Pope Leo XIII. '*Arcanum Divinae Sapientiae*', Encyclical Letter on Christian Marriage. *Acta Sanctae Sedis* 12 (1880): pp. 388–91.
Pope Pius X. '*Pascendi Dominici Gregis*', Encyclical Letter on the Doctrines of the Modernists, *Acta Apostolici Sedis* 40 (8 September 1907): pp. 593–650.
Pope Pius XII. '*Humani generis*', Encyclical Letter Concerning Some False Opinions Threatening to Undermine the Foundations of Catholic Doctrine, *Acta Apostolici Sedis* 42 (12 August 1950): pp. 561–78.
Second Vatican Council. '*Gaudium et Spes*: Pastoral Constitution on the Church in the Modern World'. In Austin Flannery, ed., *Vatican Council II: Constitutions, Decrees, Declarations*, pp. 163–282. New York: Costello Publishing Company, 2007.
Second Vatican Council. '*Lumen Gentium*: Dogmatic Constitution on the Church'. In Austin Flannery, ed., *Vatican Council II: Constitutions, Decrees, Declarations*, pp. 1–96. New York: Costello Publishing Company, 2007.

Other Works Cited

Albado, Omar César. 'La reflexión sobre la temporalidad en la teología de Henri de Lubac', *Teología* 100 (2009): pp. 465–80.
Alberigo, Giuseppe. *A Brief History of Vatican II*. Translated by Matthew Sherry. Maryknoll, NY: Orbis, 2006.
Alberigo, Giuseppe, ed. *Historia del Concilio Vaticano II*, 5 vols. Salamanca: Ediciones Sigueme, 1999–2008.
Alberigo, Giuseppe, ed. *Storia del Concilio Vaticano II*, 5 vols. Bologna: Il Mulino, 1995–2001.
Alberigo, Giuseppe and Joseph A. Komonchak, eds. *History of Vatican II*, 5 vols. Maryknoll, NY: Orbis, 1995–2006.
Aldana, Ricardo. 'Las *Notas del Concilio* de Henri de Lubac', *Toletana* 18 (2008): pp. 357–78.
Allen, A. Mrówczynski-Van. *Between the Icon and the Idol*. Oregon: Cascade Publications, 2014.
Allen, John L. Jr. *Pope Benedict XVI: A Biography of Joseph Ratzinger*. London: Continuum, 2005.
Anonymous. 'La Theologie et Ses Sources: Réponse', *Reserches de Science Religieuses* 33 (1946): pp. 385–401.
Aquinas, Thomas. *Commentary on the Book of Causes*. Translated by Vincent A. Guagliardo, O. P., Charles R. Hess, O. P., and Richard C. Taylor. Washington, DC: The Catholic University Press of America, 1996.
Aquinas, Thomas. *Compendium of Theology*. Translated by Richard J. Regan. Oxford: Oxford University Press, 2009.
Aquinas, Thomas. *Expositio super librum Boethii de Trinitate*. Edited by Bruno Decker. Leiden: E. J. Brill, 1955.

Aquinas, Thomas. *Summa contra Gentiles*, 4 vols. Translated by A. Pegis, J. Anderson, V. J. Burke, and C. J. O'Neil. Garden City: Doubleday, 1955–1956.

Aquinas, Thomas. *Summa Theologiae*. Edited and translated by Thomas Gilby, et al. New York: McGraw-Hill, 1964–1981. Reprinted by Cambridge: Cambridge University Press, 2008.

Aquinas, Thomas. *Summa Theologica*. Translated by the English Dominican Province. New York: Benziger Brothers, 1947.

Aquinas, Thomas. *De veritate*. In *Sancti Thomae de Aquino opera Omnia*, vol. 22. Leonine Edition. Rome: Editori di San Tommaso, 1975–1976.

Atack, Margaret. *Literature and the French Resistance: Cultural Politics and Narrative Forms, 1940–1950*. New York: St Martin's Press, 1989.

Augustine. *The City of God*. Edited by Boniface Ramsey. New York: New City Press, 2012.

Augustine. *Commentary on Galatians*. Translated by Eric Plumer. Oxford: Oxford University Press, 2003.

Augustine. *Confessions*. Edited by R. S. Pine-Coffin. London, Penguin, 1961.

Augustine. *Letters*, 4 vols. Translated by Roland Teske. New York: New City, 2001–2005.

Augustine. *On Christian Belief*. Translated by Matthew O'Connell. New York: New City, 2005.

Augustine. 'Sermon 57'. In John E. Rotelle, ed., *The Works of St. Augustine: A Translation for the 21st Century: Sermons 51–94*. Translated by Edmund Hill. Brooklyn, NY: New City Press, 1991.

Augustine. *Tractates on the Gospel of John: 11–27*. Edited by John W. Retting. Washington, DC: Catholic University of America Press, 1994.

Ayres, Lewis. 'The Soul and the Reading of Scripture: A Note on Henri de Lubac', *Scottish Journal of Theology* 61 (2008): pp. 173–90.

Baius, Michael. *Opuscula Theologica*. Louvain: Joannes Bogard, 1566.

Balthasar, Hans Urs von. *Apokalypse der deutschen Seele: Studien zu einerlehre von letzen Haltunger*, 3 vols. Einsiedeln: Johannes Verlag, 1998.

Balthasar, Hans Urs von. *Explorations in Theology*, vol. 3, *Creator Spirit*. Translated by Brian McNeil. San Francisco: Ignatius, 1993.

Balthasar, Hans Urs von. 'Georges Bernanos on Reason: Prophetic, Free and Catholic', *Communio: International Catholic Review* 23 (Summer 1996): pp. 389–418.

Balthasar, Hans Urs von. *Pour une philosophie chrétienne*. Paris: Sycamore, 1983.

Balthasar, Hans Urs von. *Test Everything: Hold Fast to What Is Good*. San Francisco: Ignatius Press, 1989.

Balthasar, Hans Urs von. *The Theology of Henri de Lubac*. San Francisco: Ignatius Press, 1991.

Balthasar, Hans Urs von. *The Theology of Karl Barth*. San Francisco: Ignatius Press, 1992.

Barrau, Grégory. *Le Mai 68 des catholiques*. Paris: Les Éditions de l'Atelier, 1998.

Bars, Henri. 'Gilson et Maritain', *Revue Thomiste* 7 (1979): pp. 237–71.

Barth, Karl. *The Church and the Churches*. Grand Rapids, MI: Eerdmans, 2005.

Barth, Karl. *Church Dogmatics*, III/2: *The Doctrine of Creation*. Translated by Harold Knight, et al. Edinburgh: T&T Clark, 1960.

Barth, Karl. 'The First Commandment as an Axion of Theology'. In H.-M. Rumscheidt and Allison Park, eds, *The Way of Theology in Karl Barth: Essays and Comments*, pp. 63–78. Allison Park, PA: Pickwick, 1986.

Baur, F. C. *Die christliche Lehre von der Versöhnung in ihrer geschichtlichen Entwicklung von der ältesten Zeit bis auf die neuste*. Tübingen: Osiander, 1838.

Bautain, Louis. *De l'enseignement de la philosophie en France au xixe siècle*. Paris: Derivaux, 1833.
Bellelli, Fulgenzio. *Mens Augustini de creaturae rationalis ante peccatum*. Lucerne: Anna Felicitas Hauttin, 1711.
Bellelli, Fulgenzio. *Mens Augustini de modo reparationis humanae naturae post lapsum adversus Baium et Jansenium*, 2 vols. Rome: Bernabò, 1737.
Belsole, Kurt. 'Guéranger, Prosper 1805–1875'. In William Johnson, ed., *Encyclopedia of Monasticism: A-L*, pp. 558–59. Chicago: Fitzroy Dearborn, 2000.
Benedict XVI. 'What Has Been the Result of the Council?' In Norman Tanner, ed. *Vatican II: The Essential Texts*. New York: Image, 2012.
Bergin, Liam. *O Propheticum Lavacrum*. Rome: Pontifical Gregorian University, 1999.
Bernardi, Peter J. 'Maurice Blondel and the Renewal of the Nature-Grace Relationship', *Communio: International Catholic Review* 26 (Winter 1999): pp. 806–45.
Bernardi, Peter J. *Maurice Blondel, Social Catholicism and Action Française: The Clash over the Church's Role in Society during the Modernist Era*. Washington, DC: CUA Press, 2009.
Bernauer, James. 'A Jesuit Spiritual Insurrection: Resistance to Vichy'. In James Bernauer and Robert A. Maryks, eds, *'The Tragic Couple': Encounters between Jews and Jesuits*, pp. 203–18. Boston: Brill, 2014.
Berti, Giovanni. *De theologicis disciplinis*, 10 vols. Naples: Gaetano Migliaccio, 1776–1784.
Blanchette, Oliva. *Maurice Blondel: A Philosophical Life*. Grand Rapids, MI: William B. Eerdmans, 2010.
Bloch, Ernst. *The Principle of Hope*, vol. 2. Translated by Neville Plaice, Stephen Plaice, and Paul Knight. Cambridge, MA: MIT Press, 1995.
Blondel, Maurice. *Action (1893): Essay on a Critique of Life and a Science of Practice*. Translated by Oliva Blanchette. Notre Dame, IN: University of Notre Dame Press, 2007.
Blondel, Maurice. 'Does Christian Philosophy Exist as Philosophy?' In Gregory B. Sadler, ed., *Reason Fulfilled by Revelation: The 1930s Christian Philosophy Debates in France*. Washington, DC: Catholic University of America Press, 2010.
Blondel, Maurice. *L'Etre et les êtres. Essai d'ontologie concrete et intégrale*. Paris: Alcan, 1935.
Blondel, Maurice. *The Letter on Apologetics and History and Dogma*. Translation by Alexander Dru and Illtyd Trethowan. Grand Rapids, MI: William B. Eerdmans Publishing Company, 1964.
Blondel, Maurice. *Lettre sure les Exigences de la Pensée Contemporaine en Matière d'Apologétique*. Paris: PUF, 1956.
Blondel, Maurice. *Lettres Philosophiques*. Paris: Aubier, 1961.
Blondel, Maurice. *Le Problème de la philosophie catholique*. Paris: Bloud et Gay, 1932.
Blondel, Maurice. 'The Third "Testis" Article', trans. Peter Bernardi, *Communio* 26 (Winter 1999): pp. 846–74.
Blondel, Maurice, et al. 'La notion de philosophie chrétienne', *Bulletin de la société française de la philosophie* 31 (1931): pp. 37–93.
Blondel, Maurice, et al. 'La querelle de l'athéisme', *Bulletin de la Société française de la philosophie* 28 (1928): pp. 45–95.
Bocxe, Winfried. *Introduction to the Teaching of the Italian Augustinians of the 18th Century on the Nature of Actual Grace*. Louvain: Augustinian Historical Institute, 1958.
Boersma, Hans. *Nouvelle Théologie and Sacramental Ontology: A Return to Mystery*. Oxford: Oxford University Press, 2009.

Boersma, Hans. 'Sacramental Ontology: Nature and Supernature in the Ecclesiology of Henri de Lubac', *New Blackfriars* 88, no. 1015 (May 2007): pp. 242–73.
Bonhoeffer, Dietrich. *Life Together: The Classic Exploration of Faith in Community*. San Francisco, CA: Harper San Francisco, 1954.
Bonino, Serge-Thomas, ed. *Surnaturel: A Controversy at the Heart of Twentieth-Century Thomistic Thought*. Translated by Robert Williams and Matthew Levering. Ave Maria, FL: Sapientia Press, 2009.
Bonino, Serge-Thomas. 'To Be a Thomist', *Nova et Vetera* 8, no. 4 (Fall 2010): pp. 763–75.
Bosco, M. 'Georges Bernanos and Francis Poulenc: Catholic Convergences in Dialogues of the Carmelites', *Logos* 12, no. 2 (Spring 2009): pp. 17–40.
Bouillard, Henri. *Karl Barth*, 3 vols. Paris: Aubier, 1957.
Bouyer, Louis. 'Mysticism: An Essay in the History of the Word'. In Richard Woods, ed., *Understanding Mysticism*, pp. 42–53. New York: Doubleday, 1980.
Boyer, Charles. *Cursus philosophiae ad usum seminariorum*, vol. II. Paris: Desclée De Brouwer, 1937.
Boyer, Charles. 'Nature pure et surnaturel dans le *Surnaturel* du Père de Lubac', *Gregorianum* 28 (1947): pp. 377–95.
Boyer, Charles. *Tractatus de Deo creante et elevante*. Rome: Aedes Universitatis Gregorianae, 1933.
Braine, David. 'Henri de Lubac and His Critics', *Nova et Vetera* 6, no. 3 (Summer 2008): pp. 543–91.
Brandewie, Ernest. *Wilhelm Schmidt and the Origin of the Idea of God*. Lanham, MD: University Press of America, 1983.
Bredin, Jean-Denis. *The Affair: The Case of Alfred Dreyfus*. Translated by Jeffrey Mehlman. New York: George Braziller, 1983.
Bretherton, Luke. *Christianity and Contemporary Politics: The Conditions and Possibilities of Faithful Witness*. Chichester, UK: Wiley-Blackwell, 2010.
Buckley, Cornelius. *When Jesuits Were Giants: Louis-Marie Ruellan, S.J. (1846–1885) and Contemporaries*. San Francisco: Ignatius, 1999.
Cajetan, Thomas. *Commentaria in primam partem*. Rome: Leonina, 1988–1989.
Calvez, Jean-Yves. *Chrétiens, penseurs du social*, Histoire de la morale. Paris: Éditions du Cerf, 2008.
Calvez, Jean-Yves. 'The French Catholic Contribution to Social and Political Thinking in the 1930s', *Ethical Perspectives: Journal of the European Ethics Network* 7, no. 4 (December 2000): pp. 312–15.
Calvez, Jean-Yves. 'Relire *Catholicisme* de Henri de Lubac', *Études* (Octobre 1991): pp. 371–78.
Calvin, John. *Institutes of the Christian Religion*. Edited by John T. McNeil, Translated by Ford Lewis Battles. Louisville, KY: Westminster John Knox Press, 2006.
Carraud, Vincent. 'Une oeuvre nécessairement immense', *Communio* 17, no. 5 (1992): pp. 8–12.
Cavanaugh, William T. *Theopolitical Imagination: Christian Practices of Space and Time*. New York: T&T Clark, 2002.
Cavanaugh, William T. *Torture and Eucharist*. Malden, MA: Wiley-Blackwell, 1998.
Chantraine, Georges. 'Le cardinal Henri de Lubac', *Communio* 16, nos. 5–6 (1991): pp. 155–61.
Chantraine, Georges. *Henri de Lubac, t. I: De la naissance à la démobilisation (1896–1919)*. Paris: Cerf, 2007.
Chantraine, Georges. *Henri de Lubac, t. II: Les années de formation (1919–1929)*. Paris: Cerf, 2009.

Chantraine, Georges. 'Henri de Lubac. Pourquoi ses oeuvres nous parlent', *Nouvelle revue théologique* 121 (1999): pp. 612–29.
Chantraine, Georges. 'Logique théologique chez Henri de Lubac', *Nouvelle revue théologique* 115 (1993): pp. 543–59.
Chantraine, Georges. 'The Supernatural: Discernment of Catholic Thought According to Henri de Lubac'. In Serge-Thomas Bonino, ed., *Surnaturel: A Controversy at the Heart of Twentieth-Century Thomistic Thought*, pp. 21–40. Ave Maria, FL: Sapienta Press.
Chantraine, Georges. 'Le Surnaturel. Discernement de la pensée catholique selon Henri de Lubac', *Revue Thomiste* (Janvier–Juin 2001): pp. 31–51.
Chantraine, Georges. 'La théologie du surnaturel selon Henri de Lubac', *Nouvelle revue théologique* 119 (1997): pp. 218–35.
Chantraine, Georges and Marie-Gabrielle Lemaire. *Henri de Lubac, tome IV: Concile et après-Concile (1960–1991)*. Paris: Cerf, 2013.
Charbonnier, Jean-Pierre. *Christians in China, A.D. 600 to 2000*. Translated by M. N. L. Couve de Murville. San Francisco: Ignatius, 2007.
Charles, Pierre. 'La Théologie dogmatique hier et aujourd'hui', *Nouvelle revue théologique* 56 (1929): pp. 800–17.
Chenu, Marie-Dominique. *Faith and Theology*. New York: The Macmillan Company, 1968.
Chenu, Marie-Dominique. 'La position de la théologie', *Revue des Sciences Philosophiques et Théologiques* 24 (1935): pp. 232–57.
Chenu, Marie-Dominique. *La théologie comme science aux XIIIe siècle*. Paris: Vrin, 1957.
Chenu, Marie-Dominique. *Une école de théologie: Le Saulchoir*. Paris: Cerf, 1985.
Clarke, W. Norris. *The Creative Retrieval of Saint Thomas Aquinas: Essays in Thomistic Philosophy, New and Old*. New York: Fordham University Press, 2009.
Claudel, Paul. *Interroge L'Apocalypse*. Paris: Gallimard, 1952.
Coakley, Sarah. *God, Sexuality, and the Self: An Essay 'On the Trinity'*. Cambridge, UK: Cambridge University Press, 2013.
Cointet, Michèle. *L'Église sous Vichy, 1940–1945: La repentence en question*. Paris: Librairie Académique Perrin, 1998.
Colombo, Giuseppe. 'Genesi, storia e significato dell'enciclica "Ecclesiam suam"'. In *'Ecclesiam suam' première lettre encyclique de Paul VI. Colloque internationale (Rome 24–25 octobre 1980)*, pp. 131–60. Rome: Edizioni Studium, 1982.
Congar, Yves. *I Believe in the Holy Spirit*. Translated by David Smith. New York: Crossroad, 1999.
Congar, Yves. *Journal d'un théologien: 1946–1956*. Paris: Cerf, 2001.
Congar, Yves. *My Journal of the Council*. Translated by Mary John Ronayne, et al. Collegeville, MI: Liturgical Press, 2012.
Congar, Yves. *Tradition and Traditions*. London: Burns and Oates, 1960–1963.
Contreni, John. 'Review of *Medieval Exegesis, Vol 1: The Four Senses of Scripture*', *The Medieval Review* (1999): https://scholarworks.iu.edu/journals/index.php/tmr/article/view/14822/20940
Coolman, Boyd Taylor. *Knowing God by Experience: The Spiritual Senses in the Theology of William of Auxerre*. Washington, DC: Catholic University of America Press, 2004.
Corvez, Maurice. 'De la connaissance de Dieu', *Revue Thomiste* 48, no. 3 (1948): pp. 511–24.
Cottier, Georges. *Le désir de Dieu: Sur les traces de saint Thomas*. Paris: Parole et Silence, 2002.
Courtenay, William. *Parisian Scholars in the Early Fourteenth Century: A Social Portrait*. Cambridge: Cambridge University Press, 1999.

Cuchet, Guillaume. 'Comment Dieu est-il acteur de l'histoire?' *Revue des Sciences Philosophiques et Théologiques* 96 (2012): pp. 33–55.
Cunningham, Conor. *Darwin's Pious Idea: Why the Creationists and Ultra-Darwinists Both Get It Wrong*. Grand Rapids, MI: Eerdmans Publishing Company, 2013.
Cunningham, Conor. '*Natura Pura*, The Invention of the Anti-Christ: A Week with No Sabbath', *Communio* 37 (Summer 2010): pp. 243–54.
Cyprian of Carthage. *The Letters of St. Cyprian of Carthage*, 4 vols. Translated by G. W. Clarke. New York: Newman, 1984–1989.
Daley, Brian. 'The Nouvelle Théologie and the Patristic Revival: Sources, Symbols and the Science of Theology', *International Journal of Systematic Theology* 7, no. 4 (November 2005): pp. 362–82.
D'Ambrosio, Marcellino. *Henri de Lubac and the Recovery of the Traditional Hermeneutic*. PhD dissertation: Catholic University of America, 1991.
Daniélou, Jean. 'The Conception of History in the Christian Tradition', *Journal of Religion* 30, no. 3 (1950): pp. 171–79.
Daniélou, Jean. *From Shadows to Reality: Studies in the Biblical Typology of the Fathers*. Translated by Wulstan Hibberd. London: Burns & Oates, 1960.
Daniélou, Jean. 'Les divers sens de l'Écriture dans la tradition chrétienne primitive', *Ephemerides Theologicae Lovanienses* 24 (1948): pp. 119–26.
Daniélou, Jean. 'Les Orientations présentes de la pensée religieuse', *Études* 251 (April 1946): pp. 5–21.
Daniélou, Jean. 'Traversée de la Mer Rouge et baptême aux premiers siècles', *Recherches Science Religieuse* 33 (1946): pp. 402–30.
Davison, Andrew, ed. *Imaginative Apologetics: Theology, Philosophy and the Catholic Tradition*. London: SCM Press, 2011.
Davison, Andrew. *The Love of Wisdom: An Introduction to Philosophy for Theologians*. London: SCM Press, 2013.
Dawson, John David. 'Figural Reading and the Fashioning of Christian Identity in Boyarin, Auerbach and Frei', *Modern Theology* 14, no. 2 (April 1998): pp. 181–96.
Deason, Gary. 'Reformation Theology and the Mechanistic Conception of Nature'. In David Lindberg and Ronald Numbers, eds, *God and Nature: Historical Essays on the Encounter between Christianity and Science*, pp. 167–91. Los Angeles: University of California Press, 1986.
de Berranger, Olivier. 'Lubac Henri Sonier de'. In Jean-Yves Lacoste, ed., *Dictionnaire critique de théologie*. Paris: Presses Universitaires de France, 1998, pp. 675–77.
de Broglie, Albert. *L'Église et l'Empire romain au IVe siècle*. Paris: Didier, 1857.
de Chardin, Pierre Teilhard. *Le Milieu Divin: Essai de Vie Intérieure*. Paris: Ed. du Seuil, 1957.
de Chateaubriand, François-René. *Le génie du christianisme*. Paris: Migneret, 1802.
de Finance, J. *Éthique générale*. Rome: Presses de l'Université Grégorienne, 1967.
de Lamennais, Félicité. *Défense de l'essai sur l'indifférence en matière de religion*. Paris: Méquignon Fils Aîné, 1821.
de Lamennais, Félicité. *Les paroles d'un croyant*. Paris: Eugène Renduel, 1833.
Delporte, L. 'Les principes de la typologie biblique', *Ephemerides Theologicae Lovanienses* 3 (1926): pp. 307–27.
de Mattei, Roberto. *The Second Vatican Council: An Unwritten Story*. Translated by Michael M. Miller, et al. Fitzwilliam, NH: Loreto Publications, 2012.
de Montcheuil, Yves. *Le Royaume et ses Exigeances*. Paris: Epi, 1957.

de Mortier, Jean-Baptiste, ed. *Conférences du Révérend Père Lacordaire des Frères Prêcheurs; précédés d'une notice biographique par P. Lorain*, 2nd ed. Brussels: L'Académie Royale de Médicine, 1852.

Dondyne, Albert. *Contemporary European Thought and Christian Faith*. Pittsburg: Duquesne University Press, 1962.

Donnelly, Philip. 'Baius and Baianism'. In *The New Catholic Encyclopedia*, vol. 2, 2nd ed. Detroit: Gale, 2003.

Donnelly, Philip. 'Discussions on the Supernatural Order', *Theological Studies* 9, no. 2 (1948): pp. 213–49.

Doyle, Dennis M. *Communion Ecclesiology: Vision and Versions*. Maryknoll: Orbis, 2000.

Dru, Alexander. 'From the *Action Française* to the Second Vatican Council: Blondel's La Semaine sociale de Bordeaux', *Downside Review* (July 1963): pp. 226–45.

Dulles, Avery. *A History of Apologetics*. San Francisco: Ignatius Press, 2005.

Dumas, Bertrand. *Mystique et théologie d'après Henri de Lubac*. Paris: Cerf, 2013.

Durand, Jean-Dominique. *Henri de Lubac: La rencontre au coeur de l'Eglise*. Paris: Cerf, 2006.

Fabriziani, Anna. *Blondel interprete di Tommaso: Tra rinascita del tomismo e condanna del pensiero modernista*. Padua: Antenore, 1984.

Fédou, Michel. *Henri de Lubac. Sa contribution à la pensée chrétienne*. Paris: Médiasèvres, 1996.

Feingold, Lawrence. *The Natural Desire to See God According to St. Thomas Aquinas and His Interpreters*, 2nd ed. Florida: Sapientia Press, 2010.

Feser, Edward. *Scholastic Metaphysics: A Contemporary Introduction*. Editiones Scholoasticae, 2014.

Fessard, Gaston. *De L'actualité historique*. Paris: Desclée, 1960.

Figura, M. *Der Anruf der Gnade: Über die Beziehung des Menschen zu Gott nach Henri de Lubac*. Einsiedeln: Johannes Verlag, 1979.

Flipper, Joseph. *Between Apocalypse and Eschaton: History and Eternity in Henri de Lubac*. Minnesota: Fortress Press, 2015.

Flynn, Gabriel. '*Ressourcement*, Ecumenism, and Pneumatology: The Contribution Yves Congar to *Nouvelle Theology*'. In Gabriel Flynn and Paul Murray, eds, *Ressourcement: A Movement for Renewal in Twentieth-Century Catholic Theology*, pp. 219–35. New York: Oxford, 2012.

Forte, Bruno. 'Nature and Grace in Henri de Lubac: From *Surnaturel* to *Le mystere du surnaturel*', *Communio* 23 (1996): pp. 725–37.

Fouilloux, Etienne. *Une Église en quête de liberté: La pensée catholique française entre modernisme et Vatican, 1914–1962*. Paris: Desclée de Brouwer, 1998.

Fouilloux, Etienne. 'Henri de Lubac at the Moment of the Publication of *Surnaturel*'. In Serge-Thomas Bonino, ed., *Surnaturel: A Controversy at the Heart of Twentieth-Century Thomistic Thought*, pp. 3–20. Florida: Sapientia Press, 2009.

Fowlie, Wallace. *Claudel*. London: Bowes and Bowes, 1957.

Franco Gomes, Vitor. *Le paradoxe du désir de Dieu*. Paris: Cerf, 2005.

Franzelin, J. B. *Tractatus de divina traditione et scriptura*. Rome: Collegio Romano, 1860–1864.

Freeman, Curtis W. *Contesting Catholicity: Theology for Other Baptists*. Waco TX: Baylor University Press, 2014.

Frenay, Henri. *The Night Will End*. Translated by Dan Hofstadter. New York: McGraw-Hill, 1976.

Gardeil, Ambroise. 'L'Action: Ses ressources subjectives', *Revue Thomiste* 7 (1899): pp. 23–39.
Gardeil, Ambroise. 'Ce qu'il y a de vrai dans le néo-Scotisme', *Revue thomiste* 8 (1900): pp. 531–50, *Revue Thomise* 9 (1901): pp. 407–43.
Gardeil, Ambroise. 'Les exigences objectives de l'action', *Revue Thomiste* 6 (1898): pp. 125–38, 269–94.
Gardeil, Ambroise. 'Les ressources de vouloir', *Revue Thomiste* 7 (1899): pp. 447–61.
Gardeil, Ambroise. 'Les ressources de la raison practique', *Revue Thomiste* 8 (1900): pp. 377–99.
Garrigou-Lagrange, Réginald. 'Le désir naturel du bonheur prouve-t-il l'existence de Dieu?' *Angelicum* 8 (1931): pp. 129–48.
Garrigou-Lagrange, Réginald. *God: His Existence and His Nature*, vol. 1. Translated by Don Bede Rose. St Louis, MO: Herder Book Co, 1934.
Garrigou-Lagrange, Réginald. *Grace: Commentary on the Summa Theologica of St. Thomas, Ia IIae, q. 109–114*. St Louis: Herder, 1952.
Garrigou-Lagrange, Réginald. 'La nouvelle théologie. où va-t-elle?', *Angelicum* 23 (1946): pp. 126–45.
Geroulanos, Stefanos. *An Atheism That Is Not Humanist Emerges in French Thought*. Stanford: Stanford University Press, 2010.
Gillman, Ian and Hans-Joachim Klimkeit. *Christians in Asia before 1500*. Richmond: Curzon, 1999.
Gilson, Étienne. *Christianisme et philosophie*. Paris: Vrin, 1936.
Gilson, Étienne. 'The Future of Augustinian Metaphysics'. In *A Monument to St. Augustine*, pp. 289–315. New York: Meridian Books, 1957.
Gotcher, R. F. *Henri de Lubac and Communio: The Significance of His Theology of the Supernatural for an Interpretation of Gaudium et Spes*. PhD dissertation: Marquette University, 2002.
Gratry, Auguste. *Guide to the Knowledge of God*. Translated Abby Alger. Boston: Roberts Brothers, 1892.
Gratry, Auguste. *La Morale et la loi de l'histoire*, 2 vols. Paris: Charles Douniol, 1968.
Greenstock, D. L. 'Thomism and the New Theology', *The Thomist* 13 (1950): pp. 567–96.
Grelot, Marce. *Il rinnovamento biblico nelventesimo secolo: memorie di un protagonist*. Cinisello Balsamo: San Paolo, 1996.
Grillmeier, Aloys. 'The People of God'. In Herbert Vorgrimler, ed., *Commentary on the Documents of Vatican II*, vol. 2, pp. 168–75. New York: Herder and Herder, 1967.
Groppe, Elizabeth. *Yves Congar's Theology of the Holy Spirit*. New York: Oxford, 2004.
Grumett, David. *De Lubac: A Guide for the Perplexed*. London: T&T Clark, 2007.
Grumett, David. 'Henri de Lubac: Looking for Books to Read the World'. In Gabriel Flynn and Paul D. Murray, eds, *Ressourcement: A Movement for Renewal in Twentieth-Century Catholic Theology*, pp. 236–49. Oxford: Oxford University Press, 2012.
Grumett, David. 'Yves de Montcheuil: Action, Justice, and the Kingdom in Spiritual Resistance to Nazism', *Theological Studies* 68 (2007): pp. 618–41.
Grumett, David and Thomas Plant, 'De Lubac, Pure Land Buddhism, and Roman Catholicism', *The Journal of Religion* 92 (2012): pp. 58–83.
Grygiel, S. 'Marriage, Family and New Evangelisation', *Humanitas* no. 2 (2012): pp. 124–29.
Guardini, Romano. *Welt und Person*. Würzburg: Werkbund, 1939.
Gucht, R. van der and H. Vorgrimler, eds. *Bilan de la théologie du XX siecle*. Paris: 1970.

Guéranger, Prosper. *Essais sur le naturalisme contemporain*. Paris: Julien, Lanier, Cosnard, 1858.
Guéranger, Prosper. *Institutions liturgiques*, vol. 2. Le Mans: Fleuriot, 1841.
Guilbert, Etienne. *Le mystère du Christ d'après Henri de Lubac*. Paris: Cerf, 2006.
Gutierrez, Gustavo. *A Theology of Liberation: History, Politics and Salvation*. Maryknoll: Orbis, 1973.
Hall, Douglas J. 'The Great War and the Theologians'. In Gregory Baum, ed., *The Twentieth Century: A Theological Overview*, pp. 3–14. New York: Orbis, 1999.
Hanby, Michael. *No God? No Science?* Oxford: Wiley-Blackwell, 2013.
Hansen, Valerie. *The Silk Road: A New History*. Oxford: Oxford University Press, 2012.
Harnack, Adolf von. *History of Dogma*, vol. VII. Translated by Neil Buchanan. New York: Dover, 1961.
Harrison, Carol. *Romantic Catholics: France's Postrevolutionary Generation in Search of a Modern Faith*. Ithaca: Cornell University Press, 2014,
Healy, Nicholas J. 'Henri de Lubac on Nature and Grace: A Note on Some Recent Contributions to the Debate', *Communio* 35 (Winter 2008): 535–64.
Hendrick-Moser, E. H. 'The Auguste Valensin Controversy and the Historiography of *Nouvelle Théologie*', *Ephemerides Theologicae Lovanienses* 90, no. 1 (2014): pp. 41–70.
Hennesey, J. 'Leo XIII: Intellectualizing the Combat with Modernity', *U.S. Catholic Historian* 7, no. 4 (Fall 1988): pp. 393–400.
Henrici, Peter. 'La descendance blondélienne parmi les jésuites française'. In Emmanuel Gabellieri and Pierre de Cointet, eds, *Maurice Blondel et la philosophie française*, pp. 305–22. Paris: Parole et Silence, 2007.
Hercsik, Donath. *Jesus Christus als Mitte der Theologie von Henri de Lubac*. Francfort: J. Knecht, 2001.
Hervé, J. M. and C. Larnicol. *Manuale Theologiae Dogmaticae*, vol. II. Paris: Apud Berche et Pagis, 1964.
Hick, John and Paul Knitter, eds. *The Myth of Christian Uniqueness*. London: SCM, 1987.
Hillebert, Jordan. 'The Death of God and the Dissolution of Humanity', *New Blackfriars* 95, no. 1060 (November 2014): pp. 674–88.
Hoff, Johannes. *The Analogical Turn: Rethinking Modernity with Nicholas of Cusa*. London: SCM Press, 2013.
Hollon, Bryan C. *Everything Is Sacred: Spiritual Exegesis in the Political Theology of Henri de Lubac*. Oregon: Cascade Books, 2009.
Hollon, Bryan C. 'Knowledge of God as Assimilation and Participation: An Essay on Theological Pedagogy in the Light of Biblical Epistemology', *Perspectives in Religious Studies* 38, no. 1 (Spring 2011): pp. 85–106.
Hsia, R. Po-Chi. *A Jesuit in the Forbidden City*. Oxford: Oxford University Press, 2012.
Huby, Joseph. 'Henri de Lubac, *Surnaturel*', *Etudes historiques*, *Etudes* 251 (1946): pp. 265–68.
Hughes, Kevin L. 'The Fourfold Sense: De Lubac, Blondel, and Contemporary Theology', *The Heythrop Journal* 42, no. 4 (2001): pp. 451–62.
Hughes, Kevin L. '*Ressourcement* and Resistance: *La nouvelle théologie*, the Fathers, and the Bible, against Fascism'. In Daniel Wade McClain and Matthew A. Tapie, eds, *Reading the Bible as Political Act*, pp. 221–40. Minneapolis, MN: Fortress Press, 2015.
Hultgård, Anders. 'Zoroastrian Influences on Judaism, Christianity and Islam'. In Michael Stausberg, ed., *Zarathustra and Zoroastrianism: A Short Introduction*, pp. 101–12. London: Equinox, 2008.

Hütter, Reinhard. 'Aquinas on the Natural Desire for the Vision of God: A *Relecture* of *Summa Contra Gentiles* III, C. 25 *après* Henri De Lubac', *The Thomist* 73 (2009): pp. 523-91.
Hütter, Reinhard. '*Desiderium Naturale Visionis Dei – Est autem duplex hominis beatitudo sive felicitas*: Some Observations about Lawrence Feingold's and John Milbank's Recent Interventions in the Debate over the Natural Desire to See God', *Nova et Vetera* 5 (2007): pp. 133-83.
Hütter, Reinhard. *Dust Bound* for *Heaven: Explorations in the Theology of Thomas Aquinas*. Grand Rapids, MI: William B. Eerdmans Publishing Company, 2012.
Irenaeus. *Against Heresies*. In Ante-Nicene Fathers, vol. I. Edited by Alexander Roberts and James Donaldson. Peabody, MA: Hendrickson, 1994.
Irenaeus. *Demonstration of the Apostolic Preaching*. Translated by J. Armitage Robinson. Aldershot: Ashgate, 2002.
Jackson, Julian. *France: The Dark Years, 1940-1944*. Oxford: Oxford University Press, 2001.
Jansen, Otto. *Augustinus*, 3 vols. Louvain: Jacobus Zegers, 1640.
Jodock, Darrell. *Catholicism Contending with Modernity: Roman Catholic Modernism and Anti-Modernism in Historical Context*. New York: Cambridge, 2000.
John of the Cross. 'The Ascent of Mount Carmel'. In Kieran Kavanaugh, ed., *Selected Writings*. New York: Paulist, 1987.
John Paul II. *Crossing the Threshold of Hope*. New York: Alfred A. Knopf, 1994.
John Paul II. *Rise, Let Us Be on Our Way*. Translated by Walter Ziemba. New York: Warner Books, 2004.
Johnson, Cuthbert. *Prosper Gueranger (1805-1875), A Liturgical Theologian: Introduction to His Liturgical Writings and Work*. Rome: Pontificio Ateneo S. Anselmo, 1984.
Jonas, Hans. *The Phenomenon of Life: Toward a Philosophical Biology*. Evanston, IL: Northwestern University Press, 2001.
Jonas, Hans. *Philosophical Essays*. New York: Atropos Press, 2010.
Kaplan, Grant. *Answering the Enlightenment: The Catholic Recovery of Historical Revelation*. New York: Herder and Herder, 2006.
Kaplan, Grant. 'Roman Catholic Perspectives: The Nineteenth Century'. In Sarah Coakley and Richard Cross, eds, *The Oxford Handbook of the Reception of Christian Theology*. Oxford: Oxford University Press, forthcoming.
Kennedy, A. 'Christopher Dawson's Influence on Bernard Lonergan's Project of "Introducing History into Theology"', *Logos: A Journal of Catholic Thought and Culture* 15, no. 2 (Spring 2012): pp. 138-65.
Kerr, Fergus. *After Aquinas: Versions of Thomism*. Oxford: Blackwell, 2002.
Kerr, Fergus. 'French Theology: Yves Congar and Henri de Lubac'. In David F. Ford, ed., *The Modern Theologians*, pp. 105-17. Oxford: Blackwell, 2000.
Kerr, Fergus. 'Knowing God by Reason Alone: What Vatican I Never Said', *New Blackfriars*, 91 (May 2010): pp. 215-28.
Kerr, Fergus. *Twentieth-Century Catholic Theologians: From Neoscholasticism to Nuptial Mysticism*. Malden, MA: Blackwell Publishing, 2007.
Koerpel, R. C. 'Tradition, Truth and Time: Remarks on the "Liturgical Action" of the Church'. In Craig Hovey and Cyrus P. Olsen, eds, *The Hermeneutics of Tradition: Explorations and Examinations*, pp. 173-92. Oregan: Cascade, 2013.
Koma, Élie. 'Le Milieu théologique de l'oeuvre de Henri de Lubac', *Nouvelle revue théologique* 118 (1996): pp. 539-49.

Komonchak, Joseph. 'Interpreting the Council and Its Consequences'. In James L. Heft and John O'Malley, eds, *After Vatican II: Trajectories and Hermeneutics*, pp. 164–72. Grand Rapids, MI: Eerdmans, 2012.

Komonchak, Joseph. 'La lucha por el Concilio durante la preparación'. In Giuseppe Alberigo, ed., *Historia del Concilio Vaticano II*, vol. 1, pp. 155–230. Salamanca: Ediciones Sigueme, 1999–2008.

Komonchak, Joseph. 'Theology and Culture at Mid-Century: The Example of Henri de Lubac', *Theological Studies* 51 (1990): pp. 579–602.

Körner, Bernhard. 'Henri de Lubac and Fundamental Theology'. Translated by Adrian Walker. *Communio* 23 (1996), pp. 710–21.

Krieg, Robert. *Theologians in Nazi Germany*. London: Continuum, 2004.

Küng, Hans. 'The Council: End or Beginning?', *Commonweal* 81 (1965): pp. 631–37.

Küng, Hans. 'Dialog mit Karl Barth', *Dokumente: Zeitschrift für übernationale Zusammenarbeit* 14, no. 3 (1958): pp. 236–37.

Küng, Hans. *Justification: The Doctrine of Karl Barth and a Catholic Reflection*. Translated by Thomas Collins, Edmund E. Tolk, and David Granskou. Louisville, KY: Westminster John Knox Press, 2004.

Küng, Hans. *My Struggle for Freedom: Memoirs*. London: Continuum, 2002.

Kupczak, Jarosław. *The Human Person in the Philosophy of Karol Wojtyła/John Paul II: Destined for Liberty*. Washington, DC: Catholic University of America, 2000.

Kupczak, Jarosław. 'John Paul II's Interpretation of the Second Vatican Council', *Communio* 39 (2012): pp. 152–69.

Labourdette, Marie-Michel. 'La théologie et ses sources', *Revue thomiste* 46 (1946): pp. 353–71.

Lacordaire, Henri. *Considérations sur le système philosophique de M. de Lamennais*. Paris: Derivaux, 1834.

Lacroix, Jean. *Essai sur l'indifférence en matière de religion*. Paris: Leblan, 1817.

Lacroix, Jean. *Maurice Blondel: An Introduction to the Man and His Philosophy*. Translated by John C. Guinness. New York: Sheed and Ward, 1968.

Lafosse, Fulgence. *Augustinus Theologus*, 4 vols. Toulouse: Guillaume Bosc, 1676–1683.

Larsen, Sean. 'The Politics of Desire: Two Readings of Henri de Lubac on Nature and Grace', *Modern Theology* 29, no. 3 (2013): pp. 279–310.

Lash, Nicholas. *Holiness, Speech and Silence*. Aldershot: Ashgate, 2004.

Law, Bernard, ed. *The Extraordinary Synod 1985*. Boston: St Paul Editions, 1986.

Lawler, Michael G. and Thomas J. Shanahan. *Church: A Spirited Communion*. Collegeville: Liturgical Press, 1995.

Lefebvre, Marcel. *An Open Letter to Confused Catholics*. Translated by Father M. Crowdy. London: Fowler Wright Books Ltd, 1986.

Lefebvre, Marcel. *Religious Liberty Questioned – The Dubia: My Doubts about the Vatican II Declaration of Religious Liberty*. Kansas City, MO: Angelus Press, 2001.

Le Goff, Jacques. *Intellectuals in the Middle Ages*. London: Wiley-Blackwell, 1993.

Levinas, Emmanuel. 'On Maurice Blanchot'. In *Proper Names*, 127–70. Translated by Michael B. Smith. London: The Athlone Press, 1996.

Lonergan, Bernard. *Philosophical and Theological Papers: Collected Papers (1958–1964)*. Edited by R. C. Croken et al. Toronto University Press, 1996.

Long, D. Stephen. 'Does God Have a Future? Theology and the "Future" of God'. In Trevor Cairney and David Starling, eds, *Theology and the Future: Evangelical Assertions and Explorations*, pp. 27–44. London: Bloomsbury T&T Clark, 2014.

Long, Steven A. *Natura Pura: On the Recovery of Nature in the Doctrine of Grace*. New York: Fordham University Press, 2010.
Long, Steven A. 'On the Loss, and the Recovery, of Nature as a Theonomic Principle: Reflections on the Nature/Grace Controversy', *Nova et Vetera* 5, no. 1 (2007): pp. 133–84.
Louzeau, Frédéric. 'Gaston Fessard et Henri de Lubac: leur différend sur la question du communisme et du progressisme chrétien (1945–1950)', *Revue des Sciences Religieuses* 84, no. 4 (2010): pp. 517–43.
Löwith, Karl. *Meaning in History: The Theological Implications of the Philosophy of History*. Chicago: University of Chicago Press, 1957.
MacIntyre, Alasdair. 'Aquinas's Critique of Education: Against His Own Age, Against Ours'. In A. O. Rorty, ed., *Philosophers on Education: New Historical Perspectives*, pp. 93–106. London: Routledge, 1998.
Malevez, L. 'La gratuité du surnaturel', *Nouvelle Revue Théologique* 75 (1953): pp. 561–86, 673–89.
Malloy, Christopher J. 'De Lubac on Natural Desire: Difficulties and Antitheses', *Nova et Vetera* 9 (2011): pp. 567–624.
Mangasarian, M. M. *A New Catechism*. Chicago: Open Court, 1902.
Mansini, Guy. 'The Abiding Theological Significance of Henri de Lubac's *Surnaturel*'. *The Thomist* 73 (2009): 593–619.
Mansini, Guy. *What Is a Dogma?* Rome: Gregorian University, 1985.
Marchetto, Agostino. *The Second Vatican Ecumenical Council: A Counterpoint for the History of the Council*. Translated by Kenneth D. Whitehead. Chicago, IL: Scranton University Press, 2010.
Maréchal, Joseph. *Le point de départ de la metaphysique: Leçons sur le développement historique et théorique du problème de la connaissance, Cahier V: Le Thomisme devant la philosophie critique*. Paris: Félix Alcan, 1926.
Maritain, Jacques. *Approaches to God*. Translated by Peter O'Reilly. New York: Macmillan Company, 1965.
Maritain, Jacques. *Integral Humanism: Temporal and Spiritual Problems of a New Christendom*. Translated by Joseph W. Evans. New York: Scribner, 1968.
McCool, Gerald A. *From Unity to Pluralism: The Internal Evolution of Thomism*. New York: Fordham University Press, 1989.
McDermott, John M. 'De Lubac and Rousselot', *Gregorianum* 78 (1997): pp. 735–59.
McDermott, Ryan. 'Henri de Lubac's Genealogy of Modern Exegesis and Nicholas of Lyra's Literal Sense of Scripture', *Modern Theology* 29, no. 1 (January 2013): pp. 124–56.
McGinn, Bernard. *The Calabrian Abbot: Joachim de Fiore in the History of Western Thought*. New York: Macmillan, 1985.
McInerny, Ralph. *Praeambula fidei: Thomism and the God of the Philosophers*. Washington, DC: Catholic University of America Press, 2006.
McNeil, John J. *The Blondelian Synthesis: A Study of the Influence of German Philosophical Sources on the Formation of Blondel's Method and Thought*. Leiden: E. J. Brill, 1966.
McPartlan, Paul. *The Eucharist Makes the Church*. Fairfax, VA: Eastern Christian Publications, 2006.
Mention, Léon, ed. *Documents relatifs aux rapports du clergé avec la royauté de 1682 à 1705*, 3 vols. Paris: Alphonse Picard et Fils, 1893.
Mettepenningen, Jürgen. *Nouvelle Théologie – New Theology: Inheritor of Modernism, Precursor of Vatican II*. London: T&T Clark, 2010.

Milbank, John. *Being Reconciled: Ontology and Pardon*. London: Routledge, 2003.
Milbank, John. *Beyond Secular Order: The Representation of Being and the Representation of the People*. Oxford: Wiley-Blackwell, 2013.
Milbank, John. 'The Double Glory, or Paradox versus Dialectics: On Not Quite Agreeing with Slavoj Žižek', In John Milbank and Slavoj Žižek, *The Monstrosity of Christ: Paradox or Dialectic?* Edited by Creston Davis, pp. 111–233. Cambridge, MA: The MIT Press, 2009.
Milbank, John. 'Henri de Lubac'. In David F. Ford, ed., *The Modern Theologians: An Introduction to Modern Theology since 1918*. Malden, MA: Blackwell, 2005.
Milbank, John. 'The New Divide: Classical versus Romantic Orthodoxy', *Modern Theology* 26 (January 2010): pp. 26–38.
Milbank, John. 'The Programme of Radical Orthodoxy'. In Laurence Paul Hemming, ed., *Radical Orthodoxy? – A Catholic Enquiry*, pp. 33–45. Aldershot: Ashgate, 2000.
Milbank, John. 'The Soul of Reciprocity Part One: Reciprocity Refused', *Modern Theology* 17 (2001): pp. 335–91.
Milbank, John. 'The Soul of Reciprocity Part Two: Reciprocity Granted', *Modern Theology* 17 (2001): pp. 485–507.
Milbank, John. *The Suspended Middle: Henri de Lubac and the Debate Concerning the Supernatural*, 1st ed. Grand Rapids, MI: William B. Eerdmans Publishing Company, 2005.
Milbank, John. *The Suspended Middle: Henri de Lubac and the Renewed Split in Modern Catholic Theology*, 2nd ed. Grand Rapids, MI: William B. Eerdmans Publishing Company, 2014.
Milbank, John. *Theology and Social Theory: Beyond Secular Reason*, 2nd ed. Oxford: Wiley-Blackwell, 2006.
Milbank, John and Catherine Pickstock. *Truth in Aquinas*. London: Routledge, 2001.
Milbank, John, Catherine Pickstock, and Graham Ward, eds. *Radical Orthodoxy: A New Theology*. London: Routledge, 1999.
Moffett, Samuel H. *A History of Christianity in Asia*, 2 vols. Maryknoll, NY: Orbis, 1998.
Möhler, Johann Adam. *Symbolism: Exposition of the Doctrinal Differences between Catholics and Protestants as Evidenced by Their Symbolical Writings*. Translated by James Burton Roberston. New York: Crossroads, 1997.
Möhler, Johann Adam. *Unity in the Church or the Principle of Catholicism Presented in the Spirit of the Church Fathers of the First Three Centuries*. Translated and edited by Peter C. Erb. Washington, DC: Catholic University of America Press, 1996.
Moloney, Raymond. 'Henri de Lubac on Church and Eucharist', *Irish Theological Quarterly* 70 (2005): pp. 331–42.
Montag, John. 'Revelation: The False Legacy of Suárez'. In John Milbank, Catherine Pickstock and Graham Ward, eds, *Radical Orthodoxy: A New Theology*, pp. 38–63. London: Routledge, 1999.
Moulins-Beaufort, Éric de. *Anthropologie et mystique selon Henri de Lubac*. Paris: Cerf, 2003.
Mouroux, Jean. *The Meaning of Man*. Translated by A. H. G. Downes. New York: Sheed & Ward, 1952.
Murphy, Francesca. *Art and Intellect in the Philosophy of Étienne Gilson*. Missouri University Press, 2004.
Murphy, Francesca. 'De Lubac, Grace, Politics and Paradox', *Studies in Christian Ethics* 23 (2010): pp. 415–30.

Neufeld, Karl Heinz. 'Au service du concile. Évêques et théologiens au deuxième concile du Vatican'. In René Latourelle, ed. *Vatican II. Bilan et perspectives. Vingt-cinq ans après*, vol. 1, pp. 95–124. Montréal-Paris: Bellarmin-Cerf, 1998.

Newman, John Henry Cardinal. 'Milman's View of Christianity'. In *Essays Critical and Historical*, vol. 2, pp. 186–248. London: Longmans, Green and Co, 1907.

Nicholas of Cusa. *Selected Spiritual Writings*. Translated by H. Lawrence Bond. New York: Paulist Press, 1997.

Nichols, Aidan. *Catholic Thought since the Enlightenment*. Leominster: Gracewing, 1998.

Nichols, Aidan. *From Hermes to Benedict XVI: Faith and Reason in Modern Catholic Thought*. Leominster: Gracewing, 2009.

Nichols, Aidan. 'Henri de Lubac: Panorama and Proposal', *New Blackfriars* 93 (2012): pp. 1–31.

Nichols, Aidan. *Reason with Piety: Garrigou-Lagrange in the Service of Catholic Thought*. Naples, FL: Sapientia Press, 2008.

Nichols, Aidan. 'Thomism and the Nouvelle Théologie', *The Thomist* 64 (2000): pp. 1–19.

Nietzsche, Friedrich. *Nietzsche Werke: Kritische Gesamtausgabe*. Edited by Mazzino Montinari and Giorgio Colli. Berlin: De Gruyter, 1967 ff.

Noris, Enrico. *Vindiciae Augustinianae*. Brussells: Lambert Marchant, 1675.

Novak, Michael. *The Catholic Ethic and the Spirit of Capitalism*. New York: Free Press, 1993.

Oakes, Edward T. 'Catholic Eschatology and the Development of Doctrine', *Nova et Vetera* 6, no. 2 (Spring 2008): pp. 419–46.

Oakes, Edward T. 'The Paradox of Nature and Grace: On John Milbank's *The Suspended Middle: Henri de Lubac and the Debate Concerning the Supernatural*', *Nova et Vetera* 4, no. 3 (2006): pp. 667–96.

Oakes, Edward T. 'The *Surnaturel* Controversy: A Survey and a Response', *Nova et Vetera* 9, no. 3 (2011): 625–56.

O'Collins, Gerald. *Salvation for All: God's Other Peoples*. Oxford: Oxford University Press, 2008.

Oliver, Simon. 'Aquinas and Aristotle's Teleology', *Nova et Vetera* 11 (2013): pp. 849–70.

Oliver, Simon. 'Introducing Radical Orthodoxy: From Participation to Late Modernity'. In Simon Oliver and John Milbank, eds, *The Radical Orthodoxy Reader*. London: Routledge, 2009.

O'Malley, John W. 'The Sweet Delight of Virtue and Grace in Aquinas's Ethics', *International Journal of Systematic Theology* 7 (2005): pp. 52–71.

O'Malley, John W. *What Happened at Vatican II?* Cambridge, MA: Harvard University Press, 2008.

O'Meara, T. F. *Romantic Idealism and Roman Catholicism: Schelling and the Theologians*. Notre Dame, IN: University of Notre Dame Press, 1982.

O'Sullivan, Noel. *Christ and Creation: Christology as the Key to Interpreting the Theology of Creation in the Works of Henri de Lubac*. Oxford: Peter Lang, 2009.

Ouellet, Marc Cardinal. *The Relevance and Future of the Second Vatican Council, Interviews with Father Geoffroy de la Tousche*. Translated by Michael Donley and Joseph Fessio. San Francisco: Ignatius Press, 2013.

Pabst, Adrian. *Metaphysics: The Creation of Hierarchy*. Grand Rapids, MI: Eerdmans Publishing Company, 2012.

Pecknold, C. C. and Jacob Wood. 'Augustine and Henri de Lubac'. In C. C. Pecknold and Tarmo Toom, eds, *T&T Clark Companion to Augustine and Modern Theology*, pp. 196–222. London and New York: Bloomsbury, T&T Clark, 2013.

Peddicord, Richard. *The Sacred Monster of Thomism: An Introduction to the Life and Legacy of Reginald Garrigou-Lagrange*. South Bend, IN: St Augustine's Press, 2005.
Péguy, Charles. 'Avertissement', *Cahiers de la quinzaine* 11, ser. 5 (1 March 1904).
Péguy, Charles. 'Supplément aux "Vies parallèles de M. Lanson et de M. Andler"', *Cahiers de la quinzaine* 9, ser. 14 (22 April 1913).
Pérez, Francisco A. Castro. *Cristo y cada hombre: Hermenéutica y recepción de una enseñanza del Concilio Vaticano II*. Rome: Gregorian & Biblical Press, 2011.
Pickstock, Catherine. *After Writing: On the Liturgical Consummation of Philosophy*. Oxford: Blackwell, 1998.
Pickstock, Catherine. *Repetition and Identity*. Oxford: Oxford University Press, 2013.
Portier, William L. 'Twentieth-Century Catholic Theology and the Triumph of Maurice Blondel', *Communio* 38 (Spring 2011): pp. 103–37.
Portier, William L. 'What Kind of a World of Grace? De Lubac and the Council's Christological Center', *Communio* 39 (2012): pp. 136–51.
Pottier, Bernard. 'Daniélou and the Twentieth-Century Patristic Renewal'. In Gabriel Flynn and Paul Murray, eds, *Ressourcement: A Movement for Renewal in Twentieth-Century Catholic Theology*, pp. 250–62. New York: Oxford, 2012.
Prévotat, Jacques. *Henri de Lubac et le mystère de l'Église*. Paris: Cerf, 1999.
Przywara, Erich. *Analogia Entis: Metaphysics: Original Structure and Universal Rhythm*. Translated by John R. Betz and David Bentley Hart. Grand Rapids, MI: Eerdmans Publishing Company, 2014.
Rahner, Karl. 'The Abiding Significance of Vatican II'. In *Concern for the Church*, pp. 90–102. Translated by Edward Quinn. New York: Crossroad, 1981.
Rahner, Karl. 'Chalkedon – Ende oder Anfang?'. In A. von Grillmeier and H. Bacht, eds, *Das Konzil von Chalkedon*, vol. 3, pp. 3–49. Würzburg: Echter Verlag, 1954.
Rahner, Karl. 'Current Problems in Christology'. In *Theological Investigations*, vol. 1, pp. 149–200. Translated by Cornelius Ernst. Baltimore, MD: Helicon, 1961.
Rahner, Karl. *Das Konzil. Ein neuer Beginn. Vortrag beim Festakt zum Abschluss des II. vatikanischen Konzils im Herkulessaal der Residenz in München am 12. Dez. 1965*. Freiburg: Herder, 1966.
Rahner, Karl. *Faith in a Wintry Season: Conversations and Interviews with Karl Rahner in the Last Years of His Life*. New York: Crossroad, 1991.
Rahner, Karl. *Mater Ecclesia. Lobpreis der Kirche aus dem ersten Jahrtausend*. Einsiedeln: Johannes Verlag, 1944.
Rahner, Karl, ed. *The Pastoral Approach to Atheism*. Glen Rock: Paulist Press, 1967.
Rahner, Karl. 'Toward a Fundamental Theological Interpretation of Vatican II', *Theological Studies* 40 (1979): pp. 716–27.
Ratzinger, Joseph. *Eschatlologie: Tod und ewiges Leben*. Regensburg: Pustet, 1978.
Ratzinger, Joseph. *Milestones – Memoirs 1927–1977*. San Francisco: Ignatius, 1998.
Ratzinger, Joseph. *Principles of Catholic Theology: Building Stones for a Fundamental Theology*. Translated by Mary Frances McCarthy. San Francisco: Ignatius Press, 1987.
Reardon, Bernard. *Liberalism and Tradition*. New York: Cambridge University Press, 1975.
Reid, Alcuin. *The Organic Development of the Liturgy: Principles for Liturgical Reform*. San Francisco: Ignatius, 2005.
Riches, Aaron. 'Christology and *duplex hominis beatitudo*: Re-sketching the Supernatural Again', *International Journal of Systematic Theology* 14 (2012): pp. 44–69.
Rondet, Henri. 'Nouvelle théologie'. In Karl Rahner et al., eds, *Sacramentum Mundi. An Encyclopedia of Theology IV*, pp. 234–36. London: Burns & Oates, 1969.
Rousselot, Pierre. *The Intellectualism of Saint Thomas*. New York: Sheed and Ward, 1935.

Rowland, Tracey. *Catholic Theology*. London: Bloomsbury, 2017.
Rowland, Tracey. *Culture and the Thomist Tradition: After Vatican II*. London: Routledge, 2003.
Rowland, Tracey. *Ratzinger's Faith: The Theology of Pope Benedict XVI*. Oxford: OUP, 2008.
Rummel, Erika. *The Humanist-Scholastic Debate in the Renaissance and Reformation*. Cambridge, MA: Harvard University Press, 1995.
Russo, Antonio. *Henri de Lubac*. Milan: Edizione San Paolo, 1994.
Russo, Antonio. *Henri de Lubac: Teologia e dogma nella Storia. L'influsso di Blondel*. Rome: Ediziona Studium, 1989.
Sales, Michel. *L'Être Humaine et la Connaissance Naturelle Qu'il a de Dieu dans la penseé du P. Henri de Lubac*. Paris: Parole et Silence, 2003.
Sales, Michel. 'La résistance au nazisme du Père de Lubac', *Christus* 47 (2000): pp. 155–61.
Salzman, Todd A. and Michael G. Lawler. *The Sexual Person: Toward a Renewed Catholic Anthropology*. Georgetown University Press, 2008.
Sartre, Jean-Paul. *Existentialism and Humanism*. Translation and Introduction by Philip Mairet. London: Methuen & Co, 1968.
Schillebeeckx, Edward. *Approches théologiques*, vol. 3. *Le monde et l'église*. Bruxelles: Editions du Cep, 1967.
Schillebeeckx, Edward. 'L'Église et l'Humanité', *Concilium* 1 (1965): pp. 57–78.
Schindler, D. C. *The Catholicity of Reason*. Grand Rapids, MI: Eerdmans Publishing Company, 2013.
Schindler, D. C. 'The Natural Supernaturality of Marriage', *Communio: International Catholic Review* (forthcoming).
Schindler, David L. *Heart of the World, Soul of the Church*. Grand Rapids: Eerdmans, 1996.
Schindler, David L. *Ordering Love: Liberal Societies and the Memory of God*. Grand Rapids: Eerdmans, 2011.
Schindler, David L. and N. J. Healy. *Freedom, Truth and Human Dignity: The Second Vatican Council's Declaration on Religious Freedom*. Grand Rapids: Eerdmans, 2015.
Schmutz, Jacob. 'The Medieval Doctrine of Causality and the Theology of Pure Nature (13th to 17th Centuries)'. In Serge-Thomas Bonino, ed., *Surnaturel: A Controversy at the Heart of Twentieth-Century Thomstic Thought*, pp. 203–50. Florida: Sapientia Press, 2009.
Scola, A., G. Marengo, and J. Prades López, eds. *La Persona Umana: Antropologia Teologia*. Milano: Jaca, 2000.
Scott, Joan Wallach. *Parité!: Sexual Equality and the Crisis of French Universalism*. Chicago: University Of Chicago Press, 2005.
Simmonds, Gemma. 'Jansenism: An Early *Ressourcement* Movement?' In Gabriel Flynn and Paul Murray, eds, *Ressourcement: A Movement for Renewal in Twentieth-Century Catholic Theology*, pp. 23–35. New York: Oxford, 2012.
Siri, Giuseppe. *Getsemani: Riflessioni sul Movimento Teologico Contemporaneo*. Roma: Fraternità della Santissima Verginia Maria, 1980.
Skirry, Jason. 'Malebranche's Augustinianism and the Mind's Perfection'. PhD dissertation: University of Pennsylvania, 2010.
Smalley, Beryl. *The Study of the Bible in the Middle Ages*. Notre Dame, IN: University of Notre Dame Press, 1964.
Smith, Gerard. 'The Natural End of Man', *Proceedings of the American Catholic Philosophical Association* (1949): pp. 47–61.
Smith, James K. A. *Introducing Radical Orthodoxy: Mapping a Post-Secular Theology*. Grand Rapids, MI: Baker Academic, 2004.

Spaemann, Robert. *Philosophische Esssays*. Stuttgart: Reclam, 1993.
Staley, Kevin M. 'Happiness: The Natural End of Man'? *The Thomist* 53, no. 2 (April 1989): pp. 215–34.
Sutton, Michael. *Nationalism, Positivism and Catholicism: The Politics of Charles Maurras and French Catholics: 1890–1914*. Cambridge: Cambridge University Press, 1982.
Swafford, Andrew Dean. *Nature and Grace: A New Approach to Thomistic Ressourcement*. Eugene, OR: Pickwick Publications, 2014.
Taylor, Charles. *A Secular Age*. Cambridge, MA: Harvard University Press, 2007.
Te Velde, Rudi. *Aquinas on God: The 'Divine Science' of the Summa Theologiae*. Burlington, VT: Ashgate, 2006.
Torrell, Jean-Pierre. *Saint Thomas d'Aquin, maître spirituel*. Paris: Cerf, 1996, 2002.
Vacant, Alfred, E. Mangenot, and Emile Amann, eds. *Dictionnaire de Théologie Catholique*. Paris: Letouzey et Ané, 1903–1950.
Valadier, Paul. 'Dieu présent. Une entrée dans la théologie du Cardinal de Lubac', *Recherches de Science Religieuse* 80, no. 3 (1992): pp. 345–58.
Vanneste, Alfred. *Nature et grâce dans la théologie occidentale: Dialogue avec H. de Lubac*. Leuven: Peeters, 1996.
Vanneste, Alfred. 'Review of Henri de Lubac, *Catholicisme. Les aspects sociaux du dogme*', *Ephemerides Theologicae Lovanienses* 80 (2004): p. 207.
Virgoulay, René. *Philosophie et théologie chez Maurice Blondel*. Paris: Cerf, 2002.
Voderholzer, Rudolf. 'Dogma and History: Henri de Lubac and the Retrieval of Historicity as a Key to Theological Renewal', *Communio: International Theological Review* 28 (Winter 2001): pp. 648–69.
Voderholzer, Rudolf. *Meet Henri de Lubac: His Life and Work*. San Francisco: Ignatius Press, 2008.
Vorgrimler, Herbert. 'Henri de Lubac'. In Robert Vander Gucht and Herbert Vorgrimler, eds, *Bilan de la théologie du XXe siècle II*, pp. 806–20. Tournai-Paris: Casterman, 1970.
Wagner, Jean-Pierre. *La Théologie Fondamentale selon Henri de Lubac*. Paris, Cerf, 1997.
Walker, Adrian J. 'Original Best: The "Coextensiveness" of Being and Love in Light of *Gaudium et Spes*, 22', *Communio* 39 (2012): pp. 49–65.
Wannenwetsch, Bernd. 'Liturgy'. In Peter Scott and William T. Cavanaugh, eds, *The Blackwell Companion to Political Theology*, pp. 76–90. Malden, MA: Blackwell, 2007.
Ward, Graham. *Christ and Culture*. Oxford: Blackwell, 2005.
Ward, Graham. *Unbelievable: Why We Believe and Why We Don't*. London: Tauris, 2014.
Weber, Eugen. *Action française: Royalism and Reaction in Twentieth-Century France*. Stanford: Stanford University Press, 1962.
Weigel, George. *Witness to Hope: Witness To Hope: The Biography of Pope John Paul II*. New York: HarperCollins, 1999.
White, Thomas Joseph. 'The "Pure Nature" of Christology: Human Nature and *Gaudium et Spes* 22', *Nova et Vetera* 8 (2010): pp. 283–322.
Williams, Rowan. *The Edge of Words: God and the Habits of Language*. London: Bloomsbury, 2014.
Wiltgen, Ralph M. *The Rhine Flows into the Tiber: A History of Vatican II*. Rockford, IL: Tan Books, 1985.
Wittstadt, L. 'En vísperas del Concilio Vaticano II'. In Giuseppe Alberigo, ed. *Historia del Concilio Vaticano II*, vol. 1, pp. 373–465. Salamanca: Ediciones Siguemé, 1999–2008.
Wojtyła, Karol. *Amour et responsabilité. Étude de morale sexuelle*. Paris: Éditions du Dialogue, 1965.

Wood, Susan K. *The Church as the Social Embodiment of Grace in the Ecclesiology of Henri de Lubac*. PhD dissertation: Marquette University, 1986.

Wood, Susan K. 'The Nature-Grace Problematic within Henri de Lubac's Christological Paradox', *Communio (US)* 19 (Fall 1992): pp. 389–403.

Wood, Susan K. *Spiritual Exegesis and the Church in the Theology of Henri de Lubac*. Grand Rapids, MI: Eerdmans, 1998.

Young, Frances. *Biblical Interpretation and the Formation of Christian Culture*. Cambridge: Cambridge University Press, 1997.

Young, Robin Darling. 'A Soldier of the Great War: Henri de Lubac and the Patristic Sources for a Premodern Theology'. In James L. Heft and John O'Malley, eds, *After Vatican II: Trajectories and Hermeneutics*, pp. 134–63. Grand Rapids, MI: Eerdmans, 2012.

Zaleski, Carol. 'Newman for a New Generation'. In Francesca Aran Murphy, ed., *The Beauty of God's House: Essays in Honour of Stratford Caldecott*, pp. 255–69. Eugene: Wipf and Stock, 2014.

Zimoń, Henryk. 'Wilhelm Schmidt's Theory of Primitive Monotheism and Its Critique within the Vienna School of Ethnology', *Anthropos* 81 (1986): pp. 243–60.

INDEX

act and potency 271–4
Action française 33–5, 39, 42, 62, 68, 71, 110, 112, 172, 420. *See also* Maurras, Charles
Aegidianism 106–7, 109, 114, 118
Aeterni Patris 29, 61, 84, 108–9, 295
aggiornamento 23, 132
allegory. *See under* scripture, interpretation of
Anselm 286
anti-Semitism 14–15, 168, 207–8, 262–5, 296, 420–5
anxiety 368
apologetics 10–11, 27, 46, 70, 165, 242–3, 292, 312
Aquinas. *See* Thomas Aquinas
Aristotle/Aristotelianism 106, 183, 271–8, 287, 329, 364, 410–11, 414, 428–31
atheism 142–3, 152, 225–46. *See also* humanism, atheistic
Augustine
    on the Church 171, 294
    on divine presence 254
    on the letter and spirit of scripture 221–2
    on the restless heart 188–9
    on the scope of salvation 259
    on the two cities 102, 430–1

Baius, Michael 114, 344, 384–5
baptism 166–7, 170
Barth, Karl 4, 152, 377–81, 388–92, 394, 446–7, 449
Baur, Ferdinand Christian 385
Bautain, Louis 104–6
beatitude xvi, 20, 354, 356–7, 359, 363. *See also* finality
    beatific vision 20–1, 83, 114, 188–9, 191, 198, 272, 338, 365
    different from happiness xvi, 367–8
Bellarmine, Robert 439
Benedict XVI, Pope. *See* Ratzinger, Joseph
Benigni, Umberto 35
Berengar of Tours 221, 383
Bernanos, Georges 38–9, 54–5
Berti, Giovanni 105–7
Billot, Louis 32, 34
Bloch, Ernst 305, 388, 390
Blondel, Maurice 35–9, 57–91, 109, 112–14, 203, 232–3, 267
    on apologetics 70
    on 'Christian philosophy' 75–6
    on extrinsicism 35–6, 62–3, 70–1
    the idea of the infinite 65–6
    influence on de Lubac 8–9, 72–7, 164–5
    the meaning of action 58–9, 65–6
    method of immanence 59–60
    on the supernatural 62–3, 66
    on tradition 36–7
Bloy, Leon 38
Boehme, Jacob 303–4, 389
Boersma, Hans 31–2, 46
Bonhoeffer, Dietrich 323, 378
Bonino, Serge-Thomas 30–1, 54, 184
Bosco, Mark 38
Bouillard, Henri 329, 380–1
Boutroux, Emile 69
Boyer, Charles 353–60
Bréhier, Émile 74–5
Brentano, Franz 63–4
Bretherton, Luke 461–2
Brunschvicg, Léon 74–5, 82
Buddhism 22, 247, 257, 308–9
Bultmann, Rudolf 379

Cahiers du Témoignage chrétien 15, 42, 77, 168, 175, 227, 263–4, 422
Calvin, John 114, 376–9, 383–6, 388
Chaillet, Pierre 15, 42
Chaine Declaration 263, 424
Chantraine, George 81, 113, 127, 137, 146
'Christian Philosophy' debates 74–6, 243
Christology. *See* Jesus Christ
Church 26–7, 159–79
    ecclesiology of communion 124–5, 131, 138–9, 155, 172, 174, 397, 437–8, 440, 442
    and eschatology 173–4, 296–7, 440–3
    and Eucharist (*see under* Eucharist)
    mission of xix, 6, 135, 176, 277 (*see also* mission)
    as mystery 150–1, 292
    as sacrament 11–12, 25, 125, 139, 159–60
    sinfulness of 173, 292–3, 296–7
    subsisting in the Roman Catholic Church 160–2
    and temporal power 439–40
    unifying role 162–7, 284, 437–9
    visible and invisible 377–8
Clarke, William Norris 35–6
Claudel, Paul 38–9, 50, 300, 345

Clement of Alexandria 336
Combes, Emile 33
Communio (journal) 47
Comte, Auguste 61–2, 65, 68, 229, 236–8, 299–300
Concilium (journal) 132–4, 140, 143–4, 150
Congar, Yves 13, 37, 94–6, 127, 137, 143, 150, 302–3
Coolman, Boyd Taylor 205
Cyprian of Carthage 261

Daniélou, Jean 40–1, 78, 94–5, 143, 149, 211, 313–14
Dawson, John David 321
de Chardin, Teilhard 129, 174, 227
De Fontibus Revelationis. *See under* Vatican II
Dei Filius 53, 61, 84, 270–1, 277–8, 287
Dei Verbum. *See under* Vatican II
de Lamennais, Hugues 99–101
Delbos, Victor 69
de Lubac, Gabrielle 7
de Lubac, Louise 7
de Lubac, Maurice Sonier 6–7
del Val, Merry 72
de Montcheuil, Yves 15, 42, 70, 90, 168–9, 176
Derrida, Jacques 403
Descartes, René 74, 76, 87
Descoqs, Pedro 36, 62, 71–3, 80, 108, 112–13, 197
desire for God xvi, 20–1, 66–9, 74, 87–8, 90–1, 182–6, 190–2, 231–2, 272–8, 281–5, 315–17, 319–20, 401–3
  Aegidian interpretation of 106–7, 231
  beyond claim 365–71
  elicited 272–3, 412
  spirit and 231
  in Thomas Aquinas (*see under* Thomas Aquinas)
de Solages, Bruno 146–7
destiny. *See* finality
dialectic. *See* symbolism and dialectic
Donnelly, Phillip 429
Dreyfus Affair 110–13
Dru, Alexander 32–3, 37, 46

Ebeling, Gerhard 379
epistemology 106, 269–70
Erasmus 387
eschatology 173–4, 296–306, 358–60. *See also* Church; eschatology
Eucharist
  Protestant construals 383–4
  real presence 161–2, 221
  transformative power of 173–4
  and the unity of the Church 12, 114–17, 159–60, 162, 166, 221, 292
existentialism xvii, 57–8, 60
extrinsicism 10, 16–17, 35–6, 40, 62–3, 67, 74–7, 229–31, 408–12. *See also* neo-scholasticism; pure nature

faith 10–11, 51, 61, 71, 75–6, 85–6, 104–6, 132–3, 243, 246, 258, 286, 314, 342–4, 378–81, 407–9, 439, 450–1, 454, 464–5
fate 88, 238–9
feeling 368–71
Feingold, Lawrence 49, 51, 184, 195, 198, 273, 413
Ferry, Jules 6–7, 33
Fessard, Gaston 299, 426–7
Feuerbach, Ludwig 235–6
Feuillet, André 343
Fichte, Gottleib 64, 87
Fideism 104–5
Fifth Lateran Council 355
finality 58, 64–8, 182, 193–5. *See also* teleology
  finality as ontological 20, 67–8, 282–3, 401, 412–13
  single/supernatural 8, 20, 186–95, 198, 245, 272–4, 412–13, 428–9 (*see also* beatitude; desire for God)
  twofold 18–20, 67, 186, 190, 194–5, 319, 353, 356, 359–65, 369, 414–15, 431. (*see also* pure nature)
form 410–15
Fouilloux, Étienne 18
Fourvière, 'school of' 9–10, 20–2, 275
Fowlie, Wallace 38–9
Franzelin, Johannes Baptist 31–2
freedom 81–2, 90–1, 347
  of Christ (*see under* Jesus Christ)
  consequences of the Fall upon 114
  and political liberalism 433
French Revolution 32, 103, 111

Gallicanism 100–1
Garrigou-Lagrange, Reginald 10, 29–30, 42–3, 46, 70, 78, 113–14, 117, 172, 275–6
Gaudium et spes. *See under* Vatican II)
Giles of Rome 430, 439
Gilson, Étienne 39, 45, 74–5, 78, 83–4, 91, 280
grace 44, 51–3, 100, 174–8, 197–9, 294–5, 317–20, 384–6, 399–417
  and Christology (*see under* Jesus Christ)
  condition for desiring the supernatural (*see also* desire for God, elicited) 272–3
  elevating nature 112–14, 181–6, 189–90
  as gift 66, 353, 401–5
  perfecting nature 107
  and protology 100, 114, 352–3
  recipients of 258–9
  and union with God 309–11
Gratry, Auguste 98, 106–9
Grumett, David 42, 196, 247, 408
Grygiel, Stanisław 40
Guardini, Romano 44
Guéranger, Dom Prosper 98–102, 104, 115
Gutierrez, Gustavo 170–1

Hains, Eugène 7
Hamel, Robert 72–3, 80
happiness. *See under* beatitude
Healy, Nicholas J. 49, 413–15
Hegel, Georg W. F. 69, 304–5, 358–62, 368–9, 389
Heidegger, Martin 357, 363–4, 370–1
history, theology of 11–13, 22, 25, 31, 36–7, 252–3, 280, 289–306, 360–2, 421
Hollon, Bryan 285, 436–7
Holy Spirit 244–5, 333–4
Huby, Joseph 17, 43, 71–4, 187, 231, 328
Hugh of St Victor 219–20
Humani generis, 3, 21–3, 43–4, 78, 126–7, 193, 275
humanism xiv, 25, 228, 284
  atheistic 8, 12–13, 15–16, 41–2, 54, 68, 86, 142–3, 228–9, 234–40, 425–6 (*see also* atheism)
  Christian xiv, xvii–xviii, 45–6, 86, 138–9, 178, 226, 230–3, 242–6, 306
humility 447
Hütter, Reinhard 189, 274, 412, 429

idealism 64, 73, 85–7
idolatry 65, 68, 427, 451
Ignatius of Loyola. *See Spiritual Exercises,* Ignatian
imago Dei 66–8, 87–8, 91, 167, 178, 188–9, 231–4, 245, 279, 316–17, 428–9
  image and likeness 316, 343–7
immanentism 10, 19, 61, 87, 164, 218, 228, 379, 425–7
intellect. *See* reason
Irenaeus of Lyons 200, 258, 334
Islam 265–7

Jansen, Cornelius 76, 100, 230, 329–30, 384–5, 408
  Jansenism 38–9, 52, 100, 222, 258
Janssens, Jean-Baptiste 21–3
Jesus Christ xviii, 6, 11–12, 26–7, 41, 49, 327–48, 406–7
  body of Christ 116–17, 160–2, 171, 221
  the hypostatic union 244, 335–6
  interpreter and fulfillment of scripture 212–14, 255–6 (*see also* scripture)
  and the meaning of history 12, 290 (*see also* history, theology of)
  and the mystery of nature and grace 181–2, 185, 203, 328–31
  newness of 200–1, 331–5
  relation of person and works 342–4
  the revelation of God 6, 130–1, 151–2, 309, 336, 344–6, 456 (*see also* revelation)
  the revelation of humanity 6, 41, 123–4, 185, 245, 309, 316, 442
  self-consciousness of 339–42

  sinlessness and freedom of 337–9
  unifying work of 11, 124–5, 138–9, 166
Joachim of Fiore 25, 218, 240–1, 298–305, 387–90
John XXIII, Pope 23, 53, 127, 131–4
John Chrysostom 258
John of the Cross 254, 323–4
John Paul II, Pope. *See* Wojtyła, Karol
Jonas, Hans 185
Judaism 263–5

Kant, Immanuel 48, 69, 83, 90–1, 271, 355
Kaplan, Grant 37–8, 97
Kasper, Walter 174
Kerr, Fergus 30, 46, 53–4
Kierkegaard, Søren 380
Kołakowski, Leszek 48
Kraemer, Hendrik 379
Küng, Hans 23, 54, 127, 140, 150, 380–1

Laberthonnière, Lucien 35, 62
Labourdette, Marie-Michel 314
Lacordaire, Henri-Dominique 98, 101–4
Lacroix, Jean 426
Lash, Nicholas 460
Lefebvre, Marcel 34, 131, 133–4, 145, 149
Le Floche, Henri 34
Le Guillou, Marie-Joseph 198
Le Maistre, Joseph 98–9
Leninism 249
Leo XIII, Pope 29–30, 32, 61, 79, 108, 168, 201, 295, 419–20
Lessing, Gotthold E. 304
liberty. *See* freedom
limbo 50–2, 274–5
Loisy, Alfred 61, 63
Lonergan, Bernard 45–6, 275
Long, Steven A. 318
Louzeau, Frédéric 426–7
love xv–xix, 102, 159, 200–3, 319–20, 323–4, 452, 455
  divine 124, 181, 200–3, 290, 331–8, 347, 456
Lumen Gentium. See under Vatican II
Luther, Martin 85, 303–4, 343, 376, 382, 384–9

MacIntyre, Alasdair 50–1
Malebranche, Nicholas 105
Mansini, Guy 184
Maritain, Jacques xiv, 74–6, 79, 192, 230, 420
marriage 199–202
Marty, François 142–3, 148–9
Marx, Karl 12, 143, 235–6, 293, 298–300, 304–5, 421, 426–7, 461
Mary, mother of Jesus 137–8
Mauriac, François 38–9
Maurras, Charles 33–5, 61–3, 68, 71, 77, 110, 112, 116, 172, 234, 420. *See also Action française*
McDermott, John 233

McInerny, Ralph 195
Metaphysics. *See* ontology
Milbank, John 4, 47, 274, 282, 295, 393–7, 401–9, 414–16, 434–7. *See also* Radical Orthodoxy
mission 256–61, 378–9, 423. *See also* Church, mission of
Modernism xvii, 32, 35–7, 61–3, 70–1, 164, 229, 271–3, 275
Möhler, Johann Adam 37–8, 95–7, 297, 374–6
Moltmann, Jürgen 388–90
Montini, Giovanni 3, 25, 53, 131–3, 136–7, 141, 148, 156, 240
Moore, G. E. 63–4
morality 451–3, 458
Murray, John Courtney 51–2, 432
mysticism 253–4, 307–25, 453–4
   an ecclesial mysticism 310
   of likeness 317–20
   and scriptural interpretation 320–4
   universal occurrences of 308–9

natural desire for the supernatural. *See* desire for God
Nazism 14–16, 42, 168, 207–8, 227, 247, 262, 421–3, 427
neo-scholasticism xiv, 16–17, 29–55. *See also* extrinsicism; pure nature
   anthropology 40–1
   interpretation of Aquinas (*see under* Thomas Aquinas)
   theological method 31, 45–6
   on tradition 31–3
Newman, John Henry xviii, 36, 40, 374–5
Nicholas of Cusa 145, 155–6, 407
Nicholas of Lyra 387
Nichols, Aidan 32
Nietzsche, Friedrich 68, 237–9, 279–80, 300, 309, 361–2
nouvelle théologie 5, 29–30, 43, 78, 275, 313–17
Nygren, Anders 455

Oakes, Edward T. 5, 51–2, 394
Ontologism 105
ontology 280, 397
ontotheology 278
Origen of Alexandria 118, 211–16, 297, 303, 306
Ottaviani, Alfredo 129–32, 136

paradox xiv, 19–20, 49–50, 221–3, 232–4, 242–6, 339–41, 351, 366–7, 400–7, 429, 446–7
Pascal, Blaise 87, 165–6, 176, 290
Pascendi Dominici Gregis 32, 61
Paul VI, Pope. *See* Montini, Giovanni
Pecknold, Chad 231
Peddicord, Richard 46
Péguy, Charles 38–9, 93–4, 110–15

persons 445
Pétain, Maréchal 14, 42, 116–17, 172, 247
Phenomenology 57–64. *See also* Blondel, Maurice
Philips, Gérard 138, 151
Philosophy, task of 8–9, 57–60, 74–5, 84–6, 228–9, 243, 369, 416–17
   independent of theology 354–61
Pius IX, Pope 200
Pius X, Pope 32, 61–2, 271
Pius XI, Pope 33–4, 172, 262–3, 420
Pius XII, Pope 3, 21–3, 43–4, 126–7, 160, 193, 275
Pomponazzi, Pietro 355–6
Protestantism 373–92
   ecclesiology of 383–4
   and Joachimism 388–90
   on nature and grace 384–6
   as religion of antitheses 374–9, 382
   and scriptural interpretation 386–7
Proudhon, Pierre Joseph 229, 239–40, 299, 305
pure nature 18–20, 60, 73, 86, 125–6, 183–7, 196–9, 279, 351–4, 359, 402–4, 428. *See also* extrinsicism
   and epistemology 270–3, 354–7
   and 'exclusive humanism' 8, 25, 51, 142, 229–30, 276, 294–5, 357–8, 362, 370–1, 411–12, 428
   and limbo 50–2, 274–5
   and marriage 199–202
   and political liberalism 51–2, 407, 416, 432–3

Radical Orthodoxy 5, 393–417, 434–6
   account of the secular 395–6
   metaphysics of participation 397–400
   and the paradox of nature and grace 400–7, 411–15
Rahner, Hugo 137
Rahner, Karl 24, 36, 132, 134, 140, 143–8, 246, 338, 434–5
Ratzinger, Joseph 13, 36, 41, 52, 54–5, 96, 124, 138, 153, 155, 203, 459
reason xv–xvi, 8, 11, 17, 40, 47–50, 53, 54, 61–3, 75–6, 84–7, 91, 105, 189, 228–9, 232, 243, 286, 355–7, 361, 369–70, 395, 408–9
religion xvi, 66, 71, 236, 247–68, 375–6, 378, 448–51, 454
   monotheistic 250–3
   origins of 248–50
ressourcement 4, 93–119, 121–2, 313–14
   method of 94–5
   Péguy's call for 93
   and Radical Orthodoxy 396–7
   in the writings of de Lubac 114–19, 276
revelation xviii, 8, 10, 60, 70, 88, 163–4, 417. *See also* Jesus Christ
   as historical 36–7 (*see also* history, theology of)
   natural 278–9
   two-source theory 130, 285–6

Riches, Aaron 49–50, 405, 415
Romanticism 38, 47, 63–4, 87–8, 454
Romeyer, Blaise 197
Rousselot, Pierre 17, 71–4, 83–4, 232–3, 243

Sales, Michel 334
salvation, scope of 258–61, 283–4
Schema 13. *See under* Vatican II
Schillebeeckx, Edward 24–5, 132, 134, 140, 143–4, 150, 174
Schindler, David L. 51–2, 432–4
Schmidt, Wilhelm 250
Schmitt, Paul Joseph 130
Schmutz, Jacob 400, 404
Schwalm, Marie-Bedoit 70
Scripture, interpretation of 12, 22, 118–19, 205–3
　according to Origen (*see* Origen of Alexandria)
　allegory 210–11
　Christian use of the Old Testament 205–8
　'fourfold sense' 208–9, 320–4
　history/letter and spirit 212–14
　Joachimite (*see* Joachim of Fiore)
　Protestant (*see under* Protestantism)
　School of St Victor 218–20
　typology 210–11
sin 167, 176–8, 319–20, 352, 452–3
　sinfulness of the Church (*see under* Church)
　sinlessness of Christ (*see under* Jesus Christ)
Siri, Giuseppe 123–4, 130
Social Catholicism 419
Sources chrétiennes 20, 23, 78, 94, 208, 396
Spaemann, Robert 183
Spinoza, Baruch 69
spirit 67, 90, 231–4, 445–7. *See also* Holy Spirit; spirituality
Spiritual Exercises, Ignatian 162
spirituality 453–6, 459–60
Suárez, Francisco 36, 79–80
Suenens, Leo Jozef 134
suffering 455–6
supernatural. *See under* finality
symbolism and dialectic 221–2

'teleological argument' 81
teleology 409–11. *See also* finality
theology, task of 10–11, 46–7, 242–3, 289, 325, 354–7, 396–7, 405–9, 416–17
　'mystical' approach to 312–15
Te Velde, Rudi 183
Thomas Aquinas
　'Blondelian' Thomism 79–84, 109
　on faith 454
　on Jesus Christ 341
　on knowledge 82
　on nature and the supernatural 19, 182–92, 194–5, 280–2, 319, 409–15, 428
　neo-scholastic interpretations of 30–1, 45, 47, 49, 70, 94, 108
　on participation 397–400
　transcendental Thomism 73, 79, 83
Tillich, Paul 48
Tilliette, Xavier 7, 9
Tractarianism 396
tradition 26, 31–2, 36–8, 215
traditionalism 98–9, 104–5
Trinity 245, 290–1, 309, 345–6
Tübingen School 37, 95–7, 297

Ubaghs, Gérard-Casimir 105

Valensin, Albert 9, 72
Valensin, Auguste 35–6, 42, 70, 72–3
Vatican II 121–56
　De Fontibus Revelationis 130–1
　Dei Verbum 36, 53, 130, 144, 150–2, 154, 345–6
　De Lubac's commentary on 150–5
　de Lubac's involvement in 127–45
　Gaudium et spes 41, 53, 123–4, 134–45, 152–5, 177, 240, 440–2
　influence of de Lubac's work on 53, 123–4, 137–9, 144
　Lumen Gentium 138–9, 150–5, 154–5, 160, 162, 166, 170, 178
　para-Council 24, 132, 135–6, 139–40, 144–50
　preparatory commission 128–9
　Schema Thirteen 134–5, 139–45
　la settimana nera 136–7
Voderholzer, Rudolf 46, 49–50, 228
von Balthasar, Hans Urs 9, 11, 13, 26, 48, 54, 78, 89–90, 125, 128, 152, 164, 206, 243, 247, 282, 297, 300–1, 402, 407
von Kuhn, Johannes Evangelist 37

Weber, Eugene 34, 116
William of Auvergne 256
Williams, Rowan 406
Wiltgen, Ralph 127
Wojtyła, Karol 25, 40, 41, 52–5, 124, 133, 140–1, 154, 159, 199–202
Wolff, Christian 280
Wood, Jacob 231
Wood, Susan 96, 160–1, 178, 244, 437
World War I 7–8, 48, 311
World War II 14–17, 42, 48, 172, 276, 311, 313, 421–2, 461

Zoroastrianism 251–2

www.ingramcontent.com/pod-product-compliance
Lightning Source LLC
Chambersburg PA
CBHW070005010526
44117CB00011B/1434